JOURNEY

AN ILLUSTRATED HISTORY OF TRAVEL

JOURNEY

AN ILLUSTRATED HISTORY OF TRAVEL

Foreword Michael Collins
Contributors Simon Adams, R.G. Grant, Andrew Humphreys

DK

DK LONDON
Senior Editor Angela Wilkes
Senior Art Editor Gadi Farfour
Editors Andy Szudek, Kate Taylor, Victoria Heyworth-Dunne
US Editor Karyn Gerhard
Designers Vanessa Hamilton, Renata Latipova, Nicola Rodway
Picture Researcher Sarah Smithies
Managing Editor Gareth Jones
Senior Managing Art Editor Lee Griffiths
Producer, Pre-Production Gillian Reid
Senior Producer Mandy Inness
Jacket Designer Surabhi Wadhwa
Design Development Manager Sophia M.T.T.
Jacket Editor Claire Gell
Associate Publishing Director Liz Wheeler
Art Director Karen Self
Publishing Director Jonathan Metcalf

DK DELHI
Senior Art Editor Ira Sharma
Art Editors Vikas Sachdeva, Roshni Kapur
Editors Antara Moitra, Madhurika Bhardwaj
Managing Editor Soma B. Chowdhury
Managing Art Editor Arunesh Talapatra
Cartography Coordinator Rajesh Kumar Mishra
Cartography Manager Suresh Kumar
Picture Researcher Aditya Katyal
Picture Research Manager Taiyaba Khatoon
Senior DTP Designer Harish Aggarwal
DTP Designers Rajesh Singh Adhikari, Syed Md Farhan, Pawan Kumar
Production Manager Pankaj Sharma
Pre-production Manager Balwant Singh
Jacket Designers Suhita Dharamjit, Tanya Mehrotra
Managing Jackets Editor Saloni Singh

SMITHSONIAN
Established in 1846, the Smithsonian—the world's largest museum and research complex—includes 19 museums and galleries and the National Zoological Park. The total number of artifacts, works of art, and specimens in the Smithsonian's collections is estimated at 154 million, much of which is contained in the National Museum of Natural History, which holds more than 126 million specimens and objects. The Smithsonian is a renowned research center, dedicated to public education, national service, and scholarship in the arts, sciences, and history.

SMITHSONIAN CURATOR
Dr. F. Robert van der Linden, Curator of Air Transportation and Special Purpose Aircraft, National Air and Space Museum, Smithsonian

SMITHSONIAN ENTERPRISES
Product Development Manager Kealy E. Gordon
Licensing Manager Ellen Nanney
Vice President, Education and Consumer Projects Brigid Ferraro
Senior Vice President, Education and Consumer Projects Carol LeBlanc
President Christopher Liedel

First American Edition, 2017
Publlished in the United States by DK Publishing
345 Hudson Street, New York, New York 10014

17 18 19 20 21 10 9 8 7 6 5 4 3 2 1
001–300214–Oct/2017

Published in Great Britain by Dorling Kinderley Limited.

A catalog record for this book is available from the Library of Congress.
ISBN: 978-1-4654-6414-9

DK books are available at special discounts when purchased in bulk for sales promotions, premiums, fund-raising, or educational use. For details, contact: DK Publishing Special Markets, 345 Hudson Street, New York, New York 10014 or SpecialSales@dk.com

Printed and bound in China

CONTENTS

1 THE ANCIENT WORLD

EDITORIAL CONSULTANT

Michael Collins is a native of Dublin, Ireland. He has written several books with DK and publishes articles about his travels, which have a focus on archeology, ancient cultures, and civilizations. *Journey* is based on an original idea by Father Michael about the history of travel.

LEAD CONTRIBUTOR

Andrew Humphreys is a journalist, author, and travel writer, who has written or co-written more than 35 books for DK, Lonely Planet, *National Geographic*, and *Time Out*. His journalism often involves travel with a historical focus and has appeared in *The Financial Times*, *The Telegraph*, and *Condé Nast Traveler*. He is the author of two books on the golden age of travel in Egypt. He wrote Chapters 4, 5, 6, and 7 of *Journey*.

CONTRIBUTORS

Simon Adams worked as an editor of children's reference books before becoming a full-time writer 25 years ago. Since then, he has written and contributed to more than 60 books, specializing in history, travel, and exploration. A keen jazz fan, he now lives and works in Brighton. He contributed to Chapters 1 and 2 of *Journey*.

R.G. Grant has written extensively on history, military history, current affairs, and biography. His publications include *Flight: 100 Years of Aviation*, *A Visual History of Britain*, and *World War I: The Definitive Visual Guide*. He was the consulting editor on DK's *The History Book*, which was published in 2016. He contributed to Chapters 1, 2, and 3 of *Journey*.

4

THE AGE OF EMPIRES

5

THE AGE OF STEAM

6

THE GOLDEN AGE OF TRAVEL

7

THE AGE OF FLIGHT

Foreword

"Those who sail close to the shore never discover new lands." A young American student, full of youthful enthusiasm, said this to me while I was teaching archeology at the American University of Rome. I thought how well the words, adapted from a 1925 novel by French writer André Gide, summed up the human desire to travel.

For some 60,000 years, humans have explored the world, out of necessity and curiosity. Our ancestors, who first lived in caves and makeshift shelters, hunted and foraged. The rivers were both a source of food and also a means of transport. As humans began to herd animals, they needed to travel for pasture. So began the fascinating story of humanity's journey, filled with light and shade.

The most significant inventions in antiquity were the sail, which transformed rafts into boats, and the wheel, which made it possible for our ancestors to travel wide distances. Humans also learned to harness animals to pull chariots and coaches. The Ancient Romans developed a highway system that linked their ever-expanding empire. The Ancient Greeks, meanwhile, devised a complex astrolabe to chart the seas using the stars and planets, and a system of longitude and latitude, enabling sailors to undertake lengthy voyages. Despite these astronomical advances, for centuries mariners believed the Earth was flat, but still sailed the oceans. They were aware of the dangers of their missions but resolutely continued

to push the boundaries. Others scaled the snowy heights of unknown mountains, often for the thrill and sense of adventure. Many risked and lost their lives for little more than the spectacular view from the highest peaks in the world.

Each generation has contributed to novel means of travel. Leonardo da Vinci, for example, conceived the original idea of a helicopter in 1493, but it was only in the last century that airborne travel became commonplace. Today, luxury tourism is the largest-growing industry in the world. Voyages into space continue to broaden our understanding of the vast expanses beyond our galaxy, yet the sea floor, beneath the oceans that cover 70 percent of our planet, still remains largely unexplored.

Journey explores travel in all its varied forms. In this wonderful book, we have gathered extraordinary accounts of exploration, exile, pilgrimage, refuge, crusades, trade, colonization, and conquest. I hope that as you read it and enjoy the stunning images, in your mind's eye you will leave the shores and push out into the deep. Many people have gone before us, and we can be sure that many more will pass beyond the limits of our present horizons.

Michael Collins

Introduction

Humans have always been wanderers. Our distant ancestors were nomads for thousands of years before they founded any settlements. Beyond the many practical motives for travel—the pursuit of trade, warfare, pilgrimage, the search for new lands to settle or conquer—there has always been a more primitive human urge, the impulse to find out just what lies over the next range of hills, to trace a river all the way back to its source or sail along an unfamiliar coastline, to explore ever further and deeper into the unknown.

Looking back from the present hi-tech age, the scale of the journeys once made by people who traveled only on foot, on horseback, or in small boats propelled by sails or oars is simply astonishing. The soldiers of Alexander the Great marched all the way from Greece to northern India, while the Mediterranean sailors of the ancient world ventured as far as the southern tip of Africa. Without so much as a compass to guide them, the Vikings sailed from Scandinavia to the shores of North America, and Polynesian sailors set off across vast expanses of the Pacific Ocean in search of new islands to colonize.

Long journeys to distant places were not the preserve of a bold minority of adventurers. In medieval times, thousands of pilgrims from Christian Europe undertook arduous journeys by land and sea to visit the holy places of Jerusalem, as did Muslims to Mecca, and merchants transported goods in caravans across the arid wastes of the Sahara Desert or along the mountainous Silk Road from China to Europe.

About 500 years ago, the oceanic voyages of Christopher Columbus and other European sailors made it possible for cartographers to draw up broadly accurate maps of the world for the first time. But for centuries after these voyages of discovery, many areas of the world remained a mystery. Even in the 20th century, people were still foraying across uncharted deserts or jungles, or to places where no human had set foot before, such as the Arctic and Antarctica.

As steamships, railways and, later, aircraft made long-distance journeys more common, the romance of travel was sustained by luxury and novelty, from the Orient Express and Blue Riband liners to airships and flying boats. More recently the ocean depths and outer space have provided new places to explore, and the lust for adventure has been satisfied by fresh challenges to human endurance, from treks through rainforests or across polar regions to flying around the world in balloons or solar-powered aircraft. The one thing it seems that humans will never do is stay at home.

▷ **Desceliers's world map**
This map was created around the 1530s by French chartmaker Pierre Desceliers. Made in the style of a sea chart, it has compass roses and navigation lines, but was clearly a work of art rather than for use at sea.

“ I travel not to go anywhere, but **to go**. I travel for **travel's sake**. The **great affair is to move**. ”

ROBERT LOUIS STEVENSON, *TRAVELS WITH A DONKEY IN THE CEVENNES*

CANADA
MER DE FRANCE
MER DESPAIGNE
MER OCCEANE
DE CANCER
MER DES ENTILLES
EVROPPE
AFRIQUE
LA LIGNE
LA ZONA TORRIDA
AMERIQUE
TROPIQUE
DE
MER AUSTRALLE
Riuiere de plate
estroict de magellan

THE
ANCIENT
WORLD
3000 BCE—400 CE

THE ANCIENT WORLD, 3000 BCE–400 CE

Introduction

The ability to travel swiftly over long distances is common to many species, but bipedalism, coupled with a slightness of build, hunter-gatherer instincts, and an apparently insatiable curiosity, are all hallmarks of *homo sapiens*—a creature for whom no stone, it seems, can be left unturned. Exploration—that restless need to shine light on the unknown—is the lifeblood of the species. Thanks to our ability to conceptualize, we can imagine better worlds and search for them—sometimes cooperating, sometimes warring along the way.

The first travelers

We do not know the name of the first traveler, or what journey they made, but no doubt they were a hunter-gatherer, searching for shelter, food, or water. Foraging and returning to the fold may have been a daily, weekly, or monthly routine. With the advent of farming and the domestication of animals, shepherds traveled with their flocks from winter to summer pastures and back again. Nomads moved in search of water and grazing lands, while armed warriors moved across the lands in search of booty and conquest.

International trade developed when the first cities were founded in Mesopotamia in the third millennium BCE. These cities traded goods and services with their neighbors, and their merchants traveled great distances by land and sea in search of markets. Echoes of long-distance trade around the Indian Ocean can be heard in the *Epic of Gilgamesh*, dating to around 2100 BCE. Likewise, in the Mediterranean, the Minoans of the second millennium BCE traded goods across the inland sea. Meanwhile, the

AN ASSYRIAN RELIEF c.800 BCE DEPICTS CEDARWOOD BEING SHIPPED FROM LEBANON

A ROMAN MOSAIC PORTRAYS THE GREEKS' ARCHETYPAL TRAVELER, ODYSSEUS

A 7TH-CENTURY FRESCO SHOWS CHINESE DIPLOMAT ZHANG QIAN TRAVELING IN CENTRAL ASIA

> " A man who has been through **bitter experiences** and traveled far **enjoys even his sufferings after a time**. "
>
> HOMER, THE *ODYSSEY*

Egyptians bartered with the fabulous land of Punt, and the Phoenicians, who sold dye, reconnoitered the entire coast of Africa. By the first millennium BCE, the Polynesians were already voyaging across the vast expanse of the Pacific Ocean—not for trade, but to find new islands.

The classical world

The Greeks of the 5th century BCE produced the first map of the known world. Herodotus, the "Father of History," recorded voyages to distant lands in the 4th century, while Pytheas traveled north from his beloved Mediterranean to the unknown and icy Thule (possibly Iceland) in around 325 BCE. Couriers ran an efficient long-distance postal service throughout the Persian Empire. Alexander the Great conquered vast lands, spreading Greek culture but also absorbing much from the lands which he and his armies invaded. In China, diplomacy sent Zhang Qian out into the world in the 2nd century BCE, preparing the ground for that international artery of trade, the Silk Road, which ran between China and Europe.

In their organized and efficient way, the Romans revolutionized travel. Their road system made movement around their vast empire relatively straightforward, and travelers were aided by road maps and roadside inns. Likewise, the seafarers of the Indian Ocean made use of detailed guides to the ports and coastlands along their routes, while Strabo and Ptolemy established geography as an academic subject. Slowly, the world was becoming more familiar to its inhabitants, and the possibilities of travel, not just for trade but also for adventure and pure exploration, were multiplying accordingly.

THE ROADS BUILT BY THE ROMANS INCREASED TRAVEL THROUGHOUT THEIR EMPIRE

PTOLEMY'S WORLD MAP OF c.150 CE REMAINED AUTHORITATIVE UNTIL THE RENAISSANCE

THE PURPLE DYE SOLD BY THE PHOENICIANS WAS LOVED BY EMPERORS SUCH AS JUSTINIAN I

Journeys from the cradle

In around 2340 BCE, the world's first empire arose in Sumer in Mesopotamia. Ruled by King Sargon of Agade, it traded food, ceramics, metals, and precious stones with its many neighbors in the region.

The empire created by Sargon of Agade emerged in the fertile lands between the Tigris and Euphrates rivers, in what is now southern Iraq. The rivers provided water to drink and irrigation for crops, as well as a means of travel. Apart from water, however, the raw materials required for the military campaigns and conquests of the empire were in short supply. All that its sandy soil could produce was little more than grain and other basic crops, as well as the necessary mud and straw for building houses.

All the necessities of an empire, therefore, had to be imported. Wood to construct ships and wagons came from the cedar trees of Lebanon to the west, while tin and copper to make tools, weapons, and utensils came from Anatolia to the north, Sinai to the south, or Iran to the east. Stone for building also came from Anatolia, and ceramics from India. Gold, silver, and precious gemstones came from across the region. Pearls were sourced from Bahrain in the Persian Gulf, turquoise and ivory from India, and deep blue lapis lazuli, used for jewelry and incorporated into the panels of the Standard of Ur, came all the way from distant Afghanistan.

IN CONTEXT
Sargon of Agade

The exact location of Agade (or Akkad) is still unknown, but archaeologists presume it was in southern Mesopotamia, on the banks of one of the branches of the Euphrates River. The ancient *Sumerian King List*, a stone tablet written in Sumerian that records all the kings of Sumer, names Sargon as the son of a gardener and then the cup-bearer to King Ur-Zababa of Kish, who reigned for around six years before Sargon deposed him. Sargon then ruled his new kingdom from around 2340 to 2284 BCE, although some sources suggest his reign only lasted 37 years. During this time, he conquered the whole of Mesopotamia and extended his power to the Mediterranean coast and into modern-day Turkey and Iran.

BRONZE HEAD OF SARGON, c.2300 BCE

▷ **Standard of Ur**
The Standard of Ur, a wooden box of unknown purpose, dates to around 2600 BCE. Its sides are covered with intricate, inlaid mosaics depicting scenes of war and peace.

The first travelers

Such goods were traded by merchants along recognized trade routes, the products passing from merchant to merchant as they were carried by pack animals such as donkeys, or hauled in wagons toward Sumer. Bulk goods were shipped by boat up and down the Euphrates, the Tigris being less amenable to travel. The merchants would reach a market town where they would then sell on their goods to the next merchant before returning home. It is these traders who were the journeymen of Sumer, the travelers of the empire. Most would have been foreigners bringing their goods and products for sale in Sumer. They spoke the many different languages of the region, and

▽ **The Sumerian Empire**
Sargon of Agade conquered the city-states of Mesopotamia to create a single unified empire. Trade routes spread out to India in the east, and to Europe and Africa in the west.

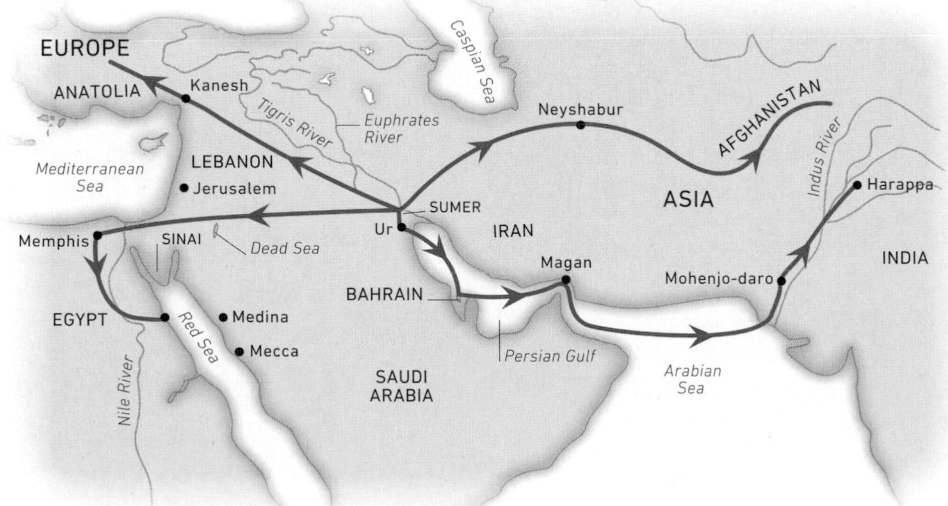

◁ **Bill of sale**
Clay tablets inscribed in a Sumerian cuneiform script have been found in the city of Shuruppak. Dating to around 2500 BCE, they record the goods bought and sold in the city, including shipments of silver for the city's governor.

although few would have been literate, their knowledge of the known world was immense.

Around the known world

The scale and scope of the journeys these merchant-travelers undertook was extensive. The resin found in the royal tomb of Queen Puabi, who ruled Ur in around 2600 BCE, came from Mozambique on the southeast coast of Africa, and clay seals recording commercial transactions have been found bearing the Indus Valley script of the distant Indus Empire in India. A detailed record of this long-distance trade is found in *The Epic of Gilgamesh*, a lengthy epic poem written about Gilgamesh, King of Uruk, who ruled around 2100 BCE.

The other travelers of the empire were the soldiers of Sumer, who sallied forth around the region for conquest and plunder. Wagons similar to those they would have used feature on the Standard of Ur, which depicts, among many things, the Sumerian army on the move. These soldiers were often abroad for many months, traveling across new lands, before returning home when their victories were won. The empire that Sargon and his soldiers created lasted for around 200 years until, in 2154 BCE, it collapsed altogether after the invading Gutians, a nomadic people from the Zagros Mountains in western Iran, overran the empire.

▽ **Sargon on campaign**
This 20th-century illustration shows Sargon leading his army in Syria. The Mediterranean gave him easy access to Europe and North Africa.

△ **Ship procession**
In this fresco from Akrotiri—a Bronze Age settlement on the island of Thera—a Minoan ship is rowed past a coastal town. The fresco has kept its strong colors, despite its great age.

Minoan seafarers

Europe's first civilization took root on Crete around 3000 BCE. It was established by the Minoans, whose voyages around the eastern Mediterranean coast made them among the first travelers in Europe.

Until the late 19th century, historians and archaeologists were unsure about the ancient history of Europe. Existing historical records dated the first European Iron Age civilization to the 8th or 7th century BCE, but the Greek myths of Homer suggest that an earlier, bronze-using civilization must have flourished somewhere. In 1870, the German archaeologist Heinrich Schliemann discovered the Bronze Age site of Troy in modern-day Turkey, and then went on to find gold at Mycenae on the Greek mainland. But the most important find took place in 1900, when British archaeologist Arthur Evans discovered the magnificent palace at Knossos, on Crete. He dated the site to around 2000 BCE, and in doing so established the island as the birthplace of European civilization. As Knossos was the legendary birthplace of King Minos of Crete, this newly discovered civilization became known as the Minoan.

Minoan travel

Crete is not the most fertile of islands, but the Minoans cultivated the hillsides to grow olives and vines for wine, and they used the limited farmland to grow wheat. Sheep roamed the hills, providing wool for a flourishing textile industry. All these commodities were traded throughout the Greek islands, and across the eastern Mediterranean. Evidence of their trade has been found in Egypt, Cyprus, Turkey, and the Levant, where Minoan artifacts have been discovered in the palace of Tel Kabri, in what is now northern Israel.

The Minoans established their first overseas colony on the nearby island of Kythira in around 1600–1450 BCE, and later settled on Kea, Melos, Rhodes, and Thera (modern-day Santorini), as well as Avaris, in the Nile Delta, around 1700–1450 BCE. To carry out trade and to travel to their overseas colonies, the Minoans built a fleet of ships. Some of these were used to suppress the pirates that preyed on their boats in the Aegean.

Unfortunately, the names of any intrepid Minoan sailors remain unknown. The first Minoan script was in hieroglyphs, recorded on unbaked clay tablets, few of which have survived. In around 1700 BCE, a new script, based on syllables and known as Linear A, was introduced. Neither of these scripts has been deciphered, which means that much of Minoan history is still to be revealed, including the origin of this great civilization. A study of Cretan place names suggests that the Minoans did not speak an Indo-European language, implying they were not Greeks—but exactly where they did come from is unclear.

The end of an era

In 1628 BCE, a massive volcanic explosion destroyed the Minoan settlements on Thera. Excavations at Akrotiri in the 1960s and '70s, however, revealed a large palace with many fine frescos that survived. Volcanic fallout damaged the palaces on Crete, but they were restored, only to be wrecked again in around 1450 BCE. No one knows the nature of that second catastrophe—it may have been an earthquake or the arrival of the Mycenaeans—but the palace of Knossos alone remained standing.

◁ **The Minoan civilization**
Minoan kingdoms were established on Crete in around 2000 BCE, and Knossos became the dominant power in around 1700 BCE. The Minoans then extended their power north into the islands of the Aegean.

◁ **Minoan ceramics**
The Minoans were skilled at creating beautiful jugs, plates, bowls, and other objects in ceramics. They would be painted or engraved for decoration.

◁ **Minoan ship**
The Minoans built simple wooden ships powered with a single sail, or by rows of oars. They used these ships to trade with other islands and to travel around the Mediterranean.

Two steering oars, located at the stern of the boat, were used to guide the ship's course.

A single mast supports a broad sail woven from linen or Egyptian papyrus.

IN CONTEXT
Bronze Age grandeur

The palace of Knossos dates from around 1900 BCE. It consists of a series of multi-story buildings containing state rooms, shrines, archives, workshops, and numerous grain and oil stores, all arranged around a central courtyard. The palace had a sophisticated drainage and sewage system. Discovered by Arthur Evans in 1900 CE, the palace has been partially restored, revealing the splendor of its decoration and richness of its contents. The palace was taken over by the Mycenaeans in around 1450 BCE and occupied until it was destroyed by fire and finally abandoned in around 1200 BCE.

KNOSSOS PALACE, RESTORED TO SHOW SOME OF ITS ORIGINAL COLOR

Travel in ancient Egypt

The ancient Egyptians were great travelers who sailed up the Nile and across the seas in sturdy wooden boats. They also used two-wheeled war chariots, both as weapons and for transport.

△ **Relief of Harkhuf**
Harkhuf was born on Elephantine, an island on the Nile, and became governor of Upper Egypt. Most of what we know about him comes from the inscriptions on his tomb at Aswan.

The Nile River was the lifeblood of ancient Egypt, providing water for drinking and cooking, and irrigation for the crops that grew along its banks. The annual flood fertilized the fields. Above all, the Nile was the highway of Egypt, the main artery of communication that held the country together. People traveled up and down the Nile in wooden boats driven by large sails, while cargo ships carried grain, livestock, and even huge blocks of granite to build new temples and palaces. The Egyptians named their ships, just as we do today; one commander started off aboard a ship called *Northern* and was later promoted to captain *Rising in Memphis*.

At first, the Egyptians restricted their voyages to the Nile, but by 2700 BCE, they were exploring both the Red Sea and the Mediterranean Sea. During the reign of Sneferu (2613–2589 BCE), a huge fleet of 40 seagoing ships sailed north across the Mediterranean to Byblos, in what is now Lebanon, to collect cedar wood. During the reign of Queen Hatshepsut (1478–1458 BCE), another large trading fleet sailed down the Red Sea and into the Indian Ocean to the land of Punt (see pp. 22–23).

The travels of Harkhuf

A lot is known about Egyptian travelers due to the *Autobiography of Harkhuf*, a series of inscriptions on a tomb at Qubbet el-Hawa, one of a number of rock-cut tombs on the western bank of the Nile, opposite modern-day Aswan. The inscriptions record that Harkhuf, who was born nearby, was appointed governor of Upper Egypt by King Merenre I (r. 2287–2278 BCE) and oversaw the trading caravans that headed south to Nubia.

Harkhuf was tasked with increasing trade with Nubia and building alliances with local Nubian leaders, to prepare the ground for Egyptian expansion into their country. He led at least four expeditions into Nubia, and brought back on one trip someone he described to the young pharaoh Pepi II as a "dwarf"—most probably a pigmy.

On one of these expeditions, Harkhuf traveled to the land of Iyam. It is not certain where Iyam was, but it was probably on the fertile plain that opens out south of modern-day Khartoum, where the Blue Nile meets the White Nile, although some historians believe it lay in the Libyan Desert to the west of Egypt.

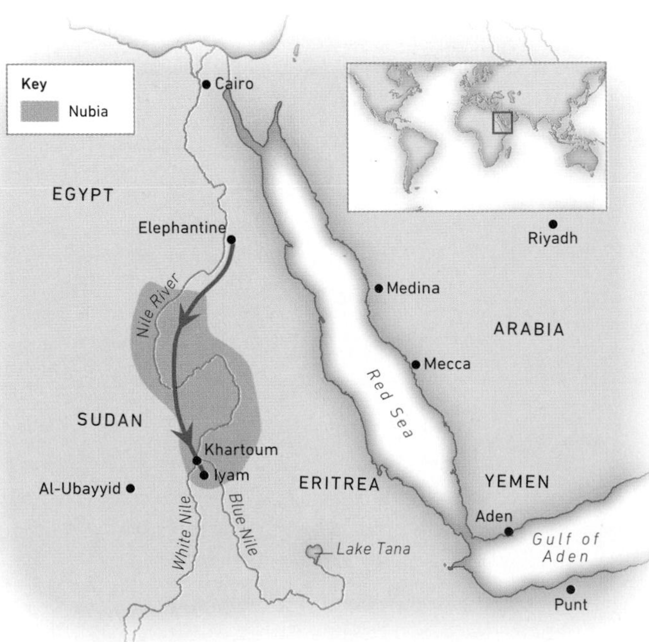

◁ **Harkhuf's travels**
Harkhuf led at least four major expeditions south into Nubia. On one of these journeys, he visited Iyam, a place many now believe is located south of modern Khartoum in Sudan.

Sails powered the boat; oars were used in poor wind.

◁ **Nubian traders**
The Nubians lived along the upper reaches of the Nile to the south of Egypt. They traded gold, ebony, ivory, copper, incense, and wild animals with the Egyptians. During the Middle Kingdom (2040–1640 BCE), the Egyptians expanded into Nubia and gradually took over the country.

Traveling by chariot

The second mode of transportation used by the ancient Egyptians was the chariot. Both the chariot and the horse were introduced into Egypt by the Hyksos invaders of the 16th century BCE. The chariot itself was a lightly built, wooden affair with two spoked wheels, manned by two soldiers and pulled by two horses.

These chariots were incredibly effective weapons of war. The chariot served as a mobile platform from which soldier-archers could fire at the enemy. During the Battle of Kadesh in 1274 BCE, near modern-day Homs in Syria, Pharaoh Ramesses II (r. 1279–1213 BCE) led about 2,000 war chariots into battle against the Hittites, who opposed him with at least 3,700 war chariots of their own. Evidence of these chariots can be seen in the tomb paintings of the pharaoh Tutankhamun (r. 1332–1323 BCE) and in the many paintings of Ramesses II at war. Away from the battlefield, chariots were used in the civilian world to transport people and goods quickly and efficiently from place to place.

◁ **On wheels**
The war chariot was used as a means of transportation. Here, a scribe is driven by a charioteer who controls two horses using long reins.

A rear steering oar kept the boat on course.

◁ **Watercraft**
The Egyptians built small riverboats and larger seagoing boats out of cedar planks nailed together. The gaps between the planks were sealed with pitch.

The expedition to Punt

About 3,500 years ago, Queen Hatshepsut of Egypt sent an expedition to the mysterious land of Punt. A record of the voyage survives, carved in stone.

The location of the country that the ancient Egyptians called Punt is an unsolved puzzle. The best guess is that it lay on the east coast of Africa, perhaps in modern-day Somalia or Eritrea. Punt had long been the source of highly valued incense used in Egyptian religious ceremonies, but it had remained an unknown, semi-mythical country. The story of the expedition is told in a bas-relief at the temple that was erected at Hatshepsut's burial site at Thebes (now Luxor), after her death in 1458 BCE. An oracle of the god Amun apparently instructed Hatshepsut to send the mission to Punt. Five boats crammed with Egyptian officials, soldiers, servants, and trade goods sailed south down the Red Sea, under the command of Hatshepsut's chancellor, Nehasi. Each boat had a square-rigged sail and 30 oarsmen. They kept close to the coast, as they were fearful of the dangers of the open sea. Arriving at Punt, they marched inland across a series of hills. The temple bas-relief depicts Punt as a place with lush vegetation, cattle grazing, and domed houses on stilts, accessed by ladders.

The unexpected visitors received a warm and respectful welcome from Punt's rulers, King Parahu and Queen Ati, who expressed amazement that they had found "this country unknown to men." They exchanged jewelry and weapons for a host of exotic products: elephant tusks, leopard skins, rare woods, and, above all, the trees from which frankincense and myrrh were extracted. These were carried back to Egypt and planted to produce their own incense. The bas-relief shows the Egyptians also returning with live animals, including pet baboons on leashes.

The expedition sailed back northward along the Red Sea coast, then journeyed overland by donkey caravan to the Nile Delta, before setting sail again and traveling up the Nile to Thebes. There the incense trees were planted in a garden dedicated to the god Amun. The existence of the bas-relief in Hatshepsut's temple testifies to the importance the Egyptians attached to the success of this bold mission beyond the boundaries of their known world.

◁ **Egyptian soldiers on the expedition**
These Egyptian soldiers taking part in the Punt expedition are depicted on a wall of Hatshepsut's mortuary temple. The ruined building is at Deir el-Bahri on the west bank of the Nile, opposite Luxor.

Polynesian navigators

Some of the most amazing journeys in the history of navigation were made by the people who left Asia thousands of years ago to sail across the Pacific and settle on the islands of Polynesia.

The story of Polynesian navigation begins more than 2,000 years ago, when people, probably originally from islands in Southest Asia, sailed across the northern Pacific and began to settle in the western islands of Micronesia. From there, they spread further, making sea journeys to settle much further south, on islands such as Samoa and Tonga. The dates of these migrations are uncertain, because the people left no written records, but it is likely that the settlement of the southern islands took place between around 1300 and 900 BCE. By the 13th century CE, all of Polynesia, bordered by Hawaii in the north, Easter Island in the east, and New Zealand in the south, had probably been settled.

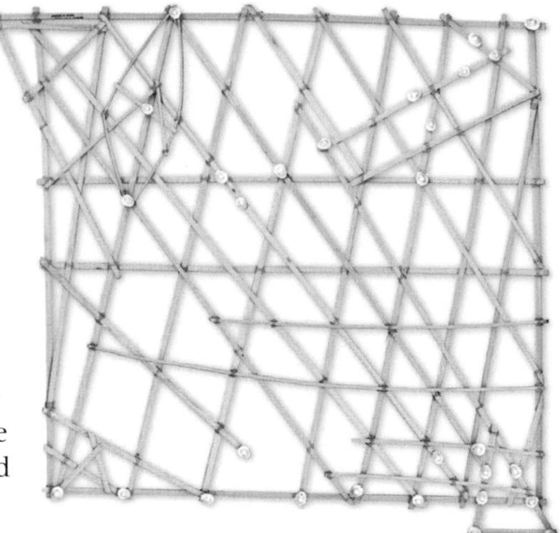

△ **Stick map**
Polynesian navigators made maps out of sticks and lengths of thread, which represented the swells and currents around islands. Shells were used to depict islands, although the precise symbols varied from one mapmaker to another.

Wind, sea, and sky

The people who made these perilous journeys traveled in outrigger canoes (canoes with stabilizing floats) made of wood. They had no navigational instruments, and early historians often explained their journeys by suggesting that they were blown off-course by storms. However, modern Polynesian sailors can navigate in the traditional way, without instruments, and their ancestors no doubt did the same. They worked out which way they were going using a combination of techniques—observing the stars, watching the ocean, and following the migration routes of birds. Polynesian sailors use similar methods today, but benefit from a knowledge of the positions of islands that their ancestors could not have had.

Like all early navigators, they took clues from the sky. The position of the rising and setting sun gave the compass directions, and stars provided other key reference points. Cloud formations also provided useful information. For example, certain types of cloud often formed above islands, and clouds moving in a V formation sometimes

▷ **Bora Bora**
This view of the island of Bora Bora, one of the Society Islands, shows one of its peaks, which is part of an extinct volcano. The island was probably first settled by Polynesians around the 4th century CE.

indicated land—a phenomenon caused by clouds reacting to heat rising from an island's surface. It was even possible to work out something about the type of land by the color of the cloud, since clouds tend to appear darker above forests and lighter above sand.

Migration routes and swells

Experience at sea also gave sailors an understanding of swell patterns. Swells are waves that are generated by distant winds and weather systems, and they can form regular patterns, which help sailors to navigate. The Polynesians would keep their canoes at the same angle to the swells they observed. Navigators would then pay close attention to any sudden changes in the motion of the canoe to indicate that they were veering off-course.

The movements of birds could also give navigators information about the position of land. Some Pacific birds migrate over long distances, and so could have helped sailors navigate to distant lands. For example, the long-tailed cuckoo might have helped people sail from the Cook Islands to New Zealand—and the Pacific golden plover follows a route between Tahiti and Hawaii.

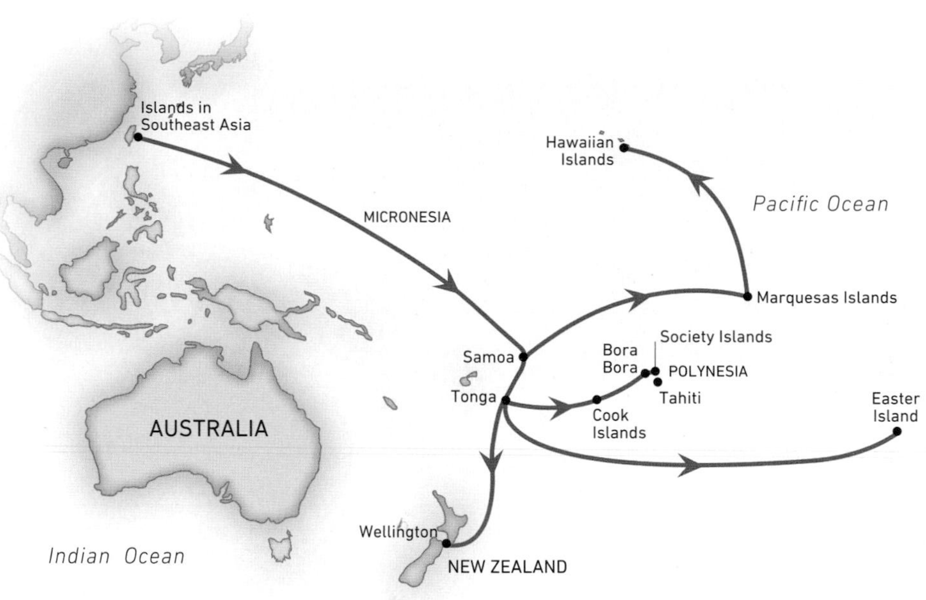

◁ **Polynesian expansion**
Polynesian navigators conquered a vast area of the Pacific known today as the Polynesian Triangle. Hawaii, Easter Island, and New Zealand form the three points of the triangle.

▷ **Long-tailed cuckoo**
The Pacific long-tailed cuckoo is shown here with its young, and a grey warbler. It is one of the birds whose migrations follow a route between the Cook Islands and New Zealand.

Inherited information

As navigators encountered islands that were new to them, they were added to their mental atlas, and their position memorized in relation to the stars. They then passed on this knowledge to their children by word of mouth and by making charts, including diagrams made of sticks and shells. By the time of the first western contact, local sailors' knowledge was vast. British explorer Captain James Cook (see pp. 172–75) reported the navigator Tupaian from Raiatea in the Society Islands, who helped Cook on his first expedition in the area, knew some 130 islands within a 1,988-mile (3,200-km) radius of his home.

IN CONTEXT
Voyaging canoes

The Polynesians were skilled boat builders. They used small canoes with dug-out hulls and outriggers for short journeys, but for long voyages a much larger, double-hulled vessel evolved. This typically had two plank-built hulls, connected by beams lashed together with plant fibers, and sometimes fitted with a deck between the hulls. The timbers were thoroughly caulked, probably with tree sap. Although fitted with large sails made of a fiber such as *hala*, the craft could also be paddled. Voyaging canoes could be up to 98 feet (30 m) long, and had enough space to carry several families, plus their belongings and supplies.

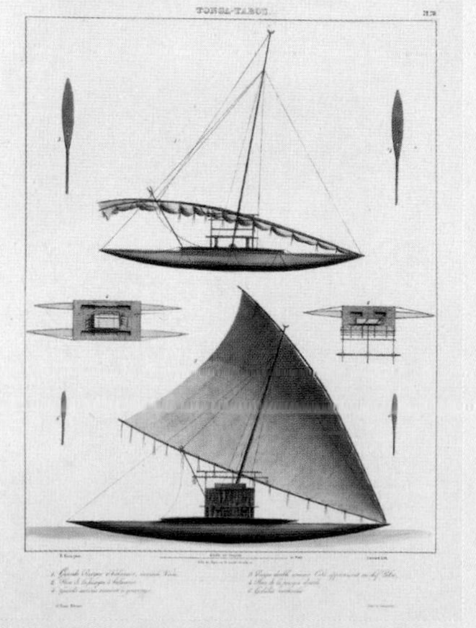

AN 1820s DRAWING OF TWIN-HULLED AND OUTRIGGER SAILING CANOES FROM TONGA

Around Africa

The Phoenicians traded across a vast maritime empire based around the Mediterranean Sea between 1500 and 300 BCE. They even sailed around Africa—the first people to accomplish this remarkable feat.

△ **Imperial purple** The purple dye discovered by the Phoenicians was highly prized as its color did not fade. It was later restricted to being used only by the Byzantine imperial court, hence its name.

The Phoenicians lived along the eastern coastline of the Mediterranean Sea, in the areas that are now Lebanon, Syria, Israel, Palestine, and Turkey. Their first capital was at Byblos, Lebanon, but was moved further south, to Tyre, in 1200 BCE. In 814 BCE, however, they transferred their capital and center of operations across the Mediterranean to Carthage, in what is now Tunisia. The Phoenicians did not create a single, unified empire with vast tracts of land. Instead, they established their expanding number of ports, which were scattered around the southern Mediterranean coastline, as independent city-states. The name of this vast empire, Phoenicia, was coined by the ancient Greeks, in reference to the "land of purple," as the Phoenicians were renowned for their trade in the purple dye derived from the Murex snail. They also developed a royal blue dye from a related snail.

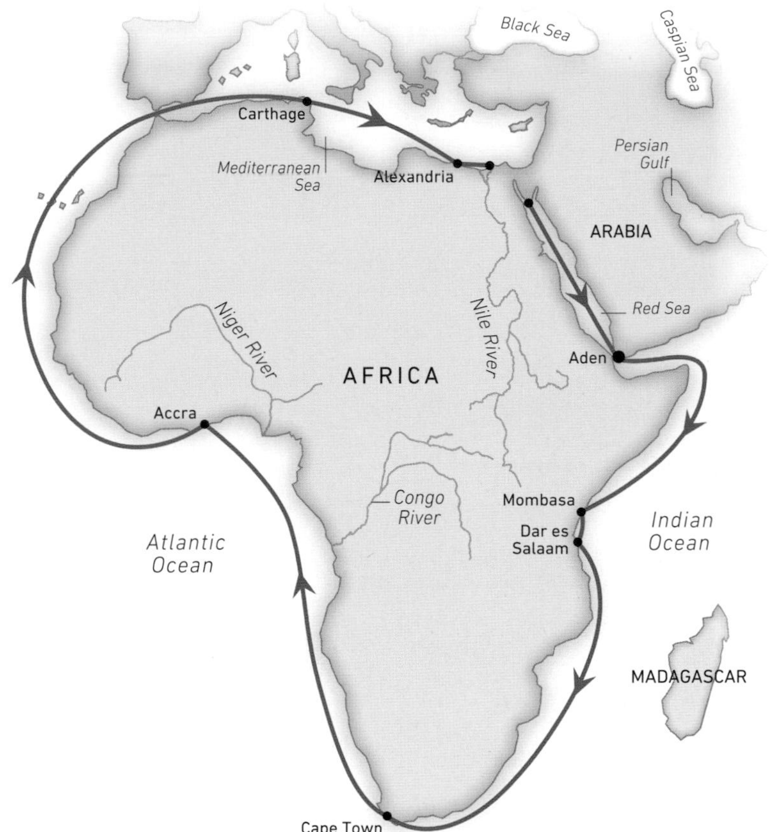

△ **Route around Africa** The exact route taken by the Phoenicians is unknown, but it is thought they sailed south into the Indian Ocean before heading west around Africa. They then went north up the Atlantic Ocean and east across the Mediterranean Sea.

Trade and culture

The Phoenicians lived by trade. They sold wine to the Egyptians in terra-cotta jars, and bought Nubian gold in return. They also traded with the Somalis of eastern Africa. With the Greeks, they traded wood and glass, as well as slaves and the fabled purple cloth. They acquired silver from Sardinia and Spain, which they traded with King Solomon of Israel. Tin was obtained from Galicia on the Atlantic coast of Spain, and even from distant Britain. They mixed this metal with copper from Cyprus to create the harder bronze alloy. The Phoenicians sailed the Mediterranean in tub-shaped merchant ships. As they traded on the seas, they spread the use of their alphabet throughout the region. The Greeks adopted this alphabet and then passed it on to the Romans, creating the Roman alphabet that is still in use around the world today.

▷ **Silver coin** This silver coin depicts the merchant ships that brought such great wealth to the Phoenicians. It also shows a mythical sea horse.

Phoenician exploration

Although there is a lot of archaeological evidence of the Phoenician's travels, there is little in the way of written evidence. Ancient Gaelic myths recount a Phoenician and Scythian expedition to Ireland led by the king of Scythia, Fénius Farsa. A Greek *periplus* manuscript listing ports and coastal landmarks also records that in the 6th or 5th century BCE, Hanno the Navigator set sail from Carthage with 60 ships to explore northwest Africa. He set up seven colonies in what is now Morocco, and possibly reached as far south as Gabon on the Equator.

The most fascinating account of Phoenician travel occurs in Herodotus' *The Histories*, in which he records that Pharaoh Necho II of Egypt, (r. 610–595 BCE), sent a Phoenician expedition down the Red Sea around 600 BCE. For three years, the fleet sailed down the Indian Ocean and

◁ **Phoenician galleys**
The ancient Greeks had two names for Phoenician ships: *galloi* (tubs) and *hippoi* (horses), as the ships were tub-shaped with horse heads on each end. This carving is from the palace of the Assyrian king, Sargon II, in Dur-Sharrukin.

> “These people ... began at once, they say, to **adventure** on **long journeys**, **freighting their vessels** with the **wares** of Egypt and Assyria.”
>
> HERODOTUS, WRITING IN *THE HISTORIES*, c. 440 BCE

around the southern tip of Africa, before sailing north up the Atlantic and back into the Mediterranean Sea to return to the mouth of the Nile. Herodotus records that as the Phoenicians “sailed on a westerly course round the southern end of Libya [Africa], they had the sun on their right”—that is, to the north of them. Herodotus heard this information by word of mouth but did not believe it because, like most people then, he did not know that Africa was surrounded by ocean and thought it was connected to Asia. There is also some doubt as to whether Necho II would authorize such an expedition. Whether or not this journey took place, the Phoenicians were nonetheless the creators of an impressive maritime empire.

IN PROFILE
Herodotus

Herodotus was born in Halicarnassus, in what was then the Persian Empire (now Bodrum, in Turkey), around 484 BCE. He was widely known as “The Father of History” because of his book *The Histories*, which he wrote in 440 BCE. This book was a record of the recent wars between the Persians and the Greeks, and included a great deal of cultural and geographical information. Herodotus was the first historian to treat historical evidence systematically and to arrange it into chronological order. Some of his stories are fanciful—or even wrong—but he does clearly state that he was only reporting what was told to him by others. Herodotus died in Macedon around 425 BCE.

MARBLE BUST OF HERODOTUS, 2ND CENTURY CE

Persian couriers

The mighty Persian Achaemenid Empire bestrode the known world in the 6th century BCE. It was connected by a series of royal roads, along which couriers carried messages, and merchants and traders moved in peace.

△ **Chariot of gold**
One of the pieces in the Oxus Treasure is this 4-in (10-cm) tall gold chariot with a driver, a passenger, and a team of four small horses (one of which has lost a leg). The wheels of the chariot would once have turned freely.

The Achaemenid Empire, founded in 550 BCE by Cyrus the Great, was the greatest empire the world had ever seen up to that time. At its height under Darius I (r. 522–486 BCE), its population of around 50 million people included at least 44 percent of the entire population of the world. This empire stretched from Greece and Libya in the west to India and Central Asia in the east. The empire was efficient and well governed. Persian satraps ruled its many provinces and one official language was used to conduct business. To speed up royal communications, Darius I built a series of roads on which mounted couriers could travel, of which the Royal Road is the most famous. That road began on the Aegean coast and headed east to the royal city of Susa. One branch extended northeast from Babylon into central Persia and on to the Silk Road, the ancient trading route between China and the West. Another branch continued southeast to the royal capital of Persepolis.

The Angarium

Cyrus made sure that official messages and instructions from the king could be transmitted quickly to officials in the distant provinces, and their reports received back again, by establishing

▷ **Darius I**
Darius I was the third of the great kings of the Persian Achaemenid Empire, which he ruled at its peak. He strengthened its government, introduced standard weights and measures, and made Aramaic the official language.

an imperial postal service. This service employed mounted couriers known as the Angarium. These couriers were well trained and were paid handsomely for their efforts on behalf of the king. Each day, the couriers and their fresh horses waited in one of 111 stations placed at intervals a day's ride apart from each other along the Royal Road. Each courier rode with the message for one day and then handed it over to a waiting courier who did the same the following day. In this way, the relay of couriers could carry a message along the entire road in a week, a journey that would have taken 90 days on foot. Herodotus, the Greek historian, noted of the Angarium that, "There is nothing in the world that travels faster than these Persian couriers." Further words of praise from Herodotus, quoted at the top right of this page, are still read today, as they are inscribed on the main post office in New York and are sometimes thought of as the creed of the United States Postal Service.

Lifeline of the Empire

The couriers were not the only people to travel these new roads. Merchants and traders carried their goods for sale, often walking for many miles. Darius I built a series of royal caravanserais, or roadside inns, along the roads, where they could stay at night and refresh themselves and their pack animals.

> " **Neither snow nor rain** nor heat nor **gloom of night** stays these **couriers** from the **swift completion** of their **appointed rounds**. "
>
> HERODOTUS, *HISTORIES*, c.440 BCE

The roads were also used by troops who had be able to move rapidly to defend the borders from Persia's enemies. Some soldiers, especially senior officials, traveled in two-wheeled chariots pulled by two to four horses. Priests of the official Zoroastrian religion traveled the roads on religious business, while farmers moved their flocks, and families walked to meet and celebrate with each other. The Royal Road and its offshoots were the lifeline of the Achaemenid Empire.

IN CONTEXT
The Oxus Treasure

Although the exact time and place remain unclear, it is known that in around 1880 BCE a vast hoard of gold, silver, and coins from the Persian Achaemenid Empire was found next to the Oxus River in central Asia. The treasure probably once belonged to a temple, where it had been left as a votive offerings to gain favor with the gods, but it is not known why it was buried. The treasure shows the huge skills of the Persian craftsmen who molded and shaped the gold and silver. It can now be seen on display in the British Museum in London.

A GOLDEN AMULET AND A SMALL SILVER STATUE OF A KING

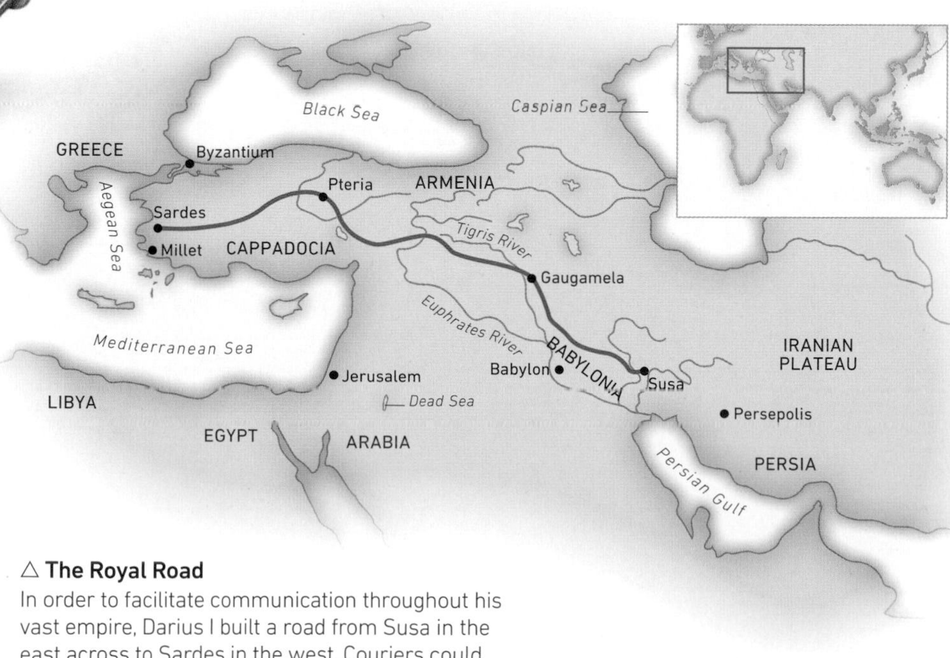

△ **The Royal Road**
In order to facilitate communication throughout his vast empire, Darius I built a road from Susa in the east across to Sardes in the west. Couriers could travel its 1,677 miles (2,699 km) in seven days.

The Temple of Hera
Greek culture spread throughout the Mediterranean. This 19th-century engraving shows the Temple of Hera in Paestum, a major Greek city on the southwest coast of Italy.

The Greek world

Over the course of many centuries, the ancient Greeks developed one of the most advanced civilizations in the world. It was a centre of philosophy, learning, ingenious architecture, and maritime exploration.

The Greeks began to build their remarkable civilization in the 8th century BCE. The old Mycenaean script had been forgotten, so the Greeks took the Phoenician alphabet and adapted it to create a new Greek alphabet. The first written records appear around this time. By 680 BCE, they had introduced a system of coinage, indicating the growth of a merchant class. The country was divided into small, self-governing communities, a development imposed by geography—mountain ranges and the sea cut off access to neighboring lands. At first, these communities were governed by aristocratic families, many of whom were later overthrown by populist tyrants. One such tyrant, Hippias, was deposed in Athens in 510 BCE, after which the Athenians set up the world's first democracy to govern themselves.

City-states

By the 6th century BCE, four city-states had emerged as the dominant forces in ancient Greece. They were namely Athens, Sparta, Corinth, and Thebes, each of which fought with the others for dominance. Athens and Corinth became major maritime and trading powers, while Sparta became a militarized state in which every male was a soldier, and slaves (known as helots) worked the land for the state.

However, when danger faced the country, rivalries were set aside. In 492, 490, and 480 BCE, the Persians invaded, forcing the Greeks to unite to fight the enemy. National institutions were also maintained, the most famous being the Olympic Games, established in 776 BCE. A rapidly increasing population and a shortage of arable land in the 8th and 7th centuries forced many Greeks to set up colonies overseas, particularly on the coasts of the Mediterranean and the Black Sea. Although independent, these colonies retained commercial and religious ties to their founding cities in Greece. They generated huge amounts of wealth from commerce »

△ **Navel of the world**
Delphi, in central Greece, was the seat of an oracle that the Greeks consulted when they had to make important decisions. They considered it the omphalos, or navel, of the world.

◁ **The touch of Asclepius**
This stone relief shows Asclepius, the Greek god of medicine and healing, tending to a patient. The sick traveled from far and wide to his temples in search of a cure.

▷ **Ancient Greece**
The first Greeks lived on the mainland and islands of what is now modern-day Greece. From 750 BCE, they established colonies in Italy, France, Spain, Turkey, Cyprus, North Africa, and the south coast of the Black Sea.

» and manufacturing, which only strengthened the Greeks' hold on the Mediterranean and the lands around it.

△ **Olympic sports**
This Greek vase shows an athlete throwing a discus. Discus throwing was one of the five sports in the Pentathlon competed for in the original Olympic Games, held in Olympia every four years from 776 BCE.

Sailing the world

As a maritime people, the Greeks were great travelers. They mapped the world they knew and explored as far as they could. In the 6th century BCE, Anaximander, a philosopher and geographer who lived in Miletus (in present-day Turkey) produced the first known map of the world. The map was circular, with the Aegean Sea at its center and the three known continents of Europe, Asia, and Libya (Africa) arranged around it. Surrounding all three was a large ocean.

The main boat of the Greeks was the three-tiered trireme, which was used for both transportation and war. In this mighty vessel, they sailed the Mediterranean and beyond. The historian Herodotus (484–c.425 BCE) records that, during the 6th century BCE, a ship from the island of Samos was blown off course through the Straits of Gibraltar and arrived at the city of Tartessos on the Atlantic coast of Spain. Friendly relations were soon established with Arganthonios, the king of Spain, who encouraged the Greeks to trade with his country. On doing so, the Greeks then learned of trade routes to Britain, the Elbe river in Germany, and as far away as the Shetland Isles north of Scotland.

> "The barbarians pointed out ... **the place where the sun lies down** ... the **night** is **very short** ..."
>
> PYTHEAS, AS RECORDED BY GEMINUS OF RHODES, 1ST CENTURY BCE

Pytheas explores

One of the most remarkable travelers of the ancient world was Pytheas, a Greek from the colony of Massalia (modern-day Marseilles) in southern France. Pytheas was that rare traveler who journeyed not for trade but for scientific interest—although he was certainly interested in the possibilities of trade. Around 325 BCE, he set sail for northern Europe, avoiding the Straits of Gibraltar, which the Carthaginians had closed to all but their own shipping. His route possibly took him up the Aude river and then down to the mouth of either the Loire or Garonne into the Bay of Biscay. From there, he explored Brittany and sailed across the English Channel to Britain, where he visited the tin mines of Cornwall and commented on the amber trade with Scandinavia. He then sailed north between Ireland and Britain, describing the latter as roughly triangular in shape and surrounded by many islands. In particular, he identified the isles of Wight, Anglesey, and Man, and the Hebrides, the Orkneys, and the Shetlands.

Pytheas was fascinated by all he saw. He noted that the tidal ranges of the north were much higher than those of the Mediterranean, and he was the

◁ **The Lighthouse of Alexandria**
The Pharos, or Lighthouse of Alexandria, was one of the Seven Wonders of the World. Built between 280 and 247 BCE, it stood more than 394 feet (120 m) tall, and was for many centuries the tallest man-made structure in the world.

first to suggest that the tides were caused by the Moon. He was also the first Greek to describe the north's long periods of winter darkness—reports of which had reached the Mediterranean centuries before, but had never been confirmed. To complement this, he provided accurate notes on the shortening of the summer nights before the 24-hour days, or "midnight sun," around the summer solstice.

Pytheas also reported a country of perpetual ice, and the existence of icebergs and other Arctic phenomena. He described the relationship between the Pole Star and the Guard Stars, and used a simple gnomon, or sundial, to calculate his latitude. It is unclear how far north he actually traveled, since he called his northernmost stopping point Thule, which could possibly be Iceland, or one of the smaller northern islands. Unfortunately, his own account of his voyage has not survived, although excerpts have been quoted or paraphrased by later authors, most notably Strabo in his *Geographica* (see pp. 42–43).

Seven Wonders

The Greeks had many reasons for traveling. Some did so to visit shrines and temples, particularly the temples of Asclepius, the god of medicine, where healing might be found. Others, such as lawyers, scribes, actors, and craftsmen, traveled for work. A few traveled for adventure or just for pleasure—the Seven Wonders of the World being the highest on a tourist's list. These were the places that both Herodotus and the scholar Callimachus of Cyrene decided, while working at the Museum of Alexandria, were the greatest man-made sites in the world.

The number seven was important because it represented plenty and perfection, and was also the number of known planets (then five), plus the Sun and the Moon. The original Seven Wonders were the Great Pyramid of Giza, the Hanging Gardens of Babylon, the Statue of Zeus at Olympia, the Temple of Artemis at Ephesus, the Mausoleum of Halicarnassus, the Colossus of Rhodes, and the Lighthouse of Alexandria. Of these, only the Great Pyramid at Giza still exists today.

▽ **The face of Zeus**
This ancient coin bears the face of Zeus, the Greek god of the sky and thunder who ruled as king of the gods on Mount Olympus. He was married to Hera, but had many romantic encounters, fathering, among others, Athena, Artemis, Helen of Troy, and the Muses.

◁ **The trireme**
The most important Greek ship was the trireme—a long, thin galley powered by three banks of oars. Fast and agile, it was the main warship of Greece, and played a crucial role in the wars against the Persians.

IN CONTEXT

Greek passports

It is not known when the first passport was issued, but an early reference to the practice can be found in the Book of Nehemiah in the Hebrew Bible, circa 450 BCE. It states that Nehemiah, an official working for King Artaxerxes I of Persia, asked for permission to travel to Judea. In response, the king granted him leave and gave him a letter addressed "to the governors beyond the river," requesting safe passage for Nehemiah as he passed through their lands. The ancient Greeks had their own form of passport. This was a clay tablet stamped with the owner's name, and was used by travelers or messengers between military headquarters. The one shown here belonged to Xenokles, a border commander in the 4th century BCE.

CLAY PASSPORT BELONGING TO XENOKLES, c.350 BCE

The travels of Odysseus

For ten years, Odysseus, the legendary king of Ithaca in Greece, traveled the length and breadth of the Mediterranean Sea, desperate to return home. His mythical adventures are related in Homer's epic poem the *Odyssey*.

△ **Monstrous Scylla**
This fragment of a Greek terracotta vase from c.300 BCE shows Scylla, a sea monster who lived on the rocks opposite another monster, Charybdis, in the *Odyssey*.

Since the earliest times, people have regaled each other with tales of extraordinary journeys, in which heroes have battled with monsters and demons in order to reach their destination. Homer's *Iliad* and *Odyssey* tell such tales, based on a masterful blend of fact and fiction.

The myths of ancient Greece relate that in about 1260 BCE, Zeus, king of the gods, held a banquet on Mount Olympus. Eris, the goddess of strife, was not invited, and in revenge threw into the banquet the golden Apple of Discord, inscribed with the word *kallistei*, meaning "for the fairest."

The three most beautiful goddesses, Hera, Athena, and Aphrodite, each claimed the apple, and so Zeus, who refused to choose between them, asked Paris, son of King Priam of Troy, to judge who was the fairest. As bribes, Hera offered him land and Athena tried to tempt him with skills. Aphrodite, however, offered him Helen, the most beautiful woman on Earth. Paris chose Aphrodite, who duly made Helen fall in love with him.

However, Helen was already married to King Menelaus of Sparta, so Paris had to raid Menelaus's house and steal her away to Troy. The Greeks were furious, and sent an army to besiege Troy and recover Helen. The war lasted for 10 years, and only ended when the Greeks broke into Troy hidden inside a giant wooden horse. Many heroes fought and lost their lives in the war, but Odysseus, king of Ithaca, survived. The Greek poet Homer records the last few weeks of the war in the *Iliad*, a tale about warrior values. In the *Odyssey*, he tells of the lengthy, exciting voyage of Odysseus and the personal quests and ordeals he had to endure in order to return home safely.

The *Odyssey*

Homer's epic begins after the Trojan War has ended. Odysseus and his men sail from Troy in 12 ships but are driven off course by storms. They visit the Lotus-Eaters, a race who eat nothing but the lotus plant, and are then captured by the Cyclops Polyphemus, from whom they

▽ **Off course in the Mediterranean**
A 16th-century map charts Odysseus's convoluted journey around the islands of the Mediterranean after the Trojan War.

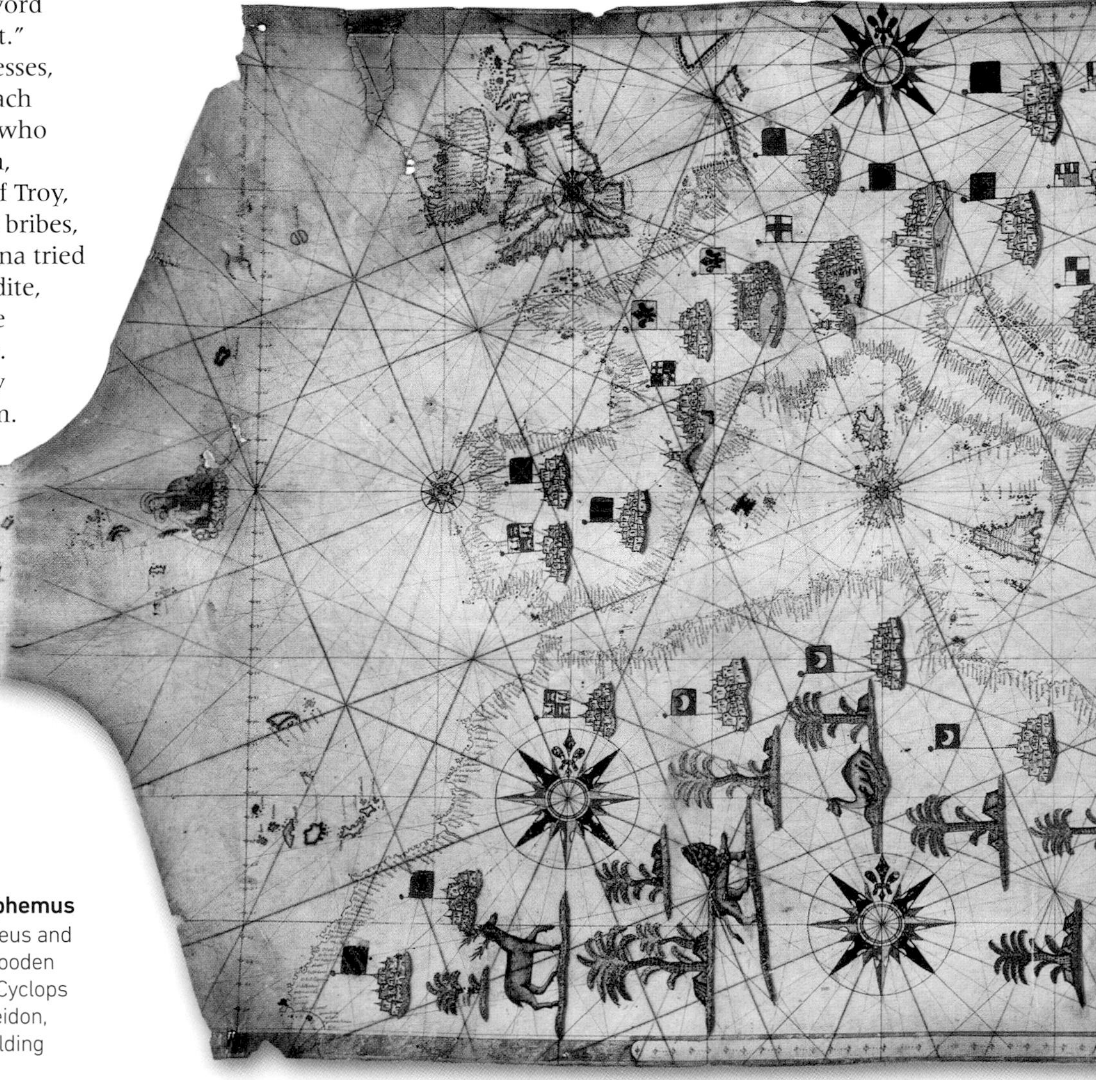

◁ **The blinding of Polyphemus**
This krater shows Odysseus and his men driving a long wooden stake into the eye of the Cyclops Polyphemus, son of Poseidon, god of the sea, who is holding them captive.

◁ **The Sirens' song**
This Roman mosaic shows Odysseus strapped to the mast of his ship to prevent him following the deathly bidding of the Sirens' song.

escape after blinding him with a wooden stake. Foolishly, Odysseus tells the Cyclops who he is, and the Cyclops tells his father, Poseidon, god of the sea. Poseidon then condemns Odysseus to spend 10 years wandering the oceans.

Further misfortunes soon befall Odysseus. He meets the Laestrygonian cannibals and visits the witch-goddess Circe, who turns his men into swine. On her instructions, Odysseus crosses the ocean and reaches the western edge of the world, where he encounters the spirits of his dead family and friends. Odysseus and his men then avoid the bewitching call of the Sirens—beautiful but dangerous creatures who try to lure them to shipwreck on the rocks—and ster their way between the six-headed monster Scylla and the whirlpool Charybdis. Finally, the sailors are shipwrecked again and everyone but Odysseus is killed.

Washed ashore on the island of Ogygia, Odysseus is held captive by the nymph Calypso for seven years. Calypso falls in love with him, but as he is already married to Penelope, he spurns her. Eventually, Calypso is ordered by Zeus to release him. Odysseus is returned to Ithaca by the Phaeacians, where he is reunited with his son, Telemachus, and rids the islands of the tyrannical suitors who have been competing for Penelope's hand.

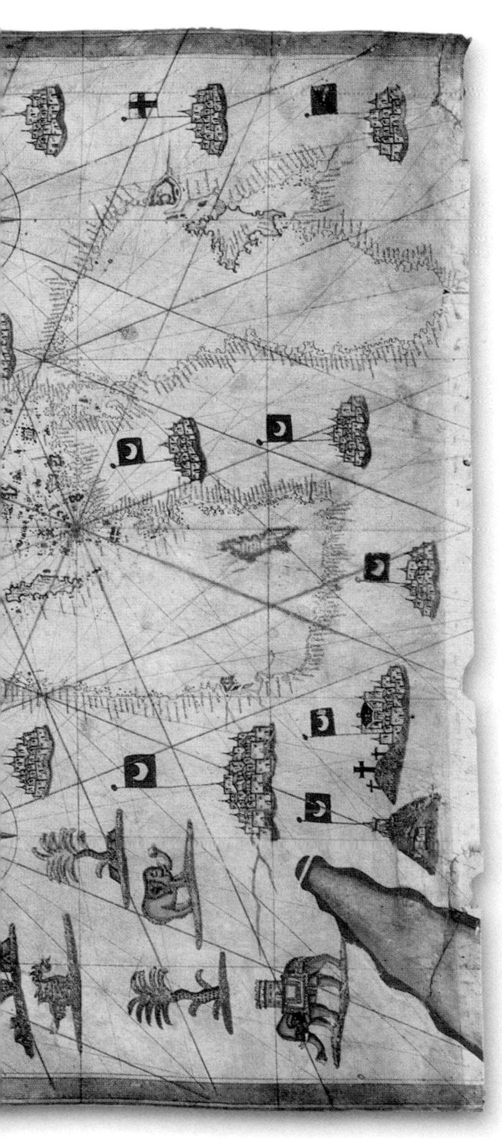

The legacy of the *Odyssey*

Although a fictional account based on myths passed down orally from generation to generation, the *Odyssey* may be partly based on events that actually took place. It also does more than recount a journey—it gives journeying itself a meaning. To go on an "odyssey" is to go on a quest—to travel in order to find oneself and come back strengthened. More than this, it means to become a hero—one who prevails against the slings and arrows of fate. Importantly, though, the *Odyssey* moves beyond the warrior-song of the *Iliad* and focuses instead on the final goals of peace, family, and home.

IN PROFILE
Homer

The ancient Greeks believed that Homer was the author of the *Iliad* and the *Odyssey*, and that he was a blind poet born in Ionia in Anatolia (in modern-day Turkey), between 1102 BCE and 850 BCE. However, it is unclear if Homer actually existed. While one group of modern scholars does believe that a single man wrote most of the *Iliad* and possibly the *Odyssey*, another claims that both poems are the work of many contributors and that "Homer" is a label for their efforts. What is generally accepted is that the poems were originally composed and handed down orally before they were written down during the 8th century BCE.

REPLICA BUST OF HOMER MADE IN THE ANCIENT ROMAN STYLE

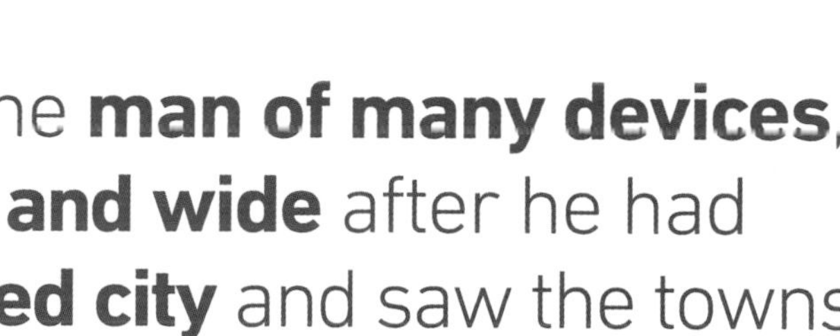

"**Tell me**, Muse, of the **man of many devices**, who **wandered far and wide** after he had sacked Troy's **sacred city** and saw the towns of **many men** and **knew their mind**."

HOMER, WRITING ABOUT ODYSSEUS IN THE *ODYSSEY*

MACEDONIAN KING, 356–323 BCE

Alexander the Great

One of the greatest empires the world has ever seen was created by a young Macedonian warrior who traveled the known world in search of fame and empire and left a legacy that still survives today.

In spring 333 BCE, Alexander of Macedon stood in the city of Gordium in central Turkey. Here, the Gordian knot bound the yoke of a ceremonial wagon to a tall pole, its ends tied so that it was impossible to untie. It was believed that whoever untied the knot would become the master of Asia. Alexander took out his sword and slashed the knot with a single blow. "What difference does it make how I loose it?" he said. He was master of Asia now.

Everything about Alexander is extraordinary. Born into the royal family of Macedon in northern Greece, he became king in 336 BCE at the age of 20. His life's mission was to carry out his father's plan to attack the mighty Persian Empire in retaliation for its invasion of Greece in 480–479 BCE.

Conqueror of the world

Over the course of the next five years, he did just that. In 334 BCE, he crossed the Hellespont that separated Greece from Persian-controlled Asia. With his highly trained, professional army, he won three decisive victories over the Persians, conquering them by 331 BCE. Then the Persian emperor Darius III was killed by his cousin Bessus, who declared himself Darius's successor. Alexander's pursuit of Bessus took him across the Hindu Kush and into central Asia, where he finally killed his foe near what is now Samarkand, in Uzbekistan, in 329 BCE.

However, Alexander was eager to journey on. Like many Greeks of the time, he believed that the world was surrounded by a great ocean, so once he had reached its shores he would have conquered the known world. To find it, he crossed the Hindu Kush again in 327 BCE and invaded India. Here, he won a great victory against a vast Indian army, but he lost the backing of his troops. He tried to persuade them that the great ocean was close, but they were not convinced.

Alexander reluctantly led his men through the Gedrosian Desert of southern Persia to Babylon, where, ill with fever, he died at 32 years old. He had conquered a vast empire and created one that was even bigger. He established cities bearing his name that still exist today, and spread Greek culture throughout the known world. Not for nothing is he known as Alexander the Great.

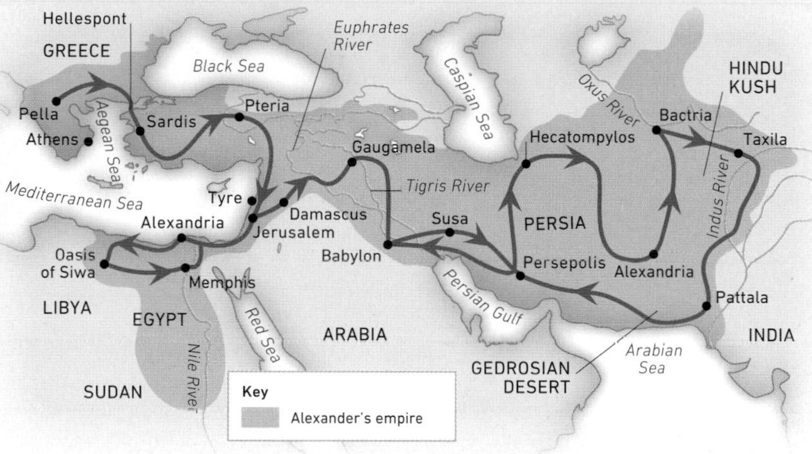

△ **Alexander's journeys**
From 334 BCE until his death in 323 BCE, Alexander traveled the breadth of the great Persian Empire, crossing into central Asia, India, and Egypt.

◁ **Alexander the Great portrait**
This detail from the *Alexander Mosaic*, c.100 BCE, shows Alexander at the Battle of Issus, where he fought his greatest foe, Darius III of Persia, and won a great victory despite having a smaller army.

◁ **Alexander and the oracle**
This bas-relief depicts Alexander dressed as a pharaoh. In 331 BCE, Alexander consulted the oracle of Amun at the Siwa Oasis. He may have believed that he was the son of Amun.

KEY DATES

- **356 BCE** Born in Pella, Macedonia.
- **343** Tutored by Aristotle.
- **336** Becomes king of Macedon after the assassination of his father, Philip.
- **335** Defeats the Thebans and takes control of Greece.
- **334** Crosses into Asia to attack the Persian Empire and wins a great battle at the River Granicus.
- **333** Defeats the Persians again at Issus and captures Palestine.
- **332** Invades Egypt and becomes Pharaoh.
- **332** Founds Alexandria and consults the oracle of Amun, claiming to be a god.
- **331** Conquers the Persian Empire.
- **329** Kills Bessus, who slayed Darius III.
- **327** Invades India.
- **325** Leaves India and marches back through the deserts of southern Persia.
- **323** Arrives in Babylon, where he dies.

GREEK COIN OF ALEXANDER AT WAR IN INDIA

ALEXANDER IN CHINA, A PLACE THAT HE NEVER VISITED, 4TH CENTURY BCE

The travels of Zhang Qian

Isolated from the rest of the world, China first opened its eyes to the West when the diplomat Zhang Qian led an expedition in 138 BCE that led to the establishment of the Silk Road.

At the time of Emperor Wu, China knew almost nothing about the countries beyond its borders. Wu wanted to find out about them and to establish commercial ties, but he was prevented from reaching them by the hostile nomadic Xiongu tribes. They encircled the Han dynasty to the west and controlled what is now Mongolia and western China. Wu therefore needed to form an alliance with the friendly Yuezhi people, who lived beyond the Xiongu. He chose Zhang Qian, a military officer and a member of his court, to lead a diplomatic mission to negotiate with the Yuezhi.

△ **Emperor Wu**
Emperor Wu (r. 141–87 BCE) was the seventh Han emperor of China. He hugely expanded the empire he inherited.

Into the unknown

In 138 BCE, Zhang Qian left the capital Chang'an with about 100 men, including Ganfu, a Xiongu guide who had been a prisoner of war, and headed west. Unfortunately, he and his party were soon taken by the Xiongu and held captive for ten years. During this period of imprisonment, Zhang Qian was given a wife by the Xiongu, who bore him a son. He also managed to gain the trust of the Xiongu leader. In 128 BCE, he, his wife, son, and Ganfu managed to escape and made their way along the north side of the inhospitable Tarim Basin. From there, they went to Dayuan in the Ferghana Valley (now Uzbekistan), where Zhang Qian first saw the powerful Ferghana horses, and then south into Yuezhi territory. The peaceful Yuezhi people had no wish to fight the Xiongu, so instead, Zhang Qian spent his time studying their culture and economy before moving west into Daxia, the Greco-Bactrian kingdom that had declared independence from the Seleucid Empire in 250 BCE. Here, he learned about Shendu (India) to the south and Anxi or Parthia (Persia) and Mesopotamia to the west, as well as the nomadic kingdoms on the steppes to the north.

△ **Zhang Qian**
This 7th-century fresco in the Mogao caves on the Silk Road in central China depicts Zhang Qian and his party leaving Emperor Wu as they set out on their first expedition in 138 BCE.

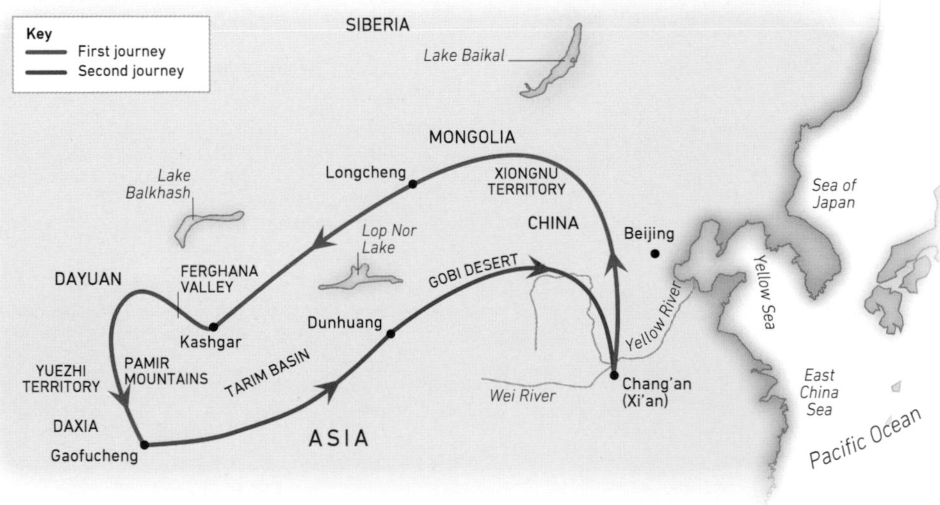

▷ **The Silk Road**
Zhang Qian's epic journey to Daxia was the first step in the establishment of the Silk Road—a network of routes that linked China to Central Asia, and eventually to the ports of the Mediterranean Sea.

Recaptured by the Xiongu

In 127 BCE, Zhang Qian and his party decided to return to China, this time traveling along the southern edge of the Tarim Basin. Once again, they were captured by the Xiongu, but their lives were again spared, as the Xiongu people appreciated Zhang Qian's sense of duty and his fearlessness in the face of death.

Two years later, the Xiongu leader died and, in the midst of the chaos and subsequent infighting for the succession, Zhang Qian, his wife, his son, and Ganfu managed to escape and return to China. Emperor Wu welcomed Zhang Qian's report that sophisticated civilizations with whom China could trade lay to the west. They valued Han merchandise and wealth, and could also supply goods, such as Ferghana horses, that China wanted. Zhang Qian's report produced immediate results, apparently: in 114 BCE, the trade routes from China into central Asia were organized into the Silk Road.

△ **Persian box**
This silver box from Persia was found in the tomb of Emperor Zhao Mo, who ruled southern China and northern Vietnam from 137 BCE until his death 15 years later. It is thought to be the earliest product imported into China.

IN CONTEXT

The Ferghana horse

The Chinese called the Ferghana valley horses "divine," as they were the finest mounts they had ever seen. After Zhang Qian reported on these horses upon his return from his epic journey in 125 BCE, the Han began to import them in such large numbers that Ferghana ended the trade. In response, Emperor Hu sent an army in 113 BCE to capture some horses, but it was defeated. In 103 BCE, he sent another army of 60,000 men, who managed to acquire 10 horses, as well as an undertaking that Ferghana would supply two heavenly horses each year. Chinese military supremacy was assured.

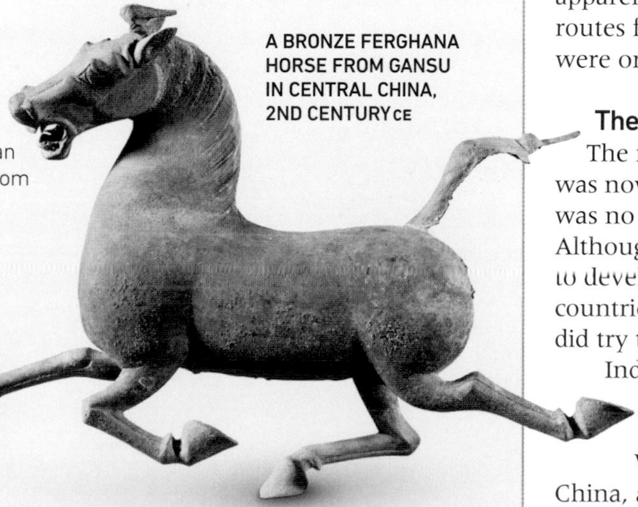

A BRONZE FERGHANA HORSE FROM GANSU IN CENTRAL CHINA, 2ND CENTURY CE

The Silk Road

The road from China to the west was now open for business, and China was no longer isolated by hostile tribes. Although Zhang Qian had been unable to develop commercial ties with the countries he had visited himself, he did try to develop trading links with India and, in 119–115 BCE, he succeeded in establishing a trading relationship with the Wusun to the far northwest of China, and thus with distant Persia. The trading future of China was now secure.

Across the Alps

In 218 BCE, Carthaginian general Hannibal Barca marched an army, including war elephants, from Spain to Italy, making an epic crossing of the Alps.

The North African city of Carthage was a bitter rival of the Roman Republic. Inheriting command of the Carthaginian army in Spain from his father, Hamilcar, Hannibal planned a surprise overland attack on Rome. Mostly recruited from the tribes of Spain, his forces also included Libyan infantry, Numidian horsemen, and 37 elephants—of a small African breed often used in battle in the ancient world. This army, more than 100,000 strong, set off from New Carthage (Cartagena) in southeast Spain in late spring. By the time it reached Roman Gaul, it was late summer and the force had dwindled to 60,000, partly because Hannibal wanted only the best troops with him for a rapid advance with lightweight baggage.

The major natural obstacle in Gaul was the Rhône. Hannibal's army, including the panicking elephants, crossed the broad river on rafts. There was some fighting with local tribes and with a Roman army sent to intercept the Carthaginians, but by November, Hannibal had reached the foothills of the Alps. His exact route over the mountains remains a matter of dispute. Mountain tribesmen harassed the Carthaginians on their ascent over the rough terrain, causing the loss of men and animals, and it took nine days to reach the snowbound crest of whichever pass was chosen.

The demoralized soldiers only agreed to start the daunting downward leg of the crossing after much exhortation from Hannibal. Horses, mules, and elephants struggled to find footing on icy tracks bordered by steep precipices. The soldiers from warmer climes suffered in the unaccustomed freezing cold. At one point, a landslide carried away the path and a new one had to be laboriously constructed amid the ice and snow. The exhausted force finally reached flat ground after a crossing probably lasting three to four weeks.

When he arrived on the north Italian plain, Hannibal began preparations for his attempt to conquer Rome. He would campaign in Italy for 15 years and inflict terrible defeats on Roman armies, but he never achieved the total victory he sought. Eventually, it was Rome that destroyed Carthage. Hannibal committed suicide in 183/182 BCE, a fugitive from Roman power.

◁ **Hannibal and his army**
This 16th-century Italian painting depicts Hannibal and his army entering battle in suitably exotic outfits. Hannibal might have mounted an elephant's back to survey the battlefield, but the animals' main use was as a shock force in the vanguard of an attack.

Strabo

The author of one of the first books of geography ever written, Strabo provided the world with an invaluable source of information about the people and places of the Roman Empire and its neighbors.

Like many prominent people from the ancient world, Strabo is a figure about whom little is known for certain. He was apparently born into a wealthy Greek family in Amaseia in Pontus (Turkey), in either 64 or 63 BCE. Pontus had only recently been incorporated into the Roman Empire, following the death of its military leader, Mithridates VI, and Strabo's family had held prominent positions in the former government. It is also known that in 44 BCE Strabo moved to Rome, where he lived for at least 13 years and studied philosophy and grammar under the Greek poet Xenarchus and Tyrannion of Amisus, a grammarian and noted geographer.

Exploring the world

Around this time, Strabo also began to travel. In 29 BCE, he visited Corinth and the small Greek island of Gyaros. He sailed up the Nile to the temples of Philae in the Nubian kingdom of Kush in around 25 BCE, and at some point traveled even further south to Ethiopia. He also visited Tuscany, in Italy, and explored his homeland of Asia Minor. At the time, the Roman Empire under Emperor Augustus (27 BCE–14 CE) was peaceful, which enabled Strabo to travel extensively.

Some time around 20 BCE, Strabo wrote his first book, *Historical Sketches*, which covered the history of the known world from the conquest of Greece by the Romans in the second century BCE. Unfortunately, only a fragment of this work survives, despite its popularity at the time (it is mentioned by several classical authors). Nevertheless, the book was only a precursor to his main work, *Geographica*—a geographical history of the world that is still in print today. It is unclear when he started work on the book, but some historians date it to around 7 BCE—others place it as late as 17 or 18 CE. The latest passage in the text that can be accurately dated refers to the death of Juba II of Mauretania, who died in 23 CE. What is clear is that Strabo worked on the book for many years and revised it as he went along.

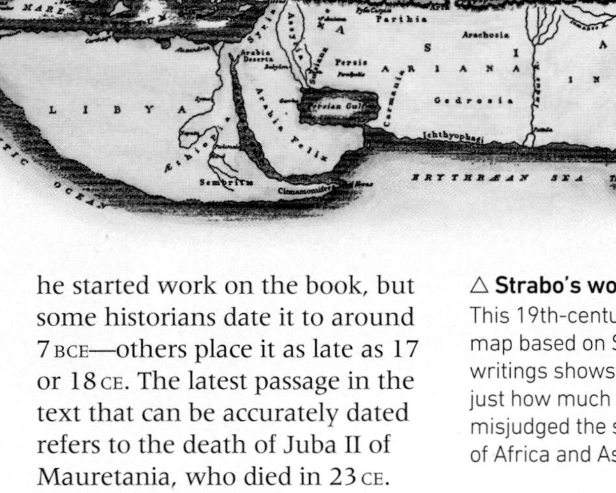

△ **Strabo's world**
This 19th-century map based on Strabo's writings shows by just how much he misjudged the size of Africa and Asia.

The shifting Earth

In *Geographica*, Strabo cites Eratosthenes, the Greek "Father of Geography" who worked out the circumference of the Earth, and Hipparchus who discovered the precession of Earth's equinoxes. However, their work was purely scientific—Strabo's aim was to take such ideas and incorporate them into a practical guide for travelers, particularly politicians and statesmen. As such, the book is full of insights, many of which are original. For example, Strabo was the first person to describe the formation of fossils and the effects of a volcanic eruption on a landscape. Most importantly, he also discussed the question of why marine shells are buried in the earth so far away from the sea. He concluded that it was not the change in sea levels that made these shells move, but shifts in the land itself, which had slowly risen up above the sea. For this thought, which anticipates plate tectonics, Strabo deserves to be known not only as a great traveler, but also as one of the founders of modern geology.

◁ **The Great Pyramids**
In around 25 BCE Strabo sailed up the Nile, passing the Great Pyramids on his way to the temples of Philae, which now lie beneath Lake Aswan in southern Egypt.

“ And it is not merely the small, but the large islands also, and not **merely the islands,** but the continents, which can be **lifted up together** ... ”

STRABO, IN *GEOGRAPHICA*, c.7–18 CE

◁ **Studying the Earth**
This 16th-century engraving provides a good idea of what Strabo might have looked like. The globe he is holding shows a disproportionately large Black Sea.

KEY DATES

- **64 or 63 BCE** Born into a wealthy Greek family in Amaseia in Pontus (modern-day Amasya, in Turkey), a region only recently assimilated by the Roman Empire.
- **c.50s** Studies in Nysa (modern-day Sultanhisar, Turkey) under rhetoretician Aristodemus. Becomes familiar with the poetry of Homer.
- **44** Moves to Rome, where he studies and writes until at least 31 BCE. His teachers include the Aristotelians Xenarchus and Tyrannia of Amisus, the latter stimulating his interest in geography. A third teacher, Athenodorus, introduces him to Stoicism, and provides much information about the further reaches of the Roman Empire.

JOANNEM WOLTER'S 1707 EDITION OF *GEOGRAPHICA*

- **29** On his way to Corinth, he visits the island of Gyaros in the Aegean Sea.
- **27 BCE to 14 CE** Travels extensively during the peaceful reign of Augustus, the first emperor of Rome.
- **25 BCE** Sails up the Nile to Philae, in the Nubian kingdom of Kush.
- **20 BCE** Writes *Historical Sketches*, almost all of which is now lost.
- **c.7 BCE** Starts writing *Geographica*.
- **23 CE** The latest historical reference made in the *Geographica*, concerning the death of Juba II of Mauretania.
- **24 CE** Dies, probably in Amaseia.

The Roman Empire

In their time, the Romans were innovative and exceptionally skilled engineers, building roads, bridges, and other structures that enabled their citizens to move quickly and safely throughout the empire.

◁ **Roman milestone**
Circular stone milestones were placed every *milia passuum*—one thousand paces, or 4,842 feet (1,476 m)—along every Roman road. Each advertised its distance along the road plus other important facts, such as the distance to the Roman Forum.

The Romans were an intensely practical people who used their skills in engineering and construction to great and lasting effect. They built dams to collect water and aqueducts to carry the water into the cities. They were also great miners. They harnessed the power of water to wash away unwanted soil from the land and water mills to crush hard ores. They developed water wheels to power flour mills and the saws they used to cut stone. They erected bridges to cross rivers and roads to connect their towns and cities.

For their delight and pleasure, the Romans built huge, tiered stadiums, such as the Colosseum in Rome, in which up to 80,000 spectators watched gladiatorial contests and other public spectacles. Roman towns contained vast public baths and huge monumental arches celebrating great victories. Most towns had efficient drainage systems and many houses had underfloor central heating. All these constructions helped to improve the daily lives of the Roman people, holding their empire together and giving them the confidence to travel great distances. The greatest achievement of the empire, however, was its road network.

The needs of Rome

The Roman Republic, and the Roman Empire that followed in 27 BCE, had to be able to move its armies rapidly in order to defend its borders from its many enemies. The government also needed to move its officials and send orders quickly and efficiently. Traders had to be able to move from town to town to buy and sell their goods, while civilians needed the roads both for work and for religious reasons. To meet all these requirements, a series of roads was begun in 300 BCE. By the height of the empire in the 2nd century CE, the network had been completed. Twenty-nine military highways radiated from Rome, connecting the 113 provinces with 372 great roads, and numerous smaller roads linked countless towns and ports. This vast network had over 248,548 miles (400,000 km) of roads, of which over 50,020 miles (80,500 km) were paved.

The art of road building

An ancient law circa 450 BCE stated that a road should be eight Roman feet wide where straight and twice that width

THE INTERIOR OF THE PANTHEON DOME IN ROME

ON TECHNOLOGY

The development of concrete

Around 150 BCE, the Romans discovered that by mixing three parts of volcanic ash and other aggregates with one part of binder of gypsum or lime, and then adding water, they had created the perfect building material. The volcanic ash, called *pozzolana*, or "pit sand," prevented cracks from spreading, making the concrete extremely durable. The Romans used it for all their buildings, facing it with stone or marble for decorative effect. They also developed a version that set under water, which was particularly useful for making bridges. Their finest concrete construction was the roof of the Pantheon in Rome. Even now, 2,000 years later, it remains the greatest unreinforced concrete dome in the world.

where curved. To build a road, a civil engineer would first survey the route, then a *gromaticus* or *agrimensor* (land surveyor) plotted its course using a vertical rod and a groma—a post with horizontal crosspieces that held plumb lines for calculating right angles.

Construction of the roads varied according to local conditions, but the standard road consisted of a base layer of rammed earth and then subsequent layers of stones, rubble, and fine cement before the top layer of regularly shaped blocks was put in place. The finished surface was smooth, and was slightly arched in the middle to allow rainwater to drain off into the ditches on either side. Today, Roman roads look rough and uneven, but this is only because their mortar has washed away.

Perhaps the most striking aspect of the roads is that they were straight wherever possible. Some stretched up to 56 miles (90 km) without a curve, running up and over hills without diversion. Not only were straight roads faster, they were safer, since nobody could hide on the road ahead—an important consideration for armies on the move. »

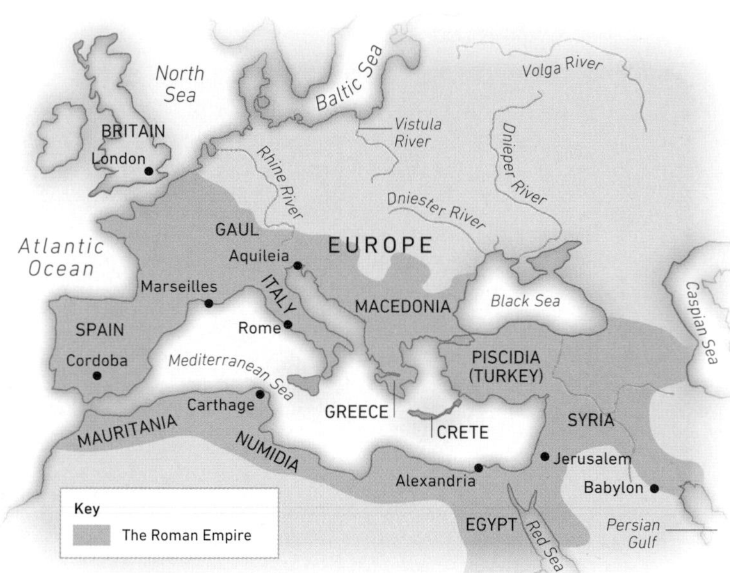

△ **The Roman reach**
At its greatest extent, under Emperor Trajan in 116 CE, the Roman Empire stretched from northern England all the way across Europe and the Middle East to the Persian Gulf. However, its eastern extremities were soon abandoned as they proved too costly to maintain.

" There is **hardly a district** to which we might expect a **Roman official** to be sent, on service either civil or military, **where we do not find roads**. "

FROM THE *ANTONINE ITINERARY*, A SURVEY OF ROMAN ROADS, c.300 CE

◁ **Appian Way**
Built in 312 BCE, the Appian Way ran 350 miles (563 km) from Rome to Brindisi. Its initial purpose was to aid the deployment of legionaries in the Romans' fight against the Samnites of southern Italy.

◁ **On wheels**
Unlike other ancient peoples, the Romans did not use chariots for warfare but for racing and parading in triumphal processions.

▽ **Pont du Gard**
Probably the greatest surviving feat of Roman engineering, the Pont du Gard aqueduct, built around 60 CE, carried water 31 miles (50 km) from a spring at Uzès to the Roman colony of Nemausus (Nîmes).

» Maps and stations

In order to find their way around this vast network of roads, the Romans produced road maps, such as the *Tabula Peutingeriana* (see pp. 48–49). Long-distance travelers on official business stayed and presented their passports at *mansiones* (staying places), which were set roughly 16–19 miles (25–30 km) apart. Other travelers stayed in *cauponae*, or private inns. In the early days of the road network, before such inns were built, houses near the road were required by law to offer hospitality on demand. These houses gave rise to the first hostels. *Mutationes* (changing stations) were built every 12–19 miles (20–30 km), and provided wheelwrights, vets, and cartwrights to service both vehicles and animals.

The traffic of empire

Roman roads were constantly busy. Soldiers marched along them from camp to camp, sometimes over great distances. A register listing people who had visited Hadrian's Wall in the far north of England between 253–258 CE records the presence of a unit of Aurelian Moors—black soldiers from Roman-occupied North Africa. In addition to the Roman legions, officials in the service of the emperor regularly used the roads—as did magistrates on their way to dispense justice, and students traveling to study in distant cities. Pilgrims needed them to reach their temples and other religious sites, as did the landowners of Rome to reach their country estates.

Merchants and traders were a regular sight on the roads, as were farmers taking their produce and livestock to market. Public couriers, with their distinctive leather caps, were also common. They ran messages in relays for the government (a horse and rider were used for special deliveries). More common still were the *tabellarii*—slaves whose job it was to deliver private mail. The only people not on the road at this time were tourists, as the concept of travel for pleasure was alien to the Roman world.

The most popular vehicle on the road was the *carrus*—a one-horsed chariot that carried a driver and one passenger. Carts and wagons drawn by horses or oxen were also commonplace. Larger chariots, pulled by two, three, or even four horses, were unusual. Even more rare were four-wheeled coaches. These were drawn by teams of oxen, horses, or mules, and had a cloth "roof" that could be put up in bad weather.

◁ **Sea travel**
This mosaic of a merchant ship was placed in the Square of the Guilds in Ostia, the main port of Rome. Such a ship primarily carried cargo, but took passengers on board as well.

Across the sea

Traveling by road was not the only means of transport open to the Romans. Originally an inland tribe, they had no tradition of seafaring, but during the protracted wars against Carthage (Tunisia) in the 3rd and 2nd centuries BCE, they developed both maritime forces and fleets of trading ships. Their merchant vessels had round hulls, were usually flat-bottomed, and were powered by a single sail. Some of these ships carried passengers as well as cargo, but a regular passenger ferry also operated on the popular route from Brindisi, in southern Italy, across the Adriatic to Greece. Passengers, like the crew, slept on the deck and brought along their own food, which was cooked in the ship's galley.

> "The **couriers** ... by making use of **relays** on **excellent horses** ... often covered **in a single day** as **great a distance** as they would **otherwise** have **covered in ten**."
>
> PROCOPIUS, GREEK HISTORIAN, c.500 CE

IN CONTEXT
Temple of Bacchus

The extent of the Roman Empire can still be seen today, preserved in the Roman buildings and structures that have survived in outposts of the empire in other lands. The temple of Bacchus at Heliopolis, or Baalbek, in Lebanon, is one such example. The temple, which was built between 150 and 250 CE, stands 102 feet (31 m) tall. Forty-two rounded and polished Corinthian columns, each nearly 66 feet (20 m) high, support an elaborate entablature (a superstructure of carvings and moldings) and the roof. Inside, a chamber depicts scenes from the sybaritic life of Bacchus, the god of wine. The building is one of antiquity's greatest achievements.

THE TEMPLE OF BACCHUS, IN LEBANON, HAS BEEN AN INSPIRATION TO ARCHITECTS FOR ALMOST 2,000 YEARS

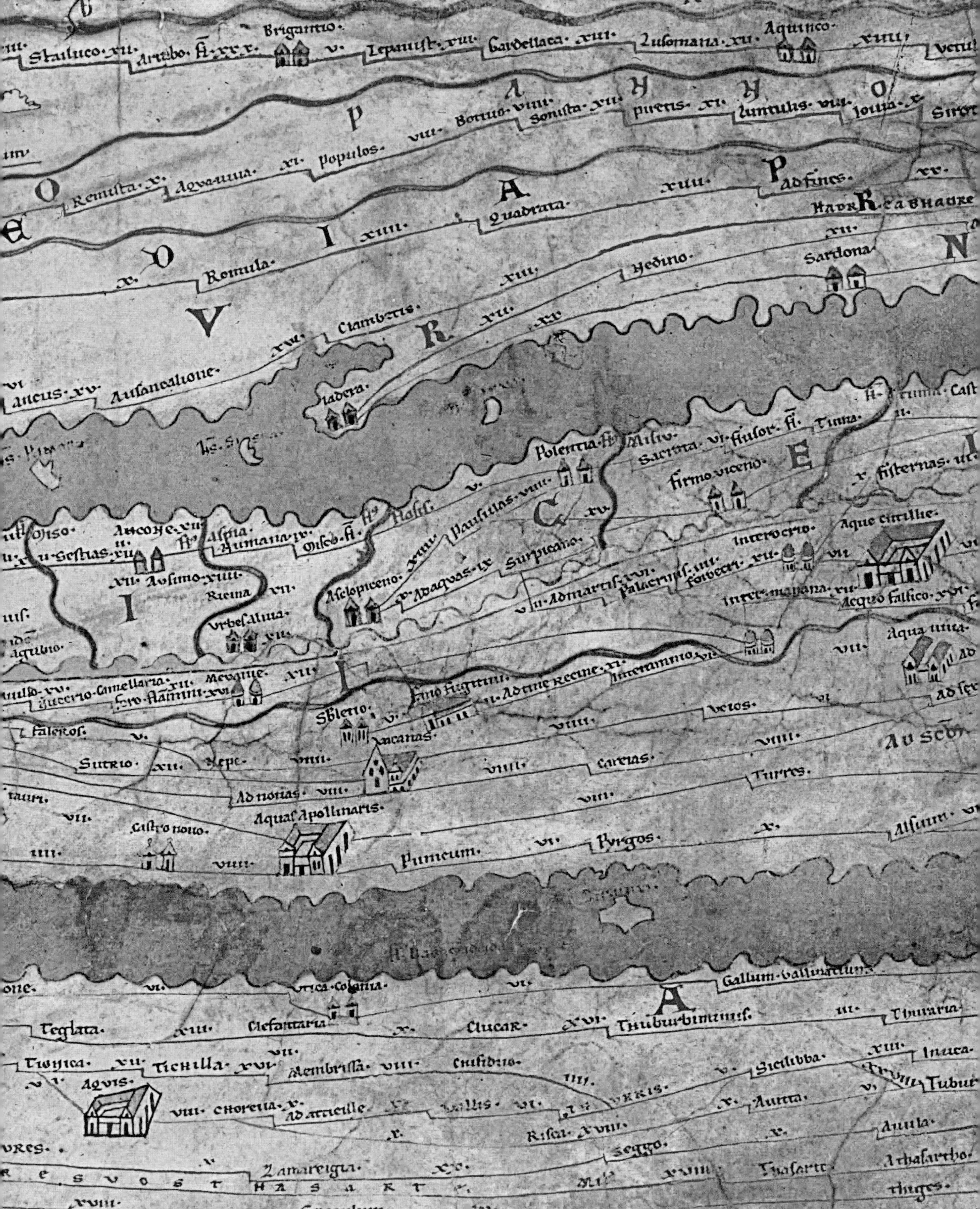

Brigantio
Aquinco
Gardellaca
Lepavist
populos
Remista
Aquaviva
Quadrata
Ad fines
Romula
Hedino
Sardona
Clambetis
Ausancalione
Iadera
Polentia
Tinna
firmo viceno
fisternas
Aque cutilliae
Ancone
Numana
Aosimo
Ricina
Urbesaluia
Asclopiceno
Surpicano
Interocrio
Foroecri
Aequo falisco
Aqua viva
Agubio
Mevanie
Foro flamini
Sbletio
Fano fugitivi
Interamnio
Veios
Faleros
Sutrio
Nepe
Careias
Turres
Ad novas
Aquas Apollinaris
Castro novo
Pyrgos
Punicum
Alsium
Gallum gallinacium
Utica colonia
Teglata
Clefantaria
Clucar
Thuburbiminus
Thuraria
Tichilla
Membrissa
Chisiduo
Sicilibba
Aquis
Risca
Seggo
Zamareigia
Thasarte

The *Tabula Peutingeriana*

The Roman road network was so complex that a map was required to understand it. Such a map was first drawn up in the first century CE, and survives today as a 13th-century copy.

Roads were the lifeblood of the Roman world, enabling legions, officials, merchants, and travelers to move swiftly around the empire. They were often paved with stone, were cambered to allow water to run off to the side, and were flanked by footpaths and drainage ditches. They were laid along surveyed lines and often cut through hills, and were carried by bridges over rivers and gorges. The whole network stretched some 249,000 miles (400,000 km). At its center was Rome, from which 29 great military highways radiated to distant provinces.

A state-run courier service known as the *cursus publicus* ran along this network. Created by Emperor Augustus (r. 27 BCE–14 CE), it transported messages, state officials, and tax revenues between the provinces and Rome. Couriers and other travelers needed a map with which to navigate the roads; such a map was first prepared by Agrippa, son-in-law of Augustus. A later version was created in the 4th or 5th century, and that has survived in the form of a copy made by a monk in Colmar, eastern France, in 1265. The map acquired its modern name, the *Tabula Peutingeriana*, from Konrad Peutinger of Augsburg, Germany, who owned it in the 1500s.

The Peutinger map is drawn on a parchment scroll 13.4 in (34 cm) high and 265 in (675 cm) long. It shows the road network of the entire Roman Empire, except for Morocco, Spain, and the British Isles (that section was probably lost), as well as the Near East, India, and Sri Lanka. Its contents are schematic, not geographic, with considerable east-west distortion, and the seas are represented by thin strips of water. More than 550 cities and 3,500 other place names are included, as well as all the roads and the distances between them. Armed with this information, a traveler would know which town was coming next, and how far away it was. For a Roman traveler, it would have been invaluable.

◁ **The center of the world**
All the roads on the Peutinger map lead to Rome (center right), the hub of the Roman Empire. In this section, modern-day Croatia lies above the Adriatic Sea at the top of the map, with North Africa below the Mediterranean Sea at the bottom.

The *Periplus of the Erythraean Sea*

For modern-day Greeks, the Erythraean Sea is the Red Sea. In ancient times, it included the Indian Ocean and the Persian Gulf. A remarkable document from the first century CE survives to tell its tale.

A periplus is a document that was used by mariners of the ancient world. It listed the ports and major landmarks that a captain would find along a given shore, plus approximate distances between them.

The *Periplus of the Erythraean Sea* was written in Greek and consists of 66 chapters, most of which are just a single paragraph. It lists the ports of the Red Sea, Arabia, the Persian Gulf, East Africa, and India during the time of the Roman Empire, and describes the type of industries pursued in those regions. Historians date the *Periplus* to the middle of the 1st century CE, and most agree that its author was probably a Greek-speaking Egyptian merchant. It is likely that he lived in Berenice Troglodytica, a seaport on the Egyptian coast of the Red Sea, since the *Periplus* describes that port at length. Although clearly well-traveled, the author was not particularly well-educated; he often confused Greek and Latin words and had little understanding of grammar.

△ **Apollo with a chelys**
The chelys was the common lyre of the ancient Greeks. Its convex body was usually made from a complete tortoise shell. The *Periplus of the Erythraean Sea* describes a thriving trade in tortoise shells, that of the hawksbill species being the best.

Arabia and Africa

The *Periplus* records friendly relations between Rome and the trading empires of the Himyarite Kingdom and the Sabaeans of Yemen. Further along the Arabian peninsula, he describes "a continuous length of coast, and a bay extending two thousand *stadia* or more, along which are Nomads and Fish-Eaters living in villages… All the frankincense produced in the country is brought by camels to that place to be stored, and to Cana on rafts held up by inflated skins after the manner of the country, and in boats." Frankincense is just one of many traded goods reported in the *Periplus*. The author pays great attention to the port of Opone in Somalia, East Africa, where much ancient Roman and Egyptian pottery has since been found. Here, the *Periplus* records that "the greatest quantity of cinnamon is produced, and slaves of the better sort, which are brought to Egypt in increasing numbers, and a great quality of tortoiseshell, better than that found elsewhere." It also mentions Aksum, in Ethiopia, as an important market place for ivory. Further south, it details the port of Rhapta, probably to the south of modern-day Dar es Salaam in Tanzania, "where there are great quantities of ivory and tortoiseshell," and where many Roman coins have been found.

India and the Greeks

Across the Indian Ocean, the *Periplus* records extensive trade with the Indian port of Barygaza, which is modern-day

" ... **just beyond the cape** projecting from this bay there is another **market-town by the shore**, Cana, of the Kingdom of Eleazus, the **Frankincense Country** ... "

AUTHOR OF THE *PERIPLUS OF THE ERYTHRAEAN SEA*

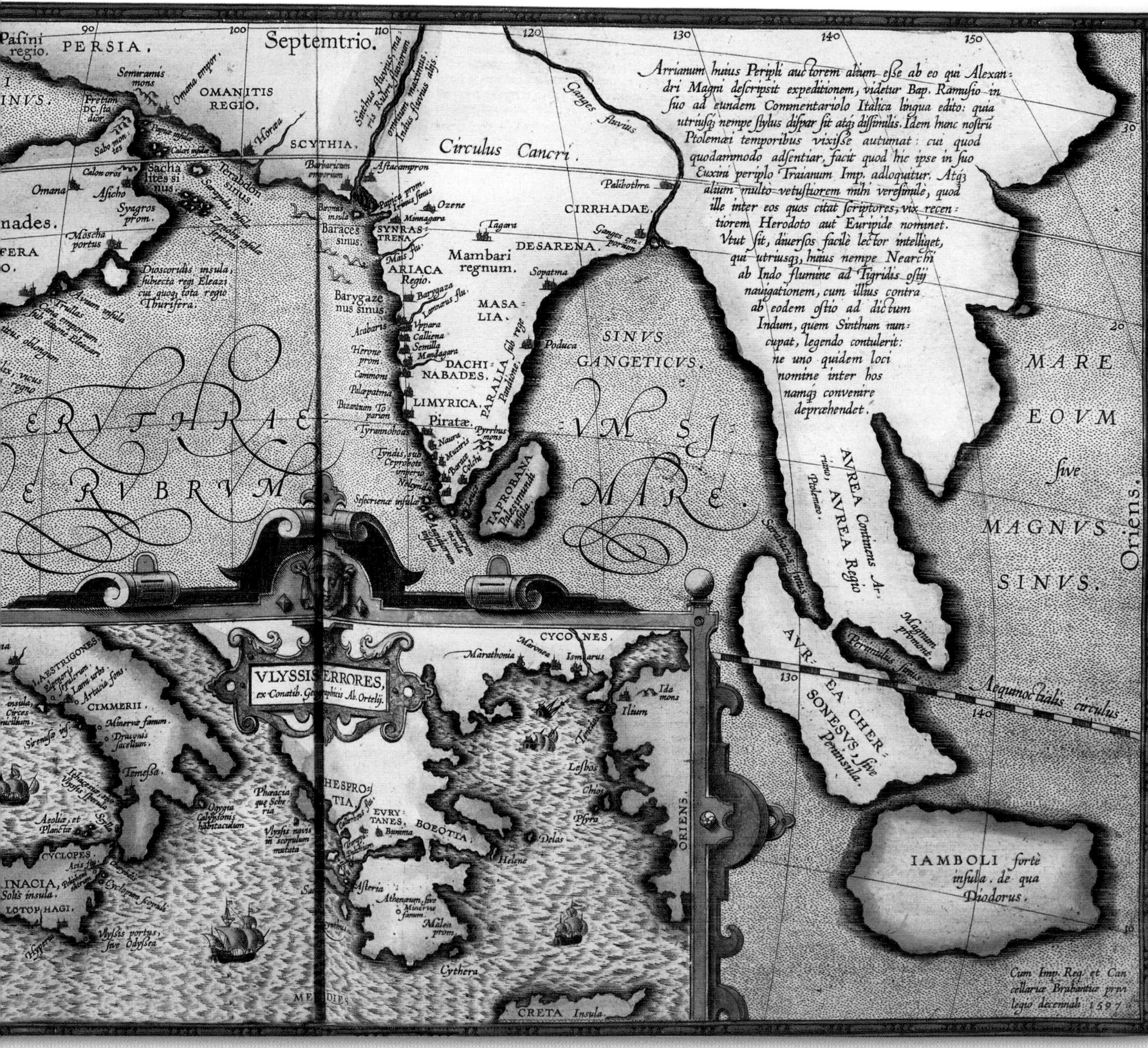

◁ **Landmarks of the *Periplus*** This 17th-century map of the lands around the Indian Ocean shows the locations identified in the *Periplus of the Erythraean Sea*. A map of Europe is superimposed at the bottom.

Bharuch in Gujarat. "It is a fertile country, yielding wheat and rice and sesame oil and clarified butter, cotton and the Indian cloths made therefrom, of the coarser sorts." Most fascinatingly, it also records that "to the present day ancient drachmae are current in Barygaza, coming from this country, bearing inscriptions in Greek letters, and the devices of those who reigned after Alexander"—evidence of the Macedonian empire of Alexander the Great (see pp. 36–37).

The *Periplus* describes a series of trading ports in southern India, and an annual fair on the Indian border with Tibet. It also mentions an extensive trade in pearls, silk cloth, diamonds, and sapphires that were brought to the coast from the Ganges River Valley. Many more reports all add up to a remarkable account of the trading world of the Indian Ocean and its shores. Of the areas outside the scope of the *Periplus*, the author writes: "The regions beyond these places are either difficult of access because of their excessive winters and great cold, or else cannot be sought out, because of some divine influence of the gods."

◁ **Frankincense** The aromatic frankincense resin used in perfumes and incense has been traded from Arabia and Somalia for more than 5,000 years. The four main species of the resin all come from various species of Boswellia trees.

IN CONTEXT

Roman merchant ship

Roman merchant ships were round-hulled or flat-bottomed vessels, curving up at the bow and stern to give a roughly symmetrical shape. The two ends, the keel, and the external planks were assembled first before the internal timbers were inserted for support. The planks running from end to end were fastened to each other with mortise-and-tenon joints and strengthened with copper nails. Most merchant ships were between 50–120 feet (15–37 m) long and weighed between 150 and 350 tonnes. As well as cargo, many ships carried passengers. The grain ships between Rome and Alexandria regularly carried as many as 200 passengers on each journey.

ROMAN MERCHANT SHIP c.200 CE

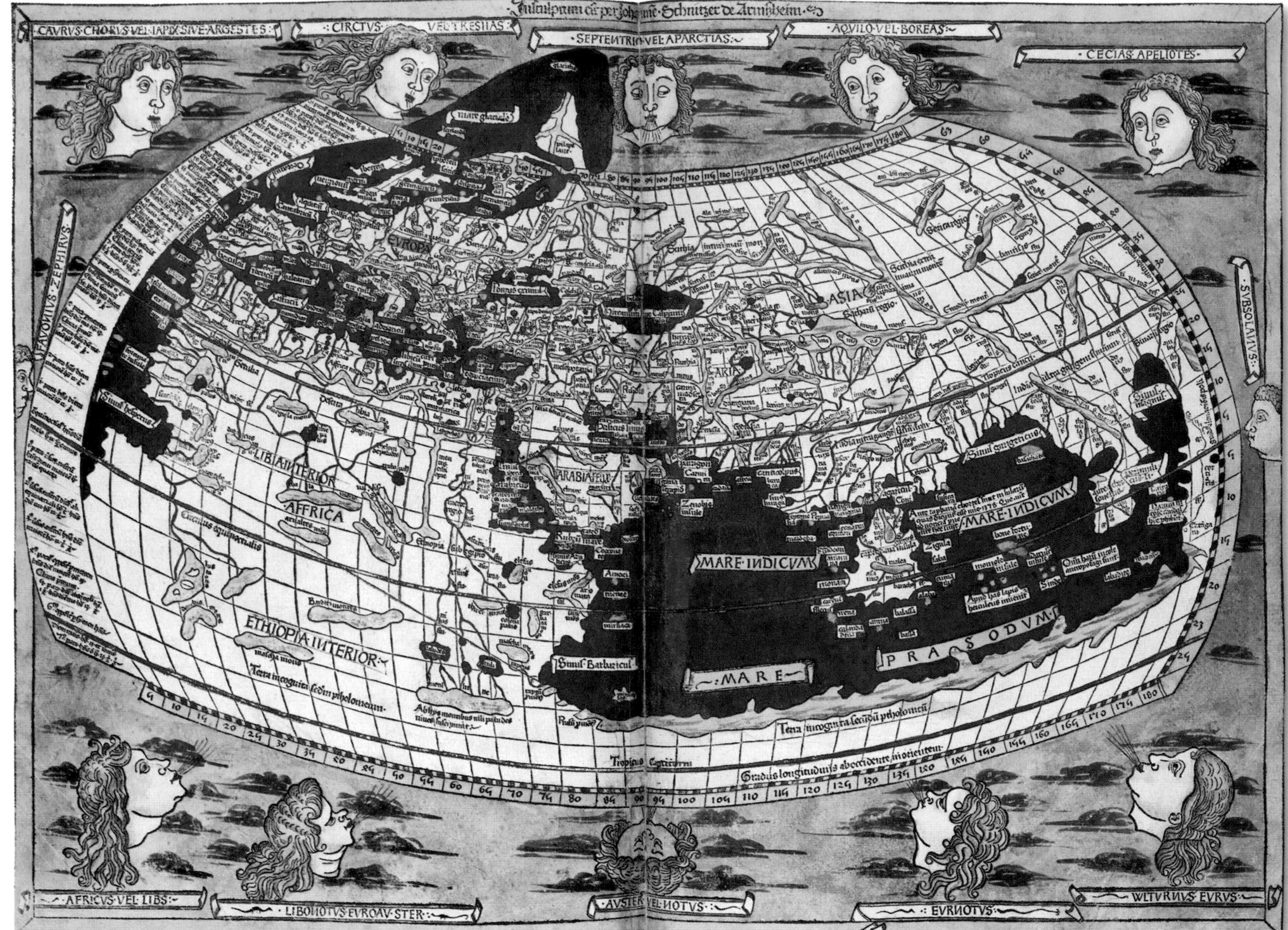

△ **Ptolemy's world** In this 15th-century manuscript copy of Ptolemy's world map, China (Sinae) is shown at the far east, beyond the oversized island of Sri Lanka (Taprobane) and the Malay Peninsula (Aurea Chersonesus). The Canary Islands are in the far west.

Ptolemy's *Geographia*

In the second century CE, a geographer and astronomer from Egypt transformed the existing knowledge of the world and the heavens above. His influence lasted for a thousand years, and is still significant today.

Very little is known about Ptolemy, other than that he was born in Alexandria, Egypt, around 100 CE, and died in the same city about 70 years later. He was a Roman citizen and a Greek, although he might have been a Greek-educated Egyptian who wrote in contemporary Greek. Despite his name, he was probably not related to the earlier pharaohs of Egypt, also called Ptolemy. It is for his writings that he is remembered, for in his lifetime he wrote three hugely important scientific works. The first, the *Almagest*, is the only ancient treatise about astronomy that survives today. The second work, the *Tetrabiblos*—its title derived from the Greek for "four books"—is a work of astrology. Most important is the third, the *Geographia*—a major discussion of the state of geographical knowledge at the time of the Roman Empire.

As an astronomer, Ptolemy believed that the Earth was at the center of the universe, a geocentric view that survived until the Sun-centered, or heliocentric, view of the universe became commonly accepted following the Copernican Revolution of the 16th century. Ptolemy thought the universe was like a set of nested spheres rotating around the Sun. From this premise, he calculated the dimensions of the universe and drew

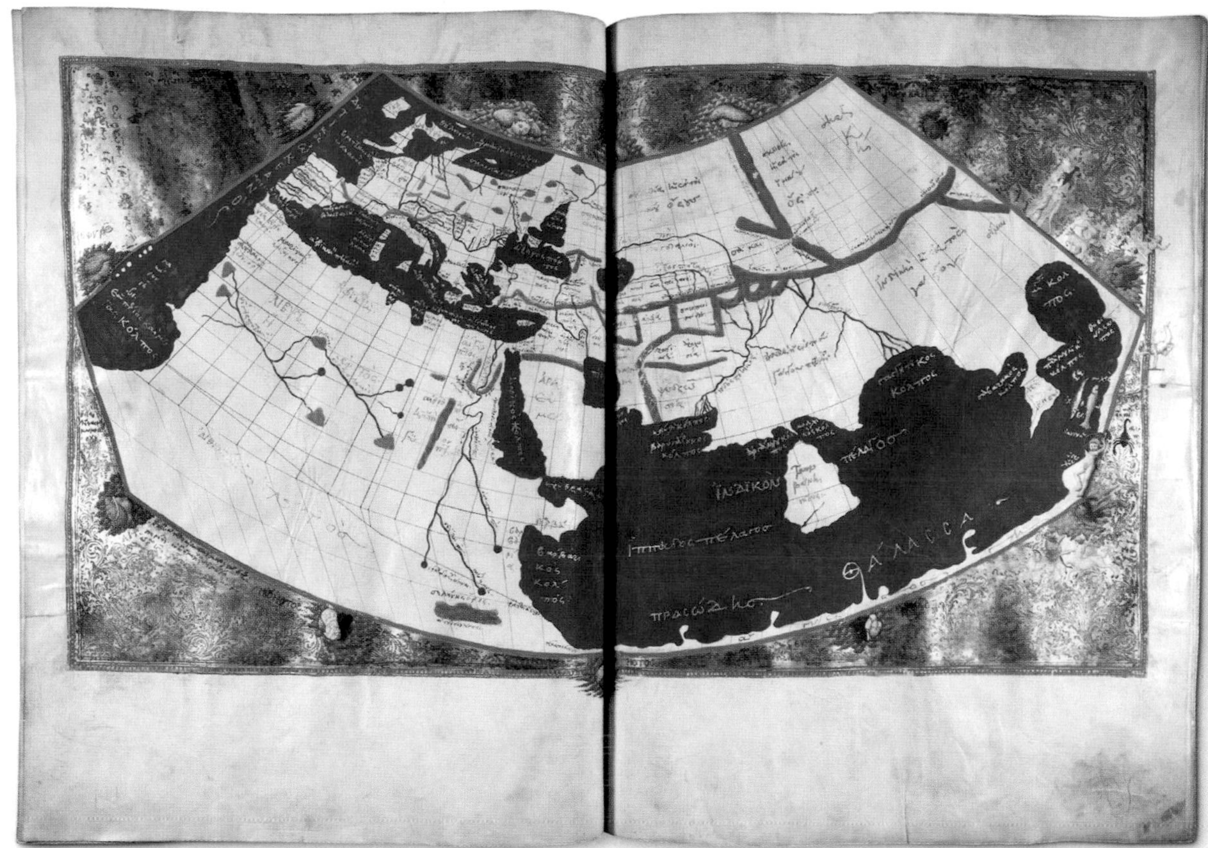

◁ **The known world**
Engraved in 1482 by Johannes Schnitzer, this map of the world shows Ptolemy's understanding of the *ecumene*—the known or inhabited world. In his time, neither the Americas nor Australasia had been discovered, the Pacific Ocean was unknown, and European sailors had yet to round the southern tip of Africa.

ON TECHNOLOGY
The sextant

This early 16th-century engraving shows Ptolemy, sextant in hand, being guided by Urania, the Greek muse of astronomy. However, the sextant was unknown to Ptolemy, as it was not invented until the early 1700s. A sextant is used by sailors to work out the angle between an astronomical object, such as the Sun at noon, and the horizon in order to calculate the ship's latitude. A measurement of the distance between the moon and another celestial object could also be used to calculate the right time, and thus longitude.

PTOLEMY GUIDED IN HIS WORK BY URANIA, THE GREEK MUSE OF ASTRONOMY

> " I know that I am **mortal** ... but when I trace ... the **windings to and fro** ... of the **heavenly bodies**, I no longer touch **earth** with my **feet**. "
>
> PTOLEMY, IN THE *ALMAGEST*, 150 CE

up a catalog of 48 major constellations. He also recorded all the data necessary to work out the positions of the Sun, the Moon, and the planets, the rising and setting of the stars, and the eclipses of the Sun and the Moon.

Ptolemy's attention to detail can be seen throughout his major work, the *Geographia*. He based it on an earlier treatise by the Greek geographer Marinus of Tyre, a work that has since been lost. Ptolemy's own book consists of three sections divided among eight books. Book I concerns cartography, while Book II to the start of Book VII is a gazetteer providing the longitude and latitude of every place in what was then the known world. Ptolemy measured latitude from the equator in Africa, but stated it in terms of hours: the equator was set with 12 hours of midsummer daylight, the Arctic with 24. The prime meridian, from which longitude is measured, runs through the Fortunate Islands in the Atlantic Ocean, which are thought to be the Canary Islands. The rest of Book VII provides details on the three different projections or perspectives needed to construct a map of the world. The final tome, Book VIII, contains a series of regional maps.

◁ **The Earth-centered sphere**
In this 15th-century painting by Justus van Gent and Pedro Berruguete, Ptolemy is shown holding an armillary sphere, a model of the objects in the sky with the Earth at its center, as he believed it to be.

The legacy of Ptolemy

Ptolemy's maps were more accurate than any others in existence at the time, although his calculations of longitude stretched the world considerably from east to west. Calculating longitude, however, remained difficult to work out until Galileo tackled the problem in the 17th century. The translation of *Geographia* into Arabic in the 9th century, and then into Latin in 1406, ensured that Ptolemy's influence lasted for a thousand years. His ideas were not superseded until the 16th century.

TRADE AND CONQUEST
400–1400

TRADE AND CONQUEST, 400–1400

Introduction

In medieval times, all long-distance travel was an adventure, undertaken at risk of life and fortune. Contemporary maps were full of blank spaces—unknown territories that were marked as sites of mythical wonders. To a Christian, it was credible that if they left Europe they might stumble upon the location of the Earthly Paradise or the kingdom of the legendary Prester John. Travelers' tales, among the most avidly read literature of the time, inextricably mixed fantastic invention with eyewitness reports.

Yet, despite the limits of formal geographical knowledge, the world was knitted together with trade routes that stretched across continents. Emperor Charlemagne in western Europe exchanged gifts with the caliph of Baghdad; the Roman popes sent ambassadors to the Mongol rulers of Central Asia. A remarkable number of people took to the primitive roads and the perilous seas in search of profit or adventure, conquest or salvation.

Faith and trade

Throughout the age, thousands of people traveled for their religion. In the 7th century, the Chinese Buddhist Xuanzang embarked on the long journey to India in search of the roots of his faith. The creed of Islam, established in the same century, obliged its believers to make the hajj, or pilgrimage to Mecca. As Islam spread, annual caravans of hajji traveled toward the Red Sea on routes across Asia and northern Africa. Christians expanded their own tradition of pilgrimage to sacred sites, drawing the faithful to a wide range of holy places near and far. The greatest wish for many Christians was to make the long journey to Jerusalem.

A 13TH-CENTURY ARAB MANUSCRIPT SHOWS A TYPICAL MERCHANT'S DHOW OF THE TIME

AS TODAY, MUSLIMS WERE OBLIGED TO MAKE THE HAJJ AT LEAST ONCE IN THEIR LIVES

THE LATEST NAVIGATIONAL AIDS ARE TESTED IN *THE TRAVELS OF SIR JOHN MANDEVILLE* (1357)

> “ It **behoves a man** who **wants to see wonders** sometimes to **go out of his way**. ”
>
> *THE TRAVELS OF SIR JOHN MANDEVILLE*, c.1350

Other voyagers were not so peaceful. None traveled more widely than the Vikings, whose thirst for adventure matched their lust for land and plunder. Viking warbands eventually sailed beyond the limits of the known world to Iceland, Greenland, and the edge of the Americas. The European Crusader knights also voyaged with sword in hand, wresting Palestine from the Muslims in 1099. The establishment of Crusader states in the Eastern Mediterranean became another stimulus to travel and trade, making the fortunes of the Italian maritime cities of Venice and Genoa.

A golden age

In the 13th century, the conquests of the Mongols under Genghis Khan and his successors imposed a measure of political unity on an area stretching from the Middle East to China, utilizing the ancient Silk Road trade routes. In the same period, camel caravans conducted a busy trade across the Sahara Desert to the source of gold in the mysterious kingdom of Mali. Seaborne commerce, benefiting from the introduction of the astrolabe and the compass as aids to navigation, linked the ports of the Red Sea to east Africa, India, Indonesia, and, ultimately, China. The Venetian Marco Polo was far from unique in making the journey from Europe to Mongol-ruled East Asia. The Muslim traveler Ibn Battuta, driven by sheer curiosity, was able to ramble the world from North Africa to Beijing. However, by the end of the 14th century, this golden age of Eurasian travel was fading as war and insecurity imposed new barriers on travel. The next great journeys would be made across the oceans.

KING (AND SOON SAINT) LOUIS IX OF FRANCE, WHO DIED ON THE EIGHTH CRUSADE IN 1270

GENGHIS KHAN, WHOSE CONQUESTS UNIFIED AN AREA STRETCHING FROM THE MIDDLE EAST TO CHINA

VENETIAN TRAVELER MARCO POLO USED THE SILK ROAD TO REACH MONGOL-RULED EAST ASIA

△ **The Mahabodhi Temple, Bodh Gaya**
This 19th-century watercolor shows the Mahabodhi Temple in India. Here, while meditating under a peepul (fig) tree, the Buddha found the answers to his questions about suffering and achieved a state of enlightenment.

Xuanzang's journey to India

Chinese scholar Xuanzang's expedition to India was one of the greatest overland journeys of its time. He discovered much about a little-known country and took back to China hundreds of texts that helped to spread Buddhism in his homeland.

The Buddhist scholar Xuanzang was born in Goushi (in what is now Henan province), China, c. 602. From an early age, he read widely, especially religious texts, and by the age of 20, he had become a Buddhist monk. His reading convinced him that the Buddhist scriptures that were available in China were either incomplete, or poor translations of the Indian originals. So, in 629, he decided to travel across Asia to India to find authentic copies of the Buddhist scriptures that he could take back to China and translate. He did this in spite

▷ **Xuanzang**
The scholar and traveler is depicted on the wall of the Dacien Temple, in China's Shanxi province, which was built to house scriptures he brought back from India.

> “I would **rather die** trying to take the **last step westward than** try to make it **back to** the **East alive**.”
>
> VOW MADE BY XUANZANG

of the fact that China's borders were officially closed, meaning that he risked being a fugitive in his country when he returned.

Xuanzang's journey turned out to be an epic 17-year expedition. First, he had to travel across northern China. Taking the Silk Road across the Gobi Desert, he followed the Tian Shan mountains into dangerous territory where he narrowly escaped being robbed. He then traveled along the Bedel Pass into Kyrgyzstan, where he met the great Khan of the Göktürks. The Göktürks were a league of nomadic Turkic people who had been at war with Tang China, but now had peaceful relations with the Chinese. Xuanzang then continued southwest through Uzbekistan to its capital, Tashkent, pushing on westward to Samarkand, where there were many abandoned Buddhist temples. Traveling further south, he came to Termez, where there was a monastery that was home to more than 1,000 Buddhist monks.

Reaching India

In Kunduz, Xuanzang was advised to make a diversion westward to Afghanistan, where he encountered another large Buddhist community. Here he began to collect Buddhist texts and found many Buddhist relics. One local monk, Prajñakara, helped him study some of these early scriptures and went with him to Bamyan, where he found a vast number of monasteries as well as the famous large Buddha statues carved into a rock face.

Traveling on to Gandhara (Kandahar), Xuanzang took part in a religious debate and met Hindus and Jains for the first time. Here, near the border of modern Pakistan, Xuanzang felt himself to be in the Indian world, and close to his goal at last. Leaving Gandhara, he began a long journey around India, meeting local rulers, staying in monasteries, talking to Buddhist monks, and collecting Buddhist texts.

Among the highlights of Xuanzang's period in India were his visits to major north Indian sites associated with the Buddha himself. This included a journey to what is now Bangladesh, where he found some 20 monasteries devoted to both the Hinayana and Mahayana traditions of Buddhism. He also stayed at the monastery at Nalanda, eastern India, a renowned center for the study of Mahayana Buddhist scriptures. At Nalanda, Xuanzang studied various subjects, especially Sanskrit, and found an inspirational master in the monastery's abbot, the renowned philosopher Silabhadra.

Xuanzang returned to China in 645. He had traveled some 9,942 miles (16,000 km) by horse and camel, collected 657 Buddhist texts, been triumphant in debates with Buddhist monks and Hindu teachers, and even, on one occasion, converted a group of criminals to Buddhism. He spent the rest of his life translating the texts he had collected into Chinese, making it possible for Buddhism to spread widely across the country. Emperor Taizong, impressed by his great achievements, not only pardoned him for making his journey but also appointed him a court adviser.

◁ **Buddhas of Bamyan, Afghanistan**
Carved into a cliff face in Bamyan, central Afghanistan, in the 6th century, the largest of these statues was 174 feet (53 m) tall. It was destroyed by the Taliban in 2001, but a reconstruction project is underway.

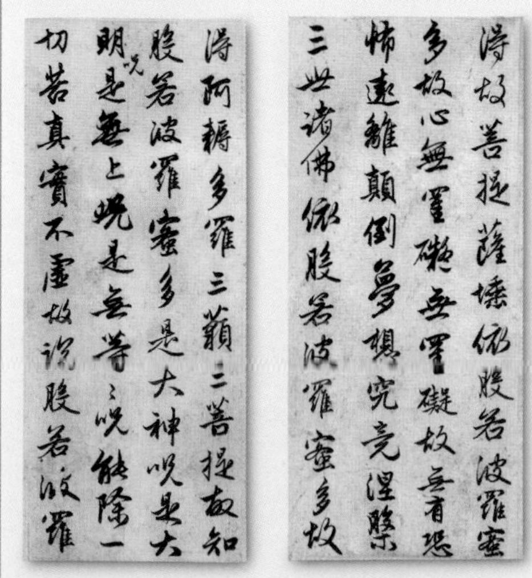

得故菩提薩埵依般若波羅蜜
多故心無罣礙無罣礙故無有恐
怖遠離顛倒夢想究竟涅槃
三世諸佛依般若波羅蜜多故
得阿耨多羅三藐三菩提故知
般若波羅蜜多是大神咒是大
明咒是無上咒是無等等咒能除一
切苦真實不虛故說般若波羅

CHINESE TRANSLATION OF *PERFECTION OF WISDOM*, BY CALLIGRAPHER ZHAO MENGFU

IN CONTEXT
Buddhist scriptures

The principal Buddhist scriptures originated in India and consisted either of the Buddha's words, or those of his close disciples. However, many of the texts available in China were incomplete or poor translations of the Sanskrit originals. Xuanzang felt compelled to travel to India, which was the source of scriptures such as the important group called *Prajnaparamita* (*Perfection of Wisdom*), and to translate them anew. When he returned to China, Emperor Taizong helped him set up a translation center in the capital Chang'an, where Xuanzang, together with a team of scholars and students, set about translating the material he had brought back from his journey.

Journey to the West

Journey to the West is a novel published in China in the 16th century, often attributed to Wu Cheng'en. The story is based very loosely on Xuanzang's great journey across Asia.

Although based on the Buddhist scholar Xuanzang's journey to India, *Journey to the West* is not a realistic account but incorporates many mythological and religious elements into the tale. The Buddha himself is at the heart of the narrative. Concerned by the sinful behavior of the people of China, he singles out Xuanzang as the person best suited to go to India to bring back the Buddhist scriptures needed to instruct the people how to live moral lives.

In the story, Xuanzang is accompanied on his journey by four disciples. These are mythical figures who are persuaded or inspired by the Chinese Buddhist deity Guanyin to travel with Xuanzang and protect him, enduring the dangers of the journey as a way of atoning for their sins. They take animal form but display human frailties. The most prominent of the four disciples is the violent and cunning Sun Wukong, or Monkey, a shape-shifting immortal who led a rebellion in heaven. The other three are: Zhu Bajie, a rapacious pig; Sha Wujing, a quiet and reliable river ogre; and Yulong, the Dragon King of the Western Sea, who takes the form of the white horse that carries Xuanzang on his travels.

The main section of the narrative describes the trip across Asia and consists of a series of adventures and mishaps in which the five travelers encounter monsters, evil magicians, and challenges such as flaming mountains. They emerge from these hazards largely unscathed and eventually reach India. There, they have more adventures before finally reaching their goal, a site called Vulture Peak, where they receive the scriptures from the Buddha himself and make their way back to China.

Containing both prose and poetry, *Journey to the West* combines comedy, adventure, and religious content in a unique way. This mixture of materials has made it one of the best-loved classics of Chinese literature. It has also helped to keep alive the memory of the great Xuanzang (see pp. 58–59) and his real-life journey.

▷ **Pilgrimage to India**
This mural depicts Xuanzang being carried by the Dragon King, Yulong, who has taken the form of a white horse. Behind them are the Monkey king, Sun Wukong, and Zhu Bajie, a half-human, half-pig monster.

△ ***Navicella***
This 1628 oil painting is based on a mosaic by Giotto di Bondone, which is located on the façade of St. Peter's Basilica. It depicts Jesus walking on water through a storm on Lake Galilee to join his disciples on a boat.

Kingdom of Heaven

Travel played a key role in the Gospels, from Mary and Joseph's trip to Bethlehem for a census, to the visit of the Magi from the East. Journeys were also crucial to the early spread of Christianity.

The Gospel accounts depict Jesus as a wandering Jewish preacher who traveled throughout Palestine, largely on foot, with a band of disciples. He was crucified by the Roman authorities around 33 CE, but his teaching was continued by his followers who traveled enormous distances around the world by sea and by land.

The spread of early Christianity was facilitated by the Roman road system. As Rome expanded and conquered new territories, well-patrolled roads enabled people to travel longer distances than ever before. Commerce followed, leading to prosperity and economic stability. Emperor Augustus (r. 27 BCE–14 CE) boasted that the world had never known such peace until his reign.

△ **Constantine I**
Roman Emperor from 306–337 CE, Constantine reversed centuries of imperial persecution and decreed tolerance for Christians, allowing them to move freely throughout the Roman Empire.

Christianity initially put down roots in towns and cities, rather than in rural areas. However, practicing Christianity was forbidden by Emperor Nero (r. 54–68 CE) and until the reign of the first Christian emperor, Constantine I, nearly 300 years later, Christians were persecuted throughout the Roman Empire. Furthermore, like Judaism, Christianity was a religion of sacred scriptures, and many ancient Greek and Roman authors disputed elements of the developing creed. Yet despite external threat and internal conflict and divisions, Christianity continued to spread rapidly, and in 301 CE, Armenia became the first nation to officially embrace the religion.

IN PROFILE

Saint Paul

Paul of Tarsus (c.5–67 CE) was one of the earliest Christian missionaries to travel long distances on Roman roads, preaching about Jesus. Greek, Latin, and Semitic languages were the dominant languages in the area of the Mediterranean basin. As a citizen of the Roman province of Cilicia, St. Paul was fluent in Hebrew and spoke the Greek *koine* dialect made popular by the armies of Alexander the Great. Translators were also available in all the ports and could be easily hired in large towns.

St. Paul recorded his journeys across Asia Minor and Europe in the *Acts of the Apostles*. The cause of his death is uncertain, but it is thought that he was executed in Rome at Emperor Nero's command.

MOSAIC DETAIL SHOWING ST. PAUL, ST. SOPHIA'S CATHEDRAL, KIEV

The spread of Christianity

Pilgrimage soon became a distinctive part of Christianity. Constantine built several churches over the tombs of saints in Rome, which became a focus for religious travelers. His mother, Helena, made a pilgrimage to Palestine in around 325 CE. Another notable pilgrim was a woman called Egeria who, in a letter known as the *Itinerarium Egeriae* (*Travels of Egeria*) recounted her visits to many sites in the Holy Land.

As a result of Roman traders traveling in the 1st century, Christianity spread rapidly through the British Isles from the 2nd to the 5th centuries. Monasteries were established by monks who were noted for their learning and writing.

The Western Roman Empire collapsed in the late 5th century, partly because of numerous barbarian invasions, but a Roman emperor continued to rule the East from Constantinople. This meant that roads were no longer maintained as they had been and aqueducts fell into disrepair. Many routes became dangerous and the ports and seas were under threat of piracy.

◁ **Rylands Library Papyrus**

In order to spread Christianity, the gospels, the letters of St. Paul, and other Christian writings were copied by hand and then disseminated. The Rylands Library Papyrus is a fragment of a copy of St. John's Gospel from around the 2nd century CE.

Christianity in Europe

During the 6th and 7th centuries, monks from Britain traveled throughout Europe, founding monasteries and centers of learning. They also re-established literacy, which had lapsed in some places. This self-imposed exile from home was called "white martyrdom."

By the 8th century, Christianity had taken hold in Europe. Many countries were ruled by Christian monarchs, and Greek missionaries, such as Methodius and Cyril, had created the Cyrillic alphabet to translate the Bible. This same alphabet still forms the basis of the modern-day Russian language.

▽ **Hagia Eirene**

From the mid-4th century, Christians began to build churches as public places of worship. Like Hagia Eirene in Istanbul, they were rectangular in shape with a rounded end, similar to the Roman basilicas used as law courts.

" Remember **Christ's disciples**. They **rowed** their **heavy ships** to shore, then abandoned everything to **follow Christ**. "

ÆLFRIC OF EYNSHAM, ENGLISH ABBOT

△ **The Qur'an**
Muslims believe that the Qur'an was revealed by God to Muhammad through the angel Gabriel. The revelations were collected into one book by Muhammad's successor, Abu Bakr, in 634. The Qur'an consists of 114 *surah* (chapters) divided into numerous *ayah* (verses).

The spread of Islam

In 632, a new religion emerged in eastern Asia. Within a few years, the armies of Islam had established an empire that stretched from the borders of India in the east to the Atlantic Ocean in the west.

Muhammad, the founder of Islam, was born in the western Arabian city of Mecca in around 570. He was orphaned at an early age and raised by his uncle. He used to hide away in a mountain cave for nights on end to pray, and in around 610 he began to receive visits from the angel Gabriel, who revealed to him the first verses of what became the Qur'an, Islam's holy book. As the revelations continued, Muhammad began to preach their message, stating that he was a prophet and messenger from God. After being warned of a plot to assassinate him, Muhammad and his followers fled Mecca for Medina in 622. This *Hijra*, or flight, marks the start of the Islamic calendar.

In Medina, Muhammad united all the tribes under his leadership, and in 630 he returned to Mecca with an army of 10,000 Muslim converts. By the time of his death in 632, most of the Arabian peninsula had converted to Islam.

▽ **The Islamic world**
Soon after its birth in 632, Islam spread throughout Arabia, reaching Palestine in 634 and Persia in 643. Westward, it swept across Egypt and North Africa, crossing over into Spain and southern France in 711.

Across the world

Muhammad's successor, Abu Bakr (r. 632–34), completed the religious and political union of the various Arab tribes, but under the next two caliphs—Umar and Uthman—a rapid expansion began that changed the face of the region. Muslim armies took Damascus in 635 and Jerusalem in 638, and defeated the Persian Sasanian Empire in 642. To the west, Muslim armies conquered Egypt in 640 and Tunisia by 680, reaching the Atlantic coast of Morocco by 683. In 711, Muslim armies attacked and conquered Spain. By now, the Islamic empire stretched from the Atlantic coast to the borders of India, creating the largest empire the world had even seen.

The limits of its expansion became clear when, between 670 and 677, and again between 716 and 717, Muslim armies failed to capture Constantinople, the capital of the Byzantine Empire. Expansion north over the Pyrenees into France was halted by the Franks at Poitiers in 732, although success over the Chinese at the battle of the River Talas in 751 opened up Central Asia to Muslim control.

> " Oh mankind! ...We **created** you from **a male and a female** and made you into **nations and tribes** that you may **know one another**. "

QUR'AN, CHAPTER 49, VERSE 13

Islamic government

◁ **Umayyad currency**
Abd al-Malik ibn Marwān was the fifth leader of the Umayyad caliphate, which was based in Damascus. During his reign, he made Arabic the state language, established a postal service, and minted a currency for the Muslim world.

At first, this vast empire was governed from Medina, but in 661 Muawiya established the Umayyad Caliphate and moved the capital to Damascus. In 750, the Umayyads were overthrown by the Abbasids, and the empire gradually broke up into different regional caliphates and emirates. Rebel Umayyads fled to Spain, where they established a new emirate based in Córdoba.

Travel in the Islamic world

Throughout the Muslim world, whether united or divided, people were constantly on the move. As the armies conquered new lands, governors and administrators followed them. Merchants and traders moved between the cities and sailed around the coasts. Scholars traveled to cities to study at the madrassas, or religious schools. The schools founded in Fez in Morocco in 859, and in Cairo in Egypt in 970, can be considered the oldest universities in the world.

The biggest group of travelers were the pilgrims to Mecca. Among the Five Pillars of Islam—the five basic acts of Islamic faith, and the foundation of all Muslim life—is the requirement that each Muslim at least once in his or her own lifetime makes a Hajj, or pilgrimage, to Mecca. Pilgrims undertook an often dangerous round trip of up to two years to fulfill this requirement (see pp. 80–83).

◁ **The Kaaba**
The Kaaba is a shrine that stands in the center of Islam's most sacred mosque in Mecca. In this Persian illustration, Muhammad is seen placing the sacred Black Stone, the eastern cornerstone, into place when the Kaaba was rebuilt in around 630.

◁ **Invasion of Spain**
In 711, the Arabs and their Berber allies crossed from Africa to begin the conquest of Spain. Their armies eventually reached Poitiers, in central France, where they were defeated by the Franks in 732.

IN CONTEXT
Islamic architecture

The first mosque ever built was constructed around the sacred Kaaba (the most sacred site in Islam) in Mecca in around 632. Mosques were then built wherever Muslim armies conquered, each with internal prayer halls, minarets from which the faithful were called to prayer, and many with a central dome. Inside was a *mihrab*, or niche, which indicated the direction of the Kaaba, and a *minbar*, or tiered pulpit, from which the imam preached. Because Islam forbids the depiction of living creatures, most mosques are decorated with geometrical patterns.

THE OCTAGONAL DOME OF THE TREASURY IN THE UMAYYAD MOSQUE IN DAMASCUS

Arab exploration

With peace established under the magnificent Abbasid Caliphate, Arab travelers could now journey safely and securely. Where traders went, travelers and explorers followed in their wake.

After a century of rapid expansion and internal turmoil, the Arab Empire was taken over in 750 by the Abbasid Dynasty. The Abbasids were descended from Muhammad's youngest uncle, Abbas, from whom they took their name. Their first capital was in Kufa, in what is now central Iraq, but in 762 the capital was moved to the newly built city of Baghdad. The city became a center of scientific exploration, invention, philosophy, and culture during what became known as the Golden Age of Islam. In the House of Wisdom, scholars were brought together to gather and translate the knowledge of the classical Greek and Roman worlds into Arabic.

◁ **The dhow**
The dhow was the main sailing ship of the Indian Ocean, Persian Gulf, and Red Sea. It is unclear whether the Arabs or Indians invented the dhow, but it proved to be a seaworthy vessel, carrying a wide range of cargoes with a crew of up to 30 men.

An empire at peace

The peace of the Abbasid empire encouraged both trade and travel. The advanced scientific knowledge of the Arabs and their use of detailed maps and rudimentary *kamals*, or sextants, for navigation made it possible for sailors to cross the Indian Ocean and they traded extensively with India and the African coast. Accounts of a number of voyages still exist today. In the 9th century, the Muslim geographer Ahmad al-Ya'qubi traveled widely, visiting North Africa, Egypt, and India, and recorded his experiences in two extensive chronicles; one a history of the world, the other an account of general geography.

Travel abroad

During the next century, the explorer al-Mas'udi visited Persia, Armenia, and Georgia, as well as Arabia, Syria, and Egypt. His voyages took him around the Caspian and Mediterranean seas, as well as across the Indian Ocean to India and down the east coast of Africa. Some of his ideas were obviously ill-informed, such as his suggestion that a northern passage from the Asian Arctic must lead to the Black Sea, but his main book, *The Meadows of Gold and Mines of Gems*, was a major contribution to the history and geography of the known world. In the second half of the 10th century, al-Muqaddasi became the foremost Muslim geographer, compiling a detailed account of all the Islamic places and regions he had visited on his travels.

In the 8th century, Muslim traders had reached the Malay Peninsula, China, and Korea. A story from the mid-800s tells how a merchant named Sulayman traded with the Chinese. Al-Masudi records Arab, Persian, and Chinese

◁ **Al-Idrisi's world map**
Muhammad al-Idrisi was born in North Africa in 1099, but worked for most of his life in Palermo, at the court of King Roger II of Sicily, where he prepared maps for the king. This is a 15th-century copy of one of his maps.

merchants meeting in the Malay Peninsula. In 953, Al-Ramhormuzi, a Persian traveler, wrote that Muslim sailors had traveled throughout Indonesia and north to China. He also remarked on the cannibals that lived in the Andaman Islands, south of Burma.

One of Al-Ramhormuzi's most famous stories is about Abhara, a renowned Arab seafarer, who made seven voyages to and from China. Found alone on a small boat off the coast of Vietnam, Abhara was taken on board an Arab merchant ship and was made its captain. He promptly offloaded all its heavy cargo, enabling the ship to survive an incoming typhoon.

To the west, Ibn Hawqal, who had traveled extensively in Asia and Africa, left detailed reports about Muslim-held Spain and Sicily. Another 10th-century traveler, Ahmad ibn Fadlan, traveled as a member of a diplomatic mission from the Abbasid caliph to the king of the Volga Bulgars—newly converted Muslims who lived on the eastern bank of the Volga, in what is now Russia. In his account of his travels, ibn Fadlan provides detailed reports of the Volga Vikings, including a fascinating account of a ship burial.

△ **Astronomy**
The Arabs were great astronomers, mapping the heavens and the movements of the planets. Taqi al-Din Muhammad ibn Ma'ruf founded one of the largest astronomical observatories of the time, the Galata observatory in Constantinople, in 1577. The orthodox clergy opposed its use for astrology, and it was closed down in 1580.

IN CONTEXT
Sinbad the Sailor

Sinbad is a fictional sailor who lived in Baghdad in the early 800s, and whose story features in *One Thousand and One Nights*. His tale begins when a poor goods-carrier rests on a bench outside a merchant's house and complains aloud about the injustice of a world that allows the rich to live in luxury, while the poor must work hard for a living. The rich merchant hears his woes and asks him inside, whereupon he discovers that they are both called Sinbad. The rich Sinbad is the titular Sinbad the Sailor, and he tells the other man that he became rich "by fortune and fate" over the course of seven voyages. The journeys are fantastical, full of magical places, terrifying monsters, and encounters with the supernatural, but elements of the tales are based on real-life voyages of Arab travelers.

19TH-CENTURY ENGRAVING OF SINBAD FROM *ONE THOUSAND AND ONE NIGHTS*

The astrolabe

The astrolabe was one of the most important aids to the early explorer. Invented by the Greeks, then developed by the Muslims, it helped travelers by land or sea determine their latitude on Earth.

Latitude is the distance north or south of the equator. Once a traveler can determine latitude, they can figure out how far north or south they are. Together with a rough estimate of the distance traveled, they can then work out how far east or west they have journeyed. Early travelers had no such knowledge of latitude, and navigated by known landmarks, using the hills and rivers to plot their course. However, this system was obviously of no use when in unfamiliar territory, or when crossing the open sea, where there were no natural landmarks. What travelers needed was some sort of mechanical instrument to help calculate latitude.

▷ **Moorish astrolabe**
This beautifully constructed astrolabe was made in Moorish Spain by Abū Isḥāq Ibrāhīm al-Zarqālī around 1015. Its rotating rings and plates could be used to establish either latitude or time.

IN PROFILE
Hypatia of Alexandria

Hypatia (c.350–415 CE) was a Greek mathematician, astronomer, and philosopher born in Egypt (which was then part of the Byzantine Empire). She ran a school of philosophy in Alexandria, where she taught astronomy and philosophy. Synesius of Cyrene, the bishop of Ptolemais in Libya, was one of Hypatia's students. He credits her with inventing the astrolabe—although it is more likely she collaborated with him to improve an existing design. Hypatia was murdered by a Christian mob in 415, after being accused of exacerbating a conflict between the governor and the bishop of the city.

PORTRAIT OF HYPATIA OF ALEXANDRIA

◁ *Mihrab*
A semi-circular niche in the wall of a mosque, a *mihrab* shows the direction of the holy Kaaba, or "House of Allah," in Mecca. This highly decorated *mihrab* is inside the late 15th-century Bara Gumbad Mosque in New Delhi, India.

Early inventors

Early astrolabes combined a planisphere (a star chart that used a rotating, adjustable disc to work out which stars were visible that day) and a dioptra, or sighting tool, to measure angles. By such primitive means, the angle of the Sun, Moon, and stars, and their position in the heavens relative to the ground, day or night, could be worked out. Armed with this knowledge, travelers could then plot their latitude to find out where they were on Earth.

It is not completely clear who invented the first mechanical astrolabe. Credit is usually given to Hypatia of Alexandria, due to a letter written to her by one of her students, Synesius of Cyrene. However, this seems unlikely, given the fact that Hypatia's father, Theon of Alexandria, had already written a treatise—sadly now lost—on the working of the astrolabe. It is also claimed that Ptolemy had used an astrolabe in his calculations for *Tetrabiblos*, his book on astrology, some two centuries earlier. Apollonius of Perga, a Greek astronomer who lived in what is now southern Turkey, is thought to have invented an early astrolabe some 350 years before Ptolemy.

All the individuals attributed to the invention of the astrolabe were Greeks living in the Roman Empire, and the Greeks continued to use and develop astrolabes during the succeeding Byzantine Empire. John Philoponus, a Byzantine philosopher from Alexandria, wrote the earliest extant treatise in Greek on the instrument around 530. By the mid-600s, Severus Sebokht, a scholar and bishop who lived in Mesopotamia, wrote a major treatise on the astrolabe, and described it as being made of brass, indicating that by then it was an instrument of some complexity.

△ **Celestial globe**
Made by Ibrahim ibn Said al-Sahli in Valencia, Spain circa 1085, this globe of the heavens is believed to be the oldest such object in the world.

Muslim advances

In the 640s, Muslim armies from Arabia occupied most of the Byzantine Empire, and knowledge of the astrolabe passed to the Arabs. They further developed it, adding new dials and discs to make it more complex and accurate. In its most advanced form, the astrolabe consisted of a mater, or base plate, marked with a degree scale around its outer rim. On top of this, two rotating plates and a ring were aligned to work out the angles of the known stars, and thus determine latitude. If the latitude was already known, the astrolabe could be used in reverse to calculate the time.

While the Arabs used the astrolabe as a navigational tool, they also discovered a more specific purpose for the instrument. When praying, Muslims have to face the holy city of Mecca, the birthplace of Muhammad. By using the astrolabe, Muslims could calculate *qibla*—the direction of Mecca. Used both as a secular and a religious instrument, the astrolabe soon became indispensable for travelers and worshippers alike.

> " It uses as its **servants geometry** and **arithmetic**, which it would not be improper to call **a fixed … truth**. "

SYNESIUS OF CYRENE (c.373–c.414 CE), WRITING TO HIS FRIEND PAEONIUS

▽ **The Ptolemaic universe**
This illustration from 1708 shows Ptolemy's geocentric view of the universe, in which Earth is orbited by the Sun, Moon, and all the planets.

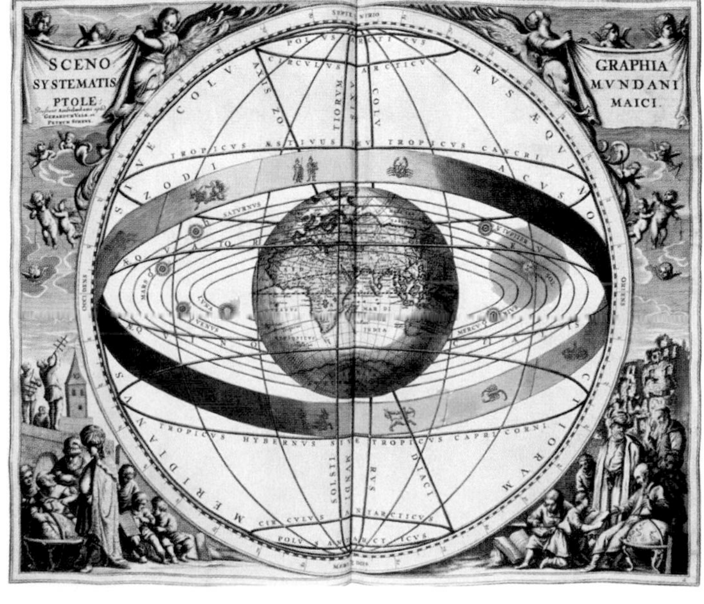

Voyages of the Vikings

The most wide-ranging voyagers of medieval Europe, Viking bands traveled as far as Iceland, Constantinople, and North America, driven by a hunger for land, plunder, trade, and a thirst for adventure.

▽ Viking travels and trade routes
Vikings ventured across the North Sea to the British Isles and down Europe's Atlantic coast; south along the rivers of Russia and Ukraine to the Black Sea; and across the Atlantic to Iceland, Greenland, and America.

▽ Viking shields
Viking warriors carried round shields made of hand-painted wooden planks riveted together. They fought with a shield in one hand and an ax, sword, or spear in the other.

The Vikings hailed from Denmark, Sweden, and Norway. In the 8th century, these were turbulent pagan areas of Europe that stood in contrast to relatively orderly Christian states such as Anglo-Saxon England or Charlemagne's empire in France and Germany. Scandinavian society was dominated by warbands—groups of warriors following a leader distinguished by his strength, courage, and success in battle. These warbands fought one another both at home and overseas. Shipbuilders in Scandinavia had developed the longship—a fast, shallow-draft war vessel capable of sailing on both seas and rivers. In 793, a Viking warband crossed the North Sea and carried out a ferocious raid on the monastery at Lindisfarne, an island off the coast of northeastern England. Two years later, Vikings sailed around the north of Scotland, raiding monasteries at Iona in the Hebrides, and others off the coast of Ireland. They also occupied the Shetland and Orkney Islands, which then became permanent bases for further raids that were carried out on the British Isles.

From around 830, the scope of Viking activity expanded dramatically. Their raiding parties, of increasing size, struck around the coast of northwest Europe and advanced deep inland along major rivers such as the Rhine, Seine, and Loire. A permanent Viking settlement on the island of Noirmoutier, off the mouth of the Loire, provided the base for a famous expedition launched in 859 by the warband leaders Björn Ironside and Hastein. Sailing their longships southward along the Atlantic coast of the Iberian Peninsula, the Vikings entered the Mediterranean through the Straits of Gibraltar. There they made a prolonged stay, plundering both Muslim and Christian states in Spain, North Africa, the south coast of France, and Italy, before returning to the Loire, in triumph and weighed down with booty, in 862.

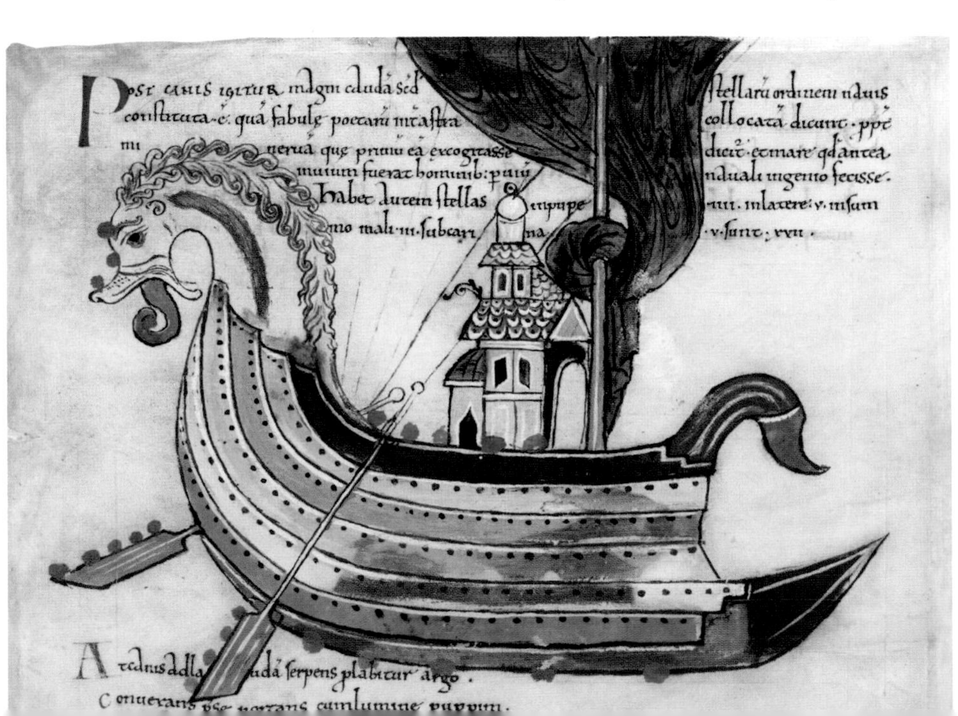

▷ Ocean voyages
This 11th-century codex illustration shows a Viking longship. Due to the shape of the prow, these ships were called "dragonships" by the Franks.

Expanding horizons

By that time, the Vikings were raising their ambitions from hit-and-run raids to conquest and settlement. In 865, a substantial force invaded eastern England and embarked on a sustained campaign of conquest. After 14 years of warfare, Alfred the Great, the Anglo-Saxon King of Wessex, stemmed the Viking advance, but Danish settlers became a permanent presence in north and eastern England. Vikings also settled in Ireland and Scotland, and as far north as the Faroe Islands. Vikings led by Rollo settled in northern France. By the early 10th century, longships crossing the North Sea were no doubt outnumbered

◁ **The Vikings attack Paris**
This 19th-century colored lithograph depicts the besieged Frankish city of Paris, France. In 845, and again in 885–886, the Vikings sailed inland up the Seine. However, the Vikings never captured the city.

by knarrs, the broader, deeper-hulled ships used for the transport of livestock, stores, and trade goods.

The Vikings who voyaged to the British Isles and western Europe chiefly came from Denmark and Norway. In eastern Europe, it was primarily the Swedes who forged new trade routes and embarked on raids. Crossing the Baltic in the course of the 9th century, they established control of an area stretching from Lake Ladoga south to Kiev, where they became known as "Rus" or "Varangians." The Rus Vikings traveled along the great rivers—the Vistula, the Dnieper, the Dniester, and the Volga—down to the Black Sea and the Caspian. This brought them into contact with two key civilizations substantially wealthier and more advanced than those of Western Europe—the Christian Byzantine Empire and the Muslim Abbasid Caliphate. Viking traders penetrated as far as the Abbasid capital Baghdad in modern-day Iraq. Thousands of Arabic silver coins, found in buried Viking treasure hoards in Sweden, attest to the importance of the trade established with the Muslim world. »

"**Never before** ... was it thought that such an **inroad from the sea** could be made."

LETTER FROM ALCUIN TO KING ETHELRED, 793

ON TECHNOLOGY
Viking longship

The famous Viking longships, used for raiding and long-distance voyages, had a sleek hull that was clinker-built—that is, constructed of overlapping planks. Lightweight and with a shallow draft, the longships traveled fast and could easily be sailed up rivers or landed on beaches. They had a square sail, but were rowed by their crew on still days. The longships employed on coastal raids were exceptionally long and thin, those intended for ocean voyages were somewhat broader and shorter. Most of the examples of longships that survive today were unearthed from ship burials, the style of interment adopted for high-status Viking warriors.

9TH-CENTURY GOKSTAD BURIAL SHIP IN THE VIKING SHIP MUSEUM, OSLO, NORWAY

△ **Viking coin**
Around the 10th century, the Vikings adopted silver coinage in imitation of the more civilized countries they raided. The images on these coins provide evidence of the design of Viking ships.

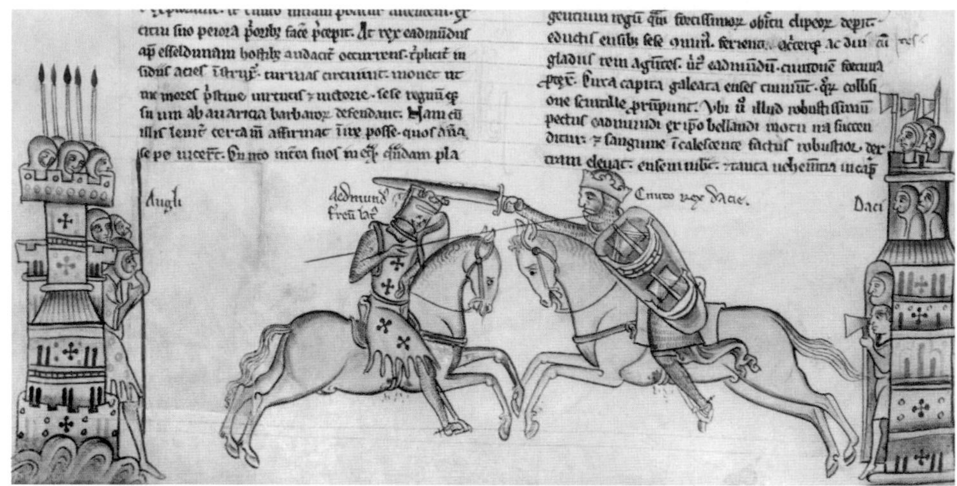

▷ **King Cnut the Great**
A medieval illustration shows Cnut, king of Denmark, defeating Anglo-Saxon king Edmund Ironside in battle. Cnut became ruler of all England in 1016, and later also added Norway to his North Sea Empire.

» Viking ambitions were rarely limited to trade alone—plunder and conquest were always a temptation. In the summer of 860, some 200 Rus Viking longships commanded by the warriors Askold and Dir sailed down the Dnieper into the Black Sea, bent upon seizing the Byzantine capital, Constantinople. They were frustrated by the city's formidable fortifications, but Viking armies returned to attack Constantinople repeatedly over the following century. A more cooperative relationship with the Byzantine Empire developed from 988, when the ruler of Kievan Rus, Vladimir I, converted to Christianity. As a gesture of peace, Vladimir sent a group of Rus warriors to enter the service of the emperor in Constantinople. These warriors founded the Varangian Guard, which became an elite mercenary element of the Byzantine army—Viking ferocity placed at the service of the Empire.

The Vikings' most extraordinary voyages of exploration were those made across the North Atlantic. The Vikings first discovered the existence of Iceland when a sea captain heading for the Faroes was blown off-course and returned to tell of a "land of snow." This inspired Danish warrior Garðar Svavarsson to make an exploratory voyage that circumnavigated Iceland in around 860. The prospect of empty lands in the north attracted Norwegian warband leaders in search of remote locations where they could live untrammeled by authority. The first attempt at a settlement was made by Flóki Vilgerðarson, but he returned declaring the country uninhabitable. The first durable Viking Icelandic settlement was established by Ingólfr Arnarson, in around 874.

Discovering North America

By the second half of the 10th century, land in Iceland was becoming scarce. In 983, Erik the Red, a notably unruly immigrant to Iceland from Norway, became probably the first European to see the ice cliffs of Greenland. He returned from an exploratory voyage to organize a fleet of colonists, leading 25 knarr transport ships with settlers and supplies back to Greenland. Around 1000, the final step in the Vikings' extraordinary adventure was taken. Traveling west from Iceland, a certain Bjarni Herjólfsson got lost in fog and missed Greenland, ending up sailing along an unknown coast. Inspired by Bjarni's report of a forested

▽ **Lindholm Hoje**
The Viking burial site at Lindholm Hoje, in Denmark, has graves marked with stones laid out in the shape of a boat. These "stone ships" reflect the importance of sea travel in the Viking world.

◁ **Icelandic sagas** Viking voyages were recorded in sagas written by Icelanders in the 13th and 14th centuries. They were based on family histories passed down by word of mouth.

land, Leif Erikson, first son of Erik the Red, sailed with 35 men in search of the new country. He sailed to Newfoundland, the Gulf of St. Lawrence, and beyond to the south, although exactly where remains disputed. He built a camp at a place he called Vinland because his men found grapes growing there. It is speculated that this may have been somewhere between present-day Boston and New York. Subsequent voyages attempted to establish a permanent Viking settlement in North America, but the effort failed, probably because of vigorous resistance by Native Americans. Yet Leif Erikson's men had almost certainly been the first Europeans to "discover" North America.

By that time, the golden age of Viking voyages was coming to an end. In the Scandinavian homelands, kingdoms evolved that established their rule over the warbands, putting an end to their raids. By the early 11th century, a North Sea Empire had taken shape, ruled by King Cnut of Denmark, who was also ruler of England and Norway. Outside Scandinavia, Viking warriors and settlers became integrated into their host societies. The Slav population of eastern Europe absorbed the Rus Vikings. In northern France, the Vikings adopted French language and customs, intermarried with local people, and became the Normans. With the collapse of the North Sea Empire after Cnut's death in 1035, the Viking era was effectively over.

◁ **Gotland stone** The lower half of this carved stone from Sweden's Gotland island shows a Viking longship. The upper half depicts a scene from Norse mythology—Viking warriors who have died in combat entering Valhalla.

KEY HISTORIC SITE

L'Anse aux Meadows

The remains of the Viking settlement at L'Anse aux Meadows in Newfoundland, Canada, were identified in 1960. They provided the first material evidence to support the story of Leif Erikson's discovery of America as related in the Icelandic sagas. Sited in a sheltered cove, the settlement consisted of eight buildings made of turf over a wooden frame. These would probably have accommodated some 90 people, as well as housing a forge and facilities for ship repair. Radiocarbon dating has confirmed that the settlement was established around 1000, a date that fits with the evidence from the sagas. The settlement seems to have been abandoned within 20 years of being founded.

AN AERIAL VIEW OF A RECONSTRUCTED LONGHOUSE AT L'ANSE AUX MEADOWS

> " Leif **set sail** as soon as he was ready ... and **lighted upon lands** of which before he had **no expectation**. "
>
> *THE SAGA OF ERIK THE RED*, c.1265

△ **Jerusalem siege**
A 13th-century image of the Crusaders' siege of Jerusalem in 1099 shows Christian soldiers defending the Church of the Holy Sepulchre, the traditional site of Christ's crucifixion.

The Crusades

Between the 11th and 13th centuries, tens of thousands of Christian soldiers from Europe made the 3,100-mile (5,000-km) journey to the eastern Mediterranean to fight for their faith against the warriors of Islam.

> “ Take **the road to the Holy Sepulchre**, rescue that land and rule over it yourselves. ... Take this road **for the remission of your sins**. ”

POPE URBAN II, SPEECH AT CLERMONT, FRANCE, NOVEMBER 27, 1095

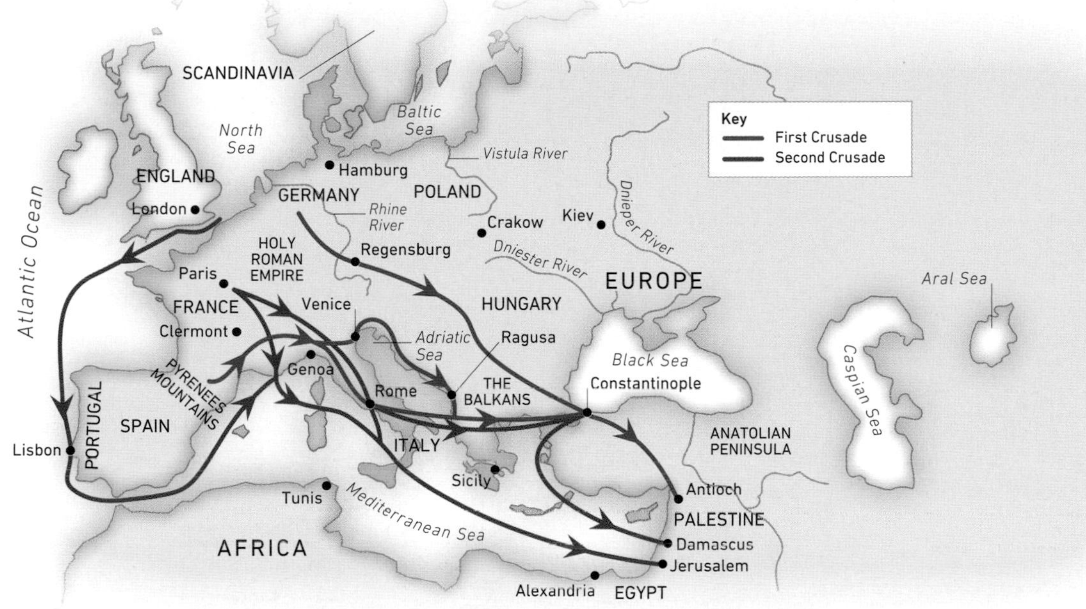

△ **Crusader routes**
Crusader armies from Germany tended to prefer an overland route to the east through Hungary, the Balkans, and Anatolia. Other countries usually sailed across the Mediterranean, often in ships provided by Genoa or Venice.

In November 1095, during a church council held at Clermont in central France, Pope Urban II delivered an impassioned appeal for a “Crusade” to liberate the holy city of Jerusalem from the rule of Muslim infidels. The response in Western Christendom was on a scale the Pope could never have anticipated. A wave of religious enthusiasm inspired rich and poor alike to “take the cross,” the symbol of the Crusades, and embark on the long, hazardous journey to Palestine. Some no doubt hoped for material advantage, but most were motivated by a sincere faith and the promise of remission of their sins.

The first Crusaders to embark for the east in 1096 were a disorganized mass of poor peasants inspired by the charismatic French preacher Peter the Hermit. In bands tens-of-thousands-strong, they rambled down the Rhine and across Hungary and the Balkans, massacring Jewish communities and devastating the countryside as they went. When they eventually reached Constantinople, the capital of the Christian Byzantine Empire, they were ferried across to Muslim-dominated Anatolia, where an army of the Seljuk Turks cut them to pieces. The official First Crusade, led by French and Norman noblemen, was far better prepared. Four armies, comprising some 40,000 knights, footsoldiers, and noncombatants, either traveling overland or taking ships across the Adriatic, met up outside Constantinople in the spring of 1097. The next stage of their journey, across Anatolia, was fraught with dangers and hardships. The Christian knights defeated the Turks in battle, but on the onerous march through the summer heat, most of their horses died and proud warriors were reduced to riding oxen.

◁ **Heraldic cross**
The Lorraine cross was the heraldic sign of Crusader Godfrey de Bouillon, who was declared ruler of Jerusalem after the First Crusade. It was later associated with the Knights Templar.

The assault on Jerusalem

On arriving at the walls of Antioch, the Crusade stalled. By the time the Christian knights had gained secure possession of the city, they had almost forgotten Jerusalem amid rows over the division of territory already conquered. But the ordinary soldiers on the expedition, who held a simpler, clearer faith, mutinied and insisted that the Crusade continue to its prescribed goal. The Crusaders finally reached the Holy City in June 1099. Now perhaps 15,000-strong, they faced a difficult task in wresting Jerusalem from its Muslim defenders. After building siege machines, including towers, catapults, and rams, they attacked the city on July 15 and took it by assault, inflicting a terrible massacre upon its Muslim and Jewish population. »

IN PROFILE
Richard the Lionheart

English King Richard I (1157–99) set out on a Crusade to the Holy Land in 1190. Traveling via Marseilles, Sicily, and Cyprus, he arrived at the Muslim-held port of Acre in 1191, joining in the siege of the city by Crusader forces. His subsequent feats in battle against the Muslim leader Saladin earned him the admiration of the Christian world, but he failed to capture Jerusalem. Traveling homeward in 1192, he was shipwrecked in the Adriatic. He was held prisoner by the Duke of Austria, a political enemy, and only returned to England in 1194 after payment of a large ransom. He was killed during a siege in France in March 1199.

RICHARD THE LIONHEART EMBARKS ON THE THIRD CRUSADE IN 1187

In Europe, the capture of Jerusalem was hailed as a triumph for the Christian faith. The crusading ideal had been successfully launched and it became the ambition of many kings, noblemen, and knights to go on a Crusade to the Holy Land at least once in a lifetime, with the aim of saving their souls and advancing Christendom.

Mixed motives

The original Crusader knights settled into the area they had seized from the Muslims. They created a Kingdom of Jerusalem and various other feudal states, built formidable castles, and founded two military orders—the Knights Templar and the Knights Hospitaller—as armed forces dedicated to religious warfare. The transport of people and goods to and from these Crusader states was controlled by Italian maritime cities, chiefly Venice and Genoa, whose merchants and sailors made fortunes ferrying pilgrims and armies across the Mediterranean.

Historians have identified nine major Crusades over two centuries, but there were also many lesser ventures. In 1107, for example, King Sigurd of Norway set off with an army aboard a fleet of 55 ships, sailing via Portugal and Sicily to Palestine and returning to Scandinavia overland from Constantinople. The whole journey lasted four years. Arguably the largest of the numbered Crusades was the Third. The Muslims had found a leader, Saladin, who was capable of leading a unified counter-offensive against the Christian intruders. In 1187, Saladin defeated a Christian army at the Battle of Hattin and retook Jerusalem for Islam. In response, the most powerful rulers in Western Europe—King Richard I ("the Lionheart") of England,

◁ **Death of St. Louis**
The pious King Louis IX of France died during his second Crusade, at Tunis in August 1270, and his body was carried back to France by sea. Louis was proclaimed a saint by Pope Boniface VIII in 1297.

▽ **Crusaders aboard**
This 15-century miniature shows the Frankish knight Godfrey of Bouillon embarking on a Crusade. Transporting an army by sea was a logistical challenge.

◁ **Crusader castle**
The Krak des Chevaliers was a mighty fortress built and garrisoned by the Knights Hospitaller in Syria. Despite its huge concentric walls and many towers, the castle fell to the Muslim Sultan Baibars in 1271.

> “ But now, O mighty soldiers, O men of war, **you have a cause** for which **you can fight** without danger to your souls. ”
>
> BERNARD OF CLAIRVAUX, LETTER PROMOTING THE SECOND CRUSADE, 1146

▷ **Imperial seal**
Emperor Frederick II led the Sixth Crusade, which regained Jerusalem from Muslim control by negotiation. An open-minded Christian ruler, he exhibited great respect for Islamic beliefs.

King Philip Augustus of France, and Frederick Barbarossa, King of Germany and Holy Roman Emperor—all embarked with armies for the Holy Land. Frederick Barbarossa, taking the overland route, died on the journey across Anatolia, while the French and English kings arrived in Palestine by sea. Richard I stayed longest, his contest with Saladin succeeding in saving the Crusader states from destruction, but failing to regain Jerusalem.

The Fourth Crusade, launched in 1202, showed the crusading spirit at its worst. The Venetians, who provided ships to transport the knights and their horses to the east, effectively controlled the Crusade and turned it into an attack on Constantinople. The city was captured and sacked in 1204, and many of its treasures ended up in Venice. The Sixth Crusade was controversial for a very different reason. Its leader, the Holy Roman Emperor Frederick II, was at loggerheads with the papacy—and being an open-minded individual he was prepared to talk with the Muslims. Using negotiation instead of force, Frederick achieved the restoration of Christian control of Jerusalem—a peaceful success that scandalized enthusiasts of holy war.

The sincere Christian faith that had initiated the First Crusade found a fresh embodiment in French King Louis IX, later canonized as St. Louis. In 1249, this pious monarch landed in Egypt to strike at the heart of Muslim power, which lay in Cairo. However, his army was defeated and he was taken prisoner, and only obtained release after payment of a huge ransom. By that time, the Crusader states were crumbling under Muslim military pressure. In 1270, Louis died on a final unsuccessful Crusade, this time directed against Tunis in North Africa.

The last Crusader stronghold in Palestine fell to Muslim forces in 1291, but this did not bring the crusading tradition to an end. Indeed, by the 13th century, the number of Crusades was increasing. In 1209, Pope Innocent III declared a Crusade against the Christian Cathars of Provence. The German order of the Teutonic Knights, originally founded in Palestine, fought Crusades against pagan peoples around the shores of the Baltic. In the 14th and 15th centuries, Crusades were launched against the Ottoman Turks in southeast Europe and against Hussite heretics in Czech Bohemia. Some historians even consider the Spanish conquests in the Americas to be a continuation of the crusading movement, spreading the Christian faith by the sword.

△ **Saladin**
A Muslim warrior born into a Kurdish family, Saladin made himself sultan of Cairo and Syria, and then pursued a holy war against the Crusader states. He was respected by the Christians for his chivalry.

IN CONTEXT
Knights Templar

The order of the Knights Templar was founded by Crusader knights based in the Temple of Solomon in Jerusalem in 1119, originally to provide armed escorts for pilgrims. Sworn to poverty, chastity, and obedience, they became the elite warriors of the Crusader armies. The Templars built and garrisoned formidable castles, and displayed discipline and courage in battle against the Muslims. Thanks to donations from Christians in Europe, the order amassed considerable wealth. In 1307, French King Philip IV, in debt to the order and tempted by its wealth, had thousands of the knights arrested on trumped-up charges. Hundreds were later burned at the stake and the order was disbanded.

FRENCH KING PHILIP IV OVERSEES THE BURNING OF TEMPLARS, INCLUDING GRAND MASTER JACQUES DE MOLAY

Prester John

The search for the fabled exotic Christian king Prester John provided a major motive for European exploration in Asia and Africa.

The first mention of Prester John appeared in a chronicle written by Otto, Bishop of Freising, in 1147. Talking to a fellow ecclesiastic from the Crusader states, Otto had learned of a powerful Christian king ruling over lands to the east of Persia who had defeated a Muslim army in battle. Today, historians believe that Otto's story relates to the exploits of the Kara-Khitai empire in Central Asia, but Otto's readers knew nothing of this region, and seized on the idea of a Christian king in the East, offering hope of aid in the Crusaders' struggle against Islam. Then, around 1165, a mysterious letter surfaced, supposedly written by Prester John himself. Circulated widely across Europe, the letter described him as king of the "Three Indias"—a vaguely conceived area of South Asia, the Middle East, and East Africa. His kingdom was a place of marvels, inhabited by giants, Amazons, pygmies, and dog-headed folk. His palace contained a fountain of youth and a magic mirror that let the king see what was happening anywhere in his lands.

In the 13th century, European travelers penetrating Asia were disappointed to report that there was no evidence of this magical kingdom. At the same time, through contact with Coptic Christians in Egypt, Europeans learned of the existence of the Christian kingdom of Ethiopia. By 1330, the travel writer Bishop Jordan Catalani had identified Prester John with the King of Ethiopia.

When the Portuguese embarked on voyages of exploration down the coast of Africa in the 15th century, one of their express goals was to locate Prester John's Ethiopia. In 1487, King John II sent Pêro da Covilhã on an expedition via Egypt and Arabia to reconnoiter the Indian Ocean. In 1493, Covilhã landed in East Africa and became the first European to reach the Ethiopian court. Covilhã addressed the Ethiopian emperor as Prester John.

> "I, Prester John, the **Lord of Lords**, surpass all under **heaven** in **virtue**, in **riches** and in **power**."
>
> PURPORTED LETTER FROM PRESTER JOHN, c.1165

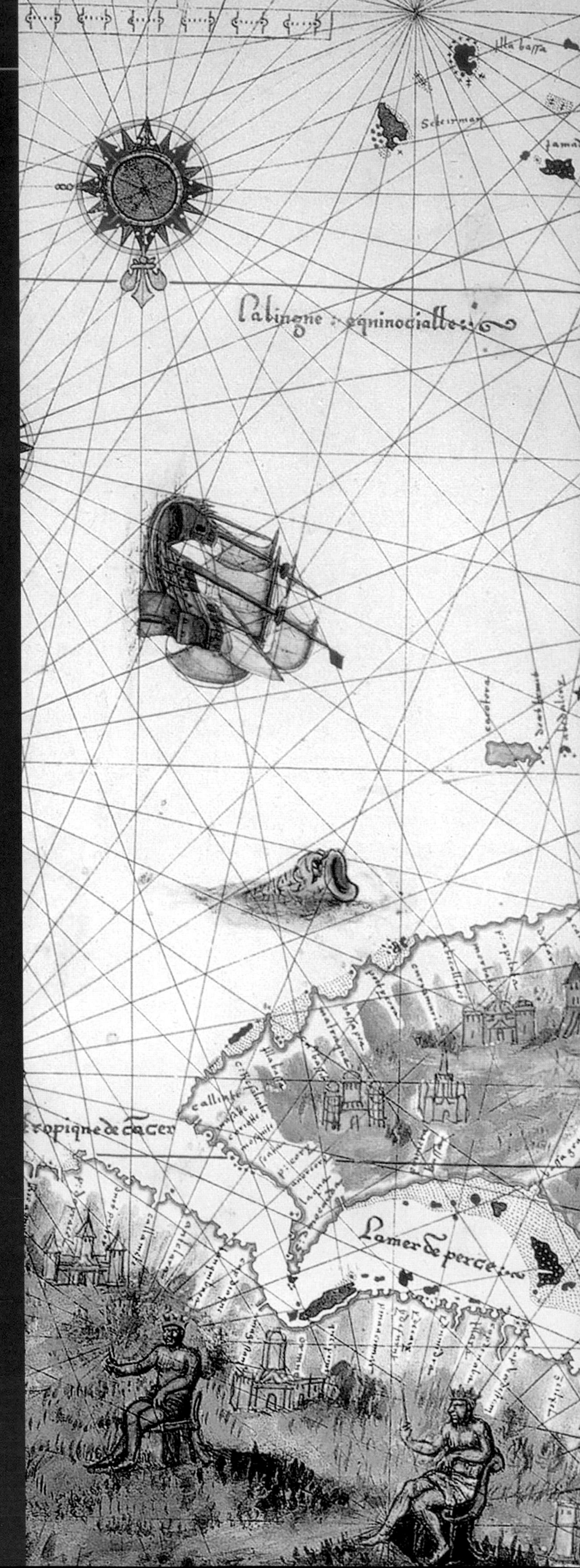

▷ **Early modern map**
The *Vallard Atlas* of 1547 shows Prester John on his throne in Ethiopia. Based on reports made by Portuguese travelers, the map accurately depicts the Horn of Africa, with south at the top.

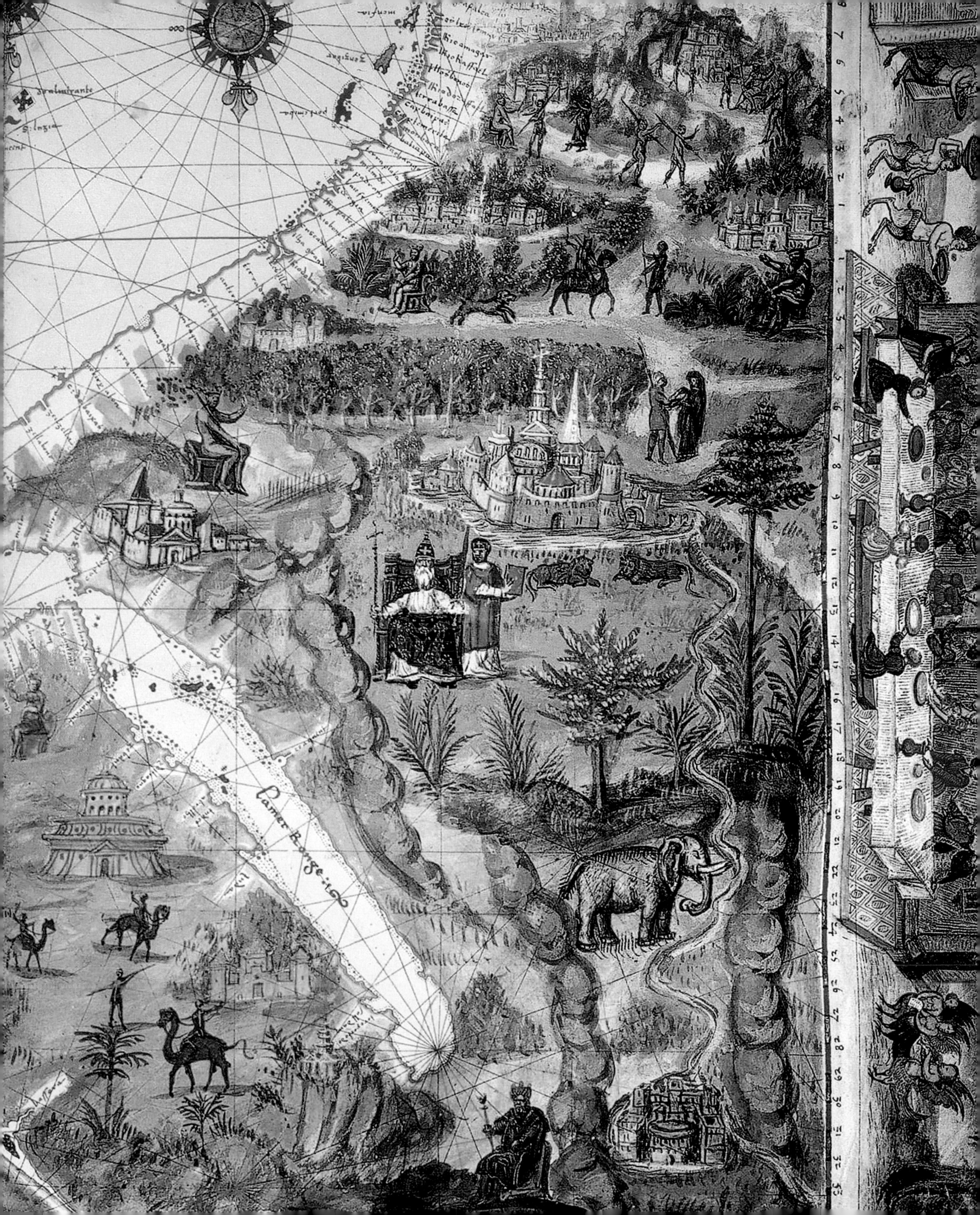
Lamer Rouge

Medieval pilgrimages

△ ***Reception of Pilgrims and Distribution of Alms***
Domenico di Bartolo's fresco, painted in 1442, is in a hospital in Siena that was dedicated to caring for pilgrims on their way to Rome. In this painting, pilgrims are being offered food and medical care.

Pilgrimage was the most common motive for long-distance travel in medieval times. Each year, thousands of believers left the safety of their homes to embark upon perilous journeys to distant sacred places.

Although all religions have had some tradition of travel to holy sites, medieval Christians were especially drawn to pilgrimage. The religious importance of visiting Palestine, revered as the setting for the life of Jesus, was established as early as the 4th century CE, when Helena, wife of the Roman Emperor Constantine, made a well-publicized trip to Jerusalem to search for relics of Christ's crucifixion, and had the Church of the Holy Sepulchre built on the alleged site of Jesus's tomb. Christian pilgrimage remained a relatively small-scale affair until the 10th century, after which it rapidly expanded and diversified.

Jerusalem was never surpassed as a goal for the Christian pilgrim, but other pilgrimage sites proliferated

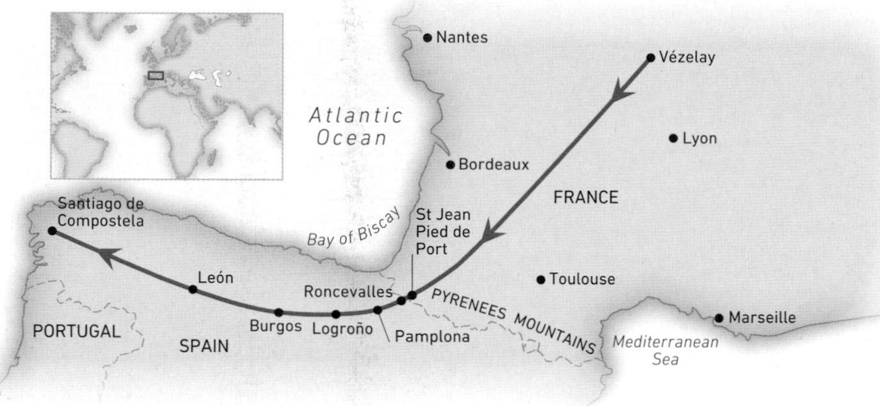

△ **The way to Santiago**
Most of the pilgrims who traveled to Santiago de Compostela followed established routes across France and northern Spain from assembly points at Vézelay, Paris, and Le Puy.

through the Middle Ages. Rome claimed the tombs of the apostles Peter and Paul, but many lesser shrines housing a sacred relic or the corpse of a saint also built up large followings. Pilgrims flocked to the Shrine of the Three Kings in Cologne Cathedral, Germany, which was said to contain the bones of the Magi from the biblical nativity story, or to the city of Santiago de Compostela in northern Spain, the alleged burial place of St. James the Apostle. In England, Canterbury became the principal pilgrimage site after the murder of the saint and martyr Archbishop Thomas Becket in the cathedral in 1170.

Pilgrims came from all levels of society and their motives were many and various. The journey might be a form of penance undertaken in expiation of a sin or crime, or even a legal punishment imposed on a wrongdoer. The pilgrim might be seeking a miraculous cure for an illness or fulfilling a vow to a saint who had been asked to intercede at some moment of peril. Some had deep religious motivation, while others, more like modern tourists, primarily wanted to see the world. For most people, the journey to Jerusalem—long, expensive, arduous, and dangerous—could only be a once-in-a-lifetime experience, but a pious Christian might make pilgrimages to more local sites several times a year.

△ **Badge of a pilgrim**
This pilgrim's cloak is bedecked with scallop shells, the emblem of St. James whose shrine drew pilgrims to Santiago de Compostela.

Catering to pilgrims

Pilgrims are usually represented with a coarse garment, staff, purse, and scallop shell, but in reality, most wore their ordinary clothes and carried a spare pair of shoes. Easy prey for robbers and wild animals, they traveled in groups for safety and mutual support. Pilgrims who were bound for Santiago de Compostela, for example, traditionally gathered at the Benedictine abbey of Vézelay in central France. From there, the route across the Pyrenees and through northern Spain was dotted with pilgrim hostels established by pious local landowners or by the Benedictine monastic order, which was very active in fostering pilgrimages. These hostels might provide a range of services, from the repair of shoes broken on the stony roads to hospital beds and barbers. Other pilgrims traveled to northern Spain by sea, hiring ships for the return journey from England or Germany, much in the same way people charter flights today.

Once the pilgrims reached their final destination, they would usually take part in a carefully stage-managed ritual designed to satisfy both their religious urge and their desire for mystery and wonder. Approaching the popular English shrine of the Virgin Mary at Walsingham in Norfolk, for example, pilgrims were instructed to take off their shoes and walk the last "Holy Mile" barefoot, singing religious songs. Reaching the shrine itself, they »

IN CONTEXT
The Canterbury Tales

Written by the English courtier Geoffrey Chaucer in the late 14th century, *The Canterbury Tales* is a collection of verse stories purportedly narrated by a group of pilgrims bound for the shrine of Thomas Becket in Canterbury Cathedral. The pilgrims range from a chivalrous knight and his son to a bawdy miller, a friar, and a raunchy widow.

As well as offering a panorama of English medieval society, Chaucer's work shows the variety of motives and attitudes found among pilgrims, some of whom are far from godly folk. The impression created is of travelers who have embarked on a jaunt, rather than an act of penance.

A WOODCUT OF THE KNIGHT FROM THE 1490 EDITION OF *THE CANTERBURY TALES*

◁ **Shrine of the Magi**
Cologne Cathedral in Germany was built to house a sarcophagus that is said to contain the remains of the biblical Magi. It still attracts hosts of pilgrims today.

"The pilgrim should carry with him **two sacks**—one right **full of patience**, the other containing **200 Venetian ducats**."

PIETRO CASOLA, *PILGRIMAGE TO JERUSALEM IN THE YEAR 1494*

▷ **Stained glass**
This window in Canterbury Cathedral shows pilgrims at the shrine of Archbishop Thomas Becket, murdered there in 1170. His death was followed by miraculous cures that guaranteed the site's popularity.

» were led through a chapel where they would kiss the finger bone of St. Peter, then went past a well and into another dimly lit chapel containing the site's most sacred relic, drops of the Virgin Mary's breast milk.

Although pilgrims benefitted from the charity of the Church and pious laymen, mass pilgrimage inevitably became a source of profit for many enterprising individuals who provided services to the religious throng. Pilgrims bought travel guides that offered advice on the journey and detailed information on the sites. Among the most famous of these, manuscripts of *Mirabilis Urbis Romae* (*The Marvels of Rome*), a guide to the monuments of Rome, remained in circulation from the 12th to the 16th century. All pilgrims wanted to return with souvenirs of their journey. These were readily provided by hawkers at pilgrimage sites, and ranged from badges to display on their clothing to replica relics with alleged healing powers. The cathedrals or abbeys controlling the shrines and the towns in which they were sited prospered on the necessary spending and voluntary offerings of the pilgrims.

A dangerous road

The pilgrimage to Jerusalem was the most difficult to undertake, both because of the distance from Christian Europe and the presence of Muslims, either in lands around the Holy City or actually in possession of it. The overland journey to the Levant through the Balkans and Anatolia was always fraught with dangers. Increasing Muslim hostility eventually made the land route effectively impossible. Sea passages became an essential part of journeys to Palestine, and from the 13th century, the maritime city of Venice developed a virtual monopoly of the pilgrim trade. However, crossing the Mediterranean on board a Venetian galley brought its own hardships and dangers. The ships were overcrowded, unsanitary, infested with rats, and poorly provisioned. They were also liable to interception by Muslim corsairs. Once in the Holy Land, visitors

△ **Rome travel guide**
This woodcut appeared as an illustration in *Mirabilia Urbis Romae*, a medieval guide to the wonders of Rome that was bought by many generations of pilgrims visiting the papal city.

▷ **The *mahmal* leaves Cairo**
This 19th-century lithograph depicts the *mahmal*—a ceremonial palanquin in which the sultan of Cairo was borne to Mecca on the annual hajj. It was first employed by the Mamluk Sultan Baybars in the 13th century.

were eager to make a thorough tour of the key sacred sites, including the Holy Sepulchre, the Mount of Olives, Bethlehem, the Pond of Bathsheba, and Mount Zion. While the Crusaders were in control of the Holy Land, pilgrims could count on the protection of the Knights Templar and the ministrations of the Knights Hospitaller. But in periods of Muslim domination, they could expect harassment and considerable expenditure on bribes and fees.

The Muslim pilgrimage

Muslims had their own tradition of pilgrimage, although it differed from that of the Christians. The hajj to Mecca was an obligation for the pious Muslim, but pilgrimages to lesser sacred sites played a relatively small part in Muslim religious practice. The hajj was highly organized, with caravans of thousands of pilgrims departing annually from gathering points at Cairo, Damascus, and Basra. Water, food, and lodging were provided along the way. The perils and hardships associated with Christian pilgrimage were certainly not unknown to Muslims, however. Caravans were preyed upon by Bedouin tribes in the desert and taxes were levied on pilgrims by the rulers of the Mecca region.

The Muslim pilgrimage has not only survived, but has expanded to the present day. The Christian tradition of pilgrimage, by contrast, has gone into severe decline since the 16th century. The rise of the Muslim Ottoman Empire made the Holy Land almost inaccessible to European Christians. The veneration of saints was rejected by the Protestant Church as a superstition and even the Catholic hierarchy eventually became suspicious of popular faith in the miraculous power of relics and shrines.

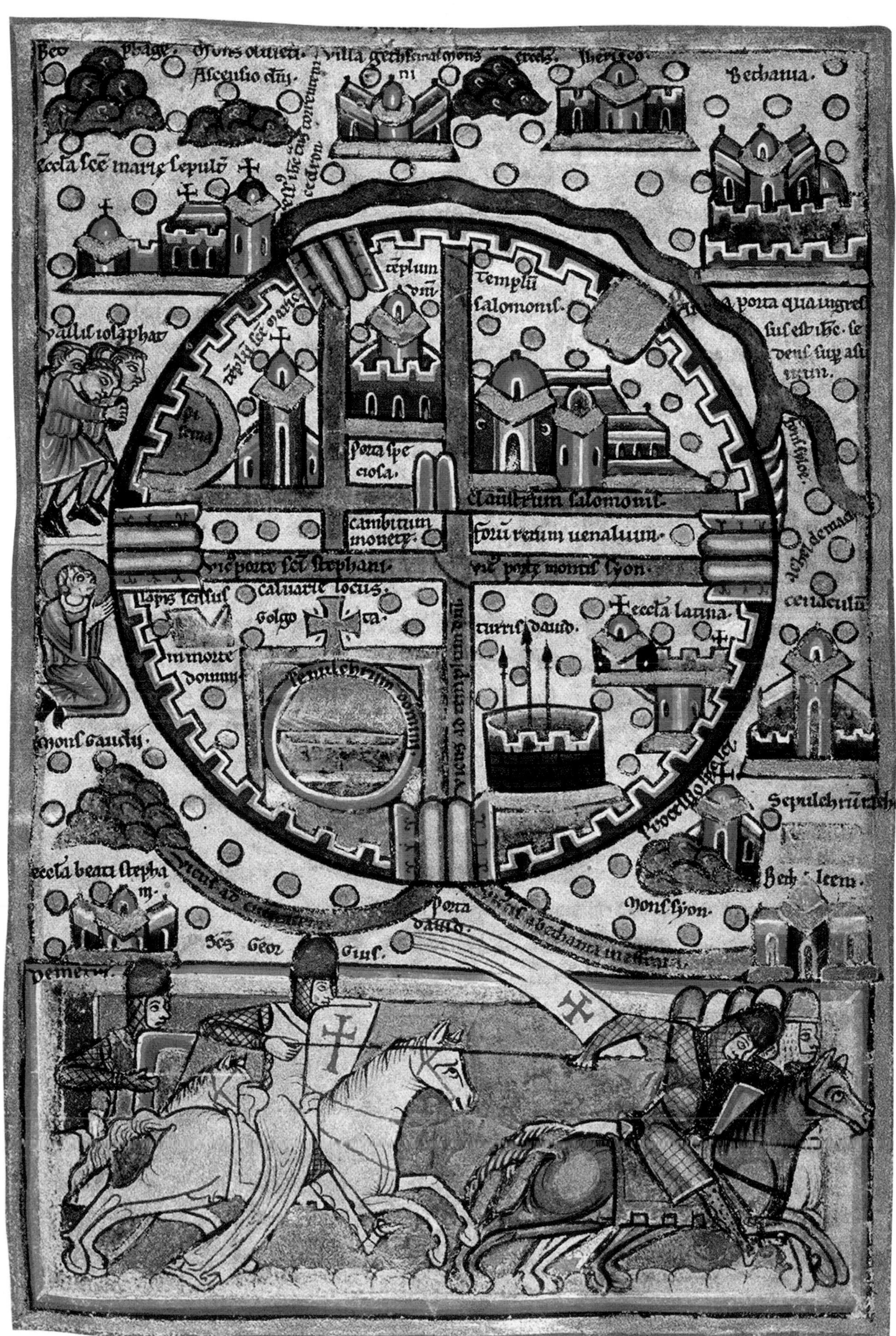

▷ **Medieval plan of Jerusalem**
A stylized plan of the Holy City, dating from around 1200, is accompanied by a scene of battle between Crusader knights and Muslims. The Crusades were partly launched in order to guarantee Christian pilgrims access to Jerusalem.

Medieval travel accounts

Medieval Europeans reveled in picturesque accounts of foreign travels. Ignorant of the wider world, they could not distinguish fact from fantasy, credulously consuming tales in which imaginary monsters appeared in otherwise accurate portraits of exotic lands.

The most influential of medieval travel writers was a man who faked his identity and who may never have traveled at all. Appearing in the mid-14th century, *The Travels of Sir John Mandeville* was one of the most widely read books in Europe. The author describes himself as a knight from St. Albans, England, but researchers have found no trace of such a person. Authorship of the book has been speculatively ascribed to, among others, a physician from Liège and a monk from Ypres, but no one really knows Mandeville's identity. Some believe the author had at least traveled to the Holy Land, as he describes Jerusalem in extensive detail, but no one thinks his supposed eyewitness accounts of India, Ethiopia, and China are authentic. For example, Mandeville describes Ethiopians as having only one leg, which they use to shelter themselves from the sun. He also claims to have passed through lands where people have the heads of dogs and dwarves thrive on the smell of apples. Yet Mandeville's text includes many not wholly inaccurate secondhand accounts of the customs of distant countries. Christopher Columbus read it, and discovered the idea that a man who travels in a straight line will end up back where he started—because the world is a sphere.

◁ **Irish boatmen**
An illustration from Gerald of Wales's *Topographia Hibernica* shows two Irishmen paddling a coracle. Gerald describes the Irish as "suffering their hair and beards to grow enormously in an uncouth manner."

" I, **John Mandeville, Knight** … have been **long time** over the sea, and have seen **many diverse lands**, and many … **kingdoms** and **isles**. "

THE TRAVELS OF SIR JOHN MANDEVILLE, c.1350

Approaching authenticity

Popular travel accounts were not necessarily of journeys to far distant places. The widely circulated *Topographia Hibernica*, written by Gerald of Wales in the 12th century, was a description of Ireland. Gerald found the Irish "a rude people … living like beasts," their hair too long and their clothes too rough. Although much of his account was firsthand, it still contained imaginary marvels such as an encounter between a priest and an articulate werewolf.

As well as the famous Marco Polo (see pp. 88–89), a number of Europeans wrote more or less accurate accounts of journeys to the East. The earliest was by Franciscan friar Giovanni da Pian del Carpine, who traveled as a papal ambassador to the court of the Mongol Khan at Karakorum in 1245–47. He was followed by another friar, William

◁ **Medieval astronomers**
This tinted version of a picture attributed to John Mandeville shows astronomers on the summit of Mount Athos, Greece, using various astronomical instruments.

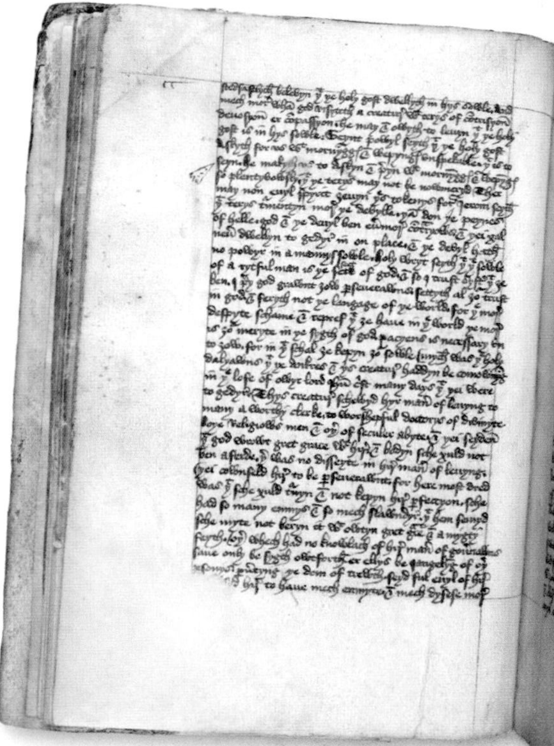

△ **Autobiographical manuscript**
The manuscript of the autobiography of 15th-century Englishwoman Margery Kempe, which relates her travels to holy sites. It was only rediscovered in 1934 after centuries of oblivion. It now resides in the British Library.

◁ **Odoric of Pordenone**
A medieval illustration of the narrative of Odoric's travels in Asia shows the Franciscan friar about to embark on his mission. He was beatified as a saint in 1755, four centuries after his death.

of Rubruck, who traveled to Mongolia and back in 1253–55. William wrote the most level-headed medieval travel account of Asia—but, being frankly skeptical about the existence of monsters and human freaks, it was not widely read.

Yet another Franciscan, Odoric of Pordenone, embarked on a journey through Asia in 1318, returning to Italy 12 years later, having visited Persia, India, Indonesia, and China. The account of his travels contains details of unquestionable veracity—such as the Chinese use of cormorants for fishing—and was highly influential, much of it plagiarized by Mandeville. For information about India, Europeans could turn to the *Mirabilia* of Bishop Jordanus Catalani, who lived on the subcontinent some time between 1321 and 1330. Jordanus is reliable on Indian customs, but resorts to marvels when writing of other parts of Asia and Africa.

An interesting contrast to these often dubious travel accounts is provided by the autobiography of Margery Kempe. Written in the 1430s, this vividly relates the fears and ecstasies of a woman from King's Lynn in Norfolk, England, during her often stressful journeys to holy sites in Palestine and Europe. Kempe's work, little known in its day, conveys the experience of medieval travel far more authentically than the more famous books of marvels.

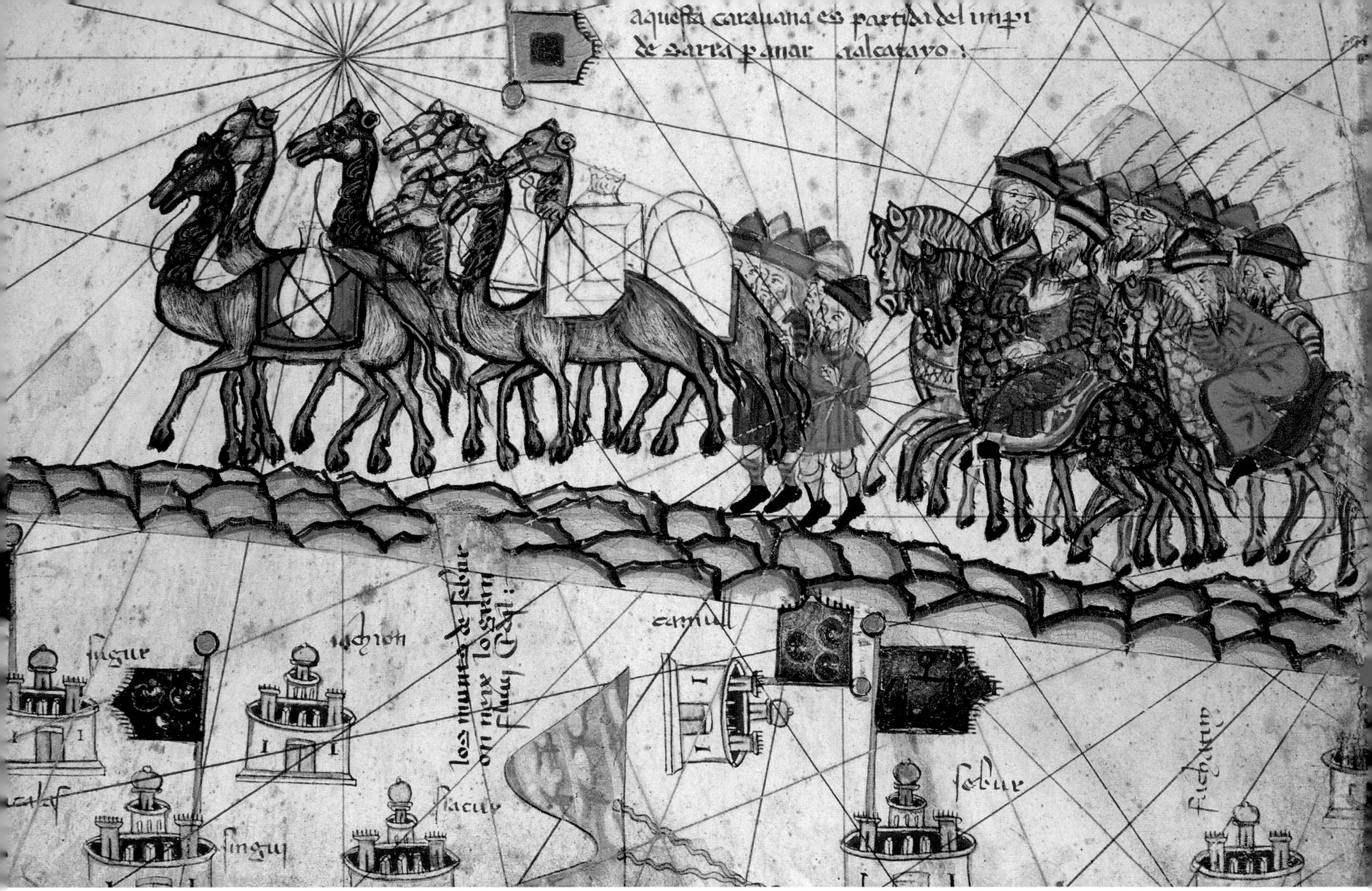

△ **Silk Road caravan**
An image from the 14th-century *Catalan Atlas* shows Marco Polo on the Silk Road crossing the rugged Pamir Mountain range. Merchants ride on horseback and their baggage is carried by camels.

The Silk Road

In the 13th century, the Mongol khans created a vast land empire that stretched across the breadth of Asia. Under their rule, travel flourished along the Silk Road linking China to the Muslim Middle East and Europe.

▷ **Genghis Khan**
Leader of the nomadic Mongol tribes, Genghis Khan was one of the most brutal conquerors in history, yet his legacy was a tolerant empire that facilitated trade and communication across Eurasia.

By the time of the founding of the Mongol Empire, the Silk Road already had a history stretching back over a thousand years—the wealthy elite of ancient Rome had worn silk imported across Asia from Han-dynasty China. But for centuries the trade route had only operated partially and intermittently, disrupted by wars, banditry, and the predations of greedy local rulers. When Genghis Khan united the Mongol tribes of Central Asia in 1206 and launched them on far-flung campaigns of conquest, the initial effect on trade was disastrous. Famous cities along the Silk Road, from Baghdad and Balkh to Samarkand and Bukhara, were left in ruins after Mongol attacks. However, by the second half of the 13th century, in control of an empire stretching from Persia to China, the Mongol rulers had learned to appreciate the value of well-maintained communication routes and the wealth that trade could bring. The peace they imposed and the religious tolerance they practiced brought a drastic rise in the number of foreign merchants traveling the Silk Road.

For merchants from Christian Europe, the main starting points for the journey east were Constantinople and the Black Sea coast, while Muslim traders set off from Cairo or Damascus. The travelers

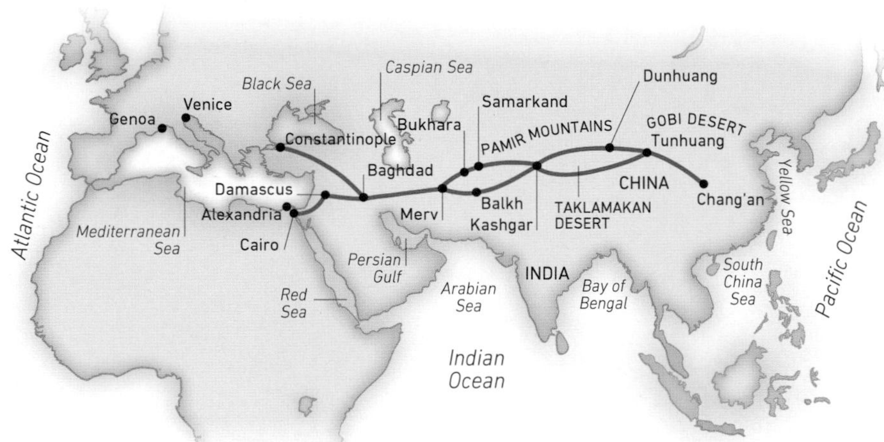

△ **Silk Road trade routes**
The Silk Road was not a single highway but a network of routes converging and diverging across Asia. Its total length has been estimated at around 4,300 miles (7,000 km).

formed caravans of hundreds—or even thousands—of merchants, porters, guides, and translators, and had long trains of pack animals. Along parts of the route, caravansaries (see pp. 92–93) provided lodging and sustenance for men and beasts alike, but in spite of these, the journey could only be arduous. The road from the Black Sea coast around the south of the Caspian Sea, followed by many European merchants, was plagued by bandits. Paying protection money to groups of armed men was a normal procedure for any Silk Road traveler. Much of the land was arid, and on particularly barren sections, all food and drink had to be carried for many days of travel. Crossing the Pamir Mountains and the Taklamakan Desert posed especially grueling challenges to travelers.

Heyday and decline

By the 14th century, travel on the Silk Road had become common enough for guidebooks to be written. Italian merchant Francesco Pegoletti had success with *The Practice of Commerce*, a book of advice for travelers to China that itemized travel times on various stretches of the route, the likely costs to be incurred, what precautions should be taken, and the most profitable trade goods to carry. Pegoletti ended with a description of Cathay (China), where paper money had to be used and the city of Khanbaligh (Beijing) which "has a circuit of a hundred miles and is all full of people and houses."

The golden age of the Silk Road came to an end with the Chinese revolt against Mongol rule, which led to the founding of the Ming dynasty in 1368. As the Mongol Empire declined, the rise of the militantly Islamic Ottoman Empire blocked Christian European access to the trade routes via Constantinople. But it was the development of oceanic trade in the 16th century, opening up sea routes from Europe to the Spice Islands and East Asia, that delivered the final blow to the Silk Road—it was one from which it never recovered.

△ **Bactrian camel**
This statue is of a sturdy Bactrian camel, native to the Central Asian steppe, which was the standard pack animal of the Silk Road caravans.

IN PROFILE

The Black Death

The Silk Road carried not only trade goods, but also disease. Plague was endemic in Central Asia, and in the 1340s it spread along the Silk Road to trading posts on the Black Sea. From there, it was distributed by ship—possibly carried by fleas on rats infesting the ships' holds—to ports in western Europe. Known as the Black Death, between 1348 and 1350 the plague epidemic killed at least a third of the entire European population, which had no immunity to this exotic disease. The Black Death also struck Syria and Egypt with equally disastrous effect.

A MEDIEVAL PAINTING OF A DOCTOR DOING HIS BEST TO TREAT PLAGUE VICTIMS

> "And from Utrar to Almalik it is **45 days** by **pack asses**. And you meet Mongolians **every day**."
>
> FRANCESCO PEGOLETTI, *GUIDE TO THE SILK ROUTE*, 1335

◁ **Desert tower**
A Chinese frontier town on the edge of the Taklamakan Desert, Dunhuang was a major stopping point on the Silk Road. Its towers and walls, now ruined, were a welcome sight to travelers arriving from the west.

The travels of Marco Polo

Marco Polo was a Venetian merchant who journeyed to China in the 13th century and lived at the court of the emperor Kublai Khan. His published account of his experiences made him the most famous traveler of his time.

△ **Venetian traveler**
Marco Polo was born into a wealthy family of Venetian merchants. He was not the only European to travel to China and back, but his compelling account of his travels by land and sea had a unique appeal.

When Marco Polo was born in 1254, the maritime city of Venice was a major player in the burgeoning trade between Europe and the East. Venetian merchants made fortunes purchasing luxury Asian goods such as silk and spices at trading posts in the eastern Mediterranean and the Black Sea, and reselling them in the European market. Marco's father and uncle, Niccolò and Maffeo Polo, were both engaged in this trade. Traveling to the Black Sea around the time of Marco's birth, they found themselves drawn even deeper into Asia. After many vicissitudes, they arrived at the court of the Mongol leader Kublai Khan, who found these European visitors an amusing novelty. He made them his emissaries and charged them with establishing communication between him and the Pope.

By the time Niccolò and Maffeo returned to Venice in 1269, Marco was an adolescent. In 1271, he accompanied his father and uncle when they set off on a second journey to Kublai's court. This time, they sailed to the port of Acre in the Crusader-controlled Levant. From there, they followed a rambing course eastward, changing direction to avoid regions rendered hazardous by war or theives. Traveling via Baghdad and the Persian port of Hormuz, they eventually picked

▽ **Travels to the East and back**
The Polos' 15,000-mile (24,000-km) journey took them through numerous dangerous territories, many of which would later become impassable. However, they returned rich, reputedly with gems sewed into their coats.

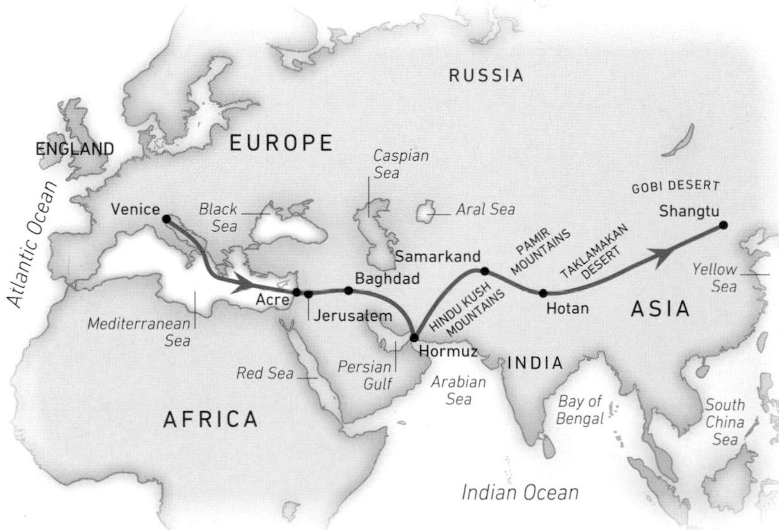

> " I did not tell **half of what I saw**, for I knew that **I would not be believed**. "
>
> MARCO POLO ON HIS DEATHBED, AS REPORTED BY JACOPO D'ACQUI, 1330

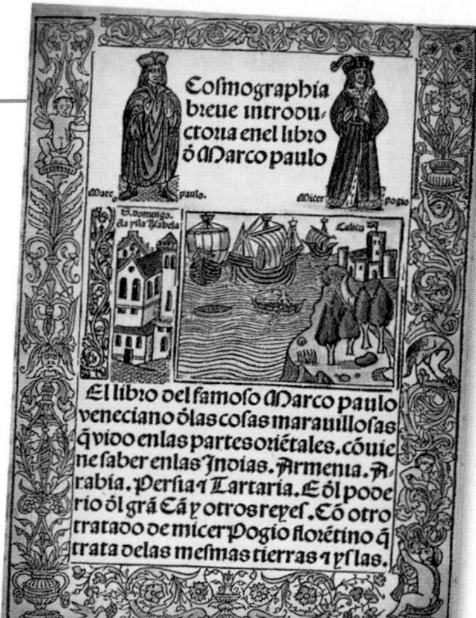

Cosmographia breue introductoria enel libro d Marco paulo

Marco paulo. Micer pogio

S. domingo. da ysla Ysabela

Calicu

El libro del famoso Marco paulo veneciano d las cosas marauillosas q vido enlas partes orietales. couiene saber enlas Indias. Armenia. Arabia. Persia y Tartaria. E d l poderio d l gra Ca y otros reyes. Co otro tratado de micer Pogio floretino q trata delas mesmas tierras y yslas.

◁ ***Il Milione***
This version of Marco Polo's *Travels* was published in 1503. The book is usually known in Italian as *Il Milione*, perhaps because it was maliciously said to contain a million lies.

up the main trail of the Silk Road (see pp. 86–87) across the formidable obstacles of the Pamir Mountains and the Taklamakan Desert. All along the route, they found cities in ruin, still not recovered from the effects of the Mongol conquest that had completely devastated the region earlier in the century.

◁ **Marco Polo leaves Venice**
A medieval illustration shows Marco and his relatives departing from their home city, bound for the court of Kublai Khan. It would be almost a quarter of a century before they saw Venice again.

Agent of the emperor

The Polos' journey from Venice to China took three and a half years. They arrived at Kublai Khan's summer residence at Shangtu, north of Beijing, in 1275, and were taken into the emperor's service. The Mongol ruler of a restive Chinese population, Kublai welcomed the chance to employ foreigners who posed no threat to his rule. As the emperor's agent, Marco was sent on many journeys around Kublai's domains, giving him the opportunity to observe local customs.

Marco and his relatives stayed in Kublai's service for 17 years, until in 1292 they found an opportunity to leave. A Mongol princess in China was pledged in marriage to a Mongol prince in Persia, and the Polos were entrusted with escorting the bride to her promised husband. They made the journey by sea, following the maritime trade routes that carried spices across the Indian Ocean from Southeast Asia to the Muslim Middle East. Landing at Hormuz, they delivered the princess to Tabriz, the Mongol capital of Persia, and continued overland to the Black Sea, where they took a ship for Venice. They arrived home in 1295.

The Travels of Marco Polo

The world would never have heard of Marco's many adventures but for a chance encounter with an author. In 1298, Marco was taken prisoner by the Genoese, who were at war with Venice. In prison, he met the Italian romance writer Rustichello da Pisa, and told him the stories of his travels. Adding fantastical elements of his own, Rustichello wrote *The Travels of Marco Polo*, which was published around 1300. Although many people were skeptical of the facts narrated in *The Travels* (doubting, for example, that the Chinese could use paper as money), it became one of the most widely read books of its day. Marco Polo died in his bed in Venice, in January 1324.

A CHINESE PORTRAIT OF EMPEROR KUBLAI, WHO EMPLOYED MARCO IN 1275

IN PROFILE
Kublai Khan

A grandson of Genghis Khan, the founder of the Mongol Empire, Kublai Khan succeeded to reign Mongol-ruled northern China in 1251. He was proclaimed Great Khan, the overall leader of the Mongols, in 1260, but in effect mutated into an emperor of China, ruling from Beijing. Founding the Yuan dynasty, he completed the conquest of southern China in 1279, and attempted several expansionist ventures, including unsuccessful invasions of Japan in 1274 and 1281. His rule in China was characterized by religious tolerance, but despite adopting the traditions of Chinese government, he remained an alien ruler to his Chinese subjects.

CHARIOT, ROME, 200 BCE

LAUFMASCHINE, GERMANY, 1817

COVERED WAGON, US, 1850

HARLEY DAVIDSON, UK, 1916

CHARABANC, UK, 1920

On wheels

For 5,500 years, people have been thinking up evermore inventive ways of using and improving wheels to make travel easier.

SCHOOL BUS, US, 1940

The first potter turned a wheel on its side as an aid to transport around 3,200 BCE, when the ancient Mesopotamians began to make horse-drawn chariots. It was another 1,600 years before spoked wheels, as strong as a solid wheel but much lighter, appeared on Egyptian chariots. These early spokes were wooden, a far cry from the steel, aluminium, or carbon composites used to make lightweight bicycles today.

Wheels work best on a smooth surface, and rudimentary roads appeared soon after chariots. Improvements in wheels and roads went hand in hand. Around the same time that spokes were invented, iron bands were first used to reinforce the wheel rims on wagons—these were the earliest tires. Macadamized roads, made from compacted broken stone aggregate, were built in the 1820s, followed in 1846 by the first pneumatic tires. Thanks to the internal combustion engine, wheels no longer needed horses to propel them, and transport hit the road fast in the 20th century. Tarmac was patented in 1901, boyhood friends William S. Harley and Arthur Davidson produced their first motorcycle in 1903, and Henry Ford brought out his “Tin Lizzie” in 1908. From its first hesitant revolutions, the wheel is still essential to transport, and the future seems inconceivable without it.

BENZ MOTORWAGEN, GERMANY, 1886

SPIDER PHAETON, UK, 1890

FORD MODEL T, US, 1908

AEC REGENT III RT BUS, UK, 1938

CUSHMAN AUTO-GLIDE MODEL 1, US, 1938

BIANCHI PARIS-ROUBAIX, ITALY, 1951

VOLKSWAGEN KOMBI, GERMANY, 1950-67

CHEVROLET BEL AIR CONVERTIBLE, US, 1957

NISSAN LEAF, JAPAN/US, 2010

Caravansary

Caravansaries were way stations along medieval Asian trade and pilgrimage routes, offering secure lodging for travelers and their animals.

For any pilgrim or merchant, the sight of a caravansary promised welcome refreshment and relief from the hardships and dangers of travel. Wayfarers entered these establishments through an arched gateway high enough to admit a heavily burdened camel, and passed into an open roofless courtyard. Around this courtyard were the sleeping rooms—bare chambers with no bed, table, or chair. The traveler was free to occupy any such room he found empty. The caravansary also provided secure storerooms for trade goods and stables for the horses, donkeys, and camels, plus a prayer room and a bathhouse.

From the outside, most caravansaries looked like forts, a high outer wall giving protection against bandits or wolves. Caravansaries were erected and maintained by local rulers obeying the religious injunction to facilitate the pilgrimage to Mecca and the commercial imperative to encourage trade. Basic lodging, food, and animal fodder were provided free. A foreign merchant might have found himself obliged to pay stiff local dues levied on trade, however.

Along the most frequented routes, there would be a caravansary every 20 or 25 miles (30 or 40 km)—the distance of a day's travel for a caravan. As well as those sited in open country, there were numerous similar establishments in towns and cities. Filled with a wide mix of travelers, the caravansaries became busy marketplaces in which goods were traded with local people and between the travelers themselves. They were also places of cultural exchange, where people encountered different ideas and beliefs. The caravansaries played an essential part in Asian life for about a thousand years, into the 20th century. Now, many survive only as spectacular ruins, although some still function as marketplaces or have been renovated as tourist hotels.

◁ **Wikalat Bazar'a** Built by a Yememi called Bazar'a in the 17th century, Wikalat Bazar'a is one of 20 caravansaries left in Cairo. Like most caravansaries, it is built around a central arcaded courtyard.

Remote ruins
Many caravansaries provided the only shelter in remote, barren terrain, like this long-abandoned building in a mountain valley in Afghanistan. Caravansaries were found all across Asia, from Turkey to northern India and Kazakhstan.

Trans-Saharan salt caravans

Seven hundred years ago, one of the world's richest trade routes led north across the Sahara desert from Timbuktu, capital of the Mali Empire. Camel caravans carried precious cargoes of gold, salt, ivory, and slaves.

▷ ***Catalan Atlas***
In the *Catalan Atlas*, drawn in 1375, Mansa Musa, Malian ruler and "most noble lord of all this region," is shown seated on his throne south of the Sahara.

A landlocked Muslim state at the southern edge of the Sahara, the Mali Empire was mysterious even in its own day. The wider world only became conscious of its existence—and of its enormous wealth—in 1324, when its ruler, Mansa Musa, embarked upon a pilgrimage to Mecca. His arrival in Cairo, where he emerged unexpectedly from the desert with thousands of followers, caused a sensation. Mansa Musa's train of camels was burdened with such a quantity of gold that it had a major impact upon the Egyptian economy—at that time the most prosperous in the Islamic world.

" There is **complete security** in their country. Neither **traveler** nor **inhabitant** has **anything to fear**. "

MOROCCAN EXPLORER IBN BATTUTA DESCRIBING THE MALI EMPIRE, 1354

Trans-Saharan trade

Founded in the 13th century, the Mali Empire drew its wealth from its control of the trans-Saharan trade. In the markets at Timbuktu and other Malian towns, gold and other products, such as copper, kola nuts, ivory, and slaves, carried up the River Niger from the forest country south of the Sahara were exchanged for salt and Berber horses brought by Tuareg nomads from the

▽ **Camel train**
Capable of surviving for long periods without water, dromedaries were essential beasts of burden in trans-Saharan trade.

desert. The Tuareg then carried the valuable goods from the south right across the desert to Sijilmasa or other Moroccan towns at the northern edge of the Sahara. From there, other traders eventually passed them on to the Islamic Middle East and Europe—the gold coinage of late medieval European states was minted from African gold.

Fiercely independent, the Berber Tuareg had survived in their harsh desert environment since ancient times, living in characteristic blue tents and herding camels, goats, and sheep. They also exploited the salt deposits found in the heart of the Sahara at Taghaza, almost midway along the 1,000-mile (1,600-km) route from the Mali Empire to Sijilimasa. Great slabs of rock salt were strapped on to the backs of camels for the desert journey, and fetched a high price in the Malian markets. Salt was so highly valued that it was sometimes known as "white gold."

◁ **Tuareg veil**
This Tuareg man wears the traditional indigo-dyed tagelmust, a combined turban and veil. It offers maximum protection from windblown sand.

Crossing the desert

The Tuareg trade caravans were impressively large. The Arab traveler Ibn Battuta, who crossed the desert southward from Sijilmasa in 1352, says a caravan typically numbered a thousand camels and could be much larger. Caravans traveled mostly by night to avoid the scorching desert heat, breaking their journey at rare oases. It took around two months to cross the desert, a hard and hazardous journey justified by the high profits to be made.

The rulers of Mali levied duties on the Saharan trade and used the revenue to make their empire a place of learning, religious piety, and architectural splendor. Timbuktu, in particular, flourished around the hub of its marketplace. In the early 15th century, its population may have reached 100,000. Scholars from across the Islamic world came to teach and study in the city, which boasted a university and one of the most extensive libraries in the world, containing tens of thousands of manuscripts.

In the course of the 15th century, the Mali Empire was supplanted by a local rival, the Songhai Empire, but the Saharan trade routes continued to flourish. In subsequent centuries, however, the vast expansion of oceanic trade, dominated by European maritime nations, reduced the interior of North and West Africa to a commercially insignificant backwater of international trade. The whole area eventually fell prey to French imperial ambitions in the 19th century.

△ **Sankore Mosque**
Timbuktu is famous for its mosques made of sun-dried mud and sand. The Sankore Mosque is part of the city's university, dating from the golden age of the Mali Empire.

TRAVELER AND SCHOLAR, 1304–1369

Ibn Battuta

In medieval times, no one traveled further than Muhammad Ibn Battuta. Born in North Africa, he voyaged across deserts, steppes, and oceans, recording the splendors of Baghdad, Samarkand, Beijing, and Timbuktu.

Born into a family of judges and educated in Islamic law, Ibn Battuta left his home in Tangier, Morocco, at the age of 21 to make the pilgrimage to Mecca. Having embarked on the journey, he fell in love with travel for its own sake. He was not to return home to Tangier for 14 years.

In the early 14th century, great opportunities were open to a Muslim traveler. The world of Islam, united by religious custom, trade, and the language of the Qur'an, extended from Spain to Indonesia, and from the Central Asian steppe to Zanzibar. After completing his pilgrimage, Ibn Battuta made ever longer journeys across this interconnected world. His first foray took him overland around Iraq and Persia. He then traveled by sea down the east coast of Africa, where traders had spread Islam as far south as modern-day Tanzania. Between these journeys, he perfected his legal studies in Mecca, making himself readily employable in any Muslim state he might visit.

◁ **Routes through the East**
Ibn Battuta's travels took him across most of the world known to Muslims in the 14th century. Only Christian Western Europe was closed to him because of its religious intolerance.

▷ **Ibn Battuta in Egypt**
An Egyptian guide shows Ibn Battuta the ruins of ancient Egypt during his visit to Cairo in 1326. Cairo was then one of the world's greatest cities.

To the ends of the Earth

In 1332, he decided to seek a place at the wealthy court of the Muslim ruler of Delhi. Instead of going to India by sea routes from Arabia, he made a vast detour overland via Christian Constantinople, along the Silk Road into Mongol-ruled central Asia, and across the snow-capped Hindu Kush. The Sultan of Delhi, Muhammad bin Tughluq, was happy to be served by a visiting scholar, but Ibn Battuta found him a capricious employer. Eventually, sent on a mission to southern India, he decided not to return to Delhi. Instead, he followed the sea trade routes from Sri Lanka around southeast Asia to imperial China.

In the known world, there was almost nowhere further to travel. In 1347, Ibn Battuta finally headed for home. His return coincided with the scourge of the Black Death, the effects of which he observed with horror. His parents had also died in his absence. Barely stopping at Tangier, he continued to travel, first into Muslim-ruled southern Spain, and then by camel caravan across the Sahara Desert to the fabled empire of Mali. Only then had he seen enough.

Having traveled some 75,000 miles (120,000 km) in 30 years, he settled in Morocco and began to dictate the story of his travels. Although the accuracy of some of the material has been queried, his *Rihla* (*Travels*) remains a key source of information about the lost world of the Middle Ages.

◁ **Hagia Sophia**
Ibn Battuta was impressed by the splendor of the cathedral of Hagia Sophia when he visited Constantinople, capital of the Byzantine Empire. He spent a month in the city in 1332.

> **"** I set out **alone**, having **neither fellow traveler**... **nor caravan** whose **part** I might **join**. **"**
>
> IBN BATTUTA, *RIHLA*, 1354

KEY DATES

- **1304** Born February 25 in Tangier, Morocco, to a family of Berber origin.
- **1325** Makes the pilgrimage to Mecca, via the coast of North Africa.
- **1326** Visits Cairo and Damascus en route to Medina and Mecca.
- **1327–28** Travels around Iraq and Iran.
- **1330–31** Sails down the Red Sea to Aden and south along the coast of Africa to Kilwa.
- **1332–34** Journeys to India via the Byzantine Empire, Central Asia, and Afghanistan.
- **1334–42** Serves at the court of the Sultan of Delhi.
- **1342–46** Travels to China via southern India, Sri Lanka, and Southeast Asia.
- **1352** Heads south across the Sahara to the Mali Empire and the River Niger.
- **1354** Returns to settle in Tangier and dictates the story of his travels.
- **1369** Dies in Tangier at age 64 or 65.

BYZANTINE EMPEROR ANDRONIKOS III PALAEOLOGOS, WHO MET IBN BATTUTA

THE PURPORTED TOMB OF IBN BATTUTA IN TANGIER, MOROCCO

Medieval maps

Medieval maps were compendiums of myth, religious tradition, and inaccurate travelers' tales. Even as familiar regions became better mapped, much of the wider world was left in obscurity.

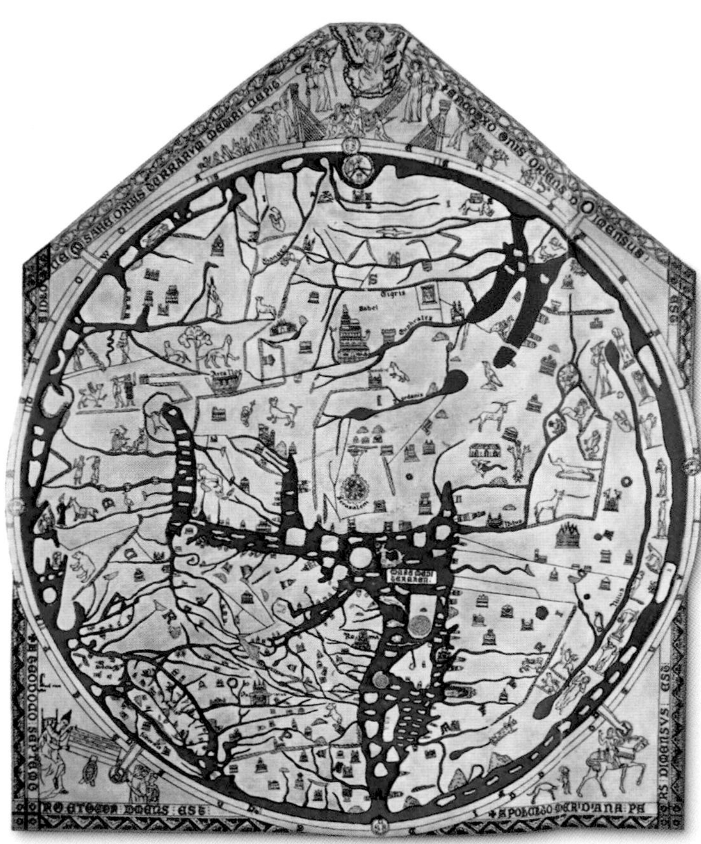

△ **Hereford Mappa Mundi**
The picture of the world presented in this mappa mundi is to a large degree mythical. Asia and Africa are peopled with monsters and figures from biblical stories and legends.

Medieval traders, pilgrims, and Crusaders setting out from Europe for the East did not consult maps. The maps which existed in Christian Europe were not intended to help travelers find their way to distant lands, but rather to represent the broad idea of the world as conceived by medieval Christians. A fine example is the mappa mundi (map of the world) in Hereford Cathedral, England, dating from around 1300. The world is shown as divided into three continents—Europe, Asia, and Africa—bordered by the Nile, the Don, and the Mediterranean, and surrounded by a circular outer ocean. The mapmakers have placed the city of Jerusalem, the site of Christ's crucifixion and burial, at the center of the circle of the world, and East is at the top. Superimposed on this general geographical scheme is a wealth of imagery relating to biblical stories and ancient legends. There are exotic animals and mythical beasts, the Garden of Eden, and the location of Noah's Ark, human monsters, and the Minotaur's labyrinth. Other medieval mappa mundi include the world map in the Béatus manuscript, made at Saint-Sever Abbey in France around 1050, and the Ebstorf map from northern Germany.

Medieval Muslim mapmakers produced more accurate world maps. They had two key sources not available to the makers of the Hereford Mappa Mundi: the works of the ancient geographer Ptolemy, long known to the Arabs but at that time still unavailable to Europeans, and information from Muslim traders and sailors who voyaged across the far-flung lands of Islam. As a result, Muhammad al-Idrisi, an Arab geographer working at the religiously tolerant court of King Roger II of Sicily in the 12th century, was able to make a map showing North Africa, Europe, and Asia with a fair degree of realism.

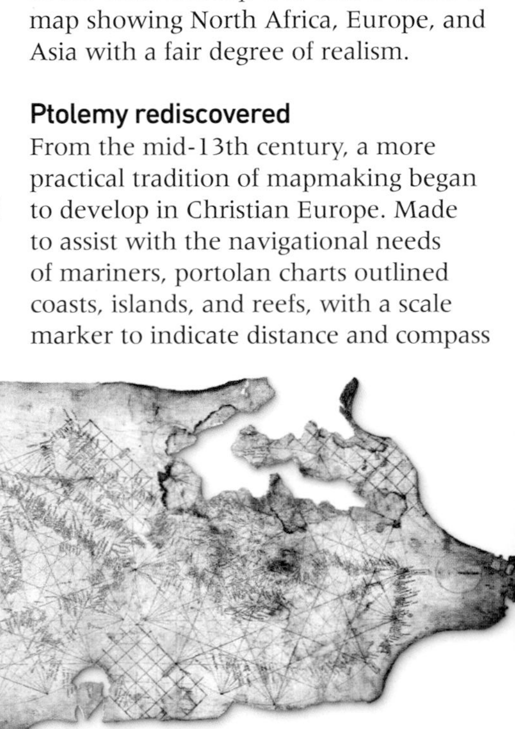

Ptolemy rediscovered

From the mid-13th century, a more practical tradition of mapmaking began to develop in Christian Europe. Made to assist with the navigational needs of mariners, portolan charts outlined coasts, islands, and reefs, with a scale marker to indicate distance and compass

> " The **globe** ... is divided into **three parts**, which are called **Asia**, **Europa**, **Africa**. "
>
> ISIDORE, ARCHBISHOP OF SEVILLE, IN *ETYMOLOGIAE*, 633

▷ ***Carta Pisana***
Dating from the late 13th century, the *Carta Pisana* is the oldest surviving portolan chart. Intended for use by Italian sailors, it accurately depicts the Mediterranean coastline and its ports.

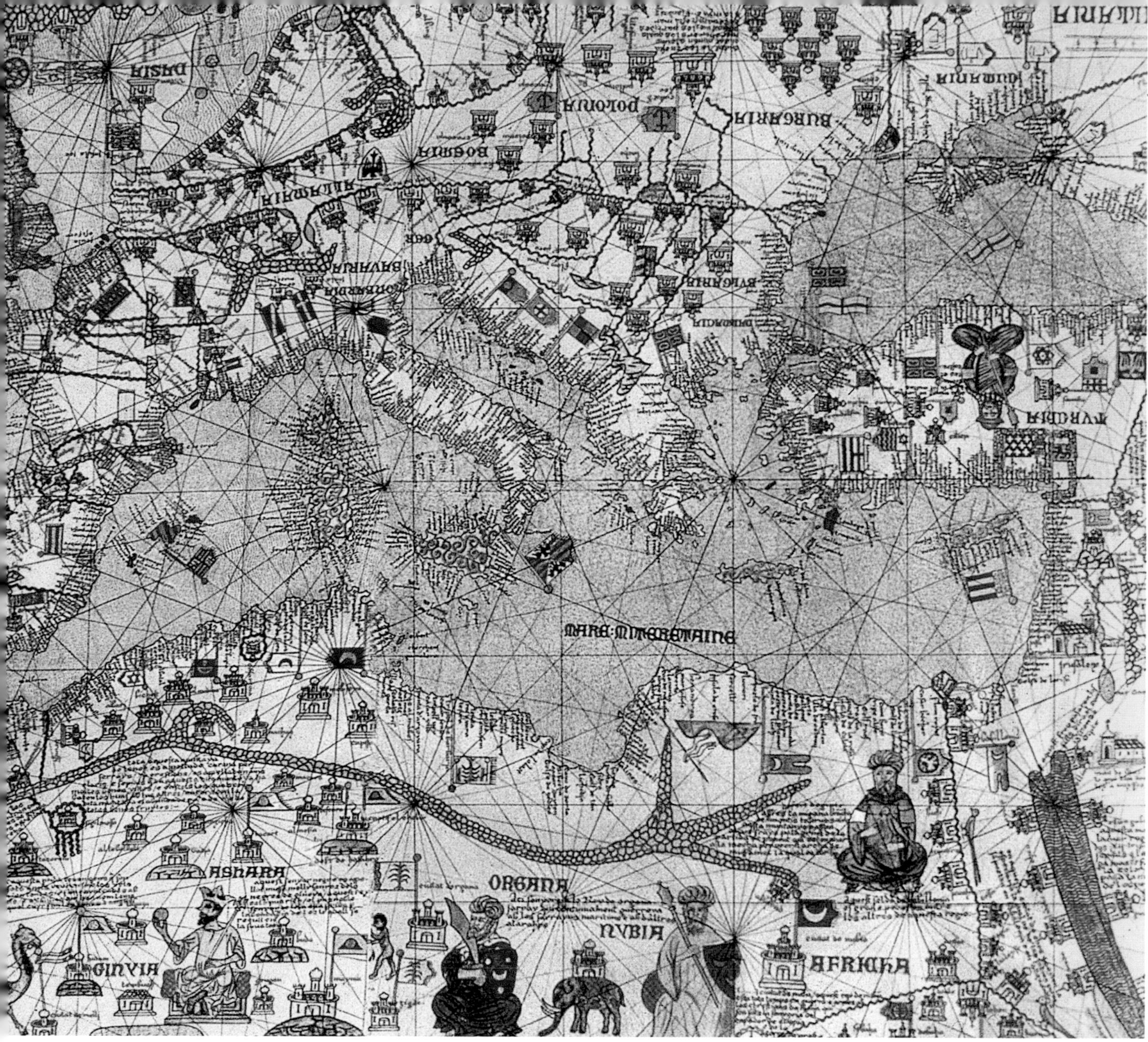

◁ ***Catalan Atlas***
Made in Majorca in 1375, the *Catalan Atlas* world map has many features of a portolan chart, with compass roses and rhumb lines. Superimposed on it are elements from medieval travelers' tales, both real and imagined.

roses to show direction. These charts were crisscrossed with networks of rhumb lines drawn from the points of the compass, to help pilots follow a precise course. Often extraordinarily accurate in tracing coastlines, given the technology available at the time, they were first produced in the maritime cities of Italy, later spreading to Catalonia and Portugal.

Portolans were practical regional maps, mostly covering parts of the Black Sea and Mediterranean coasts. Over time, however, the techniques acquired through making portolan charts fed into attempts to map the wider world. Pietro Vesconte, a Genoese cartographer working in Venice, made a reputation for himself with his portolans in the early 14th century. Around 1320, he combined his chart-making skills with the tradition of the mappa mundi to create a world map of much greater accuracy than previous efforts in Europe.

△ **Portolan charts**
This chart was made in 1559. It shows how much progress was made in cartography once the age of oceanic exploration had begun.

Another map that combined the portolan and mappa mundi traditions was the *Catalan Atlas* (1375). Produced by Jewish cartographer Abraham Cresques in Majorca, it incorporated information from the travel accounts of Marco Polo and the tales of Sir John Mandeville—including their fantastical elements.

The key event in the further development of European cartography was the rediscovery of the works of Ptolemy via Islamic sources in the 15th century. Ptolemy established the importance of defining places by coordinates of longitude and latitude. Although European mapmakers had always known the world was a sphere, Ptolemy gave them a precise estimate of its size. However, his estimation was wrong, as he had judged Earth to be only three-quarters of its true size. It was this miscalculation that would send Christopher Columbus westward in search of a passage to China.

THE AGE OF DISCOVERY
1400—1600

THE AGE OF DISCOVERY, 1400–1600

Introduction

The period between 1400 and 1600 is known as the Age of Discovery because it was the time when many navigators from Western Europe made voyages of exploration and discovered places that were previously unknown to Europeans. As a result, countries such as Spain, Portugal, France, and England formed worldwide trading networks, and founded settlements in Africa, America, and Asia. This gave them a lasting influence, not only in the countries they settled, but also globally.

Maritime pioneers

The main reason for embarking on these often dangerous journeys into the unknown was trade. European merchants already imported costly goods, such as spices and silk cloth, from the Far East, but these items came via the long overland route across Asia. A sea route could provide a more reliable, and possibly faster, way of importing goods from the east, and, it was hoped, access to valuable new markets. Members of the ruling European families, such as Prince Henry of Portugal (also known as Henry the Navigator), Ferdinand and Isabella of Spain, and Elizabeth I of England, all encouraged explorers to search for new routes to Asia.

Among the most important of these early voyagers were Vasco da Gama, who was the first European to reach India via the Cape of Good Hope, and Christopher Columbus, who crossed the Atlantic to become the first European since the Vikings to land on American soil. These pioneers and their followers established sea routes, set up staging posts on the African and Caribbean coasts, and inspired like-minded adventurers to follow their example.

IN 1492, CHRISTOPHER COLUMBUS BECAME THE FIRST EUROPEAN SINCE THE VIKINGS TO REACH THE AMERICAS

IN 1501, AMERIGO VESPUCCI DISCOVERED THAT THE AMERICAS WERE NOT ATTACHED TO ASIA

SCHOLAR ANTONIO PIGAFETTA CIRCUMNAVIGATED THE GLOBE WITH FERDINAND MAGELLAN'S CREW

> “ By **prevailing over all obstacles** and distractions, one may unfailingly **arrive at his chosen goal**. ”
>
> CHRISTOPHER COLUMBUS

Further waves of explorers included Ferdinand Magellan, whose project to circumnavigate the globe was completed by his crew after his death. At the same time, conquistadors defeated the Aztec and Inca empires, beginning the long period of European rule in Mexico and South America. These later adventurers were motivated less by trade than by the quest for resources—they expected South America to be rich in gold and silver. However, trading never ceased, and when the French began to explore Canada, they profited from the fur trade as well as from the territory they claimed for France.

Exchange of goods

Most of these expeditions were small in human numbers. Columbus made his first voyage with just three ships; Pizarro set out to conquer Peru with 180 men; Cortés had 500 soldiers. However, they had the advantage of superior technology: navigational aids, such as the backstaff and compass, helped them find their way, and plate armor and firearms ensured victory over ill-equipped natives. As a consequence, the impact of these voyages was enormous.

The transatlantic explorers in particular created an entirely new network of exchange, through which crops, livestock, and technologies crossed the world, albeit in tandem with infectious diseases. Corn, tomatoes, and potatoes came to Europe for the first time, while chickens, pigs, and horses crossed from Europe to America. Such networks ensured the eventual industrialization of America, but they also paved the way for the slave trade. The Age of Discovery profoundly changed both the old and new worlds alike.

IN 1519, HERNÁN CORTÉS BEGAN THE PROCESS OF CONQUERING MEXICO FOR SPAIN

IN THE 1530S, FRANCISCO PIZARRO DEFEATED THE INCAS AND CLAIMED THEIR LANDS FOR THE SPANISH THRONE

A MAP OF THE EAST COAST OF NORTH AMERICA BASED ON THE FRENCH DISCOVERIES OF 1534–41

Fleet commander
Admiral Zheng He, who led seven Chinese naval expeditions between 1405 and 1432, was born a Muslim—his father had made the pilgrimage to Mecca. Like all officials at the Ming imperial court, he was a eunuch.

FLEET ADMIRAL, 1371–1433

Zheng He

In the early 15th century, before the beginning of the European Age of Exploration, Chinese admiral Zheng He commanded what was then the world's largest fleet on a series of epic voyages from China to India, Arabia, and Africa.

Zheng He was a court eunuch in the service of the Yongle Emperor, Zhu Di. At the time, the newly founded Ming dynasty was full of energy, determined to assert China's international status. Zhu Di ordered a great "treasure fleet" to be built to project China's power and prestige far beyond its shores. As the emperor's most trusted official, Zheng He was selected to command this fleet.

The fleet consisted of more than 1,600 of the largest wooden sailing ships ever built. Zheng He's task was to lead expeditions around Southeast Asia and into the Indian Ocean, to impel local rulers to acknowledge the Chinese emperor as their overlord and send tribute to the Chinese court. The fleet carried some 27,000 soldiers, in case the required homage was not willingly given.

Between 1405 and 1422, Zheng He made six voyages, each taking about two years. Setting off from Nanjing on the Yangtze River, the first three voyages sailed to Sri Lanka and southern India via the coasts of Vietnam and the islands of Java and Sumatra. The fourth voyage carried on beyond India to the Persian port of Hormuz, and the fifth and sixth voyages extended to Arabia, the Red Sea, and the east coast of Africa. Each voyage returned with ambassadors from Indian Ocean states and a wealth of tribute goods—including exotic animals such as giraffes and zebras for the imperial menagerie.

When voyages were suspended in 1424, Zheng He continued to hold high office. He resumed the role of admiral for a final voyage of the treasure fleet in 1432, but died the following year. Subsequently, imperial China turned inward, banning oceanic voyages and largely erasing the memory of Zheng He's missions for five centuries. In parts of Southeast Asia, however, he was venerated by many Chinese overseas, who built temples in his honor.

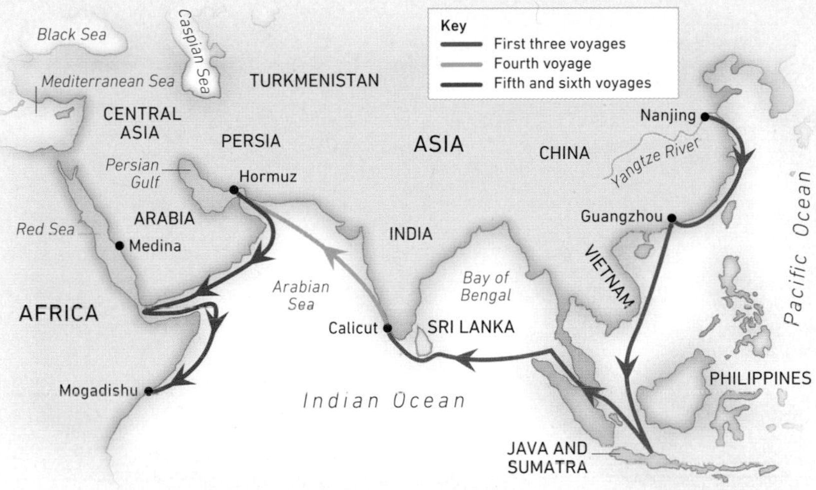

△ **Map**
Zheng He's voyages followed established coastal trade routes around the Indian Ocean from Malaysia to East Africa.

◁ **Mighty treasure ship**
This modern representation of the treasure fleet gives an impression of the size of the junks Zheng He commanded: each was almost 330 feet (100 m) long.

KEY DATES

- **1371** Born into a Muslim Hui family in the remote Yunnan region of China.
- **1381** His father is killed resisting the Ming conquest of Yunnan; he is castrated and made a servant of Zhu Di, Prince of Yan.
- **1402** Leads an army during Zhu Di's seizure of the imperial throne and is rewarded with high office at court.
- **1405** Commands the first voyage of the Chinese fleet built on Zhu Di's orders, sailing as far as southern India.

A GIRAFFE BROUGHT TO CHINA AS TRIBUTE

- **1407–19** Carries out four more voyages, traveling as far as Arabia and East Africa.
- **1422** Returns from his sixth voyage. Further sailings are suspended on the emperor's orders.
- **1422–31** Serves as military governor of the city of Nanjing.
- **1432** Embarks on a final voyage into the Indian Ocean. He dies in 1433 and is buried at sea.

TEMPLE DEDICATED TO THE VENERATION OF ZHENG HE IN PENANG, MALAYSIA

SAILING BOAT, EGYPT, 1900 BCE

MERCHANT SHIP, ROME, 200 CE

VIKING LONGSHIP, NORWAY, 800

AGAMEMNON MERCHANT STEAMSHIP, UK, 1865

WENDUR CARGO SHIP, SCOTLAND, 1884

Ships

For millennia, ships have been the primary mode of transport for carrying people and goods over long distances.

Many early civilizations depended on rivers for their survival: the ancient Egyptians on the Nile; the Mesopotamians on the Tigris and Euphrates; the earliest societies in what are now India and Pakistan on the Indus. As well as providing water for people and their crops, the rivers created an opportunity for waterborne transport.

The earliest known boats were made from animal skins and carved-out tree trunks. The Egyptians made sailing boats from papyrus reeds and the Greeks raised the art of rowing to a level that has never been surpassed. Later, the Vikings built sturdier vessels from trees and took to the oceans, propelled by wind and manpower.

In the 15th century, shipbuilders in Europe blended the best of what had gone before to construct massive, three- and four-masted vessels for the high seas, and added guns so that they could conquer other nations. Trade came in the wake of conquest, and huge merchant ships—the East Indiamen—were built to carry goods to trade with Asia.

The Age of Sail ended with the Industrial Revolution, when steam engines replaced sails to power transoceanic vessels. Steam engines have now mostly been replaced by diesel and gas-turbine engines, but many warships still use steam for propulsion, produced by onboard nuclear reactors.

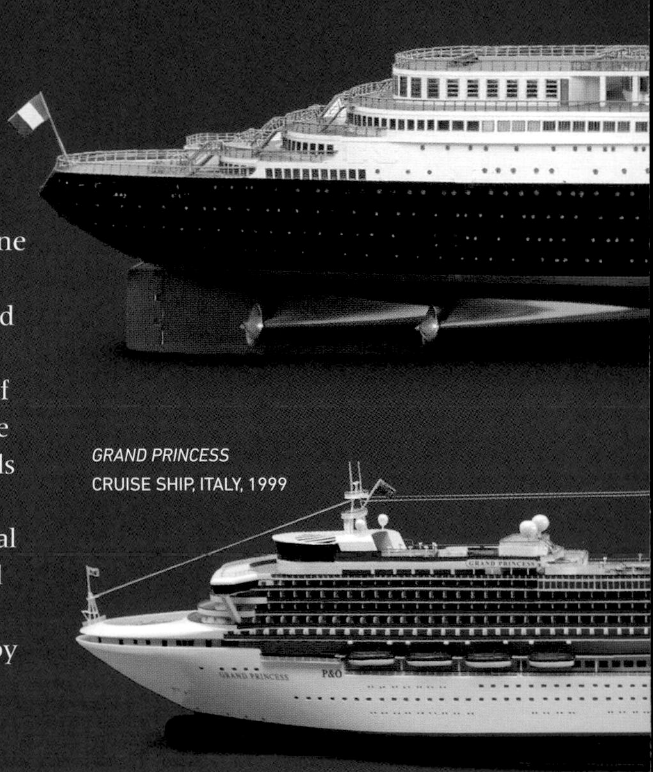

GRAND PRINCESS
CRUISE SHIP, ITALY, 1999

SANTA MARÍA CARRACK, SPAIN, 1492

SAVANNAH SAIL/STEAMSHIP, US, 1819

JUNK, CHINA, 1840

ROYAL SOVEREIGN PADDLE STEAMER, UK, 1893

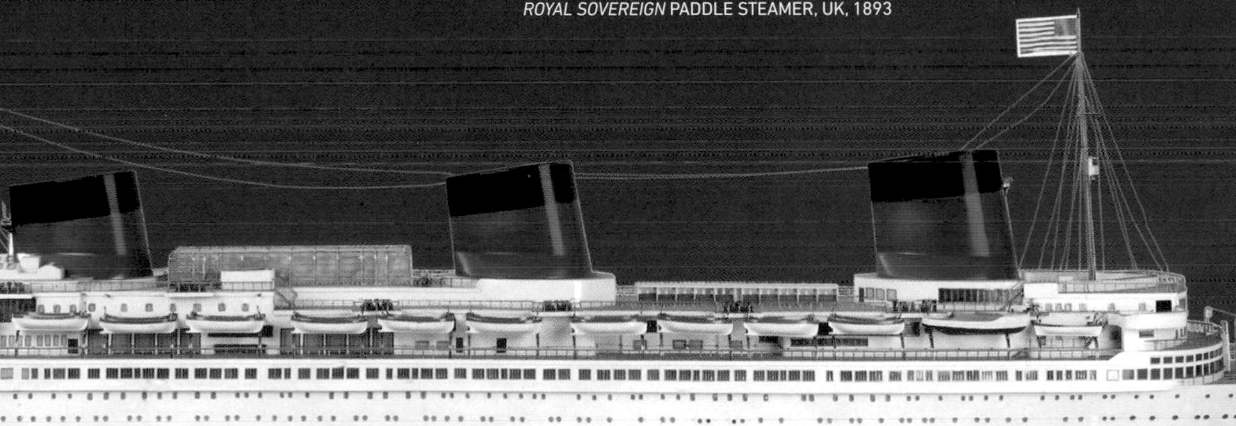
SS *NORMANDIE* OCEAN LINER, FRANCE, 1932

HIMIKO WATER BUS, JAPAN, 2010

Around Africa to India

Seeking the source of one of the most valuable items of world trade—spice—the Portuguese monarchy sent a naval expedition on a pioneering ocean voyage to India around the Cape of Good Hope.

△ **Vasco da Gama**
After his famous voyage in 1497–99, da Gama led a second fleet to India in 1502. He was appointed governor of all Portuguese territories in the east in 1524.

Portuguese exploration of the African coast began in the early 15th century, sponsored by Prince Henry the Navigator. Seeking Christian allies to fight Muslims in North Africa, and eager for the gold he knew could be found somewhere south of the Sahara, the Portuguese prince promoted voyages as far south as Sierra Leone. By the time Henry died in 1460, Portugal had begun a profitable trade in West African slaves and gold.

◁ **Portuguese caravel**
The key ship used in the Portuguese exploration of the African coast was the caravel. Small and nimble, it could sail in shallow coastal waters and up rivers.

First attempts

After a lull of two decades, the accession of King John II in 1481 triggered new voyages of exploration. Although information on Africa was scant, contemporary knowledge suggested it was possible to sail around the south of the continent into the Indian Ocean, gaining direct access to the Asian spices whose valuable trade was monopolized by Muslim powers and their Venetian trading partners. The king assembled astronomers and mathematicians to produce a manual of navigation, and sent a secret mission to Egypt to scout the lands around the Indian Ocean.

At first, the new project floundered. In 1482 and 1484, Portuguese sailor Diogo Cão traveled as far south as modern-day Namibia without finding the expected eastward turn toward India. In 1487, the king sent another maritime expedition down the African coast, led by Bartolomeu Dias. Early in 1488, lost in the ocean, Dias was carried by wind and currents around the Cape of Good Hope without seeing it, before making landfall in southern Africa.

At this point, Dias's sailors insisted on turning for home, but he returned to Lisbon with the assurance that the route to India was open.

Da Gama's triumph

A decade later, under John II's successor, Manuel I, the Portuguese were finally ready to embark for India. Commanded by Vasco da Gama, a fleet of four well-armed ships set sail from Lisbon in July 1497. Da Gama was not a sailor but a nobleman and diplomat. His mission was to act as a Portuguese ambassador, establishing trade links with Indian states. The fleet traveled to the Cape Verde Islands, then followed an oceanic route to southern Africa, spending 13 weeks out of sight of land—an impressive feat of navigation. After rounding the Cape of Good Hope, the Portuguese sailed up the coast of East Africa to Malindi. There, they met Ahmad ibn Mājid, a Gujarati sailor who was prepared to guide them across the Indian Ocean to Calicut in southern India.

Da Gama was not warmly received by the local ruler, but he succeeded in loading up with pepper and cinnamon before embarking for home.

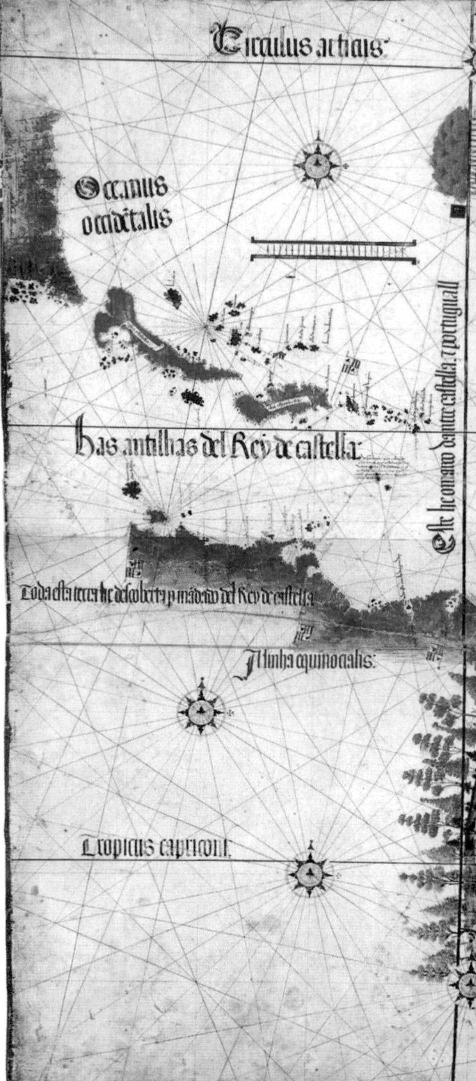

“ God alone is **the master and pilot** who had to deliver them by **his mercy**. ”

VASCO DA GAMA, ACCOUNT OF HIS VOYAGE, c.1500

◁ **Bartolomeu Dias**
Leading an expedition of two caravels and a supply ship, Dias rounded the Cape of Good Hope in 1488.

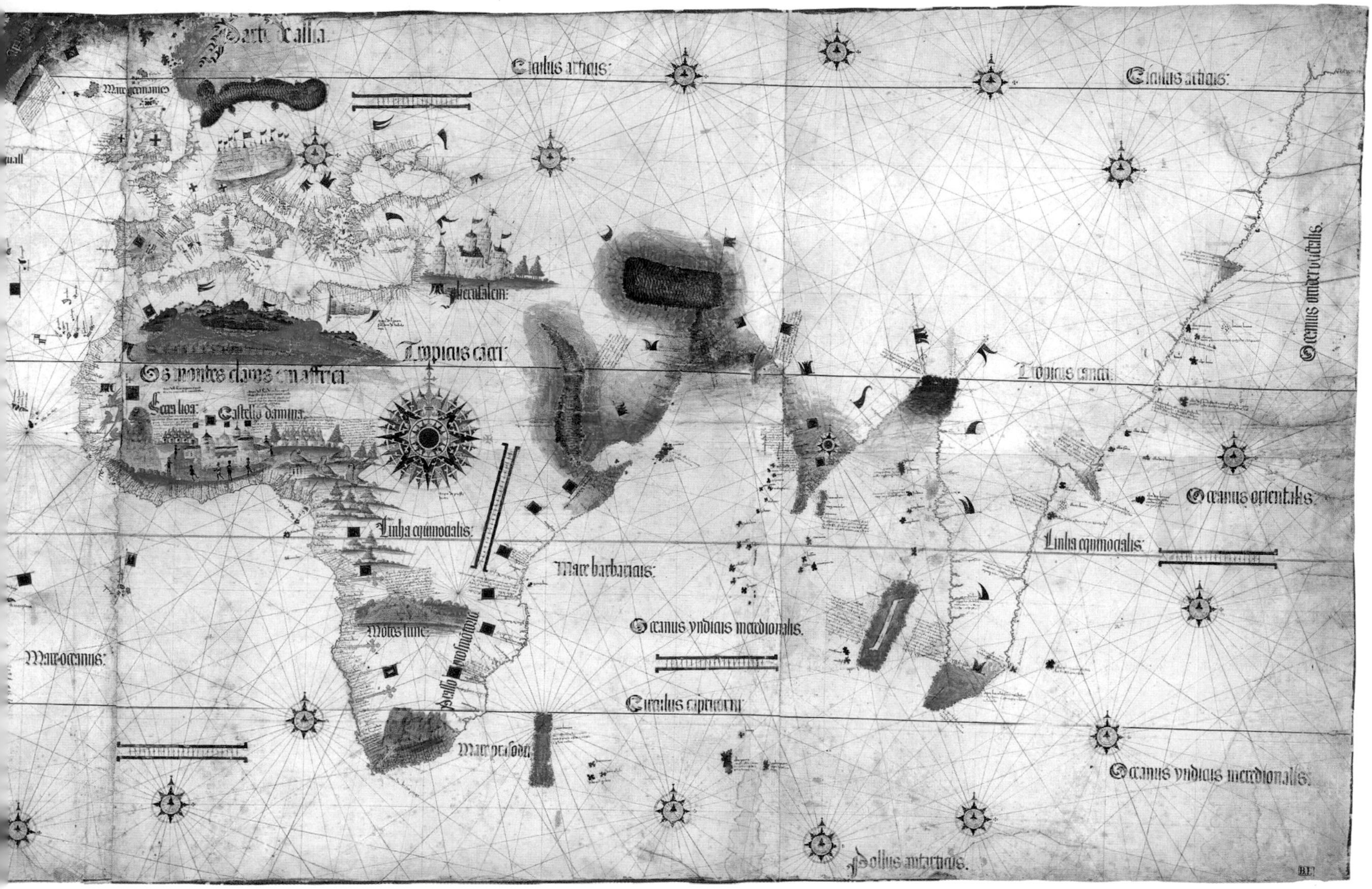

△ **The Cantino Planisphere**
Completed by an unknown cartographer in 1502, the Cantino Planisphere depicts the world as it was known to the Portuguese after da Gama's voyages of exploration.

Recrossing the Indian Ocean, the expedition was slowed by headwinds, battered by storms, and decimated by disease. Da Gama had to suppress a mutiny, and one of the ships was abandoned. When he reached Lisbon in September 1499, he had lost more than half his men. But da Gama's return was celebrated as a triumph. Subsequent expeditions cemented the Portuguese presence in India, and discovered Brazil. During the course of the 16th century, Portuguese mariners sailed as far as China and Japan, and the country grew rich on the trade in spices and other Asian goods.

◁ **Jerónimos Monastery**
This monastery at Belém, Lisbon, was built to celebrate da Gama's voyage to India, and was paid for with a tax on Portugal's trade with Africa and Asia.

Arrival on Hispaniola
Columbus's landing on Hispaniola is the subject of this 16th-century engraving by Theodore de Bry. Some of the explorer's men erect a cross by the coast, indicating their intention to convert the locals to Christianity.

A new world

From 1492 to 1502, explorer Christopher Columbus made four transatlantic voyages. These marked the beginning of the European colonization of America, and the forging of permanent links between the two continents.

Christopher Columbus was born in Genoa, an Italian city-state with a strong tradition of maritime trade. An experienced navigator, he became convinced that the best route from Europe to the Spice Islands of Southeast Asia was westward across the Atlantic.

During the 1480s, Columbus tried to find sponsors for a transatlantic expedition, but he was turned down by the rulers of Portugal, Venice, Genoa, and England, whose advisors knew that he had greatly underestimated the distance involved. However, Ferdinand and Isabella, the monarchs of Spain, decided to back Columbus, and he was able to crew and equip three ships—the *Santa Maria*, a large carrack, and two smaller caravels, the *Pinta* and the *Niña*—for the journey. The monarchs' main reason for sponsoring the explorer was to prevent others from benefitting from the lucrative trade he might open up.

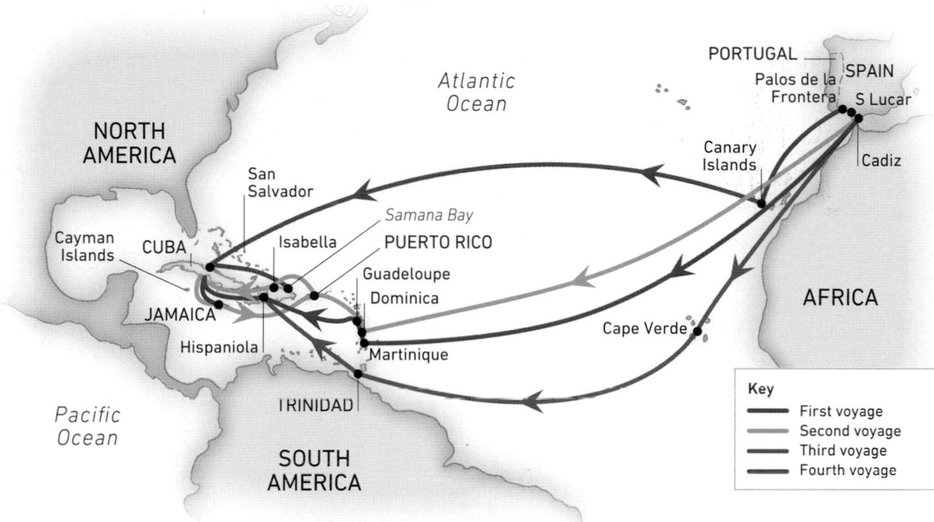

◁ **The four voyages of Columbus**
Columbus followed various routes across the Atlantic as he discovered more about the prevailing winds. The usual Spanish route westward was to go south to the Canaries and then catch the trade winds blowing toward the Caribbean.

The first voyage

Columbus's small fleet set off from Palos de la Frontera, on Spain's southwestern coast, on August 3, 1492. First, they sailed southwest to the Canary Islands, a Spanish possession, where they topped up their supplies and made repairs to the *Pinta*, which was taking on water. Columbus and his men then sailed westward into unknown waters for what turned out to be a five-week crossing of the Atlantic.

On October 12, the lookout on the *Pinta* reported that he had spotted land—an island in the Bahamas that they called San Salvador. Columbus noted that the people had only primitive weapons and would be easy to defeat if it came to a battle. However, nearly all the people Columbus met on his first voyage were friendly. He admired their gold ear ornaments and took a number of locals prisoner, hoping that they would lead him to the source of the gold. The lure of treasure led the captain of the *Pinta*, Martín Alonso Pinzón, to break away in search of an island rumoured to have lots of gold. The *Santa Maria* and *Niña*, meanwhile, carried on exploring the coast of Hispaniola until the *Santa Maria* ran aground, on Christmas Day 1492. Columbus was forced to abandon his flagship, continuing with just one vessel until the *Pinta* rejoined them on January 6, 1493.

△ **Christopher Columbus**
This portrait of the explorer was engraved about 100 years after his famous voyages to America.

Viceroy of the Indies

Leaving 39 men to start a colony—La Navidad, on present-day Haiti—Columbus continued along the Hispaniola coast. He stopped at the Bay of Rincón, where he met the local Cigüayos people. Columbus hoped to trade with them, but the Cigüayos refused and a clash »

IN CONTEXT
The carrack

Columbus's largest ship, the *Santa Maria*, was a carrack. A spacious vessel with several masts, and larger and more sturdy than his smaller caravels, a carrack was big and strong enough to survive rough seas, and was large enough to carry plenty of trade goods or supplies for a long voyage. Carracks were developed in the 14th century, and were used by Mediterranean seamen for trading voyages in the rough seas of the North Atlantic, as well as for journeys down the coast of Africa. They carried a mix of square and lateen (triangular) sails, the latter enabling them to tack against the wind, which was useful on long trips through variable winds.

MODEL OF THE THREE-MASTED *SANTA MARIA*

△ **Columbus with King Ferdinand and Queen Isabella**
After two years of negotiations, the Spanish monarchs agreed to back Columbus's 1492 voyage. They promised him 10 percent of any income from newly discovered lands.

» broke out. Some of the Spanish were injured, and Columbus took a group of Cigüayos prisoner and headed for Spain. Some of these prisoners died en route and the journey back proved a challenge. A severe storm forced them to take shelter in the Azores, where the local governor arrested a number of Columbus's men on suspicion of piracy. He released them after two days, but further storms delayed their return to Spain until March 15.

Because he had miscalculated the distance to the Spice Islands, and because no one knew about the existence of America, Columbus was convinced that he had reached the East Indies. The Spanish rulers agreed and made him Admiral of the Seven Seas and Viceroy of the Indies. A series of return journeys was planned.

A new colony

Columbus's second expedition (1493–96) was the biggest, with 17 ships carrying some 1,200 men, including farmers, soldiers, and priests, who planned to found a colony. Columbus explored the coasts of Dominica and Guadeloupe, sailed along the Lesser and Greater Antilles, and landed in Puerto Rico. He also found that La Navidad had been destroyed in disputes with locals; many colonists had been killed. Columbus therefore founded a new settlement at La Isabela on Hispaniola. Keeping the colony going proved difficult. Not all the locals wanted to be governed by Columbus, and many of the colonists were disappointed not to find the many riches they had been promised.

◁ **Coat of arms**
The coat of arms granted to Columbus in 1493 featured the lion and castle of Léon and Castile together with a group of islands.

Columbus humiliated

On his third voyage (1498–1500), Columbus sailed with six ships, three of which went directly to Hispaniola laden with supplies for the colonists. He took the other three to explore Trinidad and the South American coast. He became ill, however, and returned to Hispaniola, only to face a rebellion among the Spanish colonists. Their disillusion with their difficult life in the Caribbean, together with Columbus's authoritarian rule as governor, had finally boiled over. They put Columbus in chains and sent him back to Spain, where he was sacked from the governorship.

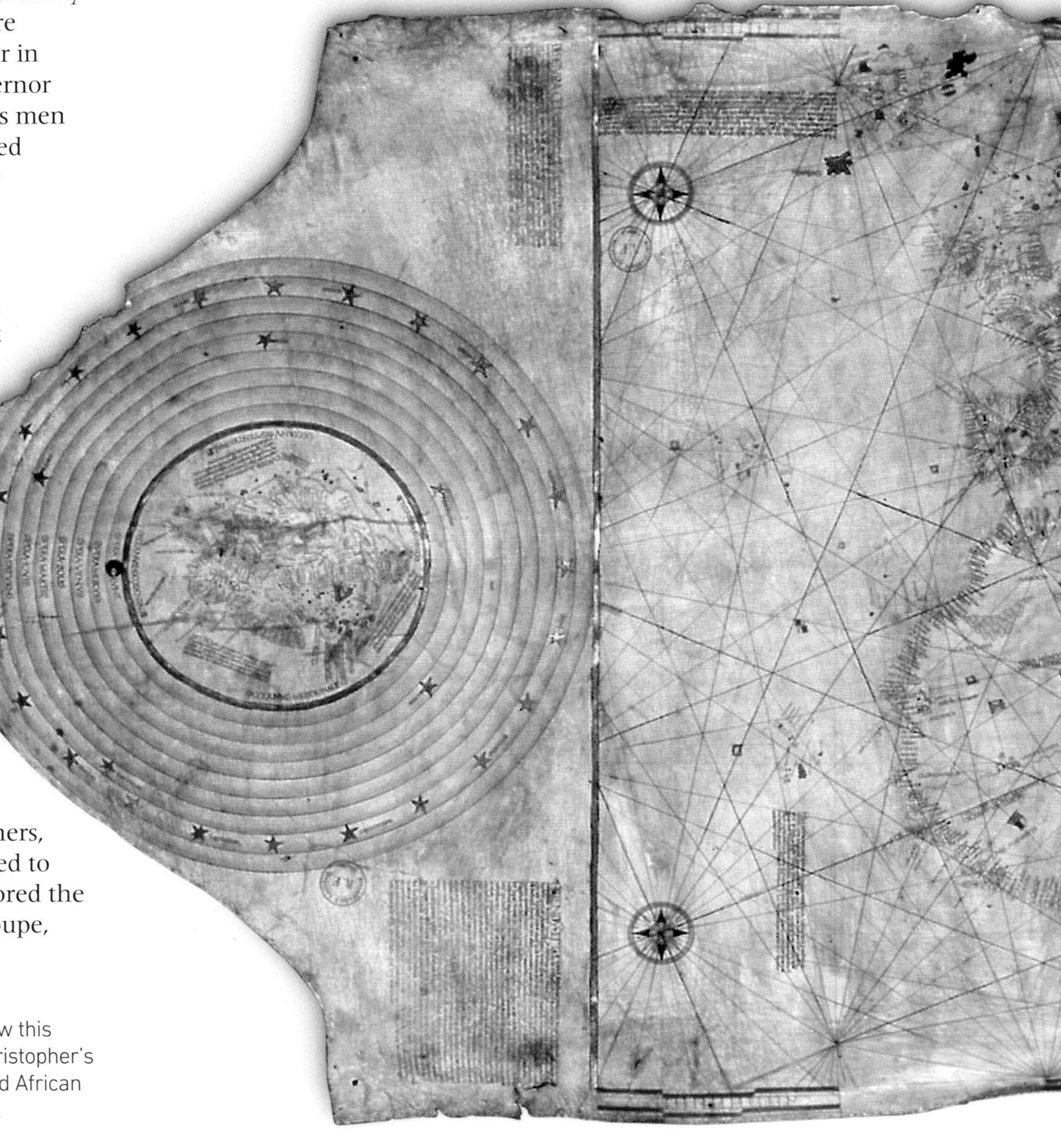

▷ **Columbus's map**
Columbus's brother Bartholomew drew this map in Lisbon around 1490, before Christopher's first voyage. It shows the European and African coasts and the eastern Atlantic Ocean.

The final voyage

In 1502, after persuading the crown to give him another chance, Columbus embarked on a fourth and final voyage. His aim was to find a route from the Caribbean into the Indian Ocean. His four ships arrived off Hispaniola as a hurricane was just beginning. The governor forbade him to enter to the harbor, so he took shelter in a nearby bay. Heedless of his own warnings, the governor then sent a fleet of 30 ships out of the harbor, loaded with treasure bound for Spain. All but one were destroyed in the hurricane, while Columbus's ships remained safe.

Columbus continued exploring, sailing along the coast between Honduras and Panama, where he established a garrison. However, his land force was attacked by locals, who also harried his ships. Returning to the Caribbean, he passed the Cayman Islands, naming them Las Tortugas, after the many turtles he spotted there. Further storms followed off Cuba, and when the ships were damaged he became stranded in Jamaica. The governor there offered no support and tried to prevent any rescue attempts, but Columbus won favor with the locals, whom he impressed when he accurately predicted a lunar eclipse. After a year, help arrived from Hispaniola and the explorer returned to Spain.

Columbus died a disappointed man in 1506. His dismissal from the governorship meant he was deprived of his expected share of the profits of his exploration. However, he always believed he had found a route to the East Indies, and he had brought back not only gold but also tobacco, potatoes, and pineapples, all new to Europe, beginning a series of trading and cultural exchanges that have continued ever since (see pp. 128–29).

◁ **Columbus fights Francisco Poraz**
In the Caribbean, Columbus often faced hostility from Spanish colonists who had not made the fortunes he had promised. Here he fights an insurrection led by Francisco Poraz.

> "I saw that they were **very friendly** ... and perceived that they could be **much more easily converted** to our holy faith by **gentle means** than by **force**."
>
> CHRISTOPHER COLUMBUS, JOURNAL, OCTOBER 11, 1492

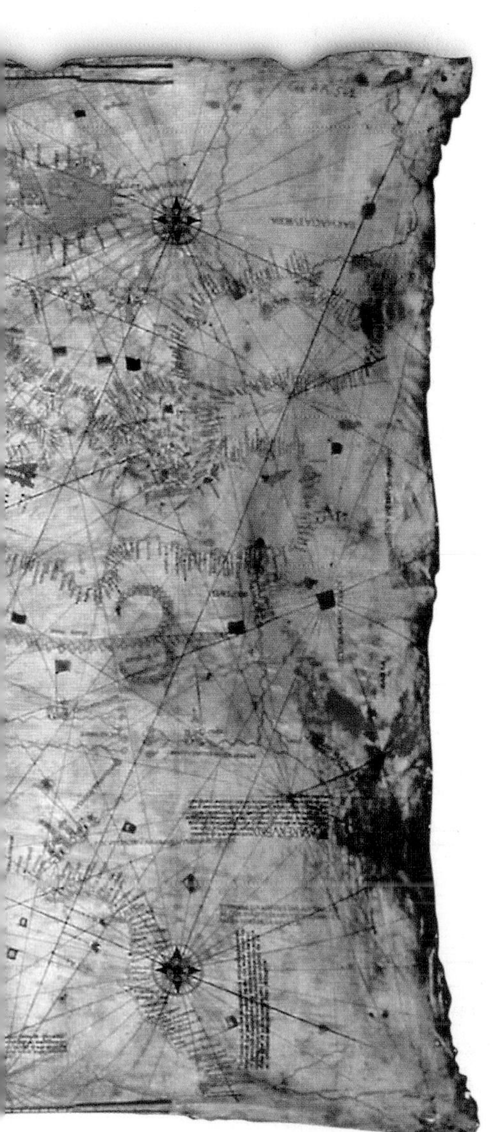

▷ **The discovery of Trinidad**
The three peaks of the island of Trinidad are clearly shown in this 18th-century engraving, which commemorates Columbus's arrival there in 1498.

After Columbus

A number of travelers followed Columbus in trying to reach Asia via the Atlantic. Thanks to navigators such as Amerigo Vespucci, however, the Europeans finally realized that the lands they were exploring were not part of Asia, but an entirely separate "New World."

The discoveries of Christopher Columbus made many people curious about the western route to the Indies. Traders, rulers, and navigators were all keen to retrace the explorer's route and find a way beyond it to gain access to the valuable silks and spices of Asia. One of the most prominent of these people was Amerigo Vespucci, a Florentine businessman and traveler whose work took him to Spain. There, in 1499, he became part of a Spanish transatlantic expedition led by Alonso de Ojeda, a seaman who had sailed on Columbus's second voyage, and by navigator Juan de la Cosa.

From Venezuela to the Amazon

They left Spain in May 1499, sailing first to the Canary Islands, and from there crossing the Atlantic in just 24 days. Arriving at the coast of what is now Guyana, South America, the expedition then split up. Vespucci sailed south along the coast of Brazil; Ojeda and Cosa traveled westward along the coast of Venezuela. Ojeda and Cosa explored the Gulf of Paria (where they obtained pearls and some gold) and carried on along the Venezuelan coast.

◁ **Amerigo Vespucci**
John Ogilby's engraving shows Vespucci, a navigator from Florence. He worked for the Medici family, running their business interests in Spain. While there, he met Columbus, who sparked his interest in exploration.

On sighting the island of Curaçao, they named it Giants' Island as they thought that the inhabitants looked enormous. Landing on the mainland, Ojeda angered the local people, and there was a clash in which there were several casualties among Ojeda's men.

Ojeda and Cosa retreated, and met up again with Vespucci, who by this time had reached the mouth of the Amazon, and then turned north to retrace his steps. Finding houses on the coast built on wooden stilts above water, Vespucci was reminded of Venice, which is one explanation of the origin of the name Venezuela—which means "little Venice" in Spanish. The reunited fleet headed home via Hispaniola, and in June 1500 they arrived back in Spain with the pearls and gold, together with a cargo of Brazilwood as well as some 200 Native Americans bound for a life of slavery.

Sailing southwards

Vespucci's second expedition was under the flag of Portugal. He left in May 1501, joining Portuguese explorer Pedro Álvares Cabral in the Cape Verde Islands and then crossing the Atlantic to Brazil. They traveled down the coasts of Brazil and Argentina, but it is uncertain exactly how far south they went. Vespucci made detailed observations of the night sky, gathering valuable information about stars visible from the southern

◁ **Alonso de Ojeda**
A skilled navigator and brave military leader, Alonso de Ojeda benefitted from having sailed on Columbus's second transatlantic voyage. His voyages along the coasts of Guyana, Trinidad, and Venezuela were important in the history of exploration.

A WOODCUT FROM 1505, BASED ON INFORMATION IN *MUNDUS NOVUS*, SHOWING VESPUCCI'S SHIPS AND NATIVE SOUTH AMERICANS

IN CONTEXT
Vespucci's writings

We know about Vespucci's voyages because of two publications that came out during his lifetime and which were attributed to him: *Mundus Novus* (*New World*), which describes a journey of 1501–2 and *Lettera di Amerigo Vespucci* (*Letter of Amerigo Vespucci*), which is an account of four voyages. These are now thought to be forgeries, although factually accurate at least in some respects. In the 18th century, three genuine letters from Vespucci were discovered, describing two voyages that correspond to his journeys in 1499 and 1501. Vespucci's conviction that he had discovered a new continent is clear from these accounts.

hemisphere. He also made clear and informative notes on the native people he encountered before returning to Europe in July 1502.

A new continent

Using the descriptions of Asia made by Ptolemy and Marco Polo, Vespucci realized that the area he had explored was not the East Indies, but a continent previously unknown to Europeans. Some contemporaries were suspicious of his claim to have discovered a "new" continent, believing he was trying to undermine the reputation of Columbus as the discoverer of the lands in the western Atlantic. However, Vespucci was soon recognized as the first European to have explored the coasts of Brazil and Argentina. Indeed, by 1507, maps of the world were naming the new continent "America"—the Latinized (and feminized) version of Vespucci's first name.

◁ **World map by Juan de la Cosa**
Cosa made his world map in 1500. It is the earliest surviving world map to feature the Caribbean. It also includes information gathered by Vasco da Gama on his 1498 voyage to India.

▽ **Hostile encounters**
Ojeda and Vespucci sometimes came into conflict with native peoples. This early engraving shows a clash between Vespucci and the people of an unknown island, which he called "Ity" in a letter.

First map of the New World

By including America as a separate continent, Waldseemüller produced a map that came close to showing the world as we know it today.

German geographer Martin Waldseemüller produced his world map in 1507. A large map, more than 8 feet (2.4m) in overall length, it divides the globe up into 12 areas, each represented on a separate woodcut. Waldseemüller drew it as part of an attempt to combine the information gathered by recent explorers, such as Amerigo Vespucci, with existing knowledge of the countries and oceans of the world dating back to Ptolemy, the 2nd-century scholar from Alexandria (pp. 52–53).

Waldseemüller's map was designed to accompany a book, *Cosmographiae Introductio* (*Introduction to Cosmography*), which was also published in 1507. The author of the book was probably Matthias Ringmann, who worked with Waldseemüller in St. Dié, in the Vosges region of eastern France. The purpose of the book and map are described on the book's title page as "A description of the whole world … with the insertion of those lands unknown to Ptolemy discovered by recent men."

The map combines a conventional and recognizable picture of Europe, Africa, and Asia with representations of the Caribbean islands discovered by Columbus and the coasts of Central and South America as described by Amerigo Vespucci. Like Vespucci, Waldseemüller realized that America was a separate continent. He made a guess at its overall shape, deducing that beyond it was a large ocean separating it from eastern Asia. Waldseemüller was the first to name the new continent, calling it "America," from the Latinized form of Amerigo Vespucci's name, Americus.

Although around a thousand copies were printed, only a single copy of the map is known to have survived, making it a unique document showing the state of knowledge of the globe in the early 16th century. It is not only the first map to name America, but the first to discard the old notion of a world made up of three parts (Europe, Africa, and Asia), adding a fourth part made up of America and the ocean that later explorers would name the Pacific.

▷ **Remapping the West**
Much of the eastern hemisphere on the map was copied from Ptolemy's second projection, whereas the western hemisphere was largely redrawn using new geographical discoveries.

ASIA
AFRICA
AQVILO
SEPTENTRIO
MARE GLACIALE SIVE CONGELA
MARE GLACIALE
SERICA REGIO
SCITHIA EXTRA IMAV
SCITHIA INTRA IMAVM
ASIA
MARE HIRCANVM SIVE CASPIVM
SINVS PERSICVS
ARABIA FELIX
INDIA EXTRA GANGEM
SINVS GANGETICVS
TAPROBANA INSVLA
EQVINOCTIALIS
MARE INDICVM
OCEANVS INDICVS MERIDIONALIS
TROPICVS CAPRICORNI
MADAGASCAR
MARE PRASODVM
ETHIOPIA INTERIOR
AFRICA
NOTVS
AVSTER
90
80
120
130
140
150
160
170
180
190

Circumnavigating the globe

Portuguese navigator Ferdinand Magellan launched the first full round-the-world sea expedition. He did not survive the journey, but a few of his seamen made it home, achieving a complete circumnavigation of the globe.

△ **The *Victoria***
The sole ship in Magellan's fleet that made the full journey, the *Victoria* was a carrack of 85 tons, with a crew of 42. Magellan named it after the Santa Maria de la Victoria de Triana Church in Seville.

The transatlantic voyages of Christopher Columbus, Amerigo Vespucci, and other explorers proved that there were lands on the western side of the Atlantic. Columbus believed that these lands were the Spice Islands of Southeast Asia, but Vespucci realized that they were in fact part of a new continent, which geographers named America (see pp. 116–17). However, some navigators were still convinced that if they could find a strait through America, they would reach Asia and the riches of the Spice Islands. One of these was the Portuguese seaman Ferdinand Magellan.

Magellan changes sides

Magellan was a very experienced sailor. From 1505 to 1514, he spent several years in India fighting in battles on the Portuguese side, sailed to Malacca with the first Portuguese embassy, and later served his country in Morocco, before falling out with the Portuguese government when he was accused of doing illegal trade deals with the Moors. He then tried to interest the Portuguese Crown in a westward journey in search of the Spice Islands. If the route was an easier one than the eastward route around Africa and India, this would potentially give Portugal greater profits in the spice trade. However, Magellan was out of favor, and King Manuel I rejected the plan.

◁ **Ferdinand Magellan**
Having served his native Portugal over many years, Ferdinand Magellan lost favor with the Portuguese court and decided to sail under the flag of its rivals, Spain.

Still keen to get his voyage underway, Magellan turned to Portugal's rival, Spain. The Spanish were eager to find a western passage to Asia because, under the Treaty of Tordesillas (1494), the eastern route (and therefore, in effect, the spice trade) was allotted to Portugal. So, in 1518, Magellan was authorized by Spain's ruler Charles I (later known as Holy Roman Emperor Charles V) to journey westward. Magellan was given royal funds and a number of benefits, including a 10-year monopoly on the resulting trade and the governorship of any lands he discovered.

Crossing the Atlantic

Magellan set sail with five ships and a crew of around 237. Key people on the voyage included Spanish merchant ship captain Juan Sebastián Elcano; Venetian scholar Antonio Pigafetta, who kept a record of the journey that is an invaluable source for historians; and Juan de Cartagena, who was in charge of the trading side of the expedition. The mix of nationalities on board brought Magellan trouble, because many of the Spanish resented being led by a Portuguese captain.

The five ships left Spain on September 20, 1519. The Portuguese King Manual I immediately sent ships in pursuit—Magellan was seen as a traitor for having mounted an expedition with the backing of Spain. However, the Portuguese did not catch Magellan's ships and, after they stopped at the Canary Islands for provisions, they sailed toward Cape Verde. Bad storms delayed them off the coast of Africa, but eventually they set a course southwest toward Brazil. They sighted Brazil on December 6, 1519, but this was a Portuguese possession, so they sailed south, putting down their anchors when they reached what is now Argentina, near modern-day Rio de Janeiro.

Trouble in the South Atlantic

Continuing southward, they anchored for the winter in a natural harbor in Patagonia that Magellan called Puerto San Julián. Here, over Easter 1520, Magellan hit his first major problem: three of the five captains staged a mutiny. Their revolt was partly the result of continuing tension between the Spanish and Portuguese, and partly an unwillingness to sail further into the unknown, icy South Atlantic waters. Magellan suppressed the rebellion rapidly. Some of the rebel leaders »

IN CONTEXT
Wildlife

Magellan and his crew were the first Europeans to sail down the eastern coast of South America into the Pacific. On their way, they noticed a number of animals and birds that were unknown to European naturalists. Antonio Pigafetta noted them in his journal, which is the main source for information about the voyage. One was described as a camel without humps, which was probably a guanaco, although it may have been a llama, vicuna, or alpaca. Perhaps the most notable bird was the penguin, which they called a "goose" because it had to be skinned rather than plucked. Later, scientists named one species the Magellanic penguin, in honor of their discoverer.

MAGELLANIC PENGUIN

◁ **Juan Sebastián Elcano**
Like Magellan, Elcano had been out of favor with his sovereign, having surrendered a Spanish ship to the Genoese to pay off a debt. He joined Magellan's dangerous expedition to gain a pardon from Charles I.

> " **Unlike** the mediocre, **intrepid spirits** seek **victory** over those **things** that **seem impossible**. "
>
> FERDINAND MAGELLAN

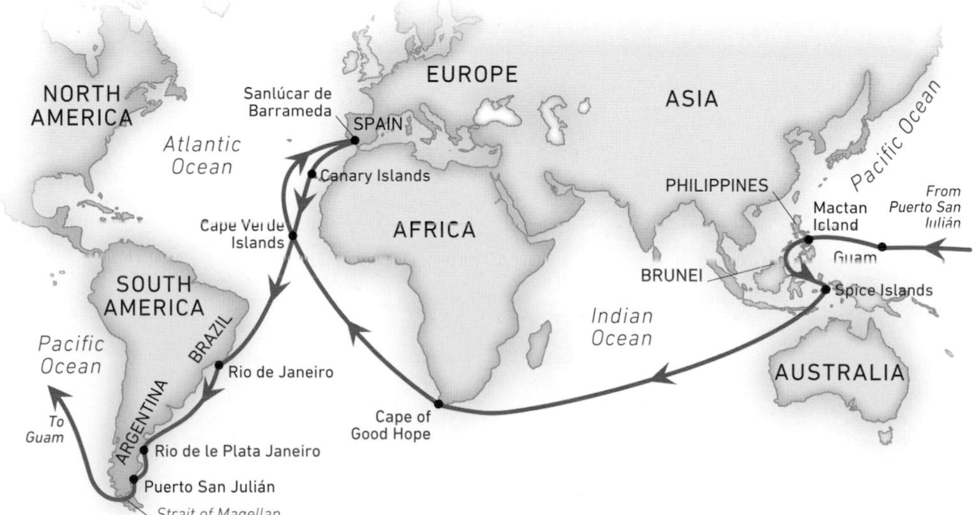

◁ **Magellan's route**
By starting with an Atlantic crossing and locating the strait into the Pacific, Magellan proved that Southeast Asia could be reached by a westerly route. The survivors of the trip made it home via the Indian Ocean.

were executed, and one of the rebel captains, together with the expedition's chaplain, was marooned. Their followers were pardoned and they continued southward. Finally, on October 21, 1520, they found the strait that would take them west toward Asia. By the end of November, all the ships were through the 370-mile (600-km) passage and into the comparative calm of the waters beyond. Grateful for this respite from storms, Magellan named the sea *Mar Pacifico* (Pacific Ocean).

△ **Antonio Pigafetta**
The Venetian scholar Pigafetta took notes on plants, animals, people, languages, and geographical features during the voyage. His *Report* was of great value to future navigators.

◁ **Battle of Mactan**
This illustration from a 1626 book by Lenvinus Hulsius shows the Spanish fighting native peoples on the Philippine island of Mactan, where Magellan met his death.

The Philippines

Sailing northwest, they crossed the Pacific, visiting Guam (where locals stole one of their ships' boats) and arriving in the Philippines on March 16, 1521. Magellan had a Malay indentured servant who helped him speak to the local people. At first, relations were peaceful, gifts were exchanged, and a local leader, Humabon of Cebu, was converted to Christianity. However, another leader, Lapu-Lapu, who was the enemy of Humabon, refused to convert and Humabon persuaded Magellan to launch an armed attack on him. The battle took place on April 27, 1521, when 49 Europeans landed on the island of Mactan and faced a much larger force of locals. Magellan was recognized as the European leader, injured with a spear, and attacked by islanders, who killed him. The rest of the Europeans escaped in their boats.

The voyage home

The expedition was now much reduced. Casualties on the way and in the Battle of Mactan left them with only enough men to sail two ships, so they burned one and the rest of the team set sail in the *Trinidad* and *Victoria*. They sailed to Brunei, where they saw the splendid court of the ruler and such wonders as tame elephants. On November 6, they finally reached the Spice Islands and were able to trade with one of the local sultans who had not already made a trading alliance with the Portuguese.

Set to return to Spain loaded with valuable spices, they had a further mishap—the *Trinidad* sprung a leak.

> "**All** at once **rushed upon him** ... so that they slew our **mirror**, our **light**, our **comfort**, and our **true guide**."
>
> ANTONIO PIGAFETTA, ON MAGELLAN'S DEATH, IN *REPORT*, 1525

CARTAGENA IS PUT IN THE STOCKS BY MAGELLAN AS PUNISHMENT FOR MUTINY

IN PROFILE
Juan de Cartagena

Juan de Cartagena traveled on Magellan's expedition as Inspector General. This role gave Cartagena the task of overseeing any trading activities and reporting directly to King Charles. Although Cartagena was an accountant and not an experienced seaman, Magellan appointed him captain of one of the ships, the *San Antonio*, as a mark of his importance. However, the pair clashed—Cartagena criticized Magellan over food rationing when they were delayed and had to ration supplies—and he was removed from his command. Cartagena resented this, and organized the mutiny of April 1520. Cartagena's punishment was to be marooned on an island off Patagonia, along with the priest Pedro Sanchez de la Reina.

It looked as if it would take a long time to repair, so some of the men stayed with the *Trinidad* (which was later lost to the Portuguese); the *Victoria*, under the command of captain Elcano, returned across the Indian Ocean toward the Cape of Good Hope and Europe. The *Victoria* and a small crew completed their journey on September 6, 1522, so it was Elcano who was the first to complete a successful circumnavigation of the globe, bringing with him not only a cargo of spices but also information about the Pacific Ocean, proof that the Spice Islands could be reached by a westward route, and more precise knowledge about the size of the Earth. However, the costs were heavy: of the original contingent of around 237 sailors on the expedition, some 219 died en route.

◁ **Strait of Magellan**
Magellan called the waterway through which he passed from the Atlantic to the Pacific the *Estrecho de Todos los Santos* (The Channel of All Saints). Seven years later, it was renamed the Strait of Magellan.

▽ **Magellan's death**
This 19th-century engraving illustrates how Magellan was killed on Mactan by native people. The locals recognized Magellan as the leader and began to attack him with spears, before finally dispatching him with cutlasses.

Meeting with Moctezuma
Cortés meets Aztec Emperor Moctezuma at Tenochtitlan on November 8, 1519. The Aztecs offer gifts, believing Cortés to be a god, while Moctezuma's feet are kept from touching the ground by a servant.

Cortés and the conquest of the Aztecs

The explorer and soldier Hernán Cortés led the Spanish conquest of the Aztecs, an event that proved to be a turning point in the history of Mexico and the surrounding regions.

After the voyages of Christopher Columbus and the first Spanish settlements in America and the Caribbean (see pp. 118–21), the Spanish Crown authorized several individuals—explorer-soldiers known as "conquistadors"—to explore parts of the New World. One of these was Diego Velázquez, who conquered Cuba for Spain, becoming its governor, and who was given the right to control further exploration of the American mainland. Another was Hernán Cortés, who moved to the Caribbean in 1504 and took part in the Cuban conquest. In 1518, Velázquez gave Cortés approval to explore Mexico, but he then had second thoughts, questioning Cortés's motives for exploring this reputedly rich area, and cancelled the commission. However, Cortés left for Mexico anyway, beginning a series of events that transformed the Mexican mainland forever.

△ **Hernán Cortés**
Cortés, a child of lesser nobility, was a Spanish conquistador who overthrew the Aztec Empire in the 1520s and helped to inaugurate the Spanish colonization of the Americas.

Ally and turncoat

Landing on the Yucatán Peninsula, Cortés defeated the locals, among whom was a woman called Malintzin, or La Malinche, who spoke both Maya and the Aztec language of Nahuatl; she

◁ **Conquistadors' route to Mexico**
This contemporary map shows the route taken by Cortés and his men during their conquest of Mexico. It begins with their landing on the Yucatán Peninsula in the east and ends with their arrival in Tenochtitlan.

IN CONTEXT
The Aztec Empire

The Aztec Empire was an alliance of three city-states (Tenochtitlan, Texcoco, and Tlacopan), which dominated the Valley of Mexico and surrounding areas from 1428 until the Spanish conquest in 1521. Tenochtitlan was the senior partner in the alliance, and the vast city was the empire's capital. The Aztec emperors expanded their territory by conquest, and by the time of the last native ruler, Moctezuma, it covered much of central Mexico together with parts of Honduras, El Salvador, and Guatemala. The Aztecs' large cities featured pyramidal temples to their gods, the principal deity being Huitzilopochtli, the sun god. Their crops included tomatoes and chocolate, which were unknown in Europe at the time.

MASK BEARING THE FACE OF THE AZTEC MAIZE GOD

became his main translator. He then made an alliance with the Totonac people of the eastern coastal area, who supported him and helped him build the new town of Veracruz. However, some of the Spanish who still felt loyal to Velázquez started a conspiracy to take one of their ships and return to Cuba. Cortés dealt with the rebellion swiftly, hanging the conspirators and then scuttling the ships. The Spanish were effectively stranded on the mainland, and had little choice but to follow Cortés.

After making another alliance with a local people, the Tlaxcalans, Cortés marched on Cholula in the Mexican highlands, where the people offered no resistance. However, he ordered the Cholulans to be massacred and their town to be burned—either as a premeditated attack to scare the Aztecs he was planning to conquer, or in response to a story of planned local treachery. There was a very high death toll, although the exact numbers are still unknown.

Tenochtitlan

By November 1519, Cortés was ready to march on Tenochtitlan, the capital of the most powerful Mexican people, the Aztecs. It was a tough march over difficult country, to what was probably the largest city in the world at the time—the population may have been as high as 300,000. It is said that there had been an Aztec prophecy about a pale-skinned god arriving from the east, so when the Spanish arrived they were welcomed and offered expensive gifts. However, tensions mounted and Cortés took the Aztec ruler, Moctezuma, hostage. Then, news came of a force sent by Velázquez to capture Cortés, who left the capital to confront them. While he was away, the Aztecs rebelled, and when Cortés returned, Moctezuma was killed, and Cortés and his men were expelled from the city. They returned in 1521, laid siege to Tenochtitlan for three months, and finally destroyed the city.

With the powerful Aztecs crushed and a new Spanish city rising on the site of Tenochtitlan, the conquerors controlled Mexico, and by 1523, Cortés was made governor and captain general of New Spain, the Spanish territory in the New World north of the Isthmus of Panama. However, fearing that he was becoming too influential, the Crown removed the title of captain general, greatly limiting his power. Mexico and much of Central America remained in Spanish hands, however, bringing huge wealth to Spain. The native people, by contrast, were unable to govern their own lands and were decimated by devastating European diseases.

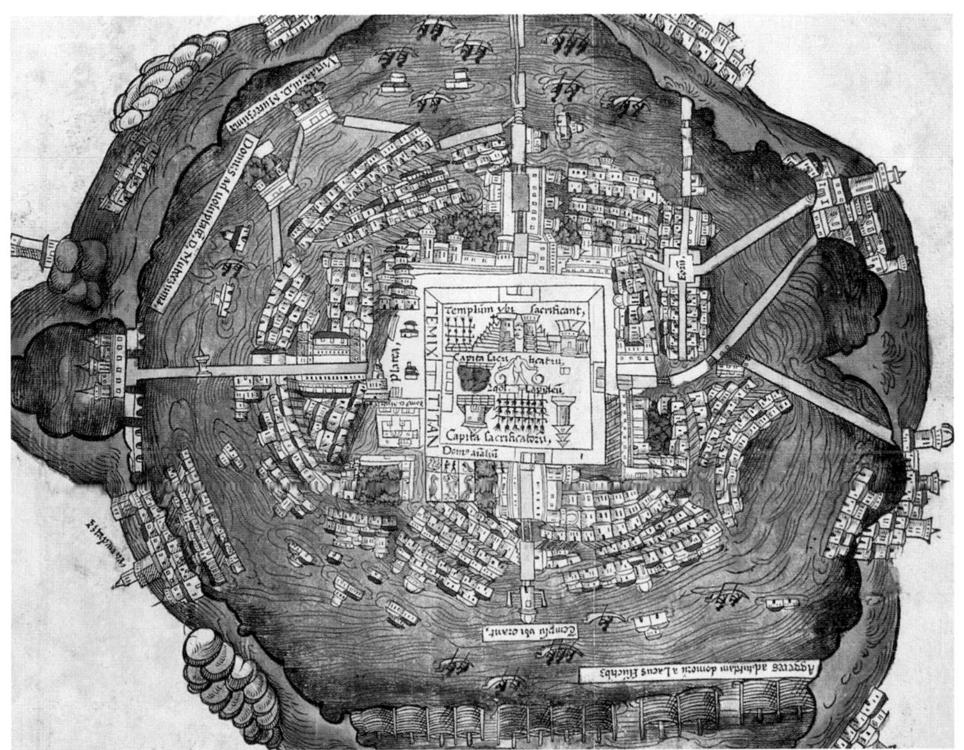

◁ **A city of islands**
This 16th-century map of Tenochtitlan shows the twin-towered ceremonial district in the center, surrounded by numerous palaces and houses, variously accessed by canals, roads, and causeways.

Pizarro's conquest of Peru

The Spanish conquest of Peru is a story of difficult journeys over harsh terrain, with limited backup, followed by one of the most surprising victories ever recorded. It changed the course of South American history.

△ **Francisco Pizarro**
This portrait of the Spanish explorer, from 1835, is by Amable-Paul Coutan. As a young man from a poor family, Pizarro went to live in the Spanish colony of Hispaniola, which gave him a taste for travel and adventure.

Francisco Pizarro was a Spanish adventurer who went to the New World with the navigator Alonso de Ojeda in 1509. He also took part in an expedition led by the explorer Vasco Núñez de Balboa in 1513, and crossed the Isthmus of Panama to become one of the first Europeans to see the Pacific Ocean. In the mid-1520s, enthused by the Spanish conquest of Mexico and rumors of the riches of Peru, he launched two expeditions to this part of South America.

The first journeys to Peru

Pizarro's first expedition was unsuccessful, as poor preparation and bad weather dogged the Spaniards' progress. The second, in 1526–28, proved more promising, although it did not go well at first, being hampered by poor weather, lack of supplies, and the swampy terrain in the coastal areas of Colombia. A detachment turned back to get reinforcements, but ran into hostile locals. When it was then sent to Panama for yet more reinforcements, Pedro Arias Dávila, the Governor of Panama, refused, and called Pizarro back. Pizarro stood his ground and urged his companions to stay—but only 13 remained.

It was this small group, plus another force ostensibly sent to recall Pizarro, that pushed further south to the Tumbes region of northwest Peru. Here they found welcoming native tribes, saw llamas for the first time, and discovered tantalizing evidence of riches, particularly silver and gold. This convinced Pizarro that the months of hardship had been worthwhile, and he soon began planning a third expedition to conquer Peru's Inca rulers in order to gain access to the country's riches.

◁ **Inca gold plate**
Inca metalworkers could make gold ornaments quite easily as the material is so soft. The feathers on this bird are suggested by the chevron and line patterns incised into the metal.

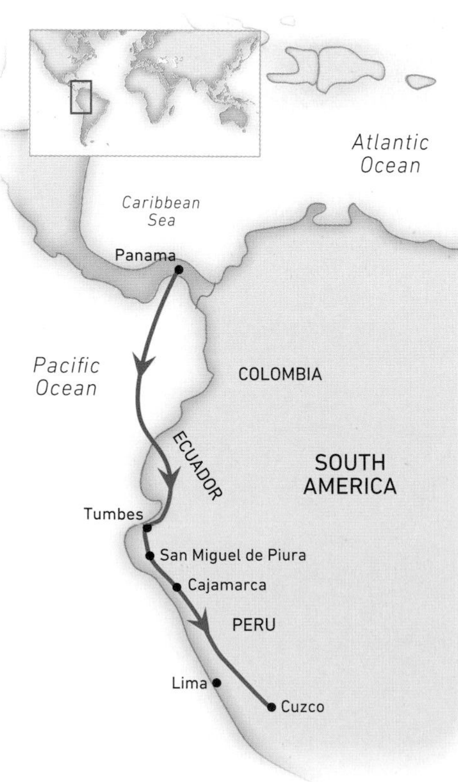

▷ **Journey of conquest**
In 1531–32, Pizarro sailed across the Pacific Ocean to the coast of Ecuador, then went south by land to Tumbes. Next he undertook a long overland journey through largely mountainous territory.

The conquest

Pizarro returned to Peru in 1531 with a new licence for conquest from the Spanish crown. Arriving in Tumbes, he found the settlements he had previously visited destroyed by rival Punian tribes, meaning the allies he had hoped for were gone. Pizarro therefore pushed on into the Peruvian interior, and founded a settlement which he named San Miguel de Piura. By November 1532, he had secured an audience with the Inca ruler, Atahualpa, at Cajamarca.

When they met, Atahualpa refused Pizarro's demands to pay tribute to Spain. He must have felt secure in his defiance, since he had 6,000 men with him (and tens of thousands more elsewhere in Peru), while Pizarro had a force of less than 200. However, the Spaniards attacked the Inca army and defeated them, thanks to superior weapons and a divided opposition. They then took Atahualpa hostage. The ruler produced the required tribute—a roomful of gold and silver—but he was executed anyway. Pizarro took his army to the principal Inca city of Cuzco, entering the town in November 1533. His conquest complete, he set up a provisional capital before founding Lima in 1535.

▷ **Saksaywaman citadel, Cuzco**
This stone structure, on the outskirts of Cuzco, shows the kind of architecture Pizarro found in Peru. The Incas built with huge stone blocks, cut so that they fitted together without mortar.

◁ **Pizarro meeting the Inca king** Felipe Guaman Poma de Ayala was a native of Peru who wrote a book about the conquest of his country. This illustration, from around 1600, shows Pizarro's first meeting with Atahualpa.

IN CONTEXT

Arms and armor

One reason that the Spanish were able to defeat the native peoples of South America with relatively small armies was their superior arms and armor. The conquistadors had metal plate armor and helmets, which protected them from arrow and spear points. They wielded heavy, iron-tipped lances that could fell a horseman, and their swords were strong and very sharp—blades made in Toledo were among the finest Europe produced in this period. They also had firearms. Although slow to load and not very accurate, they were effective in scaring the enemy and putting them off their guard.

FRANCISCO PIZARRO IN BATTLE GEAR

Spanish South America

Pizarro's success was remarkable. He sailed and marched long distances, coped with tough local conditions, and defeated a huge Inca army with a very small force. His conquest was no doubt aided by internal divisions among Peru's people, and the fact that they were succumbing to diseases introduced by the Europeans, to which they had no immunity. He laid the foundations for the Spanish domination of much of South America, influencing the history of the region to the present day.

" There lies **Peru with its riches**; here, **Panama and its poverty**. Choose, each man, what best becomes **a brave Castilian**. For my part, **I go to the south**. "

FRANCISCO PIZARRO, CONQUISTADOR, 1526

The discovery of the Amazon

Francisco de Orellana was a member of an expedition that was sent in search of spices in the area to the east of Quito, Ecuador. By chance, his journey was diverted, and he became the first European to travel along the Amazon.

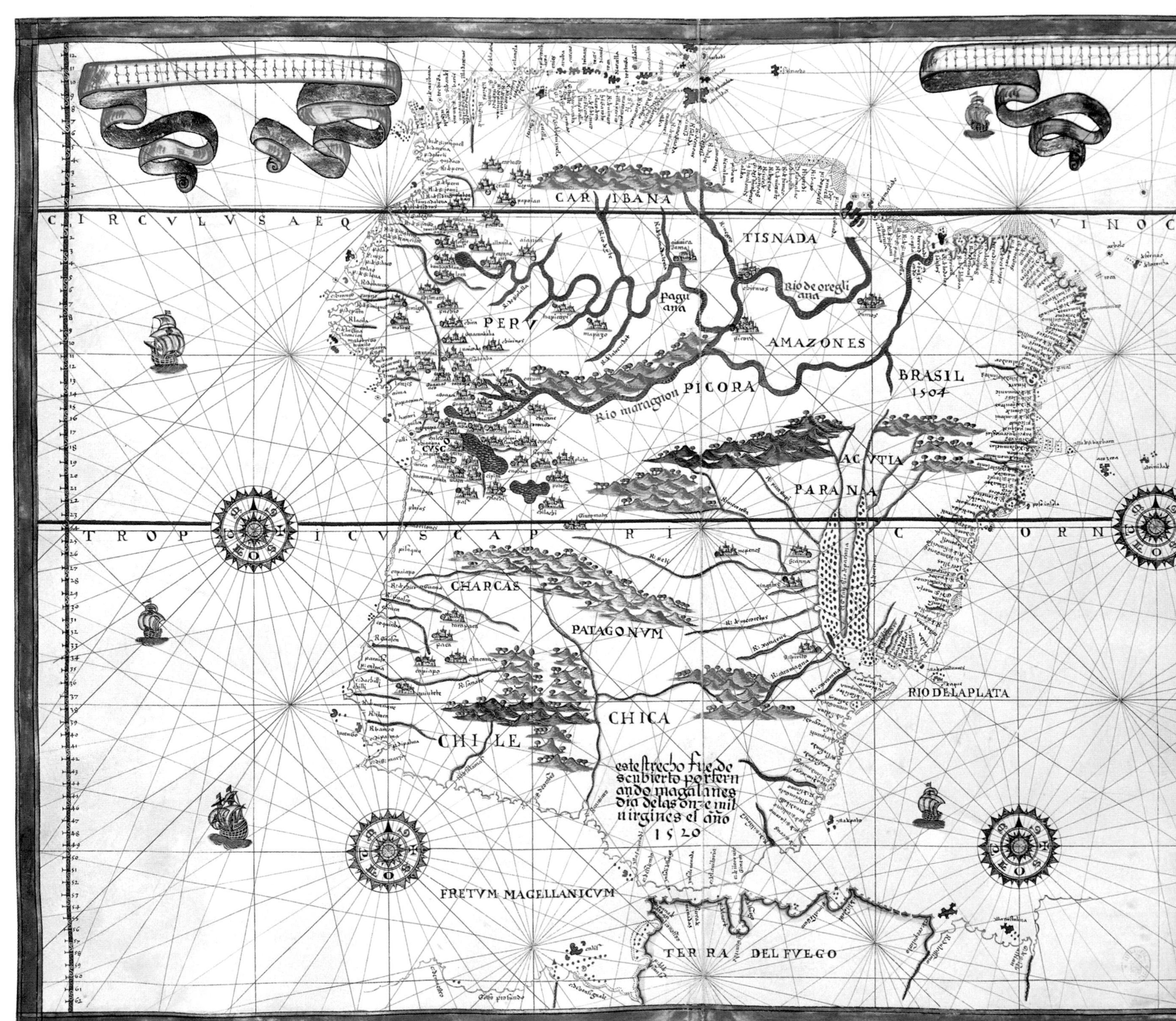

The leader of the 1541 Spanish expedition to Ecuador was Gonzala Pizarro, the younger brother of Francisco, the conqueror of Peru (see pp. 124–25). Francisco de Orellana joined him as a captain and they set out from Quito with a large party, including native people from South America. Although their main aim was to find spices such as cinnamon, some were motivated by the search for gold and the mythical land of El Dorado.

The expedition had a disastrous beginning. While working their way through unknown forests, they swiftly ran low on supplies, and by the time they had covered 250 miles (400 km), they had used up most of their food and lost thousands of their company to disease, starvation, and desertion. Having consumed all of the pigs they had taken with them, the survivors began to eat their dogs. Finding the Rio Coca, they built a boat, and Orellana and 60 men were sent downstream to find food.

The journey downriver

To begin with, they fared no better than before, and soon they were eating the soles of their shoes and the roots of forest plants, some of which were poisonous. Meanwhile, the current became so fast that they were unable to turn back, and were soon beyond hope of rejoining Pizarro and their comrades. Luckily, when they met a warlike band of locals, Orellana was able to speak to them (he was an accomplished linguist) and they managed to exchange European goods for food. Pressing on, they reached the Rio Negro, near modern-day Manaus, where they found human heads displayed on posts—a clear warning to keep away from the local people.

Eventually, the river on which they were traveling emptied into a much larger one, which they named the Orellana. They survived by raiding pens of turtles kept by local people, and clashed with a tribe that included fair-skinned warrior-women, who were apparently naked to the waist. They named these warriors "Amazons," after the female warriors of Greek myth (indeed, geographers later named the entire river after them), although the fighters may well have been men dressed in skirts. There were casualties, but most of the expedition survived the fight. The river proved to be vast, flowing past islands on which they stopped to make further repairs to their boats. Then the wind picked up, a hint that the ocean might be near. When they reached the Atlantic, Orellana and his companions sailed northward up the coast toward Guyana. Their boats were separated, but eventually they reunited on the island of Cubagua, off Venezuela. Orellana decided to return to Spain from here, hoping to lead a further expedition and eventually become governor of the Amazon region.

◁ **Orellana's boat on the Amazon**
This 19th-century American wood engraving shows Orellana's boat, under a combination of oars and sail, making its way down the Amazon. The rocky, tree-covered banks made landing difficult.

△ **Francisco de Orellana**
Based on a 16th century woodcut, this portrait shows Orellana after he had lost an eye in Peru with Pizarro.

The aftermath

Orellana did indeed lead an expedition, which embarked in May 1545. However, it ended in disaster, with the deaths of most of its participants, including Orellana himself. Orellana is nevertheless remembered for his Amazon voyage which brought the world's longest river to European notice for the first time. A Dominican friar called Gaspar de Carvajal had traveled with him, and his record of events includes descriptions of the native peoples they encountered, detailing their customs, rituals, and methods of warfare—a treasure-trove of information about the Amazon region at the time of the first European contact.

◁ **16th-century South America**
Joan Martines, cosmographer to Philip II of Spain, used information from Orellana's Amazonian expedition to produce this map of South America for his atlas of 1587.

IN PROFILE
El Dorado

The story of El Dorado (literally "the golden one") grew up among Europeans in the 16th century. It concerned a South American king who covered himself in gold dust as part of a ritual that was centered on a sacred lake. Eventually, the name El Dorado was applied not just to a person but also to the country in which he lived. Many travelers hoped to find El Dorado and come home rich with golden treasure, so the search for gold motivated both the conquistadors and many early explorers. A possible place of origin for the story is Guatavita in the Colombian Andes, where a number of gold artifacts have been found in a lake.

GOLD FUNERARY MASK FROM PERU, c.9TH–11TH CENTURIES

The Columbian Exchange

The arrival of Europeans in the Americas meant that animals, plants, goods, and diseases also traveled between the two worlds. This series of transfers is known as the Columbian Exchange.

The Columbian Exchange affected life on both sides of the Atlantic. The transfer of plants and animals brought new food crops to Europe and led to changes in agriculture in the New World. Among the tools that the Europeans brought with them was the plough, which enabled farmers to cultivate on a much wider scale than before. Firearms, unknown in the Americas before Christopher Columbus landed in 1492, transformed not only warfare, but also hunting, enabling Native Americans to kill larger animals easily.

Columbus himself brought horses, pigs, cattle, sheep, and goats across the Atlantic. These too transformed the lives of many—especially the horse, which gave Native North Americans a beast of burden for the first time. Writing was also introduced, the Europeans being keen to propagate Christianity, which relied on reading the Bible. This led to the spread of the English, Spanish, and Portuguese languages that are so widely used today. Unfortunately, slavery was also imported—on a huge scale—especially in the Caribbean and the southern parts of North America where sugar cane plantations were established.When they returned home, the Europeans brought a variety of new food plants back from America, including beans, tomatoes, avocados, pineapples, corn, and potatoes.

A number of infectious diseases also came to America with the settlers, including smallpox, chickenpox, measles, and influenza. Most of these were spread very easily, and local people had no defense against them. Huge numbers of Native Americans were killed as a result. There were also diseases that traveled the other way, including syphilis (especially prevalent at the time of the Columbian Exchange) and polio.

▷ **Roger Williams lands in the New World**
Based on a painting by Alonzo Chappel, this engraving shows a group of Native Americans offering the pipe of peace to British theologian and future founder of Rhode Island Roger Williams as his boat comes ashore.

“ For the **natives**, they are neere all **dead of Small poxe**, so as the **Lord** hathe **cleared our title** to what we **possess**. ”

JOHN WINTHROP, FIRST GOVERNOR OF MASSACHUSETTS

Cartier's North America
This map of North America's east coast was made in the early 1540s, using information provided by Jacques Cartier. Its coverage of the mouth of the St. Lawrence River is especially detailed. Technically, the map is upside-down, with north pointing toward the bottom of the map.

New France

The French involvement in North America began in the 1520s and 1530s with pioneering coastal and river expeditions backed by François I. These were led by explorers Giovanni da Verrazzano and Jacques Cartier.

After the Viking navigators of the 10th century, Giovanni da Verrazzano was the first European to explore the east coast of North America. Although born near Florence, Italy, Verrazzano settled in Dieppe, where he became a seafarer, making several voyages in the Atlantic and Mediterranean. In the 16th century, François I of France, aware of the Spanish and Portuguese interest in the lucrative Asian spice trade, and learning of Magellan's circumnavigation of the globe, did not want France to be left behind. He therefore commissioned Verrazzano to explore the North Atlantic in search of a route through to the Pacific Ocean.

The east coast

After landing at Cape Fear, North Carolina, in March 1524, Verrazzano sailed past various inlets, including Pamlico Sound, which he thought at first was an entrance to the Pacific. Continuing north, he seems to have missed Chesapeake Bay and the mouth of the Delaware, but sailed along Long Island and entered Narragansett Bay, where he stopped at the site of modern Newport, Rhode Island. Here, he met and traded with the Wampanoag, the same tribe, in fact, that would meet the Pilgrims about 100 years later.

After a stay in this area, Verrazzano sailed north again and reached Newfoundland, from where he returned to France in July 1524. He left a full record of his voyage and made two further expeditions—one landing in Brazil and another ending in the Caribbean, where he lost his life (eaten by cannibals on Guadeloupe, according to some accounts). The information he collected about North America encouraged later French explorers, such as Jacques Cartier.

△ **Giovanni da Verrazzano**
An experienced seaman, Verrazzano was also a geographer, astronomer, and mathematician. On his travels, he learned all he could about America and its people.

The Gulf of St. Lawrence

Jacques Cartier was born in St. Malo, France, into a family of experienced seamen, in 1491. He worked as a master pilot and joined several fishing voyages to Newfoundland. Then, in 1534, he received a royal commission to sail across the Atlantic to find a northern passage to Asia. Taking two ships, he explored the coast of Newfoundland and the Gulf of St. Lawrence, naming many of the islands there, and meeting and trading with the local people. On one island (one of the Îles aux Oiseaux), his men killed some 1,000 birds, including many great auks, for food. At Gaspé Bay, Cartier planted a cross to claim the area for France. In September 1534, he returned to France, accompanied by two Native Americans, whose chief only allowed them to go on condition that the French bring them back, along with European goods to trade.

The promise of Saguenay

François I sent Cartier back to the Gulf of St. Lawrence the following year. This time, Cartier was given the task of finding precious minerals as well as searching for the elusive

»

▽ **Jacques Cartier**
Cartier made three voyages of exploration to North America, opening up the St. Lawrence River as a route into the interior of the continent for European traders.

passage to Asia. He was joined by the Native Americans from the first voyage, who (perhaps to mislead him) told him stories of a fabled kingdom called Saguenay, which was reputed to be very rich. When he arrived at the St. Lawrence River, Cartier explored the Gulf, looking in vain for Saguenay, before traveling upriver and stopping at Stadacona, the Iroquois capital, near the site of modern-day Quebec City. From here, they went upriver, but progress was slow. Impeded by rocks, ice, and rapids, it took them two weeks to reach Hochelaga (present-day Montreal)—a distance of only 155 miles (250km). Defeated by the conditions, they retreated to Stadacona, where they built a fort and prepared to spend the winter. From November 1535 to April 1536, their ships were trapped in river ice 7 feet (2m) thick, and during that time, many of the men contracted scurvy. Some of them were cured, thanks to a local remedy, but 25 Frenchmen and many Native Americans died. When the time came to return to France in the spring, Cartier had only 85 men left. Without enough people to crew his three ships, he scuttled one before setting sail for France. Again, he took with him members of the local tribe, including their chief, Donnacona.

IN CONTEXT
The St. Lawrence Iroquois

Most of the native peoples that the early Canadian explorers encountered were from the Iroquoian group of tribes, who lived along the St. Lawrence River and on either side of Lake Ontario. These St. Lawrence Iroquois were distinct from the other Iroquois tribes of northeastern North America. Their homeland had rich soil and plentiful fish, and so, like their Iroquois neighbors, the St. Lawrence people had evolved a settled lifestyle. Cartier described their villages, which were surrounded by defensive wooden palisades, and the long houses in which the people of Hochelaga lived.

A TYPICAL BARK-COVERED IROQUOIS LONGHOUSE, AS DESCRIBED BY CARTIER

The first settlement

Rumors of Saguenay and the potential riches of Canada fired the imagination of François I, so a third expedition was soon planned, this time with a permanent settlement in mind. Although Cartier was to take part, a new commander was appointed, a courtier and friend of the king called Jean-François de La Rocque de Roberval. However, Roberval was unprepared on the departure date, so Cartier went ahead of him with five ships, leaving Roberval to catch up with three.

Cartier arrived on August 23, 1541 and immediately began building a settlement, called Charlesbourg (after the king's eldest son), a few miles upriver from Stadacona. He then left to travel upriver in search of Saguenay again. However, as on the first expedition, he was stymied by fierce rapids and forced to retreat.

When he returned to Charlesbourg, Cartier found that unrest had broken out between the settlers and the local Huron. It is not clear what started it, but a number of French settlers had been killed and Cartier decided that the settlement was no longer viable. And so, in the summer of 1542, he abandoned Charlesbourg and sailed for Newfoundland, where he found that Roberval and his three ships had finally arrived. Roberval told Cartier to return to Charlesbourg, but Cartier, aware that the situation there was hopeless, sailed instead for his native St. Malo, arriving in October 1542.

In the meantime, the remaining settlers at Charlesbourg held out for the winter, but many of them succumbed to the cold, disease, and attacks by local Iroquoians. In the spring of 1543, the survivors abandoned the colony.

Fool's gold

Cartier returned to France with a bountiful cargo of what he believed to be gold and diamonds that he had gathered in the St. Lawrence area. However, the gold turned out to be simple iron pyrites and the diamonds were, in fact, quartz crystals.

In terms of finding riches, Cartier's voyage had been somewhat of a disaster (the mythical land of Saguenay was never discovered), and the settlement that he founded had failed to prosper. Nevertheless, he is remembered as a pioneering explorer, who managed to establish France's presence in Canada, and inspired further exploration, trade, and settlement.

◁ **Cartier and Donnacona**
Cartier encountered Mi'kmaq, Beothuk, and Iroquois tribesmen at various stages on his North American journeys. This meeting was at Hochelaga, near the site of present-day Montreal.

▽ **Cartier on the St. Lawrence**
Cartier's discoveries paved the way for the French presence in Canada. Even 300 years after the event, French painters such as Jean Antoine Théodore de Gudin were celebrating Cartier's voyage up the St. Lawrence.

IN CONTEXT

Exploration and trade

The first French explorers survived by exchanging their own goods for food. By doing so, they laid the foundations for later French travelers (often people who had started out as Atlantic fishermen) who came to Canada to trade, bringing metal goods and textiles and returning to France with furs. Many forged lasting alliances with indigenous peoples, and such links helped later settlers establish themselves. Trade was encouraged by an increasingly popular fashion for beaver hats in late-16th century Europe, which created a strong demand for beaver pelts. By the early 17th century, traders were settling permanently in Canada.

NATIVE PEOPLE WITH BEAVER PELTS TO TRADE WITH WHITE TRADERS

NAVIGATOR, 1574–1635

Samuel de Champlain

French navigator Samuel de Champlain played a leading role in the exploration of Canada and in the setting up of French colonies there. He made important early maps of the region and wrote accounts of his findings, including his meetings with the native people.

Samuel de Champlain was born in France into a family of seafarers. As a young man, he served as a geographer at the court of the French king, Henry IV, visiting numerous French ports where he spoke to sailors about their travels across the Atlantic.

In his late twenties, he began to travel to North America himself, sailing with his uncle, François Gravé du Pont, a traveler and fur-trader. Inspired by Cartier's accounts of his voyages, Champlain was keen both to see what his predecessor had seen and to go further. He explored and mapped the St. Lawrence River, met Native Americans, and established friendly relations with them. On returning to France, he published an account of his journey, which included portraits of the Montagnais people of the St. Lawrence.

The following year, Champlain returned to Canada, joining an expedition led by Pierre Dugua de Mons, who planned to found a colony there. As cartographer, he was charged with investigating areas to find a potential site for a settlement. He explored the Bay of Fundy and the St. John River, and sailed down the Atlantic coast, traveling south as far as Cape Cod (he was the first person to describe this section of the coast in detail). In 1608, de Mons decided that the St. Lawrence would make a better site for a settlement, and sent Champlain upriver to build a fort at Quebec. This was the first permanent settlement on the site of Quebec City and it soon became an important trading center.

From his base in Quebec, Champlain developed a widespread trading network and formed alliances with several native peoples, particularly the tribes of the Ottawa River area, the Montagnais, and the Wendat (also known as the Huron) of the Great Lakes. Champlain was busy exploring new territory during this period of his life, especially the lakeside country of the Huron and the shores of Lake Champlain.

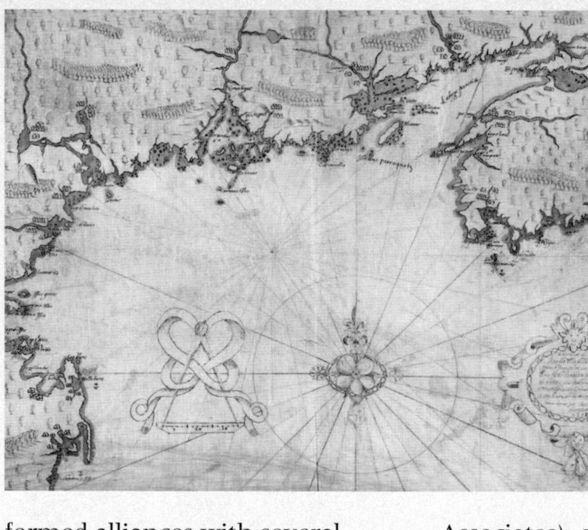

◁ **Champlain's map of New England**
This map shows the coast of New England from Cape Cod (bottom left) to Nova Scotia. Although not as accurate as modern maps, Champlain's work of 1607 is remarkably detailed for its time.

Father of New France

Champlain was ambitious for Quebec, and wanted not only to develop the settlement as a trading center but also to exploit the region's potential for farming and industry. He was one of the hundred investors in the Compagnie des Cent-Associés (the Company of One Hundred Associates), set up by the French minister Cardinal Richelieu to trade in the area, by then known as New France.

However, by the end of the 1620s, colonists from Britain had also set their eyes on Canada. In 1629, Quebec was attacked by a heavily armed force led by some Scottish merchants—the Kirke brothers—who forced Champlain to surrender the colony. Between 1629 and 1632, Quebec was occupied by British forces, but the French reclaimed control of Quebec and Champlain returned in 1633 with the backing of Cardinal Richelieu, who appointed him Lieutenant-General of New France.

He began his work of leading and promoting the colony, but fell ill with paralysis and died in 1635. He is remembered as the "Father of New France," a master navigator (in 25 round trips across the Atlantic he didn't lose a single ship), and a pioneering explorer of the North American coast and the Great Lakes.

◁ **Fighting the Iroquois**
Champlain's alliance with the Huron brought him into conflict with their enemies, the Iroquois. The explorer took part in several battles against them, including this one near the banks of Lake Champlain.

> " It is this **art** that **drew** me to **love the sea** at a **very young age** and that **compelled** me to **challenge** its **treacherous waters**... "

SAMUEL DE CHAMPLAIN, ON THE ART OF NAVIGATION

◁ **Ruler of New France**
This image of Champlain shows him toward the end of his life, when his exploring days were almost over and he was Lieutenant-General of New France.

KEY DATES

- **1574** Born into a seafaring family in the province of Aunis, southwestern France.
- **1603** Makes his first transatlantic voyage.
- **1604** Joins a voyage led by Pierre Dugua de Mons, on which he is able to record the coast of New England.
- **1608** Founds Quebec City on the site of a fort previously built by his predecessor, Jacques Cartier.

CHAMPLAIN'S *VOYAGES DE LA NOUVELLE FRANCE*, 1632

- **1609** Leads an expedition up the Richlieu River and discovers Lake Champlain.
- **1615–16** Spends a winter exploring the Lake Huron area, becoming the first European to gain firsthand knowledge of the Great Lakes.
- **1632** The treaty of St. Germain-en-Laye restores Quebec City to the French from the British. Champlain returns to the settlement as Lieutenant-General.

CHAMPLAIN JUDGING HIS LATITUDE WITH AN ASTROLABE

Early missionaries

When trade routes opened between the Americas and Europe, Christian missionaries, mostly Catholic clergy, accompanied the naval expeditions to spread the Gospel throughout the Americas, and later, parts of Asia.

△ **Jesuits in India**
This lithograph by Théophile Fragonard comes from the 19th-century book *The Dramatic History of the Jesuits*. It shows a Jesuit priest, in a distinctive black robe, preaching to Hindu Brahmins.

The first Catholic missionaries were mainly Dominican and Franciscan friars, who set up "missions," or communities, in the places where European traders had settled in the Caribbean and North America. In 1493, Spanish Pope Alexander VI instructed the friars to convert the native people in these areas, and the following year he divided the New World between Spain and Portugal. Under the Treaty of Tordesillas, signed on June 7, 1494, Spain received all the lands to the west of a meridian that cut vertically through South America, while Portugal received everything to the east. As a result, Brazilians speak Portuguese, while the rest of Latin America speaks Spanish.

◁ **Missionary church in Samoa**
The early missionaries built churches wherever they could. These were generally modeled on European buildings, but incorporated elements of local architecture.

Catholics and Protestants

The principal missions to the north were established along the coast of California—San Francisco, Los Angeles, and Santa Cruz were all missionary settlements. However, during the 16th century, other Catholic orders arrived to spread the faith throughout South America. Together, these missionaries taught Spanish, Portuguese, Bible stories, and prayers to the native people, and learned the local languages in return. By the mid-16th century, parts of the Bible had been translated into 28 South American languages. Protestant missionaries also started to arrive, most notably the French Huguenots, who had settled in Brazil by 1550.

Although the missionaries adapted to local customs, many retained their European bias. Few, for example, tried to put an end to slavery, although there were notable exceptions, such as the Dominican friar Bartolomeo de las Casas. The invasion of the conquistadores disrupted civilizations that had flourished undisturbed for centuries, sowing lasting resentment among native people (see pp. 122–25). In 1562, Diego de Landa, the Spanish-born Archbishop of Yucatán, destroyed the libraries of the Maya civilization, obliterating centuries of Mayan thought and tradition. For such reasons, missionaries were not always welcomed. In fact, in 1583, five Jesuit missionaries were executed in Goa, a Portuguese colony on the west coast of India, and several were killed by Mohawks in North America in 1649.

Lasting legacy

These early missionaries did more than spread the Gospel. They were among the first Europeans to cross-fertilize European, Native American, and Asian cultures. In around 1600, the first Portuguese-Chinese dictionary was created, and in 1603, the Jesuits published the first Japanese-Portuguese dictionary. However, in 1638, the Japanese Shogunate enforced a total ban on Christianity, imposing the death penalty on anyone who converted. All missions were then curtailed until the 19th century, when freeing slaves became a focus of missionary activity.

18TH-CENTURY PORTRAIT OF FRANCIS XAVIER

IN PROFILE
Francis Xavier

Spanish nobleman Francis Xavier was at Paris University when he met Ignatius of Loyola in 1529. Ten years later, with five other friends, they established the Jesuit Order, which was approved by Pope Paul III in 1540. In 1542, at the behest of John III of Portugal, Francis embarked on a missionary journey to India and spent three years preaching the Gospel in Tamil along the coast of Goa. Although he struggled with the language, he was convinced of the need to adapt to local customs. After traveling through Ceylon, the Moluccas, and the Malay Peninsula, he spent several years in Japan, but died at the age of 46, as he prepared to enter China.

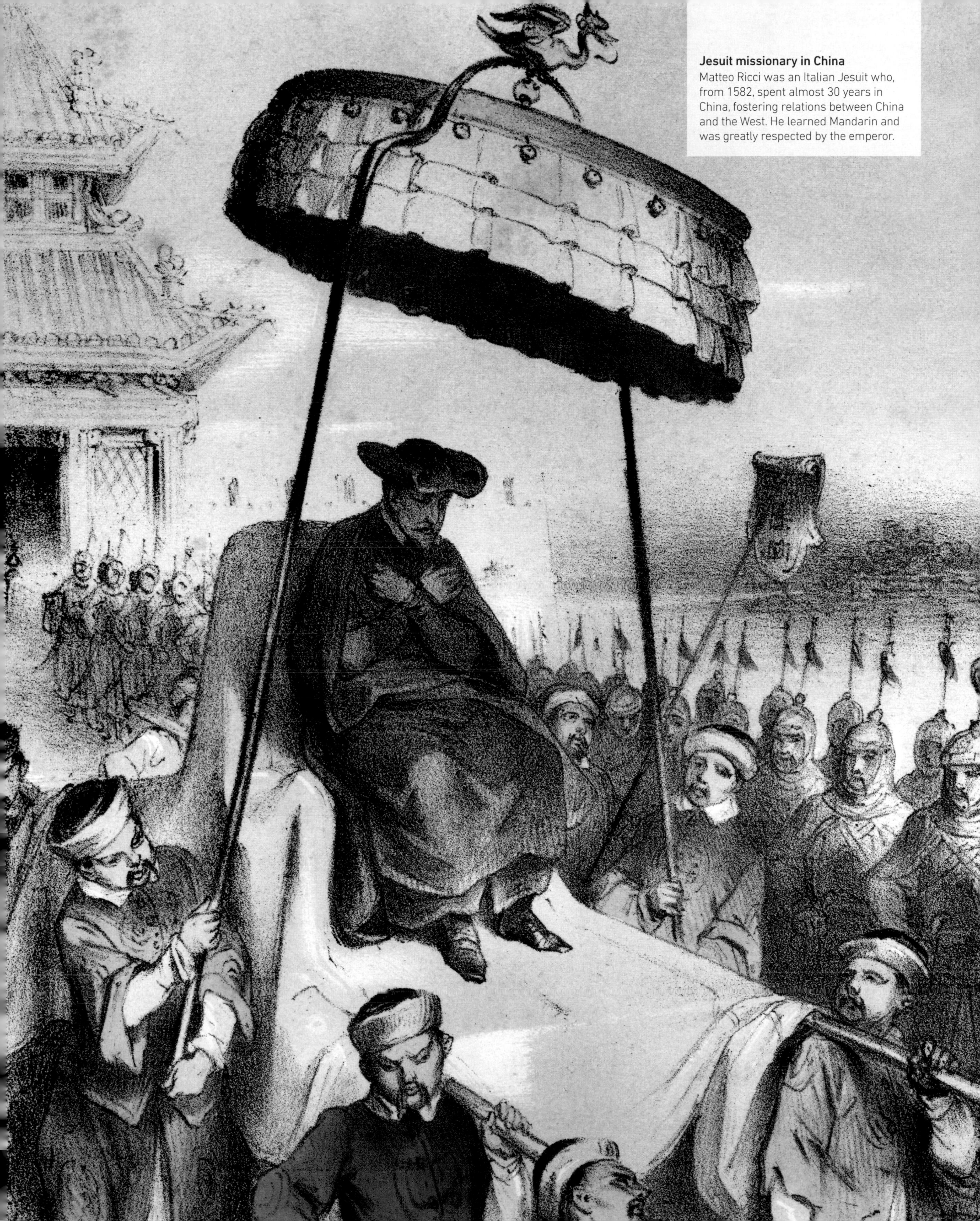

Jesuit missionary in China
Matteo Ricci was an Italian Jesuit who, from 1582, spent almost 30 years in China, fostering relations between China and the West. He learned Mandarin and was greatly respected by the emperor.

The Northwest Passage

In the 16th century, several explorers tried to find a northern passage from Europe to the spice markets of Asia. Although this route promised to be faster than the journey around Africa, it was fraught with danger.

Among the first Europeans to sail the Atlantic Ocean in search of the Northwest Passage was British navigator Martin Frobisher (c. 1535–94). Frobisher crossed the ocean in 1576, losing two of his three ships in a storm before reaching the coast of Labrador. He explored the waters around Baffin Island, becoming the first European to visit the large inlet now called Frobisher Bay. However, he clashed with the local Inuits, who took five of his men prisoner. Frobisher failed to get them released, and returned to England with just one Inuit prisoner. He also took back a sample of black rock that he thought was coal.

Frobisher led two further expeditions, in 1577 and 1578, both with several ships and a large number of men, including miners. They had been ordered to investigate the potentially valuable ores and minerals that Frobisher thought could be found on Baffin Island. As well as setting the miners to work, Frobisher continued his navigation of the waters around Greenland and Baffin Island, adding to European knowledge of the area that might lead to the discovery of the Northwest Passage. He took back to England a large amount of rock, including some that he thought was gold, but which turned out to be worthless iron pyrites. After this disappointment, Frobisher made no more attempts to find the Northwest Passage, but sailed as a privateer with English sea captain Sir Francis Drake.

▽ **Map of routes**
Martin Frobisher and Henry Hudson explored the eastern fringes of the Arctic archipelago. The map below shows the routes taken by the two explorers.

CANADA
Baffin Bay
GREENLAND
Greenland Sea
LABRADOR
Davis Strait
ICELAND
Baffin Island
Frobisher Bay
Hudson Bay
Hudson Strait
Labrador Sea
James Bay
NORTH AMERICA
London
Amsterdam
Atlantic Ocean
EUROPE
Albany
Nova Scotia
Hudson River

Key		
Martin Frobisher	First voyage	Second voyage
Henry Hudson	First voyage	Second voyage

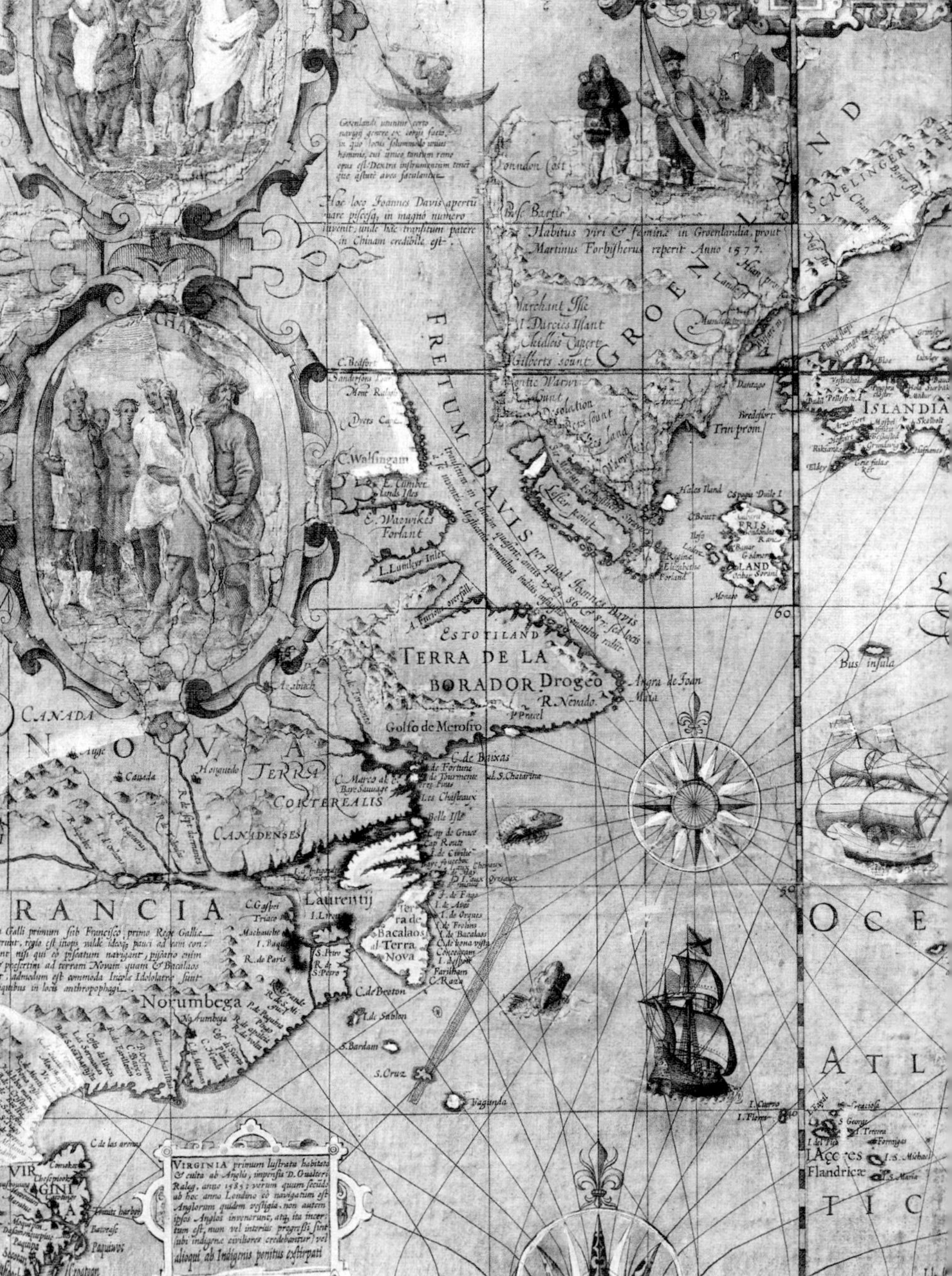

▷ **World map on Mercator's projection**
A detail from a map by Dutch cartographer Jodocus Hondius, made in 1608. Only the southeastern coast of Greenland is visible, but there is some detail around Nova Scotia and Baffin Bay.

Henry Hudson

Among the most intrepid of all northern navigators was British explorer Henry Hudson (c. 1565–1611). In 1609, he was hired by the Dutch East India Company to find a Northeastern Passage by sailing north of Russia. However, his route was blocked by thick ice and so he turned back. Instead of returning home, however, he crossed the Atlantic and looked for a Northwest Passage across North America to the Pacific. Arriving in Nova Scotia, Hudson sailed south, finding the river now named after him, and then traveled up it as far as the site of the modern city of Albany. He traded with local people, purchasing furs, and established the Dutch claim on this part of North America.

▷ **Skirmish with Inuits**
Relations between European explorers and the native people were sometimes difficult, as is shown in this watercolor by the artist John White, who accompanied Frobisher on his journeys. Some explorers, such as Hudson, however, managed to establish trading relations with them.

Hudson's last voyage

The following year, Hudson undertook a further transatlantic voyage, this time with funding from the British East India and Virginia companies. He crossed the North Atlantic and found the northern tip of Labrador. From there, he followed the strait to the northwest—now the Hudson Strait, the bay that today bears his name. It took Hudson some months to explore the waters and coasts of this vast bay, together with its southeastern extension, James Bay. By the time he had mapped the eastern coast of Hudson Bay, winter had arrived and his ship was trapped in the ice in James Bay. He stayed the winter there, but in the spring lost his life as the result of a mutiny.

Although they failed to find the Northwest Passage, Frobisher and Hudson greatly expanded European knowledge of the seas north of Canada. Hudson also opened up a valuable trade in furs with the native people of North America. The stories of these men live on in the names of various places, from Frobisher Bay to the Hudson River.

IN PROFILE
Henry Hudson

British explorer Henry Hudson made a series of voyages in search of northern passages to Asia, including two attempts to find a northeastern route north of Russia, and two northwestern voyages into the waters of Canada. Hudson's final voyage in search of the Northwest Passage, however, ended in tragedy. Trapped by thick ice, Hudson and his crew were forced to spend the winter of 1610–11 in Hudson Bay.

When the ice melted in the spring, Hudson planned to further explore Hudson Bay, hoping to find the Northwest Passage. However, many of his crew wanted to return home, and when Hudson refused, they mutinied and forced their leader off his ship. Hudson, his teenage son, John, and a few loyal crew members were left to perish in an open boat.

PAINTING SHOWING HUDSON AND HIS SON ABANDONED IN AN OPEN BOAT

حصارلر
ایاصوفیه
طوپقاپو

THE
AGE
OF
EMPIRES
1600—1800

THE AGE OF EMPIRES, 1600–1800

Introduction

As the world was explored, the challenge became how to profit from it. In the mid-17th century, the maritime dominance of Spain and Portugal was superseded by the skill and enterprise of Dutch and British seafarers. With the founding of the Dutch and British East India Companies—which became vast trading corporations—these two nations established outposts and colonies all over the world, from the East Indies and India to North America. They divided up the globe between them, little imagining the consequences. The Dutch secured parts of Southeast Asia, while handing over to Britain control of a fledgling outpost on an island called Manhattan. They initiated a global age of shipping trade, which introduced tea, coffee, tobacco, spices, and sugar to Europe, and approximately 12 million African slaves to the Americas.

Changing tastes and fashions

With the new goods came new places to meet, such as coffeehouses and intellectual salons. People wanted to know about the far-off lands from which these new goods originated, and it became fashionable among the wealthy to collect mementoes of distant lands. These small, private collections, known as *Wunderkammern* (cabinets of wonder), were symbols of status and identity, but also signs of a growing curiosity about the natural order of the world and man's place in it.

Science increasingly became a motive for exploration. Russian tsar Peter the Great sent sailor and cartographer Vitus Bering to the northern Pacific to chart the Siberian coastline and discover if there was a land bridge to Alaska. Catherine the Great sent him back to Siberia as part of the 3,000-strong Great Northern

BRITISH OFFICERS OF THE EAST INDIA COMPANY SECURED LUCRATIVE RESOURCES IN INDIA

COFFEEHOUSES BECAME PLACES WHERE CURRENT AFFAIRS WERE HEARD AND DISCUSSED

CAPTAIN COOK OPENED UP SEA ROUTES ACROSS THE WORLD, FROM ANTARCTICA TO POLYNESIA

> " Do just once **what others say you can't do**, and you will **never pay attention** to their limitations again. "
>
> CAPTAIN JAMES COOK

Expedition. At the time, this was the largest scientific venture ever undertaken, and it marked the beginning of Russian expansion into the east.

Voyages of learning

Smaller in size but even wider in scope were the expeditions headed by Captain James Cook on behalf of Britain's Royal Society. Over the course of three lengthy voyages, Cook crisscrossed the Pacific, circumnavigated Antarctica, and charted previously unknown parts of Australia and New Zealand. However, it was the onboard scientists, such as Joseph Banks, who really made the voyages so momentous. They discovered thousands of new species, all of which were carefully collected, cataloged, and taken back to Britain for examination. Cook's expeditions also produced a staggering collection of drawings and paintings of places, flora, and fauna, which together made a massive contribution to the study of the natural history of the world.

Generally speaking, however, it was not necessary to journey as far as Captain Cook to improve one's knowledge; a trip to Rome would do. The Italian capital was the ultimate goal for the multitudes who embarked upon what came to be known as the Grand Tour. In the 18th century, it was thought that there was no better finishing school for a young gentleman than to send him off with a chaperone to visit the major cultural capitals of Europe, in the hope that he would find enlightenment along the way. War in Europe brought the Grand Tour to a halt at the end of the 18th century. However, the notion of traveling for no other reason than self-fulfillment had taken root.

VITUS BERING TWICE EXPLORED THE NORTHERN PACIFIC FOR RUSSIA, AND MADE LANDFALL IN ALASKA

FOR MANY, THE GRAND TOUR ENDED IN NAPLES, WITH ITS VIEW OF MOUNT VESUVIUS

THE FIRST BALLOON FLIGHT WAS MADE IN PARIS IN 1783, PRESAGING A NEW MODE OF TRANSPORTATION

The spice trade

There have been many reasons for mankind's constant voyaging, but in the exploration of the Southeast Asian seas there was one goal above all, the quest to find the source of the treasure of the age—spice.

When the sole surviving ship of the Magellan expedition finally limped into port after completing the first circumnavigation of the world, among the meager treasures contained in its hold were 381 bags of cloves, acquired in the Far East. Taking into account the four ships that had been lost en route, the advances paid to the 237 sailors who had set out, the back pay for the 18 who survived, and all the other expenses, selling the bags of cloves enabled the three-year-long expedition to still turn a small profit.

Spices were immensely valuable commodities. It was not just the pep they brought to the table—cinnamon, cloves, ginger, mace, nutmeg, and pepper were also believed to help combat illness, guard against pestilence, dispel demons, and even to act as aphrodisiacs. Few knew exactly where the spices originated from, only that they came to Europe via a complicated route which involved passing through the hands of a succession of middlemen in Asia and the Middle East, who each ratcheted up the price.

▷ **Trading post in Hooghly, Bengal**
This painting, dating from 1665, depicts one of the numerous Dutch trading posts in Asia. Two ships can be seen on the Ganges, ready to carry goods back to the Netherlands.

Portuguese takeover

By the end of the 15th century, Portugal had established maritime dominance along the west coast of Africa—the next step was to voyage eastward in search of the source of the spices. Vasco da Gama successfully reached Calicut on the southeastern coast of India in 1498, and was delighted to find a thriving market where the Chinese delivered spices to Arab and Italian merchants for transportation overland to the Mediterranean. Within a year of his return to Lisbon, a fleet commanded by Pedro Álvares Cabral was dispatched with the express purpose of taking the spice trade out of their hands.

Cabral essentially turned the Indian Ocean into a "Portuguese lake." The pace of expansion accelerated, with successive expeditions pressing deeper into the heart of maritime Asia. In 1505, the Portuguese extracted tribute from Sri Lanka. Six years later, their galleons crossed the Bay of Bengal and seized control of Malacca, the richest port in the Far East at the time. Using this as a base, the Portuguese were eventually able to locate the heart of the fabled Spice Islands—a small archipelago called the Moluccas, which lies off the coast of modern Indonesia.

Although the Portuguese lost little time exploiting the wealth of the islands, their empire was already in decline. When English and Dutch ships began to appear in Asian waters at the close of the century, Portuguese domination was over. The first Dutch ships called at the Moluccas in 1599, and returned to Amsterdam laden with cloves. Two years later, in 1601, they were joined by ships sailing under the auspices of the newly formed British East India Company.

▷ **Company shields**
On the left, the Dutch East India Company's coat of arms, flanked by Neptune and a mermaid. The other shield shows that of Batavia, flanked by Dutch lions.

> " After the year **1500** there was no **pepper** to be had at **Calicut** that was not dyed **red with blood**. "
>
> VOLTAIRE, COMMENTING ON THE PORTUGUESE CONQUEST OF INDIA, 1756

◁ **Chinese porcelain**
In addition to spices, the Europeans traded in Asia for tea, textiles (especially silks), and porcelain.

East India rivalries

In 1602, the Dutch formed their own East India Company, known as the Vereenigde Oost-Indische Compagnie, usually abbreviated to VOC. In Asia, the company established a fortified base at Batavia (now Jakarta, the capital of Indonesia), with hundreds of subsidiary posts around the region. The Dutch had a far larger merchant fleet and navy than the British, and the VOC managed to edge the English East India Company out of the spice trade, thereafter enjoying huge profits from its monopoly.

Around the middle of the 17th century, the balance of power began to shift as England invested heavily in its navy to support its growing imperial ambitions. The result was a series of Anglo-Dutch wars. The second of these was brought to an end by the Treaty of Breda (1667), in which the English agreed to renounce claims to any of the Spice Islands. In return, the Dutch acknowledged English sovereignty of a territory called New Netherland that England had seized from them. The English subsequently renamed it New York.

The VOC went on to become the world's largest trading company. At the height of its wealth and power, it owned more than half the world's sea-going shipping, but was finally declared bankrupt in 1799.

◁ **British officials in India**
Outmaneuvered by the Dutch in Southeast Asia, the British contented themselves with a commercial monopoly in India and the new territories of America.

Wonder cabinets

Stocked with exotic artifacts collected from distant lands, cabinets of curiosities were the predecessors of the modern museum.

Before there were museums, there were *Wunderkammern*, or cabinets of wonder. First created in the 16th century, these were private collections containing all manner of marvelous and exotic objects brought back from places unknown, and often associated with the discovery of "new worlds." Ideally, the collections displayed three main themes: *naturalia* (products of nature, such as fossils, shells, and preserved exotic animals and marine life), *arteficialia* (the products of man, including native arts and crafts), and *scientifica* (scientific or mechanical objects, such as astrolabes, clocks, and other instruments). Some *Wunderkammern* had specific themes, such as the one created by Dutch anatomist Frederik Ruysch (1638–1731), which displayed body parts and preserved organs alongside exotic birds, butterflies, and plants.

These collections were displayed in multi-compartmented cabinets and vitrines. By displaying such items together, people believed that viewers could make connections between objects, leading to an understanding of how the world functioned and what humanity's place in it was. As time passed, the small private cabinets were absorbed into larger ones. In turn, these were bought by aristocrats and even royalty, and merged into cabinets so large that they took over entire rooms. Frederik Ruysch's *Wunderkammer*, for example, was bought by Tsar Peter the Great and now forms part of the Kunstkammer Museum in St. Petersburg; the cabinet of the London apothecary James Petiver (c. 1665–1718) became the basis of the British Museum. A *Wunderkammer* known as The Ark, assembled by naturalist John Tradescant Senior (c. 1570–1638) and regarded as one of the wonders of 17th-century London, ended up as part of the Ashmolean Museum in Oxford.

" **Such a collection** of … many **outlandish and Indian curiosities**, and things of nature. "

ENGLISH DIARIST JOHN EVELYN IN MILAN, 1646

▷ ***Cabinet of Curiosities*** **by Andrea Domenico Remps**
Remps's painting shows the types of object typically found in a cabinet of curiosity, such as archaeological items, scientific objects, animal specimens, and religious artifacts.

New Holland

As the great European commercial companies established themselves in the East, investigations were made into Terra Australis Incognita—the Unknown Southern Land.

△ **Abel Tasman**
An experienced merchant skipper employed by the Dutch East India Company, Tasman was charged with exploring the uncharted tracts of the southern hemisphere.

In 1606, Captain Willem Janszoon of the Dutch East India Company was dispatched from Bantam in Java to explore the coast of New Guinea in search of economic opportunities. Bearing south, he missed the Torres Strait and continued down along what he thought was an extension of New Guinea's southern coast. It was, in fact, the western coast of the Cape York Peninsula in modern Queensland. He put ashore, but after a hostile reception from the native people that resulted in the deaths of several of his men, he turned around and headed back to Java. Without knowing it, he and his crew had been the first Europeans to step foot on the land that would later be called Australia.

Over the next 160 years, many more crews from a range of European nations sighted, and sometimes set foot on, this uncharted and unexplored landmass. Most of these were merchant ships from the Dutch East India Company, and the new territory first appeared on one of the company's maps in 1622, erroneously labeled "Nueva Guinea." One notable visitor was Jan Carstensz, commissioned by the Dutch East India Company to follow up on the reports made by Janszoon in his 1606 voyages to the south. Carstensz named the large shallow sea he sailed in 1623 the Gulf of Carpentaria in honor of Pieter de Carpentier, governor-general of the Dutch East Indies. Four years later, another Dutchman sailed south and mapped the lower reaches of Australia from what is now Albany on the very southwest tip, halfway along to what is now Cebuna.

◁ **Maori club**
The Maori that Tasman encountered were armed with stone and hardwood weapons, such as this elaborately carved club, shaped to look like a bird's head.

Abel Tasman

Nearly 20 years passed before, in August 1642, the Dutch East India Company dispatched sea captain Abel Tasman on a voyage to explore the region that it now called the Great South Land. Sailing west with the prevailing winds from Batavia (present-day Jakarta), and then southeast, he actually missed Australia altogether, and alighted instead on a landmass he named Van Diemen's Land after another governor-general of the Dutch East Indies. It was not until well over a century later that explorers established that it was in fact an island, and it was renamed Tasmania in honor of the Dutchman.

Tasman sailed on eastward, becoming the first European to reach New Zealand. He anchored his ships off the northern end of South Island, but quickly departed again after they were attacked by the Maori tribesmen. He returned to Batavia via several Pacific Island groups (now known as Fiji, Tonga, and the Solomon Islands) and New Guinea.

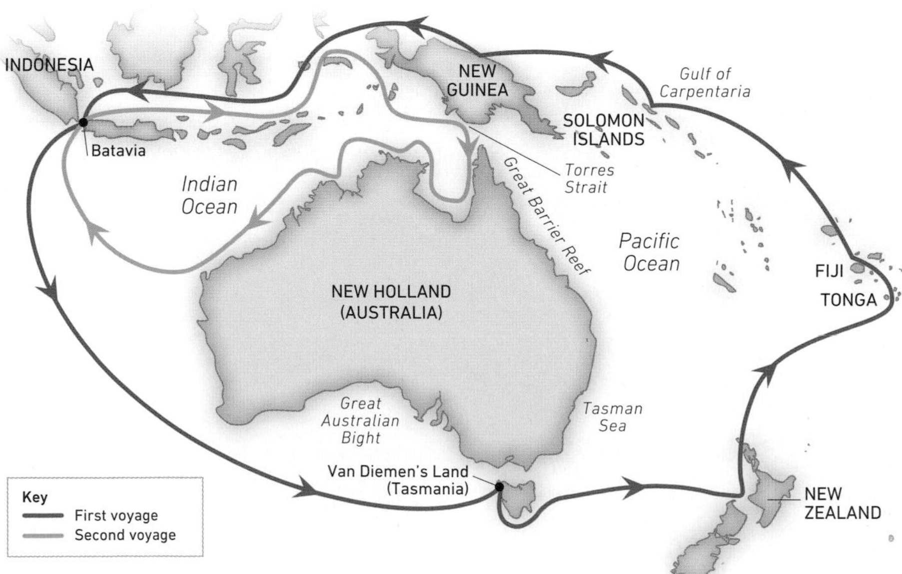

▷ **The voyages of Abel Tasman**
Tasman made two exploratory voyages. On the first, he discovered Van Diemen's Land and New Zealand; on the second, he mapped the northwest coast of Australia.

◁ **Murderers' Bay**
This drawing, made by Abel Tasman's artist, shows the Dutch skirmishing with Maori warriors at what became known as Murderers' Bay (present-day Golden Bay).

New Holland

In 1644, Tasman made a second voyage, this time following the south coast of New Guinea eastward and then south. Again, he failed to find the Torres Strait, which would have provided the direct access east to South America the Dutch were hoping for. Instead, he sailed back west along the north coast of the Great South Land. He mapped the continent's coastline and made observations on its geography and inhabitants. He also named it New Holland.

From the point of view of the Dutch East India Company, however, Tasman's explorations had proved to be a disappointment. He had not found a new shipping route, and New Holland offered nothing in the way of trading opportunities. The Dutch interest in the continent had dissipated, and Tasman's would be the last voyage to Australia until those of William Dampier and James Cook, 55 and 126 years later respectively (see pp. 172–75).

▷ **Coronelli globe**
The globes made by Venetian Vincenzo Coronelli depicted the world of the late 17th century. New Holland already appears on it, but there is no detail on its eastern coast, which was not explored until the arrival of James Cook in 1770.

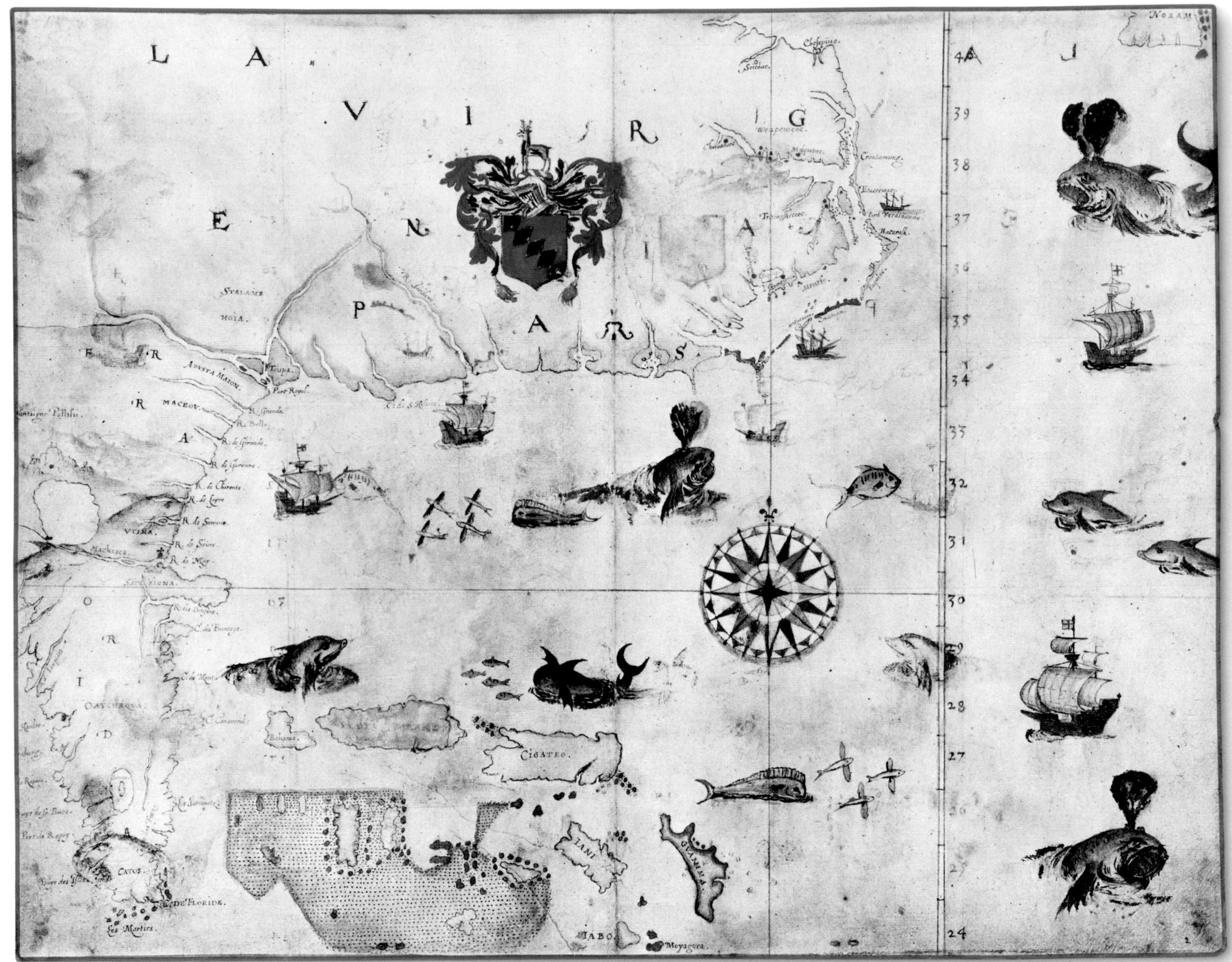

△ **Here be monsters**
John White produced this map (complete with ships and sea-monsters) showing the American coast from Chesapeake Bay down to the Florida Keys during an expedition to Virginia with Sir Walter Raleigh in 1585.

Settling America

Once Portugal and Spain had laid claim to most of Central and South America, the powers of northern Europe were left to contest the colder and seemingly less promising coastline of North America.

By the end of the 16th century, North America had been well and truly "discovered." After Christopher Columbus (see pp. 110–13), the Spaniard Ponce de Leon had landed in what is now Florida, in 1513, and the Portuguese Estêvão Gómez had sailed along the Maine coast and may have entered New York Harbor in 1525. The conquistador Hernando de Soto had also explored deep inland, becoming the first European to ever cross the Mississippi River, which is where he died in 1542.

So far, however, the hardships involved in settling this New World had largely proved too daunting, and the rewards meager. By 1600, the only permanent colony in America was the one established by the Spanish at Saint Augustine in Florida in 1565.

Colonizing North America

The English had attempted to establish a colony on Roanoke Island off North Carolina in 1585, but it vanished without trace, a mystery that has never been solved. Undaunted, in 1606 a group of merchants founded the Virginia Company of London and raised money for a new expedition in the hope that the new colony would provide profits in the form of gold, silver, and gems. The company duly dispatched three ships carrying 104 settlers which reached the east coast of America in May 1607; they founded a settlement named Jamestown after the English king.

The colony struggled. There was no gold, and all attempts to farm potentially lucrative cash crops failed. Of the 500 men in the colony in October 1609, only 60 were left when spring arrived. For the next few years, the settlement was only able to survive thanks to fresh supplies sent from England. Its fortunes changed in 1612, however, when the colony managed to cultivate and export tobacco. By 1619, the settlement was considered permanent and sufficiently family-friendly for a ship to be sent over carrying "respectable maidens."

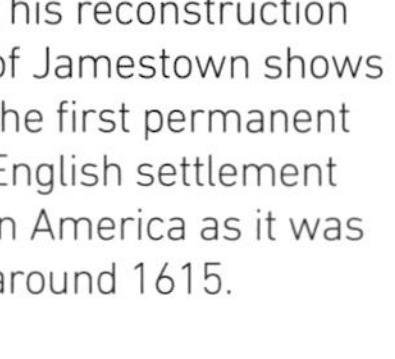

◁ **Jamestown**
This reconstruction of Jamestown shows the first permanent English settlement in America as it was around 1615.

▽ **Secotan Indians**
When the first English settlers built a fort at Roanoke, John White painted the local Secotan warriors. No Englishman had ever painted anything in North America before.

The Pilgrims

Commercial gain was not the only motivation for people to settle. Modern America's boast of being the land of freedom is rooted in its foundation. From the very beginning, it was a place of refuge for those who were fleeing religious persecution in Europe. As early as 1564, an expedition of around 300 French Huguenots fled certain death at home to form a short-lived settlement called Fort Caroline, near what is now Jacksonville in Florida. The following year, they were brutally massacred by a Spanish force from Saint Augustine that was keen to nip any French territorial ambitions in the bud.

The English Puritan evangelists met with more success. They viewed their nation's church as beyond redemption because of its Catholic past, and set out for a new and untainted country in which they could practice a "purer" form of worship. In November 1620, their ship, the *Mayflower*, landed on the shores of Cape Cod, in present-day Massachusetts. After scouting locations, the group, who came to be known as the Pilgrims, eventually landed at Plymouth Harbor in December. Despite suffering similar hardships to those experienced by the Jamestown settlers (by February 1621, half of the group were dead), the Pilgrims were able to raise a harvest in their first summer, which they supplemented with abundant fish.

In the next few years, as life for Puritans became increasingly difficult in England, more of them made the journey across the Atlantic. »

▷ **Jamestown Church**
A ruined brick tower is all that survives of Jamestown Church, built by the settlers in 1639. It replaced several earlier structures, but remains one of the oldest buildings in the US.

▷ ***Gezicht op Nieuw Amsterdam*, 1664**
This painting, by Johannes Vingboons, shows New Amsterdam in the same year that the English would seize it from the Dutch and rename it New York.

» By 1630, some 10,000 Puritans had arrived to form new colonies in Massachusetts, a number swollen that year by the arrival of a fleet of 11 ships that carried around another 1,000 people and their livestock. This group formed a settlement that would soon become the thriving port of Boston.

New Netherland

In the meantime, other European groups were arriving to settle America: the French, in what is now Canada; scattered bands of Finns and Swedes along the mid-Atlantic coast; the Spanish in Florida and the far southwest (today's New Mexico); and the Dutch on the east coast in what they were calling New Netherland. In 1609, Henry Hudson, an English explorer employed by the Dutch East India Company, sailed along the coast of North America exploring inlets on a mission to find a northwest passage through to the Indies. He traveled up the river that nowadays bears his name, as far as modern-day Albany, and claimed the territory for his employers. He did not find a Northwest Passage, but the territory proved to be an excellent source of fur—a valuable trading commodity.

The Dutch began arriving in North America soon after Hudson's voyage. In 1614, Dutch merchants formed the New Netherland Company, and the following year they established a post called Fort Orange, near Albany, to trade with Native Americans, exchanging cloth, alcohol, firearms, and trinkets for beaver and otter pelts. Six years later, the newly incorporated Dutch West India Company began organizing a more permanent Dutch settlement, and in 1624, the ship *Nieu Nederlandt* (New Netherland) departed with the first wave of settlers.

New York

Once in America, these new Dutch immigrants spread out over several settlements in the territory claimed by the company. Some of these outposts proved impossible to sustain, and others were too dangerous because of the local Native Americans. So, in the early summer of 1626, the Dutch purchased the island of Manhattan from the Native Americans for around 60 guilders' worth of trinkets. There, they started building Fort New Amsterdam, which became the hub of a province that by 1655 numbered 2,000 to 3,500 inhabitants. One significant way in which the

▽ ***The Landing of the Pilgrim Fathers***
This 19th-century engraving by John C. McRae depicts the Pilgrim Fathers arriving on the shores of North America on November 21, 1620. Their ship, the *Mayflower*, is seen in the background.

◁ **Pilgrim hat**
Beaver fur was a source of income for the settlers. It was processed into felt to make hats like this one, said to have belonged to Pilgrim Constance Hopkins.

◁ **New Amsterdam**
This 1916 redrawing of a map of 1660 called the *Castello Plan* shows the Dutch settlement of New Amsterdam at the southern tip of Manhattan. The town was renamed New York in 1664.

New Netherland province differed from the British colonies to the north was demographics. Up to one half of the New Netherland population was not Dutch, and included Germans, Swedes, and Finns, as well as French, Scots, English, Irish, and Italians. All of these nationalities lived under Dutch rule.

As New Netherland prospered, the British set their sights on it. Back in 1498, the Genoese-born John Cabot, who was in the employ of Britain, had explored the coast of America from Newfoundland down to Delaware, and as this trip predated Hudson's by more than a century, the British felt they had prior claim to the land. In 1664, a fleet under the command of the King of England's brother, the Duke of York, was sent to seize the colony, and the settlement of New Amsterdam and the entire colony of New Netherland were both renamed New York.

Spain and France held far larger parts of North America, and the English settlements were confined to a narrow strip along the Atlantic coast, but as most immigrants arrived along the eastern seaboard, English speech and common law became dominant in American life.

> “On the **island** of **Manhate** there may well be **four** or **five hundred** men of **different sects** and **nations**.”
>
> FATHER ISAAC JOGUES, A VISITOR TO NEW AMSTERDAM IN 1643–44

سلیمانیه جامعی
حصارلر
بسم الله الرحمن الرحیم
اولیا چلبی
آیا صوفیه
اسکدار
مهرماه سلطان

Evliya Çelebi spent most of his life journeying and left behind one of the greatest works of travel literature ever written.

Evliya Çelebi (*çelebi* means "gentleman" in Turkish) was a courtier to the sultans when the Ottoman Empire (or Sublime Porte) was at the height of its power. He was born in Istanbul in 1611, and from his first expedition in 1640 to his death around 1682, he spent most of his life traveling. By the time he died, he had visited the lands of 18 monarchies from Russia to Sudan, witnessed 22 battles, and heard 147 different languages. All of this was meticulously described in his *Seyahatname* (*Travelogue*), a sprawl of a biography and journal that runs to 10 volumes.

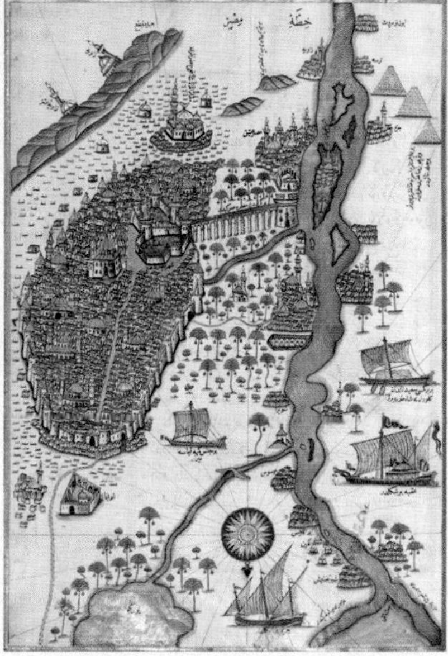

◁ **Piri Reis map of Cairo**
Maps by Ottoman admiral Piri Reis, including this early 16th-century map of Cairo, were commonly used by 17th-century travelers, including Evliya.

Childhood dream

By his own account, it all started at the age of 20 with a dream in which the Prophet Muhammad blessed his intention to travel the world. However, the first volume of Evilya's account begins at home, with a depiction of Istanbul and the area around it. In the second volume, he travels to Anatolia, the Caucasus, Azerbaijan, and Crete.

With his inherited wealth and powerful family connections (his father had been an imperial goldsmith), Evliya could well afford to travel, but he worked his passage, often accompanying diplomatic delegations as a minor functionary. In 1665, for example, he went to Vienna as part of the delegation sent to sign a peace treaty with the Habsburgs. Although a devout Muslim—he was able to recite the Qur'an from memory and did so every Friday—Evliya expressed great admiration for St. Stephen's Cathedral in Vienna, where, he reports, the choir fills "one's eyes with tears." However, he also made scurrilous claims about other cultures, such as: "Hungarians are more honorable and cleaner infidels. They do not wash their faces every morning with their urine as the Austrians do."

Evliya's path crossed Buddhists, sorcerers, snake charmers, and tightrope walkers, but he was not above embellishing his work—he included, for example, a story about a Bulgarian witch who transformed herself into a hen and her children into chickens. Despite these flourishes, his book remains an important guide to life in the Ottoman Empire of the 17th century.

◁ **Writer at work**
This modern-day miniature shows Evliya at his desk writing an account of his travels.

▷ **Travel by sea**
This three-masted, Ottoman passenger ship is typical of the kind of vessel Evliya would have used on his voyages.

KEY DATES

- **1611** Born in Istanbul to a wealthy family from Kütahya.
- **1631** Dreams of a visit from the Prophet Muhammad in which he is told to travel.
- **1640** Makes his first journeys to Anatolia, the Caucasus, Azerbaijan, and Crete.
- **1648** Visits Syria, Palestine, Armenia, and the Balkans.
- **1655** Visits Iraq and Iran.
- **1663** While a guest in Rotterdam, he claims to have met Native Americans.
- **1671** Undertakes the hajj to Mecca.
- **1672** Visits Egypt and the Sudan, and settles in Cairo.
- **1682** Dies in either Cairo or Istanbul.
- **1742** Manuscript of *Seyahatname* discovered in a Cairo library and taken to Istanbul, where it achieves renown.

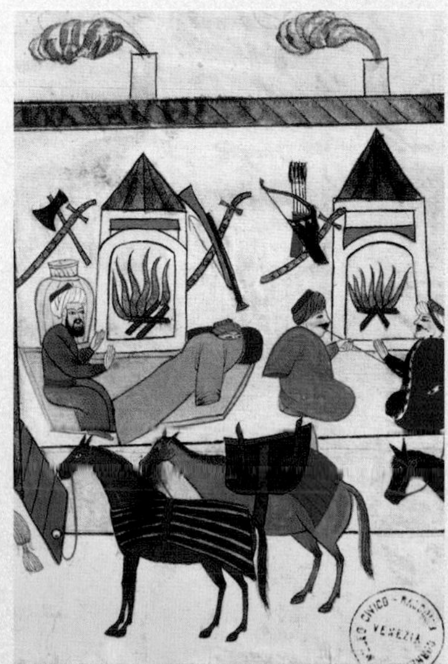

TRAVELERS SPEND THE NIGHT AT A TYPICAL 17TH-CENTURY CARAVANSARY

Coffee

Few commodities illustrate the growing global interconnections of the 17th century better than the coffee bean.

Many legends surround the discovery of coffee, but all agree that it took place in Ethiopia, or possibly Yemen. All also extol the invigorating effects of this bitter, brown brew, created by boiling up roasted berries. From its origin in the ports of the Horn of Africa, the drink is recorded as being enjoyed in Mecca as early as 1511, and it was the beverage of choice across much of the Middle East and Turkey by the end of the century—spread, no doubt, by the thousands of pilgrims visiting the holy city each year from all over the Muslim world.

Coffee was drunk in the home, and more significantly, in the new public coffeehouses. Here, coffee-drinking and conversation were complemented by itinerant musicians, professional storytellers, and games such as chess. The coffeehouses were sources of gossip and news, places people went to if they wanted to know what was going on. Not surprisingly, the authorities saw them as places of potential sedition, and coffee-drinking was frequently banned. In fact, when the absolutist Murad IV claimed the Ottoman throne in 1623, he forbade coffee. Anyone found brewing or drinking it received a beating—and anyone caught a second time was sewn into a bag and thrown into the Bosphorus.

It did not take long for coffee to travel to Europe. Initially it was viewed with suspicion because of its whiff of Islam, but this was quickly overcome, particularly when no less a personage than Pope Clement VIII gave the drink his blessing. From around 1650, coffeehouses sprang up all over Europe. Just as in the Arab and Turkish worlds, they became forums for lively discussion and outlets for streams of newsletters and pamphlets. So influential was their role in fostering intellectual debate that coffeehouses were nicknamed "Penny Universities," a penny being the cost of a coffee. By 1675, there were thought to be more than 3,000 coffeehouses in England, many of which, in a nod to coffee's origins, bore names such as the Turk's Head, The Saracen's Head, or The Sultan.

▷ **A coffeehouse in Constantinople**
This watercolor painting of 1854 by Amadeo Preziosi shows all kinds of characters including two Greeks in red caps, a whirling dervish in his conical hat, a Persian in purple robes, and an African boy attending to the pipes. In the corner, two large coffee pots stand on a stove.

Slave ships in the Atlantic

One of the greatest mass movements of people in history was brought about by enforced slavery, when up to 12 million Africans were forcibly taken from their homelands and shipped across the Atlantic in chains.

"The first object which saluted my eyes when I arrived on the coast was the sea, and a slave ship, which was then riding at anchor and waiting for its cargo. These filled me with astonishment which was soon converted to terror when I was carried on board." These words were written by Olaudah Equiano, who was captured in Nigeria and transported to Barbados aboard a slave ship at the age of 11. Published in 1789, his account was one of the most influential books written by a former African slave, and it helped garner support for the campaign to abolish slavery.

A colonial workforce

By the time of Equiano's book, Europe's trade in African slaves was over 250 years old, stretching back to 1526, when the Portuguese completed the first transatlantic slave voyage from Africa to the Americas. Several other European nations were quick to get into the business, notably the British, the French, the Spanish, and the Dutch. These nations did not invent slavery, which had been practiced within Africa itself for centuries, but they took to it with an efficiency that had not been seen before. A slave kept in Africa might hope to return home some day—those shipped overseas had no such consolation.

The Europeans acquired most of their slaves from local dealers who traveled the interior gathering captives, whom they force-marched to the coast. Ships from Europe arrived off Africa loaded with goods that were traded for the slaves. Then, fully laden, they set sail across the Atlantic with their human cargo crammed below decks, the men secured in leg irons. In the early days, up to one in five slaves died during the two-month voyage—later, doctors were employed to help reduce this loss of life and profit.

The trade was driven by European colonists who were exploiting territories in the New World, and who were desperately short of labor. The first enslaved Africans were delivered to Portuguese and Spanish colonies in South America—later, they were sent to the Caribbean and North America. The first African slaves arrived in the English colony of Jamestown in 1619.

Triangular trade

The 17th century saw a massive increase in Atlantic slaving activity, with more than five times as many slaves

△ **Slave auction**
This is a colorized version of an image that originally appeared in the *Illustrated London News* in 1861. It shows an auction of slaves in the town of Richmond, Virginia.

▽ **Shackles**
Nothing is more emblematic of the slave trade than the shackles and handcuffs that were used to restrain the slaves. They remained in use on plantations in America until the early 1860s.

▷ **The *Brookes* slave ship**
This model shows the interior of the British slave ship, the *Brookes*. It illustrates the appalling conditions suffered by the 609 men, women, and children on board. It was widely reproduced to raise awareness about the evils of the trade.

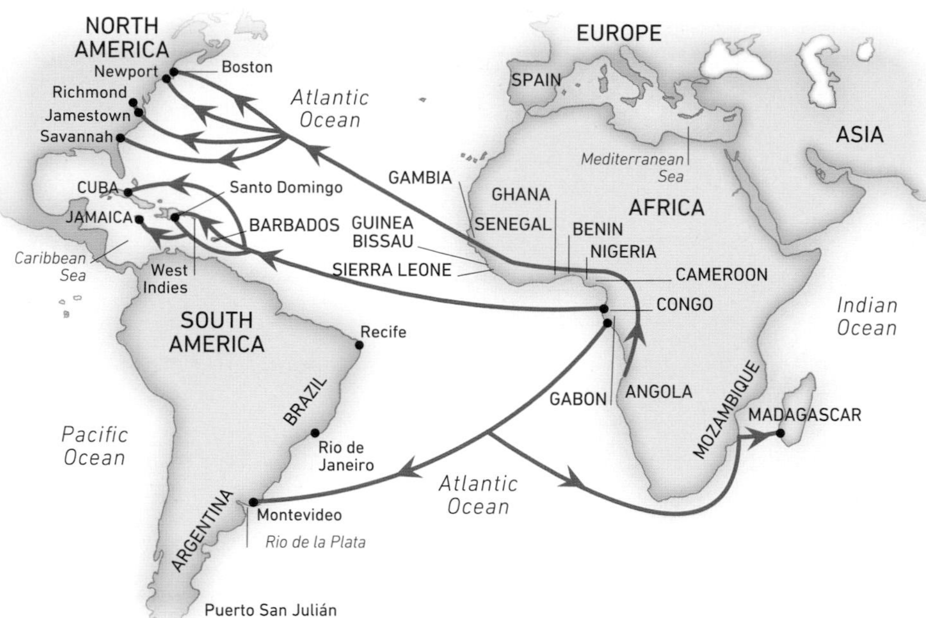

◁ **Deadly crossings**
The transatlantic slave trade was the biggest deportation in history, and possibly the most costly in terms of human life. Some 12 million slaves were shipped from Africa, but only around 11 million arrived in the Americas.

▽ **Plantation life**
Slave labor drove the sugar plantations in the Caribbean and the cultivation of tobacco and cotton in North America. By 1860, the US had four million slaves, 60 percent of whom worked in the cotton industry.

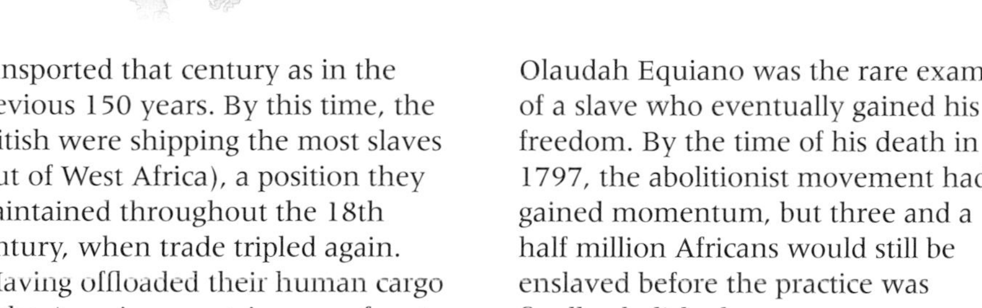

transported that century as in the previous 150 years. By this time, the British were shipping the most slaves (out of West Africa), a position they maintained throughout the 18th century, when trade tripled again.

Having offloaded their human cargo in the Americas, captains were free to restock their ships with fresh loads of goods from the New World, which were then imported to Europe. In this manner, the slavers typically made three journeys, making a profit on each one: goods from Europe to Africa; slaves from Africa to the Americas; goods from the Americas to Europe—operations that became known as "triangular trade."

Olaudah Equiano was the rare example of a slave who eventually gained his freedom. By the time of his death in 1797, the abolitionist movement had gained momentum, but three and a half million Africans would still be enslaved before the practice was finally abolished.

> " I expected every **hour** to **share the fate** of my **companions**, some of whom were almost **daily** brought upon deck at the **point of death**. "
>
> OLAUDAH EQUIANO, FORMER SLAVE

Close quarters
This painting by Flemish artist Lorenzo Castro shows a naval engagement between Dutch ships and Barbary corsairs. It was painted in the late 17th century, when piracy was at its height.

A life of piracy

Although usually associated with tales of pillage and plunder, several of the figures involved in high-seas piracy made some extraordinary journeys in their quests for pieces of eight.

"For a person never to get out of his native country, and to be ignorant how the rest of the Earth stands, appear'd to me a matter that should be appropriate to a woman only." Sexism aside, what is interesting about the globe-trotting ambitions of the Frenchman Raveneau de Lussan is the way in which he fulfilled them: he became a pirate.

Legalized theft

The second half of the 17th century could be regarded as something of a golden age of piracy, particularly if the term "golden age" is taken to mean a time of accruing wealth. For an educated gentleman like Lussan, piracy as a means of earning a living offered travel, adventure, and, of course, riches. It did not even necessarily mean criminality, as pirates (or buccaneers or freebooters, as they were also known) frequently operated with the backing of national governments, which gave them license to attack and loot the ships and ports of enemy states.

Francis Drake, who carried out the second circumnavigation of the world, raided Spanish possessions along the western coast of the Americas in the late 16th century, and was knighted for his efforts by Elizabeth I of England. Henry Morgan, who sacked Panama City, and whose life inspired the fictional tales of Captain Blood, was duly made Governor of Jamaica.

Born in 1663, Lussan had, by the time he was 16, made his way to the French-controlled Caribbean island of Hispaniola, where he joined the crew of Dutch pirate Laurens de Graaf. By his early 20s, he was leading his own crew. After a few years raiding in the Pacific—sacking towns and ambushing the Spanish navy—he and his fellow buccaneers decided that they had seized enough treasure to return home, so set off on a journey back across Guatemala. It took 59 days, during which 84 of the 480 men perished of disease or were lost in the jungle. Eventually, they reached the Caribbean and sailed back to Hispaniola. There they were given a warm welcome by the governor, who described their adventures as: "the greatest and finest voyage of any in our age."

△ **Gold doubloon**
This gold coin, minted in 1714, was one of thousands of pieces of gold stolen from the Spanish colonies by pirates.

The Barbary Coast

After the Caribbean, the other great region of piracy was the Barbary Coast of North Africa, where Muslim pirates terrorized the Mediterranean, West Africa's Atlantic seaboard, and the North Atlantic. Their main purpose was to capture Christians for the Ottoman slave trade. One of the more colorful Barbary pirates was, in fact, a Dutchman, Jan Janszoon van Haarlem, who also went by the name of Murat Reis. Janszoon captured the island of Lundy off western England and held it for five years. He also raided Iceland, and in 1631, landed at the small town of Baltimore in western Ireland, where he abducted some 108 people, only two of whom ever saw their homeland again. In honor of his endeavors, he was made Grand Admiral of the Corsair Republic of Salé, a pirating enclave in what is now Morocco.

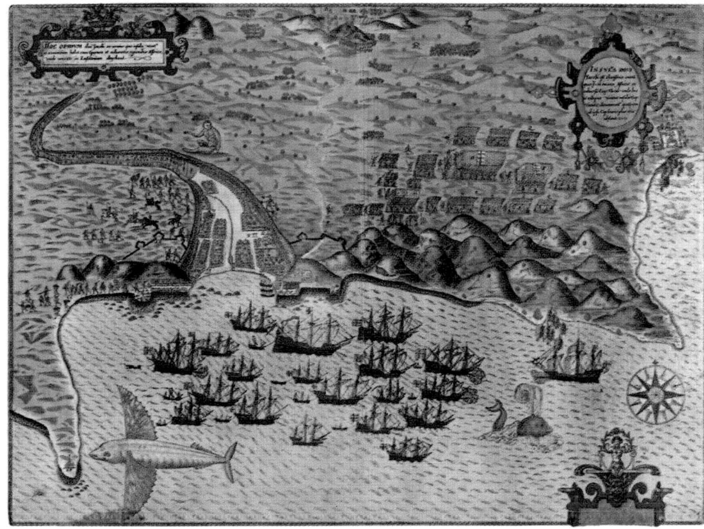

△ **Sacking the Spanish**
To the English, Francis Drake was a hero—to the Spanish, he was merely a pirate. In 1585, he raided several Spanish bases in the Caribbean, including Santiago, shown besieged on this illustrated map.

PIRATES ANNE BONNY AND MARY READ DRESSED AS MEN, READY FOR WORK

IN CONTEXT
Pirate queens

Women were not allowed aboard pirate ships. However, Irish-born Anne Bonny countered this by dressing and acting as a man while first mate on Calico Jack's ship. She also happened to be his lover. Another cross-dresser was Englishwoman Mary Read, who joined the British military as Mark Read. Sailing to the West Indies, the ship she was on was captured by pirates and she joined their ranks. She was sailing with Anne Bonny and Calico Jack on their ship *Revenge* in 1720, when the ship was captured by pirate hunter Captain Jonathan Barnet. Bonny's last words to Jack were allegedly: "Sorry to see you there, but if you'd fought like a man, you would not have been hang'd like a Dog."

Travels in the Mughal Empire

As India became more accessible to Europeans in the 16th and 17th centuries, a succession of travelers reported back on the glories, sophistication, and architectural magnificence of the Mughal Empire.

Before Marco Polo's travels in the 13th century (see pp. 88–89), the European view of India consisted largely of myths and fables. This began to change during the next 200 years, as more European travelers arrived in India to see the place Polo had described as "the richest and most splendid province in the world."

First impressions

One of the first Europeans to write a detailed account of India was Niccolò de' Conti, an Italian merchant, who from 1419 traveled in the footsteps of Marco Polo, including a spell in India. Half a century later, a Russian merchant named Afanasy Nikitin traveled via Azerbaijan and Persia to India. He spent three years there, and recorded his observations in a book called *The Journey Beyond Three Seas*, a rich source of information on the people and customs of India at the time.

De' Conti's travels provided a source for the 1450 Fra Mauro map, which suggested that there was a sea route from Europe around Africa to India. When the Portuguese proved this route existed, trade and cultural exchanges between Europe and India grew.

▽ **Diaries of a gem merchant**
Jean-Baptiste Tavernier was a French gem merchant who became famous for his six voyages to the East. His account of his travels included diagrams of the diamonds he found in India.

△ **Elephant fight at Lucknow**
This engraving from François Bernier's *Travels in the Mogul Empire* shows an elephant fight in Mughal India. Elephants were used for hunting, military campaigns, and sport.

Inevitably, conquest and exploitation were high on the European agenda, and soon the Portuguese had staked a claim to large swathes of southern India. Trading rivalries among the seafaring powers spurred the British, the Dutch, and the French to establish outposts in India over the following century. However, not everyone went there purely for profit.

Italian Cesare Federici traveled to India in 1563 to "see Eastern parts of the world." He spent 18 years in Asia and published an account of his travels in Venice in 1587. Jean-Baptiste Tavernier (1605–89) was a French gem merchant who combined business with a yearning for travel that took him to Persia and India. He documented his career in *The Six Voyages of Jean-Baptiste Tavernier* (1675). Perhaps most interesting of all was François Bernier (1625–88), a Frenchman who arrived in India during the reign of the Mughal emperor Shah Jahan, the builder of the Taj Mahal.

Court physician

Born the son of a farmer, and educated in Paris, Bernier managed to become a medical doctor on the strength of a three-month intensive course.

> " It should not escape **notice** that **gold and silver** ... come at **length** to be **swallowed up** in **Hindoustan**. "
>
> FRANÇOIS BERNIER, COMMENTING ON THE WEALTH OF INDIA

IN CONTEXT

Indians in Europe

When European ships first reached Asia, they also provided a new route for Indians trading with Europe. From around 1600, many Indians headed west, but it was not until much later that any of them wrote about it. The first three to do so wrote in Arabic or Persian, but the fourth, Sake Dean Mahomed, wrote in English. Mahomed was born in northeast India, and became a trainee surgeon working for the British East India Company. In 1782, he traveled to England, where it is claimed he opened England's first Indian restaurant and introduced the concept of "shampoo" baths. In 1794, he published *The Travels of Dean Mahomed*, the first Indian travelogue in English.

SAKE DEAN MAHOMED

Impressively, he entered service as physician to the Mughal court, and when Shah Jahan died, he was kept on by his successor, the Emperor Aurangzeb. Bernier was a keen observer of the proceedings of the court, with its fusion of different cultures and religions, and of the bitter rivalry between Shah Jahan's sons, all of whom squabbled for their father's throne. As part of the court, Bernier traveled far and wide across northern India, the Punjab, and Kashmir, where he was the first, and for a long time the only, European to venture. He later recounted his experiences in *Travels in the Mogul Empire, AD 1656–1668*.

▷ **The young Aurangzeb**
This painting of 1635 shows the three younger sons of Shah Jahan. Aurangzeb (middle), was the last great ruler of the Mughal dynasty. He reigned for 49 years, from 1658 to 1707.

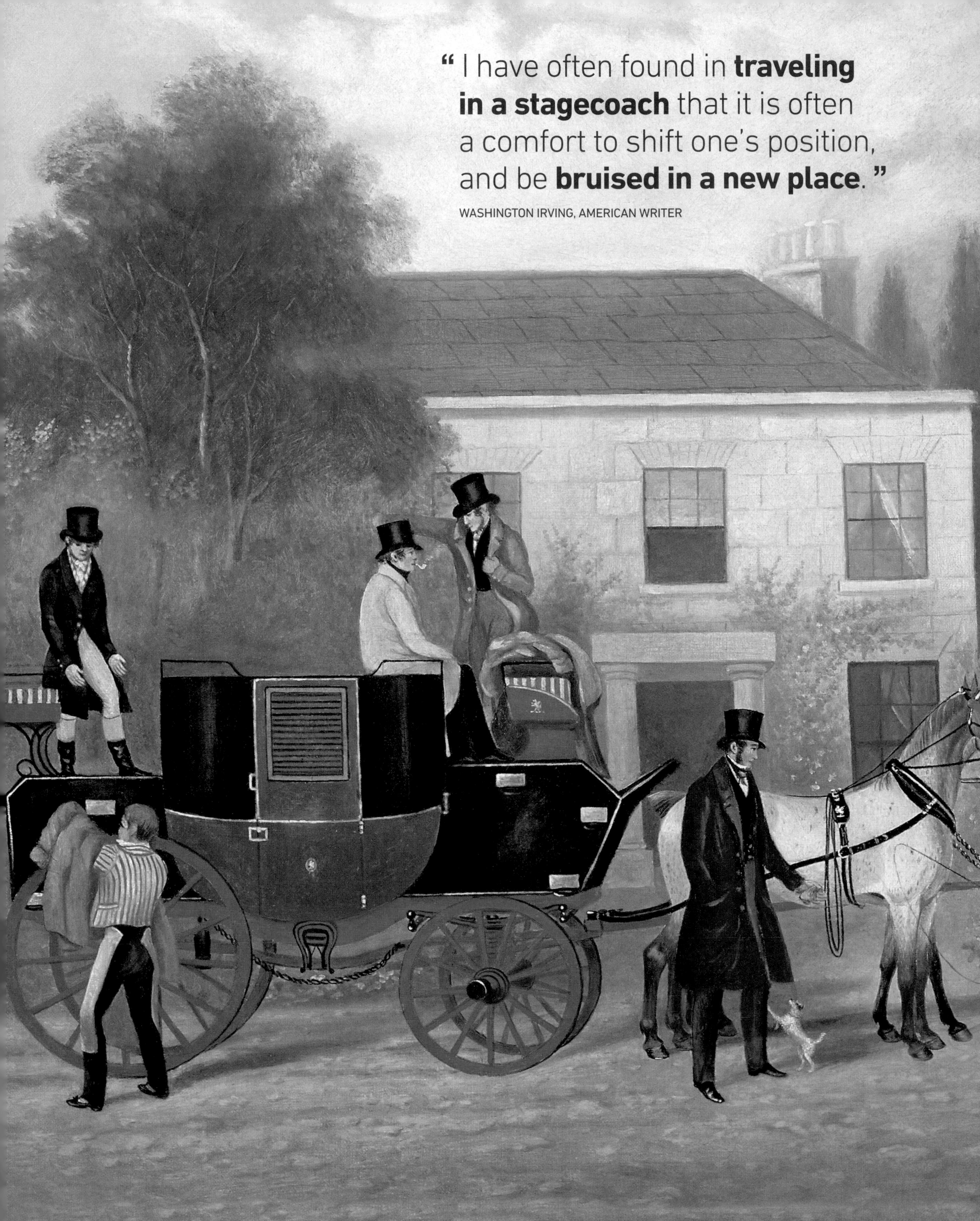

“I have often found in **traveling in a stagecoach** that it is often a comfort to shift one’s position, and be **bruised in a new place**.”

WASHINGTON IRVING, AMERICAN WRITER

The stagecoach

In the 16th century, coach services began running between towns, sparing people the discomforts of traveling on foot or on horseback.

Early travelers over land had no choice but to ride on horseback or to walk. Carriages or coaches were reserved for royalty, and generally female royalty at that. Such people had the resources to send servants out beforehand to scout the most passable routes, and, where necessary, to clear and repair the rutted cross-country tracks that passed for roads. Elizabeth I of England is recorded to have spent a fortune on coaches during her reign (1558–1603), and it is perhaps for this reason that coaches subsequently became fashionable with the gentry—although it was generally considered effeminate for a man to prefer a coach to a horse.

The popularity of the coach was not confined to England. By the mid-17th century, horse-drawn stagecoaches had begun to travel between many European cities. It is around this time these vehicles became known as stagecoaches—a reference to the fact that they traveled in stages of 10–15 miles (16–24km). This was one of the reasons that journeys on the road were painfully slow. In England, in 1657, the 182 miles (292km) from London to Chester took six days. It was also uncomfortable. Carriages lacked suspension, up to eight people might be crammed inside, second-class travelers sat in a large open basket attached to the rear of the coach, and third-class passengers risked being bounced off perches on the roof.

Then, in the 18th century, turnpike trusts were established to provide better roads, charging a toll for usage, and a network of coaching inns emerged to provide travelers with overnight lodgings. These developments were spurred on by the innovation of carrying the mail by coach, so roads were now used not only by stagecoaches, but also by mail coaches. Stagecoaches themselves became more comfortable. A German design, known as the Berlin, featured curved-metal spring suspension and a coach body for four with a door on each side. Later improvements included glass windows to keep out the wind and rain, where previously there had been only blinds. In the US, the Concord coach had leather straps for suspension, prompting Mark Twain to describe it as "a cradle on wheels." The stagecoach remained the common form of long-distance transportation until the arrival of the railways in the 1830s.

◁ ***The Stage Coach Preparing to Depart***
In its day, the stagecoach offered the most comfortable way of traveling long distances. This painting by Charles Cooper Henderson shows passengers embarking from a coaching inn sometime in the early 19th century.

The frozen east

Unable to expand further to the west, in the late 16th century Russia turned its gaze to the east. Intrepid explorers set out to explore and colonize the vast frozen expanse of Siberia.

During the reign of Ivan the Terrible (r. 1547–84), Russia's first tsar, Russian imperial ambitions had been thwarted to the west by Poland and Sweden, and to the south by the Crimean Tatars. Seeking new lands to conquer, Russia turned to the east, to the Ural Mountains and the vast expanse of Siberia beyond. While in the West, the colonization of North America from coast to coast would take some 250 years, Russian explorers went from the Urals in the west to the Pacific Ocean in the east in about 65 years.

The movement into Siberia was spearheaded by Russian Cossacks hunting for ermines, foxes, and sables. As in America, early explorers tended to follow river routes, and one of the first Russian settlements, Tobolsk (created in 1585), was founded at the meeting of the Irtysh and Tobol rivers. Also as in America, the colonizers encountered many tribes of indigenous people as they advanced. Some of these offered assistance, including sharing geographical knowledge, while others were more hostile. Whether friendly or not, the Russians viewed it as their colonial right to claim all territory as their own and to civilize these "savages." These people would be decimated by slaughter, disease, and alcoholism.

Reaching the Pacific Ocean

In 1627, the Russians, led by Cossack explorer Pyotr Beketov, reached the region of Buryatia in central Siberia. Five years later, they founded Yakutsk as a far and lonely base camp, over 3,032 miles (4,880 km) east of Moscow. At this point,

Lake Baikal
It was not until 1643 that a Russian, the Cossack Kurbat Ivanov, first set eyes on Lake Baikal. The lake freezes in the winter months between January and May, and the temperature on the land around the lake can fall to as low as -2°F (-19°C).

▷ **Siberian Route**
A road was built connecting European Russia to China, known as the Siberian Route or *Sibirsky trakt*. Its surface was often frozen in the winter, so dogsleds were used, as shown here.

they were only about 500 miles (800 km) from the eastern coast of Siberia, but it would not be until August 1639 that explorer Ivan Moskvitin and his party became the first Russians to reach the Pacific Ocean. Their reports were used to prepare the first map of the Russian Far East, which was drawn in 1642 by Kurbat Ivanov.

Ivanov was an explorer himself, and was keen to fill more of the empty spaces on his charts. He undertook his own expedition the following year, leading a party of 74 men up the Lena river in search of a rumored vast body of water. This was Lake Baikal, the world's deepest lake, and the largest freshwater lake by volume. Ivanov became the first Russian to chart and describe it.

In a very short time, Russia had added new territory of around 5 million sq miles (13 million sq km), or about a twelfth of the total land surface of the globe, stretching from the Arctic to Central Asia, and from the Urals to the Sea of Japan. However, there was plenty more exploring to do.

Beyond the Stanovoy Range

Little of the territory found so far was suitable for agriculture, so in 1643, an administrator from Yakutsk, Vassili Poyarkov, was sent south to explore the lands bordering China. He set off from Yakutsk with 133 men, following various rivers south up into the Stanovoy Range. Beyond these mountains, he discovered Siberia's great southern river, the Amur, and a fertile plain fit for farming. However, as they crossed over the Stanovoys, Poyarkov and his men were driven back by the Chinese, and it was not until 1859 that the area was annexed by Russia.

By the mid-17th century, Russian conquests in the frozen east had ensured that its borders were roughly similar to those of modern-day Russia. What remained uncharted was the Arctic coastline and the northeastern peninsula of Kamchatka. These would not be completed until the Great Northern Expedition in the following century.

IN CONTEXT
A place of exile

Almost as soon as Siberia was colonized, it became a place of banishment. It was both a convenient way to cleanse European Russia of those deemed undesirable, and a way to populate the eastern wilds. "In the same way that we have to remove harmful agents from the body so that the body does not expire, so it is in the community of citizens," declared the bishop of Tobolsk in 1708. "That which is harmful must be cut out."

Exiles had to walk to Siberia, a journey that could take up to two years, spent shuffling in chains along the *Sibirsky trakt*. At Tobolsk, 1,100 miles (1,770 km) from Moscow, the prisoners' leg irons were removed—at this point they were so far into the wilderness that there was nowhere for them to run. Their sentences began only once they had arrived at their designated place of exile.

CHAINING PRISONERS, SAKHALIN, RUSSIA, 1890s

The Great Northern Expedition

With the colonization of Siberia underway, the Russian tsars commissioned two major expeditions to probe the far northern and eastern limits of their expanding empire. The second became known as the Great Northern Expedition.

△ **Vitus Bering**
Although Danish, Bering served the Russian tsar in his explorations of what became known as the Bering Strait. He prepared the way for a Russian foothold on the North American continent.

Peter the Great (r. 1682–1725) was the tsar who transformed Russia into a major European empire. He made modest territorial gains during his reign, mainly at the expense of the Ottomans and the Swedes, but arguably his greatest military achievement was the development of a modern Russian navy. For the navy to be effective, it needed detailed maps of the country's coastline, but at the time, there were still a considerable number of blank areas on the charts.

The man selected to rectify this was Vitus Bering, a Danish cartographer and seaman who had joined the rapidly-expanding Russian navy in 1704 and then served for 20 years. On the orders of Peter the Great, in 1725 he traveled to the northern Pacific to see if there was land connecting Siberia with Alaska.

The first two years of the project were spent moving men and materials from the new capital of St Petersburg across Siberia. It was not until July 1727 that Bering reached the shanty settlement of Okhotsk on the Pacific. Two small ships were built from materials transported for the purpose—ropes, sails, and iron parts, including the anchor (everything except wood). These ships carried the expedition to the remote Kamchatka Peninsula in northeastern Russia, where the men constructed another ship, the *Archangel Gabriel*, in which they took to the open sea. Bering kept so close to the Russian coast that he did not notice Alaska, which was a mere 68 miles (110 km) away. Nevertheless,

▷ **Shipwreck**
Bering's ship was wrecked on one of the barren Commander Islands, 109 miles (175 km) off the coast of Kamchatka. Bering and 30 of his crew died there, and the island was later named after Bering.

◁ **The Russian discoveries**
This English map is based on a 1754 map published by the St Petersburg Academy of Science, showing the sea routes taken by Bering and Chirikov during the expedition.

he had discovered that there was no land bridge connecting Russia and Alaska, but just open sea.

In the summer of 1730, Bering returned to St Petersburg, where he was criticized by admiralty officials for failing to see the American coast. Three years later, however, Peter's successor, Catherine I, commissioned Bering to make a second voyage.

A tragic adventure

This second expedition involved some 3,000 men, making it perhaps the largest scientific venture to date. It was organized into three groups: one to chart the northern coast of Siberia; one to make a scientific survey of Siberia; and another (Bering's) to map the North American coast and establish Russia's interests in the wider Pacific.

After 10 years of preparation, the Pacific explorers left Kamchatka in June 1741 in two ships built at Okhotsk—the *St Peter*, commanded by Bering, and the *St Paul*, commanded by Aleksei Chirikov, his lieutenant. Within days, the two ships had lost sight of each other in fog, but on July 16, Bering saw land. Two days later, a small landing party, including German naturalist Georg Wilhelm Steller, went ashore on Kayak Island, becoming the first Europeans to set foot on Alaskan soil.

Still separated from the *St Paul*, and with supplies running low, Bering decided to head back west. Battered by storms, and with a crew sick with scurvy, the *St Peter* finally saw land on November 4. Tragically, what they hoped was Kamchatka turned out to be an uninhabited island. The crew spent the winter there, living in driftwood huts dug into the permafrost, but 31 men died, including Bering. When the weather improved, the 46 survivors built a boat from the wreckage and made it back to Kamchatka. The *St Paul* also returned, and discovered new islands en route, but lost half of its crew. Despite its losses, the Great Northern Expedition mapped much of the Arctic coast of Siberia and discovered Alaska, the Aleutian Islands, and the Commander Islands. Bering was commemorated by having not only the Bering Strait named after him, but also the Bering Sea and Bering Island. The reports, maps, and samples from the expedition paved the way for Russian expansion into Alaska, which it occupied until it was sold to the US in 1867.

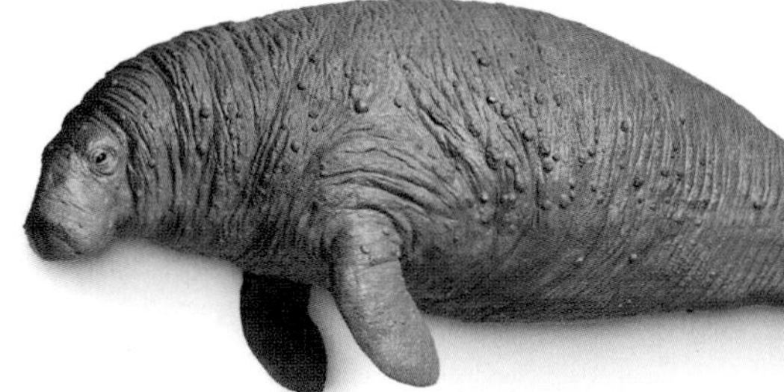

△ **Steller's sea cow**
Named for expedition naturalist Georg Wilhelm Steller, this large mammal was hunted to extinction just 27 years after its discovery.

▽ **Kamchatka**
This sketch by German naturalist Georg Wilhelm Steller, a member of Bering's expedition, depicts the remote volcanic peninsular of Kamchatka in northeastern Russia. It was the launching point for both of Bering's expeditions.

> “We have **only** come to **America** to take **water** to **Asia**.”
>
> GEORG WILHELM STELLER, ON BEING TOLD THAT THEY WERE ONLY STAYING ON KAYAK ISLAND LONG ENOUGH TO TAKE ON WATER

Calculating longitude

Due to difficulties in calculating longitude, many of the great voyages of discovery owed as much to luck as to skill. It took a humble carpenter to provide the means for sailors to know exactly where they were.

▽ **The Scilly Isles disaster**
When four ships and over 1,300 men were lost in 1707 due to a navigational error, the British government promised a reward to anyone who could solve the problem of measuring longitude.

Considering the many great voyages of discovery that were made in the 15th, 16th, and 17th centuries by the likes of Christopher Columbus, Ferdinand Magellan, and Vasco da Gama, it seems extraordinary that once they were out of sight of land, sailors were quite literally "all at sea." Despite charts and compasses, their inability to determine longitude with any reliability left even the most experienced captains largely at the mercy of luck or the grace of God.

Dead reckoning

Determining position at sea requires knowing both latitude and longitude. Latitude gives the north-south position, and longitude the east-west. Any sailor could calculate the former by the height of the sun or known guide stars above the horizon. Christopher Columbus simply followed a straight line of latitude on his historic journey of 1492.

However, to gauge their distance east or west of a home port, sailors relied on a method called "dead reckoning," by which a navigator threw a log overboard and observed how quickly it receded from the ship. This crude estimate of the ship's speed, combined with the direction of travel (taken from the stars or a compass), and the length of time the ship had been on a particular course, plus or minus ocean currents and winds, gave a sailor a rough estimate of his longitude—of how far west or east he had traveled. It was a very imprecise method, and all too often fatally so. On October 22, 1707, four homebound British warships miscalculated their position and ran aground on the Scilly Isles near the southwestern tip of England, and more than 1,300 men lost their lives.

△ **John Harrison**
Harrison was a self-educated English carpenter turned clockmaker who invented the marine chronometer, which enabled sailors to calculate longitude at sea. Thanks to Harrison, mariners could know their location anywhere on Earth.

The solution

The problem of longitude had taxed the wisest of minds for centuries. In theory, the best solution was for sailors to compare the time aboard ship with the time at the port they had left, since one hour's difference in sunrise represents 15 degrees of longitude—a distance of some 1,035 miles (1,666 km). An onboard clock could be set to local time by setting it to noon when the sun was directly overhead; the problem lay in keeping track of the time in their original time zone. In the 1700s, when ships were being sent out to explore new territories, and ever more wealth was being floated on the oceans, there were no clocks that could withstand either the changes of temperature or the motions of ships at sea. Understandably, the governments of the leading maritime nations were desperate to find a solution—and in the wake of the Scilly Isles disaster, the British Parliament set the highest reward of all. The Longitude Act of 1714 promised a sum of £20,000 (around $3.4 million today) to anyone who could find a "practicable and useful" means of determining longitude. The solution came from an unlikely source—a self-educated woodworker from Yorkshire named John Harrison. With no training as a watchmaker, he completed his first pendulum clock before he was 20, constructing the whole thing almost entirely out of wood. He went on to design and build a series of friction-free clocks that required no lubrication, were made from materials that were not susceptible to rust, and kept their moving parts perfectly balanced in relation to one another, regardless of external movement. He combined different metals in such a way that when one component expanded or contracted with changes in temperature, the others counteracted accordingly.

◁ **Marine Timekeeper H1**
This is the first experimental marine timekeeper made by John Harrison between 1730 and 1735 as a first step toward solving the problem of calculating longitude.

Harrison's clocks were not trusted by the scientific commissioners charged with awarding the longitude prize, who were convinced the solution lay with some astronomical device. In fact, it took 40 years before Harrison, with the backing of King George III, was able to claim his monetary reward. However, proof of his success is that Harrison's clocks became standard aboard ships. They were eventually mass-produced, and ultimately evolved into the modern wristwatch. When, after his return to Earth, astronaut Neil Armstrong dined at 10 Downing Street, home of the UK Prime Minister, he raised a glass to John Harrison, "the one who started us on our journey."

△ **Harrison's longitude watch**
Harrison realized that the answer to the problem of longitude lay not with large timepieces but with smaller watches. He completed this prize-winning watch in 1759.

" It is by **God's Almighty Providence** and **great chance** that there are **not** a great **many more misfortunes** ... in navigation than there are. "

ENGLISH DIARIST SAMUEL PEPYS, COMMENTING ON HIS 1683 VOYAGE TO TANGIERS

▽ **Prime meridian**
To establish a ship's longitude, an agreed zero point, or prime meridian, is required. In 1851, it was agreed this would be at Greenwich, also home of Britain's great naval college, shown below.

The voyages of Captain Cook

Over the course of three lengthy voyages, Captain James Cook explored more of the Earth's surface than any other person in history. His discoveries and methods inspired future generations of explorers.

△ **National hero**
From humble beginnings as a grocer's apprentice, James Cook became one of the world's greatest explorers. He was an excellent navigator, and proved to be an inspiring leader, particularly in adversity.

When a remarkable English pirate-turned-naturalist named William Dampier was sent by the British Admiralty to investigate New Holland (modern Australia) in 1699, the gist of his report was that there was little there worth exploiting. It was only when commercial rivalry turned to war between Britain and France that the race to fill in the remaining blanks on the map was renewed.

James Cook first went to sea at the age of 18, working in the merchant navy, shipping coal along the east coast of England. In 1755, he joined the Royal Navy and gained surveying experience during the Seven Years War, when Britain and France fought over their North American colonies. Later, in the years of peace that followed, he was given command of a ship and tasked with charting the coastline of Newfoundland.

The first voyage

Cook's navigational skills brought him to the attention of Britain's Royal Society, which, in 1768, commissioned him to lead a scientific expedition to Tahiti to observe the transit of the planet Venus across the Sun. The transit would not recur for over a hundred years, and measuring it was considered vital for the improvement of navigation. Cook was given command of a new ship, HMS *Endeavour*, with a crew that included astronomer Charles Green and a small retinue of scientific assistants and artists, including botanist Joseph Banks (see pp. 176–77).

From Tahiti, Cook then carried out a further, more secretive, mission on behalf of the British Admiralty, which had asked him to voyage south where "there is reason to imagine that a Continent or Land of great extent may be found." It was commonly thought that there must be a huge continent in the southern hemisphere to balance out those of the north, and the Admiralty wanted Cook to claim it for Britain. If no land could be found, Cook was to sail on to New Zealand and claim that instead.

The *Endeavour* sailed sufficiently far south for Cook to assure himself that no habitable land lay beyond. Then, in compliance with

△ **A skilled navigator**
On his third Pacific voyage, Cook used this sextant to find the height of the Sun above the horizon and so calculate latitude. He also took a clock to calculate longitude.

◁ **Cook's voyages**
In his three voyages, Cook sailed great distances across largely uncharted parts of the globe. He mapped the coasts of Australia and New Zealand, explored Hawaii, and became the first to cross the Antarctic Circle.

△ **Native cultures**
Cook's expeditions gathered information and wooden artifacts relating to Polynesian and other Pacific cultures, including this bowl in the shape of a seal, possibly from Alaska.

his instructions, he headed west and charted the coasts of New Zealand, confirming Abel Tasman's theory that the country was made up of two islands and was not connected to any larger landmass.

From there, Cook sailed the *Endeavour* toward the unexplored eastern parts of New Holland (Australia). On April 19, 1770, a landing party went ashore, and Banks was so thrilled by the new plants he found that Cook named that part of the coast Botany Bay. Cook surveyed the whole eastern coastline, successfully navigating the dangers of the Great Barrier Reef, and claimed the land for the British Crown. He then sailed through the Torres Strait, settling the dispute as to whether New Holland and New Guinea were joined, and finally turned for home.

Cook's second voyage

The British Admiralty, however, were still concerned about the possible existence of a great southern continent, so, in 1772, Cook was sent off again, this time commanding HMS *Resolution*, and accompanied by its sister ship, HMS *Adventure*. His mission was to sail further south than anyone had sailed before.

In his three years away, Cook sailed below the Antarctic Circle and reached the Antarctic ice shelf. He was unable to breach the ice, but came closer to the South Pole than any previous navigator. He circumnavigated the frozen land to prove definitively that there was no further continent there. Then he returned north, exploring Tahiti and New Zealand again, and for the first time he visited Easter Island,

▽ **Easter Island**
In March 1774, Cook visited Easter Island and marveled at its "Colossal Statues," like the ones depicted in this 19th-century hand-colored engraving. "Each Statue had on its head a large Cylindrical Stone," he noted.

△ **Exotic fauna**
On Cook's second voyage, onboard artists painted some of the animal life they encountered in the Pacific, including this manta ray.

» the Marquesas Islands, Tonga, and the New Hebrides. Most of these had already been discovered by earlier explorers, but Cook was the first to chart them with any accuracy. He had brought with him one of John Harrison's timepieces (see p. 170), so he was able to establish longitudinal coordinates, laying the groundwork for modern maps of the South Pacific.

The final, fatal voyage

Cook returned to a hero's welcome and was given honorary retirement from the Royal Navy. However, he could not keep away from the ocean. Although now almost 50, his thoughts turned to the North Pacific and to another holy grail of seafaring—finding a navigable Northwest Passage between the Pacific and Atlantic oceans across the top of America.

In command of the *Resolution* once more, Cook set out in July 1776 on a route that took him back to Tahiti. From there, he bore north to the unknown Hawaiian Islands, which he named the Sandwich Islands after his sponsor, the Earl of Sandwich. Cook's crew were the first Europeans to land there, and they were warmly welcomed by the inhabitants. Cook then headed north and spent the summer surveying the North American coast from Vancouver Island to the Bering Strait, where he searched in vain for a navigable passage.

In 1779, Cook bore south and returned to Hawaii—but this time he met with disaster. On February 14, while he was investigating the alleged

◁ **The third voyage**
The lands that Cook named the Sandwich Islands (today known as Hawaii) initially gave the sailors an enthusiastic welcome, as pictured here. A second visit, however, had a far from friendly outcome.

▽ ***The Resolution and Discovery off Hawaii***
This painting by John Cleveley the Younger (from the 1780s) depicts Cook's arrival at Hawaii in 1779. To the right, the ships *Resolution* and *Discovery* are at anchor in Kealakekua Bay.

theft of a boat by an islander, Cook was stabbed to death by an angry local tribe. The expedition continued under the command of Charles Clerke, but it failed yet again to discover a Northwest Passage, and returned to England the following year.

Lasting legacy

Cook's expeditions played an important role in the development of natural history, oceanography, ethnology, anthropology, and other fields of science. He also left a lasting legacy in the standards of behavior that were expected of seamen, both aboard ship (his men were remarkably well treated and fed for the time, and few died from scurvy) and, despite the circumstances of his death, on shore as well. He came to embody a spirit of peaceable, scientific exploration.

LA PÉROUSE PAINTED IN 1785, SHORTLY BEFORE HIS FINAL VOYAGE

IN PROFILE

La Pérouse

In 1785, Jean-François de la Galaup, also known as the Comte de la Pérouse, commanded a major French expedition intended to build on the work of James Cook. Accompanied by scientists and surveyors, he sailed the ships *L'Astrolabe* and *La Boussole* across the Atlantic, then rounded South America to reach Easter Island. The expedition continued to the Hawaiian Islands and the North Pacific, where it surveyed the Canadian coast and, like Cook, failed to find the elusive Northwest Passage. After visiting Kamchatka, from where reports were dispatched west, La Pérouse sailed south to investigate British activities in Australia, and reached Botany Bay in January 1788, just as the First Fleet was disgorging its initial settlement of convicts (see pp. 186–87). On March 10, La Pérouse set sail for New Caledonia, and was never seen again. Forty years later, it was discovered that his ships had been wrecked on the Santa Cruz Islands.

> “**Ambition** leads me not only **farther** than **any other man** has been **before** me, but as **far** as I think it **possible** for **man to go**.”
>
> CAPTAIN JAMES COOK, JOURNAL ENTRY FROM MARCH 1774

△ ***The Odyssey of Captain Cook***
This 2005 lithograph, by artist Marian Maguire, depicts an imaginary meeting between the ancient Greeks and the Maori of New Zealand, brought about by the arrival of the *Endeavour*.

The new naturalists

The notion of setting out on a voyage of exploration for scientific purposes alone is common enough today, but in the 18th century it was unheard of—until the voyage of HMS *Endeavour*.

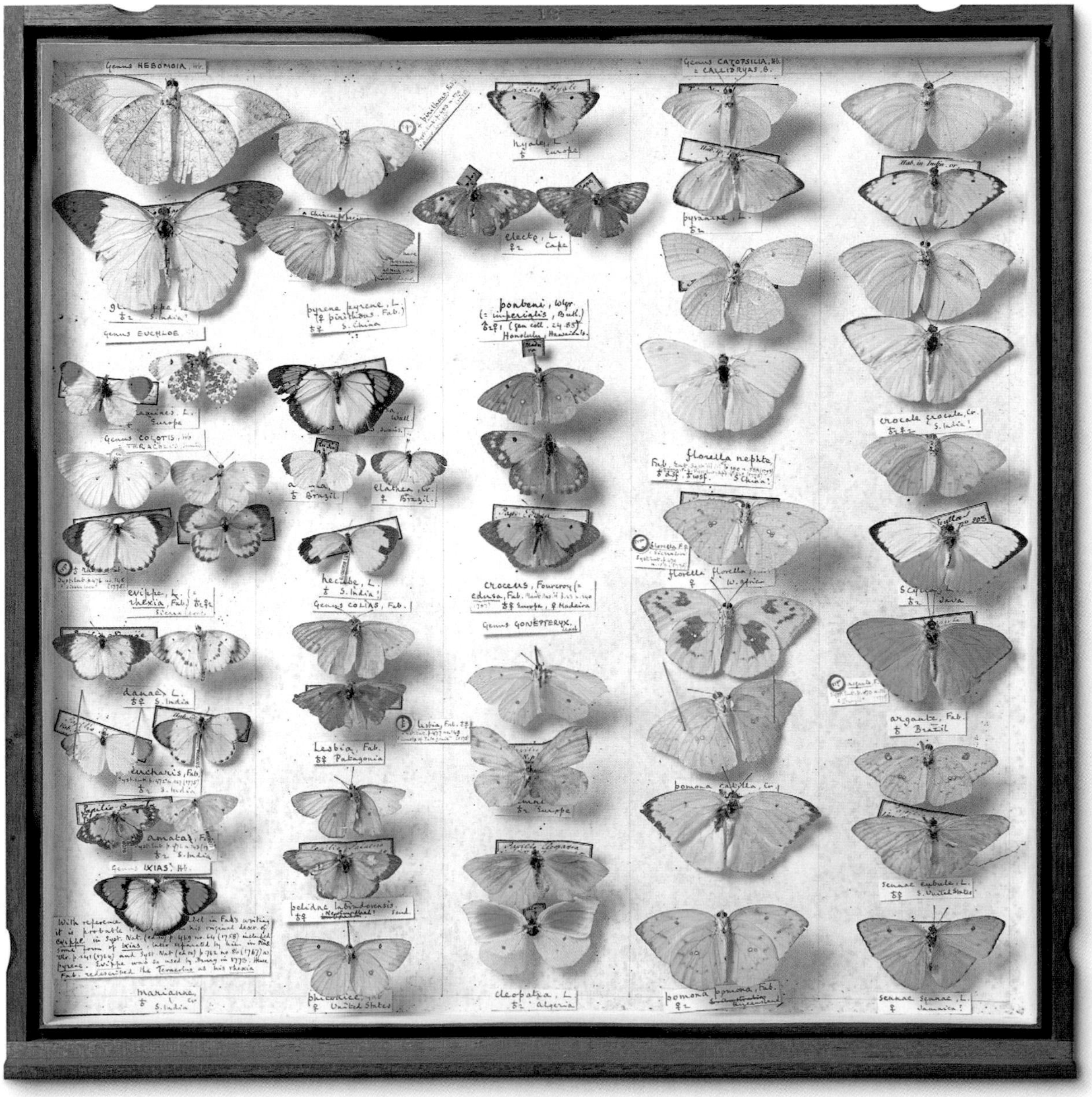

▽ **Box of bugs**
Among Joseph Banks' haul from the *Endeavour* expedition were more than 4,000 insects, including this cabinet of butterflies now kept at London's Natural History Museum.

With a few notable exceptions, such as Tsar Peter I's Great Northern Expedition in 1733–43, most voyages of discovery were designed to swell a country's coffers rather than its banks of scientific knowledge. This is what made the voyage of HMS *Endeavour* (see pp. 172–75) unique. From the start, Captain James Cook's expedition had science at its core. The primary aim of its visit to Tahiti was to record the transit of Venus; a secondary mission was to record the island's plant and animal life, and bring back samples. To achieve this, Cook took with him a young man from Lincolnshire, England, named Joseph Banks.

Banks was a passionate naturalist. As a youth, he had compiled a study of the flora of his own home county, and he later served as a naturalist on a voyage to Labrador and Newfoundland. He also happened to be very rich, having inherited extensive lands and great wealth. Although only 25, Banks supplied an estimated £10,000 of his own money to equip the *Endeavour*—which was more than three times the cost of the ship itself. "They have got a fine library of Natural History: they have all sorts of machines for catching and preserving insects; all kinds of nets, trawls, drags and hooks for coral fishing; they have even a curious contrivance of a telescope, by which, put into the water, you can see the bottom at a great depth, where it is clear," wrote John Ellis, one of the scientists aboard the *Endeavour*.

One of Banks's inspirations was Carl Linnaeus, a Swede who, through his travels in Lapland, pioneered the scientific study of native peoples and their use of plants for medical, religious, and other purposes, a discipline now known as ethnobotany. Although not a great traveler, his botanical ideas were far-reaching. One of his correspondents was the young Joseph Banks, and another member of the *Endeavour* team, Daniel Solander, was a former pupil. Erasmus Darwin, grandfather of Charles Darwin, later translated many of Linnaeus's works from Latin into English.

Cataloging the world

On Tahiti, while the *Endeavour*'s astronomers set up their observatory, Banks and his assistants began to collect everything they could, from birds and plants to local costumes and weapons. They continued gathering material when they reached New Zealand, and did so again in Australia. When the *Endeavour* finally docked in Dover in

" **No people** went to sea better fitted out for the purpose of **Natural History**, nor more **elegantly.** "

JOHN ELLIS, NATURALIST AND VOYAGER ABOARD THE *ENDEAVOUR*

July 1771, she had more than 1,000 zoological specimens on board, including strange pouched animals that had never been seen in Europe before. There were 30,000 pressed and dried botanical specimens, including 1,400 species that were new to science. No previous expedition had ever brought back collections of such size and importance.

Banks did not accompany Cook on his subsequent voyages, but in his role as president of the Royal Society, he continued to fund expeditions. One such expedition was to investigate whether breadfruit could be used as a nutritious source of food, which meant transferring masses of the plants from its native Tahiti to British islands in the Caribbean. The ship fitted for the mission was the HMS *Bounty*, captained by William Bligh, but famously the mission was never accomplished due to a mutiny led by Fletcher Christian.

Subsequent generations of intrepid naturalists carried on the work begun on the voyage of the *Endeavour*, notably Alexander von Humboldt (see pp. 192–93), who in his youth traveled to England to meet Joseph Banks. Banks was also patron to William Jackson Hooker, who explored, collected, and cataloged in Iceland, France, Italy, and Switzerland, before becoming director of Kew Gardens. His son, William Jackson Hooker, became one of the greatest botanists of the 19th century and was a close friend of Charles Darwin. It is no exaggeration to say that the work begun by Joseph Banks laid the groundwork for Darwin's world-changing theory of evolution.

◁ **New species**
Expedition artist Sydney Parkinson drew a sketch of a kangaroo on which this painting is based.

△ ***Banksia serrata***
Discovered on the east coast of Australia, *Banksia serrata* (old man banksia), is one of several plants, not to mention islands, named in honor of the eminent English naturalist.

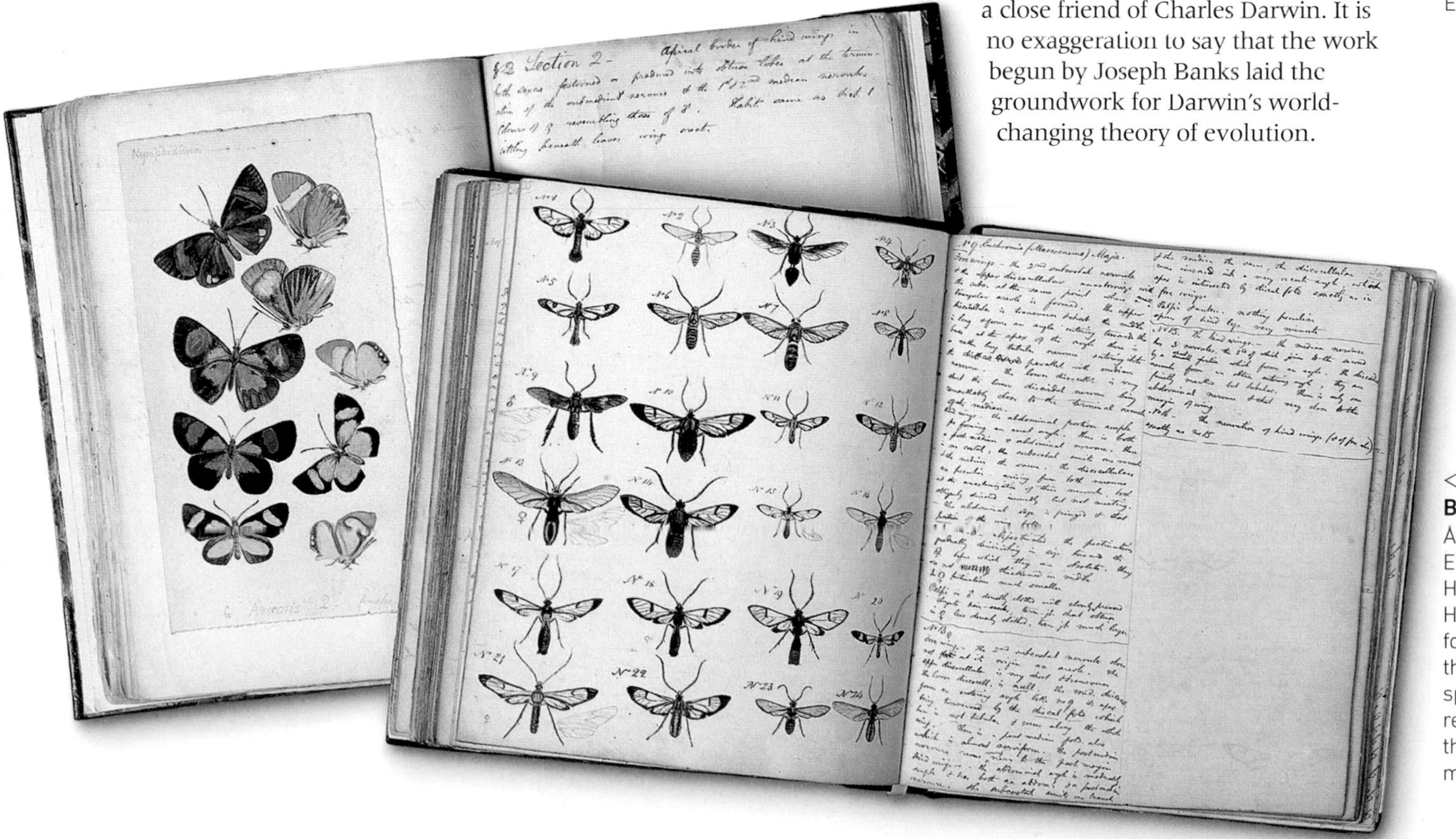

◁ **Henry Walter Bates's notebooks**
Another notable English naturalist was Henry Walter Bates. He was most famous for his expedition to the Amazon, where he spent 11 years, returning with more than 14,000 species, mostly insects.

Spectacled caiman and false coral snake
Merian became a master of watercolor painting and copper-plate engraving (guild restrictions prevented women from painting in oils). This exquisite study was painted in watercolor and gouache on vellum c.1705–10.

Artist in the rainforest

As explorers sallied forth on voyages of discovery, amateur artists also embarked on a grand engagement with the natural world.

Throughout the 17th and 18th centuries, a steady influx of wonderful plants and animals from overseas provided European artists with new subjects to paint. Some of them decided they needed to see these wonderful things in their native settings. One of the first of these adventurous traveling artists was, unusually for the time, a middle-aged divorced woman.

Maria Sibylla Merian was born in 1647 in Germany to a Swiss printmaker and draftsman and his wife. From an early age, Merian was passionate about both insects and painting, and lovingly painted fruit, flowers, and the insects she captured and bred. Married at 18, she had two daughters, and combined looking after them with working as an artist and teacher, until she left her husband to live in a commune in Denmark. Later, she moved to Amsterdam, and then, at the age of 52, she sold everything she owned, wrote a will, and set out with her younger daughter for the Dutch colony of Surinam in South America.

There, Merian made her own way. With great difficulty, she ventured deep into the rainforest to collect plants and insects: "One could find a great many things in the forest if it were passable: but it so densely overgrown with thistles and thorn bushes that I had to send my slaves ahead with axe in hand to hack an opening for me." Eventually, malaria or yellow fever forced Merian to return to Amsterdam, where she raised the money to publish her work in a series of portfolios, including *The Metamorphoses of the Insects of Surinam*, published in 1705. The resulting, mostly life-sized, paintings are phenomenally beautiful, and every bit as colorful and astonishing as the life of the woman who painted them.

" The **heat** in this **country** is **overwhelming**. It nearly **cost me** my **life**. Everyone is **amazed** that I **survived** at **all**. "

MARIA SIBYLLA MERIAN ON HER TIME IN SURINAME

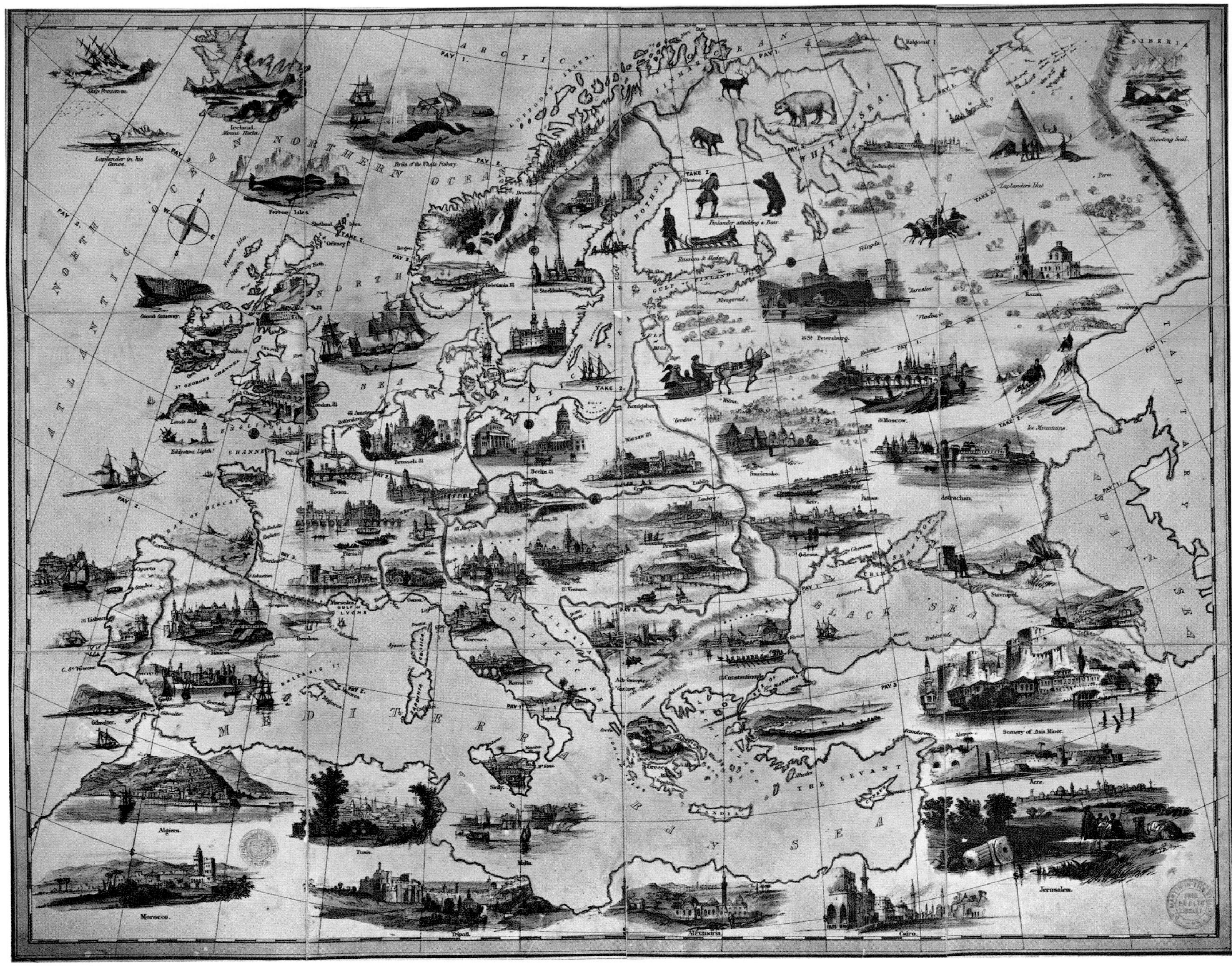

△ **A world of learning**
The Grand Tour of Europe began as a way for the sons of wealthy British families to gain a cultural education through acquaintance with the great art and architecture of the past.

The Grand Tour

From the 17th century onward, wealthy young Englishmen began traveling across Europe to discover the roots of Western civilization—which, it was generally agreed, lay in Rome.

"A man who has not been in Italy is always conscious of an inferiority," proclaimed English man-of-letters Samuel Johnson. This was somewhat self-effacing considering Johnson had never visited the country. He was, however, acknowledging a belief widely held at the time, namely that an extended trip to Italy was fundamental to a man's education.

Italy, and Rome in particular, had been a popular destination for northern European artists, intellectuals, and diplomats since at least the 17th century, and a good education invariably meant training in the classics, with a working knowledge of Latin and Greek. Both ancient and Renaissance Rome were thought to be the source of all that was important in Western civilization, and a trip there was considered a sort of finishing school.

Cultural pilgrimage

In 1670, a book called *Voyage of Italy*, or *A Compleat Journey Through Italy*, was published, in which its author, Englishman Richard Lassels, called this phenomenon of cultural pilgrimage the "Grand Tour." The Grand Tourists were almost exclusively male and, at least in the beginning, mostly British. As the world's wealthiest nation, Britain had a substantial upper class with enough money and leisure time to travel. Usually accompanied by a tutor or guardian, called a Bear Leader, the young aristocrats might spend anything from a few months to several years journeying across Europe.

ANCIENT ROME, GIOVANNI PAOLO PANINI (c.1691–1765)

IN CONTEXT
By invitation only

There were no public museums in the 17th and 18th centuries, so as well as visiting churches, palaces, and other sites of artistic merit, travelers also made calls on the homes of nobles who were known to have collections of art. It was often possible to gain access with the right credentials, which generally meant a letter of introduction. In France, it was even possible to visit the Palace of Versailles, the permanent residence of the royal family. It was necessary to look like a gentleman, which meant being immaculately dressed and carrying a sword—although those lacking a sword could hire one at the palace.

The experience was intended to broaden their intellectual horizons and teach them about art, architecture, history, and politics in preparation for a career in public life back home. However, distance from home loosened social conventions and, particularly later in the 18th century, the tour often saw any pretense at education jettisoned in favor of sex, gambling, and drinking.

As with conventional pilgrimages, the route and destinations of the tour were fairly well-defined. After crossing the English Channel, the first stop was Paris, then straight on through provincial France to cross over the Alps into Italy. Here, the great cities of Rome, Florence, Naples, and then Venice were visited (in that order of importance) before the return home, typically via Switzerland, Germany, and the Netherlands.

THE
VOYAGE
OF
ITALY;
OR
A Compleat Journey through
ITALY.
In Two Parts.
With the *Characters* of the *People*, and the Description of the Chief *Towns*, *Churches*, *Monasteries Tombs*, *Libraries Pallaces*, *Villa's*, *Gardens*, *Pictures*, *Statues*, and *Antiquities*.
AS
Also of the *Interest*, *Government*, *Riches*, *Force*, &c. of all the *Princes*.
With Instructions concerning *Travel*.

By *Richard Lassels*, Gent. who Travelled through *Italy* Five times, as Tutor to several of the *English* Nobility and Gentry.

Never before Extant.

Newly Printed at *Paris*, and are to be sold in *London*, by *John Starkey*, at the *Mitre* in *Fleet-street* near *Temple-Barr*, 1670.

▽ **Inventing the Grand Tour**
Richard Lassels earned a living acting as a guide for travelers in Europe. He first coined the phrase "Grand Tour" in his guide to Italy, published in 1670.

"Led by hand he saunter'd **Europe round**, And gather'd every **vice** on **Christian ground**."

ALEXANDER POPE, POET AND GRAND TOUR SCEPTIC (1688–1744)

Practicalities

By the mid-18th century, when Grand Tourism was at its peak, travel was surprisingly well organized. There were regular cross-Channel sailings, and travelers could, for example, arrange for transportation across »

▽ **A grand souvenir**
It was fashionable for Grand Tourists to have their portrait done. This painting is by Louis Gauffier, a French artist living in Italy, who made a living selling his work to British visitors.

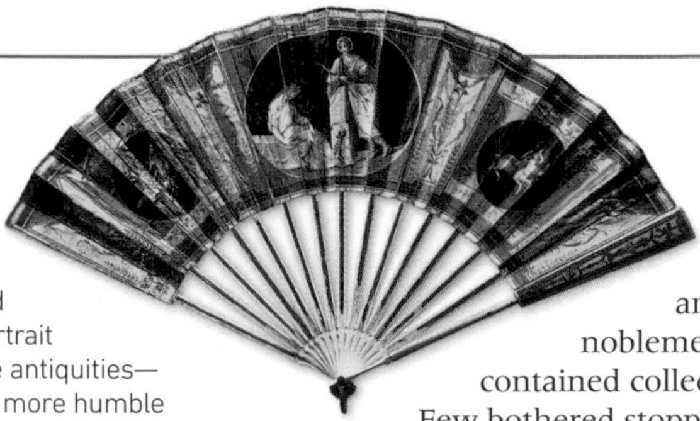

» much of the Continent from either London or Paris. There were even guidebooks, such as Thomas Nugent's *Grand Tour* (1749), offering descriptions of Europe's major cities and essays of moralistic advice in four volumes.

Once on the Continent, there were several options for continued travel. The wealthiest could purchase or hire a private carriage and horses. It was, however, more common to rent a carriage and travel "post," which meant hiring horses and a driver at designated points along main routes. This had the advantages of a private carriage without the expense of keeping horses. There were also the public coach services, which were cheap but slow.

▷ **Modest memento**
Not every tourist could afford to have their portrait painted or to purchase antiquities—some had to settle for more humble mementoes, such as this hand-painted goatskin fan.

The itinerary

Paris was still a medieval city at the time—smaller and more densely populated than London. Grand Tourist Horace Walpole, son of Robert Walpole, the British prime minister who toured the Continent in the early 1740s, called it, "the ugliest beastliest town in the universe." Even so, tourists would stay for several weeks, visiting churches, palaces, and any homes of noblemen that contained collections of art.

Few bothered stopping anywhere else in France, going straight from Paris to the Alps, where carriages were dismantled and hauled by pack animals over the Mont Cenis Pass into Italy. The travelers would traverse the mountains in a sedan chair carried by porters.

Once on the other side, Turin was the first stop, although most tourists considered it too provincial to detain them for long. By contrast, the birthplace of the Renaissance, Florence, was one of the most popular cities, worthy of a stay of several weeks.

" No one who **has not been** here can have **any conception** of what an **education Rome is**. "

JOHANN WOLFGANG VON GOETHE, 1816

▽ **The eternal city of Rome**
Englishman Charles Thompson spoke for many Grand Tourists when, in 1744, he said he was "impatiently desirous of viewing a country so famous in history"—namely Italy. The treasures of Rome are depicted here by Bernardo Bellotto.

Even in the mid-18th century, there was already a considerable English community here, so visitors could spend time socializing with their fellow countrymen.

Visiting Rome

A brief stop in Siena was usually all that then lay between the tourists and their ultimate goal of Rome. A popular guidebook recommended six weeks as a minimum to view all of the city's ancient ruins and more recent sights. William Beckford, a writer who visited Rome in 1782, thought even five years was not enough. For assistance, the visitor could call upon the services of a small army of tour guides, both Italian and foreigners who had settled in Rome. Generally speaking, the city lived up to expectations. In the opinion of German writer Goethe: "Here the most ordinary person becomes somebody, for his mind is enormously enlarged even if his character remains unchanged."

Eager to procure mementoes, many Grand Tourists had their portrait painted, often in a studio against the backdrop of some famous monument. Some bought art or antiquities, perhaps statuary and fragments of ancient buildings. Many private art collections in Britain were launched with artworks bought on a Grand Tour, and over time, many of these collections found their way into national museums.

◁ **The end of the tour**
Naples, seen here in a painting from the end of the 17th century, was as far south as most travelers went. Here they visited the lava-trapped remains of Pompeii and Herculaneum, but also just luxuriated in the balmy climate.

A change in sensibility

The furthest south most tourists went was Naples. Apart from visits to the archaeological excavations at Herculaneum and Pompeii (begun in 1738 and 1755 respectively), most of those arriving in Naples simply enjoyed themselves. They reveled in the Mediterranean climate and the exotic and colorful local coastal villages. Many also enjoyed the hospitality of William Hamilton, the British ambassador there from 1764 to 1800, who was known for his entertaining as well as for his beautiful wife, Emma, who later became the mistress of Admiral Horatio Nelson.

The tradition of the Grand Tour came to an abrupt halt with the French Revolution and the Napoleonic Wars. Europe had become far too dangerous. By the time that peace returned in 1815, the Grand Tour was essentially a thing of the past. What remained was the idea of travel for enlightenment and pleasure, which, with the advances in technology in the 19th century, would lead to the expansion of "tourism."

IN CONTEXT

Building on the Grand Tour

As well as the tangible acquisitions made on the Grand Tour, there were also intangibles: new ways of thinking about history, civilization, aesthetics, and, especially, architecture. Time spent in Italy, in particular, engendered an appreciation of Classical architectural forms, especially the work of 16th-century Venetian architect Andrea Palladio. In his book *Italian Journey*, Johann Wolfgang von Goethe describes Palladio's unfinished Convent of Saint Maria della Carità in Bologna as the most perfect work of architecture. In England, aristocrats applied what they learned in Italy to their own country houses and gardens, inspiring a movement known as Palladianism, which evolved into Neoclassicism. The influence of Palladio even spread to America: Thomas Jefferson was an admirer, and the US Capitol building was inspired by Palladio's work.

THE NEOCLASSICAL CAPITOL BUILDING, WASHINGTON, D.C.

First flight

In 1783, man's dream of flying was finally realized when hot air and hydrogen balloons were invented. These liberated people from what Victor Hugo called "the ancient, universal tyranny of gravity."

◁ **The birth of modern ballooning**
The balloon designed by the Robert brothers, shown here taking off from the Tuileries, was filled with hydrogen and had a valve in the crown to release gas for the descent.

The year 1783 was a milestone for sheep, ducks, and roosters. That September, one of each of these animals was secured in a basket and sent aloft above the Palace of Versailles in a hot air balloon. The escapade lasted eight minutes—then the balloon came down in some woods a few miles away. The three, possibly bemused creatures had just taken the first ever passenger flight. The animals did not seem to be harmed by the experience, so two months later, on November 21, 1783, two French men, Jean-François Pilâtre de Rozier, a young Parisian doctor, and the Marquis d'Arlandes, a military officer, undertook the world's first untethered hot air balloon voyage, ascending from the outskirts of Paris and traveling nearly 6 miles (9 km).

▷ **Balloon game**
Ballooning was something of a craze in the late 18th century, as can be seen in this c. 1784 French game. The illustrations of different early balloons include those made by the Montgolfier and Robert brothers.

An unpredictable ride

Both of these balloons had been built by the Montgolfier brothers, world pioneers in the field of aviation. The brothers, Joseph-Michel and Jacques-Étienne, came from a family of papermakers. Not coincidentally, their prototype balloons were made of layers of paper, covered by buttoned-together sackcloth. The brothers described their creation as "putting a cloud in a paper bag." The balloons that carried the animals and humans aloft were grander affairs of silklike taffeta, gloriously decorated with designs by wallpaper manufacturer Jean-Baptiste Réveillon.

Just 10 days after the Montgolfier's manned flight, on December 1, 1783, another pair of French brothers, *les frères* Robert, launched the world's first manned hydrogen balloon. A reported 400,000 spectators watched it rise from the Tuileries Gardens in Paris, including Benjamin Franklin, the great inventor and the diplomatic representative of the United States.

The following year, the Robert brothers attempted to tackle a major deficiency of the balloon—the fact that it would only go where the wind blew it—by making one that was elliptical and, it was hoped, could be steered with oars and umbrellas. The experiment was not a success. Other flights achieved better results, however. In 1785, for example, when the wind was blowing in the right direction, a Franco-American team successfully ballooned across the English Channel. Unfortunately, Pilâtre de Rozier had died attempting the same trip just a few months earlier, making him one of the first air-crash fatalities.

▽ **The first manned flight**
This painting shows Jean-François Pilâtre de Rozier and the Marquis d'Arlandes becoming the first people to fly. Their hot air balloon had been designed by the Montgolfier brothers.

A specialist role

This unpredictability meant that the balloon had little future as a means of public transportation, but its value

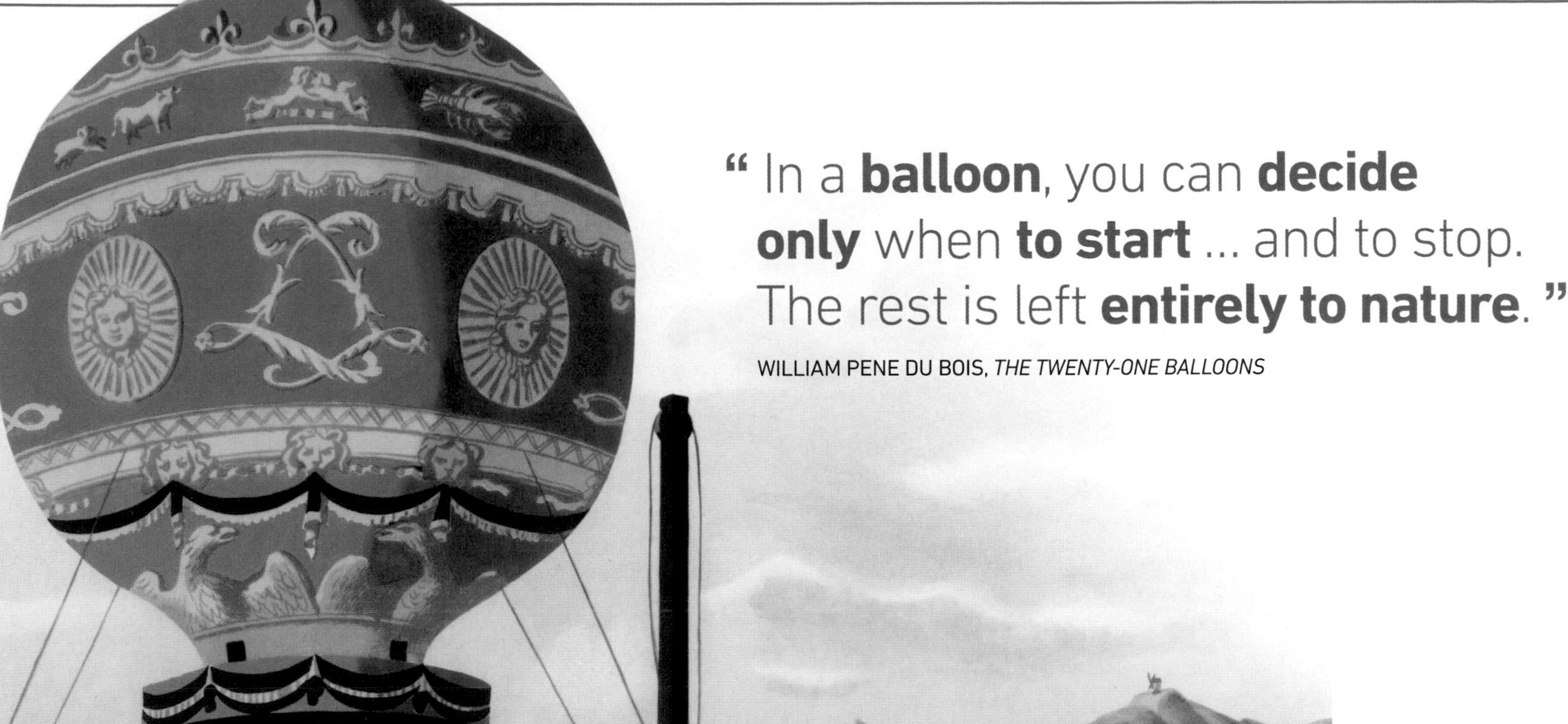

> “ In a **balloon**, you can **decide only** when **to start** ... and to stop. The rest is left **entirely to nature**. ”
>
> WILLIAM PENE DU BOIS, *THE TWENTY-ONE BALLOONS*

was recognized in other fields. During the American Civil War, the Union Army deployed a corps of balloons to spy on enemy positions, and in 1870–71, more than 60 balloons managed to fly away from Paris during the siege of the city by the Prussians.

Balloonists pioneered the science of meteorology, taking airborne readings and discovering from experience the limits of human endurance, including the effects of frostbite. This became pertinent when balloons were used in a tragic attempt to reach the North Pole in 1897. The novelist Victor Hugo even believed in the political power of the balloon, claiming that it had not only freed people from the effects of gravity but could go on to play a role in “the liberation of all mankind.”

Even if ultimately the balloon proved to be of limited use, it did provide the first ever aerial view of the world—one that showed the curvature of the Earth, the patterns of the landscape below, and the extent of man’s impact upon it. It had been thought that the balloon would reveal the secrets of the heavens, but instead, it revealed the secrets of the world below.

▽ **Polar tragedy**
In 1897, Swedish explorer S. A. Andrée attempted to reach the North Pole by hydrogen balloon. The balloon came down, as seen here, and its passengers soon perished.

Bound for Botany Bay

In 1787, the British Government attempted a new experiment—sending a fleet halfway around the world to turn an unexplored continent into a penal colony. In doing so, it laid the foundations for a new country.

▽ **Arthur Phillip**
A Royal Navy admiral when he founded the penal colony that later became the city of Sydney, Arthur Phillip was appointed the first Governor of New South Wales.

On December 13, 1786, Francis Fowkes appeared before a judge at the Old Bailey, London's central criminal court, accused of stealing a coat and a pair of men's boots from a tavern in Covent Garden. He was pronounced guilty. The sentence was severe: he was to be "transported for seven years."

Exile overseas

To be "transported" meant being sent into exile. In the second half of the 18th century, crime in Britain was rampant, as there was no professional police force. Transportation was an attempt to purge the country of petty criminals by packing them off to serve their sentences in a distant penal colony (perpetrators of more serious crimes were simply executed). Until then, the British had used North America for this, but the 1775–83 American War of Independence eliminated that option.

Of the possible alternatives, the east coast of New Holland, recently visited and mapped by Cook's expedition (see pp. 172–75), was deemed the most suitable, and a colonization party was duly sent forth in 11 ships under the command of Admiral Arthur Phillip. This "First Fleet" left Portsmouth on May 13, 1787, and sailed, via Rio de Janeiro and Cape Town, the 15,900 miles (25,588 km) to its destination of Botany Bay, where it arrived on January 20, 1788.

△ **Native inhabitants**
On landing, the naval officers were shown where to find water by local Aboriginals. Thereafter, relations swung between cooperation and armed conflict.

▽ **Port Macquarie Penal Station**
Established in 1822, this isolated island colony, in what is now Tasmania, took the worst convicts and those who had escaped from other settlements on the mainland.

> **“From rectitude’s path we did stray, So they shipped us across the salt ocean, To do time at Botany Bay.”**

PART OF THE AUSTRALIAN FOLK SONG, *PINK ’UN*, 1886

△ **Port Jackson**
A 1788 map drawn by Francis Fowkes, one of the first convict settlers, shows the origins of Sydney. The remains of the Governor’s Mansion (the large red building) can still be visited today.

Botany Bay was swiftly judged unsuitable for settlement, and after some reconnoitering, the fleet moved to Port Jackson, a more promising bay a little further to the north, which had been charted by Cook. This became the site of the first permanent European colony on Australian soil.

△ **Manacles from Port Arthur**
By the time Britain stopped penal shipments in 1868, around 164,000 convicts had been sent to Australia.

Convict settlers

Among the 732 convict settlers, accompanied by 247 marines and their families, was the unfortunate Francis Fowkes. He had considerable skill as an artist and produced a hand-drawn map of the new colony that illustrates the very beginnings of the new state and what would become its capital city, Sydney.

Many of the new settlers died in the early days as they struggled to grow enough food to feed themselves, but their diminishing numbers were replenished by waves of new arrivals. Two more convict fleets arrived in 1790 and 1791, and the first free settlers arrived in 1793.

The last convicts

By the mid-1800s, convicts were also being sent to other newly founded colonies in Australia, including Port Macquarie and Moreton Bay further up the east coast, Van Diemen’s Land (modern-day Tasmania), western Australia, and tiny Norfolk Island in the South Pacific. The vast majority of the convicts sent to Australia were English, Welsh, and Irish, but some were also sent from British outposts such as India, Canada, and Hong Kong. Of those transported between 1788 and 1852, around one in seven were women. Good behavior qualified a convict for a “ticket of leave,” which was, in effect, the freedom to live independently and earn a living in Australia, or to return to Britain if they so wished.

By the time of the last shipment of criminals in 1868, roughly 164,000 men and women had been transported. The total population of the colonies was now around one million and they were completely self-sustaining. The convicts had served their purpose.

IN CONTEXT
Ten Pound Poms

After World War II, Australia needed workers for the country’s booming industries. The government subsidized the cost of traveling for emigrants from Great Britain, charging them only £10 for the fare and promising employment. Many were only too happy to seize the opportunity of an escape from post-war austerity, and as a result, the scheme attracted more than one million migrants from Great Britain to Australia from 1945 to 1972. The scheme was also extended to migrants from other countries, including Italy and Greece.

POSTER FOR AN AUSTRALIAN GOVERNMENT SCHEME PROMOTING IMMIGRATION, 1957

BENSON
LONDON TIME

THE
AGE
STEAM
OF
1800—1900
18 201

THE AGE OF STEAM, 1800–1900

Introduction

The 19th century was an age of wonder. The achievements of mankind seemed boundless: iron towers reached to the heavens; vast factories thrummed with power; electricity lit up cities. But of all the inventions of the industrial age, the harnessing of steam had the most profound impact. Steam drove the engines that powered the factories, which created the wealth that enabled the colonial powers of Europe to extend their reach ever deeper into Africa, Asia, and Australia. In these far-flung lands they harvested and mined raw materials that were then sent back to feed the factories and add to the wealth of the nations. Britain, France, and numerous other countries dispatched explorers to blaze trails through deserts and jungles, and sail up mighty rivers, such as the Mekong, the Niger, and the Nile, in search of further treasures.

By this time, America had emerged victorious from a war of independence in which it had shrugged off the rule of the British. It was now engaged in exploring, consolidating, and exploiting its own ever-expanding territories, which had various riches in abundance. In California, for example, a wealth of gold was discovered in 1849, prompting thousands of Americans to migrate to the West Coast.

Iron roads

Steam trains and steam ships revolutionized the economies of Europe. In America, the effect was even greater. River steamers opened up swaths of territory in the Midwest to settlement, while the completion of the first transcontinental railway line in 1869 literally bound the new nation together. Most importantly, steam travel was fast.

NAPOLEON'S EXPEDITION TO EGYPT IN 1798 PROMPTED MANY TO EXPLORE THE NILE RIVER

THE FIRST COMMERCIAL STEAMBOAT, *CLERMONT*, TOOK TO THE HUDSON IN 1807

THE FIRST COMMERCIAL STEAM TRAIN OPENED BETWEEN LIVERPOOL AND MANCHESTER IN 1830

> " The prejudices which **ignorance has engendered** are **broken by the roar of the train** and the whistle of the engine awakens thousands from **the slumber of ages**. "
>
> THOMAS COOK, 1846

A journey from the Atlantic to the Pacific used to take months; now it took days. In Europe, this opened up new travel possibilities for a growing class of people with the money and leisure time to indulge themselves. Few people could spare the months that were previously needed to tour the Continent, but with railways connecting nearly every country in Europe, the trip could be made in a matter of weeks. And as Napoleon's armies had occupied and exhaustively documented Egypt, many people took steamers from Italy and followed the general's footsteps up the Nile.

Inspiration for such journeys came from poets and novelists who rhapsodized over the romance of southern climes, ancient ruins, and untamed landscapes. Many early travelers also went with journal in hand, and returned home to add their own accounts to the rapidly proliferating library of 19th-century travel literature. These included Isabella Bird and Charles Dickens in Europe, and Washington Irving and Mark Twain in America.

The business of travel

By the mid-19th century, the desire to travel was such that several shrewd entrepreneurs spotted the potential for a profitable business. Grand new hotels and railway stations were built in major cities, and in 1841, Thomas Cook launched his eponymous tour company, initially in the hope that offering people day trips would broaden their horizons. Not long afterward, Messrs. Murray and Baedeker became wealthy pioneers in the guidebook business. By the end of the century, there were few places in the world that Thomas Cook & Son did not take people, or to which Karl Baedeker did not publish a guide.

ROMANTIC POET PERCY BYSSHE SHELLEY INSPIRED MANY TO MAKE A TOUR OF EUROPE

THE DISCOVERY OF GOLD IN SAN FRANCISCO DREW THOUSANDS OF IMMIGRANTS TO CALIFORNIA

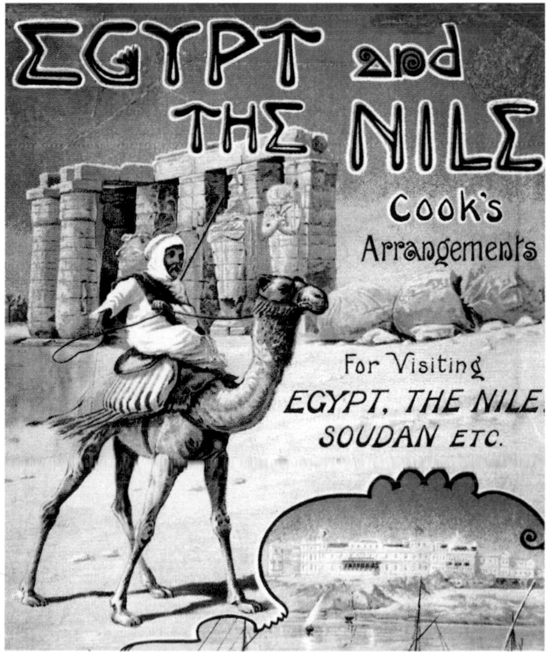

ENTREPRENEURS THOMAS COOK & SON BROUGHT VACATIONS TO THE MASSES

Humboldt at work
This portrait, made by Friedrich Georg Weitsch in 1806, shows the explorer at the age of 37. He had made his survey of South America, but was yet to make his epic crossing of Russia.

NATURALIST, 1769–1859

Alexander von Humboldt

Charles Darwin called him the "greatest scientific traveler who ever lived" and he has more plants, animals, minerals, and places named after him than anyone else, but Alexander von Humboldt's most significant contribution of all may be as the first prophet of climate change.

That there is a Humboldt lily, a Humboldt crater on the Moon, and a Humboldt squid that swims in the cold Humboldt Current off the coast of Peru indicates the breadth of interests pursued by the polyglot genius who was born in Berlin in 1769. The second child of an aristocratic Prussian family, he lost his father when he was nine, and had a cold and distant mother. He sought solace in collecting plants, insects, and rocks.

Sent away to college to study finance, Humboldt met Georg Forster, a naturalist who had accompanied Captain Cook on his second voyage (see pp. 172–75). The two traveled to Europe where Humboldt met another of Cook's scientific compatriots, Sir Joseph Banks, with whom he developed a close friendship.

After college, Humboldt became an inspector in the Ministry of Mines, which allowed him to indulge his interest in geology. It was not until his mother's death in 1796, when he inherited a windfall, that he was properly able to pursue his wider scientific interests.

◁ **Mount Chimborazo** Humboldt's 1807 drawing of this volcano in Ecuador showed for the first time how different zones of vegetation are linked to altitude and temperature.

Latin American expedition

In 1799, Humboldt set off for South America with botanist Aime Bonpland. Landing in what is now Venezuela, they canoed up rivers, trekked through the rainforest, and scaled some of the highest peaks in the Andes. In her 2015 biography *The Invention of Nature*, Andrea Wulf portrays Humboldt as insanely intrepid: trekking barefoot when his shoes disintegrated; swimming in crocodile-infested waters; and conducting experiments on electric eels bare-handed.

In the course of his adventures, Humboldt kept detailed journals and measured everything he could, from rainfall levels and soil composition to the blueness of the sky. He identified 2,000 new plant species and crossed the magnetic equator. While on Mount Chimborazo in today's Ecuador, he was struck by the idea that the Earth was one single great living organism in which everything is connected. He also reasoned that by disrupting this natural order, man might bring about catastrophe—a message so far ahead of its time that many still have trouble accepting it even today.

Returning to Europe, he wrote a monumental 30-volume account of his findings. It was this work that introduced Charles Darwin to the idea of scientific exploration. When he boarded the *Beagle* on his own voyage of discovery in 1831, Darwin took with him seven volumes of Humboldt's work.

Crossing Russia

Most scientists would be content to devote themselves to a lifetime studying the fruits of such an extended trip (Humboldt returned with 60,000 specimens), but the Prussian was not one to sit still.

In 1829, at the age of 59, he embarked on a six-month expedition to the Ural Mountains and Siberia. When he died, aged 90, his funeral in Berlin drew tens of thousands of mourners, and American newspapers lamented the end of the "Age of Humboldt."

◁ **Humboldt penguin** This South American penguin is named after the icy cold current in which it swims, itself named after Humboldt.

KEY DATES

- **1769** Born September 14 in Berlin.
- **1799** Sails from Spain to what is now Venezuela in the company of botanist Aimé Bonpland.
- **1800** Sails to Cuba, with Bonpland, where they conduct scientific surveys for three months.
- **1804** Travels to the United States and has an audience with President Jefferson.
- **1814** Publication in English of the first volume of the *Personal Narrative of Travels to the Equinoctial Regions of the New Continent.*

HUMBOLDT'S DRAWING OF *MELASTOMATACEAE*

- **1829** Crosses almost 10,000 miles (16,100 km) of Russia in six months.
- **1845** Publication of the first volume of *Cosmos*, a multi-part work that drew on all of Humboldt's observations to propose that the Earth is a living organism. James Lovelock's famous Gaia theory, formulated in the 1960s, bears remarkable similarities.

HUMBOLDT IN HIS STUDIO, PAINTED BY EDUARD HILDEBRANDT IN 1845

Rediscovering Egypt

In 1798, a failed invasion of Egypt led by Napoleon Bonaparte of France fired up European and American passions for the wonders of a forgotten ancient civilization.

The French First Republic had been at war with Britain and several other European monarchies since 1792. The territory of Egypt was shortly to become a pawn in this game of empires. Napoleon and his advisors saw that by occupying this distant province of the declining Ottoman Empire, they could divide Britain from its colonial interests in India.

▽ **An ancient world**
An illustration from the *Description de l'Égypte*, a collection of observations made by scholars during Napoleon's expedition to Egypt, shows the portico of the Temple of Isis on Philae.

The French occupation

On July 1, 1798, some 40,000 soldiers of the Armée d'Orient put ashore at Alexandria, on Egypt's Mediterranean coast. The occupation was not a success. Early victories against Egyptian forces on land, including the capture of Cairo, were undermined by the British sinking the French fleet at its moorings. Now stranded in Egypt, the French army had to combat local insurgents who were aided and abetted by the British and the Ottoman Turks. Napoleon secretly fled back to France in October 1799. His abandoned and subsequently defeated army was repatriated by the British two years later.

What might be regarded as an inglorious episode was, in time, more than redeemed by the efforts of over 160 scholars, scientists, engineers, botanists, cartographers, and artists who had travelled with Napoleon to Egypt. Their mission was twofold: to bring European Enlightenment ideas, such as liberty and progress, to Egypt, and to study a country which, until then, had only had minimal contact with the West. They were sent out to survey and document all that they saw, both ancient and modern, and to gather specimens and artifacts. It was a mission that represents the greatest scientific undertaking of its kind, the painstaking documentation and categorization of an entire land and its people. It also stands as perhaps the most extreme expression of the colonial impulse to catalogue acquired possessions.

△ **Egyptian fountain**
Napoleon's Egyptian campaign inspired many artists to explore ancient Egyptian styles. This neo-Egyptian statue at 52 rue de Sèvres, Paris, was made by sculptor Pierre-Nicolas Beauvallet in 1806.

Description de l'Égypte

The results were gathered in the encyclopedic *Description de l'Égypte*, which ran to 23 outsize volumes, published in 1809–29. At the same time, one of the artifacts found by

▷ **Rosetta Stone**
Found in 1799, the Rosetta Stone is a rock stele on which a decree was inscribed in 196 BCE on behalf of King Ptolemy V of Egypt. The decree was written in three scripts, the comparison of which gave modern scholars the key to understanding Egyptian hieroglyphs.

the French in Egypt, a stele containing an inscription in three languages, provided the key for a young French scholar, Jean-François Champollion, to finally unlock the code of the ancient Egyptian script known as hieroglyphics. Together, these laid the foundations for the science of Egyptology, and sparked a fascination in Europe and America for all things Egyptian and Oriental.

For the remainder of the 19th century, what is now the Middle East (but was then better known as the Near East) became an extension of the Grand Tour. Travelers were now given license to push on from Italy and cross the Mediterranean to Constantinople (now Istanbul), Jaffa in Palestine, and Alexandria in Egypt. The sense of awe engendered by such a journey was perfectly captured by the English poet Percy Bysshe Shelley in his sonnet *Ozymandias,* with its famous opening line: "I met a traveler from an antique land." Further discoveries were soon to follow, including the discovery of the great temple of Rameses II (Shelley's Ozymandias) at Abu Simbel, and, in neighboring Jordan, the rediscovery of the rock-hewn Nabataean city of Petra.

Egyptian-inspired architecture and decoration became popular across Europe and the US. The Americans even named two new settlements after Egypt's ancient and medieval capitals: Cairo, Illinois, founded in 1817, and Memphis, Tennessee, established in 1819. The fascination proved enduring, peaking in 1922 with the discovery of the tomb of Tutankhamun.

IN CONTEXT
Stocking national museums

The study of ancient artifacts took a great leap forward in the 18th century with the creation of large national museums, notably the British Museum in London in 1759 and then the Louvre in Paris in 1793. Egypt was ruthlessly plundered to help stock such institutions. Many antiquities collected by the French were seized by the British Navy and ended up in the British Museum, including the Rosetta Stone. Treasure hunters continued to cart off whatever they could transport, making a tidy profit by selling them off to the cultural institutions of Europe and then, later, North America.

A HEAD OF RAMESES II IS ROLLED TO THE NILE, EN ROUTE TO BRITAIN, IN 1815

▷ **Napoleon before the sphinx**
The French campaign in Egypt was an attempt by Napoleon Bonaparte, depicted in this painting by Jean-Léon Gérôme c.1858, to obstruct Britain's access to India.

" From the **heights** of these **pyramids, forty centuries** look **down** on us. "

NAPOLEON, IN A SPEECH TO HIS TROOPS BEFORE BATTLE, JULY 21, 1798

Painting the East

Throughout the 19th century, the lands of the Orient provided a rich profusion of exotic subjects for artists of the Western world.

The Orient—which includes Turkey, North Africa, and the present-day Middle East—had been exerting its charm on Western artists long before Napoleon landed in Egypt (see pp. 194–95). However, the French expedition certainly increased the fascination with the Orient. Among the painters subsequently inspired were Scotsman David Roberts and Englishman John Frederick Lewis, who captured the region's archeology and architecture in the 1830s and '40s, respectively. Others, such as French Romantic artist Eugène Delacroix, who traveled to Spain and North Africa in 1832, shortly after the French had conquered Algeria, were fascinated by the people and their dress. For Delacroix, the Arabs evoked an earlier, purer age: "The Greeks and Romans are here at my door, in the Arabs who wrap themselves in a white blanket and look like Cato or Brutus."

Other artists went further in their imaginings. The associations between the Bible and the Orient were important for artists such as William Holman Hunt and David Wilkie, who traveled to find authentic settings for their biblical paintings. Jean-Léon Gérôme, who undertook numerous trips to the eastern Mediterranean in the second half of the 19th century, painted large, theatrical canvases redolent with sensuality and violence. However, these were usually made back in his Paris studio with the aid of models and props, resulting in a realistic style of painting that suggested an unwarranted accuracy. One scene he surely never witnessed was a women's bathhouse, a subject that he painted more than once, complete with nude concubines. He was not alone in his fantasy: in 1862, for example, the highly respected French neoclassical painter Jean-Auguste-Dominique Ingres produced his erotic ideal in *The Turkish Bath*, and he had never even visited the East.

The taste for Orientalism—as this style of painting would come to be known, particularly in its more lurid form—remained into the 20th century, with artists including Paul Klee, Henri Matisse, and Auguste Renoir taking up its themes. The genre came under attack in the 1970s from cultural critic Edward Said, who saw such paintings as a means of exerting Western authority over Arab culture. Ironically, some of the biggest collectors of Orientalist work today come from the Arab world.

◁ ***The Midday Meal, Cairo***
John Frederick Lewis lived in Cairo from 1841–51. On his return to England, he continued to paint scenes of the city, including this peaceful composition of 1875.

Charting the American West

In 1804, Meriwether Lewis and William Clark were sent to find a route across the central United States to the Pacific, creating a pathway for the new nation to spread westward from ocean to ocean.

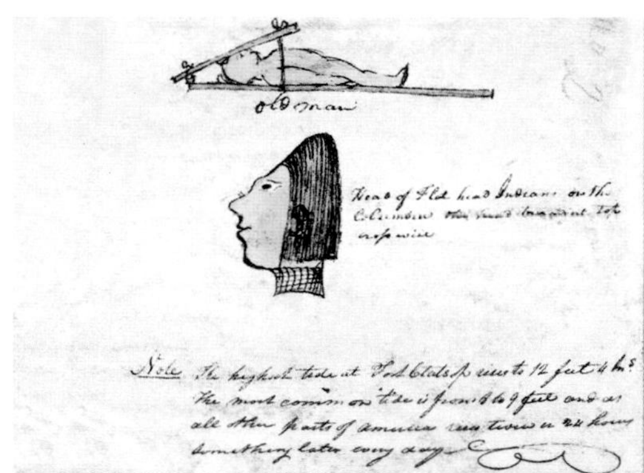

▷ **Flathead Indians**
Sketches in William Clark's diary show the practice among some Native American tribes of altering the shape of their heads by pressing their skulls during infancy.

▷ **Expedition journal**
A reproduction of William Clark's diary shows the detail with which he documented the expedition. Thanks to his and Lewis's observations, their adventure became a founding tale of the young United States.

In the first years of the 19th century, North America was roughly divided into thirds: the eastern third was the territory of the fledgling United States, the middle third was owned by France, and the western third was Spanish, apart from a region to the northwest, bordering the Pacific and Canada, which was unclaimed. In 1803, President Thomas Jefferson negotiated the purchase of the whole of what was known as the Louisiana Territory from France's Emperor Napoleon, effectively doubling the size of the United States.

Jefferson immediately commissioned a survey party to explore the new territory, as well as the unclaimed lands beyond the "great rock mountains" in the west. The hope was that a river route could be found to connect the Mississippi with the Pacific beyond the mountains, making it possible to open the land for settlement.

The Lewis and Clark expedition

Jefferson appointed his personal secretary, Meriwether Lewis, a man who combined learning with frontier skills, as expedition leader, and selected another frontiersman, William Clark, to help him. Together they assembled a team of 33 men, and in May 1804, this "Corps of Discovery" began to make its way up the Missouri River in a fleet of three boats. They traveled all summer until the first snowfall, then put ashore and built a fort, Fort Mandan, in which they could wait out winter. These were potentially hostile lands, where no non-Native American had ever ventured, so the expedition hired as an interpreter and guide Toussaint Charbonneau, a French-Canadian fur trapper, and his Shoshone Native American wife, Sacagawea.

In spring 1805, when the ice on the Missouri broke, the expedition resumed. In the last week of May, the party had its first sighting of the Rockies, the great mountains that it would have to cross. On June 13, it reached what Lewis described as "the grandest sight I ever beheld"—the Great Falls of the Missouri River, an obstacle that would take a month to pass. At the foot of the Rockies they encountered the Shoshone tribe, with whom they bartered for the horses necessary to cross the mountains. It was an arduous journey, during which the expedition had to resort to eating three of the animals. Eventually, they descended to the banks of the Clearwater River. The Rockies were behind them, the Pacific Ocean in front.

> " **Ocian in view!** O! the **Joy**... This **great Pacific Octean** which we been **So long anxious** to **See.** "
>
> WILLIAM CLARK, ON GLIMPSING THE PACIFIC OCEAN, NOVEMBER 7, 1805

▷ **American odyssey**
Lewis and Clark traveled 8,000 miles (12,000 km) by boat, on foot, and on horseback. For part of the return trip they split up to explore more territory.

To the Pacific and back

On November 7, 1805, Clark wrote in his journal, "Ocian in view! O! the Joy," although in fact, they were at the estuary of the Columbia, still 20 miles (32 km) from the coast. By mid-November, however, they had made it to the Pacific. They spent the winter there, building Fort Clatsop, named after the local Clatsop tribe, and by the third week in March the expedition was ready to retrace its steps and journey back across the continent.

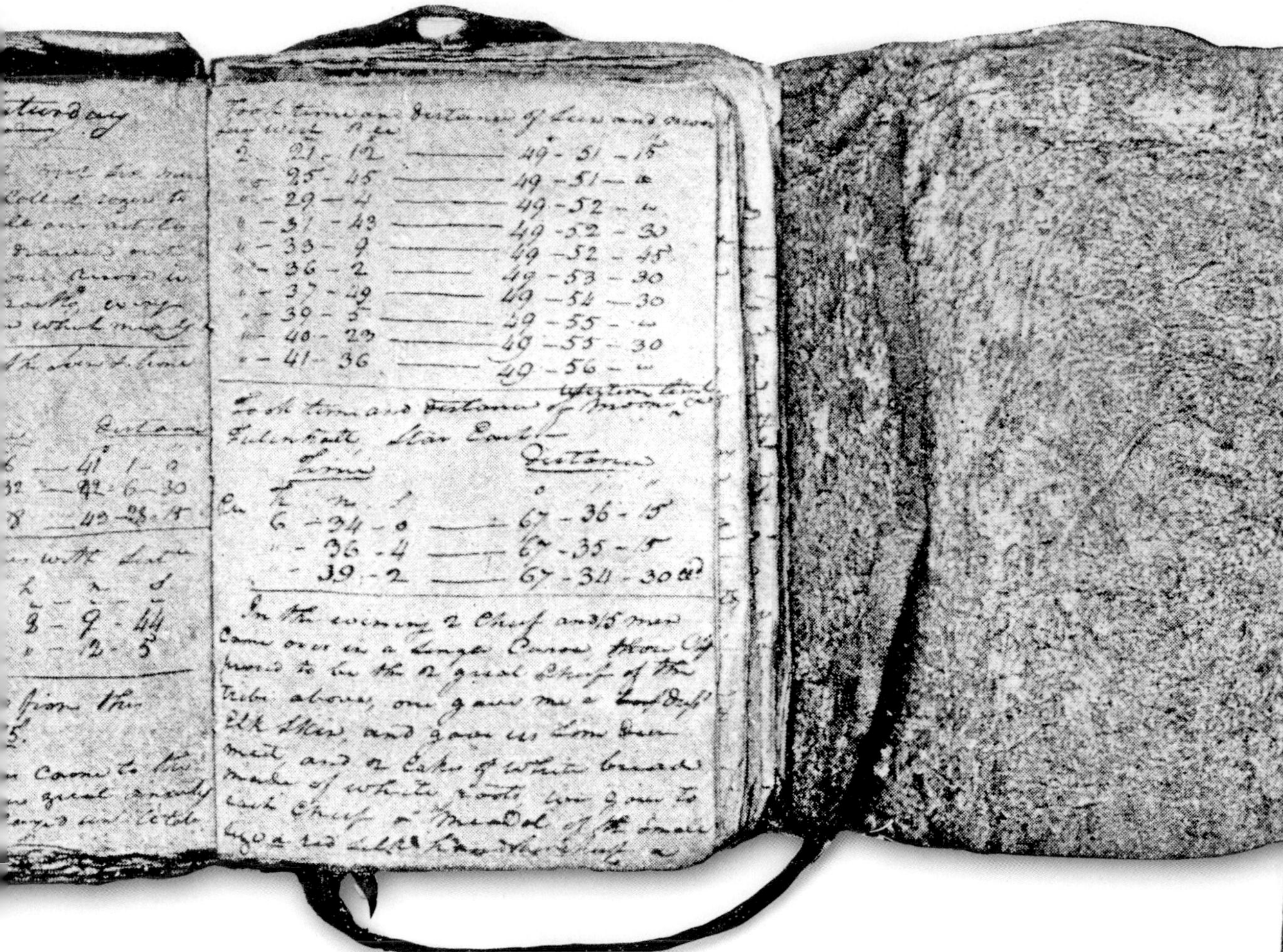

On the morning of September 23, 1806, Lewis and Clark arrived back at their starting point of St. Louis, two years, four months, and 10 days after they had left. They had been feared dead, and over a thousand people greeted their return. With them they carried records of their contact with the Native Americans, maps drawn by Clark, and information on over 300 species of new flora and fauna. Over the forthcoming decades, thousands of Americans followed their lead and crossed the central and western portions of the US, transforming the landscape, displacing wildlife, and corraling the native tribes into reservations.

▽ **Heading west**
The Corps of Discovery sets up camp beside the Columbia River. Charbonneau and Sacagawea (carrying their son Jean-Baptiste) stand behind Lewis and Clark, who study the land ahead.

IN CONTEXT
The Lewis and Clark Trail

Today, a series of marked highways, that mostly run parallel to the Missouri and Columbia rivers, serves as an official Lewis and Clark Trail. More in keeping with the original spirit of adventure is the Lewis and Clark National Historic Trail, which is part of the National Trails System, and extends some 3,700 miles (6,000 km) from Wood River, Illinois, to the mouth of the Columbia River in Oregon. Administered by the National Park Service, it provides opportunities for hiking, canoeing, and horse riding. The most unchanged part is the White Cliffs section of the Missouri River in north-central Montana, a protected area only accessible by boat. For Lewis, the sandstone formations here afforded "scenes of visionary enchantment."

FORT MANDAN, THE WINTER HOME OF THE CORPS OF DISCOVERY IN 1804–05

△ **Salmon trout**
This sketch of a white salmon trout by Clark shows the detail with which the expedition catalogued its findings. The picture is surrounded by a transcript of Lewis's diary entries.

Go west, young man!

In the wake of Lewis and Clark, ever greater numbers of Americans began to migrate west, following an arduous and often deadly route that would enter history as the Oregon Trail.

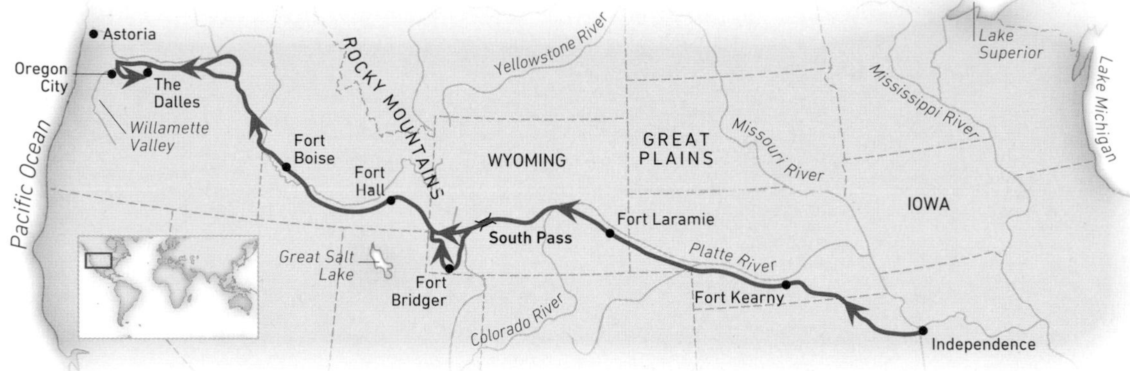

△ **Emigration route**
The route of the Oregon Trail stretches some 2,170 miles (3,490 km) from the town of Independence, Missouri, to the Willamette Valley, Oregon, in the west.

The oft-quoted phrase at the top of this page (usually attributed to newspaper man Horace Greeley) may not have been uttered until the middle of the 19th century, but a route from established settlements in the Midwest to valleys in Oregon was laid by fur trappers and traders between 1810 and 1820. John Jacob Astor, who would become the US's first multimillionaire and the owner of swaths of real estate in New York City, established a fur trading post that he called Astoria on the West Coast in 1811. His agent, Robert Stuart, located the South Pass, which provided a navigable route through the Rockies.

Early emigrants

By the 1830s, the trappers and traders were being joined by missionary groups, who sent back word of the northwest's agricultural potential. The US did not have sovereignty over the territory of Oregon at this time, but settlers were finding it difficult back east, hit hard by economic depression and diseases such as malaria. In 1839, a group set out from Peoria, Illinois, to claim Oregon country on behalf of the US government, and the following year, two families became the first pioneers to make the journey west in wagons. Further wagon trains set out in 1841 and 1842, to follow what the pioneers were now calling the Oregon Trail. In May 1843, in what is known as the Great Migration, a massive wagon train with up to a thousand emigrants, plus cattle, departed from Independence, Missouri, beginning a journey that would end that August in the Willamette Valley, Oregon. Hundreds of thousands more would follow, especially after gold was discovered in California in 1848.

The Oregon Trail

The first section of the 2,170-mile (3,490-km) trail ran through the rolling country of the Great Plains. Obstacles were few, but just a day or two of heavy rain could turn the land into a quagmire and render rivers impassable. In summer, water sources dried up, while snow could close passages through the mountains in winter. Some experienced starvation when they brought insufficient food

◁ **A child's shoes**
Guilford and Catherine Barnard traveled the Oregon Trail in 1852. These hand-made shoes belonged to their two-year-old son, Landy, who died along the trail and was buried in Kansas.

◁ **Journey's end**
For many, the sight of Mount Hood, in northwest Oregon, signaled that their journey was nearly over. This view of the mountain from Barlow Cutoff was painted by W. H. Jackson in 1865.

supplies and found it impossible to live off the land. The most dreaded danger was cholera, which claimed many lives. In total, it is thought that at least 20,000 people died along the Oregon Trail. According to the historian Hiram Chittenden: "The Trail was strewn with abandoned property, the skeletons of horses and oxen, and with freshly made mounds and headboards that told a pitiful tale."

On crossing the mountains, the trail became increasingly difficult, with steep ascents and descents over rocky terrain. The pioneers also risked injury from overturned and runaway wagons. There might have been some celebration at South Pass, which was the natural crossing point of the Rockies, from where the land dipped toward the Pacific, but hundreds of miles still lay between there and the wagoners' final goal.

Although traffic declined after 1869, when the Transcontinental Railroad was completed (see pp. 236–37), around 300,000–500,000 people made the four-to-six-month journey. It is small wonder that even today, ruts from the wagon wheels remain etched into the soil of the Midwestern landscape.

> “ **Keep traveling**! If it is only a few miles a day. **Keep moving**. ”
>
> MARCUS WHITMAN, AMERICAN MISSIONARY AND DOCTOR

▽ **Taking a break**
Travelers set up camp beside their wagons, somewhere along the Oregon Trail, c.1890.

IN CONTEXT
Carved in stone

Of the many natural landmarks that served as navigation aids to those on the Oregon Trail, including Courthouse Rock, Chimney Rock, and Scotts Bluff, there is one in particular that has great resonance. A popular campsite for the emigrants traveling along the Sweetwater River in Wyoming was next to a vast, whale-shaped, granite outcrop known as Independence Rock. It was so-called because the schedules of many wagon trains brought them to this place around the Fourth of July. Many of those passing by left their names or initials chiseled into the rock, many of which remain clear and legible to this day.

INDEPENDENCE ROCK, BY THE SWEETWATER RIVER, ON THE OREGON TRAIL, WYOMING

Full steam ahead

After the wheel, the greatest revolution in the way humans traveled came with the exploitation of the power of steam. It delivered the potential to travel further, faster, and in greater numbers than ever before.

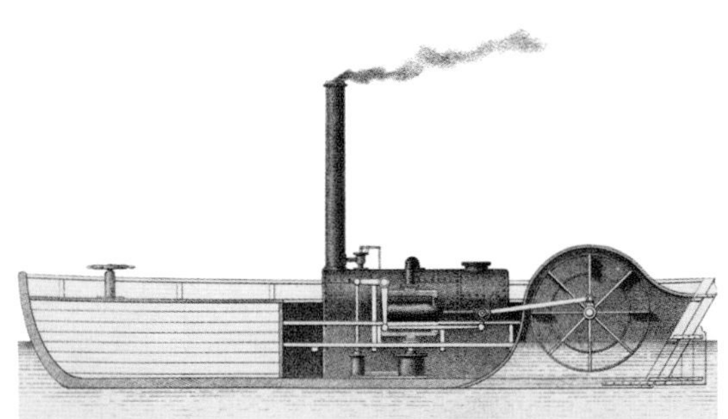

△ **Charlotte Dundas**
A lithograph by C. F. Cheffins shows the mechanics of the *Charlotte Dundas*—brainchild of the steam pioneer William Symington.

On the afternoon of August 17, 1807, a strange-looking vessel, long and sitting low in the water, pulled away from its moorings on the East River off Greenwich Village in New York. As it did so, clouds of smoke billowed out of a chimney set amidships, and two large paddlewheels mounted on the boat's sides began to turn and churn the water. Aboard was Robert Fulton, a former portrait painter who had designed the boat, his patron Robert Livingstone, and a group of their friends. The boat, with the odd hiccup, sailed on up the Hudson River at a speed of about 5 mph (8 kph), reaching Albany, which lay 150 miles (240 km) to the north, the following day. There, it took on two paying passengers and began its return voyage to New York.

◁ **Racing on the Mississippi River**
Steamboats *Baltic* and *Diana* run neck and neck during a race in 1858, as depicted by George F. Fuller.

◁ **Historic voyage**
Robert Fulton's *Clermont* makes its maiden voyage—a 150-mile (240-km) trip from New York to Albany. Built with the backing of Robert Livingstone, it was the first ever steamboat to see commercial service.

Beginnings of the steamboat

The vessel was called the *Clermont*, but although historic, it was not the first ever steamboat. As early as 1787, Fulton's fellow American John Fitch had sailed a steamboat on the Delaware River, and in 1803, Scottish engineer William Symington had built and sailed the *Charlotte Dundas* on the Forth and Clyde Canal, towing two barges. What Fulton proved, however, was that the steamboat was in fact a commercially viable and technically superior alternative to sailing.

At the age of 21, Fulton had taken himself off to London and Paris, which were then the centers of the scientific world, to learn more about canals and the recently invented steam engine. While in France, he designed the first working submarine, the *Nautilus*, and in Britain, he pioneered designs of naval mines for the Royal Navy. He returned to the US with an English steam engine, which he adapted for the *Clermont*, and after his first successful trial, Fulton's boat made trips between New York and Albany every four days, sometimes carrying as many as a hundred passengers.

The Mississippi riverboats

Together with Livingstone and Nicholas Roosevelt, Fulton designed a new steamboat, which they called the *New Orleans*. In 1811–12, they sailed it from Pittsburgh in Pennsylvania along the Ohio and Mississippi rivers, all the way to the boat's namesake city on the Gulf of Mexico. The impact of this was enormous. Steam enabled the settlers who had flooded the Western Plains following the signing of the Louisiana Purchase (1803) to travel upstream on the river as well as downstream. The *New Orleans* was the first of what would be hundreds of steamboats to open the Mississippi and Ohio valleys to trade, and to further open up the continent to exploration, settlement, and exploitation.

In May 1819, steam made an even bigger impact on American history, when the *Savannah*, a sailing ship with an auxiliary engine, crossed the Atlantic Ocean. The ship sailed under steam for only 80 of the 633 hours it took to reach Liverpool, but the achievement encouraged support for the steamship. The following year, a steamship sailed from Liverpool to South America, the first from Europe to cross the Atlantic, and in 1825 the *Enterprise* sailed all the way from England to Calcutta, India. The age of steam on river and at sea was well underway.

IN PROFILE
Mark Twain

Born Samuel Langhorne Clemens in 1835, the man who became Mark Twain, one of America's best-loved writers, left his home in Hannibal, Missouri, at the age of 17. For several years, he traveled the country working as a journeyman printer before taking passage on a boat from Cincinnati to New Orleans in 1857, intending to embark for the Amazon River to seek his fortune in the cocoa trade. His plans changed when he met pilot Horace Bixby. Before reaching New Orleans, the young Clemens's boyhood dream of becoming a steamboat pilot had been revived. Clemens convinced Bixby to take him on as a trainee pilot, and the job gave him his writer's name—"mark twain" being the pilot's cry for a river depth of two fathoms, which was a safe depth for a steamboat.

MARK TWAIN IN 1890

The Romantics

The Romantic movement is usually associated with art, poetry, and philosophy, but it was essentially a different way of looking at the world, and encouraged people to go traveling in search of new experiences.

▽ **Byron in Italy**
Lord Byron did much to popularize Europe as a travel destination, particularly Italy, where he lived for seven years.

It seems strange now, but to the majority of 18th-century travelers, particularly those who had set out on the Grand Tour (see pp. 180–83), the Alps were a nuisance. At the time, people valued order and symmetry, and humankind's ability to tame nature and shape civilization. The mountains in southern France were simply a massive barrier of rock that stood in the way of getting to Italy. Toward the end of the century, however, a growing number of travelers began to look for beauty and spiritual inspiration in such places.

In search of the picturesque

The change in attitudes was influenced by a group of intellectuals, especially the Swiss philosopher and writer Jean-Jacques Rousseau, whose novel *La Nouvelle Heloïse* (1761) rhapsodized the Swiss landscape and helped to ignite a 19th-century passion for Alpine

△ ***Landscape*, Willian Gilpin**
Unusually for the time, Gilpin's work was purely aesthetic and focused entirely on the beauty of its subject—nature—rather than trying to express a moral principle. Gilpin described this style as "picturesque."

▷ **Alone with nature**
Caspar David Friedrich's *Wanderer Above the Sea of Fog* (c.1818) encapsulates Romantic ideas about the isolation of the individual when faced with the sublime forces of nature.

scenery. In England, the works of a minister named William Gilpin were also instrumental in fostering a growing appreciation of untamed nature. His book, *Observations on the River Wye* (1782) sent hordes of tourists to south Wales, and his subsequent books on the Lake District and Scotland did much the same for those regions. Gilpin popularized the term "picturesque," which he defined literally as the kind of beauty that "would look well in a picture."

The sublime

Thomas West's *Guide to the Lakes* (1778) was a bestselling work on where to find the finest views in that famously picturesque part of northwest England. It also capitalized on the growing popularity of the "sublime," a feeling of wonder and awe that people sometimes experience when they see vast, majestic landscapes. This was part of a movement, later known as Romanticism, which renounced the rationalism and order characteristic of the Enlightenment, and stressed the importance of pure emotion and elevating imagination above reason.

An integral part of the sublime was the idealization of raw, rugged landscapes, such as mountains, heaving seas, and wild moors. This was exemplified in the work of the poet William Wordsworth, who had spent his childhood in the Lake District and moved back there in later life. Wordsworth's poetry linked the beauty of nature with the divine, imbuing landscapes with power and mystery.

Byron and Shelley abroad

One reason why English writers and artists had become so interested in the landscapes of their homeland was that two decades of war with France had prevented them from crossing the English Channel. When peace was restored to Europe in 1815, Romanticism influenced how travelers perceived the Continent. Among those who took advantage of peacetime to travel were the poets Byron and Shelley, two of the most prominent Romantics. Byron wrote one of the most revolutionary travelogues of the early 19th century, which, unusually, took the form of a poem. *Childe Harold's Pilgrimage* (1818) is an account of a voyage of self-discovery based on an extensive journey that Byron made through Portugal, Spain, Greece, and Albania. It made its author one of the most famous poets in Europe—and travelers took to using *Childe Harold* like a guidebook, its passages of high drama heightening the romance of the lands through which they passed.

> "Man is **born free**, and everywhere he is in **chains**."
>
> JEAN-JACQUES ROUSSEAU, *THE SOCIAL CONTRACT*, 1762

The glories of Italy

Both Byron and Shelley made Italy their home. They delighted in its ruins, natural beauty, and glorious weather (Byron delighted even more in its women), and exalted all in their work. Although their antics brought the poets notoriety (it was famously said of Byron that he was "mad, bad and dangerous to know"), it was ultimately their strong belief in the importance of nature that had the more lasting effect.

△ ***Childe Harold's Pilgrimage***
This frontispiece, illustrating Canto I, is from the 1825–26 edition of *Childe Harold's Pilgrimage* by Byron. The engraving is by I. H. Jones.

◁ **Shelley in Italy**
Percy Bysshe Shelley wrote many of his greatest poems, including *Prometheus Unbound*, in Italy. He moved from one Italian city to another, and was finally buried in Rome.

The voyages of the *Beagle*

In 1831, a small ship left Plymouth, England, with a young naturalist on board, taken along in part to keep the captain company. His keen observations made during the voyage would later reshape our understanding of humankind.

▷ **Charles Darwin**
This watercolor by George Richmond shows Charles Darwin in 1840, at only 31 years old. His voyage on the *Beagle* turned him into an eminent natural scientist.

Launched in May 1820, the HMS *Beagle* was just one of more than a hundred ships of its type, a modestly sized twin-masted warship. Originally outfitted for battle with ten guns, she was never called to action and instead was adapted as a survey vessel, sent off in 1826 to explore the coastline of South America. Along the way, the ship's captain sank into depression and committed suicide, possibly from the isolation of the lengthy voyage. His successor, Robert FitzRoy, assumed command and returned the ship to England. There, he was asked to take the ship on a second voyage to continue the work of the first. FitzRoy decided he would like to take along a scientist to help with the surveying and, perhaps more importantly, provide some company on the long journey.

A surprise invitation

Charles Darwin (1809–82) was a student with a passion for natural history who had just finished his final exams and was intending to return to Cambridge for theological training. A letter from one of his professors, inviting him to join the *Beagle*, changed everything. Lacking experience and scientific credentials, Darwin was proposed for his enthusiasm and enquiring mind, but his presence on board ultimately made the *Beagle* one of the most famous ships in history. The expedition left England on December 27, 1831, and reached South

▽ **The *Beagle* in the Murray Narrow**
HMS *Beagle* anchors at the island of St. Helena in this painting by the ship's artist, Conrad Martens, in 1836. Darwin formulated a theory about the formation of volcanic islands here.

" The **voyage of the *Beagle*** has been by far the **most important event** in my life, and has **determined my whole career**. "

CHARLES DARWIN, *THE AUTOBIOGRAPHY OF CHARLES DARWIN*, 1887

▷ **Discovering new species**
Darwin preserved specimens of numerous species that were new to science—including this parrot fish from the Pacific.

America the following February. Darwin was able to spend considerable time on land, collecting specimens and making observations in notebooks. At the beginning, Darwin, a keen hunter, enjoyed shooting the birds and other wildlife he encountered, before coming to the realization that "the pleasure of observing and reasoning was a much higher one than that of skill and sport."

Intimations of evolution

In September 1835, the *Beagle* reached the Galápagos Islands, where Darwin was intrigued to learn that the shells of giant tortoises differed from place to place, and that these differences allowed locals to tell which specific island a creature came from. He collected samples of mockingbirds, and noted that these birds too were slightly different on each island.

The expedition sailed on, dining on Galápagos tortoises, and arrived at Tahiti in November 1835, then New Zealand in late December. In January 1836, they reached Australia, where they explored coral reefs, and by the end of May 1836, they passed the Cape of Good Hope at the southern tip of Africa. Rather than heading straight for Europe, Captain FitzRoy wanted to make further hydrographic surveys, which involved a return trip across the Atlantic to Bahia in Brazil. It was not until October 2, 1836, that the *Beagle* finally arrived at the port of Falmouth in Cornwall.

"As far as I can judge of myself, I worked to the utmost during the voyage from the mere pleasure of investigation, and from my strong desire to add a few facts to the great mass of facts in natural science," noted Darwin. In the following years, he wrote extensively on his travels, contributing the third volume of the *Narrative of the Voyages of H.M. Ships Adventure and Beagle*. Due to its popularity, this single volume was republished many times, first as Darwin's *Journal of Researches*, published in 1839, and later as *The Voyage of the Beagle*, printed in 1905. The observations recorded in the book would ultimately lead him to formulate his theory of evolution, outlined in his masterwork *On the Origin of Species*, which was published in 1859.

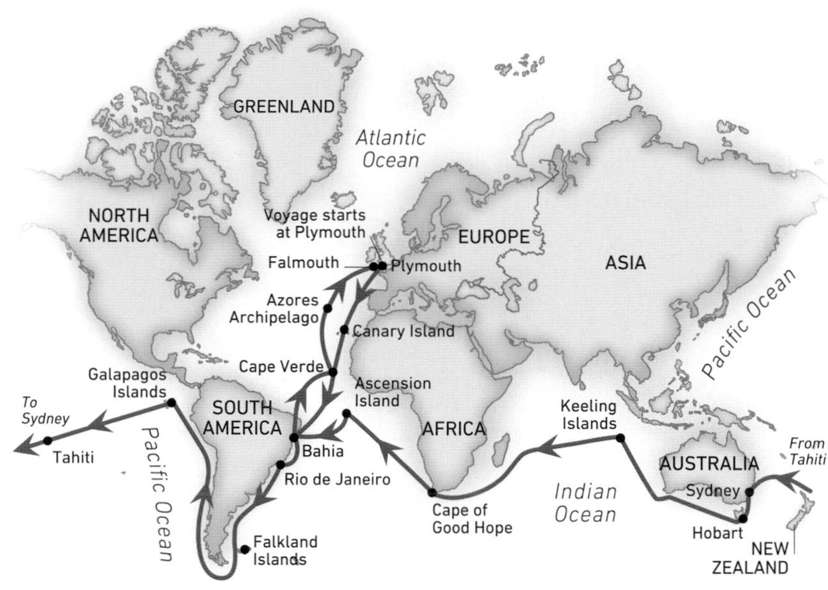

△ **Exploring the natural world**
This map shows the route that the *Beagle* expedition took around the world. The journey took nearly five years.

IN CONTEXT
Darwin's notebooks

Charles Darwin kept a detailed account of his travels aboard the *Beagle*. He filled out 15 small notebooks, writing about 116,000 words and drawing roughly 300 sketches. However, Darwin's account of his journey is anything but dry science. His writing is lively and charming, with vivid descriptions of the places and people he encountered. In places, it is even funny.

Darwin also carefully recorded the various types of flora and fauna he found. The records of the species he came across on his journey were crucial to his later work on evolution. Visiting South America, Darwin encountered and sketched a bird called a "rhea", which he learned had "a very close general resemblance" to another ostrich species. Such observations led him to conclude that "one species does change into another."

ILLUSTRATION OF DARWIN'S RHEA

Travelers' tales

In the 19th century, explorers' records of their journeys took on a new slant. As well as documenting scientific or geographical discoveries, many travelers began to keep more informal accounts.

Even if he had never written his groundbreaking work about evolution, *On the Origin of Species*, Charles Darwin would probably still be remembered as a notable travel writer. Following his voyage on the *Beagle*, he contributed to the official scientific reports, but he also wrote his own informal account, full of perceptive sketches of the places he visited and observations about the people he had met. This account was typical of travel writing of the age, which was based largely on the journals kept by scientists. Sometimes a personal narrative would emerge and prove quite thrilling.

One such account is John Franklin's *Narrative of a Journey to the Shores of the Polar Sea* (1823), which details his 1819–22 mission to chart the north coast of Canada, in which more than half of his expedition of 20 died. His account almost revels in the hardships: "We enjoyed the comfort of a large fire for the first time since our departure from the coast," he writes. "There was no *tripe de roche*, and we drank tea and ate some of our shoes for supper."

Francis Parkman's majestic account of the American migrant route through the Rockies, *The Oregon Trail* (1849), provides a similarly enthralling personal account. "A month ago," he comments, "I should have thought it rather a startling affair to have an acquaintance ride out in the morning and lose his scalp before night, but here it seems the most natural thing in the world."

Outdoing them all, though, was explorer Henry Morton Stanley. His lively accounts, including *In Darkest Africa* (1890), are full of violent clashes with native tribes, episodes of flogging disobedient porters to death, leaving the lame to die on the trail, and hanging deserters in trees.

The lure of the Orient

While Stanley was on his mission to subdue a continent, a new breed of more cerebral travel writer was emerging, one whose response to visiting foreign lands and cultures was to question civilization, beliefs, and cultural identity. Many of the Victorian travel classics were produced by such writers. Egypt and the Islamic world were of great interest at the time, and featured in many books, notably *Eothen* (1844), Alexander Kinglake's graceful account of a trip from Belgrade to Cairo. Gérard de Nerval's *Journey to the Orient* (1851) offered a more whimsical account of the East, heady with the fumes of hashish—but then its author was an eccentric who enjoyed walking his pet lobster in the gardens of Paris.

In contrast to the sensualist Nerval, English explorer Isabella Bird was driven to travel and write by her evangelical Christian beliefs. She rode—often alone—on horseback across Persia, Japan, Korea, and many other countries, taking her own photographs. Although dismissive of the "false creeds" that she encountered, she showed what, for the time, was a rare empathy with the people she met.

The traveling novelist

Travel writing had become so popular by the mid-19th century that many authors of note felt compelled to write

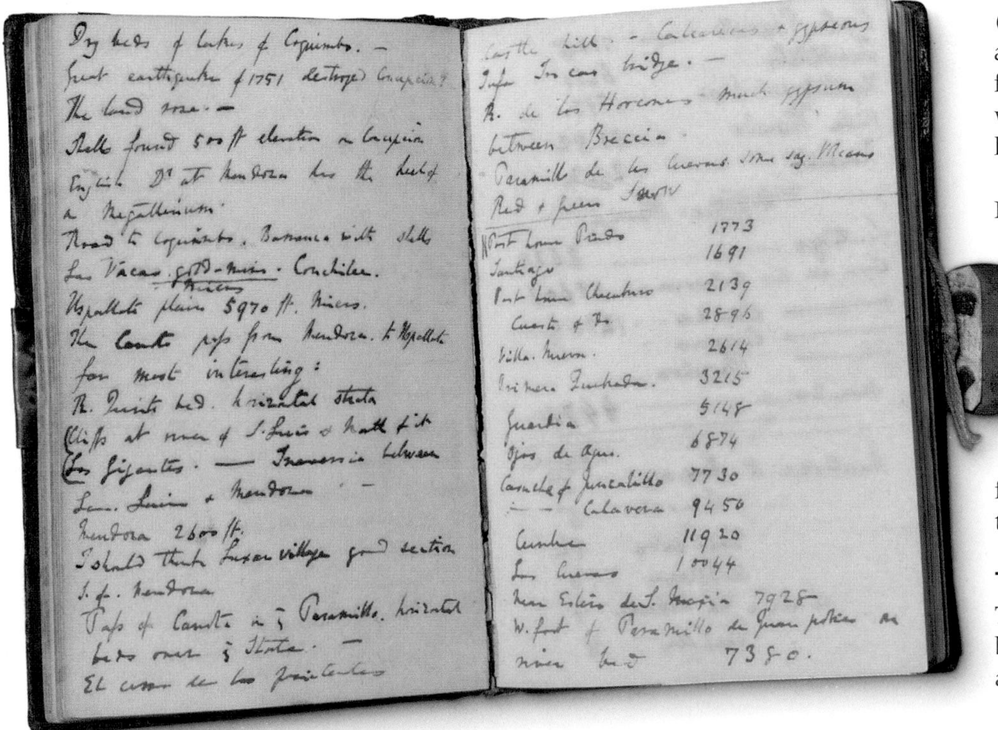

▷ **Book-keeping**
During the voyage of the *Beagle*, Charles Darwin recorded his observations in small notebooks such as this one. He copied up his notes every evening, forming a 750-page journal that would become the basis of his published work.

◁ **Imperial adventurer**
In his day, Henry Morton Stanley's feats in Africa enthralled the public. However, he later fell from favor and was viewed as a ruthless imperialist who hacked and shot his way across Africa.

◁ **Harsh terrain**
This engraving from John Franklin's *Narrative of a Journey to the Shores of the Polar Sea* brings to vivid life the forbidding landscapes through which the author traveled.

their own travel accounts. In 1844, Charles Dickens set off for southern Europe, a pleasurable jaunt related in *Pictures from Italy* (1846). Henry James turned tourist for *A Little Tour in France* (1884), and the *Treasure Island* author Robert Louis Stevenson became a pioneer of outdoor literature with his wry account of a walk taken to recover from heartbreak, *Travels with a Donkey in the Cévennes* (1879).

The most entertaining book of all, perhaps, is Mark Twain's *The Innocents Abroad* (1869), in which he humorously recounts the weeks he spent on board the chartered ship *Quaker City*, visiting the sights of Europe and the Holy Land in the company of a group of fellow American travelers. "The gentle reader will never, never know," he writes, "what a consummate ass he can become until he goes abroad." With timeless observations such as this, it is little wonder that *The Innocents Abroad* is still one of the most successful travel books of all time.

> "**Charitable views** of men **cannot** be **acquired** by vegetating in one **little corner** of the **earth**."
>
> MARK TWAIN, *THE INNOCENTS ABROAD*

▷ **The Game of Innocence Abroad**
Capitalizing on the popularity of Mark Twain's *The Innocents Abroad*, in 1888 Parker Bros produced this slyly titled game. The board illustrates activities that tourists might engage in as they traveled around Europe.

△ **Mark Twain**
Perhaps to Mark Twain's surprise, his account of a trip to Europe and the Holy Land was his bestselling book—more popular, even, than *The Adventures of Tom Sawyer* and *Adventures of Huckleberry Finn*.

Shooting the world

Soon after photography was invented, cameras went on sale to the public and people began to go on journeys with a single goal in mind—using this incredible new machine.

△ **Ancient Egypt**
The temple of Abu-Simbel was one of hundreds of sites photographed by Maxime Du Camp and Gustave Flaubert on their two-year tour of the Orient.

The two leading pioneers of photography, Frenchman Louis Daguerre and Englishman Henry Fox Talbot, made their first photographic images in the late 1830s, using a process that became commercially available in 1839. The following year, India hosted its first photography exhibition, and in 1841 Captain Lucas of Sydney took the first ever picture of Australia. Such was the speed with which photography was embraced.

Oriental landscapes

One of the most celebrated early photographers of travel was a man now better known for his novels—Gustave Flaubert, the future author of *Madame Bovary*. In 1849, he set off with his wealthy Parisian friend Maxime Du Camp to tour and photograph the ancient monuments of the Middle East. The two of them traveled through Egypt and Palestine, and published the results in *Memories and Landscapes of the Orient* (1852)—the first travel book to be illustrated with photographs. Egypt also provided rich subject matter for photographer Francis Frith, who visited three times, and Francis Bedford, the official photographer of the Prince of Wales on his 1862 royal tour of the Middle East.

Capturing the unknown

In the mid-19th century, the standard photographer's kit was a very large, heavy camera, a tripod, glass plates, plate holders, a tentlike portable darkroom, chemicals, and tanks for developing the pictures. It was cumbersome, to say the least. However, advances in technology soon

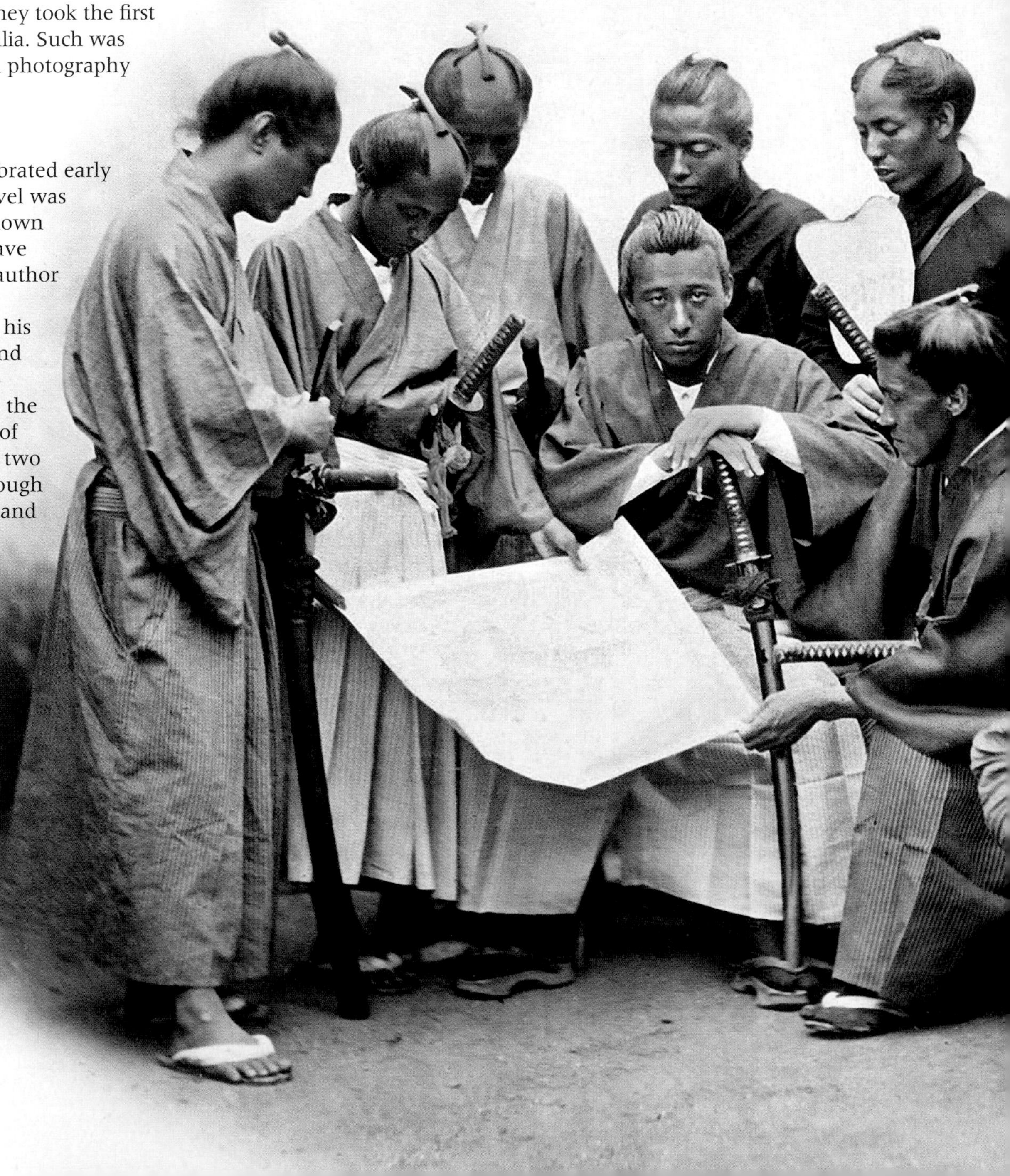

▷ **Glimpse of Japan**
The Samurai, portrayed here by Felice Beato in the 1860s, were Japan's elite warriors. Beato had privileged access to Japanese society, which was little known to Westerners at the time.

◁ **Mammoth plate camera**
Initially, prints had to be the same size as negatives, so in 1861, Carleton E. Watkins commissioned this huge camera so he could do justice to scenes of the American West.

enabled studios, particularly in Europe, to develop large numbers of images for photographers, who were then able to leave their darkrooms behind.

In 1857, the French government commissioned Claude-Joseph Désiré Charnay to go to Mexico. He spent four years there and was the first to photograph the Mayan ruins. Another Frenchman, Émile Gsell, worked in Indo-China, and took the first pictures of the temple of Angkor Wat, in what is now Cambodia. The Italian-British photographer Felice Beato became one of the first to work in China. He took pictures of the Second Opium War and of Japan during its isolationist Edo Period—images that were not only of immense scientific interest at the time, but which also now provide an invaluable insight into a bygone age.

The American West

In the United States, the invention of photography gave many citizens the opportunity to see what was in the rest of their own country for the first time. Frontiersman John Charles Frémont made several failed attempts to use a camera on his early expeditions, so for his fifth crossing of the continent, in 1853, he took along Solomon Nunes Carvalho, who was possibly the first person to photograph the American West and its native people. Others swiftly followed, including William Bell, John K. Hillers, Carleton E. Watkins, and Timothy H. O'Sullivan. Each of them returned with plates which, when developed, produced such beautiful photographs that they helped to inspire the establishment of the United States' first national parks.

△ **Cathedral Rocks**
This 1865 picture of a landmark in Yosemite Valley was taken by Carleton E. Watkins when he was working for the California Geological Survey.

> " There is no **effectual substitute** for **actual travel**; but it is my **ambition** to **provide** for those to whom **circumstances forbid** that **luxury**... "
>
> FRANCIS FRITH, PHOTOGRAPHER

IN CONTEXT
On the road

At first, travel photography was very much a group enterprise. Francis Frith, for example, traveled with a large entourage of guides and assistants, and set out across Egypt in a caravan of carts and wagons. He was one of the first to experiment with glass negatives, introduced in 1851, but he had to process them on-site, either in a stuffy, dark tent or in an ancient tomb—despite the danger of using explosive materials such as liquid ether and gun cotton. The English war photographer Roger Fenton used a similar technique, but developed his pictures in a specially rigged, horsedrawn darkroom. He also used volatile chemicals, even on the battlefields of the Crimean War.

ROGER FENTON'S ASSISTANT, MARCUS SPERLING, WITH THEIR PORTABLE DARKROOM

Into Africa

At the beginning of the 19th century, the European grasp of African geography was confined mainly to the coast. This deficit in knowledge was only slowly eroded by a succession of intrepid European explorers.

As far back as the 15th century, the Portuguese had mapped the outline of Africa as they extended sea routes into the East. It was the Portuguese, too, who initiated the transatlantic trade in African slaves, soon joined by other European powers. With the advent of the Enlightenment in Europe, and its principles of freedom, democracy, reason, and a belief in scientific investigation, the tide turned against slavery, and instead toward exploration. Africa, known to be a vast landmass twice the size of Europe, now became a particular focus of attention. There was great interest in establishing the sources of two of Africa's great trading arteries, the Niger and Nile rivers.

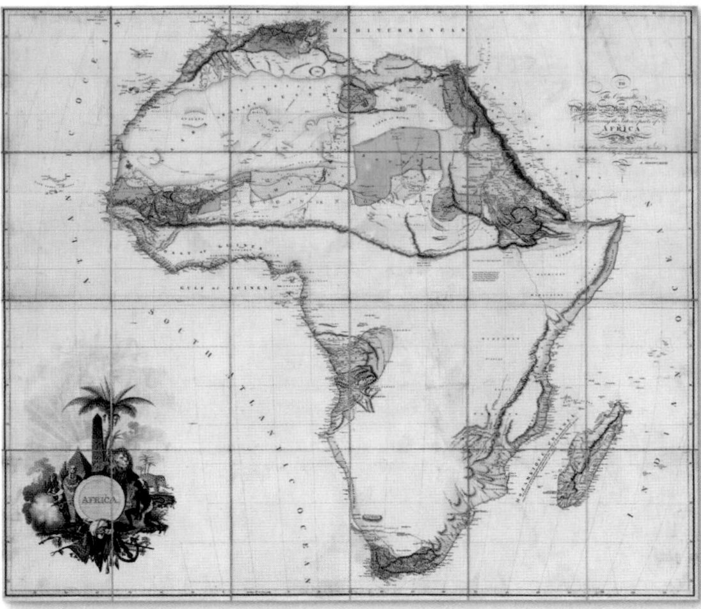

▷ Uncharted territory
This map by Aaron Arrowsmith, from 1802, shows the extent to which the center of Africa was a great unknown for European explorers.

▷ Mungo Park
Scottish-born Park had been expected to enter the Church, but a fascination for the natural world led him to travel to Africa in search of the Niger River.

The search for the Niger

The African Association was founded in London in 1788, with the aim of locating the origin of the Niger. A young Scotsman named Mungo Park, who had trained in medicine but now had the patronage of the influential botanist Joseph Banks (see pp. 176–77), was dispatched to West Africa in May 1795. Putting ashore at Pisania in Gambia, Park headed for the interior accompanied only by a local guide, a porter, a horse, and two mules. At one point, he was thrown into prison for four months by a local Muslim ruler, but he managed to escape with a horse and compass.

He eventually located the Niger, becoming the first European to set eyes on the middle stretch of the river. He then returned to the Gambian coast and to England, where his diaries, under the title *Travels in the Interior of Africa*, were published to acclaim. In 1805, he accepted a second mission to the Niger, this time in charge of more than 40 men. Tragically, they attempted

◁ Into the interior
In December 1795, Park left Gambia on his journey to find the Niger, which he located in July of the following year. It took another 11 months to make the return journey.

the expedition at the height of the hot season, and only Park and four others actually reached the Niger—the rest lost their lives to illness. The five survivors took to the river in a boat, but were attacked by hostile locals, and Park drowned while trying to swim to safety.

In 1818, British naval officer George Francis Lyon was dispatched to chart the course of the Niger and locate the fabled city of Timbuktu, which was known only from historic accounts. Inadvisably, his party started out from Tripoli, in the north, in what is now Libya, meaning they had to first cross the Sahara. The mission was a failure.

◁ **Locating Timbuktu** Réné Caillé was the first to reach Timbuktu, in 1828, followed by the German Heinrich Barth in 1853. This illustration, by Johann Martin Bernatz, is based on a sketch made by Barth.

Success at last

It was not until 1830 that the Niger was successfully mapped. Richard Lander was a born adventurer. At the age of nine, he is said to have walked 232 miles (373 km) from Truro in Cornwall to London. In 1825, he was an aide to the Scots explorer Captain Hugh Clapperton, who went on a trade mission to Sokoto, in what is now Nigeria. Once again, illness wiped out almost the whole group, and Lander had to make a seven-month walk on his own to reach the coast and a ship home. Undaunted, he returned to Africa in 1830, along with his brother John, and together they finally succeeded in visiting the Niger Delta and mapping the route of the river. »

▽ **Mungo Park's second expedition** A second expedition to the Niger, which sought to assess its potential for European settlement, ended in the death of the whole party, including Park himself.

“... if I **ever** travel **again**, I shall **trust** to **none but natives**, as the **climate** of **Africa** is **too trying** to **foreigners**.”

JOHN HANNING SPEKE, ON AFRICA'S CLIMATE

△ **Speke's sketchbooks**
John Hanning Speke filled sketchbooks with countless drawings of the flora and fauna he encountered, creating a remarkable record of his travels.

» The prize for being the first European to visit Timbuktu—a literal prize of 10,000 francs offered by the Paris-based Société de Géographie—had been claimed two years earlier by a Frenchman, René Caillié. A Scotsman, Alexander Gordon Laing, had found and visited the city in 1826, but was killed by local tribesmen as he journeyed home. Mungo Park may also have reached the city, but he died before telling anyone. Caillié traveled alone, disguised as a Muslim, and was able to return home safely to claim both glory and the prize money.

Tracing the source of the Nile

In East Africa, finding the illusive source of the Nile proved an irresistible lure to many explorers. The Royal Geographical Society in London commissioned Richard Burton and John Hanning Speke to go off and locate it. Burton was a swashbuckling adventurer and a brilliant linguist who had gone on the hajj to Mecca disguised as an Arab. He would later translate the *Kama Sutra* and the *Arabian Nights*. Although more conventional, Speke was also an experienced explorer, having already traveled with Burton on an earlier African expedition.

▷ **Captain John Hanning Speke**
This portrait depicts Speke standing in front of Lake Victoria, which he claimed was the source of the Nile river. His theory was confirmed in 1875 by Henry Morton Stanley.

The pair set off from the coast to cross present-day Tanzania in June 1857, following a map supplied by a recently returned missionary. The going was arduous, and along the way they both contracted tropical infections: Speke lost his hearing in one ear, Burton became unable to walk, and both went temporarily blind. Even so, by June 1858, they had succeeded in reaching Lake Tanganyika. They backtracked to the town of Tabora to recuperate and stock up on provisions, but Burton was too ill to travel, so Speke headed north with a party to investigate claims of another great lake. On discovering the waters of what locals called the N'yanza, he renamed it Lake Victoria, in honor of his queen. Speke was convinced that this was the source of the Nile. Burton disagreed, and the two fell out publicly.

Back in England, in 1864, Speke was killed in a hunting accident the day before a debate appointed to bring the two men and their theories together.

David Livingstone

Perhaps the most famous explorer of all was David Livingstone, the first European to cross the continent from west to east. He arrived at the southern tip of Africa in 1841 as a Christian missionary, but it is thought that he only ever managed to convert one person. Instead, he became fascinated with exploring the African interior.

△ **Livingstone at Lake Ngami**
David Livingstone became Victorian England's most famous explorer, even if, ultimately, he failed in his quest to discover the source of the Nile.

With a young family in tow, his first trip took him north to Lake Ngami in present-day Botswana. Continuing north, he reached the Zambezi River, which he followed west before striking off to reach the coast at Luanda, the modern capital of Angola. Returning to the Zambezi, he then headed east to find out whether the river was navigable for trade, and discovered its greatest natural obstacle, the Victoria Falls, making him the first European to set eyes on it.

After 1866, he became obsessed with finding the source of the Nile, a task that filled the final seven years of his life. He was out of contact with the outside world for so long at one point that an American newspaper dispatched correspondent Henry Morton Stanley to find him, resulting in their famous encounter in the jungle.

Livingstone was ill for the last four years of his life. When he died of malaria in 1873, two African assistants carried his body a thousand miles to the coast so it could be returned to Britain for burial. It was sent with a note: "You can have his body, but his heart belongs to Africa." The heart had been cut from the body and buried where he died.

◁ **David Livingstone's cap**
As a British consul, Livingstone wore the Consul's Cap. He was wearing this distinctive headgear on the day he met Stanley.

IN PROFILE
Mary Kingsley

Captivated by her father's tales of his trips overseas as a traveling doctor, ethnographer and explorer Mary Kingsley set off for her own adventure in 1892, at the age of 30. Her ambition was to discover new species of animals. She headed for Angola and then into the Congo, traveling on the River Gabon. She returned to England in 1893 with a collection of tropical fish for the British Museum.

On her second sojourn to Africa, she spent time with a tribe that was known to practice cannibalism and fell into a game pit, but was saved by her voluminous underskirts. Her subsequent book, *Travels in West Africa* (1897), became a Victorian bestseller. She died of typhoid in South Africa in 1900.

MARY KINGSLEY ON THE FRONTISPIECE OF HER SECOND BOOK, *WEST AFRICAN STUDIES* (1899)

The Railway Age

Until the 19th century, most people lived their lives in the area in which they had been born, and no one had ever traveled faster than a horse could gallop. The arrival of the railways changed everything.

△ **Early rail travel**
This woodcut of the 1830s shows passengers traveling along the Baltimore and Ohio Railroad in a horse-drawn carriage.

Before the 19th century, steam engines were cumbersome objects, used only in industry and, later, in boats (see pp. 202–03). However, in the early 1800s, they became small enough to be mounted on wheels. Experiments in putting steam engines on rails culminated in the first railway to run solely on steam power, the Liverpool and Manchester line, which opened in 1830. It was masterminded by engineer George Stephenson and employed an engine, *Rocket*, designed by his son, Robert. Robert would go on to construct a far longer line connecting London and Birmingham, and assist in constructing lines in Belgium, Spain, and Egypt. When the line celebrated its 150th anniversary in 1980, the then-chairman of British Rail, Peter Parker, observed: "The world is a branch line of the Liverpool and Manchester."

The first American railroads

The United States was quick to embrace the railway, or railroad, as it would come to be called. The country was vast and travel was slow. Steamboats were the best form of travel, but they only gave access to certain parts of the country. Otherwise, it was still horse and wagon. The original American railroad pioneer, Colonel John Stevens, was a steamboat operator. The first US railway carriages were pulled along the tracks by horses, as had also been the case in England.

It took a legendary race between a locomotive, the *Tom Thumb*, and a horse in 1830, to convince sceptics that the future lay with steam. Trains started running on completed stretches of the Baltimore and Ohio and Charleston and Hamburg lines by the end of that same year. Within a decade, 2,750 miles (4,425 km) of railroad were in operation across the US. The spur was freight, but increasingly passengers began to benefit from this innovation too. Every town wanted to be connected to the railroad, because it was considered vital for their prosperity.

◁ **Steam vs horse**
The *Tom Thumb* races a horse-drawn carriage in 1830. It lost the contest due to a mechanical failure, but proved that steam locomotion was both a viable and particularly fast form of travel.

> " A bell indicates the start and the **locomotive begins to groan** and the **wheels revolve first slowly** and then **faster and faster**, and then **the train flies**. What **fun** it is to travel now. "
>
> PUBLISHER KARL BAEDEKER, ON HIS FIRST TRAIN TRIP, 1838

Tracks across Europe

Europe was not far behind England and the US. By 1832, France was running locomotives on a line that stretched between Saint-Étienne and Lyon. Originally intended to convey coal, it quickly expanded to carrying passengers. In 1834, building started on a line in Belgium, and Germany's first railway opened the following year. The German line was only 4 miles (6.5 km) long, but unlike most of the early lines, it was built specifically for passengers. This was also the case with the inaugural line in Holland, laid to connect Amsterdam and Haarlem, which opened in 1839.

The rapidly growing railway networks across Europe and the US not only simplified travel, but also cut travel costs, as increased speed and better routes meant less time and money spent on traveling. Early entrepreneurs, who had expected the rails to be used for goods, were surprised to find that passenger traffic accounted for more than half of their revenue. The bulk of this traffic came from the lower and middle classes, the sort of people who had never before had the opportunity to travel. The arrival of the railway amounted to nothing less than a revolution.

◁ **Changing landscapes**
This English viaduct was erected for the Liverpool and Manchester Railway, under the direction of George Stephenson. Made of brick with stone facings, its 50 ft- (15 m-) wide arches rise from slabs of local sandstone.

▽ **The *Adler***
The first successful steam locomotive to operate in Germany, the *Adler* (meaning "eagle" in German) was built by pioneers George and Robert Stephenson in 1835.

Trains

It was a simple idea—to use steam to turn wheels that ran on tracks—but it was one that transformed transportation.

ROCKET, UK, 1829

The steam engine was the great invention of the Industrial Revolution, and its greatest application was the creation of the railways. Robert Stephenson's *Rocket* (1829) was not the first steam locomotive, but its design, which featured a blastpipe, was the most advanced of its day. When it won the Rainhill Trials, held by the world's first railway (the Liverpool and Manchester), the *Rocket* became the template for locomotive design. Its top speed was 35 mph (56 kph), which was amazing for its time.

Trains were powered by steam for more than 130 years, during which time they became increasingly large and powerful. There were many modifications to the basic design: American locomotives, for example, were given huge smokestacks that prevented sparks from escaping into the air, as well as "cowcatchers" at the front to clear obstacles from the track. The steam engine perhaps reached its peak with the streamlined *Mallard*, which achieved a speed of 126 mph (203 kph) in 1938, a record that stood for decades.

Although electricity had been used to power small trains as early as the 1880s, it did not begin to supplant steam until the 1950s. Since then, trains have become more streamlined—notably the Japanese *Bullet*, which borrowed elements from aircraft design—and have been given tilting mechanisms to improve performance. These and other innovations have created trains that are fast, economical to run, and can carry a vast number of passengers.

PIONEER ZEPHYR DIESEL LOCOMOTIVE, US, 1934

MALLARD STEAM LOCOMOTIVE, UK, 1938

DELTIC ELECTRIC TRAIN PROTOTYPE, UK, 1955

BULLET HIGH-SPEED ELECTRIC TRAIN, JAPAN, 1964

STEAM LOCOMOTIVE, US, 1880

N.E.R. ELECTRIC LOCOMOTIVE, UK, 1905

KING EDWARD II STEAM LOCOMOTIVE, UK, 1927

EMD GP9 DIESEL-ELECTRIC LOCOMOTIVE, US, 1949

THALYS PBKA HIGH-SPEED ELECTRIC TRAIN, FRANCE, 1996

WUPPERTAL ELECTRIC ELEVATED RAILWAY, GERMANY, 2015

The Gold Rush

The discovery of gold in 1848 brought tens of thousands of immigrants to California, both from elsewhere in the United States and from countries as far away as China.

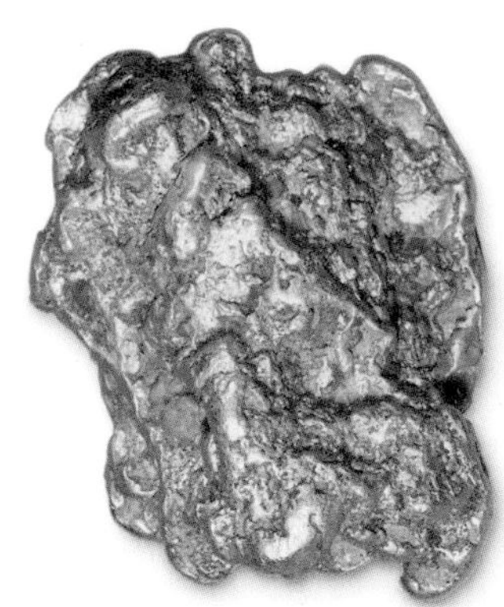

◁ **Golden future**
"It made my heart thump, for I was certain it was gold," said Californian carpenter James Marshall, on discovering gold in 1848. It is estimated that some $2 billion worth of the metal was extracted in the subsequent rush.

On the morning of January 24, 1848, a carpenter was inspecting the water flow at Sutter's Mill on the banks of the American River in Coloma, California, when he saw something gleaming on the bed of the stream. He reached in to pluck it out and found he had a small nugget of gold in the palm of his hand. It did not take long for the news to spread.

When a newspaper in the formerly Mexican township of Yerba Buena, claimed by the Americans the previous year and renamed San Francisco, published reports of several local gold finds, prospectors began to flock to the area. No expensive tools were required. All the early prospectors needed was some sort of sieving pan to wash off the dirt and expose the precious metal.

An enterprising merchant named Samuel Brannan bought up all the mining supplies he could find to stock his store at the settlement of Sutter's Fort, then took a bottle of gold flakes to San Francisco where he walked through the streets, waving his bottle and shouting, "Gold, gold, gold in the American River!" He went on to make more money than any prospector and became California's first millionaire.

The California Trail

By mid-1848, the news had reached the East Coast, drawing prospectors first from up in Oregon, and then from all over the Midwest. They traveled in covered wagons and followed what became known as the California Trail, an offshoot of the Oregon Trail (see pp. 200–201). Many more came by ship, sailing down the east coast

▽ **Panning for gold**
Prospector Peter Moiss pans for gold with his donkeys and meager supplies at Burro Mine in Death Valley, California.

▷ **Setting up shop**
This 1926 lithograph shows the booming town of San Francisco as it was in 1849. Between the various commercial buildings, two ships lie at anchor, having brought supplies for the many "forty-niners" seen in the foreground.

from New York and Boston, and then down and round the tip of South America. During the following year, 1849, some 80,000 prospectors arrived and were nicknamed "the forty-niners."

The lure of gold

By the 1850s, miners were flocking from all over the world—from South America, Europe and, notably, China. They headed out into the wilderness and established mining communities, where conditions were basic and lawlessness was rife. The digging and panning from early dawn until dusk was backbreaking work, and poor diet and exposure to harsh weather meant that illness was widespread. The stories of others striking it rich, however, spurred the prospectors on. The peak year for finds was 1852. Every year after that, less and less gold was found, even as more and more people arrived to claim a share in the dwindling supply.

" Many, **very many**, that come here meet with **bad success** & **thousands** will **leave their bones** here. "

SHELDON SHUFELT, MINER, IN A LETTER TO HIS FAMILY, MARCH 1850

▽ **Land of opportunity**
The discovery of gold in California turned a little-known part of America into an almost mythical land of opportunity. By 1870, the population of San Francisco had increased from 850 to just under 150,000.

Gold to oranges

Thousands of gold seekers returned home with nothing to show for their efforts, and thousands more perished. Many people stayed on, and turned to farming. In San Francisco, the population had swelled from 850 in 1848 to over 21,000 by 1850. The growth in California's overall population was so rapid that it soon reached the figure of 60,000 that was needed to petition for statehood. By 1850, it had become the 31st US state.

The Gold Rush is generally considered to have drawn to a close in 1858, by which time it had dramatically changed the population of California forever, making it one of the most ethnically diverse states in the US. The pioneering inhabitants found the warm Mediterranean-style climate kind and the land fertile. Ultimately, the bountiful wealth of California came not from gold, but from its farms and, in particular, from growing oranges.

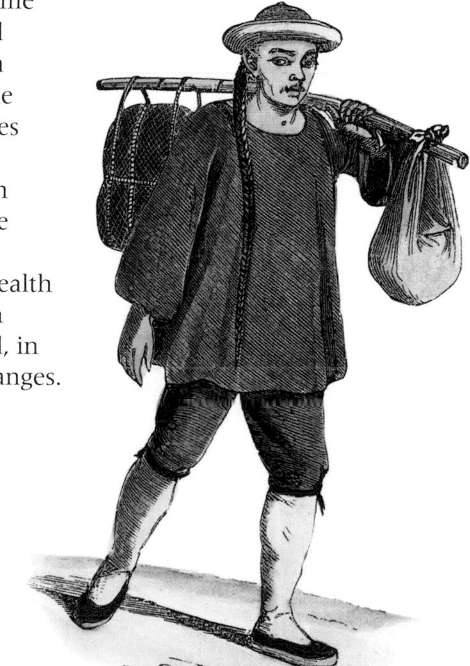

▷ **Chinese fortune-seeker**
The Gold Rush triggered a wave of emigration to the West Coast, particularly from China. Chinese miners often disguised their gold by melting it and turning it into household goods.

Thomas Cook

A prohibitionist who began organizing railway excursions to keep people away from alcohol, Thomas Cook became the unlikely father of international mass tourism.

Born on November 22, 1808, in Derbyshire in the English Midlands, Thomas Cook was only four years old when his father died. To help support his mother, he left school at the age of 10 and went to work first as a gardener's boy, then as an apprentice wood-turner, and then as an apprentice printer of books for the Baptist Association. It was while working with the latter that he found his calling as a teenage missionary, a job that saw him traveling from village to village distributing religious tracts and assisting in setting up Sunday schools. He married in 1833, and the following year his wife gave birth to a son, which obliged him to live a more settled existence.

◁ **Seeing the world**
Thomas Cook's first excursion was an 11-mile (18-km) train journey from Leicester to Loughborough and back. Made in 1841, its chief purpose was to wean people off alcohol—by getting them out and expanding their horizons and taking them to temperance meetings.

And so he redirected his energies into alleviating what at the time was viewed as one of the worst of all social ills—drunkenness. In 1841, he joined a nationwide temperance movement that was dedicated to weaning the working classes off their wasteful indulgence in beer and spirits.

Cook's devotion to God's work was matched by an equally firm faith in the virtues of progress and industry, and at the age of 33, he saw a way to combine these potentially conflicting beliefs. On Monday July 5, 1841, he made arrangements for 570 workers from Leicester to travel a distance of 11 miles (18km) on the new railway to Loughborough, where they would attend a temperance meeting and be entertained by a band. The trip went well and, having established that social reform could be compatible with profit, Cook planned more excursions. He led his first professional trip in the summer of 1845, to Liverpool, and a second the following year, to Scotland.

In 1851, Cook made good business ferrying tourists down to London for the Great Exhibition (see pp. 230–31). He made his first forays across the English Channel to mainland Europe in 1855, and his first proper trip to Paris in 1861. In June 1863, he took his first party to Switzerland. Subsequent trips included Italy in July 1864, and America in the spring of 1866.

The traveling chaperone

By 1868, Cook claimed to have organized the travel of some two million people. Using the promise of large numbers of sales, he secured discounts that were passed on to his customers, who received the benefit of a single payment covering all travel and transit costs, plus vouchers for hotel accommodation and meals. He would go on to lead tours to Egypt and the Holy Land, India, Japan, and even around the world. He set up offices in the capitals of several countries, including in New Zealand, and published his own newspaper, *The Excursionist*, to inform customers of his program.

As well as opening up travel to classes of people who could otherwise never have afforded or even considered such a thing (at the time, travel for pleasure was the preserve of the idle rich), Cook also altered the perception of travel as a largely male-only pastime. His excursions and tours appealed particularly to women, who felt able to sign up for his tours, either alone or with a companion. To this end, Cook cannily promoted himself as "the traveling chaperone."

◁ **New horizons**
By 1870, Cook's Conducted Tours had expanded to include most of Western Europe. The tours attracted customers of all classes.

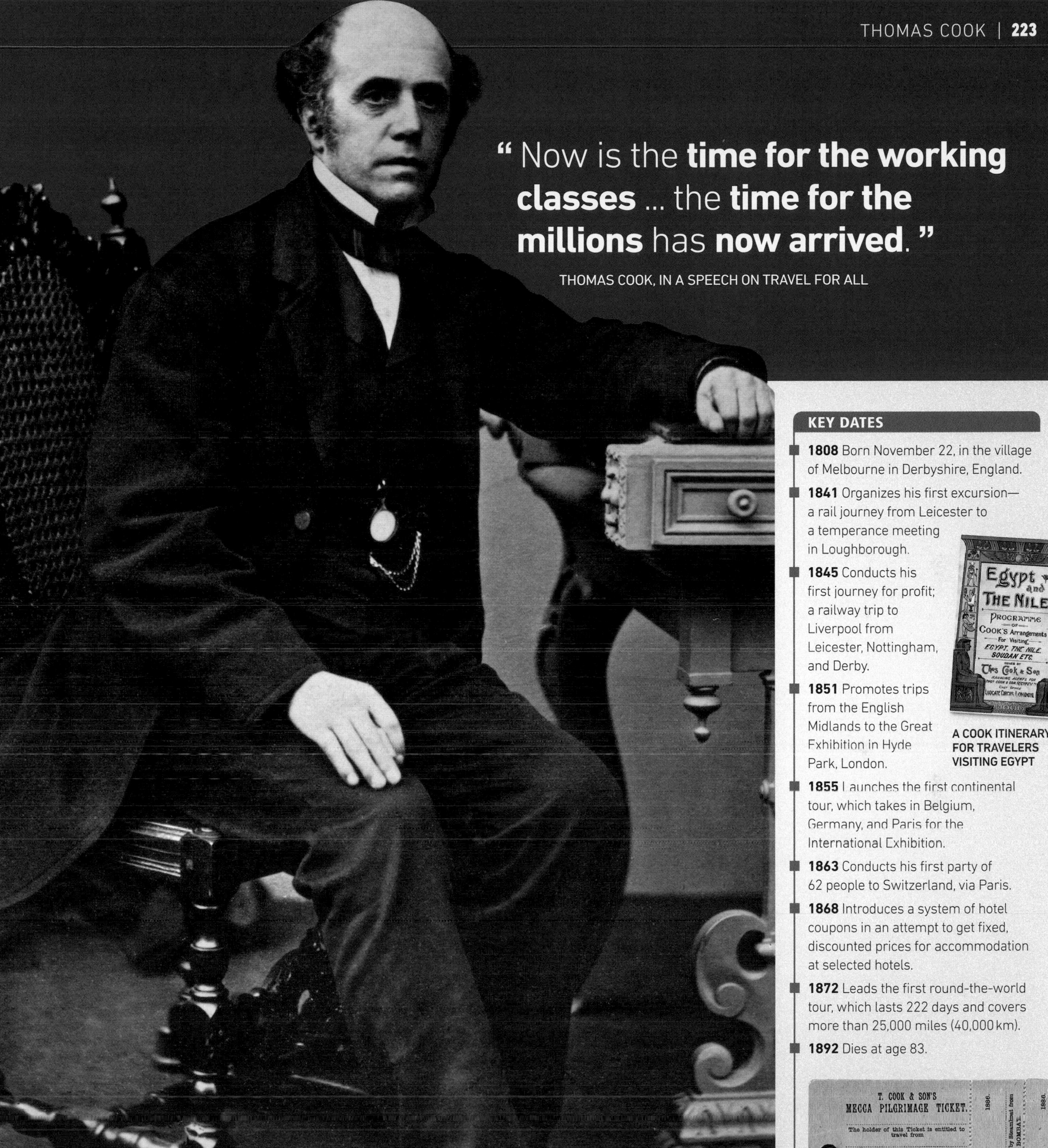

" Now is the **time for the working classes** … the **time for the millions** has **now arrived**. **"**

THOMAS COOK, IN A SPEECH ON TRAVEL FOR ALL

KEY DATES

- **1808** Born November 22, in the village of Melbourne in Derbyshire, England.
- **1841** Organizes his first excursion—a rail journey from Leicester to a temperance meeting in Loughborough.
- **1845** Conducts his first journey for profit; a railway trip to Liverpool from Leicester, Nottingham, and Derby.
- **1851** Promotes trips from the English Midlands to the Great Exhibition in Hyde Park, London.
- **1855** Launches the first continental tour, which takes in Belgium, Germany, and Paris for the International Exhibition.
- **1863** Conducts his first party of 62 people to Switzerland, via Paris.
- **1868** Introduces a system of hotel coupons in an attempt to get fixed, discounted prices for accommodation at selected hotels.
- **1872** Leads the first round-the-world tour, which lasts 222 days and covers more than 25,000 miles (40,000 km).
- **1892** Dies at age 83.

A COOK ITINERARY FOR TRAVELERS VISITING EGYPT

A TICKET FOR A THOMAS COOK PACKAGE TOUR TO MECCA, 1886

Spas

From the ancient Greeks to 19th-century invalids, people have always traveled in search of healing waters—from hot-water springs to spas.

Although 19th-century historian Jules Michelet condemned the Medieval period as *un mille années sans un bain*, or "a thousand years without a bath," he was not entirely correct. Christian morals ended the Roman tradition of communal bathing, but thermal springs attracted health pilgrims throughout the Middle Ages. Well-known hot water springs existed at Bath in England, Aix-les-Bains in France, and Spa in what is now Belgium. At the latter, according to one 17th-century account, the waters could "extenuate phlegm; remove obstructions in the liver, spleen, and the alimentary canal; dispel all inflammations; and comfort and strengthen the stomach."

The popularity of these institutions grew massively during the period of the Grand Tour (see pp.180–83), when recuperative pit stops developed as an essential part of the itinerary. This gave rise to the grand spa towns of Central Europe—places like Baden-Baden, Bad Ems, Bad Gastein, Karlsbad, and Marienbad. Here, doctors administered regimes of imbibing water from mineral sources, bathing in thermal pools, and exercising.

Given the social nature of the Grand Tour, the spas became more akin to exclusive country clubs. In time, they offered not only luxurious accommodation but also gardens, theaters, dance halls, casinos, and racecourses, as well as busy programs of concerts, operas, grand balls, and fêtes. In their heyday, which was virtually the whole of the 19th century, the grandest spas were bywords for glamour, and they competed to attract royalty, heads of state, and figures of political and cultural eminence. For 20 years, the German writer Goethe spent around four months annually at a spa, famously encountering Beethoven during one of his stays at Karlsbad. Baden-Baden, which promoted itself as "Europe's summer resort," was where Brahms wrote his *Lichtenthal Symphony*, and was favored by Russian novelists Fyodor Dostoyevsky and Ivan Turgenev. A stay at a spa was considered not only good for health, but also beneficial for mental wellbeing and excellent for one's social standing.

◁ **Spa fountain, Karlsbad**
Named after Charles IV, Holy Roman Emperor, who visited this site of hot springs in the 1350s, Karlsbad became the most visited spa town in what is now the Czech Republic. Here, attendants pose for a photograph in 1910.

Going by the book

The Grand Tourists of old had unlimited time and money, and traveled with servants who could do everything for them. In the 19th century, "modern" travelers were less well-off and had to journey far more efficiently, so a new kind of guide emerged to help them.

▽ ***The Honeymoon*** This 19th-century engraving by Roberto Forell shows a couple holding a Baedeker guidebook. These books not only acted as a guide to local attractions, but also advised on how to behave when abroad.

▷ **Murray's handbooks** London publisher John Murray launched its first handbook in 1836, setting the template for modern-day guidebooks.

In E. M. Forster's novel *A Room with a View,* Lucy Honeychurch, the heroine, faces difficulty when she has to venture out in Florence without her Baedeker guidebook. It is a name that is now forgotten, but for almost a century, the words "travel" and "Baedeker" went hand in hand, so much so that for many, it was unthinkable to visit anywhere without the famous travel guide.

Guidebooks, like general travel literature, have existed in some form since the time of the ancient Greeks. They flourished in the era of the Grand Tour (see pp. 180–83), when numerous travelers had written, advising those who followed on places to visit. However, toward the middle of the 19th century, when tourism became a significant industry, driven by rapid improvements in transport and the increasing rise of a wealthy middle class, publishers saw the need for a new kind of travel book.

Handbooks for travelers

John Murray was renowned as the publisher of Lord Byron, among others. In 1820, the company issued *Travels on the Continent* by Mariana Starke, an Englishwoman who had grown up in India and who now lived in Italy. Whereas previous travel guides aspired to the literary, Starke's book was essentially practical. It included advice on what to pack and how to deal with bureaucracy, as well as on what things cost. Starke also introduced a ratings system of exclamation marks to highlight key sights. Her book was very popular with British travelers, and ran to eight editions, each updated by the author (in one she notes the introduction of streetlamps in Italy, which, she says, has put a stop to

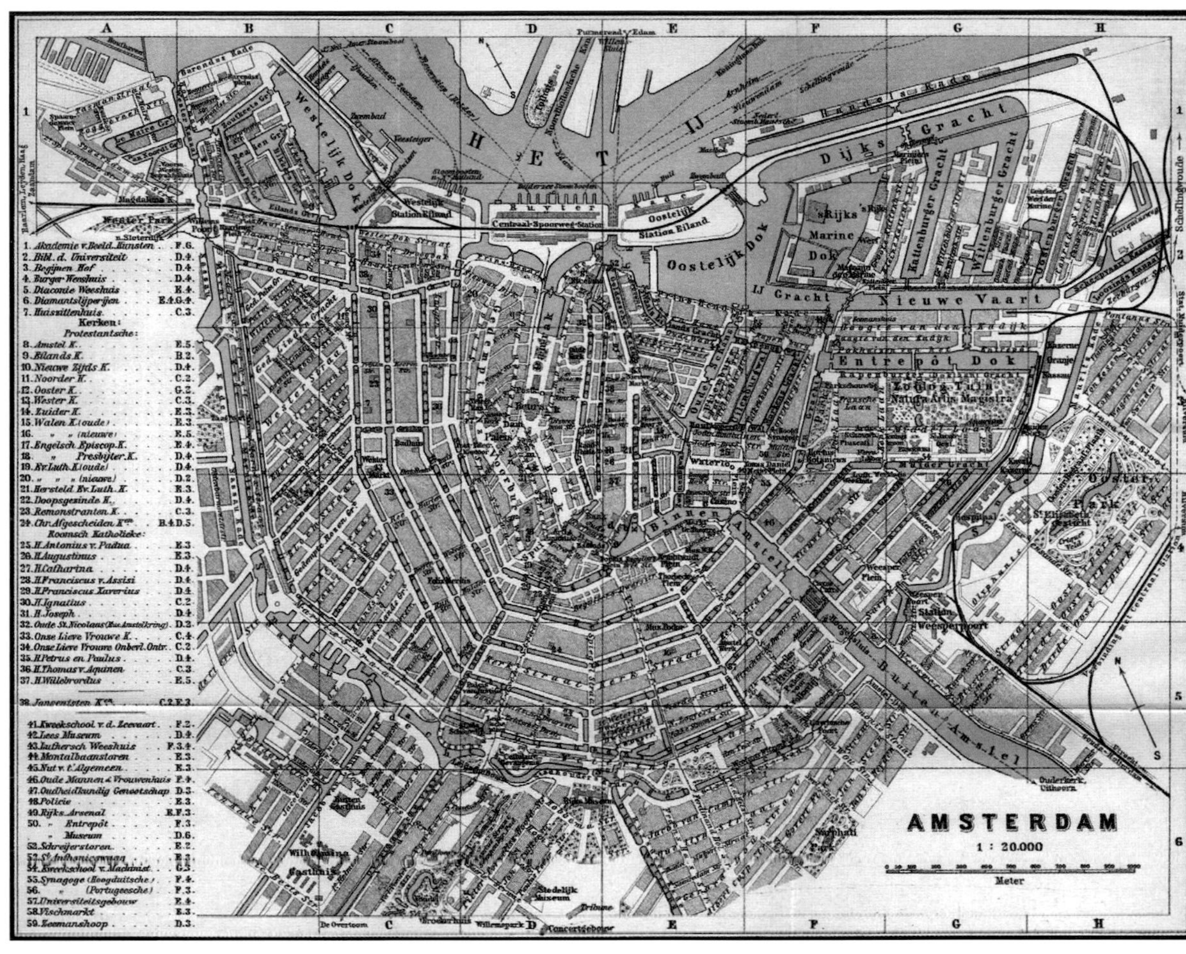

▷ **Baedeker maps**
From the beginning, Baedeker guidebook maps were famed for their detail and reliability. According to English travel writer Eric Newby, they were "made as if by spies for spies."

"the dreadful practice of assassination"). Arguably, Starke set the template for the guidebook as it exists today.

Murray capitalized on the book's success, following it with the *Handbook for Travellers on the Continent* (1836), which covered Holland, Belgium, and north Germany, and was written by the publisher himself. This was quickly succeeded by handbooks to South Germany (1837), Switzerland (1838), and France (1843). The books were standardized, made small to fit in the hand, printed on thin paper to keep down both cost and weight, and were updated on a regular basis. When the *Handbook to New Zealand* was published in 1893, one magazine commented: "Mr Murray has annexed what remained for him to conquer of the tourist world." By this time, however, Murray's handbooks were second in popularity to those published by Karl Baedeker.

Baedekers

Released by the German publishing house in 1839, the first Baedeker guides were modeled on Murray's, and were soon published in French and English as well as in German, all in a distinctive red cloth cover. Over time, they grew in popularity for the quality and concision of their information, their excellent maps, and the star-system that told travelers which sites were the most important. The books became so popular that Kaiser Wilhelm of Germany was quoted as saying that he stood at a particular window in his palace each noon, because: "It's written in Baedeker that I watch the changing of the guard from that window, and the people have come to expect it."

Less obligingly, in 1942, during World War II, several historic English cities were carpet-bombed in what became popularly known as the "Baedeker Raids," after a spokesperson for the German Air Force declared, "We shall go all out to bomb every building in Britain that is marked with three stars in the Baedeker guides". The following year, Allied bombers destroyed the publishing company's headquarters and archives in the city of Leipzig.

> " Murray's Guide-books now cover **nearly the whole Continent**. Since Napoleon, no man's empire has **been so wide**. "
>
> GEORGE STILLMAN HILLARD, IN *SIX MONTHS IN ITALY*, 1853

◁ **Karl Baedeker**
Descended from a line of publishers and printers, Baedeker saw the potential of Murray's handbooks, and soon outsold them with his own guides.

◁ **Advertising**
With the rise of tourism, guidebooks began to feature ads for specific locations, such as hotels and shops. This engraving is an ad for the Hôtel de L'Union in Brussels.

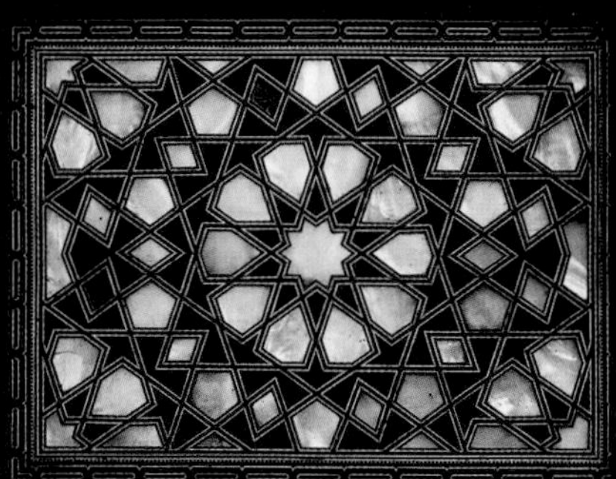

WOOD AND MOTHER-OF-PEARL QUR'AN BOX THAT BELONGED TO SULTAN SELIM II, 16TH CENTURY

PLYMOUTH ROCK FRAGMENT WITH PAINTED INSCRIPTION, US, 1830

LADY'S FAN COMMEMORATING CENTENNIAL EXHIBITION, PHILADELPHIA, 1876

DOUBLE OCTAGON SHELLWORK SAILOR'S VALENTINE, MID-19TH CENTURY

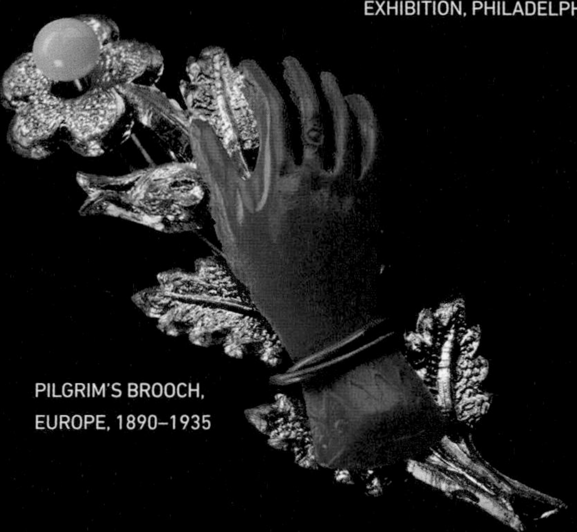

PILGRIM'S BROOCH, EUROPE, 1890–1935

JAPANESE NETSUKE (KIMONO ORNAMENT) OF OLD MAN

ENAMELED GOLD SNUFFBOX IN THE SHAPE OF A BUTTERFLY, WITH CARILLON AND WATCH

RUSSIAN NESTING DOLL, MASS-PRODUCED AFTER WINNING AWARD AT WORLD'S FAIR, PARIS, 1900

BOOKMARK ADVERTISING BUTLIN'S HOLIDAY CAMPS, UK, 1950s

BABOUCHES (EMBROIDERED MOROCCAN SLIPPERS)

DISH OF PAINTED LACQUERED SHELLS, WITH PHOTO OF A MALTESE HARBOR, MALTA c.1965–75

NEW YORK CITY NOVELTY PLASTIC SUNGLASSES

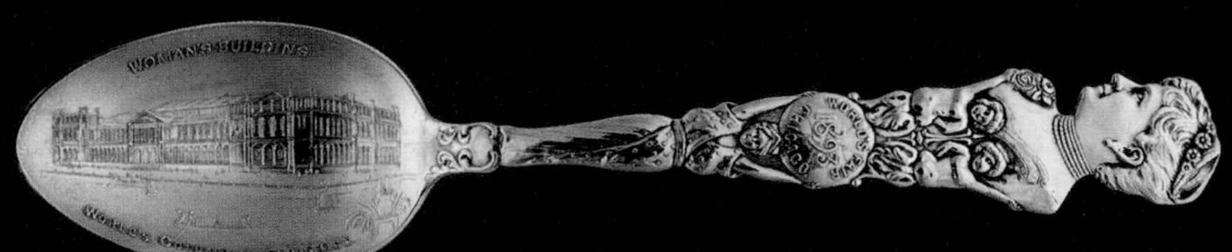

WORLD'S FAIR SILVER SPOON WITH IMAGE OF BERTHA PALMER (AMERICAN BUSINESSWOMAN AND SOCIALITE), CHICAGO, 1893

GLASS VIAL HOUSING COLORED SANDS FROM ALUM BAY, ISLE OF WIGHT, UK, 19TH CENTURY

CHINA CREAMER DEPICTING KINEO HOUSE AT MOOSEHEAD, LAKE MAINE, US, 1890s

TRAVEL GUIDES TO THE ITALIAN CITIES OF FLORENCE, CAPRI, AND MILAN, c.1926

SWEDISH DALECARLIAN HORSES, TRADITIONAL WOODEN TOY MASS-PRODUCED AFTER WORLD'S FAIR, PARIS,1937

Souvenirs

Meaning "memories" in French, souvenirs remind the owner of a place or event, and often have great sentimental value.

The first souvenirs were relics taken from a sacred or historic site such as Plymouth Rock, where the Mayflower Pilgrims were said to have first touched American soil. To preserve sites, as what was left of Plymouth Rock had to be fenced off in the 1880s, officials began to sell trinkets instead.

Souvenirs came into their own during the Grand Tour. In the 18th century, wealthy Europeans shipped home ancient sculpture, artifacts from archaeological digs, and views of Venice by the artist Canaletto that were forerunners of the postcard. Soon there was a market for manufactured keepsakes: Mt. Vesuvius erupting on porcelain and fans, bronze replicas of the Colosseum, even a "selfie" by Pompeo Batoni, who specialized in painting English lords lounging in classical settings. Starting with the 1851 British Great Exhibition, world's fairs attracted thousands of visitors in the late 19th century, and many of them took home a silver spoon, a china jug, or a penny trinket. Souvenirs could also be gifts, such as a sailor's shellwork valentine shaped with a heart and a tender message—"Think of me" or "Home again."

While love tokens, scenic tableware, and commemorative spoons are still popular, today's mass-produced souvenirs are a far cry from the handmade Qur'an and snuff boxes of earlier days. Russian dolls, snowglobes, slippers, novelty sunglasses, and bookmarks all make cheap and cheerful holiday mementos to bring home.

SNOW GLOBE (INVENTED IN VIENNA IN 1900) DEPICTING NEW YORK CITY

The works of all nations

Called variously Great Exhibitions, Expositions Universelles, and World's Fairs, a series of itinerant celebrations of industry, technology, and arts inspired those who visited to marvel at all the world had to offer.

△ **Javanese dancers** Exhibitions always featured ethnic attractions, ranging from exotic foods to costumes and dance, as here in Paris, 1889.

The full title of the very first international exhibition, which was held in London in 1851, described it as "The Great Exhibition of the Works of Industry of All Nations." This spectacular event, held in a glittering glass-and-steel "Crystal Palace" designed by Joseph Paxton, was a celebration of the achievements of the Industrial Revolution, as well as the success of the British Empire. It was the first of many exhibitions that, as well as aiming to glamorize the host city, became a platform for promoting wares from countries all around the world.

The world comes to town

In the 1851 Great Exhibition, there were exotic goods from Europe, the Near and Far East, the British colonies, and the US. Exhibits from the latter included Colt revolvers, false teeth, and a large model of the Niagara Falls. It is not recorded how many visitors were inspired to cross the Atlantic by such a display, but people from all across Great Britain flocked to the capital for the exhibition. It provided a huge boost for the new business of Thomas Cook & Son (see pp. 222–23), who organized the tickets, travel, and accommodations for 165,000 visitors from the Midlands.

Cook had a similar success when he launched his first Continental tours to the Paris Exposition Universelle of 1855. A second Paris exposition in 1867 was the first of its kind to introduce the idea of national pavilions, as well as a parade of ethnic restaurants where customers could experience different cuisines served by staff in national costume. One of its most popular exhibits was a large-scale model of the Suez Canal, complete with ships, and the Italians brought a model of the entrance to the Mont Cenis Tunnel, which was due to open the following year as part of the world's first mountain railway.

No expense spared

By this time, a pattern for Great Exhibitions had emerged: a large park was filled with a small city's worth of buildings that boasted every conceivable type of innovation, commodity, and activity. Each country was invited to take part, with no expense spared, and then after six months, the whole thing was razed to the ground, with maybe just the odd landmark surviving.

▷ ***Rue des Nations*** In Paris, in 1900, participating countries were invited to build national pavilions on the banks of the Seine river.

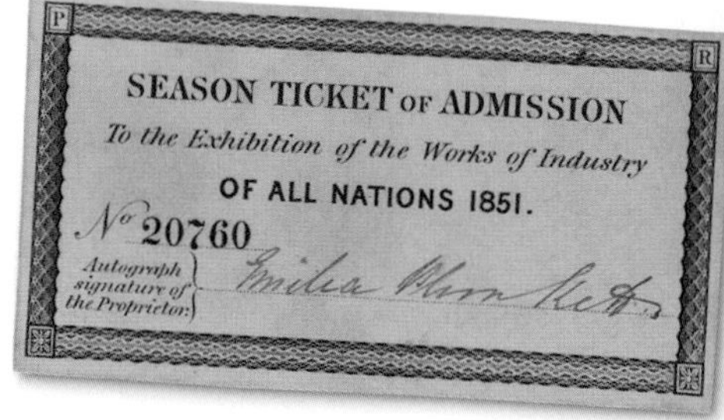

SEASON TICKET OF ADMISSION
To the Exhibition of the Works of Industry
OF ALL NATIONS 1851.
№ 20760
Autograph signature of the Proprietor.

△ **One ticket for all** Right from 1851, the Great Exhibitions drew enormous crowds of visitors on a scale that was only rivaled by the Olympic Games.

The 1878 Paris Exposition introduced a *Rue des Nations* (street of nations), a long promenade lined with facades of buildings exemplifying the architecture of numerous countries. In the 1889 Paris Exposition, this was developed into a large colonial section, complete with native villages, reproductions of parts of the Angkor Wat temples, and an entire Cairo street.

This street was so successful that the massive World's Columbian Exposition, which marked the 400th anniversary of Christopher Colombus's discovery of America and was held in Chicago in 1893, also featured an Egyptian Street, where Thomas Cook displayed models

▽ **Flying the flags**
Following the pattern set in London in 1851, the International Exhibition in Dublin, 1865, filled its halls with displays from around the world.

of its new fleet of Nile steamboats. At this exhibition too, the Syrian wife of a local Chicago restaurant owner scandalized American visitors by introducing the belly dance.

The years from 1875 to 1915 were the golden age of the Great Exhibitions, during which time over 50 of them were held in cities all over Europe and the US, as well as in Sydney and Melbourne. Millions of people flocked to see the glittering displays of pavilions and wares and were mesmerized by it all. The Great Exhibitions attracted some of the largest gatherings of people ever and, more significantly perhaps, represented one of the finest examples of international cultural and intellectual exchanges in modern history.

" A place where **young people** can see **how rich the world is in ideas**, how much there is yet to do, and **the point at which we need to begin**. "

HENRY FORD, CAR MANUFACTURER

▷ **The world from on high**
Held in Chicago, Illinois, in 1893, the World's Columbian Exposition featured the original Ferris Wheel, which stood 263 feet (80 m) high. The dome and minaret of the mosque on Cairo Street can be seen in the background.

Across Australia

Robert Burke and William Wills set out to be the first men to cross Australia, from Melbourne in the south to the Gulf of Carpentaria in the north—an epic undertaking that ended in tragedy.

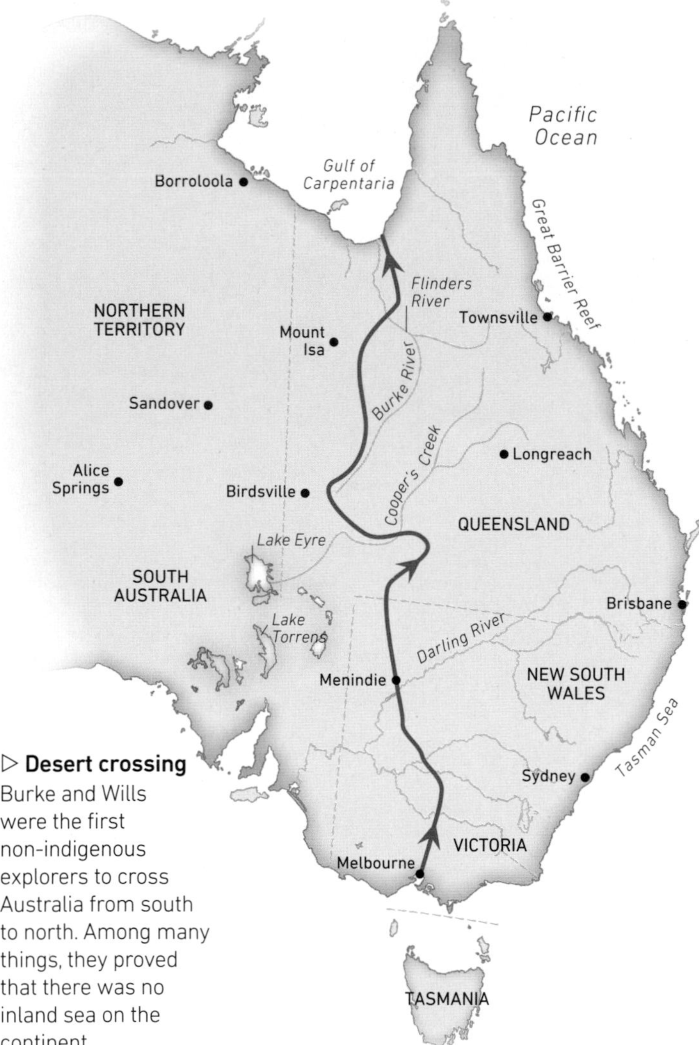

▷ **Desert crossing** Burke and Wills were the first non-indigenous explorers to cross Australia from south to north. Among many things, they proved that there was no inland sea on the continent.

On November 3, 1861, the Melbourne daily newspaper *The Argus* ran the following dispatch: "Sandhurst, Nov. 2. Mr. Brahe, of the Exploration Contingent, arrived here this afternoon, from Cooper's Creek. The remains of Burke and Wills, who both died on the same day from starvation, [supposed on or about the 28th of June] near Cooper's Creek, have been found. Gray, another of the party, also perished. King is the only survivor. They had crossed the continent to the Gulf of Carpentaria."

Bragging rights

The notion of taking on roughly 2,000 miles (3,220 km) of grueling terrain and extreme conditions was borne out of one-upmanship. The state of Victoria had recently split away from New South Wales and was eager to prove itself by winning the race to cross the continent. There was also the possibility of discovering new lands suitable for farming and grazing, and the challenge of confirming whether or not Australia had an inland sea.

An official exploration committee invited applications for the expedition, and appointed a party of 18 men, headed by Irish-born ex-army officer and policeman Robert O'Hara Burke. On August 20, 1860, cheered on by thousands, the convoy of 23 horses, 26 camels (most imported specially from Afghanistan), and six wagons laden with supplies and equipment departed. Over the next nine months, the expedition traveled north in stages from Melbourne to Menindie to Cooper's Creek to the Gulf of Carpentaria. This was not without incident. By the time the party reached Menindie, on the Darling River, on October 12, two officers had quit and 13 men had been fired and replaced with eight new hires. A journey that took the regular mail coach a week had taken almost two months.

◁ **Burke and Wills monument** A rough stone cairn, erected in 1890, marks the expedition's departure point from Royal Park, Melbourne, on August 20, 1860.

Irritated by the slow pace and afraid of being beaten in the race to the north, at Cooper's Creek, Burke decided to continue with just three companions: his second-in-command William John Wills, John King, and Charlie Gray. They took six camels, a horse, and provisions for three months and left the rest of the men at camp under the command of William Brahe.

The Dig Tree

Although they were prevented from reaching the sea by mangrove swamps, the small group reached the north coast. Getting back, however, was harder.

▷ **Cooper's Creek** The expedition reached Cooper's Creek—the boundary of unknown territory—on November 11, 1860. Here the party split, and Burke, Wills, and two others set off across the interior.

◁ **Carved in wood**
After successfully reaching the north coast, Burke and Wills managed to return only as far as Cooper's Creek, where they died of starvation. There, a tree was carved with an image of Burke in 1898.

They had to shoot and eat most of their animals, and Gray died of exhaustion. The other three made it back to the camp, but in a spectacular stroke of bad luck, after 18 weeks away, they arrived just half a day after Brahe had given them up for dead and headed back south. Brahe had buried a cache of supplies near a tree marked with the word "Dig," which was recovered by the trio. Rather than follow Brahe to Menindie, they headed for settled outposts in South Australia, which were much closer. They became lost in the bush and, suffering from starvation, exhaustion, and dehydration, Burke and Wills died. King survived and was discovered living with Aboriginals by a rescue party.

IN PROFILE
Robyn Davidson

Even in the late 20th century, the Australian interior remained formidable, which is why it seemed foolhardy when, in 1977, 27-year-old Robyn Davidson set off from Alice Springs for the west coast, alone except for a dog and four camels. Her journey covered 1,700 miles (2,735 km) and took nine months. "Why cross it by camel?" she pondered in *Tracks* (1995), the book she wrote about the expedition, "I have no ready answer. On the other hand, why not? Australia is a vast country, and most of us who live there see only a small fraction of it. Beyond the roads, in the area known as the outback, camels are the perfect form of transport. One sees little by car, and horses would never survive the hardships of desert crossings."

DAVIDSON AT THE 2014 PREMIERE FOR THE FILM ADAPTATION OF *TRACKS*

◁ ***Return of Burke and Wills to Cooper's Creek***
This painting by Nicholas Chevalier depicts Burke and Wills's desert trek. Their journey is one of Australia's great stories, the subject of countless books and images.

Charting the Mekong

Stretching from the Himalayan Plateau to Vietnam, the Mekong River flows for over 2,700 miles (4,350 km), yet almost nothing was known about it until an ambitious French expedition took to the river in 1866.

▽ **Royal Temple**
This picture by Louis Delaporte of the 16th-century Royal Temple at Luang Prabang, in Laos, featured in Doudart de Lagrée's account of the expedition.

In the middle of the 19th century, while the British were absorbed in the continued exploits of their imperial adventurers in Africa (see pp. 212–15), the French were about to undertake an equally ambitious foray into the heart of Southeast Asia.

It began in 1859, when French naval forces seized Saigon, a Vietnamese town at the mouth of the Mekong River which, it was hoped, could serve as a trade route into China via Siam (present-day Thailand). The French first needed to assess whether the river was navigable, so they assembled a seven-man Mekong Exploration Commission. Headed by Ernest Doudart de Lagrée, and including surveyor Francis Garnier, artist Louis Delaporte, and photographer Émile Gsell, the Commission set off from Saigon on June 5, 1866, in two small steamboats, each heavily laden with guns, trade goods, and huge quantities of wine and brandy. They stopped for a month to investigate the ancient Khmer temple complex of Angkor Wat in Cambodia, then re-embarked at Phnom Penh on July 7. However, only 36 hours later, near the river-port of Kratie, the waters were deemed too dangerous for the steamboats and the team transferred to eight dugout canoes. Although roofed

> “ Each **bend of the Mekong** as added to my map seemed an **important geographical discovery** ... I was **mad about the Mekong** ... ”
>
> FRANCIS GARNIER, MISSION SURVEYOR

◁ **Khmer temple art**
In Cambodia, the expedition discovered numerous Hindu temples, some dating as far back as the Khmer period (9th–15th centuries).

with bamboo to keep out any heavy monsoon rain, the canoes were still far from comfortable: “The roof being too low to let me sit up, I had to stay half lying down, and the rain accumulating in the bottom of the boat continually invaded my person,” wrote one man.

At Preatapang, the expedition encountered rapids, and only managed to get through them by threatening the native boatmen at gunpoint. However, threats were of no avail at the Falls of Khon, where thunderous, precipitous waterfalls barred their way, forcing them to leave the river.

On into China

At this point, the expedition could have returned to Saigon to report its findings, but instead it pushed on in new canoes they procured on the far side of the falls. When they reached Bassac, in Laos, they learned that northeastern Cambodia had erupted in rebellion against the French, which prevented them returning the way they had come: the only route home was ahead.

On June 18, 1867, the men reached Tang-ho and faced what was rumored to be some 60 miles (100 km) of rapids. They therefore decided to abandon the river for good, transferred the baggage to 12 bullocks, and continued on foot in increasingly treacherous conditions. With no river to follow and no map, they had to rely on compass readings and navigating by the stars to keep them on course. This they managed successfully, for on October 1, they finally reached Jinhong, on the threshold of China. From there, the going became easier, but in Dongchuan, Yunnan, Lagrée succumbed to illness and died. Garnier took charge and led the group to the Yangtze River, along which they sailed all the way to Shanghai, and then eventually back to Saigon. In all, the expedition traveled over 6,800 miles (11,000 km), which is greater than the length of Africa, and suffered all manner of personal dangers. It failed to produce the political advantages that France had hoped for, but its surveys and observations ran to thousands of pages, and helped to fill in what had up until then been gaping blanks on Western maps of this part of the world.

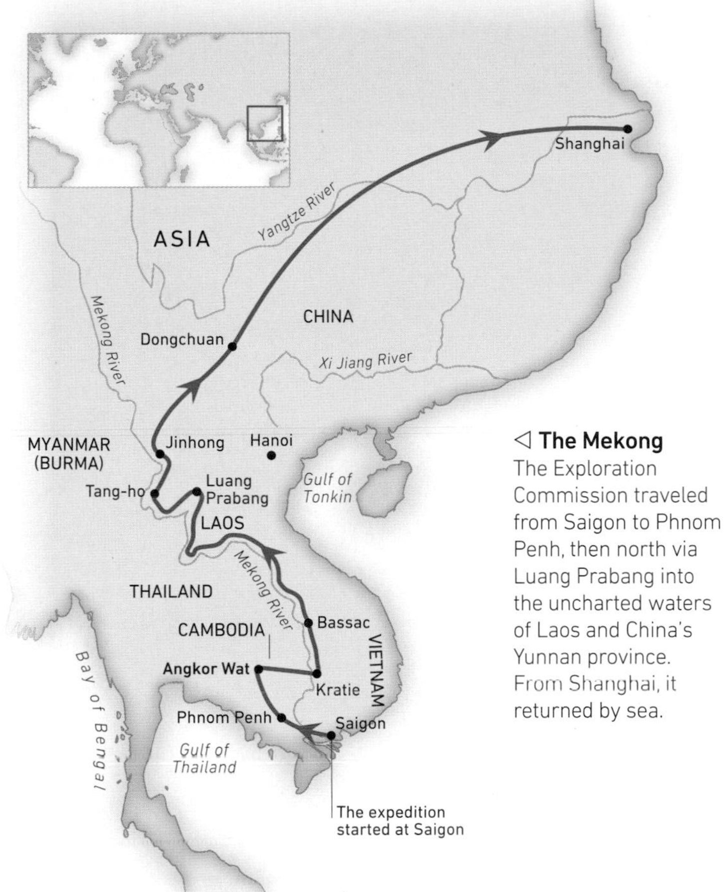

◁ **The Mekong**
The Exploration Commission traveled from Saigon to Phnom Penh, then north via Luang Prabang into the uncharted waters of Laos and China’s Yunnan province. From Shanghai, it returned by sea.

◁ **Expedition party**
This engraving, based on a photograph by Émile Gsell, shows Doudart de Lagrée (in white trousers) as well as five other members of the expedition, including Delaporte and Garnier (far right).

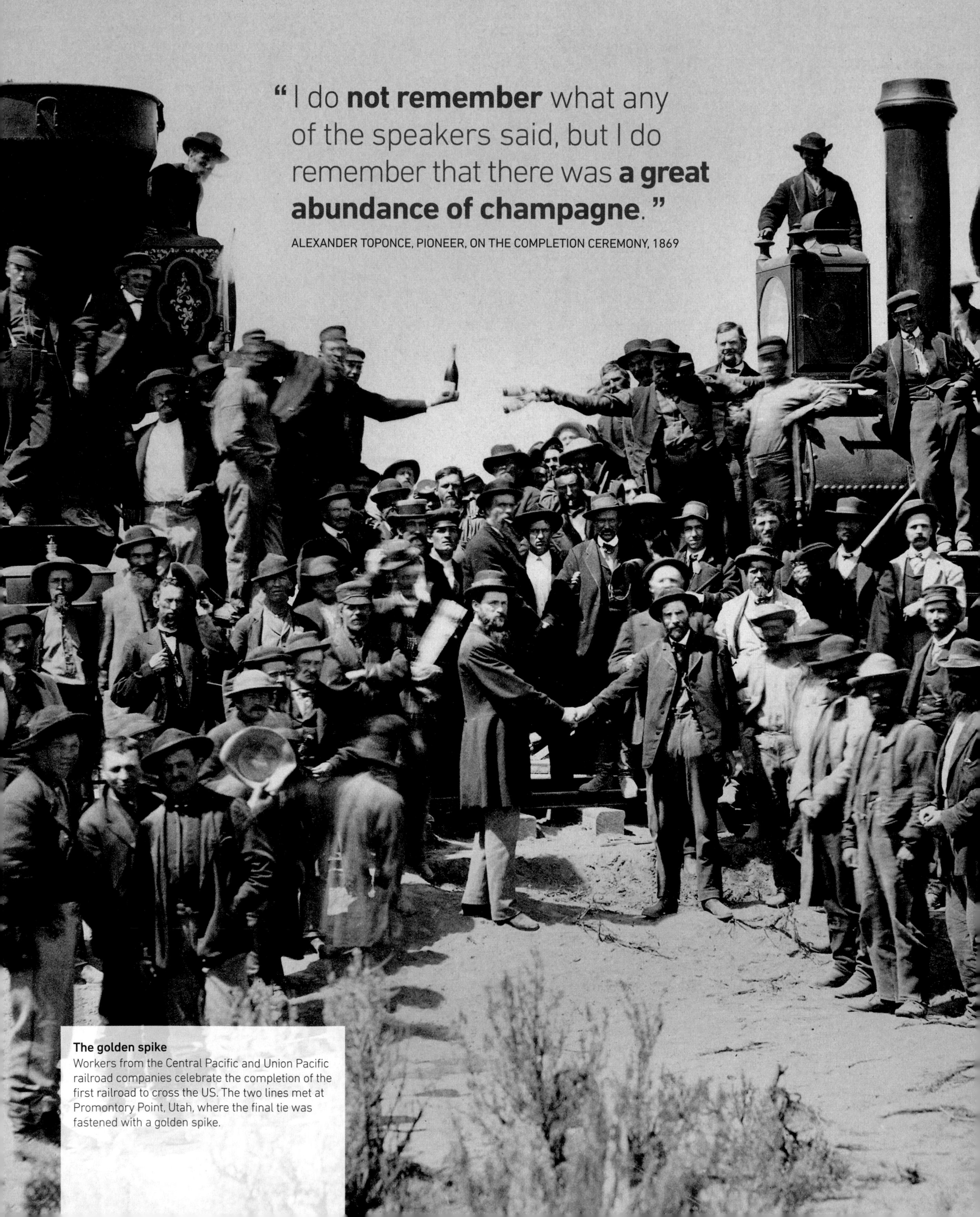

“I do **not remember** what any of the speakers said, but I do remember that there was **a great abundance of champagne**.”

ALEXANDER TOPONCE, PIONEER, ON THE COMPLETION CEREMONY, 1869

The golden spike
Workers from the Central Pacific and Union Pacific railroad companies celebrate the completion of the first railroad to cross the US. The two lines met at Promontory Point, Utah, where the final tie was fastened with a golden spike.

Ocean to ocean

The completion of America's first transcontinental railroad was a landmark not just in transportation but in nation building.

The United States had been quick to grasp the benefits of the railroad. Even so, in 1860, 30 years after the first lines had been laid, the only way to get from one coast to the other was still either by wagon or to sail round South America. To remedy this, in 1862, President Abraham Lincoln signed the Pacific Railroad Act. The legislation granted financial subsidies and land rights to railway companies in order to construct a continuous transcontinental railroad between the eastern side of the Missouri River at Council Bluffs, Iowa, to the Sacramento River in California.

In the west, four businessmen came together to back Theodore Judah's Central Pacific Railroad Company, which won the contract to build the line out of California. Progress was slow, but by 1867, the toughest engineering challenge was overcome with the completion of a passage through the Sierra Nevada mountains at the Donner Pass, 7,086 feet (2,160 m) above sea level. In the east, work was delayed by the ongoing Civil War, but once this ended in 1865, the Union Pacific Railroad Company, which held the contract for that end of the line, was boosted by the addition of ex-soldiers and freed slaves to its army of railway builders.

To build the railroad, an advance party first surveyed the route, then graders smoothed out the terrain, leveling earth, clearing rocks, and creating embankments and bridges. Lastly came the tracklayers, who put down the sleepers and rails. The government contracts paid for each mile of track completed, so both companies competed to lay as much as possible. Eventually, Promontory Summit in Utah was agreed on as the place to join the tracks—so it was there that company representatives took turns hammering a golden spike into the final tie on May 10, 1869. It was not just a railroad that had been united, but a country, and a journey that had previously taken six months was now possible in just a matter of days.

▷ **The great event**
A poster announces the opening of the railroad connecting the Pacific and Atlantic oceans. The service opened the West to settlers of all kinds, and to people traveling for pleasure.

The grand hotel

Around the middle of the 19th century, hotels blossomed from basic resting places to grand, and often luxurious, destinations in their own right.

△ **Grand arrival**
People arrived at the grand hotels in style. In this 1931 photo, hotel porters at the Bayerischer Hof in Munich load up new arrivals' suitcases and bags.

On May 5, 1862, Empress Eugénie of France was invited to the inauguration of the Grand Hôtel, Paris. Occupying a vast triangular plot next to the site on which Garnier's spectacular opera house would soon rise, the Grand was possibly the largest hotel in the world at the time, boasting 800 rooms and 65 salons. It had a spectacular glass-roofed courtyard, a cellar holding a million bottles of wine, décor by a host of well-known artists, and a vast ballroom. It was, said the Empress, "like home."

Until the middle of the 19th century, hotels in the modern sense were rare. Travelers generally stayed in boarding houses or rented lodgings in cities and put up at coaching inns while on the road. However, as the numbers of travelers increased and stays became shorter, it became impractical to rent lodgings—what people needed were modern hotels.

Two of the first great hotels of note were built in the rapidly expanding cities of North America. The Tremont House in Boston, built in 1929, was soon followed by the first luxury hotel in New York City, Astor House, which opened in 1836. Both establishments offered unimaginable luxuries such as indoor plumbing, heating, gas lighting, locked rooms for guests, free soap, and dining rooms with extensive menus.

◁ **Swiss bellboy**
Many fine early hotels were established in Switzerland, where winter sports kept them busy year round. The staff were immaculately dressed, in keeping with the status of the hotels.

Beds for the crowds

Some of the earliest large hotels in Europe were built next to stations by railway companies. The first railway hotel was completed at Euston in London in 1839, and even larger hotels were constructed soon after at Paddington in 1854, Victoria in 1861, and Charing Cross in 1864. Several hotels were also built specifically to accommodate the crowds anticipated for the Great Exhibitions (see pp. 230–31),

▷ **The Grand Hôtel, Paris**
The luxurious Grand accommodated royalty and a host of celebrities, including actress Sarah Bernhardt, composer Jacques Offenbach, and opera singer Enrico Caruso.

◁ **The Waldorf Astoria**
American hotels led the way in terms of comfort and amenities. New York's Waldorf Astoria was the first hotel to be completely electrified and offer each guest a private bathroom.

notably the Grand Hôtel du Louvre, which was built for the 1855 Paris Exposition, the Langham Hotel (London, 1862), and the Continental (Paris, 1878).

Initiated by the splendors of the Paris Grand, the late 19th century issued in a golden age of hotels. Benefitting from new inventions such as the elevator, first publicly demonstrated at the New York World's Fair of 1854, and then electricity, hotels became even larger and more grand. The Americans led the way—European travelers to the United States often remarked on the size and comfort of the hotels they found there. Hotels in Europe, in turn, attempted to attract American visitors by improving amenities, notably the number of bathrooms. When London's Savoy was under construction in the 1880s, its financier, Rupert D'Oyly Carte, requested one bathroom for every two bedrooms, leading his contractor to ask if D'Oyly Carte was expecting his guests to be amphibious.

One of D'Oyly Carte's smartest moves was to enlist the services of Swiss-born César Ritz as manager of his new hotel. In the late 1890s, Ritz left the Savoy to launch his own eponymous hotel, situated on the fashionable Place Vendôme in Paris. Behind an 18th-century façade, it boasted a private bath for each room, setting a standard for luxury that was to become the benchmark for every grand hotel that followed.

IN PROFILE
César Ritz

Born in Switzerland's upper Rhône Valley in 1850, César Ritz went to Paris to look for work during the 1867 Exposition. He worked in a succession of restaurants before returning to Switzerland to work at the Hotel Rigi-Klum, near Lucerne. In 1877, he moved to the Grand Hôtel National in Lucerne, which, although the most luxurious hotel in Switzerland, was suffering financial difficulties. In a single season, he turned it around. He struck up a partnership with chef Auguste Escoffier, and together they established the dining room as the hotel's social center, a destination not just for guests but for all of fashionable society.

CÉSAR RITZ IN 1900, TWO YEARS AFTER OPENING THE HOTEL RITZ IN PARIS

SAVOY HOTEL

Menu.

PETITE BOUCHÉE WLADIMIR
CONSOMMÉ AUX NIDS D'HIRONDELLES
SUPRÊME DE SOLE NANTUA
CAILLE ROYALE AU RAISIN DE MUSCAT
NOISETTE D'AGNEAU À LA MASCOTTE
PÂTÉ DE FOIE GRAS DE STRASBOURG
SALADE ISABELLE AUX ASPERGES
PLUM PUDDING FLAMBÉAU RHUM
FANTAISIE PARISIENNE
FRIANDISES.

New Years Eve 1908. Savoy Hotel, London.

◁ **Haute cuisine**
This 1908 New Year's menu from the Savoy Hotel Grand shows that the grand hotels were not just places to stay, but venues where high society could dine, dance, and be seen.

> " When I **dream of** afterlife in **heaven**, the **action** always **takes place** in the **Paris Ritz**. "

ERNEST HEMINGWAY, IN A LETTER TO A.E. HOTCHNER

GRAND HOTEL DE LYON, FRANCE

KYOTO HOTEL, JAPAN

HOTEL LUNA, ITALY

VILLARS PALACE, SWITZERLAND

HOTEL DE LA MAMOUNIA, MOROCCO

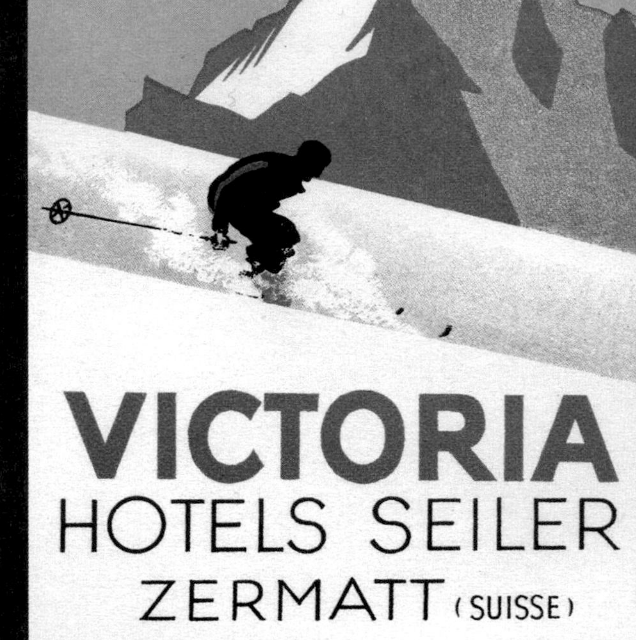

VICTORIA HOTEL, SWITZERLAND

CAISTER HOTEL, SOUTH AFRICA

HOTEL TIMES SQUARE, US

SEA VIEW HOTEL, SINGAPORE

HOLDEN'S AIR SERVICES, NEW GUINEA

STATION HOTEL, MALAYSIA

OVERLAND DESERT MAIL, MIDDLE EAST

GRAND HOTEL RICHTER, FRANCE

COSULICH LINE, ITALY

HOTEL REGIS, MEXICO

Luggage labels

Beautiful and practical, luggage labels indicated where a traveler's luggage was to go, and where it had been.

HOTEL RUHL, FRANCE

Labels were first issued by shipping companies as an aid to dockside handling, indicating which items were wanted in cabins and which could be stored in the baggage hold. They were later adopted by the hotel industry. Porters at the railway station or harbor stuck them onto travelers' luggage to make sure all items were delivered to the correct hotels. In later years, hotels handed them out to guests as souvenirs of their stay, and as a cheap and effective early form of advertising.

The artists who designed hotel labels typically sought to encapsulate the exoticism and romance of the local area, so they usually included landmarks set against dusky sunsets or brilliant blue skies. Some of these labels are mini masterpieces, resembling classic travel posters from the golden era of travel—unsurprising, given that the same artists produced designs for both posters and labels.

A well-stickered piece of luggage also advertised its owner's worldliness, wealth, and status. "Traveling in a compartment with my hat-box beside me, I enjoyed the silent interest which my labels aroused in my fellow-passengers," wrote essayist Max Beerbohm in 1909.

The advent of flight forced travelers to travel with far less luggage, and the tradition of the luggage label came to an end.

HOTELS ESSENERHOF AND SCHLICKER, GERMANY

Measuring India

In India, the British undertook the most arduous map-making expedition ever launched. It took nearly 70 years to complete, and cost more lives than many wars, yet it is all but forgotten today.

By the end of the 18th century, the British East India Company was in control of large swaths of India, but knowledge of the country was limited. Frontiers, districts, and infrastructure had yet to be established, but this was difficult without good maps. So, shortly after a victory over Tipu Sultan, the ruler of the Kingdom of Mysore in southern India, a scientific survey of the country was initiated.

The Great Trigonometrical Survey

What became known as the Great Trigonometrical Survey of India began at Madras, on the east coast, on April 10, 1802, under the command of surveyor William Lambton. It involved taking the most precise measurement possible along the ground between two fixed points, and then sighting a third fixed point from either end of this line. The distance to the third point could then be calculated using trigonometry. This new line then served as the baseline for another sighting, and so on until a given area was measured. All calculations were checked against the positions of the stars, using a huge custom-made theodolite (a kind of telescope), which weighed half a ton. By this rigorous and arduous process, the survey made its way, triangle by triangle, westward from Madras across the newly acquired territory of Mysore, via Bangalore in central India, to Mangalore on the Arabian Sea.

Logistical problems

This first portion of the survey took four years, and established that the width of India at that latitude was 360 miles (580 km), which was 40 miles (64 km) shorter than had previously been thought. The survey then worked south from Bangalore to the southern tip of India, and north up the spine of the country to Delhi and beyond, in a

◁ **Lambton's theodolite**
Weighing over 1,100 lb (508 kg), this huge piece of surveying equipment was taken to India by William Lambton in 1802. Its sturdiness helped surveyors make accurate readings.

> " We have for some years known that **this mountain is higher** than **any** hitherto **measured in India** and most probably it is the **highest in the whole world**. "

ANDREW SCOTT WAUGH, SURVEYOR-GENERAL OF INDIA, SUCCESSOR TO GEORGE EVEREST, 1850

△ **Surveyors at work**
This 19th-century lithograph shows an Indian team—stake, tripod, and line in hand—taking part in the Great Trigonometrical Survey.

vast arc roughly corresponding to the 78-degree meridian (or north-south line of longitude). However, the project was beset by problems. The most challenging was how to obtain lines of sight in jungles and landscapes hazy with dust and thousands of cow-dung cooking fires. One solution was to deploy highly visible flares at night, and to view these from specially built observation towers. Less easy to solve were the outbreaks of malaria and other diseases that claimed hundreds of lives—not to mention tiger attacks, which spread terror far and wide.

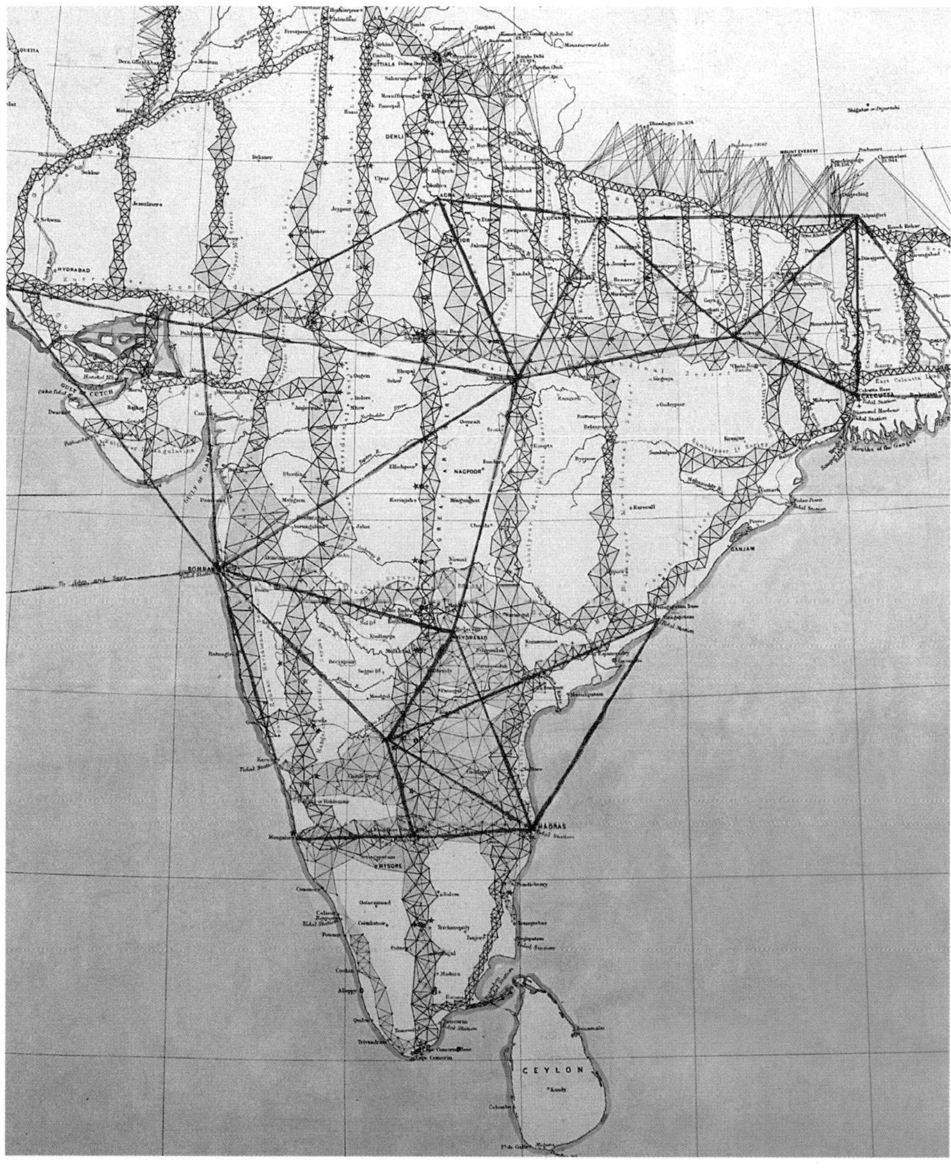

◁ **India mapped**
This chart of the Great Trigonometrical Survey shows William Lambton's network of measurements across India. Each large triangle contains numerous smaller ones.

Mount Everest

With the death of Lambton, the project came under the leadership of George Everest, who became Surveyor-General of India from 1830 to 1843. An ambitious man with a temper, Everest was not liked by his staff. Even so, when the survey reached the Himalayas in 1856 and an Indian mathematician called Radhanath Sikdar calculated the height of the tallest peak in the world, the peak was named after the former Surveyor-General. Everest himself objected (he thought a local name should be used) but his protests were overruled. It is also true that he was most annoyed when his name was mispronounced—it was "EVE-rest," he insisted, not "EVER-est." The mountain's Tibetan name is *Chomolungma*, which means "Goddess mother of the world."

▷ **The top of the world**
In 1856, the height of Mount Everest (then known as Peak XV) was recorded as 29,003 ft (8,840 m) high. Today, the official height of Earth's highest mountain is 29,029 ft (8,848 m) .

The early alpinists

With much of the known world explored and mapped, the next challenge was to conquer inhospitable regions where no-one had gone before—mountain peaks.

▽ **Top of Europe**
French photographer Auguste-Rosalie Bisson was the first person to take photographs from the summit of Mont Blanc, in the summer of 1861. He needed 25 porters to carry all his equipment.

A few days before Christmas in 1857, a group of around 20 men gathered at a hotel in London's Covent Garden for the inaugural meeting of the Alpine Club. Under the chairmanship of Edward Kennedy—a "gentleman of independent means", who two years previously had been part of the first expedition to climb Mont Blanc du Tacul in the French Alps—the club's members were to become instrumental in developing the new sport of mountaineering.

Alpinism in a contemporary sense arguably began in 1760, when a young geologist from Geneva, Horace-Bénédict de Saussure, offered a reward to the first person to climb Mont Blanc, the highest peak in Europe at 15,774 feet (4,808 m). It took 25 years for the prize to be claimed, but it eventually went to Michel-Gabriel Paccard, a doctor from Chamonix, in 1786. A year later, de Saussure reached the summit himself.

Ascents of other peaks were made during the next 60 years, but the beginning of a golden age of alpinism,

when the more difficult Alpine peaks were conquered for the first time, is generally dated to the ascent of the Wetterhorn in 1854 by Alfred Willis—the high court judge who famously jailed Oscar Wilde for "acts of gross indecency." This was not the first ascent of the mountain, but Willis's account of the expedition did much to popularize climbing. He was one of those present at the founding meeting of the Alpine Club.

◁ **Edward Whymper**
English artist, mountaineer, and explorer Edward Whymper made the first ascent of the Matterhorn. He also climbed in South America and the Canadian Rockies.

Peak season

In the early years of the golden age, British climbers, accompanied by Swiss, Italian, or French guides, scaled one after another of the high peaks of Switzerland. For some, the ascent was linked with a quest for knowledge; physicist John Tyndall, who was a member of the first team to reach the top of the Weisshorn, in 1861, took the opportunity to study glaciers and their motion. The crowning achievement was the first ascent of the Matterhorn in July 1865, by a party led by 25-year-old English artist, Edward Whymper. Unfortunately, tragedy struck on the descent over snow- and ice-covered rocks, when one of the party slipped and took three other men with him, tumbling over a precipice 4,002 feet (1,220 m) to their deaths.

By 1870, all the principal summits in the Alps had been scaled, and climbers began to look for challenges elsewhere. Initially, this was the Pyrenees and the Caucasus Mountains, but by the end of the 19th century, mountaineers had turned to the Andes in South America, the North American Rocky Mountains, and Africa's peaks. Mount Aconcagua, the highest peak of the Andes, was first climbed in 1897, and Grand Teton in the Rocky Mountains was ascended in 1898. Mount Kilimanjaro in Africa was climbed in 1889 by Ludwig Purtscheller and Hans Meyer, and Mount Kenya in 1899 by Halford Mackinder. In 1913, an American, Hudson Stuck, ascended Mount McKinley in Alaska, which is the highest peak in North America. It would, however, still be quite some time before the final bastion, Mount Everest in the Himalayas, was ascended.

Edward Whymper went to Ecuador where he made first ascents of several peaks and climbed Chimborazo, the volcano that had previously been visited by Alexander von Humboldt (see pp. 192–93). Whymper amassed data for a study of altitude sickness, and also collected amphibians and reptiles, which he handed over to the British Museum. He later climbed in the Canadian Rockies, where Mount Whymper is named in his honor.

△ **Painting Mont Blanc**
Canadian-British John Auldjo climbed Mont Blanc in 1827. His account of the ascent, which featured several watercolor paintings, was an instant bestseller.

△ **Climbing the Rockies**
General John Charles Fremont, a pioneer in American exploration, planted this "Fremont Flag" on the crest of the Rocky Mountains in August 1842.

> "We remained on the **summit for one hour**. One **crowded hour** of **glorious life**."
>
> EDWARD WHYMPER, MOUNTAINEER, ON ASCENDING THE MATTERHORN, 1865

Creating the national parks

As settlers tamed America, there was a realization that this came with a terrible cost—the destruction of land and extermination of wildlife. A handful of individuals became determined to rescue portions of the landscape before it was too late.

In 1851, during the height of the California Gold Rush (see pp. 220–21), a group of state militia soldiers on a hunt for native people entered a valley in the western Sierra Nevada mountains. One member of the party, a young doctor named Lafayette Bunnell, was astonished by the beauty of the place: "As I looked, a peculiar exalted sensation seemed to fill my whole being," he wrote, "and I found my eyes in tears with emotion." He suggested they give the valley a name: believing that it was the name of the native tribe who lived in the area, they called it "Yosemite." In fact, the word was one that other local tribes used to refer to the tribe living in the valley whom they feared; it meant, "They are killers."

△ **The first national park**
Yellowstone, shown here in a 1910 poster advertising the region, was not only the first national park in the US, but also the first national park in the world. It achieved this status in March 1872.

Four years later, failed gold prospector James Mason Hutchings led a group of visitors to the valley with the idea of making his fortune by setting up a hotel there. With the aid of drawings by illustrator Thomas Ayers, he spread the word of Yosemite's beauty and encouraged tourism in the area. The designer of New York's Central Park, Frederick Law Olmsted, was one such visitor. He described Yosemite as "the greatest glory of nature ... the union of the deepest sublimity with the deepest beauty." Olmstead was also one of the people who expressed fear at what might happen if entrepreneurs like Hutchings were not kept in check. Already, at this early stage in the nation's history, its most famous natural landmark, Niagara Falls, had almost been ruined by private developers spoiling the site with unregulated buildings and cordoning off access, except to those willing to pay.

In May 1864, therefore, a bill was proposed—the first of its kind in the world—that would set aside 60 sq miles (155 sq km) of land around the Yosemite Valley for "public use, resort, and recreation." It was made into law that June by President Abraham Lincoln.

Six years later, a group co-led by a former entrepreneur, vigilante, and tax collector named Nathaniel P. Langford

JOHN MUIR WITH PRESIDENT THEODORE ROOSEVELT IN YOSEMITE

IN PROFILE
John Muir

When an industrial accident almost cost him his eye, Scottish-born American John Muir decided to follow his dreams of exploration. He walked from Kansas to Florida, and eventually ended up in San Francisco, where he immediately set off for the Yosemite Valley. He spent several years there, living a life of simplicity, and becoming an expert on the area's flora and geology. He wrote articles to support himself financially. In one, he theorized that the spectacular Yosemite formations had been formed by glaciers—a theory now generally accepted. His writings proved highly influential in swinging public opinion in favor of national forest reservations, and inspired the conservation programs initiated by President Theodore Roosevelt who, in 1903, accompanied Muir on a camping trip to Yosemite.

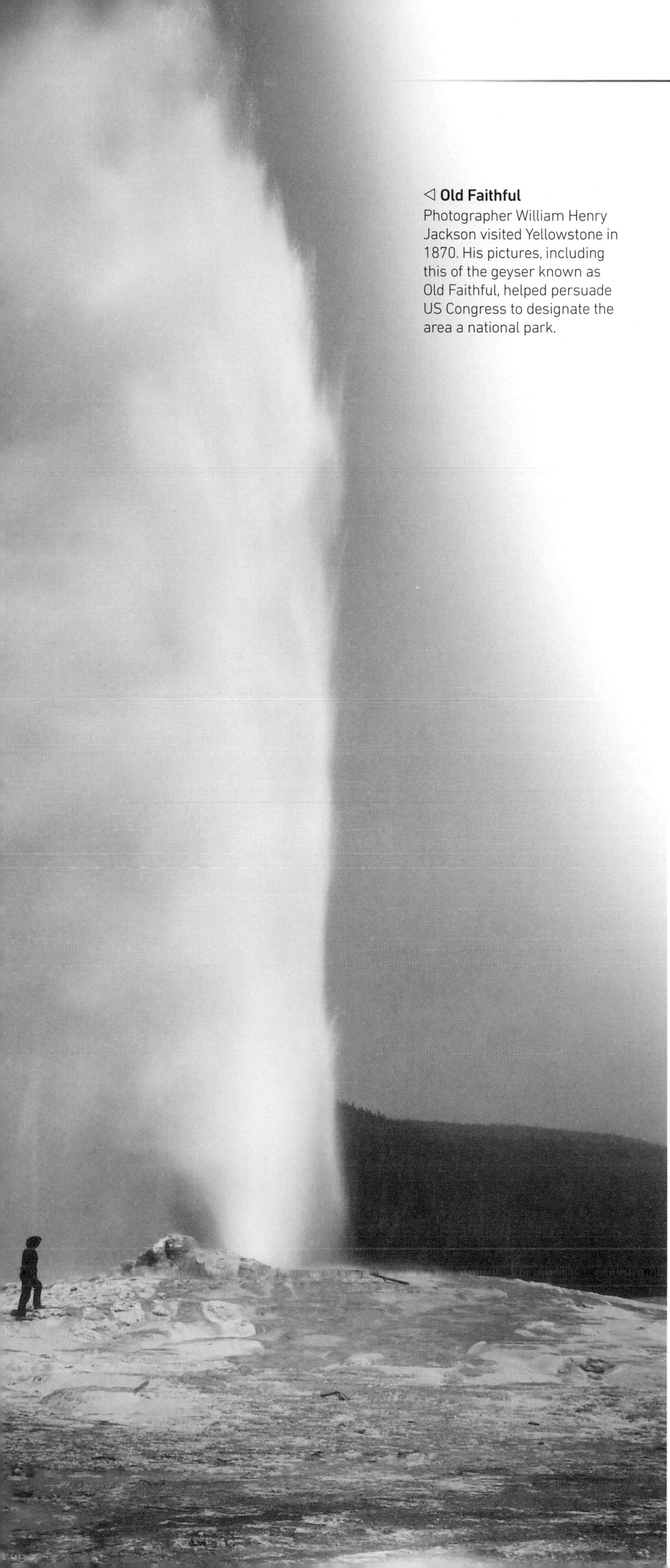

◁ **Old Faithful**
Photographer William Henry Jackson visited Yellowstone in 1870. His pictures, including this of the geyser known as Old Faithful, helped persuade US Congress to designate the area a national park.

△ **Yosemite**
Glacier Point, photographed here in 1877, was one of the rugged wonders that amazed Frederick Law Olmsted during his visit to Yosemite.

set out to investigate tales of a place in northwest Wyoming, at the headwaters of the Yellowstone River, where water and steam spouted out of the ground. The party eventually found what it was looking for. After struggling through dense forest and snow, they came across a large clearing where they witnessed the eruption of an immense geyser, causing them to toss up their hats and shout for joy.

The following year, the area was visited by a party of scientists who prepared a report that was submitted to Congress. On March 1, 1872, President Ulysses S. Grant signed the bill, creating Yellowstone National Park. Unlike Yosemite, which was administered by the state of California, this would be a national park, the first in history.

Following campaigns by naturalist John Muir, who was dismayed by the Californian state's inability to look after Yosemite, this area of outstanding national beauty was also elevated to the status of national park in 1890.

▷ **Cook's Tours**
As early as 1873, Thomas Cook was personally leading groups of tourists on trips around the world. This poster dates from 1890.

Around the world

By the end of the 19th century, thanks to improved transportation and the opening of the Suez Canal, intrepid tourists were able to travel around the world.

△ **Ida Pfeiffer**
Austrian author Ida Pfeiffer looked like a conventional 19th-century wife, but was, in fact, an adventurous traveler.

Ida Pfeiffer was an extraordinary woman. Born in Vienna in 1797, a time when women were meant to devote themselves to "Kinder, Küche, Kirche" (children, kitchen, church), she traveled the world alone, not once but twice. What is more, she paid for her travels with her writing.

Her early life was fairly conventional. Although she grew up with several brothers and was treated as one of the boys by her father (she was even dressed in boys' clothes), she was married at the age of 22 and had two sons. It was only after she and her husband had separated and the sons had grown up and left home that Ida, then age 45, decided to travel.

She went first to the Holy Land and Egypt, ostensibly on a pilgrimage, knowing that this would meet with less disapproval from family and friends. She followed her foray into the Middle East with a trip to Iceland and then, in 1846, with an around-the-world tour that took in South America, China, India, Iraq, Iran, Russia, Turkey, and Greece. She traveled with almost no luggage—just a leather pouch for water, a small pan for cooking, and some salt, rice, and bread. She returned home in 1848, staying just long enough to write a bestselling account of her voyages. Then she sallied forth again, heading for South Africa and then on to Asia.

Ida was not just unique in being a woman traveling on her own. In the mid-19th century, few people traveling for pleasure ventured farther than Europe, the Middle East, and the eastern part of America. Beyond these familiar places, there was little in the way of scheduled transportation or tourist accommodation, and traveling farther afield required fortitude and the ability to cope with the unexpected, the uncomfortable, and even the outright dangerous. Ida lodged with local people, slept outside on the decks

▷ **Media darling**
Nellie Bly's youth, sex, and daring led to fame. Here, she is depicted on the cover of an 1890 "Round the World" board game.

of crowded ships, dined with cannibals, and was even imprisoned in Madagascar, where she was accused of conspiring against the queen.

World travel

By the end of the 1860s, this situation was beginning to change. The Suez Canal opened in 1869, enabling direct steamship services between Europe and Asia. The opening of Japan to foreign trade in the 1850s had already led to similar services across the Pacific.

Unsurprisingly, the man who had taken advantage of the new steam railways to launch his guided-tour business, Thomas Cook (see pp. 222–23), was quick to spot the possibilities of world travel. By 1872, his company had already escorted parties all around Europe, and to America, Egypt, and the Holy Land. In spring that year, he announced an ambitious around-the-world excursion that he would lead himself. His route went across the Atlantic and the United States to Japan, China, Singapore, Ceylon, India, and Egypt. Travelers then took a steamer across the Mediterranean, and crossed Europe by rail to return to London. In all, the tour covered 25,000 miles (40,234 km) and took 222 days. It was such a success that it became an annual event from then on.

> " It is easy **to make plans in this world**, even a cat can do it; and when one is out on **those remote oceans**, it is noticeable that a cat's plans and a man's are **worth about the same**. "
>
> MARK TWAIN

◁ **Tourist in Shanghai, 1900**
For the well-traveled who had been to Europe, the Middle East, and America, the cities of the Far East provided novelty and new experiences. London publisher John Murray published his first "handbook" to Japan in 1884.

Over the coming decades, the route established by Cook became the standard itinerary for world travelers. It remained expensive, but thanks to ever-improving and better-connected transportation systems, traveling farther became more feasible. By the end of the 19th century, tours of Japan and India were becoming popular as journeys in their own right. Japan's fear of foreign influence on its culture meant that it continued to restrict access for tourists, but it was still possible to visit Yokohama, Tokyo, Kobe, Osaka, Kyoto, and Nagasaki. By the 1890s, Cook's itineraries included Australia, New Zealand, and South Africa.

Record journey

In January 1873, *Around the World in Eighty Days,* an adventure novel written by Jules Verne, was published in France to great acclaim. It was an entertaining work of fantasy about an impossible journey. Just 16 years later, in 1889, Elizabeth Cochran, a 22-year-old American journalist who wrote under the name of Nellie Bly, decided to follow in the footsteps of Phileas Fogg, Jules Verne's protagonist. She set herself the goal of traveling around the world in just 75 days and did so by ship, train, donkey, and any other means possible. She made it back home in 72 days, setting a world record for the time. Travel seemed to have shrunk the world.

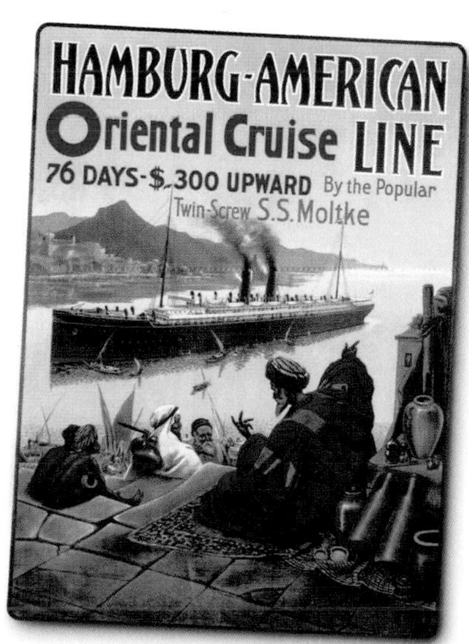

△ **The Orient lines**
By the early 20th century, round-the-world travel no longer meant hardship, and several shipping lines offered comfortable passage to far-flung destinations.

Mapping the oceans

Modern oceanography began with the *Challenger* voyage of 1872–76. It was the first expedition organized specifically to gather data on the oceans and marine life, and to investigate the geology of the ocean floor.

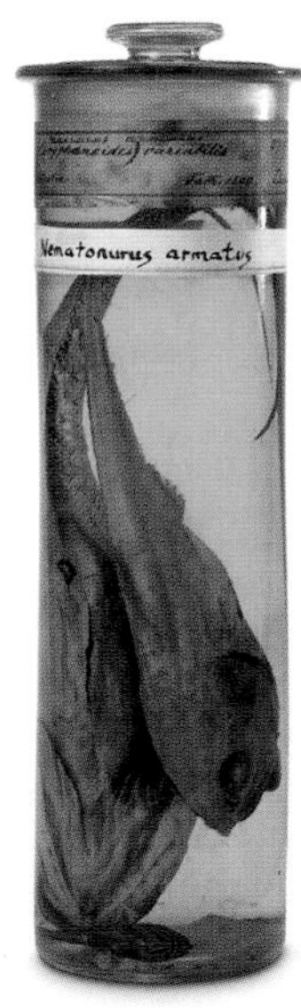

△ **Rattail fish**
This rattail fish, kept in a specimen jar, was discovered by the *Challenger* team in waters south of Australia in 1874.

As recently as the mid-19th century, the oceans and seas were regarded as vast, empty spaces that had to be crossed to get from one place to another. Naturalist Charles Darwin had even referred to them as "a tedious waste, a desert of water." Little was known of the ocean depths, but that began to change when the first transatlantic telegraph cable was laid across the seabed between western Ireland and Newfoundland in 1858. Engineers planned to lay more cables beneath the world's oceans, giving rise to an interest in what lay beneath the waves.

Into the unknown

In 1870, prompted by Scottish natural historian and marine zoologist Charles Wyville Thomson, the Royal Society of London, in collaboration with the Royal Navy, raised an expedition that would put Britain at the forefront of oceanic exploration. The venture was lent a Royal Navy frigate, HMS *Challenger*, a three-masted, square-rigged wooden ship with auxiliary steam engines. All but two of its 17 guns were removed to make room for two laboratories full of the latest scientific instruments. Some of the equipment had been specially invented or modified to suit the requirements of the expedition. The commanding officer was Captain George Nares, and as well as the crew of about 240, there were six scientists on board, including Wyville Thomson, naturalists John Murray and Henry Mosely, and the official artist, John James Wild.

▷ **On-board laboratory**
The *Challenger* was fitted with two fully equipped laboratories, one for chemistry (shown here) and another for biology.

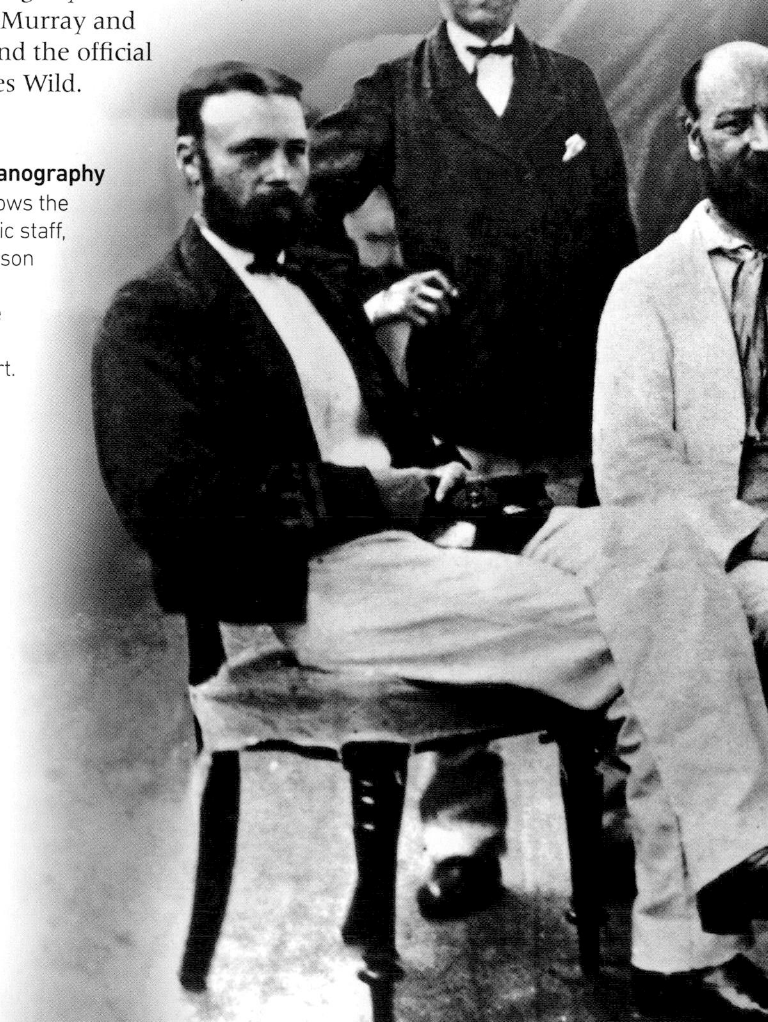

▷ **Pioneers of oceanography**
This photograph shows the *Challenger*'s scientific staff, led by Wyville Thomson (third from the left). John Murray (on the floor) was the main author of their report.

▷ **HMS *Challenger* in Antarctica**
During its three-and-a-half-year voyage, HMS *Challenger* visited every continent on the planet. This contemporary engraving depicts the vessel in Antarctica in 1874.

The ship set sail from Sheerness, Scotland, in December 1872, starting a journey that would last three and a half years. The *Challenger* sailed some 68,890 nautical miles (127,600 km) during that time, touring the North and South Atlantic and Pacific Oceans, and entering the Antarctic Circle. At regular intervals, the ship would make a sample stop (362 in all), to measure the exact depth of the water and to take temperature readings at different depths. The scientists used special devices that trawled the sea floor to gather samples of rocks, sediment, and seabed fauna, and nets to capture marine life. They also collected samples of the water at different depths, and recorded atmospheric and other meteorological conditions.

◁ **Thermal map of the oceans**
This map of HMS *Challenger*'s historic circumnavigation shows temperature readings of the oceans at different depths. It was the first time that such comprehensive data had been compiled.

"The **greatest advance** in the **knowledge** of our **planet** since the **celebrated discoveries** of the **fifteenth and sixteenth** centuries."

NATURALIST JOHN MURRAY ON THE FINDINGS OF THE *CHALLENGER* EXPEDITION

A new science

The findings of the voyage were finally presented in a mammoth 50-volume, 29,500-page report that took 19 years to compile, and which was published between 1877 and 1895. It proved definitively that life existed at the bottom of the oceans—4,700 new species of plants and animals were discovered. It also investigated the astonishing topography of the ocean floor. It recorded, for the first time, one of the deepest parts of the ocean, the Marianas Trench in the western Pacific, which is more than 4 miles (6 km) deep. The expedition made countless contributions to many different branches of science—hydrography, meteorology, and geology, as well as botany and zoology. It marked the birth of the modern science of oceanography, a term that was invented to describe the work of the *Challenger*'s scientists. It is fitting that NASA named both the 1972 Apollo 17 lunar module and its second space shuttle after the humble Royal Navy frigate that took its crew so far into the unknown.

◁ **New life forms**
Over 4,700 new species of marine animals were discovered by the *Challenger* expedition. Many were painstakingly painted and then published in the expedition's report.

Fantastic voyages

As new technologies pushed the possibilities of travel ever further, fiction writers faced the danger of being overtaken by current events.

Writing in 1869, a Sacramento newspaper noted: "Now that the Pacific Railroad is complete, few of our readers are aware that a journey around the world can be made in eighty days." Was this statement the inspiration for French author Jules Verne, who just three years later published *Around the World in Eighty Days*? Perhaps, except that Verne did not usually write about the possible—he preferred the fantastical. He favored tales of wildly imaginative exploration, such as *Journey to the Center of the Earth* (1864), *From the Earth to the Moon* (1865), *A Floating City* (1870), and *Twenty Thousand Leagues Under the Sea* (1870). In all of these, Verne celebrates the 19th-century mastery of science and technology, and looks ahead to future possibilities. Today, we call this genre "science fiction." We have to suppose that Verne's readers would have treated *Around the World in Eighty Days* as one of his usual, amusing conceits, not something that could really happen. Except the challenge was soundly met and bettered just 17 years later, by a young woman called Nellie Bly (see pp. 248–49).

Given the swift evolution of technology, new vehicles were needed to make the fantastic voyage, and they needed to reach ever more fantastical places. In the last few years of the 19th century, English author H.G. Wells took up the challenge with *The Time Machine* (1895), which opened up tourism to the limitless vistas of the future. Wells also sent men to the moon in *The First Men on the Moon* (1901), using a device that reversed gravity. Two decades earlier, in *Across the Zodiac* (1880), English writer Percy Greg took a spacecraft to Mars, propelled by a force called "apergy." Wells also thought of these voyages inversely: in *The War of the Worlds* (1898), the Martians visited Earth and liked it so much that they decided to take it. Luckily, some of these early science fiction tales were more off the mark than others.

" How much **further** can we **go?** What are the **final frontiers** in this **quest for travel?** "

JULES VERNE, FRENCH AUTHOR

Imaginary landscapes
In this lithograph made in 1882, French artist Albert Robida imagines travel in the year 2000, showing upper-class Parisians, dressed in fashionable French attire, leaving an opera. Robida creates a city skyline filled with futuristic flying vehicles, from private taxis and limousines to buses and police cars.

rican CR

THE
GOLDEN AGE
OF TRAVEL
1880—1939

THE GOLDEN AGE OF TRAVEL, 1880–1939

Introduction

By the end of the 19th century, the only parts of the world still left to explore were those that were extremely remote and inhospitable, such as the frozen expanses of the polar caps and the burning heart of the Arabian Desert. But people did go to them, with journeys such as the race to the South Pole yielding stories as thrilling as any in the history of exploration. It was in 1912 that British explorer Robert F. Scott trudged to the South Pole, only to find that Norwegian Raold Amundsen had beaten him to it. On his journey back, Scott perished, just 11 miles (18 km) short of a cache of supplies. Fourteen years later, Amundsen also reached the North Pole, albeit in an airship (the *Norge*), making him the first person to reach both poles.

Even on more familiar terrain, travel remained a considerable undertaking. Railways connected major towns and cities, but most journeys were made on foot, or at best in a horse-drawn coach. Dedicated travelers were venturing as far afield as Japan and New Zealand, but reaching the other side of the world often involved hardship and a willingness to sleep rough on occasion. Beyond Europe, many guidebooks still advised travelers to pack a gun for self-defense.

Bicycles, cars, and airplanes

For all its simplicity, the bicycle revolutionized people's lives when it first appeared. People living in cities could get out into the country easily, and those in rural areas could travel from one village to another. The motorcar liberated people even more, especially when Henry Ford started mass-producing the affordable Ford Model T. The greatest freedom of all, however, came when two bicycle manufacturers from Ohio, Orville and

THE BICYCLE WAS LIBERATING, GIVING PEOPLE THE FREEDOM TO TRAVEL UNDER THEIR OWN STEAM

WITHIN 10 YEARS OF ITS INVENTION, THE AIRPLANE HAD REVOLUTIONIZED TRAVEL

THE FORD MODEL T MADE IT POSSIBLE FOR MANY PEOPLE TO BUY A CAR FOR THE FIRST TIME

> “ We find ourselves still **dreaming** of impossible **future conquest**. ”
>
> CHARLES LINDBERGH

Wilbur Wright, built and flew the world's first real airplane. They made their historic, inaugural flight in 1903, and within 20 years, airlines launched the first passenger flights.

The early aviators were hailed as heroes as they smashed one record after another. One of the first pilots was Alan Cobham, who flew from London to Australia and back in 1926. Amy Johnson made the flight from England to Australia in 1930. In 1927, Charles Lindbergh became the first aviator to fly solo across the Atlantic, followed by Amelia Earhart in 1930. These young aviators, male and female, gave flying a glamour that cast its spell on passenger flights too. For those who could afford it, flying became a heady world of refreshments served at 4,000 feet (1,200 m) in the sky, games of bridge in the lounge, and sleeping overnight in comfortable bunks.

Inequality

This was the age of luxury travel, whether in the opulent carriages of the Orient Express, steaming across Europe, or in the ballrooms and tea salons of Cunard, White Star, and other transatlantic liners. Few people, however, traveled in such comfort and style. For every passenger in a cabin above decks on a liner bound for the US, six or more were hunkered down in the hold, enduring the most primitive conditions. Many of them, driven by poverty, had fled their homes forever, and were hoping for better lives in America.

Such radical inequalities in the nature of travel continued after World War I, which proved to be a mere hiatus in the traditional order of things. This was not true of World War II, however, which triggered massive changes in society, transportation, and the way people traveled.

ROBERT F. SCOTT'S *TERRA NOVA* TEAM WAS ONE OF THE FIRST TO EXPLORE ANTARCTICA

IN 1926, ROALD AMUNDSEN FLEW OVER THE NORTH POLE IN THE AIRSHIP *NORGE*

THOUSANDS OF EUROPEANS TRAVELED TO AMERICA IN SEARCH OF A BETTER LIFE

Central Asia

Even in the late 19th century, there were still areas of the Eurasian landmass that were nothing but white spaces on maps, challenging explorers to try and fill in the blanks.

△ **Ármin Vámbéry**
The Hungarian (1832–1913) was the first European to undertake the long and arduous journey to the interior of Asia.

The outskirts of an area—the points farthest east, west, north, and south—are usually the last to be explored. A territory identified as "central" would normally be charted first. This was never the case with Central Asia, which, for a long time, existed as a blank in the middle of the map. During the era of the Mongols, this ill-defined no-man's-land had provided a conduit for trade. But with the decline of the Mongol Empire after 1259, and particularly once Europeans had discovered a sea route to the Far East, Central Asia became depopulated and splintered into small Islamic city-states, with the steppes, deserts, and mountains roamed by nomadic tribes.

From about the 17th century, both Russia and China began to expand into Central Asia (or Turkestan, as it was also known). By the 19th century, both countries had asserted some element of control, but most of the land remained untamed frontier territory.

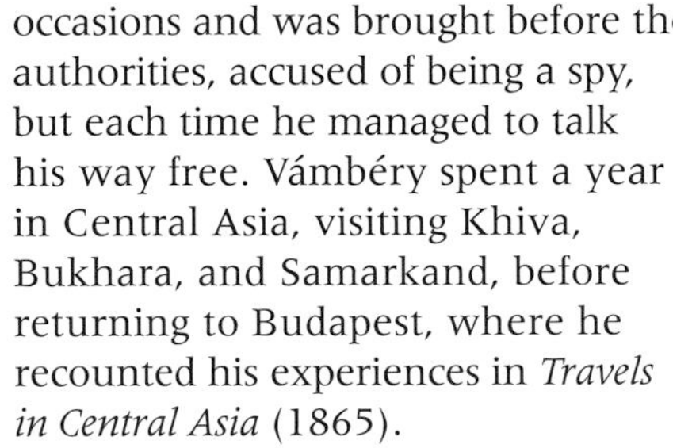

△ **Bronze-age vessel**
This 3,500-year-old tripod-footed vessel was unearthed in central Iran by Aurel Stein, who donated it to the British Museum.

Heading into unknown territory

This was still the case in March 1863, when Hungarian Ármin Vámbéry made his way on land from Tehran into the heart of Central Asia, where few Westerners had set foot since the 1600s. To prepare for this, he had spent many years in Constantinople learning over 20 Turkic dialects and studying the Qur'an. He disguised himself as a Muslim pilgrim, worried that if he were to be recognized as a European, he would be imprisoned or even executed. He aroused suspicion on several occasions and was brought before the authorities, accused of being a spy, but each time he managed to talk his way free. Vámbéry spent a year in Central Asia, visiting Khiva, Bukhara, and Samarkand, before returning to Budapest, where he recounted his experiences in *Travels in Central Asia* (1865).

◁ **Tibetan tribesmen**
Sven Hedin traveled with a camera and took some of the earliest photographs of Tibet and its people, including this hand-tinted slide of mounted tribesmen.

Sven Hedin

As Vámbéry published his work, the life of another Central Asian explorer was just beginning. The Swede Sven Hedin witnessed as a child the triumphant return of Adolf Erik Nordenskiöld after his navigation of the Northeast Passage, and this inspired him to become an explorer. He traveled in Russia, the Caucasus, and Iran while he was a student, before setting off on the first of three major expeditions to Central Asia in 1893. From 1894 to 1908, he explored and mapped parts of Chinese Turkestan (officially Xinjiang) and Tibet, much of which was completely unknown to Europeans. He nearly died in the Taklamakan Desert after gravely miscalculating his party's water supplies, but went on to discover the site of the lost city of Taklamakan, where he collected hundreds of artifacts.

Sven Hedin's writings about his explorations went on to inspire

△ **Shigatse Dzong**
In 1907, Hedin slipped unseen through the gates of Tibet's second city. The inhabitants were outraged when they found him. He later painted this image based on earlier sketches of the city.

SIBERIA
MONGOLIA
Lake Baikal
KAZAKHSTAN
Ulan Bator
UZBEKISTAN
Tashkent
TAKLAMAKAN DESERT
CHINA
Caspian Sea
TURKMENISTAN
Kashgar
Lop Nor Lake
Beijing
Yellow Sea
LOP NOR DESERT
IRAN
TIBET
ASIA
Arabian Sea
INDIA
South China Sea
Key
First journey
Second journey

△ **Hedin's route**
The Swede's first visit to Central Asia took him from China through Mongolia, into Russian Turkmenistan, and finally to the Taklamakan Desert. On his second visit, he traveled along the desert's northern edge to reach the Lop Nor lake.

“I was content with nothing less than **to tread paths** where **no European had ever set foot.**”

SVEN HEDIN

another Hungarian, Marc Aurel Stein (1862–1943). In 1900, Stein set out on the first of his own expeditions to Chinese Turkestan, traveling to places Hedin had not reached.

Journeys of rediscovery

During the 30 years Stein spent exploring, however, his most significant achievements were actually rediscoveries. He uncovered evidence of a lost Buddhist civilization and long-forgotten stretches of the Chinese Great Wall, and also established how the routes of the ancient Silk Road (see pp. 86–87) were connected. In this respect, Hedin's journeys set a template for much of the exploration that was to come in the following century, with a focus on retracing where people had gone before. These journeys would take the form of archaeological discoveries, such as those of Machu Picchu in 1911 and of Tutankhamun's tomb in 1922.

▷ **Disguised as a pilgrim**
Like Vámbéry before him, Hedin disguised himself as a pilgrim in order to travel freely. He dressed as a Buddhist in an attempt to get to Lhasa, whereas Vámbéry had passed himself off as a Muslim dervish.

On skis across Greenland

In 1888, Fridtjof Nansen became the first man to cross Greenland on skis. In doing so, he paved the way both for polar exploration and for the advancement of winter sports.

According to Roland Huntford, the author of *Two Planks and a Passion: The Dramatic History of Skiing*, it is the Norwegians who should be thanked for the staple of winter sports. It is they, he writes, a nation of native skiers, who invented modern skiing, having developed both the equipment and techniques that are used today. The first known public ski races were held near Tromsø in northern Norway in 1843, and the Norwegians were the first to organize ski marathons and ski touring. Huntford also claims that skiing was first introduced to central Europe by young Norwegians who were studying in Germany—and it is widely known that Norwegian immigrants were the first to use skis in North America, possibly as early as the 1830s.

◁ **Early skis**
Skis have been used in Scandinavia since the Middle Ages. In the late 19th century, they were refined by the Norwegians, who introduced many refinements to create the modern ski.

Taking to the skis

The greatest milestone in Norwegian ski history, however, came in 1888. Five years earlier, a Finnish-born Swede named Adolf Erik Nordenskiöld had attempted to cross Greenland on foot, and failed. With him had been two Lapps on skis who were able to traverse the snowy terrain far more easily than Nordenskiöld, suggesting that this was a better mode of travel. Fridtjof Nansen, an accomplished Norwegian skier, took up the challenge. He had already twice skied across the mountains from Bergen to Christiana (Oslo), a distance of over 310 miles (500 km). The distance across Greenland was similar, but the only settlement was on the coast at the far side, and the terrain and temperatures were likely to be a good deal worse than in Norway. One critic in the press commented: "the chances are ten to one that he will uselessly throw his own and perhaps others' lives away." Nevertheless, on August 10, 1888, Nansen and his small team of six came ashore on the east coast of Greenland and began a 93-mile (150-km) trudge upward to the summit of the ice cap. It was only there that they could finally don skis, and even then the going proved hard, as they had to haul sledges behind them. On downhill slopes, they rigged sails made from their tents to the sledges, so that they only had to steer them.

▽ **Ready for adventure**
Fridtjof Nansen poses with his Greenland expedition team: three fellow Norwegians and two Lapps from Finland, Samuel Balto and Ole Nielsen Ravna.

IN CONTEXT
The first ski resort

Isolated high in a Swiss valley, the settlement of Davos found itself booming in the 1860s as word spread of the recuperative qualities of its climate for those suffering from tuberculosis. Soon, visitors outnumbered the inhabitants, and Davos became the first alpine winter spa. The first clients were German, but in the late 1870s, the English began to arrive and soon colonized the place. The invalids were supplanted by healthy holidaymakers, lured to the spot by accounts of novel new sports such as tobogganing, horse-drawn sledging, and skiing. When Arthur Conan Doyle, journalist and creator of Sherlock Holmes, visited in 1893, Davos was well on its way to becoming Europe's first winter-sports resort.

TRAVEL POSTER FOR DAVOS, 1918

▷ **Dogskin gloves**
In *The First Crossing of Greenland*, Nansen described his expedition clothing, including gloves made of dogskin, with the hair on the outside.

The value of skiing

On September 21, 1888, the skiing came to a stop when the group reached the fjords of the west coast. By early October, they had arrived at their destination, Godthaab (now Nuuk), the Danish settlement that served as the capital of Greenland. Having missed the last boat out, they had to spend the winter there, and didn't return to Norway until the following spring. "Without skis," wrote Nansen, "this expedition would have been an absolute impossibility. We would never have returned alive." By this, he meant that the speed and economy of effort conferred by the skis saved them from running out of supplies.

From then on, skis were vital in polar exploration. News of Nansen's exploits spread around the world and he became the spiritual father of skiing, popularizing the sport from the Alps to the Rocky Mountains of North America.

◁ **Hard going**
Nansen was all too aware of the dangers of Greenland, such as deep crevasses hidden in the ice.

▽ **Conquering the ice sheet**
Nansen photographed his team struggling up the Greenland Ice Sheet, sledges in tow, in August 1888. They could not use their skis until they reached the summit.

> " For the first time, the polar explorer had revealed to him a **new means of transport** [skis], which ought to **ease his task** fantastically. "
>
> ADOLF ERIK NORDENSKIÖLD, ARCTIC EXPLORER

△ **Penny-farthing**
This kind of bicycle, developed from 1869 onward, was also known as a "high-wheeler" or an "ordinary," to distinguish it from the safety models that followed.

The bicycle craze

For the vast majority of the population who did not own horsedrawn vehicles, the invention of the modern bicycle meant that they had their own personal means of transportation for the first time.

The distinguished historian Eric Hobsbawm believed that the bicycle was one of the greatest inventions ever. It gave people true mobility in a way that was beneficial to all classes, not just the rich. He also thought it was one of the rare inventions that had no bad side effects and could not have any malicious use.

Although the bicycle had existed in one form or another since the early 19th century, it had to evolve through a series of technical improvements before it became popular. By the 1870s, it had reached the stage of the so-called "penny-farthings," bicycles that had an oversized front wheel and a tiny rear wheel, but these were heavy, cumbersome, and dangerous. From the mid-1880s, these awkward contraptions were gradually replaced with what was called the "safety bicycle," a model that had most of the hallmarks of what was to become the modern bicycle—two equal-sized wheels on a diamond-shaped frame, a chain-driven rear wheel, and inflatable tires (invented by the Scot John Dunlop in 1886).

Increasing popularity

These improvements made cycling less hazardous and more enjoyable. As cheaper models became available, bicycle fever took hold. In Britain, it was estimated that by the 1890s, some one and a half million men and women

▽ **Bicycle clubs**
The boom in cycling led to the formation of hundreds of clubs across the US. The first to form was the Boston Bicycle Club in 1878. This picture shows the Brighton Bicycle Club in Cincinnati, lined up at the start of an annual race.

> “ Every time I see an **adult on a bicycle**, I **no longer despair** for the **future of the human race**. ”
>
> H.G. WELLS, AUTHOR

▷ **The new woman**
The practicalities of cycling led to new fashions for women. Restrictive layers of petticoats and trailing dresses were replaced by loose knickerbockers and protective headwear.

were cycling on roads that had yet to be monopolized by the arrival of the motor car. In America, in 1897 alone, more than two million bicycles were sold.

Cycling was not confined to Britain and America—it was a worldwide craze. An edition of *The Egyptian Gazette* in January 1894 reported on an excursion undertaken by some 30 cyclists who rode from central Cairo out to the Pyramids one morning. “Amongst them was a lady riding astride and garbed in female knickerbockers,” the correspondent noted. “She rode very well.”

Social change

The impact the bicycle had on society was remarkable. In rural communities, it dramatically increased the distances people could travel and the places they could visit. It also increased the numbers of other people one could meet, including potential marriage partners. Steve Jones, a respected biologist, argued that the bicycle played an important role in combating genetic disorders, because people from different towns were marrying, which led to a greater and healthier genetic mix. Contemporary commentators also variously linked the bicycle to changing fashions, a drop in church attendance, and even a decline in piano playing. However, perhaps the most notable social change brought about by the bicycle was in the lives of women. Many people initially found the idea of a female sitting astride a machine “unbecoming,” but that did not stop young women from taking to the road by the thousands.

Clothes for cycling

As well as the mobility that the bicycle offered, it also led to more personal freedom of movement. The accepted clothing of the era—long, heavy skirts worn over stiff petticoats—was totally unsuitable for cycling, which required something less restrictive, such as the knickerbockers mentioned by the Egyptian newspaper. These were baggy trousers, sometimes called a divided skirt, that were cinched at the knee. Indeed, the women’s movement of the 1890s and the cycling craze became so closely intertwined that in 1896, women’s rights activist Susan B. Anthony told Nellie Bly of the *New York World* (see p. 249) that cycling had “done more to emancipate women than anything else in the world.”

▷ **Rover Safety Bicycle**
The safety bicycle was developed in the 1880s as a “safer” alternative to the unwieldy penny-farthing. The “Rover” created by John Kemp Starley was one of the most commercially successful designs.

△ **Open country**
Part of the appeal of the bicycle was that it put the countryside within easy reach of city dwellers, as illustrated in this poster for a “bicycle camp” on the banks of the Connecticut River.

IN PROFILE
Annie Londonderry

Cycling the world seems a very modern challenge, but it was a feat completed for the first time in 1885, by Englishman Thomas Stevens, riding a penny-farthing. Two Boston gentlemen bet that no woman could do it. Annie Cohen Kopchovsky, mother of three, took them up on it. She had only just learned how to cycle, when she set out from Boston on June 27, 1894. To finance her attempt, she wore a placard advertising Londonderry Lithia Spring Water Company and even agreed to change her name to promote the business. On March 23, 1895, she arrived back in the US at San Francisco and cycled west, reaching Chicago in September, to collect her $10,000 winnings.

ROUND-THE-WORLD CYCLIST ANNIE “LONDONDERRY” COHEN

Escape to the open air

As industry wreathed cities with increasing amounts of smog, a movement arose that encouraged working men and women to head for the open air. It was the beginning of a craze for camping.

△ **Liberating technology**
Numerous innovations freed people to go camping. After the bicycle, none was more important than the portable Primus stove, invented in Sweden in 1892.

Of all the travel literature published toward the end of the 19th century, there is probably no work more popular than Jerome K. Jerome's *Three Men in a Boat* (1889). In late-Victorian England, there was a fashion for recreational boating, particularly on the Thames, and Jerome's book was originally intended as a river guide. In fact, it ended up as a comic novel. There were many reasons for its success, including that it was extremely funny, but most of all it was topical. It dealt with scenarios that were increasingly familiar to readers, such as boating, holidays in the countryside, and camping. In Britain, in particular, the rapid growth of cities and the often harsh conditions in which

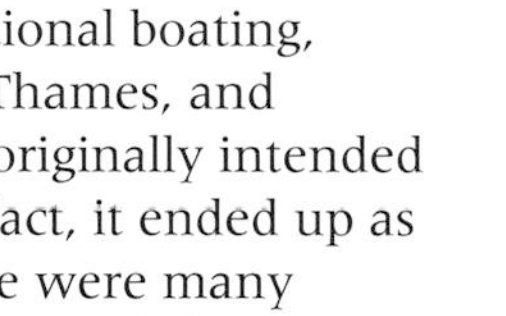

◁ **Camping pioneer**
Thomas Hiram Holding, the author of *Cycle and Camp* (1898) and *The Camper's Handbook* (1908), is widely regarded as the founder of modern recreational camping.

▷ **Camping club**
Camping was already popular in Britain in the 19th century, as is clear from this picture from the 1890s. In 1901, the Association of Cycle Campers formed. It soon had Robert Scott, the future Antarctic explorer, as its president.

people worked inspired many to seek the simplicities of rural life. It was always possible to get away by train, but the newly invented bicycle brought real countryside within easy reach of the average worker.

Camping fever

The man who popularized what became known as cycle camping was Thomas Hiram Holding, born in England in 1844 to Mormon parents. The family emigrated to Salt Lake City, Utah, in 1853, and Thomas's first experiences of camping came on the long trek across America. Tragically, two of the Holding children died en route, and the family returned to England. Thomas became a tailor, but in his spare time he traveled and camped. He took a canoe and tent off to the Scottish Highlands, then a bicycle and tent to Ireland. In 1901, he formed the Association of Cycle Campers, which later became known as the Camping and Caravanning Club. He cemented his position as the father of camping with the publication of *The Camper's Handbook* in 1908. Camping fever spread across the classes and professions—and the sexes. The *Handbook* included a guest essay by a Mrs F. Horsfield titled "Ladies and Cycle Camping." Holding advised on how to assemble lightweight, easy-to-transport kits for weekends away, and his campers often made their own tents and gear. This did not always mean kit was modest. Writing of a visit to "an ideal family camp," Holding notes it consists of "the eating tent, the sleeping tent, the servants' tent, the cooking tent for wet weather and the overboat tent."

◁ **The Thames Rowing Club**
Camping in England evolved in part from boating for leisure, particularly on the Thames river. Boaters carried tents so they could spend the night on the river bank, as shown in this 1878 illustration.

The American wilderness

During the 19th century, American settlers were mostly too busy living off the land to sit back and enjoy its finer qualities. Nevertheless, Ralph Waldo Emerson's seminal essay "Nature" (1836) had a profound influence on how Americans perceived the wilderness. So did the writings of his friend Henry David Thoreau—even if, prior to publishing *Walden, or Life in the Woods* (1854), Thoreau accidentally destroyed 300 acres of prime timber with a campfire.

A guide to camping in the Adirondacks was published in 1869, but it was far ahead of its time. Those who ventured into the mountains at this early date found no infrastructure, but plenty of black flies, mosquitoes, and dangerous animals. A turning point came in 1903, when President Theodore Roosevelt spent two weeks camping in Yellowstone National Park. In his wake, thousands of campers were drawn to the national parks, and their numbers rapidly increased as the century progressed. The first camping club, calling itself the "Tin Can Tourists," was formed in 1910, and by 1912, the Forest Service was reporting 231,000 campers in the parks.

> "We **pitch** our tents **far apart** so that **our hearts stay closer together**."
>
> BEDOUIN PROVERB

▷ **Middle-class pursuits**
Pleasure-boating, cycling, and camping were pastimes reserved for those with money and leisure time. Manufacturers catered to these hobbyists with specialized products, such as this Edwardian picnic basket.

Far-flung railways

The last quarter of the 19th century was an adventurous period for railway building that saw extraordinarily ambitious lines and services created across Asia, Africa, Europe, and the US.

The Trans-Siberian Railway
Lamentable transportation connections between European Russia and the tsar's Far Eastern territories provided the impetus to build a railway across Siberia. It was the most ambitious railway project ever attempted.

It was all very well for the tsar in St Petersburg to lay claim to all the lands from the Baltic Sea to the Pacific Ocean, but Russia's ability to govern and protect its Far Eastern territories was questionable. The distances and conditions involved made communication almost impossible. For half of the year, the rivers that served as transportation highways were frozen, and most of the rivers in eastern Siberia ran from north to south, rather than from east to west. By road, along the roughshod *Sibirsky trakt*, it could take up to nine months to reach Irkutsk from Moscow, and that was barely two-thirds of the way to Vladivostok, Russia's main Pacific port. The US had linked its two coasts by railroad in 1869 (see pp. 236–37), and it was obvious that Russia needed to do the same.

The Trans-Siberian Railway

A railway across Siberia had been discussed as early as the 1850s, but the cost and scale of the undertaking were prohibitive. However, by the 1880s, fear of American influence in Russia's Pacific region prompted the tsarist government to go ahead with the scheme. Even then, thanks to stifling bureaucracy, five years passed before anyone stuck a spade in the ground.

The difficulties facing the railway's builders were immense. These included the sheer length of the route, below-freezing temperatures for a good part of the year, and a dearth of local people to use as labor. Also, in addition to two mountain ranges, the vast Lake Baikal in the middle of Siberia had to be negotiated. Looping around the north of the lake was too much of a detour, but the southern way was blocked by rocky terrain. Initially, the two tracks (from east and west) stopped at the lake and a ferry transferred the trains across the water. Then a series of shelves and tunnels were blasted through the southern route to carry the railway around.

△ **Hard labor**
Workers lay tracks for the central portion of the Trans-Siberian Railway in the Krasnoyarsk region. The laborers included Russians, Iranians, Turks, and even Italians.

It was not until 1916 that the final stretch was completed, forming a continuous 5,748-mile (9,250-km) track that crossed seven time zones between Moscow and Vladivostok. In the early days, the journey could take up to four weeks, due to problems with the track, but no one doubted its value. It was a national symbol—an iron ribbon binding sovereign Russian territory.

An African dream

Similarly, imperial ideals of stamping authority on a map and accessing the resources of a continent fueled an even more ambitious plan in Africa. Cecil Rhodes, the Prime Minister of Cape Colony (in what is today South Africa), dreamed of linking all of Africa with a railway that traveled through British colonies alone. Its terminals would be Cape Town at the southern tip of Africa and Cairo in Egypt, from where a line already ran to the port city of Alexandria on the Mediterranean.

Initially, the track was laid at an astonishing rate of 1 mile (1.6 km) a day, heading north. In 1904, it reached the Zambezi River, where the railway crossed the Victoria Falls via a 656-ft (200-m) suspension bridge. The bridge had been built in northern England, and then taken apart, shipped to Africa, and reconstructed in situ. »

▷ **The Lake Baikal train ferry**
Until the 110-mile (180-km) Circum-Baikal stretch of railway was finished, passengers (and train) had to take an ice-breaking ferry across Lake Baikal.

△ **Bridging Africa**
This suspension bridge over the Zambezi River at Victoria Falls was the brainchild of Cecil Rhodes, as part of his Cape-to-Cairo railway scheme. He instructed engineers to build the bridge "where the trains, as they pass, will catch the spray of the Falls."

» However, in 1891, Germany secured large tracts of East Africa for its empire, and thereby blocked the path for the railway. Forced to rethink their route, the builders turned west into the Belgian Congo (where the British had permission to build), but here the project foundered, owing to difficulties negotiating the mountainous terrain. By this time, Rhodes had died, and Britain's influence in Africa was waning, so the idea of a trans-African railway was abandoned. However, 100 years later, the concept is not entirely dead and has been recently discussed by African leaders.

The Orient Express

The great railway-building projects in Russia and Africa were spurred on by politics and commerce. In Europe, however, the most significant development was all about service. By the late 19th century, every European nation was crisscrossed by its own national network of railways. What Belgian engineer Georges Nagelmackers wanted was to link them with a single service that ran *sans frontières*. In 1872, he launched a service that ran from Ostend on the North Sea coast of his native Belgium to Brindisi in southern Italy. It was a success, so he began work on a new line to connect Paris with Constantinople (Istanbul), a 1,857-mile (2,989-km) route that would cross Europe—Germany, Austria, Hungary, Serbia, Romania, and Bulgaria.

To make this happen, Nagelmackers had to deal with the railway companies of six nations, negotiating which locomotives and lines would be used, and making sure that all the tracks were a standard gauge.

▷ **Cecil Rhodes**
English administrator Cecil Rhodes, pictured here, dreamed of a railway stretching up the west coast of Africa. He died 12 years into the project, which was never completed.

The inaugural service of the Orient Express left the Gare de l'Est in Paris on October 4, 1883, and was scheduled to take three-and-a-half days to reach Constantinople. The route was undoubtedly unique, but what really captivated the public was the sheer opulence of the train. The sleeping cars were panelled with teak inlaid with marquetry, and had seats that could be opened out into beds with silk sheets. There was a library and a smoking room, and a coach in the rear that had showers with hot water. On this inaugural trip, the last leg of the journey was made by boat because the line was unfinished. Six years later, however, the train went all the way to Constantinople.

The Orient Express became popular because it was quicker and far more convenient than traveling by boat. Alternative routes were soon added, including one via Milan and Venice. At Constantinople, travelers could make connections for destinations further east, including Tehran, Baghdad, and Damascus. And if the patchwork of countries the train passed through was unstable, the occasional hold-up by thieves, kidnapping, or a day-long halt in snow only seemed to add to the trip's romance.

The Florida coast

The United States may have connected the Atlantic and Pacific by rail back in 1869, but at the end of the century there were still vast swathes of the country to be opened up. Oilman Henry Flagler saw potential in Florida and set about unleashing it with a self-financed railway line from New York. He took it all the way down to Biscayne Bay, a beautiful spot protected from the Atlantic by a barrier island and watered by the Miami River. There, he founded a settlement and gave it the river's name. He then extended his railway farther south, creating one of the most astonishing lines, which was carried on 17 miles (27 km) of bridges to reach

> " **Anything can happen** and **usually does** on the **Orient Express**. "
>
> MORLEY SAFER, CANADIAN-AMERICAN JOURNALIST

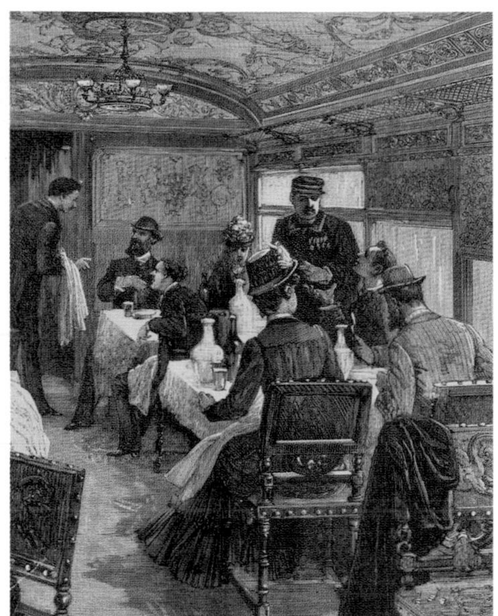

the far-flung island of Key West. Unfortunately, the railroad went bankrupt in 1932, but Flagler's bridges still support the southernmost section of Highway 1, which remains one of the most breathtaking drives in the world.

◁ **Luxury on wheels**
The Orient Express was the world's most glamorous train service. It operated on several routes, each of which offered lavishly appointed facilities. This wood engraving of 1885 shows passengers in the dining car.

▽ **Legendary train**
The Orient Express was immortalized by many writers, most notably Agatha Christie. It was also the subject of an opera by Oscar Sachs and Henri Neuzillet, which was performed in Paris in 1896, as advertised below.

IN CONTEXT
Great railway literature

Some of the greatest modern travel books are set on trains. *The Great Railway Bazaar* (1975) chronicles Paul Theroux's journey across Europe and Asia, while *The Old Patagonian Express* (1979) sees him on train after train crossing the US and South America.

British travel writer Eric Newby spent weeks on Russian rails for his *The Big Red Train Ride* (1978), and Jenny Diski spent months in Amtrak smoking cars exploring America for *Stranger on a Train* (2002). Meanwhile, Andrew Eames traveled on the same tracks as Agatha Christie for his book *The 8.55 to Baghdad* (2004).

PAUL
THEROUX
THE
GREAT RAILWAY
BAZAAR
BY TRAIN THROUGH ASIA

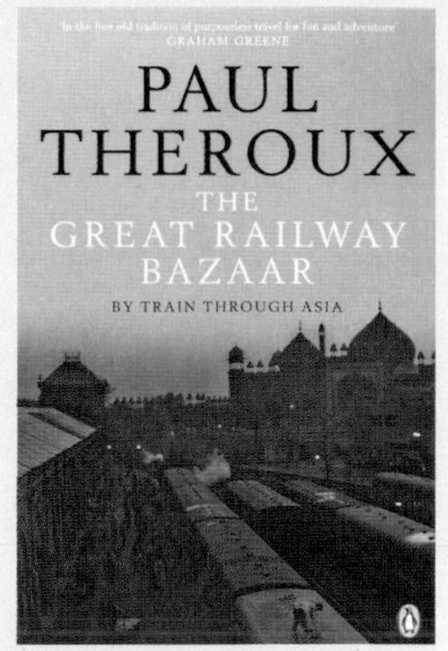

PAPERBACK EDITION OF *THE GREAT RAILWAY BAZAAR*

Ancien ÉLYSÉE MONTMARTRE
TRIANON Concert
80
Bd ROCHECHOUART
Ancien ÉLYSÉE MONTMARTRE
COMPAGNIE INTERNATIONALE DES WAGONS LITS
ORIENT EXPRESS
VOYAGE EN 2 TABLEAUX de Mr Oscar SACHS MUSIQUE de Mr Henri NEUZILLET
DÉPART tous les soirs à 10 heures ½

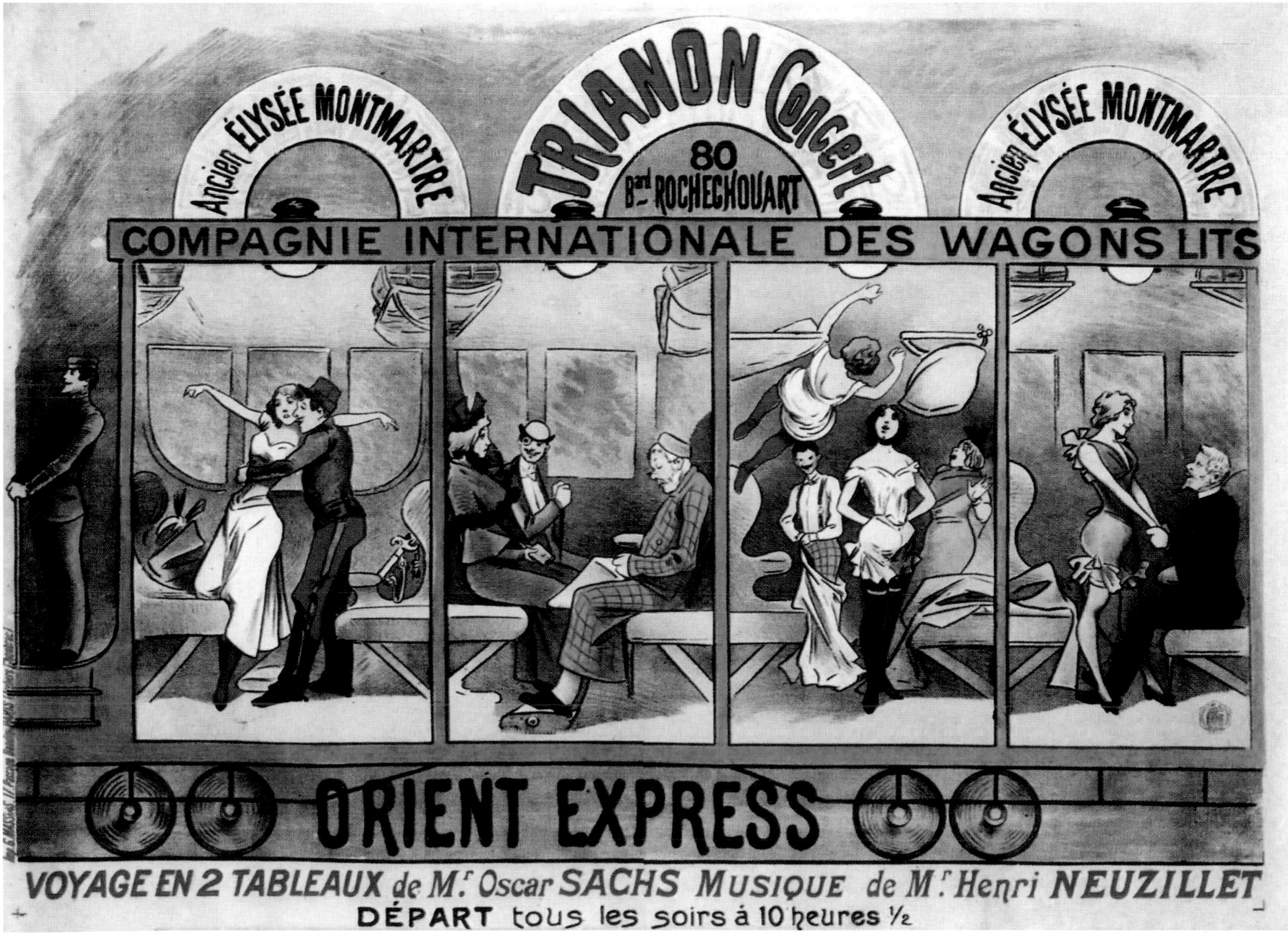

△ **Lady Liberty**
The Statue of Liberty (officially titled *Liberty Enlightening the World*) was dedicated on October 28, 1886. Placed at the entrance to New York Harbor, she welcomed travelers arriving from abroad.

The American Dream

For more than 200 years, the United States has embraced immigrants from all over the world—some fleeing persecution and others seeking riches, but all looking for a better life, regardless of social class.

In 1849, American author Herman Melville sailed out of Liverpool on a ship carrying 500 emigrants bound for New York. The journey he described was horrific. Bad weather made many people ill. Those in cabins could at least suffer in private, but for the poorer passengers—by far the majority—there was no such consolation. Traveling in the hold, or "steerage," they were "stowed away like bales of cotton, and packed like slaves in a slave-ship." Sealed in the darkness, they had nowhere to be sick but their beds. He writes: "We had not been at sea one week, when to hold your head down the fore hatchway was like holding it down a suddenly opened cesspool."

Such vessels, of course, were not designed for passengers. They were cargo ships, bringing cotton, tobacco, and timber to England from the colonies. To maximize profits, their owners filled the holds with emigrants, who served as freight for the journey home. Enduring such voyages for weeks on end, particularly in bad weather, made sickness unavoidable, the worst arising from poor sanitation and meager food. As a consequence, many died en route. Even so, from 1846 to 1855, emigration to North America boomed. In those 10 years, it is estimated that more than 2,300,000 people crossed to the US and Canada, compared to 1,600,000 over the previous 70 years. The attraction was that anyone could go. All they needed was the steerage fee to board a commercial ship.

Land of opportunity

Melville's mention of slave ships was a reminder that until 1808, when Congress banned slavery, the greatest number of people living in a new place because they were forcibly brought across the Atlantic in chains were Africans. Now, the greatest number were Irish or German, with smaller numbers of English, Scots, and Italians. The main points of arrival were New York and the eastern seaboard ports. There was also San Francisco, on the west coast, which had a huge influx of foreigners, particularly Chinese, when, in 1850, news of the Gold Rush spread around the world.

The Irish came to escape a devastating potato famine at home. From 1845 to 1852, a blight on the country's staple crop claimed the lives of around 1,000,000 people. The same number emigrated, all risking the brutal Atlantic voyage and the uncertainty of what lay ahead. For them, the US and Canada were far more welcoming than Britain. North America needed farmers, carpenters, masons, haulers, and unskilled laborers—the trades of the lower classes—to help construct its countries. It positively welcomed the poor, as long as they were willing to work. »

△ **Poor of all nations**
In the early 19th century, the largest numbers of immigrants came from Ireland and Germany. There were numerous Italians too, such as this family, who were fleeing poverty at home.

◁ **Inspection card**
Immigrants on steamships were subjected to a daily health inspection by the ship's surgeon, who recorded the check-ups by stamping each passenger's health card.

◁ **Huddled masses**
Immigrants to America gather on the decks of the SS *Patricia* in December 1906. The ship carried 408 second-class passengers and 2,143 in steerage.

" The only **encouragements** we hold out to **strangers** ... are **good laws, a free government**, and **a hearty welcome**. "

BENJAMIN FRANKLIN, ONE OF THE FOUNDING FATHERS OF THE UNITED STATES

△ **Arrival at Ellis Island**
In 1892, Ellis Island opened as New York's federal immigration station, a purpose it served for more than 60 years. Millions of new arrivals passed through the station during that time.

The Germans came to escape economic hardship, and the political unrest caused by riots, rebellion, and eventually a revolution in 1848. Unlike the Irish, who settled in east coast cities such as New York, Boston, Philadelphia, and Pittsburgh, many Germans had enough money to travel to the Midwest in search of farmland and work. After New York, some of the largest settlements of Germans were in Cincinnati, St. Louis, and Milwaukee.

◁ **American liberty**
In this World War I poster, immigrants are reminded that America has given them liberty; now it was their duty to buy bonds to help preserve that liberty.

Shaping the New World

Not every immigrant dream came true, but there were enough rags-to-riches tales to keep the influx of labor flowing. One such tale was Paddy O'Dougherty's, as related in the *New York Illustrated News* in 1853. O'Dougherty, the article said, entered the US a pauper but was taken on by the railways. After working hard for nine months, and spending nothing on drink or tobacco, he had enough money to bring over his wife and children and buy a house for the family. "Few more gentlemanly in appearance can this day be seen in Water Street than this same Paddy O'Dougherty," the paper concluded. It was a good advertisement for life in their new home.

As steamships replaced sailing ships, the transatlantic journey became faster and cheaper. Now the hopeful streamed in not just from northern Europe but from all over the world, including eastern Europe, the Mediterranean, and the Middle East. In the 1880s alone, nine percent of the total population of Norway emigrated to America. The Chinese were not so lucky. They were banned from entering the US by the Exclusion Act of 1882, which remained in force until 1943.

▷ **Immigrant city**
From 1870 to 1915, New York's population more than tripled. In 1900, when this picture of Mulberry Street in Little Italy was taken, foreign-born immigrants and their children made up 76 percent of the city's population.

From 1880 to 1930, more than 27 million people entered the US. About 12 million of that number passed through the federal immigration station on Ellis Island in New York Harbor after it opened in 1892. Among the masses, there were Jews fleeing pogroms in Russia, Mexicans displaced by revolution, and Armenians fleeing genocide. However, after the outbreak of World War I, American attitudes toward immigration began to change. Nationalism was on the rise, and quotas were introduced to slow the flow of

" **New York**, indeed, resembles a **magic cauldron**. Those who are **cast into it** are **born again**. "

CHARLES WHIBLEY, IN *AMERICAN SKETCHES*, 1908

arrivals. Numbers were reduced even further during the Great Depression of the 1930s, and again during World War II. In the wake of that global conflict, however, the US renewed its commitment to the "tired ... poor ... huddled masses" referred to on the Statue of Liberty. Over 400,000 new immigrants were accepted through the Displaced Persons Act of 1948.

In 1965, President Lyndon Johnson removed the quota system, and Asian immigration quadrupled in just five years. In recent times, immigration has continued to rise, especially from Asia, Mexico, and the Caribbean.

Today, one in eight people in the US are immigrants. Given that less than two percent of citizens have Native American ancestry, almost everybody came from somewhere else.

IN PROFILE

Annie Moore

Annie Moore was the first immigrant to be processed at Ellis Island. She was a 17-year-old Irish girl from County Cork traveling with her two younger brothers. She stepped ashore on January 1, 1892, and was presented with a $10 gold piece by an official. She then joined her parents, who had immigrated earlier, and settled on the Lower East Side. She married a bakery clerk, and had 11 children, five of whom survived. She lived a poor immigrant's life, and died of heart failure in 1924 at the age of 47, but her descendants multiplied and prospered. They married other immigrants and took on Irish, Jewish, Italian, and Scandinavian surnames. In that sense, Annie is a poster child for American immigration: she arrived bearing little more than her dreams and stayed to help build a nation enriched by diversity.

BRONZE STATUE OF ANNIE MOORE AND HER BROTHERS, IN COBH, COUNTY CORK, IRELAND

Splendor at sea

The end of the 19th century marked the beginning of a golden age of sea travel. Ships became bigger and ever more luxurious, and more people voyaged greater distances around the world than ever before.

△ **New liners**
At the turn of the 19th century, Europe's shipping lines competed to produce impressive ocean liners, such as the RMS *Lusitania* (above), which was launched in 1906.

Originally, the term "ocean liner" simply meant a ship that sailed a regular route, or line. It was a merchant shipping term, and liners were mail and cargo ships, but they also carried passengers as an extra service, especially over to America, when the decks would fill with immigrants en route to new lives.

There was nothing luxurious about these early liners. Most passengers traveled in steerage—below-deck cargo holds that were stacked with triple-decked bunks, had no amenities, and certainly had no privacy. When the SS *City of Glasgow* relaunched after a refit in 1852, her owners were proud to advertise that she had the luxury of a bath. Just the one, filled with pumped seawater.

Change was quick to come. By 1871, the White Star Line guaranteed a separate berth for each adult, as well as a 10-cubic-foot (0.3-cubic-meter) baggage allowance. The fare also included three meals a day. These were probably more luxurious arrangements than many passengers were used to back at home. The company's RMS *Oceanic* set even higher standards by setting its first-class cabins amidships and giving them the added luxuries of large portholes, electricity, and running water.

△ **The Cunard Line**
Cunard, whose steam sailing ship services were advertised on this 1875 poster, was one of the first companies to offer regular Atlantic sailings, starting in 1840.

Increasing competition

Liners were built ever larger to meet the demands of increasing immigration to America and Australia. By the 1880s, the switch to steam power was complete, so ships were no longer fitted with auxiliary sails. White Star's most famous ships had names ending in "ic", such as the *Britannic, Teutonic, Germanic,* and *Majestic,* all of which carried around 1,000 third-class and 160 first-class passengers. Several of these liners won the coveted Blue Riband, which was awarded to the ship that could cross the Atlantic fastest. Six days was the record at the time.

White Star's chief competitor was Cunard, which launched Blue Riband winners of its own. All of its ships had names ending in "ia", which in the 1880s and '90s included the *Umbria, Etruria, Campania,* and *Lucania*. New rival lines emerged, such as the German Hamburg-American Line and Norddeutscher Lloyd, which, in 1897, launched the *Kaiser Wilhelm der Große*, the first of a new breed of bigger, faster "superliners."

◁ **Ocean-going palaces**
To attract and retain the richest and most fashionable clients, shipping companies fitted their liners with opulent interiors. This is the grand staircase on the *Titanic*.

"Say, when does this place **get to New York?**"

BEATRICE LILLIE, ACTRESS, ON BOARD THE *QUEEN MARY*

△ **Silver-spoon service**
Many passengers were loyal to specific lines and ships, and regulars forged bonds with staff. Company identity was reinforced with branded items, such as this White Star spoon.

Hamburg-American responded in 1900 with the *Deutschland*, which took the Blue Riband, making the passage from Eddystone Lighthouse off the south coast of England to Sandy Hook, New York, in five days, 15 hours, and 45 minutes.

Floating five-star hotels

The new liners were not just huge and fast—they symbolized the height of civilized travel. The lines competed fiercely, particularly with regard to beauty, comfort, and service, and the ships were designed to resemble grand five-star hotels. "There is a winter garden on board, a Ritz restaurant, a Roman swimming bath, a ballroom, a gymnasium ... Luxury is being carried almost too far," commented one British journalist on board Hamburg-American's SS *Imperator* in 1913.

Such criticism, of course, could not be leveled at steerage. First-class passengers brought prestige to the shipping lines, but the real money was still made from immigrants, who filled the lower decks. The classes were kept well apart, and some liners carried signs asking the upper-deck passengers not to throw food down to those on the decks below.

Disaster brought a temporary halt to competition between the liners—White Star's *Titanic* sank on its maiden voyage, and its *Britannic* and Cunard's *Lusitania* were sunk during World War I—but this just spurred the lines on to even greater ambitions. The 1930s saw the launches of some of the most extraordinary ships ever built, such as the RMS *Queen Mary* and the SS *Normandie*. By this time, however, air travel was already in the ascendant and the days of splendor at sea were numbered.

▷ **The White Star Line**
Cunard's major rival in the early days was the White Star Line, founded in 1845. It was best known for its Olympic-class ocean liners, as advertised on this 1911 poster.

The elusive North Pole

Arctic exploration goes back to the Middle Ages, when the first attempts were made to find the Northwest Passage. It was only in the 19th century that expeditions set off to reach the elusive North Pole.

The North Pole lies 435 miles (700 km) from the nearest land. It is in the Arctic Ocean, in a region almost permanently covered by shifting sea ice. The first attempts to reach the Pole were made by expeditions sailing in search of the fabled Northwest Passage connecting the Atlantic and Pacific oceans. In 1827, after failing to find any such route, William Edward Parry set his sights on the Pole. He got as far as 82°45′ north, a record that stood for almost five decades, until it was beaten by a British Arctic expedition led by Albert Markham, which reached as far as 83°20′ north in 1876.

Norwegian explorer Fridtjof Nansen, who had previously crossed Greenland on skis (see pp. 260–61), had a theory that polar ice was carried by ocean currents from east to west. He believed that, if frozen in the right spot, a ship could float across the Pole. With this in mind, he set off in a specially constructed ship, which he called *Fram* (meaning "forward"). When Nansen left Christiania (Oslo), Norway, in June 1893, he found that his route was blocked by ice near Cape Chelyuskin, the northernmost point of Russia, and was forced to let the ship freeze into place at a latitude of 78–79°. After 18 months adrift, he realized that the ship would miss the Pole, so, along with fellow expedition member Hjalmar Johansen, he left the ship and set off on skis. The pair reached a new northernmost point of latitude 86°14′ before turning back, defeated by the conditions.

It was a further 14 months, eight of which were spent wintering in a hole in the ice, surviving on walrus and seal, before the pair chanced upon a British expedition and were rescued.

In 1897, Swedish explorer Salomon August Andrée tried to reach the Pole by hydrogen balloon, but he and his companions all died during the attempt (see p. 185). Two years later, an expedition led by Luigi Amedeo, an

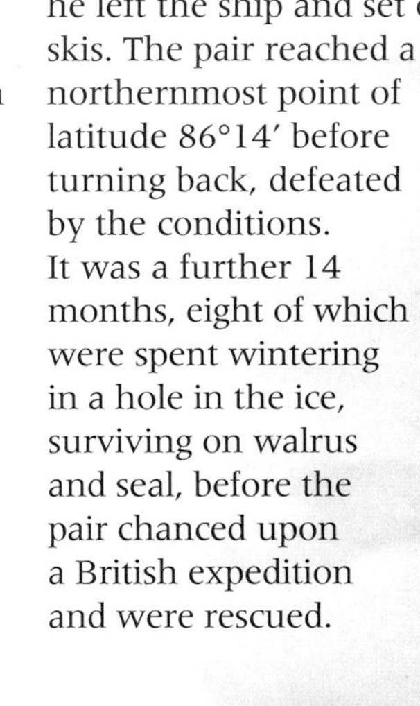

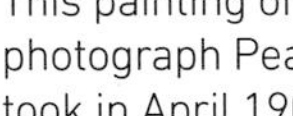

▽ **Rival claim**
This painting of a photograph Peary took in April 1909 shows his team at what they believed was the North Pole. Experts remain divided as to whether or not they reached the right location.

" I demolish my **bridges behind me**, then there is **no choice** but **forward**. "

FRIDTJOF NANSEN, ARCTIC EXPLORER

Italian prince, sailed out of Christiania, transferring to skis at the ice pack, and making it as far north as 86°34′, some 25 miles (40 km) further than Nansen had gone.

Disputed claims

On September 7, 1909, the *New York Times* carried the front-page headline: "Peary Discovers the North Pole." What made the news all the more surprising was that only a week earlier, the *New York Herald* had run the headline: "The North Pole is Discovered by Dr. Frederick A. Cook."

Cook's expedition had set out in July 1907, and it claimed to have reached the Pole on April 21, 1908. While Cook was making his way back, and before anyone knew about his claim, American explorer Robert Peary set out on his own expedition. On his return, Peary stated that he had reached the Pole on April 6, 1909. In the event, neither man was able to prove for certain that he had reached the Pole. Despite this, for many years Peary was believed rather than Cook, but his claim is disputed even to this day.

◁ **Robert Peary**
A commander in the US Navy, Peary made several expeditions to Greenland and the Canadian Arctic before launching his attempt on the North Pole. At that point, he had already lost eight toes to frostbite.

The first scientifically proven claim to have reached the North Pole was in May 1926. It was achieved by three men: the Norwegian explorer Roald Amundsen (see pp.280–81); American financier Lincoln Ellsworth; and Italian engineer and aviator Umberto Nobile. They crossed the Atlantic from Norway to Alaska in the airship *Norge*, which was piloted by Nobile. As they flew over the Pole, they dropped the national flags of Italy, the US, and Norway onto the ice. Amundsen was unimpressed when he saw that the Italian flag was the largest, and later claimed that Nobile had turned *Norge* into a "circus wagon in the sky."

◁ **Pole contender**
American explorer Frederick Cook, on the right, had been the doctor on Robert Peary's 1891–92 Arctic expedition. His claim to have reached the North Pole in April 1908 has been viewed with scepticism.

Le Petit Journal
SUPPLÉMENT ILLUSTRÉ
5 CENT.
DIMANCHE 19 SEPTEMBRE 1909
PÔLE NORD
LA CONQUÊTE DU POLE NORD
Le docteur Cook et le commandant Peary s'en disputent la gloire

△ **Arch rivalry**
A French magazine of 1909 depicts Americans Cook and Peary in a fistfight at the North Pole. The encounter is fantasy—as is the idea that there are penguins in the Arctic.

Ice grotto
Herbert Ponting was a member of the *Terra Nova* expedition. He captured some of the greatest images of Antarctica, including this shot of the scientists T. G. Taylor and C. S. Wright taken from inside an ice grotto.

Claiming the South Pole

As scientific expeditions from numerous countries probed one of the last remaining unexplored regions on Earth, two headstrong individuals set out on a grueling, frozen dash for glory.

Antarctica was the last major landmass on Earth to be explored and charted. Following the first expedition there, launched by the Belgian Geographical Society in 1897, some 17 major expeditions were sent to the region by 10 countries in a mere 20 years. It is a period known as the Heroic Age of Antarctic Exploration.

The ultimate prize, of course, was to reach the South Pole. Two expeditions set off in 1910 to achieve this goal: one from Norway, led by Roald Amundsen (see pp. 280–81), and the other from Britain, led by Robert Falcon Scott. Scott was a former Royal Navy officer who had left the service to lead the Royal Geographical Society's National Antarctic Expedition of 1901–04 aboard the research ship *Discovery*. This expedition penetrated further south than anyone had ever ventured before. On his return, Scott immediately planned a second venture, this time to the South Pole.

Winners and losers

In June 1910, the *Terra Nova*, Scott's converted whaling ship, left Cardiff, Wales, with a crew of 65, including six veterans of the *Discovery*. For transport on the ice, he took ponies, which he preferred to dogs, and some new and largely untested motorized sleds. The team spent the first winter at the most southerly point they could sail to, where the Ross Sea met the Ross Ice Shelf. They waited out the harshest weather in a hut at Cape Evans (named after one of the group), and set up supply caches on the route to the pole.

By October 24, 1911, the start of the Antarctic summer, everything was ready. It quickly became apparent that the motorized sleds and ponies could not cope with the harsh conditions, so the expedition proceeded without them. On December 21, they reached the high expanse of the Polar Plateau, where Scott selected four men to accompany him on the final leg of the journey: Henry Bowers, Edgar Evans, Lawrence Oates, and Edward Wilson.

◁ **Scott at Cape Evans**
For three years the *Terra Nova* expedition lived in a large, prefabricated hut at Cape Evans. Here, Scott sits in his private room, pipe in hand, writing his journal.

Slowed down by bad weather and Scott's insistence that the men haul their sleds, they reached the South Pole on January 17, 1912. Awaiting them was a Norwegian flag and marker tent—proof that Amundsen had arrived before them. Their dreams of glory shattered, Scott's exhausted party now faced an 808-mile (1,300-km) journey back to Cape Evans.

Final words

On February 17, a month into their return trip, Evans died after a fall. On March 17, Oates, realizing that his frostbitten and gangrenous feet were handicapping the rest of the party, uttered the most gallant words in the history of polar exploration: "I am just going outside and may be some time." He stumbled out of the tent into a blizzard and was never seen again.

On March 21, with only two days' rations left, Scott, Wilson, and Bowers, faint with hunger and ravaged by scurvy, pitched their tent in a gale. They had walked 740 miles (1,190 km) from the Pole. They were still 140 miles (225 km) short of Cape Evans, but One Ton Depot, where ample food and fuel was cached, was only 11 miles (18 km) away.

"We are weak..."

Eight months later, a search party from Cape Evans found the small green tent. Three frozen corpses lay inside, tucked into their reindeer-hide sleeping bags. Scott's journal was next to his body. "We are weak," he had written, "but for my own sake I do not regret this journey, which has shown that Englishmen can endure hardships ... and meet death with as great a fortitude as ever in the past." A sheaf of letters was also found, including one to his wife, which began, "Dear widow."

◁ **Second place**
Battered and frostbitten, Wilson, Scott, Evans, Oates, and Bowers pose for a portrait at the South Pole in January 1912. Behind them stands the marker tent left by Roald Amundsen.

Roald Amundsen

Norwegian explorer Roald Amundsen was the first man to reach the South Pole, the first to visit both poles, and the first to navigate the Northwest Passage between the Atlantic and Pacific oceans.

As a child, growing up a son of shipowners, Amundsen dreamed of being a polar explorer, his imagination fired by the exploits of fellow Norwegian Fridtjof Nansen. His mother did not want him to go to sea and encouraged him to become a doctor. Amundsen dutifully studied medicine, but when his mother died when he was 21, he left college and joined a sealing expedition to the Arctic.

In 1897, he sailed as first mate on an expedition to Antarctica aboard the ship RV *Belgica*. On his return in 1899, he set his sights on the Northwest Passage. Since the 16th century, seafarers had been searching for an Arctic route between the Atlantic and Pacific oceans (see pp. 138–39). Among those who had tried and failed to find it were Henry Hudson, James Cook, and John Franklin, whose disappearance in the icy seas of the far north fascinated Amundsen.

▽ The South Pole
Amundsen stands before the Norwegian flag he planted at the South Pole on December 14, 1911. With him are some of the huskies that gave his expedition the edge over his rival, Robert Falcon Scott.

The Northwest Passage

In June 1903, Amundsen and his crew of six set off from Christiania (Oslo) aboard a small fishing vessel called *Gjøa*. After crossing the Atlantic, they set up base on King William Island to the north of the Canadian mainland, where they spent two winters carrying out scientific studies and spending time with the local Inuits. Here they learned Arctic survival skills, including how to build snow huts, drive sled dogs, and make clothes from animal skins.

◁ Pocket watch
This pocket watch, made by US watchmaker Elgin National Watch Company, was used by Amundsen. It is now held in St. Petersburg's Arctic and Antarctic Museum.

In August 1905, the *Gjøa* weighed anchor and sailed on. Amundsen took a westward course through uncharted channels until the boat became ice-bound, forcing them to spend the winter just short of Alaska. They finally reached the Alaskan town of Nome in 1906, becoming the first crew to navigate the Northwest Passage. However, the journey had taken over three years, and parts of the route had only just been deep enough to give Amundsen's small fishing boat clearance. The Northwest Passage had no commercial viability.

The South Pole

After his return to Norway, Amundsen began to prepare for an attempt on the North Pole, using Fridtjof Nansen's old polar vessel, *Fram*. Then he received news that Frederick Cook and Robert Peary had beaten him to it, so he switched his attention to the South Pole. Robert Scott had already announced his expedition, so Amundsen telegraphed him with the courtesy message: "BEG TO INFORM YOU FRAM PROCEEEDING ANTARCTIC."

The *Fram* arrived in the Antarctic in January 1911, and the party dug in for the winter until October, when Amundsen judged the time was right to set off. His party consisted of five men and four sleds, with 13 dogs for each sled. The skills learned from the Inuits proved invaluable, and Amundsen swiftly reached the pole on December 14, 1911—more than a month before his English competitor.

▷ Called to the wild
This photograph from 1923 shows Roald Amundsen dressed in a fur parka. Unlike others who had attempted expeditions to the poles, Amundsen and his Norwegian crew were used to the freezing climate. They were also more skilled at skiing.

> "With **sufficient planning**, you can almost **eliminate adventure** from an **expedition**."
>
> ROALD AMUNDSEN, POLAR EXPLORER

KEY DATES

- **1872** Born into a ship-owning family in Borge, in southern Norway.
- **1897** Joins the crew aboard the RV *Belgica* led by Adrien de Gerlache, which becomes the first expedition to winter in Antarctica.
- **1903–06** Becomes the first to navigate between the Atlantic and Pacific oceans via the Arctic.
- **1910–12** Sails aboard the *Fram* to the Antarctic, where he beats Robert F. Scott in a race to the South Pole.
- **1926** Passes over the North Pole aboard the airship *Norge*, piloted by Italian Umberto Nobile. As previous claims are disputed, this makes them the first verified explorers to reach the Pole. Amundsen becomes the first to visit both poles.
- **1928** Disappears with five crew on June 28 while flying on a rescue mission to find Umberto Nobile. His body has never been found.

A YOUNG AMUNDSEN POSES FOR A STUDIO PHOTOGRAPHER

THE AIRSHIP *NORGE*, WHICH CARRIED AMUNDSEN OVER THE NORTH POLE

The Model T

Henry Ford's revolutionary Model T automobile forever changed the way that America—and the rest of the world—lived, worked, and traveled.

When Henry Ford entered the automobile business in the late 19th century, he was in the company of countless other inventors and entrepreneurs who were all experimenting with various technologies. Some of these inventions were having success, such as the gas-powered automobile developed by Karl Benz in 1886. Benz's automobile might even be considered the first "production" vehicle, as he made several identical copies. However, nobody did production like Henry Ford.

Henry Ford launched his company in 1903 in Detroit, Michigan. Over the next five years, he produced Ford Models A, B, C, F, K, N, R, and S, most of which only sold in the hundreds or low thousands a year. This changed in 1908, when Ford introduced the Model T, which would go on to sell substantially more. The first vehicle left the factory on September 27, 1908. On May 26, 1927, Ford watched as the 15 millionth Model T rolled off the assembly line.

Ford's revolutionary vehicle was the first automobile mass-produced on a moving assembly line with interchangeable parts. It was therefore cheap to make in comparison to other early automobiles, so it could be sold for far less than its competitors. Coupled with its ease of maintenance and availability, the Model T suddenly made motoring possible for people who had previously been unable to afford it. By 1915, the Model T accounted for 40 percent of all cars sold in the US.

The Model T came in several body styles, including a five-seat touring car, a two-seat runabout, and a seven-seat town car. A choice of colors was originally available, but from 1913 to 1925 the car was made in one color only: black. Eventually, it was superseded by larger, more powerful cars, but by that time the Model T had helped Ford realize his dream to "democratize the automobile."

" I will build a car for the **great multitude**. "

HENRY FORD (1922)

◁ **Ready for delivery**
This photograph, taken in a Ford factory in 1925, shows rows of Model Ts lined up in preparation for delivery. The automobile was assembled in Detroit, Michigan, and in Manchester, England.

The discovery of Machu Picchu

Inspired to explore South America by reading the accounts of Alexander von Humboldt, Hiram Bingham made one of the most sensational archaeological finds of the 20th century.

How does an explorer find an ancient lost city? Hiram Bingham, the organizer of the Yale Peruvian Expedition of 1911, simply asked everyone he met in Peru if they knew of any ruins. While investigating the Urubamba Valley, near Cuzco, he met a farmer who said he knew about such a site. None of the rest of the group was interested in joining Bingham, so he set off with just his translator and the farmer, who acted as a guide. They hiked in persistent drizzle for a couple of hours, hacking their way through dense tropical vegetation and having to clamber on all fours at times because the terrain was so steep, but eventually Bingham and his guide found themselves in an overgrown maze of walls. "Surprise followed surprise until there came the realization that we were in the midst of as wonderful ruins as any ever found in Peru," he wrote.

△ **Man and mule**
Yale academic and explorer Hiram Bingham and his mule, pictured shortly after he made his first trip to Machu Picchu in 1911, with the guidance of a local farmer.

A growing obsession

Bingham was born in Hawaii in 1875 to American missionaries. He studied at Yale and Harvard, where he pursued his interest in Latin American history. Later, he was appointed a lecturer at Yale, but he was more interested in

> “It is possible that **not even the conquistadors** ever saw this **wonderful place**.”
>
> HIRAM BINGHAM

exploring than teaching. In 1906, Bingham traced the footsteps of Simón Bolívar, the 19th-century hero of South American independence, through Venezuela and Columbia. In 1909, he rode a mule along an historic trade route from Buenos Aires to Lima in Peru. When he saw the spectacular ruins of the ancient imperial city of Cuzco in Peru, Bingham resolved to discover more of the legacy of the Incas. His quest in 1911 was to seek out the "lost city" of Vilcabamba, the last refuge of the Incas, who fought against the Spanish conquistadors in the 1530s.

What Bingham found that rainy day, on July 24, 1911, was Machu Picchu ("old mountain peak" in the language of the Incas), a citadel built for the Inca emperor some time during the 15th century. He came across some local peasants living in a hut among the ruins, farming some of the ancient terraces, and one of them showed him around. Bingham was astonished by the flights of beautifully constructed stone terraces and structures of the "finest quality of Inca stonework." He was also captivated by the stunning setting of the citadel, which was surrounded by majestic mountains.

▽ **Mountain retreat**
Bingham thought he had discovered Vilcabamba, the lost city of the Incas, but Machu Picchu is now believed to have been the mountain retreat of the Inca emperor Pachacutec, abandoned at some point after his death in 1472.

△ **Excavating the site**
On Bingham's second visit to Machu Picchu in 1912, he began an extensive excavation of the site, which was "covered with trees and moss and the growth of centuries."

Documenting the discovery

Later, there were claims that other travelers had been to Machu Picchu before Bingham. He himself admitted that "it seemed almost incredible that this city, only five days' journey from Cuzco, should have remained so long undescribed." But if others had been there before him, they did not record their journeys. When he returned to the site in succeeding years, Bingham took extensive photographs, made accurate site drawings, and took thousands of objects to the United States for study. His discoveries were meticulously documented and brought him great acclaim: "The greatest archaeological discovery of the age," the *New York Times* called it.

Bingham was always convinced that Machu Picchu was Vilcabamba, and expounded on this theory in his 1948 book *Lost City of the Incas*. In 1964, however, American explorer Gene Savoy established the true remains of Vilcabamba at nearby Espíritu Pampa, a site that Bingham had visited, but had rejected as being of minor importance.

▽ **Inca pendant**
Bingham excavated more than 45,000 artifacts from Machu Picchu, including this golden pendant. Yale University has since agreed to return the artifacts to Peru.

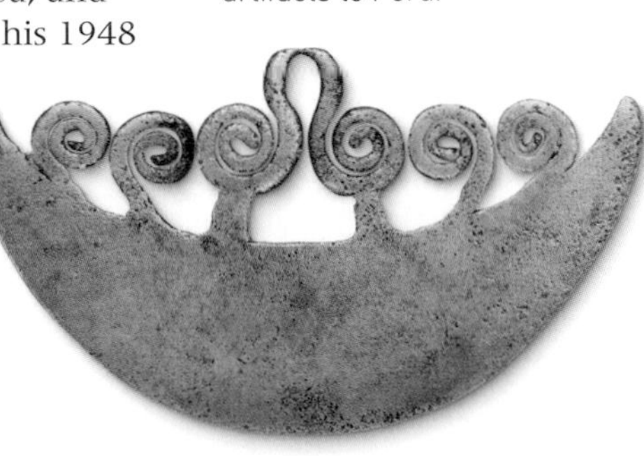

Taking flight

In 1908, on a race track in western France, Wilbur Wright took to the air with the words, "Gentleman, now I'm going to fly." His flying machine laid the foundation for a revolution in travel.

Most aviation historians refer to December 17, 1903 as the day travel changed forever. That was when Wilbur and Orville Wright, two American bicycle manufacturers, made their first controlled, sustained flight of a heavier-than-air aircraft at a site near Kitty Hawk, North Carolina.

After this feat, the brothers continued to work on their designs for another couple of years. Then, on October 5, 1905, Wilbur piloted the *Flyer III* for 39 minutes and covered some 24 miles (39 km). Fearful that competitors might steal their ideas, the Wrights carried out their experiments in relative secrecy, so there were few witnesses. Naturally, this led to scepticism. As an editorial in the *New York Herald* in February 1906 noted: "It's easy to say, 'We have flown'."

By way of response to their critics, the brothers carried out more flights in May 1908, this time in front of the American press. All of their flights up until then had been solo flights, but this time, the aircraft had been modified to carry a passenger—another historic first. The same feat was repeated later the same year in France, when Wilbur piloted the aircraft in figure-eights above a crowd of thousands. But the Wrights were far from alone in experimenting with flying machines, and they were only just ahead of the competition. One of the people in the crowd that day in France

▷ **AT&T**
In 1919, the Aircraft Transport and Travel company launched the world's first regular, daily international air service, between London and Paris. It used a de Havilland DH.16 aircraft, pictured here, which carried just four passengers.

> “ **Some day** people will be **crossing oceans** on **airliners** like they do on **steamships** today. ”

THOMAS BENOIST, PIONEER AIRPLANE BUILDER

△ **First flight**
Wilbur Wright (pictured here on an early test flight of a glider, in October 1902) and his brother Orville made the first ever controlled, sustained flights at Kill Devil Hills, near Kitty Hawk, North Carolina, in 1903.

was the inventor Louis Blériot, who, the very next year, became the first person to fly across the English Channel, and did so in an aircraft that he had designed himself.

The first airlines

Incredibly, a mere six years after the Wright brothers' international demonstration, the first aircraft capable of carrying several passengers made its debut. The four-engined *Ilya Muromets*, designed by Russian engineer Igor Sikorsky, was the first aircraft to have heating and electric lighting—not to mention a passenger saloon complete with a bedroom, lounge, and toilet.

▷ **Rapid progress**
Fewer than 20 years after the Wright brothers' first flight, there were aircraft that could carry more than 150 passengers. These people are on board a giant 12-engined DO-X flying boat crossing Lake Geneva.

It took off on a demonstration flight on 25, 1914, with 16 people aboard. In June, it flew from St. Petersburg to Kiev in 14 hours and 38 minutes, and returned in less time than that. However, due to the onset of World War I, the plane was never used as a commercial airliner.

The world's first scheduled airline had commenced its operation just one month earlier. The St. Petersburg to Tampa Airboat Line began operating across Tampa Bay, Florida, in January 1914. The service only lasted for a few months, but during that time, its two flying boats had flown more than 1,200 passengers across the bay.

Airlines come of age

Technological innovation sped up during the war, so by 1918, there were many new and improved aircraft that could be adapted for civilian service. On August 25, 1919, the Aircraft Transport and Travel company (AT&T) launched the first regular international service in the world—a daily flight between London's Hounslow Heath Aerodrome and Le Bourget in Paris.

AT&T only flew until December 1920 before it went bankrupt, but within a year, no fewer than six companies were operating a London-to-Paris service. On May 17, 1920, another new airline had its inaugural flight from London to Amsterdam. The Dutch company behind it was Koninklijke Luchtvaart Maatschappij, better known as KLM.

These airlines transformed travel just as radically as the steam engine had 100 years earlier. Journeys that had once taken weeks, or even months, now took a matter of hours. The idea of spending months at sea to travel from one place to another became unthinkable, not just to the rich, but to businessmen and many other people too. By the 1950s, flying had become the principal way to travel long distances.

◁ **KLM**
KLM, the Dutch airline that made its inaugural flight in 1920, has been in service for longer than any other airline. This poster from 1929 states: "The Flying Dutchman—A Legend Becomes Reality."

Adventurers of the skies

Early aviation history is a roll call of leather-hatted and goggled adventurers who risked life and limb—all too often with fatal results—to push back the boundaries of air travel.

In modern times, flight has become merely the fastest way of getting from one place to another. This was not always so. At the beginning of the 20th century, taking to the air was an incredible, almost mystical experience, and airmen were the heroes of the day. The most exciting time was the period between the wars, when engineers were revising aircraft designs almost weekly, and pilots were shattering speed and distance records. For every success there were many failures, and often deaths, but the pioneers believed that flying was a calling that justified the risks.

Explaining his decision to become an airmail pilot, Frenchman Antoine de Saint-Exupéry (who vanished over the Mediterranean in 1944) could think of no better comparison than entering a monastery. He wrote about his experience in books such as *Wind, Sand and Stars* and *Flight to Arras*. Death in the air came in unexpected ways. Alan Cobham was a pioneer of long-distance aviation, and in March 1926 he completed a flight from London to Cape Town and back. Three months later he set off again from London, this time bound for Australia. While flying over Iraq, a sandstorm forced Cobham to fly low and the aircraft was shot at by tribesmen. His co-pilot was hit, and although Cobham landed at Basra and got him to a hospital, he died later that night.

Long-distance hero
This photograph shows Alan Cobham landing on the Thames river, in London, on October 1, 1926. He had just made a 26,703-mile (42,974-km) flight from England to Australia and back.

△ **The *Spirit of St Louis***
The aircraft in which Lindbergh flew across the Atlantic was a single-engine, single-seat monoplane, built by Ryan Airlines of San Diego. Today, it is on display at the Smithsonian Institution's National Air and Space Museum.

> " Sometimes, **flying feels too godlike** to be attained by man. "
>
> CHARLES LINDBERGH, AVIATOR

Across the Atlantic

In the annals of aviation history, nearly all flights are overshadowed by the one made by Charles Lindbergh on May 20–21, 1927. The 25-year-old military and airmail pilot achieved worldwide fame when he flew solo non-stop from Long Island, New York, to Paris, traveling the 3,600 miles (5,800km) in 33½ hours. However, he was not the first to cross the Atlantic by air. In May 1919, Lieutenant Commander Read of the US Navy flew from Newfoundland to Portugal by way of the Azores. Two weeks later, Captain John Alcock and Lieutenant Arthur Brown flew nonstop from Newfoundland to Ireland. In fact, by 1927, over 100 other men had flown across the Atlantic. Lindbergh's achievement was to do it solo, and to fly from New York to Paris, thus linking two key cities.

The following year, Australian Charles Kingsford Smith and his three-man crew were the first to fly across the Pacific, from Oakland to Brisbane. The headlines that year, however, were made by Amelia Earhart, who became the first woman to cross the Atlantic by air, albeit as a passenger. "I was just baggage, like a sack of potatoes," she said in an interview after landing—adding, "Maybe someday I'll try it alone." That day came on May 20, 1932, when, five years to the day from Lindbergh's flight, the 34-year-old set off from Newfoundland. Four minutes shy of 15 hours later, she touched down in a field in Northern Ireland, becoming the first woman to fly the Atlantic solo.

Around the world

Ironically, perhaps the greatest aviation achievement of all is the least known. Wiley Post, a native of Oklahoma, worked in the oilfields, spent a year in prison for armed robbery, and lost an eye in an accident before he became the personal pilot of a wealthy oilman. On June 23, flying the oilman's aircraft (a Lockheed Vega named *Winnie Mae*), Post and his navigator, Harold Gatty, set off from New York, heading west. They arrived back in New York on July 1, after circling the world in 8 days, 15 hours and 51 minutes.

△ **Amelia Earhart**
In 1932, Earhart became the first woman to fly solo across the Atlantic. She has been an inspiration to aviators ever since.

This smashed the previous around-the-world record of 21 days, which had been set by a Zeppelin.

In July 1933, Post took the *Winnie Mae* around the world again, this time solo, becoming the first person to do so, and in just 7 days, 19 hours. Two years later, his extraordinary career came to an end when the engine of his seaplane failed and he plunged into a lake in Alaska.

MORE PICTURES, MORE NEWS AND MORE SPORT

Daily Mirror

THE DAILY PICTURE NEWSPAPER WITH THE LARGEST NET SALE

28 PAGES

MONDAY, MAY 30, 1927

One Penny

CROYDON BATTLE TO WELCOME ATLANTIC HERO

▷ **Hero's welcome**
This front page of Britain's *Daily Mirror* records Charles Lindbergh's arrival at Croydon Airport, London, in the *Spirit of St Louis*, following his historic flight across the Atlantic.

Travels in Arabia

Over the centuries, a succession of lone maverick travelers from the West have been drawn to Arabia. They often traveled disguised in Arab dress, and adopted local ways.

▽ **When in Rome**
Bertram Thomas is pictured here, in 1930, with warriors from the Shahari tribe in Oman. He gained the trust of local people by observing their customs.

As the heartland of Islam from the 7th century onward, Arabia was familiar to Muslim travelers from all over the world as a place of pilgrimage. However, for non-Muslims, Mecca and Medina were part of a list of forbidden cities—including Lhasa and Timbuktu—that for centuries captured the imagination of the West. Although strictly forbidden to non-Muslims, intruders were not uncommon. By the early years of the 20th century, some 25 Westerners had visited Mecca and written about it.

The first known traveler was an Italian named Ludovico di Varthema. In 1503, he left Damascus, where he had spent two years studying Arabic, in a pilgrim caravan bound for Mecca. He was the first Westerner to describe the rituals of the Hajj.

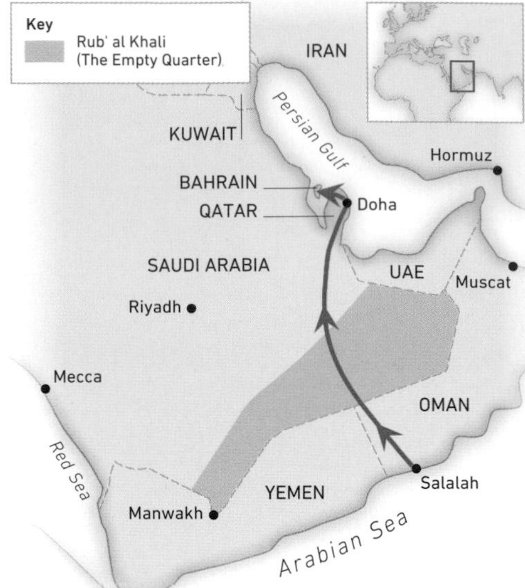

△ **Expeditions of Bertram Thomas**
In 1930, Bertram Thomas set off from Salalah, Dhofar, along with Sheik Saleh bin Kalut. They arrived in Doha—the other side of the Empty Quarter—60 days later. They then boarded a dhow and finished their journey in Bahrain.

◁ **Dressing up**
Like many Westerners who aimed to visit Mecca, Richard Burton studied Islam, learned Arabic, and dressed as a Muslim pilgrim, as shown here.

Another Westerner to travel in Arabia was the Swiss Johann Ludwig Burckhardt, who discovered the ancient rock-hewn city of Petra, in what is now Jordan. In 1814, he spent two months in Mecca, mapping the city and gathering information on the little-known Arabian Peninsula.

The best documented account came from adventurer Richard Burton. Britain's Royal Geographical Society refused to give Burton a grant to explore Arabia on the grounds that it was too dangerous, but he decided to go anyway. The resulting three-volume account was published in 1855.

Burton originally intended to use Mecca as a starting point to cross the Arabian Desert, but that did not happen. That expedition was left instead to the scholarly explorer Charles Montagu Doughty. In 1876, after overhearing a conversation in an Arab coffeehouse, Doughty learned of the existence of an ancient city in Saudi Arabia. He was determined to find it. Like all Europeans in Arabia, he adopted local dress to conceal his nationality, and joined a pilgrim caravan. Doughty was found out and shunned, but he still managed to discover the rock-cut facades of Mada'in Saleh, a smaller, sister city to Petra, and made a wide loop into the desert to Jeddah. In total, he traveled for two years, recording the details in his two-volume work *Travels in Arabia Deserta* (1888).

Crossing the Empty Quarter

In the first decades of the 20th century, with the Ottoman empire in terminal decline, the British regarded Arabia as part of their imperial sphere of influence. Bertram Thomas was a British civil servant employed as financial advisor to the sultan of Muscat. While working for the sultan in Arabia, he began planning his crossing of the Rub' al Khali, or the Empty Quarter—250,000 sq miles (650,000 sq km) of uninhabited, shifting desert.

△ **Lost desert city**
Arabian explorer Charles Doughty succeeded in visiting the rock-carved ruins at Mada'in Saleh, formerly the second most important city of the ancient Nabataean kingdom.

On December 10, 1930, Thomas set off from Salalah, Dhofar, arriving 60 days later in Doha, Qatar. He was the first European to traverse this inhospitable southeastern corner of Arabia.

Thomas's achievement did not please everyone. Harry St. John Philby, a British advisor to the king of Saudi Arabia, had been planning his own crossing of the Empty Quarter when he heard that he had been beaten to it. Still, he forged ahead. In the course of crossing 1,700 miles (2,700 km) of hostile desert, he discovered the previously unknown Wabar craters—large craters formed by meteorite impacts.

Although he was not the first to cross the Empty Quarter, Philby's achievements were recognized by a generation of later explorers, notably Wilfred Thesiger (see pp. 316–17), who said, "I shall always be proud to have followed in Philby's footsteps."

> "What remained for me but **to prove**, by **trial**, that what might be **perilous** to other travelers was **safe to me?**"
>
> RICHARD FRANCIS BURTON, 1855

△ **Philby's coffee pot**
After a long day's travel, the appearance of the coffee pot signaled rest. Philby wrote cheerfully of "coffee to cheer the heart of man."

The sunseekers

With the advent of steamships and trains, wealthy Victorian Britons no longer had to suffer the gloom of long winter months at home, but could set off to sunnier Mediterranean climes instead.

The idea that anyone would want to take a dip in the sea is a modern one. For much of history, the sea had been regarded as violent and unpredictable, something to be feared and conquered. This all changed with the Romantics (see pp. 204–05), who believed that spending time communing with nature was beneficial to the soul. Doctors also began to suggest that fresh air, exercise, and a warm climate were good for the health. Bathing machines (changing huts on wheels) began to appear on the beaches of Britain and Europe, and vacationers tentatively dipped their toes into the water. The rise of the middle classes following the Industrial Revolution, along with improvement in wages and the spread of railways, combined with this new-found enthusiasm for the sea, and led to the first seaside resorts. In the early 19th century, Brighton, a coastal resort favored by royal patronage, became one of the fastest-growing towns in England. When, in the 1840s, a railway was built connecting the factory towns of northern England to Blackpool, it became the world's first working-class seaside resort. But while English seaside towns began to flourish, some people,

△ **Showing off in swimwear**
In order to enjoy the seaside fully, many 19th-century tourists donned bathing suits, although modesty ensured that swimwear was hardly more revealing than normal daywear.

including a former English Lord Chancellor, were enjoying a spot of sun further away from home.

The French Riviera

In 1834, a cholera epidemic in Marseilles forced Lord Brougham to remain in a tiny fishing village called Cannes. Delighted by the brilliant skies, balmy climate, and sparkling sea, he bought a plot of land and built a villa. Soon, other Britons followed and the Riviera was born. It was, in effect, a Mediterranean extension of Brighton.

It rapidly became the world's first major coastal resort, albeit one of an exclusive nature. Places such as Antibes, St. Raphael, Juan-les-Pins, Cannes, Nice, and Monaco flourished, and by the 1920s, that stretch of coastline had become the most glamorous playground in the world. It was the haunt not only of millionaires, royalty, and film stars, but also of prominent artists and intellectuals, from Renoir, Matisse, and Picasso, to Charlie Chaplin, Coco Chanel, and F. Scott Fitzgerald. The latter, who rented a seaside house in Juan-les-Pins with his wife Zelda, said that the French Riviera was where he wanted "to live and die," and he used it as the setting for the hedonism of his final novel, *Tender is the Night* (1934).

From 1922, the region was served by the exclusively first-class Blue Train, which ran from Calais to Menton in the South of France via Paris. An elegant locomotive painted blue with a gold trim, it became known as the "millionaire's train." Its passengers made suntans fashionable, swimwear stylish, and popularized outdoor sports such as swimming, tennis, and golf.

Beyond France

The French Riviera was undoubtedly the most high-profile resort, but it was not the only beach retreat. By the mid-19th century, Rimini was already one of several Italian seaside resorts. They also developed along the northern French and Belgian coasts, and the Baltic coast of north Germany, and soon afterward reached the coasts of Spain. In the US, entrepreneur Carl G. Fisher, who had purchased mangrove swamps in Florida and drained them, ran a billboard in wintery Times Square, New York, that read: "It's June in Miami."

The lure of the Riviera faded after World War II, as the rich began to travel elsewhere for their sun-soaked freedom. However, the idea of the vacation abroad caught on, and in the second half of the 20th century, the growth of cheap air travel made it possible for millions of people a year to pack their suitcases and escape to sunnier climes.

△ **Bathing machines**
The first female bathers used mobile changing huts to change as a way of preserving their modesty. As shown in this postcard from 1908, the huts were pushed into the sea so women could enter the water with a degree of privacy.

◁ **The Riviera**
This photocrom from around 1890 shows Menton, in France. The seaside promenade was an important social setting, allowing people to show off their finest clothing.

◁ **Migrating south**
While northern Europe had plenty of coastline, it lacked sunshine. Ads, such as this poster from 1930, encouraged wealthy tourists to head south for the summer, to places such as the French Riviera.

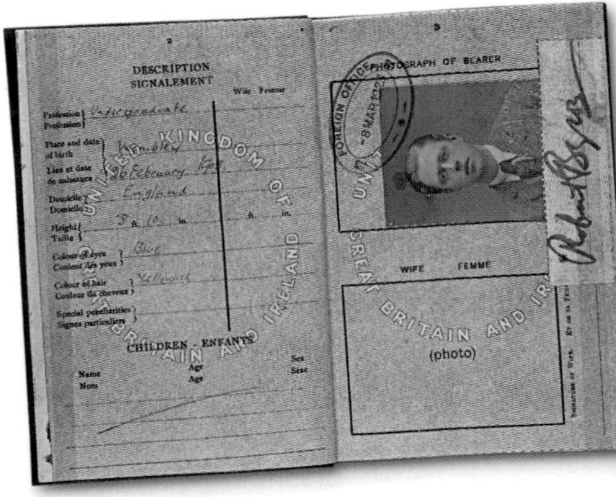

△ **Robert Byron's passport**
Listed as an "undergraduate" with "yellowish" hair, travel writer Robert Byron (1905–41) attended Merton College, Oxford, when this passport was issued in 1923.

Beyond Baedeker

Although much of the world had been thrown into turmoil by the Great Depression followed by World War II, the 1930s and '40s witnessed a second golden age in travel writing.

△ ***Brazilian Adventure***
Despite his verdict that "nothing of importance was achieved," Fleming's book is as thrilling a read today as it was in the 1930s.

The first boom in travel writing occurred when railways and steamships opened up the world. The general public had a compelling desire to read about the far corners of the Earth, even if they could not visit them themselves. It was a similar story between the great wars—this time with aviation as the catalyst. However, the new type of travel writing was different from what had gone before.

A new breed of travel writer

The archetypal 19th-century traveler had written heroic narratives about his own feats of stamina and courage. While Robert Byron shared many of the attributes of a 19th-century traveler, in that he was well-educated, wealthy, and free to indulge his passions in a way the average working man was not, his writing did not. Instead of glorifying himself and his travels, Byron wrote with warmth and humour about the people he met. He acknowledged that after centuries of ruling foreign lands, Europeans might be able to learn a thing or two from others, and his view of foreign cultures was largely positive. *The Road to Oxiana* (1937), his account of travelling to Persia (Iran) and Afghanistan in search of the origins of Islamic architecture, is commonly regarded as the first great example of modern travel writing.

Another prestigious travel writer of this period, Peter Fleming began his literary career when he joined an expedition to South America to search for missing explorer Percy Fawcett, on which his first book, *Brazilian Adventure* (1933), was based. The trip was a farce and Fleming delighted in his own and his party's incompetence and non-heroism. "It requires less courage to be an explorer than to be a chartered accountant," he explains. He went on to write books on Central Asia, China, and Russia.

Amateur archaeologist Freya Stark displayed a similarly blasé attitude to adventure as she recounted her journey

▽ **Freya Stark**
Known to have worn Dior in remote parts of Asia and Arab dress in London, Freya Stark's spirit of adventure and travels to exotic places transcended her gender and era.

" There is **no foreign land**; it is the **traveler only** who is foreign. "

ROBERT LOUIS STEVENSON, AUTHOR

across Persia, dodging bandits and police, in her breakthrough book *The Valley of the Assassins* (1934). Some two dozen more works followed, which did much to inspire women to venture into exotic climes. "To awaken quite alone in a strange town is one of the pleasantest sensations in the world," she enthuses in *Baghdad Sketches* (1932).

Although men still outnumbered women when it came to travel writing, Rebecca West's *Black Lamb and Grey Falcon* (1941), a complex portrait of Yugoslavia and Europe on the brink of war, was another of the most significant books of the period.

Most travel writers at this time looked to venture where the Baedeker guides did not, but others combined travel writing with reportage to present new angles on familiar places. The young teacher and essayist Eric Blair wrote about Paris from the vantage point of a kitchen worker in his book *Down and Out in Paris and London* (1933), which was published under the pseudonym George Orwell. The French poet and pilot Antoine de Saint-Exupéry vividly described the Sahara and South American Andes as seen from his airplane as he flew delivering the mail in the classic flying adventure *Wind, Sand and Stars* (1940).

The end of an era?

Few writers were able to resist the ease with which people could now travel. The mountaineer H.W. Tilman wrote sarcastically in the preface to his book *China to Chitral* (1951), "Comparatively few travelers have visited Chinese Turkestan; which is perhaps just as well because of those fortunate few, not many have refrained from writing a book." However, in 1946, Evelyn Waugh suggested that travel writing had had its day, stating that he did not "expect to see many travel books in the near future". He called his new collection of travel writing *When the Going Was Good*: to him, the joy of journeys was over.

◁ **Antoine de Saint-Exupéry**
Author of the classic book *The Little Prince* (1943), daring aviator Antoine de Saint-Exupéry (left) attempted to break the speed record for flying from Paris to Saigon in 1935. Unfortunately, the plane crashed.

EXPLORER AND NATURALIST, 1884–1960

Roy Chapman Andrews

Considered by many to be the original Indiana Jones, Roy Chapman Andrews was an explorer, educator, and naturalist whose adventures took him to the Gobi Desert, where he became the first person to discover dinosaur eggs.

Roy Chapman Andrews was born in the small town of Beloit, Wisconsin, in 1884. As he wrote in his autobiography: "I was born to be an explorer. There was never any decision to make. I couldn't be anything else and be happy."

After graduating from college in 1906, Amdrews went to New York to pursue another thing that he had always wanted: a job at the American Museum of Natural History. When told that there were no jobs available, he volunteered to scrub the floors. He was taken on as a cleaner in the taxidermy department, then as a taxidermy assistant, but he soon moved on to the type of adventurous fieldwork he had hoped for. The museum assigned him to measure and study different whale species, and to collect their skeletons. This required him to travel throughout the Pacific, including to Alaska, China, Japan, and Korea. From 1909 to 1910, he sailed around the East Indies on the USS *Albatross*, observing marine mammals and collecting snakes and lizards. In 1913, he went to the Arctic, where he filmed seals.

It was apparently always in Andrews' nature to tackle challenges head-on. "In [my first] fifteen years [of field work] I can remember just 10 times when I had really narrow escapes from death," he wrote. "Two were from drowning in typhoons, one was when our boat was charged by a wounded whale, once my wife and I were nearly eaten by wild dogs, once we were in great danger from fanatical Lama priests, two were close calls when I fell over cliffs, once I was nearly caught by a huge python, and twice I might have been killed by bandits."

◁ **Action man**
This water bottle is similar to the one Chapman took with him on his adventures. Other items included a ranger's hat and a revolver.

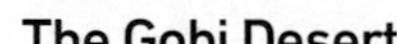

The Gobi Desert

In 1922, Andrews embarked on the first of the expeditions for which he is best known. These were to Mongolia's Gobi Desert, where Henry Fairfield Osborn, the director of the American Museum of Natural History, hoped he might find evidence that supported his theory that humans originated in Central Asia rather than Africa. No such evidence was found, but on the first trip, the team uncovered several complete fossil skeletons of small dinosaurs, as well as parts of larger dinosaurs. A second expedition in 1923 led to even more exciting finds, including the skull of a small mammal that had lived alongside the dinosaurs—few mammal skulls had been found from that period. Even more exceptional, though, was a nest of fossil dinosaur eggs, the first to be scientifically recognized. Until then, no-one had been sure how dinosaurs reproduced. To everyone's great excitement, 25 eggs were found altogether. Andrews even appeared on the cover of *Time* magazine.

Andrews' stories were just as thrilling as his discoveries. He told how, on one extremely cold night in the desert, a huge number of poisonous pit vipers slithered into the Americans' camp in search of warmth. The men killed 47 snakes in just a few hours.

In 1930, the political situation in Mongolia and China forced the museum to suspend expeditions there. This meant that one phase of Andrews' career was over, but another was about to begin. In 1934, he became director of the American Museum of Natural History, a post that he held until 1942, when he retired.

◁ **Inspecting fossils**
Andrews and his team examine mammal fossils in Mongolia, in 1928. The expedition had initially set out to look for traces of "pre-dawn man" in Asia. No such evidence was found, but Andrews did discover a wealth of mammal fossils.

" **Always** there has been an adventure **just around the corner**—and the world is still **full of corners**. "

ROY CHAPMAN ANDREWS

◁ **A shining career**
A determined and resourceful man, Andrews went from sweeping floors at the American Museum of Natural History to becoming its director. During his career, he led many successful expeditions, which he wrote about in bestselling books.

KEY DATES

- **1884** Born in Beloit, Wisconsin, to a father who sells pharmaceutical drugs wholesale.
- **1906** Begins work as a taxidermist's assistant at the American Museum of Natural History in New York.
- **1908** Goes on his first expedition, to Alaska. On this trip, and until 1914, he specializes in the study of whales and other aquatic mammals.
- **1916** Serves as the museum's chief of Asiatic exploration, leading three trips: to Tibet, southwest China, and Burma (1916–17); to Outer Mongolia (1919); and to Central Asia (1921–25).

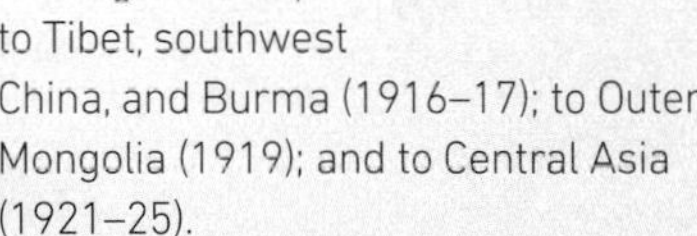

ANDREWS IN TRADITIONAL DRESS IN KOREA

- **1935** Becomes director of the American Museum of Natural History. He resigns in 1942 in order to write.
- **1943** Publishes the autobiographical *Under a Lucky Star*, which is followed by *An Explorer Comes Home* (1947) and *Beyond Adventure* (1954).

SKELETON OF A WHALE IN THE AMERICAN MUSEUM OF NATURAL HISTORY

Zeppelin fever

In the first decades of the 20th century, the airship was hailed as the glamorous and luxurious future of flight.

In the 1930s, people were so convinced that the future of travel lay with the airship that the spire of the iconic Empire State Building, the tallest building in the world when completed in 1931, was designed as a mooring mast for anticipated passenger airships.

All manner of gas-filled, engine-propelled airships had been tested by inventors around the world in the 19th century, but the most successful one took to the air in July 1900. This was designed by German Count Ferdinand von Zeppelin, whose name rapidly became synonymous with all giant airships. Designed to carry passengers in a sealed cabin beneath it, his airship began commercial operations in 1910, and by the middle of 1914, it had made over 1,500 flights and carried over 10,000 fare-paying passengers. At the time, this put the airship far ahead of the airplane as the model for any sort of viable aviation industry.

In 1929, the *Graf Zeppelin* made its most famous flight, an around-the-world voyage covering 20,651 miles (33,234 km) in four stages: from Lakehurst, New Jersey, to Friedrichshafen in Germany; from Friedrichshafen to Tokyo; from Tokyo to Los Angeles; and from Los Angeles back to Lakehurst. The longest leg of the journey was the 6,988-mile (11,247-km) flight from Friedrichshafen to Tokyo, which passed over the vast emptiness of Siberia. However, a planned flight over Moscow had to be cancelled due to adverse winds, prompting an official complaint from the government of Joseph Stalin, who felt slighted by the change in plan. In Tokyo, a crowd of some 250,000 people greeted the airship's arrival, and Emperor Hirohito personally met the captain and crew. The entire journey, including stops, took 21 days, five hours, and 31 minutes. It was the first passenger-carrying flight around the world and received massive coverage in the world's press—in part because the flight was partly sponsored by American newspaper publisher William Randolph Hearst, and had journalists from several countries on board. Tragically, the disaster in which the airship *Hindenburg* burst into flames and crashed on May 6, 1937, killing 36, was even bigger news. It effectively put an end to the idea of passenger airships.

◁ **The *Hindenburg* over New York**
The LZ-129 *Hindenburg*, built by the Zeppelin company, flies over lower Manhattan and Battery Park. It was the longest and largest airship ever built, and came into service in March 1936. It was destroyed by fire just 14 months later.

The airline of empire

When Imperial Airways flew from Britain to Australia, it was the longest airline journey in the world, taking a couple of weeks and stopping at dozens of places en route.

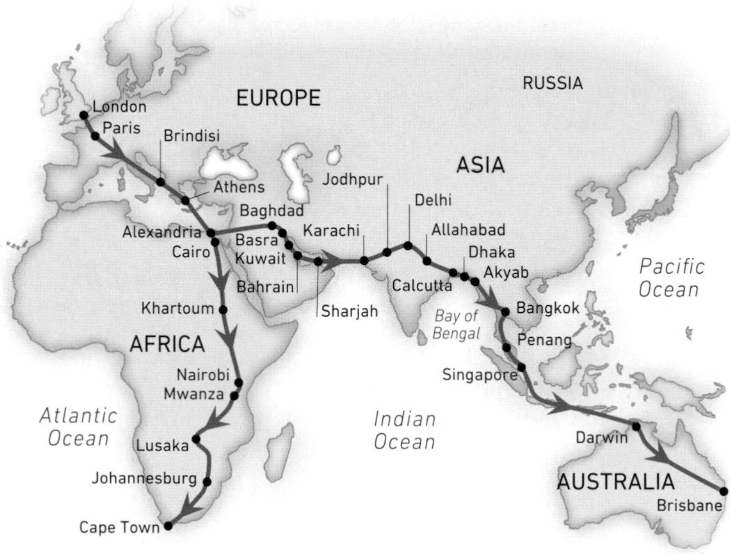

△ **Imperial Airways** This map shows the initial route taken by Imperial Airways. The service began in 1935, flying between London, England, and Brisbane, Australia.

▷ **High-class travel** The posters made long-distance air travel look alluring, but it was not available to everyone. In 1934, Imperial Airway's fare from London to Singapore was £180, the equivalent of about £10,900 ($13,500) today.

Britain's long-range Imperial Airways only operated from 1924 to 1939, but in those 15 years it made a mark on aviation history. It was the airline of the British Empire, connecting Britain with her far-flung colonies in South Africa, India, Hong Kong, and Australia.

Imperial's very first services, in 1924, were from London to Paris, but by the end of 1929, regular scheduled services extended as far as Delhi. From 1935, it became possible to buy a ticket all the way from London to Brisbane.

London to Alexandria

The journey started at Victoria railway station in central London, where Imperial had its check-in center. From there passengers were taken south by bus to Croydon, London's principal airport before Heathrow. The first leg of the 13,000-mile (20,920-km) journey was the Silver Wing service to Paris, which departed daily at 12:30pm. This was made in a Handley Page 42 biplane, which could seat just 18 passengers and was handsomely fitted with carpeted floors and chintz-covered armchairs. Stewards waited on the passengers and pointed out places of interest en route.

Paris was the first of 35 stops, but the next, Brindisi, on Italy's Adriatic coast, could only be reached by train because Mussolini had banned foreign planes from flying over Italy. At Brindisi, passengers boarded a seaplane, the second of five types of aircraft used along the route. This took them via Athens across the Mediterranean to Alexandria, where the route divided: the African service flew south, while the eastern one flew to India.

Eastern and African services

From February 1931, Imperial ran a weekly service between London and Mwanza on Lake Victoria. The following year, this was extended to Cape Town. On leaving Alexandria, in Egypt, the aircraft flew via Cairo, Khartoum, Nairobi, Lusaka, and Johannesburg, fulfilling aeronautically the dreams of Cecil Rhodes, who, 40 years earlier, had wanted to build a Cape-to-Cairo railway (see pp. 267–68). Passengers on both routes traveled

▷ **Short Empire flying boats** In 1937, Imperial Airways took delivery of its first Short Empire flying boat (a seaplane that uses its fuselage as a hull to land on water). This one could carry 24 passengers.

between Alexandria and Cairo by train, but those on the Eastern service now made a beeline across the desert for Baghdad. The next morning, the pilot bore southeast to the port city of Basra, and from there hugged the coast down to Kuwait, Bahrain, Sharjah, and Karachi. Flying was only attempted in daylight, so passengers stayed at a hotel each night. Pilots were advised to always keep the coast within gliding distance, in case of emergencies.

Australia

Beyond Karachi there was no coast to hug, as the route cut across the north of India, via Jodhpur, Delhi, Allahabad, and Calcutta to Dhaka in present-day Bangladesh. Now well into Southeast Asia, the service flew on, skirting the coasts of Burma, Thailand, and Malaysia before touching down in Singapore. The last stretches were flown by aircraft of Qantas Empire Airlines, a joint venture between Imperial and the Australian airline that started out in 1920 as the Queensland and Northern Territory Aerial Services. When the first flight was made from Darwin, Australia, to Singapore to connect with the Imperial Airways service, Qantas co-founder Hudson Fysh wrote: "The old isolated and constricted environment of our people was destroyed that day."

End of an era

In 1939, the introduction of the new Short Empire flying boats reduced the flying time between England and Australia even further, with three services a week, each taking just 10 days of flying, including nine overnight stops. However, this was short-lived. The same year, Imperial was merged with British Airways Ltd to form BOAC (British Overseas Airways Corporation), and the outbreak of war put an end to its long-distance civilian passenger services. There had been nothing before like the Imperial Eastbound service, and there never would be again.

▷ **Silver service**
Flying boats were used on some Imperial routes. These had spacious cabins, dining rooms, and lounges. Here, a steward on the *Canopus*, flying between Alexandria and Athens, serves breakfast.

TRAVEL BY TRAIN POSTER, NEW MEXICO, c.1920

ART DECO SKI POSTER, FRANCE, ROGER BRODERS, 1929

AUTUMN IN NIKKO POSTER, JAPAN, c.1930

POSTER ADVERTISING INDIA WITH A VIEW OF THE TAJ MAHAL, c.1930

FRENCH POSTER DEPICTING A CAR ALONG A ROAD IN GREECE, c.1930

NORD EXPRESS POSTER, A.M. CASSANDRE, 1927

POSTER ADVERTISING CORSICAN RESORT, WILLIAM SPENCER, c.1932

ITALIAN LINE POSTER FOR SOUTH AFRICA, GIOVANNI PATRONE, 1935

HOLLAND-AMERICAN LINE POSTER, WILLEM TEN BROEK, 1936

BOAC AIRLINE POSTER, TOM ECKERSLEY, 1947

Travel posters

The glamour of passenger travel was the perfect subject matter for colorful advertising posters.

At the end of the 19th century, the color lithographic process transformed graphic art and coincided with the growing popularity of travel for pleasure. Large, bold, brightly colored posters could be mass-produced, with words and images skilfully combined to entice passersby to set off on an adventurous trip by boat, train, car, or airplane.

Posters advertising travel and exotic holidays catered for every taste and season. Station billboards encouraged passengers to explore the vast expanses of North America by train. Images of chic ski resorts helped make alpine sports popular. For those who preferred sunnier climes, Mediterranean beach hotels and the exotic allure of India and Africa were on offer, as were the cooler charms of autumn in Japan. Railway and airline operators, travel agents, and tour organizers seized on the colorful graphic posters as modern marketing tools.

Artists were quick to spot the potential of commercial art. A.M. Cassandre led the way in Paris in the mid-1920s with his Art Deco posters inspired by the Machine Age. The geometric shapes of his streamlined, speeding trains and looming ocean liners caught the public imagination, and his style influenced the posters of the 1940s and '50s in Europe and the US.

CANADIAN PACIFIC TRAVEL POSTER, 1956

The Long March

In 1934, the Chinese Red Army made an epic trek to escape the clutches of its enemies. The year-long journey that it made created a founding myth for modern China.

In the mid-1930s, China was ruled by Chiang Kai-shek, the leader of the Kuomintang, or Nationalist Party. However, he faced a threat from the Red Army—the armed forces of the Communist Party. It had mounted a rebellion that was centered in the southeastern province of Jiangxi, with a base in the city of Ruijin.

In September 1933, Kuomintang forces encircled the communists in Ruijin. After an 11-month siege, it was clear to the besieged communists that they could not hold out for much longer, so they planned a diversionary attack. Military leader Fang Zhimin charged enemy lines with a small group of troops, taking the enemy by surprise and allowing most of the Red Army to escape. Some 86,000 communists crossed the barrier of the Yudu River on makeshift pontoon bridges built from doors and bed boards.

Over the following year, the Red Army trekked west and north, constantly harried by Kuomintang forces. Numerous battles ended in defeat, such as the Battle of the Xing River, in which it lost 45,000 men—over 50 percent of its fighting force. However, these defeats were punctuated with the occasional morale-raising victory. In May 1935, for example, the Red Army managed to capture an 18th-century bridge across the Dadu River, in the remote town of Luding. It only managed this, however, because one detachment made a harrowing march of 75 miles (121 km) in 24 hours over mountain roads. Elsewhere, the communists, who were only wearing light clothes and straw sandals, suffered terribly as they marched across the icy mountains in Sichuan.

Mao Zedong, who had become chairman of the party, declared the Long March over when it reached the province of Shaanxi. Mao claimed that his army had covered a distance of about 7,770 miles (12,500 km). Of the 86,000 communists who broke out of Jiangxi, only a few thousand remained, but they had secured some kind of victory simply by surviving this arduous journey. Furthermore, on learning of their heroism, thousands of young Chinese people enlisted in the Red Army. In 1949, Mao came to power and proclaimed the People's Republic of China.

▷ **Mountain-crossing in Sichuan**
It is estimated that the Red Army marched just over 4,000 miles (6,400 km) in the 12-month Long March. Some of their greatest obstacles were the mountains in Sichuan, which took a terrible toll on the men.

TWA
TWA

THE AGE OF FLIGHT

1939—PRESENT

THE AGE OF FLIGHT, 1939–PRESENT

Introduction

The early 20th century had, in many ways, been a golden age of travel for the leisured and wealthy, who could enjoy the first passenger flights, cruises on luxury ocean liners, and train journeys across continents. However, everything was changed by World War II. By the time the war broke out, thousands of Jews and ethnic minorities had already fled persecution in central Europe, and millions of refugees were on the move around the world, seeking new homes.

When the war was over, intrepid adventurers began once more to venture forth and investigate far-flung corners of the globe. Jacques Cousteau plumbed the ocean depths, Wilfred Thesiger explored inhospitable regions of the Arabian Desert, and Edmund Hillary and Tenzing Norgay were among the many who risked their lives to try and conquer the highest mountain on Earth. Meanwhile, with the postwar economic recovery gathering pace, traveling was becoming an option for more than just the most wealthy in society. The postwar boom in car manufacturing made it possible for many people in the West to own a car for the first time, releasing them from reliance on public transportation. It gave them the freedom to drive wherever they liked. This found unique expression in the US, where the sheer size of the continent led to a passion for the road trip, as evoked by Bobby Troup in his 1946 song, *Route 66*.

The jet age

In 1952, the Comet, the first commercial jet airliner, took to the skies, instigating a revolution in aviation. The jet engine made it possible to build bigger, faster, and lighter aircraft, which could fly higher, making flying more economical.

TRAVEL WRITERS SUCH AS WILFRED THESIGER WROTE ABOUT LIFE IN EXOTIC PLACES

AFFORDABLE CARS, SUCH AS THESE CHEVROLETS, GAVE MANY PEOPLE THE FREEDOM OF THE ROAD

IN 1953, EDMUND HILLARY AND TENZING NORGAY REACHED THE SUMMIT OF EVEREST

> “ I think **humans will reach Mars**, and I would like to see it happen **in my lifetime**. ”
>
> BUZZ ALDRIN, ASTRONAUT

It took a while for the cost benefits to filter through to passengers, but keen competition between airlines, the subsequent slashing of air fares, and the advent of budget airlines, such as Laker Airways and Southwest Airlines, finally brought the price of tickets down. For the first time, flights and package holidays abroad became affordable for the masses.

Leaving Earth

The Space Race, which began with the launch of the Sputnik satellite in 1957, was a competition between two superpowers—the US and the USSR. It ended in 1969, when astronauts Neil Armstrong and Buzz Aldrin became the first humans to land on the Moon. As Armstrong memorably said, it was a "giant leap for mankind." Since then, space exploration has become a collaboration between international space agencies. By 1994, Russia and the US were collaborating on the Shuttle-*Mir* program, which led to the construction of the International Space Station (ISS). Finally completed in 2012, the ISS has since been manned by crews from 10 different countries and has hosted visitors from 18 lands. Meanwhile, since 1977, the Voyager program, often called the greatest feat of human exploration, has sent two probes past the great planets and beyond into the outer reaches of the solar system, from where they are continuing to send back remarkable data.

Today, it may seem as if there is nowhere left to explore. However, adventurers are all around us, constantly discovering new places or finding out astonishing information about places that we thought we already knew. Who knows where they will go next or what they will uncover.

CHEAP FLIGHTS HAVE MADE HOLIDAYS ABROAD AVAILABLE TO MANY PEOPLE

BUZZ ALDRIN (PICTURED) AND NEIL ARMSTRONG WALKED ON THE MOON ON JULY 20, 1969

AFTER 136 SPACE FLIGHTS, THE INTERNATIONAL SPACE STATION WAS FINALLY COMPLETED IN 2012

The great displacement

Throughout history, war and conquest have resulted in the mass movement of people, but conflicts in the 20th century led to forced migrations on an unprecedented scale.

The 20th century was scarcely underway when World War I uprooted millions of European civilians. Meanwhile, revolution and civil war in Russia from 1917 to the early 1920s led to an exodus of more than one million people opposed to the Bolshevik regime. And from 1915–23, the Ottomans set about eradicating 1.5 million Armenians from the territories of the Ottoman Empire. But as far as forced displacement of people goes, all of this was only the start.

The rise of nationalism

When the political map of Europe was redrawn in 1919 after the fall of the Austrian and Russian empires, many countries suddenly found themselves hosting large populations of ethnic minorities who had previously lived in a neighboring country. This created sectarian tensions and fueled the rise of nationalism, ultimately setting the stage for World War II, as Adolf Hitler began to claim territory that was inhabited by ethnic Germans. When Hitler's National

▽ Leaving home
This photograph from June 1945 shows people packed into every available space of a train leaving Berlin. By May 1945, in the wake of 363 Allied air raids, 1.7 million people (40 percent of the total population) had fled Berlin.

◁ **Refugee camp**
From 1945 to 1947, more than 700 refugee camps were set up all over Europe. In these, homeless people were given shelter, food, and medical treatment and then repatriated or sent to build new lives elsewhere.

Socialist German Workers' Party gained power in Germany in 1933, it targeted and actively persecuted the Jewish population, resulting in hundreds of thousands of Jews fleeing central Europe to safety elsewhere. Many of them headed for the US, and about 250,000 made their way to Palestine between 1929 and 1939. Some 10,000 children under the age of 17 were also rescued from German and German-annexed territories and taken to Britain on the Kindertransport (children's transport).

The legacy of war

When World War II broke out in 1939, Jews from all over northern Europe fled the threat of German occupation. After the invasion of Poland in 1939, the Germans set about "cleansing" parts of the country of its indigenous population. They deported 2.5 million Polish citizens, resettled 1.3 million ethnic Germans, and killed some 5.4 million Polish Jews. The Soviet Union, similarly, deported tens of thousands of Estonians, Latvians, and Lithuanians to Siberia when it annexed the Baltic States in 1941.

However, it was the end of the war in 1945 that brought about the largest mass migrations in European history. The number of civilians who were displaced from their homes during World War II has been estimated at 11–20 million. They included prisoners of war, workers who had been brought into Germany by the Nazis for wartime labor, survivors of concentration camps, and those who had simply fled the destruction. All of them had to be sent back to their homelands or resettled somewhere else.

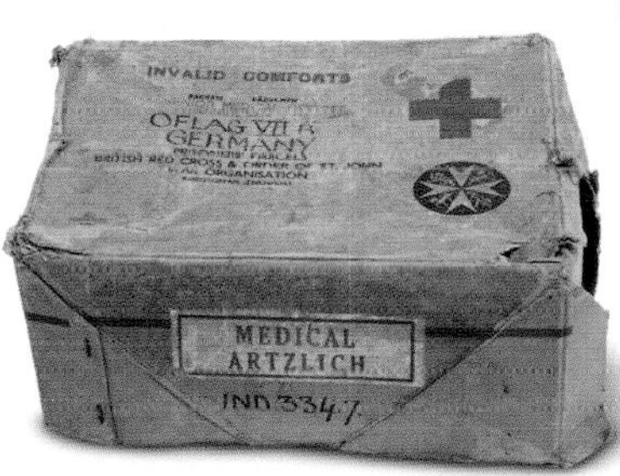

△ **Food parcels**
Red Cross parcels were a lifeline for prisoners of war. Up to 20 million packages containing medical supplies and food were dispatched from Britain.

Sent home

Meanwhile, the Allies were instigating their own form of ethnic cleansing. At the Potsdam Conference in July 1945, British, American, and Russian leaders agreed that the Germans who were still living in Czechoslovakia, Poland, and Hungary would have to be sent back to Germany. As a result, more than 11 million people were expelled from their homes and forced to move to Germany over the next five years.

Refugees' rights

The international response to the refugee crisis took legal form with the Universal Declaration of Human Rights of 1948, which guaranteed the right "to seek and to enjoy in other countries asylum from persecution."

Three years later, the 1951 Geneva Convention on Refugees accorded refugees specific rights. Among those, it expressly prohibited the forcible return of refugees to the countries from which they sought to escape. This principle was evoked at the time by many citizens of east European states that had become part of the newly formed Soviet Union. And although the creation of the State of Israel in 1948 finally provided a secure place for the Jews who had been hounded from their homes in central and eastern Europe, around 700,000 Palestinians then became refugees during the war that led to the creation of Israel.

IN CONTEXT
Partition

In August 1947, the British Raj, which had ruled India for 100 years, was dissolved and India was given independence. As a result, the country was divided into two new states along religious lines (Partition): Hindus and Sikhs were to live in India and Muslims in Pakistan. This triggered one of the greatest and bloodiest migrations in history, involving up to 15 million people, as Muslims trekked from India to Pakistan, and millions of Hindus and Sikhs went the other way. There was extensive and appalling sectarian violence, during which it is estimated that between 1–2 million people were slaughtered, and refugee crises were created in both countries.

MAHATMA GANDHI VISITS MUSLIM REFUGEES AT PURANA QILA, DELHI, IN 1947

▽ **Debris of war**
By 1946, bombed German cities were full of piles of rubble. Prisoners, ex-Nazis, and local women volunteers helped to clear it, the latter for extra food coupons.

EMPIRE
WINDRUS

Arriving in Britain
In this photograph taken for the *Daily Herald*, a crowd waves as it approaches the dock. The ship had sailed from Kingston, Jamaica, carrying 490 men and two women.

The *Windrush*

When the *Empire Windrush* arrived in London from Jamaica in 1948, it marked the start of a postwar immigration boom that changed British society.

On the morning of June 22, 1948, the former troop carrier *Empire Windrush* arrived at Tilbury Docks in Essex, near London, having sailed from Kingston, Jamaica. Aboard were 492 immigrants who had arrived at the invitation of His Majesty's Government. When World War II ended, the government realized that reconstructing the British economy would require a large influx of immigrant labor, so the British Nationality Act 1948 was passed to give Commonwealth citizens (citizens of British colonies) free entry to Britain. The *Empire Windrush* arrivals were the first wave of immigrants to come and staff vital jobs at institutions like the National Health Service. Of the arrivals, 236 were temporarily housed in a deep air-raid shelter under Clapham Common. Others, many of whom had served in the British forces during World War II, had organized accommodations for themselves beforehand.

Not everybody, however, was convinced that importing Jamaicans was the correct solution to the country's problems. Prime Minister Clement Attlee was obliged to reassure a group of Members of Parliament that "it would be a great mistake to take the emigration of this Jamaican party to the United Kingdom too seriously." He thought that immigration would be limited by the fact that not many people in the Caribbean would be able to afford the £28 10s ($358) fare to England. In fact, over the next 14 years, some 98,000 West Indians made Great Britain their home.

As well as Caribbeans, large numbers of workers and their families from other Commonwealth nations, notably India and Pakistan, emigrated to Britain after World War II. Many hundreds of thousands of people came during the 1950s, not just for short-term work, but to settle for good. Immigration has continued ever since, resulting in a multicultural diversity that would have been unthinkable in 1945.

" **London** is the **place for me**. London this **lovely city**. "

LORD KITCHENER, A FAMOUS TRINIDADIAN CALYPSO SINGER WHO WAS A PASSENGER ON THE *EMPIRE WINDRUSH*, 1948

The *Kon-Tiki* expedition

Norwegian anthropologist Thor Heyerdahl went to extreme lengths to prove his theories of migration, most famously sailing a handmade raft from South America to Polynesia.

△ **Thor Heyerdahl**
In this photograph from 1947, the anthropologist is climbing the mast of the *Kon-Tiki*. The large figure of the Inca sun god on the sail behind him was painted by his crewmate Erik Hesselberg.

As a student with an interest in the civilizations of the South Pacific, Thor Heyerdahl traveled to Fatu Hiva in the Marquesas Islands in French Polynesia in 1937. During his one-and-a-half-year stay, he became convinced that the islands had been initially populated by South Americans rather than, as commonly believed, people from Asia who came to the West. It was no coincidence, he thought, that the huge stone figures of the mythical Polynesian leader Tiki resembled the monoliths left behind by pre-Incan civilizations. He concluded that the original Polynesian inhabitants had crossed the Pacific on rafts, 900 years before Columbus traversed the Atlantic.

Heyerdahl presented his theory to a group of leading American academics, who were skeptical. One of them went so far as to challenge Heyerdahl: "Sure, see how far you get yourself sailing from Peru to the South Pacific on a balsa raft!" So that is exactly what Heyerdahl did. He built a raft using only materials and techniques that were available to the pre-Columbians, so no nails, spikes, or wires. Working from illustrations made by the Spanish conquistadors, he used balsawood logs for the base, mangrove wood for the mast, and braided bamboo for a cabin, then roofed it with large banana leaves.

Gone fishing

On April 28, 1947, Heyerdahl and his crew of five, plus a parrot, sailed out from Callao, Peru. They named their raft *Kon-Tiki*, after the Inca sun god. None of the crew, made up of five Norwegians and one Swede, were sailors—Heyerdahl could not even swim. Other than some essential modern equipment, such as radios, watches, shark repellant, and a sextant, they carried nothing that would have been unavailable to ancient sailors. Heyerdahl counted on easterly winds and the Humboldt Current,

◁ **The sole loss of life**
The expedition consisted of Heyerdahl, five other crew, and a Spanish-speaking green parrot named Lorita. Unfortunately, she was washed overboard partway through the voyage.

▷ **Balsawood raft**
Heyerdahl's crew spent around 15 weeks on board the 40 sq ft (3.7 sq m) *Kon-Tiki*. It was built from nine balsawood logs, which were covered with a deck made of bamboo. A bamboo cabin provided some shelter.

△ **Shark baiting**
Sharks were numerous as the *Kon-Tiki* sailed across the Pacific. The crew even caught some, as in this photograph, in which Heyerdahl is holding one by its tail.

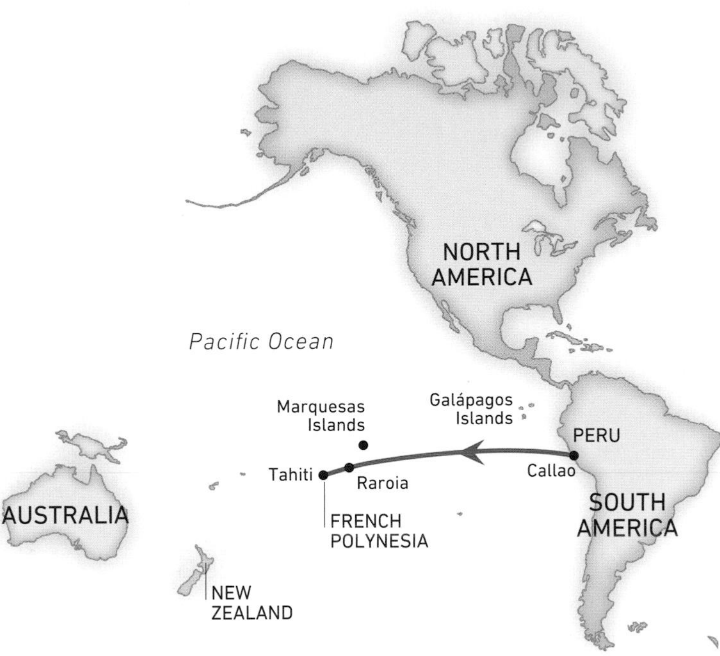

△ **The *Kon-Tiki* voyage**
From Callao in Peru, the *Kon-Tiki* set off west across the Pacific Ocean. It traveled for 101 days and covered around 4,340 miles (6,980 km), before reaching French Polynesia.

a cold-water current in the southeast Pacific Ocean—to carry the raft in the right direction.

Critics were convinced that the crude *Kon-Tiki* would break up after a week or two, but it proved highly seaworthy. The hand-woven ropes that bound the logs swelled with seawater, embedding themselves into the soft wood and strengthening the vessel, rather than weakening it. It was, Heyerdahl wrote in his log, "a fantastic seagoing craft."

According to Heyerdahl's account, when the seas were rough, the crew were sometimes waist-deep in water, and had to hang on to avoid being washed away. To supplement their rations of coconuts, sweet potatoes, and fruit, the crew caught plenty of fish, particularly flying fish, yellowfin tuna, and bonito. For amusement, they dangled fish overboard for the ever-present sharks to snap at.

Reaching French Polynesia

After 101 days at sea, the *Kon-Tiki* struck a coral reef and was beached on an uninhabited islet off the Raroia atoll. The raft had finally reached Polynesia, and had traveled a distance of around 4,340 miles (6,980 km). After spending a few days marooned, the crew was rescued by inhabitants of a nearby island, before being collected by a French schooner bound for Tahiti.

Heyerdahl's expedition had successfully demonstrated that South American peoples could, in fact, have journeyed to the islands of the South Pacific by balsa raft. Subsequent DNA tests have shown that the Polynesian people are, in fact, of Asian descent. However, the expedition brought Heyerdahl immense fame, and even triggered a craze for Tiki bars, motels, and cocktails, and a hit track released in 1961 by English band The Shadows.

" **Borders**? I have **never** seen one. But I have **heard** they **exist in the minds** of **some people**. "

THOR HEYERDAHL

EXPLORER AND TRAVEL WRITER, 1910–2003

Wilfred Thesiger

Arguably the last of the great explorers, Thesiger was an Englishman who rejected the modern world in favor of the tribespeople of Africa and the Arabian deserts.

Wilfred Thesiger was born in Addis Ababa, in Imperial Abyssinia (modern-day Ethiopia), where his father was the chief British representative. He was sent to England for his education, but was unhappy there. During his first summer holiday from college, he worked for his passage on a boat to Istanbul. He spent his second summer on a fishing trawler off the coast of Iceland.

Sudan, Syria, and the SAS

As soon as he was able to, Thesiger returned to Africa. Here, at the age of 23, he decided to explore a remote region of Abyssinia. Two years later, he found work as an assistant district commissioner in the Sudan, where one of his roles was to shoot lions that attacked the farmers' herds. He served in Darfur, where he learned how to travel by camel. It was in Sudan that he had his first real experience of the desert: "I was exhilarated by the sense of space, the silence, and the crisp cleanness of the sand. I felt in harmony with the past, traveling as men had traveled for untold generations across the deserts."

During World War II, Thesiger fought with the British Army against Italian forces in Abyssinia, as part of the Special Air Service (SAS) in North Africa, and against the Vichy French in Syria.

Arabian sands

After the war, Thesiger began to work with the United Nations in Arabia. In 1946, ostensibly on a search for the breeding grounds of locusts, Thesiger made a 1,500-mile (2,414-km) circuit of the Rub' al-Khali—or Empty Quarter—a famously inhospitable region of desert. Although he was not the first to cross it, he was the first to explore it thoroughly, and the first outsider to visit the oasis of Liwa and the quicksands of Umm al Samim. A second expedition two years later penetrated even further into the desert, during which time he was arrested by the Saudi authorities and became caught up in inter-tribal hostilities.

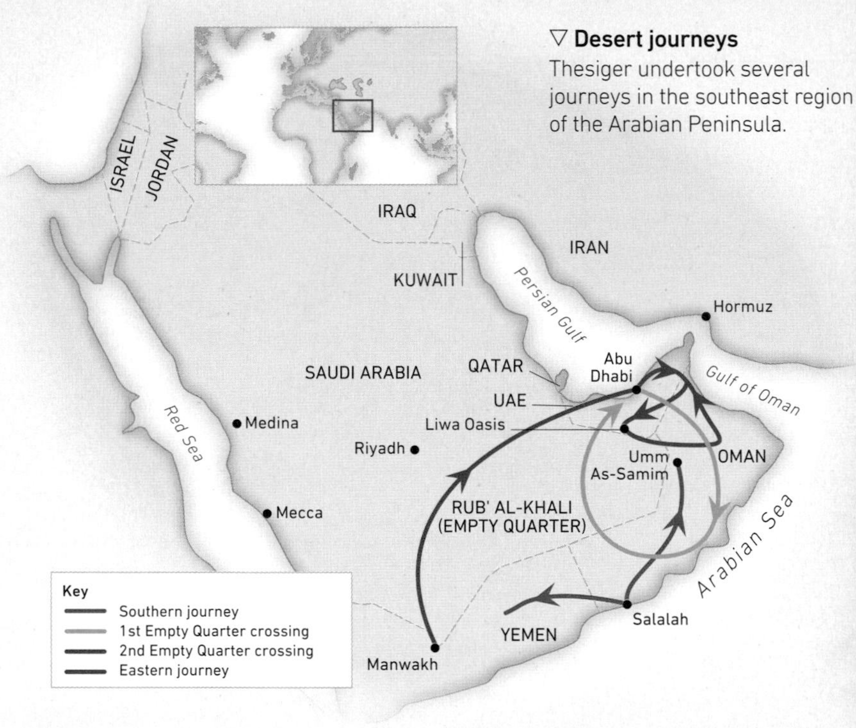

▽ Desert journeys
Thesiger undertook several journeys in the southeast region of the Arabian Peninsula.

These journeys represented the last, and possibly greatest, expeditions of Arabian travel. Thesiger later said he found the experience humbling because he rarely matched the standards of endurance and generosity of his Bedouin traveling companions.

In 1950, Thesiger made a new base among the Marsh Arabs in southern Iraq, where he lived for eight years. Every summer, he left to go trekking in the mountains of the Hindu Kush, the Karakorams, or Morocco. In 1959 and 1960, Thesiger took two journeys by camel to Lake Turkana, in northern Kenya. He lived and traveled in Kenya for much of the next 35 years.

With his health failing, Thesiger reluctantly returned to England for good in the mid-1990s. However, his heart remained with the tribespeople in whose company he had spent his life. He resented much of modern technology, and regarded cars and aircraft as "abominations." In Thesiger's autobiography, *The Life of My Choice*, published in 1987, he expressed his belief that Western civilization was a corrupting force that had robbed the world of its rich diversity.

◁ Crossing the Empty Quarter
One modern invention Thesiger did approve of was the camera. This photograph shows him crossing the Awarik sands in the Empty Quarter.

▷ Last of his kind
This portrait of Thesiger was taken in Abu Dhabi in March 1948, during the British explorer's second journey across the Empty Quarter. He wears typical Arab garments, including a *thawb* (shirt) and a headscarf.

" Here in the desert I had found **all that I asked**: I knew that I should **never find it again**. "

WILFRED THESIGER, *ARABIAN SANDS*, 1959

KEY DATES

- **1910** Born in Addis Ababa, Ethiopia, the son of the British minister Wilfred Gilbert Thesiger.
- **1945–46** Makes the first of his legendary journeys, crossing the Empty Quarter of Arabia by camel in the company of four Bedouin.
- **1950** Travels to the southern marsh regions of Iraq where he lives intermittently for seven years.
- **1959** Publishes a book about his travels, called *Arabian Sands*. The book brings him acclaim as a writer and photographer, and becomes an international bestseller.

THESIGER'S 1959 TRAVEL ACCOUNT, *ARABIAN SANDS*

- **1964** Publishes his second great work, *The Marsh Arabs*, another portrait of a world on the verge of vanishing.
- **2003** Dies in England. His collection of 38,000 travel photographs is donated to the Pitt Rivers Museum, Oxford.

THESIGER WITH COLONEL GIGANTES IN THE WESTERN DESERT IN LIBYA, 1942

The jet age

If time is money, then the jetliner made the world a much richer place. It drastically reduced flying times and slashed costs for a new generation of air travelers.

On May 2, 1952, the first commercial jet airliner took to the skies. A de Havilland Comet flying for BOAC (the British Overseas Airways Corporation) took off from London for Johannesburg, South Africa. It was a four-engine aircraft capable of carrying 36 passengers at a cruising speed of 450 mph (720 kph). Truly innovative, it traveled faster and higher than propeller aircraft and gave passengers a quieter and smoother journey. At the time, it was nothing short of revolutionary. In the words of Juan Trippe, founder of Pan American Airways, the jetliner was the most important development in aviation since Lindbergh's transatlantic flight.

However, after 18 months of service, design weaknesses led to metal fatigue, resulting in three catastrophic accidents. The faults were duly corrected, but the Comet's reputation was damaged.

The aircraft that truly began the jet age appeared six years after the Comet's launch. Just as Henry Ford's Model T had popularized the car late in the day, it was the Boeing 707 that brought jet travel to the masses. The 707 was almost half again as fast as the Comet, and carried five times as many people. This made it commercially more viable than any previous aircraft. In October 1958, Pan Am flew the first commercial service of a 707, from New York to Paris. Trippe proclaimed that a trip to Europe was every American's birthright.

▷ **Graphic appeal**
Airlines used contemporary graphics and branding to woo customers. This 1960s poster suggests that the glorious sun and cool modern architecture of Miami are just a quick flight away.

" In **one fell swoop**, we have **shrunken the earth**. "

JUAN TRIPPE, FOUNDER OF PAN AM, ON THE INTRODUCTION OF JET AIRCRAFT

▽ **The future is now**
Eero Saarinen's dynamic, winglike TWA terminal at New York's Idlewild Airport opened in 1962. It was a symbol of the advances in design and technology that jet travel helped to promote.

The Boeing 707

With its sleek body and swept-back wings, the 707 rolled out before a public that was already in love with air travel. Just that year, Frank Sinatra had released his album *Come Fly with Me*, its cover showing him gesturing with his thumb to a TWA airliner on a runway. President Eisenhower himself had already ordered three Boeing 707s to serve as the very first Air Force Ones.

The popularity of the 707 and the new generation of aircraft it spawned led to rapid developments in almost every aspect of aviation infrastructure and design, from the terminal buildings to cabin crew uniforms. The heady

Silver bird
Photographed on a world tour in December 1955, the de Havilland Comet 3 was the first passenger jet airliner. It had sleek wings containing powerful jet engines.

optimism of the jet age was epitomized by Eero Saarinen's 1962 TWA Terminal at what later became JFK Airport. Air carrier Braniff employed advertising executive Mary Wells, who touted the airline as "The End of the Plain Plane," and introduced futuristic flight attendant uniforms designed by Emilio Pucci. While hot meals had been introduced in the 1930s, in-flight meals as we know them—eaten from a fold-down seatback tray—first became standard in the 1960s.

▷ **Come fly with me**
"Just say the words, and we'll beat the birds down to Acapulco Bay", sang Frank Sinatra in 1958's *Come Fly with Me*. It was an invitation for millions to take to the air.

The bestselling book of 1968 was Arthur Hailey's *Airport*, which spent 30 weeks at number one on the *New York Times* bestseller list.

Airlines come of age

Flying was an adventure, and one that increasing numbers of people could share. The world's first "tourist" fare, later to become "economy," was introduced in the 1950s, and by 1959, more people were crossing the Atlantic by air than by sea. Airlines were also quick to exploit the advantages of jet travel for businesses. By 1965, the annual number of US air passengers reached 100 million, double the figure for 1958. The next turning point was the launch of the Boeing 737 in 1968. This soon became the most numerous jetliner. The Boeing 747, nicknamed Jumbo Jet, followed in 1970. Its vast size and efficiency allowed fares to decrease further. By the end of the century, there were around 1,250 747s in the air at any time—which meant that one was either landing or departing somewhere in the world every five seconds. By this time, the word "jetliner" had fallen out of use. Jet technology had replaced the propeller-driven planes of old to such an extent that the new machines were now simply known as airliners.

◁ **TWA cabin crew**
Air stewardesses became poster girls for the glamor of flying. They were chosen for their good looks and attractive manner, and decked out with fashionable uniforms.

▽ **Fast food**
In-flight pre-packaged airline meals on trays were introduced as standard in the 1960s, just one example of the many innovations of the jet age.

WRIGHT FLYER, US, 1903

TRAVEL AIR 4000, US, 1929

SARO A.19 CLOUD, UK, 1930

STITS SA-2A SKY BABY, US, 1952

AVRO 652A ANSON C19, SERIES 2, UK, 1946

Planes

As soon as the Wright brothers achieved takeoff in 1903, engineers set about producing larger and ever-faster aircraft.

The initial goal was to give airplanes more power. The greater the thrust, the greater the lift, which made it possible to build larger planes that could carry heavier loads. That heavier load was sometimes fuel, which enabled aviators to make record-breaking long flights, such as Charles Lindbergh's crossing of the Atlantic in the *Spirit of St. Louis*. Larger planes were developed to carry passengers. One of them was the Boeing 247, an early airliner with many features that later became standard, including an all-metal airframe, cantilevered wings, and retractable landing gear. Aircraft were subsequently designed in all shapes and sizes, from the world's smallest plane, the 1952 Sky Baby, to Howard Hughes's giant flying boat, the H-4 Hercules of 1947.

The jet engine, introduced in the 1950s, revolutionized flight. Its extraordinary thrust made passenger air travel truly viable for the first time. Today, ever-larger aircraft carry increasing numbers of passengers with greater fuel efficiency, as exemplified by the Airbus A380.

BLÉRIOT XI,
FRANCE, 1909

RYAN NYP *SPIRIT OF ST. LOUIS*, US, 1927

BOEING 247, US, 1933

DE HAVILLAND DH87B HORNET MOTH, UK, 1934

MORAVAN NÁRODNÍ PODNIK ZLÍN
Z.226T, CZECHOSLOVAKIA, 1956

BOEING 727-200, US, 1967

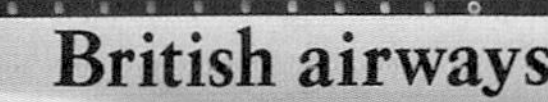

CONCORDE, UK/FRANCE, 1969

AIRBUS A380, EUROPE, 2007

PC-AERO ELEKTRA ONE,
GERMANY, 2011

The roof of the world

In May 1953, Edmund Hillary and Tenzing Norgay became the first people to stand on the summit of Mount Everest. Their achievement was only possible thanks to those who had failed before them.

In 1856, the Great Trigomometric Survey of India determined that an obscure Himalayan mountain, known as Peak XV, was the highest mountain in the world (see pp. 242–43). Named Everest shortly afterward, attempts to climb it could not begin until 65 years later, when the forbidden kingdom of Tibet first opened its borders to outsiders.

In 1921, the British led an expedition to scout a northern approach to the mountain. The following year, they returned for a proper attempt on the summit, reaching a record altitude of 27,316 ft (8,326 m). The next expedition came in 1924. After an initial aborted attempt, two British climbers, George Mallory and Andrew Irvine, made another push for the summit. They were last seen disappearing into the clouds that perpetually swirl around the mountain. No one knows if they reached the top. Mallory's frozen body was found 75 years later, in 1999. Irvine's has yet to be located.

Such are the dangers of Everest. At 29,029 ft (8,848 m), its peak is hostile to life. At that height, the air contains only a third of the oxygen found at sea level, increasing the chance of fatal cerebral edemas, which occur when the oxygen-starved brain swells up. In such conditions, non-essential body functions shut down, so digestion and sleep are impossible. The temperature at the summit is -33°F (-36°C), making frostbite and hypothermia likely. There are also constant threats of avalanches, crevasses, and storms. And yet, when explaining his reasons for climbing, Mallory said: "What we get from this adventure is just sheer joy. And joy is, after all, the end of life. We do not live to eat and make money. We eat and make money to be able to live."

The southern route

In all, there were seven attempts to climb Everest before World War II halted expeditions. They were all carried out by the British, who deliberately used their position of power in India and Tibet to deny other nations the chance to climb the mountain. Access to Everest was closed in 1950, after China invaded Tibet, but by that time Nepal was open, after being closed to foreigners for 100 years. In 1950, an exploratory expedition was made from the south, along the route that has now become the standard approach. In 1952, a Swiss expedition following this route reached a new, record height of 28,199 ft (8,595 m). The following year, a ninth British expedition traveled to Nepal. The first pair of climbers failed to reach the summit, but planted backup caches of oxygen for a second pair, New Zealand beekeeper Edmund Hillary and Nepali Sherpa Tenzing Norgay. At 11:30am local time on May 29, 1953, they became the first people to reach the summit. They took photographs, buried a few sweets and a cross in the snow, and then began their descent.

Reporting the achievement, Britain's *Manchester Guardian* concluded that the mountain "is in its nature a terminal point. ... It is doubtful whether anyone will ever try to climb Everest again." Of course, far from signaling an end, the ascent opened a whole new chapter in mountaineering history—one in which hundreds of climbers flock to the mountain each year.

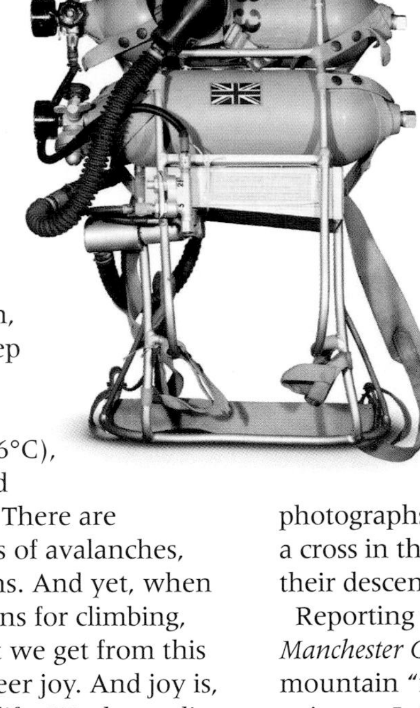

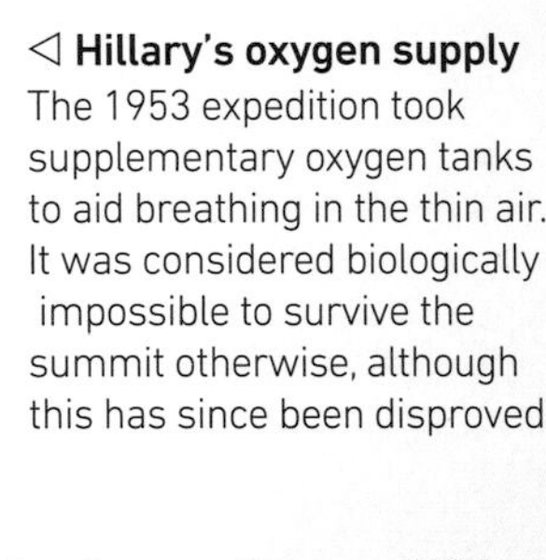

◁ **Hillary's oxygen supply**
The 1953 expedition took supplementary oxygen tanks to aid breathing in the thin air. It was considered biologically impossible to survive the summit otherwise, although this has since been disproved.

▽ **Ascending Everest**
This photograph, from 1953, shows one Sherpa using ropes to guide another across a log bridge over a crevasse in the Western Cwm. Both wear crampons—metal plates with spikes fixed to boots.

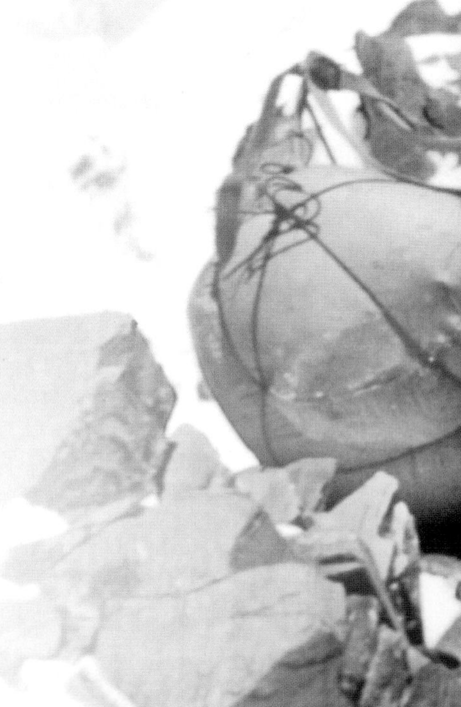

"Nobody climbs for **scientific reasons**. You really **climb** for the **hell of it**."

EDMUND HILLARY, MOUNTAINEER

▽ **On the southeast ridge**
This image shows Edmund Hillary (left) and Tenzing Norgay preparing to make for the final camp on their way up Everest. The following day, they became the first people to stand on the summit.

IN CONTEXT
Climbing Everest today

Since Hillary and Tenzing conquered Everest, the summit has been reached over 7,600 times by around 4,460 climbers. The numbers have rocketed recently, partly because fixed ropes and ladders have made the climb easier. In just one day in 2016 (May 19), 209 climbers scaled the mountain, which is more than the number who made it in the 33 years after the first ascent.

In 1990, just 18 percent of attempts on the summit were successful, but in 2012 that figure was 56 percent. However, the climb is not necessarily any safer. 282 people have died on Everest since 1921, and 18 died in 2015 alone, following a massive earthquake. Nor is it cheap. The British Mountaineering Council puts the minimum spend for an Everest climb at $35,000, but climbers can pay as much as $65,000.

PERMANENTLY FIXED ROPES AND LADDERS HAVE MADE EVEREST EASIER TO CLIMB

The open road

The mass manufacture of cars after World War II made it possible for even more families to take to the road on vacation. In the US, the road trip became synonymous with freedom and romance.

△ **Growth in car ownership**
During World War II, manufacturing was restricted. After the war, there was a boom in consumer goods, which included cars.

The great American road trip was born in 1903, when former doctor Horatio Nelson Jackson, mechanic Sewall Crocker, and a dog called Bud set out in a red Winton touring car across the US. At the time, there were fewer than 150 miles (240 km) of paved road in the entire country. A gentleman bet Jackson $50 that it would take him at least 90 days to drive from San Francisco to New York. In fact, the 4,500-mile (7,242-km) journey took just 63 days, 12 hours and 30 minutes. Jackson won his wager, but with the cost of the car, the trip cost him $8,000.

Sixteen years later, a military convoy led by Major Dwight D. Eisenhower traveled from Washington, DC to San Francisco, at an average speed of only 5 mph (8 kph). Improving the highways became a key issue for Eisenhower as president, and his response was to create the Federal Aid Highway Act of 1956 and to construct the Interstate Highway System.

By the 1950s, one in six Americans was employed either directly or indirectly in the car business. The US was the largest car manufacturer in the world, and it was also its greatest buyer. There were 25 million registered cars on the road at the beginning of the decade and by 1958, that number had more than doubled to 67 million. It did not hurt that the cars of the time were some of the most powerful and stylish ever made, culminating in the '57 Chevy, one of America's iconic cars. But more than anything, the new multi-lane highways spurred car-owning Americans to take to the open road. Anyone with a car could go almost anywhere, with just a driver's licence as a passport.

Drivers and drive-ins

Motoring for pleasure was not restricted to the Americans. Tire manufacturers André Michelin and his brother Edouard had been publishing a guide for French motorists since 1900, and Britain's AA (Automobile Association) had a million members by 1950. As the US was developing its highway system, Europe too was becoming criss-crossed by motorways, autobahns, autoroutes, and autostrada.

▷ **Quick break**
Car culture led to the drive-in restaurant, such as this seafood diner in California, designed to catch the eye of speeding passers-by.

▽ **Roadside manuscript**
The cross-country road trip is quintessentially American, and no book captures it better than Jack Kerouac's *On the Road*. He taped his manuscript pages into a long scroll of paper.

However, Europe's many borders and passport controls meant that motoring freedom was more restricted.

In the US, businesses emerged to cater specifically for motorists, such as roadside motels, drive-in restaurants, and drive-in cinemas. In the 1950s, with considerable backing from the car industry, the first Holiday Inn opened (by 1959 there were a hundred of them), as did the first Howard Johnson's Motor Lodge, and the first franchises of a roadside hamburger restaurant called McDonald's.

◁ **Michelin men**
In Europe, the French Michelin brothers built a successful tire business. They promoted it with rubber men who showed motorists where to find the best places to eat.

The road in art

As a metaphor for freedom, the great American road trip was, and still is, a source of inspiration for writers and filmmakers. The year after Eisenhower's Highways Act, *On the Road* (1957), Jack Kerouac's iconic, freewheeling celebration of youth and a journey to find America, was published. Around the same time, celebrated novelist John Steinbeck came to a startling conclusion: "I discovered I did not know my own country." He went on the road at the age of 58 accompanied by his pet poodle, Charley. His road trip of discovery was published as *Travels with Charley: In Search of America* (1962).

That most American of cultural media, the cinema, has glorified the open road repeatedly, from the film that is more LSD trip than road trip, *Easy Rider* (1969), through feminist fable *Thelma and Louise* (1991) to the wine-trip buddy movie *Sideways* (2004).

▷ ***Easy Rider***
The cult 1969 film reinvented the road trip, replacing the car with motorbikes, but still celebrating the timeless American urge to hit the road and head out west.

" The cross-country trip is the **supreme example** of the **journey** as the **destination**. "

PAUL THEROUX, TRAVEL WRITER

Route 66

Stretching from Chicago to Los Angeles, Route 66 is the quintessential American highway. Covering more than 2,451 miles (3,900 km), it is rightly considered the mother of all road trips.

In 1946, Bobby Troup set off on a cross-country drive from Pennsylvania to California, where he wanted to try his hand as a Hollywood songwriter. The trip began on highway US 40, and he thought about writing a song about the road. However, inspiration did not strike until the route reached US 66, which, Troup's wife noted, rhymed with "Get your kicks." The resulting song, *(Get your kicks on) Route 66*, became a hit for Nat King Cole later that year, and has since been recorded by artists including the Rolling Stones, Bruce Springsteen, and Depeche Mode.

However, although the road was now enshrined in popular culture, Route 66 was famous long before Troup turned his key in the ignition and headed west.

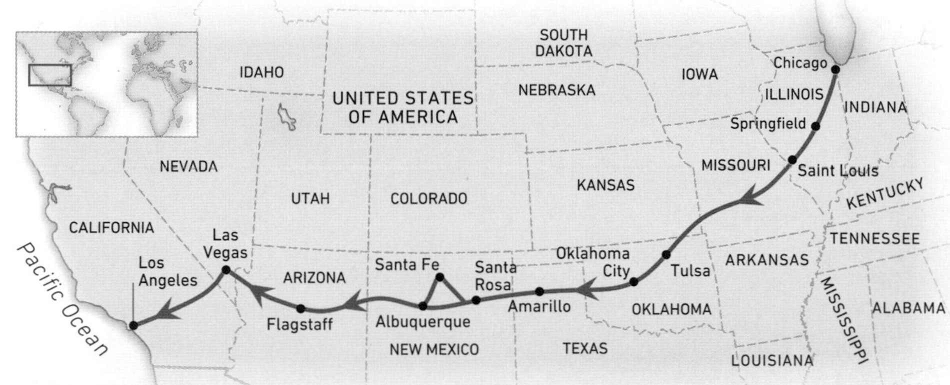

▽ **Historic route**
When Route 66 opened in 1926, its purpose was to link hundreds of rural communities in Illinois, Missouri, and Kansas to Chicago. During the Depression, it became the route that many took to seek better lives in the west.

Road of dreams

Route 66 was not the first US transcontinental highway—that was the Lincoln Highway, which was dedicated in 1913, and ran from New York to San Francisco. Established 13 years later, in 1926, US 66 followed a different route, starting in Chicago, and then turning southwest, down into the heartlands of the Midwest, traversing eight states and three time zones to end at Los Angeles. The route was deliberately intended to give many small towns their first access to a major road.

▽ **Route of freedom**
No other road has symbolized the American spirit and captured the popular imagination like Route 66. Nearly a century after its construction, it still exerts a pull on Americans and foreigners alike.

> “ 66 is the **mother road**, the **road of flight**. ”
>
> JOHN STEINBECK, *THE GRAPES OF WRATH*

One of the main supporters of the highway was Cyrus Avery, a businessman from Oklahoma, who was determined that the route should pass through his home state and deliver the economic benefits of connectivity.

Ironically, a highway that was meant to bring wealth to middle America ended up becoming famous as an escape route. It was completed just in time for the families who were forced to leave their homes and farms in the Midwest during the Great Depression and the Dust Bowl crisis of the 1930s. Route 66 was the road they hoped would take them to better lives out west. Almost from the start it was a "road of dreams."

Route 66 reached the height of its popularity in the 1950s, when the boom in car ownership led to great numbers of vacationers hitting the road to find out what the rest of the US looked like. And so, a little later than originally planned, the highway finally brought prosperity to businesses all the way along it.

Mother Road

Ironically, it was the very legislation that encouraged long-distance car travel in the US—President Eisenhower's 1956 Federal Highway Act—that led to the demise of Route 66. The new four-lane interstate system bypassed it. Towns suffered from the loss of through traffic, and businesses closed down as parts of the route were abandoned altogether. By 1985, Route 66 was decommissioned and officially ceased to exist.

However, the role Route 66 played during the Depression has given it iconic status. It is sometimes referred to as the Mother Road. Thus, in recent times, non-profit organizations and the US National Park Service have mobilized support and provided funding to conserve what is left of the route. Stretches of the former highway are now promoted as a heritage site. Once again, people come from all over the US and from around the world to drive along this historic road and experience a slice of Americana.

△ **Route 66 today**
An extensive nostalgia industry has grown up around US 66. Visitors can stay in old-style motels all along the route, such as the Blue Swallow Motel in Tucumcari, New Mexico.

No-frills flying

The jet engine made passenger flights fast and convenient, but it was not until the prices of airline tickets were dramatically slashed that flying became affordable for most people.

△ **Peanut airlines**
Southwest was the first of a new generation of airlines to undercut established rivals by doing away with the "frills." It served snacks instead of full meals, which earned it the nickname "peanut airlines."

In 1977, Freddie Laker, a former teaboy for the flying-boat builders Short Brothers of Rochester, made airline history by launching Skytrain, a pioneering cheap daily flight between the US and Britain.

Until that time, international flights were largely the privilege of the rich. After World War II, it was thought that competition between airlines would compromise passenger safety, so commercial aviation was strictly regulated by the IATA (International Air Transport Association). This left state airlines free to run monopolies, offering identical services at high prices.

There were exceptions to the rule. The Icelandic airline Loftleiðir declined to join IATA, and in the 1960s it offered cut-price fares between the US and Europe via Reykjavik, earning it the nickname "the hippie airline." Charter flights were also available, but generally they only operated on package holidays to Spain and other places where there were resorts.

Skytrain and Southwest Airlines

Freddie Laker proposed a system in which passengers who wanted cheap flights could line up for tickets at the airport, like at a train or bus station.

▽ **Freddie Laker**
The launch of Laker's London-to-New York Skytrain in September 1977 was the first low-cost operation of its type. Other airlines lowered their fares in response.

△ **Grabbing the headlines**
To stand out from the competition, Southwest had stewardesses wear orange hot pants and white boots, and serve drinks called "love potions." The airline's slogan was "Long legs and short nights."

After six years of negotiations with the British and US governments, the first Skytrain took off for New York in September 1977. The service had no frills (such as meals), but its fares were a third of those of rival airlines.

Another budget-fare pioneer was Texas-based Southwest Airlines, which was launched in 1971. It promoted its cheap flights with sensational posters featuring leggy stewardesses in hot pants and white boots. Its success convinced the Civil Aeronautics Board to relax its regulations on airfares, and more competitive pricing was introduced in 1978. Airfares fell by a third, and traffic more than doubled in the 1980s as more low-cost American carriers were launched. Ironically, having championed cheap fares, Skytrain went out of business when British Airways and Pan Am slashed their transatlantic fares.

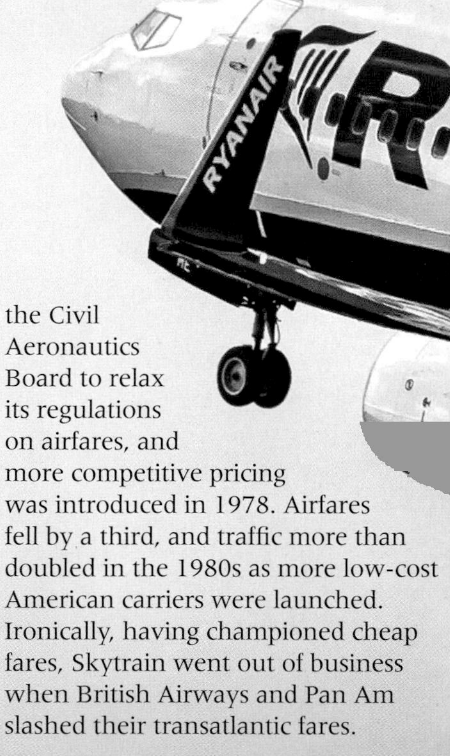

Ryanair and easyJet

The success of the budget American airlines caught the attention of aspiring aviation executives across the Atlantic.

In 1990, a small loss-making Irish airline called Ryanair reinvented itself as a no-frills airline offering cheap flights to secondary European airports. A few years later, a similar business began in a cramped office at Luton Airport in the UK. Known as easyJet, it began advertising flights to Edinburgh and Glasgow, in Scotland, that were "as cheap as a pair of jeans." These two airlines, and the many copycat businesses that followed, revolutionized European air travel.

By stripping their product to the bare minimum—having a single cabin in which all the seats were the same, charging for food, and dispensing with free baggage allowance—low-cost carriers offered flights that everyone could afford. In just over 25 years, low-cost airlines became not just a fixture of the travel industry, but also a vital part of contemporary life in Europe, the US, and around the world.

◁ **Global revolution**
"Now everyone can fly" is the slogan for Air Asia. It is just one of the many budget airlines seen in this photograph taken at an airport in Kuala Lumpur, Malaysia.

Flight for all

Cheap fares, frequent schedules, and flights to places where no one had flown before have made it feasible for people to commute between their homes and businesses in different parts of the world, and to enjoy short, spur-of-the-moment city breaks. Today, people talk of the "nanobreak," a single night away in another city, a phenomenon that was created by the airline revolution. Ever more flights at ever cheaper rates have created an unprecedented freedom of movement for people everywhere.

△ **Low fares model**
Inspired by the success of Southwest Airlines, Ireland's Ryanair lowered fares by cutting costs wherever possible. It crammed in more flights each day, used smaller airports with cheaper landing charges, and operated just one aircraft model, the Boeing 737.

" What railways have **done for nations**, airways will **do for the world**. "

CLAUDE GRAHAME-WHITE, AVIATION PIONEER, 1914

Into the abyss

People have spent centuries exploring the surface of the Earth, but it was only in the 20th century that advances in technology made it possible to investigate the oceans.

△ **New technology**
Divers Jacques Cousteau (right) and Terry Young prepare to dive with Aqua-Lungs strapped to their backs. The apparatus was soon renamed the SCUBA system.

Rarely has one man dominated a field of study so completely as Jacques-Yves Cousteau. Not only was he a pioneering marine explorer, but he also invented the technology that allowed divers to swim underwater.

The Aqua-Lung

Experiments in breathing underwater date back as far as the 17th century, when English physicist Edmond Halley (of Halley's Comet fame) patented a design for a diving bell. In the 1930s, American naturalist and undersea explorer William Beebe used the newly invented bathysphere to explore the oceans to what was then a record depth of 2,638 feet (804m). At the time, Jacques Cousteau was only in his early twenties. He had originally joined the French Naval Academy to become a pilot, but a car accident put an early end to this ambition, and instead he began to explore the underwater world of the Mediterranean from the beaches around the naval base at Toulon in France.

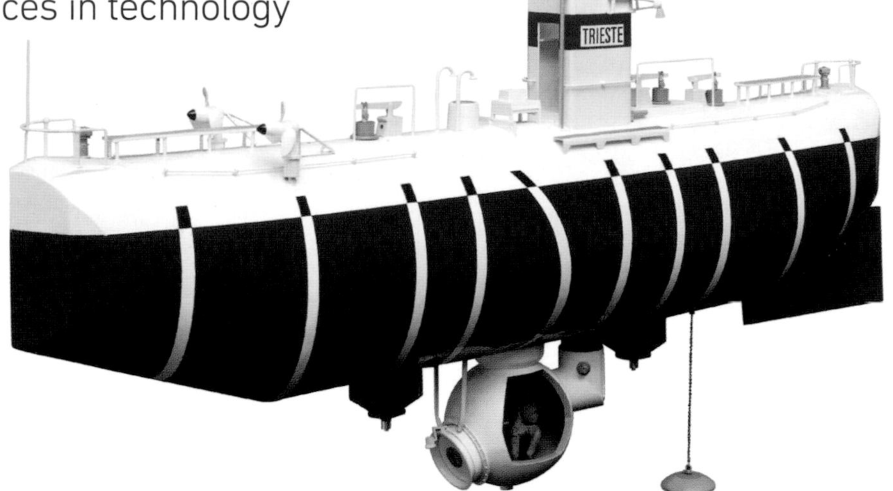

△ **Bathyscaphe *Trieste***
On January 23, 1960, Jacques Piccard and Don Walsh descended to the bottom of the Mariana Trench in a bathyscaphe called *Trieste*. A window cracked on the way down, but they still spent 20 minutes on the sea floor.

At this time, diving suits were heavy and cumbersome, and the diver received oxygen through an air line connected to a ship above, which greatly restricted movement. With help from his colleagues, Cousteau developed an alternative, which was a canister of compressed air strapped to the diver's back, with a regulator to control air flow. So successful was this Aqua-Lung, as he called it, that the US Navy bought it and renamed it the SCUBA (Self-Contained Underwater Breathing Apparatus) system.

In the 1950s, Cousteau adapted the first of several ships, each called *Calypso*, to operate as a research station, creating a base from which he could dive. A few years later, he invented a diving saucer for two people, and in 1962 built an experimental underwater living capsule, which he called the "Conshelf." He documented all of these inventions in books and television films that made him a household name worldwide.

The origin of life

Another key figure in oceanography was Jacques Piccard, a Swiss engineer who developed underwater vehicles for studying ocean currents. In 1960, aboard the bathyscaphe *Trieste*, Piccard and a companion became the first people to reach the deepest location on Earth—the floor of the Mariana Trench, in the Pacific Ocean, which lies 36,070 feet (10,994m) below sea level.

◁ **Hydrothermal vent**
Hydrothermal vents are fissures in the Earth's crust, from which water erupts due to volcanic activity. These vents are so rich in various life forms that many believe that they were crucial to the origin of life on Earth.

In 1969, Piccard also joined a team that spent 30 days drifting 1,444 nautical miles (2,674 km) in the *Ben Franklin PX-15* subsurface research vessel. They were investigating the path of the Gulf Stream, a current in the Atlantic Ocean, but they also studied how they reacted to being cooped up for so long—something NASA was interested in at the time.

In 1977, oceanographers made a discovery that overturned one of our most cherished beliefs—that the Sun played a key role in the origin of life. When the submersible ALVIN descended 6,890 feet (2,100 m) to the East Pacific Ocean floor, its cameras revealed chimney-like structures channeling superheated water and minerals up from the mantle beneath. Large communities of sea creatures were thriving there, in utter darkness, using heat for energy and minerals for food. Many now believe that life on Earth began in such conditions.

IN CONTEXT

Underwater archaeology

Robert Ballard discovered the *Titanic*. In 1985, using a small unmanned submersible called *Argo*, he found wreckage on the floor of the Atlantic Ocean and followed it until he reached the infamous liner. Since then, entire historic cities have been uncovered on the seabed. In 2000, for example, Franck Goddio, diving off the coast of Egypt, discovered the ruins of Thonis-Heracleion (and Canopus in 1997). Built at the mouth of the Nile river in the 8th century BCE, Thonis-Heracleion was submerged by geological and cataclysmic phenomena some 1,200 years ago. During the Late Period of ancient Egypt, it was Egypt's principal port of international trade.

A DIVER INSPECTS A BARNACLED STATUE IN THE SUNKEN CITY OF HERACLEION

" The sea, **once it casts its spell**, holds one in its **net of wonder forever**. "

JACQUES COUSTEAU, MARINE EXPLORER

▽ **Jacques Cousteau**
Aided by his many inventions, Cousteau became a pioneering underwater explorer and conservationist. His adventures were televised in the series *The Undersea World of Jacques Cousteau* (1968–75).

Flight to the Moon

In 1903, humans took to the air for the first time in a flight that lasted 12 seconds. Less than 70 years later, aviation had become space travel, and astronauts were walking on the Moon.

△ **Test launch**
An early rocket designed by Robert H. Goddard is winched onto its launch pad in Roswell, New Mexico, in 1935.

Leonardo da Vinci sketched flying machine designs back in the 15th century, but it took more than 400 years for the Italian's dreams to become reality. Yet, from the first experimental flights with liquid-fueled rockets, it took just 33 years to reach the Moon.

Space race

American scientist Robert H. Goddard, with support from the Smithsonian Institution, ushered in the era of space flight when he successfully launched a rocket on March 16, 1926. He successfully launched a total of 33, but, in 1941, Nazi Germany took the lead in rocket research. Hitler wanted to make the rocket into a weapon, and the result was the V-2, the world's first long-range guided ballistic missile. The V-2 also became the first man-made object to leave the Earth's atmosphere when it was launched on June 20, 1944.

During the Cold War, the V-2 became the model for both American and Soviet rocket designs, which in turn became the basis of their space exploration programs. The two powers competed to be the first into space, the Americans employing captured German scientists, such as Wernher von Braun.

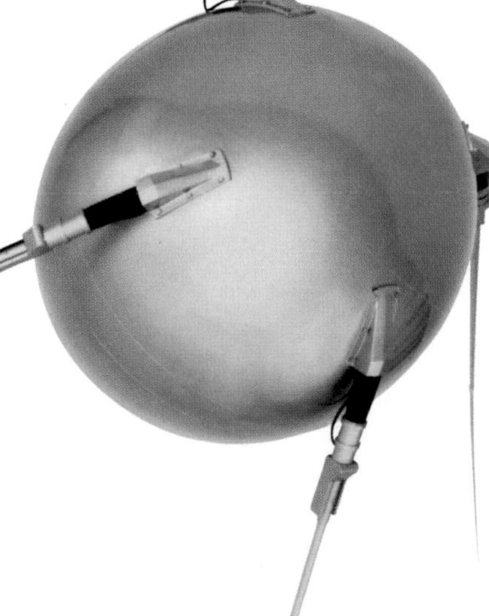

▷ ***Sputnik I***
Launched by Russia on October 4, 1957, *Sputnik 1* was the first artificial Earth satellite. Its position was broadcast by its four radio antennae.

▷ **One step beyond**
A Russian poster celebrates Yuri Gagarin's historic achievement of becoming the first human in space. "Cosmonautics Day USSR," it reads, with the date of the flight in the rocket's exhaust plume: "12, IV, 1961."

In orbit

The first goal was to launch a satellite. The Soviets got there first: on October 4, 1957, they received the distinctive "beep... beep... beep... " from radio transmitters signaling *Sputnik I* was in orbit. Two years later, in 1959, the Soviets became the first to land an unmanned craft, the *Luna 2*, on the Moon. Later that year, the *Luna 3* took pictures of the far side of the Moon.

△ **Space dog**
Before sending a man into space, the Soviets sent a dog named Laika. A stray from the streets of Moscow, she orbited the Earth aboard *Sputnik 2*, but soon died from overheating.

On April 12, 1961, the Soviets finally launched a human into orbit, in a craft called *Vostok I*. The cosmonaut on board was Yuri Gagarin, a former fighter pilot, who initiated the launch with a shout of "*Poyekhali!*" ("Let's go!") This momentous first space journey took just 108 minutes, which was just as well for Gagarin, since he was crammed into a compartment just 7½ feet (2.3 m) in diameter. In that short time, however, he circumnavigated the Earth.

Almost a year later, on February 20, 1962, astronaut John Glenn became the first American to orbit the Earth. Both nations now stepped up their efforts to be the first to land a man on the Moon. However, in 1967, both the Apollo (American) and Soyuz (Russian) programs suffered fatal disasters. The Americans lost the crewmen of Apollo 1 when a fire swept their spacecraft cabin during a ground test, and the Russians lost a Soyuz 1 cosmonaut when his capsule crashed due to a parachute failure.

Man on the moon

The Soviets took 18 months to recover from their disaster. The US, on the other hand, rallied more quickly, and on July 16, 1969, the crew of Apollo 11—mission commander Neil Armstrong, Michael Collins, and pilot Edwin "Buzz" Aldrin—entered their capsule at the top of a colossal Saturn V rocket. At 9:32am, the rocket took off from Kennedy Space Center in Florida, beginning its epic space flight.

Four days later, on July 20, Collins remained in the command module as Armstrong and Aldrin embarked in the *Eagle*, the lunar-landing craft, and touched down on the Moon. "Houston, Tranquility Base here, the *Eagle* has landed," reported Armstrong. Shortly afterward, he took his first tentative step onto the surface and said the immortal words: "That's one small step for a man, one giant leap for mankind."

Aldrin joined Armstrong, and the two explored their surroundings, staying within a short distance of the *Eagle*. They took soil and rock samples, and left an American flag and a Soviet medal in honor of Yuri Gagarin. After about 21 hours on the Moon's surface, they returned to the landing craft and started on the long journey home.

◁ **Reaching Pluto**
On January 19, 2006, NASA's *New Horizons* spacecraft took off from Cape Canaveral Air Force Station in Florida. It traveled 4.67 billion miles (7.5 billion km) to Pluto, arriving on July 14, 2015.

Last man on the Moon
Apollo 11 was followed by six other manned flights to the Moon, culminating in Apollo 17, which landed in 1972. Eugene Cernan, pictured here, was the last man to stand on the lunar surface.

The Hippie Trail

In the 1960s, hoards of idealistic youths took off from cities across Europe to hitchhike or bus their way through central Asia to India and beyond, in search of peace, love, and enlightenment.

▽ Hippie Trail route
The point of the Hippie Trail was not just the destination (e.g. India), but the journey itself. Unlike traveling by boat or plane, the overland route exposed travelers to numerous local cultures, and gave them time to explore.

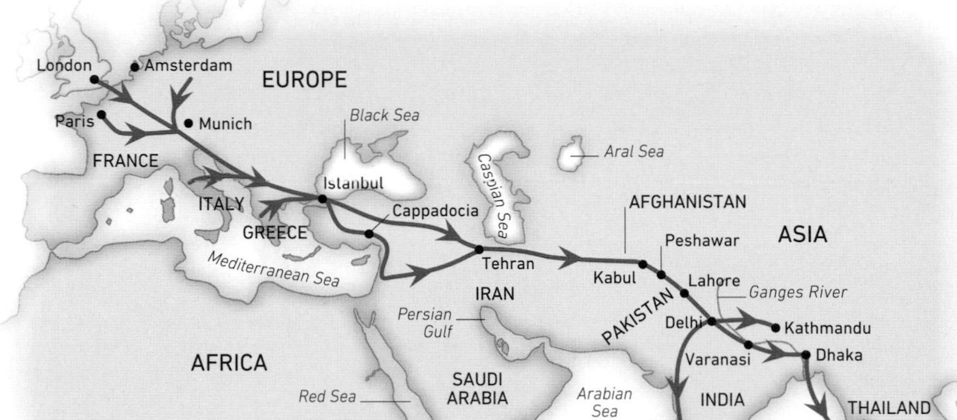

For two decades, in the second half of the 20th century, the spirit of the Grand Tour was briefly revived (see pp. 180–83). But where once-wealthy young aristocrats had roamed Europe to bolster their education, the young people who took to the road in the Sixties, on what became known as the Hippie Trail, traveled in search of spiritual enlightenment.

The overlanders' inspiration came from figures like American author Jack Kerouac and his fellow adventurers of the "alternative" scene. Kerouac had traveled the US in a quest for fulfilment, and turned the experience into a bestselling novel, *On the Road* (1957). The Hippie Trail was the European counterpart to the great American road trip. Its end point was India, the home of ancient eastern philosophy. "The east was not only a country and something geographical but it was the home and youth of the soul," wrote German author Hermann Hesse in *Journey to the East* (published in English in 1956).

▽ Kombi mural
Various companies ran buses along the Hippie Trail from Europe to India. Many travelers used their own vehicles, the most popular being the VW Kombi van.

Hitting the road

From starting points in major cities across Europe, the path to India followed the Silk Road of old, through Istanbul and on into Iran, Afghanistan, and Pakistan (see pp. 86–87). After India, many went further, through Southeast Asia to Bangkok, and even to Australia.

One of the key elements of the trip was to travel as cheaply as possible, mainly to extend the length of time away from home. Cheap, private buses provided transportation. According to Rory Maclean, author of *Magic Bus: On the Hippie Trail from Istanbul to India* (2006), the first European tourist bus to follow the route took 16 passengers from Paris to Bombay in the spring of 1956. The following year, Irishman Paddy Garrow-Fisher established the first regular coach service from Europe to the subcontinent. For almost a decade, Garrow-Fisher's Indiaman Tours operated the world's longest bus route from King's Cross, London, to Calcutta. Dozens of similar operators followed in his footsteps. Travelers also hitchhiked, or drove their own vehicles, typically trucks, minibuses, or camper vans that doubled as accommodation.

△ Backpacking
The modern phenomenon of backpacking—traveling with everything you need in a backpack—began with the Hippie Trail to India.

A support network grew along the Trail, and certain cafes, restaurants, and hotels became marshaling points where travelers wearing Apache headbands, paisley shirts, or Afghan coats congregated. These also served as pre-internet forums, with bulletin boards full of information on travel, offers of lifts, or hookups along the lines of: "Gentle deviant, 21, seeks guitar-playing chick ready to set out for mystical East." In Istanbul, the Pudding Shop became the place to meet; in Kabul, it was Sigi's on Chicken Street; in Tehran, it was the Amir Kabir Hotel; and in Kathmandu, it was an entire road, nicknamed "Freak Street" because of the thousands of hippies who passed through.

Journey's end

After Istanbul, the first major stop was Cappadocia in central Turkey, an area that was unknown to western Europeans until the 1950s. Its volcanic

> " All you've got to do is **decide to go** and the **hardest part is over**. "
>
> TONY WHEELER, FOUNDER OF *LONELY PLANET*

landscapes of fantastically shaped rock chimneys riddled with caves provided pleasingly alternative accommodations for travelers, who squatted there for days or even months at a time. Iran was regarded as a repressive police state, so few lingered there. Instead, they pushed on into Afghanistan, which became something of a hippie paradise thanks to native hospitality.

Pakistan was another "passing" country that could be crossed in 48 hours—then there was India, which had all the ashrams a pilgrim could need. The most popular destinations were the holy city of Varanasi on the Ganges, Goa in the west, and Kathmandu in Nepal.

The Trail came to an end in 1979. Following the Islamic revolt, Iran's borders were closed to tourists, while a Soviet invasion had the same effect in neighboring Afghanistan. By this time, the idea of "backpacking," as this kind of budget independent travel had become known, was well established. Some of those who had taken the Hippie Trail had written notes on the best places to stay, things to see, and how to get around, and they published these to great success, reinventing the travel guidebook. Such writers included Tony and Maureen Wheeler, founders of the *Lonely Planet* guidebooks. The idealistic travelers on the Hippie Trail may not have changed the world, but they did create a very successful modern travel publishing industry.

▽ **Heading east**
The term "hippie" was shorthand for anyone with long hair (i.e. "to the hips"), which is why the journey east became known as the Hippie Trail.

“ I’ve always thought of the Concorde as a **magical object**, a symbol, a **miracle**. ”

ANDREE PUTMAN, FRENCH DESIGNER

Concorde

Once man had walked on the moon, anything seemed possible, including flying commercial passengers at twice the speed of sound.

Concorde, introduced in 1976 after decades of development by France and Britain, was unique. Although engineers in the US and the Soviet Union had worked on supersonic airliners of their own, the American Boeing 2707 never made it off the drawing board, while the Soviet Tupolev TU-144 was abandoned because of performance and safety problems.

Concorde was the only commercial airliner to fly faster than the speed of sound. A Machmeter on the bulkhead told passengers when they were hitting Mach 1, then Mach 2. At this point they would be traveling at twice the speed of sound, or about 1,350 mph (2,180 kph), compared with 485 mph (780 km/h) on a commercial Boeing 737. It was the closest most people came to space flight.

Nothing else looked like Concorde, with its dart-like delta wings, and adjustable pointed nose that could be lowered to give pilots better visibility on takeoffs and landings. Inside, it was not overly luxurious. The aircraft was created by engineers who, it was said, built a narrow metal tube that flew very fast and then grudgingly bolted seats in afterward. But it was exclusive. Only 14 of the aircraft ever entered service, seven each with Air France and British Airways. Tickets were expensive, but some international businesspeople were inclined to splurge on the fare because of the time saved; Concorde could cross the Atlantic in just three hours, compared to seven on a Boeing 747. With twice-daily services from London to New York, it was possible to fly over, do business, and be back home in time for a late dinner.

For most of its service, Concorde had an exemplary safety record. This changed on July 25, 2000, when an Air France flight burst into flames and crashed shortly after taking off. 113 people died. The damage this caused to Concorde's reputation, combined with low passenger numbers following the 9/11 terrorist attacks in the US, and escalating maintenance costs, meant that in the summer of 2003, the supersonic fleet was permanently retired.

For many, the end of Concorde was a step backward in technology. As the English broadcaster and Concorde regular David Frost once said: "You can be in London at 10 o'clock and in New York at 10 o'clock. I have never found another way of being in two places at once." We may never have that possibility again.

◁ **Concorde air stewardesses**
Air stewardesses from a variety of airlines from around the world stand in front of a scale model of Concorde. In fact, only Britain and France had airlines that operated this supersonic service.

New horizons

In 1946, Evelyn Waugh predicted the death of travel writing. As he saw it, everywhere had been written about. Yet not only is travel literature still alive, it appears to be in remarkably good health.

In the early 1970s, a young American novelist suggested to his publisher that he write a book about a train journey. The publisher agreed and Paul Theroux set off from London's Victoria railway station, bound eventually for Tokyo Central. *The Great Railway Bazaar* was published in 1975 and went on to sell more than 1.5 million copies in 20 languages. Theroux followed up his great train ride with others in South America (*The Old Patagonia Express*, 1979) and China (*Riding the Iron Rooster*, 1988), as well as plenty of excursions by boat, bus, and car.

A rapidly growing roster of names joined Theroux on the bookshop travel shelves, notably Bruce Chatwin (who debuted with *In Patagonia*, 1977), Colin Thubron (whose breakthrough was *Among the Russians*, 1983), and Jonathan Raban (*Arabia Through the Looking Glass*, 1979), followed by many others. All achieved both commercial success and critical acclaim. A huge resurgence in the travel writing genre, which had enjoyed its first peak in the late 19th century and its second in the 1930s, was afoot.

Once again, the increase in the popularity of writing about foreign places coincided with a revolution in the methods of getting to them—in this case, international air travel was just becoming widely affordable. The new travel writers addressed this new market with books that were faster paced, hipper, and more inventive than those that had gone before.

△ ***In Patagonia***
Unforgettable and influential, Bruce Chatwin's account of his journey across "the uttermost part of the earth" became an instant classic.

◁ ***A Walk in the Woods***
Nick Nolte (shown here as hiker Stephen Katz) stars alongside Robert Redford and Emma Thompson in *A Walk in the Woods*, the 2015 comedy biopic based on Bill Bryson's 1998 memoir of the same name.

The endearingly grumpy Theroux filled his books with spiky encounters and diplomacy-be-damned honesty. Chatwin, a former art auctioneer, created high-concept travelogues that read like slightly surreal fiction—*In Patagonia* centers on a quest to find a piece of a brontosaurus. It has been said that you fall into Chatwin's travel stories, and stay there.

Breaking boundaries

Other new authors pushed travel literature in different directions, not just geographically. The naturalist Redmond O'Hanlon introduced black humor into the Amazon in his book *In Trouble Again: A Journey Between the Orinoco and the Amazon* (1988), gleefully detailing episodes when he shared hallucinogens with tribesmen and the effects of invasive parasites. Bill Bryson, an expatriate journalist living in the UK, went back home to poke fun at America ("I come from Des Moines. Somebody had to") for *Lost Continent* (1989). He then used the same approach for the UK, Europe, and Australia, becoming a bestselling author as a result.

Writers such as the American Tim Cahill (*Jaguars Ripped My Flesh*, 1987; *A Wolverine is Eating My Leg*, 1989) put a sense of adventure back into travel writing, often in an extreme manner, recounting exhilarating tales of harvesting poisonous sea snakes in the Philippines and dining on baked turtle dung in the Australian Outback. For *Holidays in Hell* (1988), P.J. O'Rourke traveled the world's blackspots from war-torn Lebanon to Heritage USA, a vast theme park for Christians run by famous television evangelists.

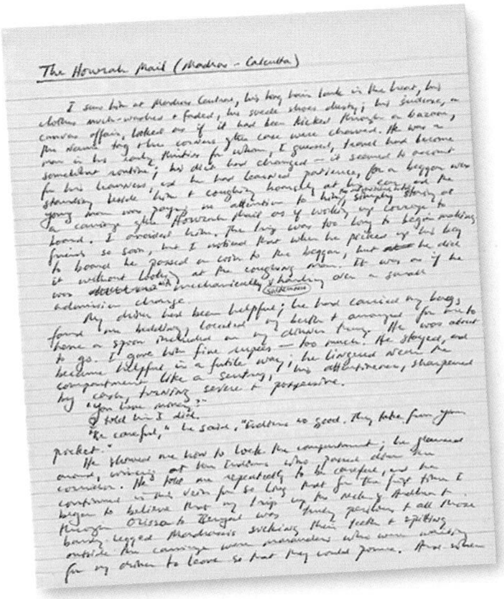

> "As long as there are **writers**, there will be travel writing **worth reading**."
>
> SAMANTH SUBRAMANIAN, AUTHOR OF *THIS DIVIDED ISLAND: STORIES FROM THE SRI LANKAN WAR*

◁ **Notes for *The Great Railway Bazaar***
As well as notes for *The Great Railway Bazaar*, the Paul Theroux Collection at the Huntington Library in California contains correspondence from V.S. Naipaul and many other writers.

Fresh perspectives

For a long time, V.S. Naipaul, the Trinidadian author of the Indian travelogues *An Area of Darkness* (1962), *A Wounded Civilization* (1977), and *A Million Mutinies Now* (1990), was a solitary non-Western voice in the field of travel literature. Then, in 1983, Indian author Vikram Seth published *From Heaven Lake: Travels Through Sinkiang and Tibet*, and Indian novelist Amitav Ghosh wrote an affectionate portrait of the time that he spent in an Egyptian village, which was published in 1992 as *In an Antique Land*. More recently, the Indian-American Suketu Mehta returned to the city of his youth to write *Maximum City: Bombay Lost and Found* (2004).

These titles suggest possibilities for a rich new form of travel writing. In the last 150 years, we have grown accustomed to reading about the journeys of Westerners who have ventured out into remote corners of the globe and then reported back. Now, it will be fascinating to read the travel accounts of the millions of migrants who travel in the other direction and head to Europe and America each year.

◁ **V.S. Naipaul**
Nobel Prize-winning writer V.S. Naipaul (right) and "Rolling Stone" magazine editor Hunter S. Thompson (left) report on Grenada after US involvement in 1983.

▽ **Steam locomotive, India**
In a scene that may have been familiar to V.S. Naipaul, railway workers move a steam locomotive at the railway yard near the Taj Mahal in Agra, India, in 1983.

Exploration today

In the 21st century, it may seem that there is nothing left to explore, but adventurers are still finding new places to discover and learning things about Earth that were not known before.

People have visited the North and South Poles, stood on the highest peaks, and looked down on Earth from space, but there are still caves and mountains that have not been explored. Above all, the oceans are yet to be fully charted. According to US deep-sea explorer Robert Ballard, humans have seen only "one tenth of one per cent" of what is below the sea.

Deep beneath the Earth

In 2012, film director James Cameron, of *Titanic* fame, put his fascination with wrecks on the ocean floor to scientific use when he became only the third person to descend to the Challenger Deep, the deepest known point on Earth, in the western Pacific's Mariana Trench. This was part of an ongoing survey of the planet's most remote spot to find new animal species (using a "slurp gun" to suck up small creatures) and bring back images of rocks between the two tectonic plates that could further understanding of how tsunamis start.

Perhaps the most extreme example of underground mapping is that of Krubera Cave—a chasm on the edge of the Black Sea some 7,208 feet (2,197 m) below sea level, and thus the deepest known cave on Earth. Ukrainian diver Gennady Samokhin explored Krubera in 2007. He plunged into its aptly named "terminal sump", reaching record-breaking depths, and found out that the cave was 150 feet (46 m) deeper

▷ **Record depth**
On 26 March 2012, Canadian film director James Cameron descended to the Challenger Deep, 35,756 feet (10,898 m) below sea level, aboard *Deepsea Challenger*, a single-person vessel. He trawled the sea floor, videoing and collecting samples of sediment.

> " That there is an **inner urge** [to do this] is **undeniable**. "
>
> SIR RANULPH FIENNES, ON CROSSING THE ANTARCTIC IN WINTER

◁ **Old techniques**
Today, explorers have all kinds of state-of-the-art equipment, including light, breathable clothing. Physical challenges remain tough, however. Crevasses are still crossed the hard way—using small, precarious-looking ladders.

than previously imagined. Three years later, new species were discovered, one of which—the tiny, eyeless *Plutomurus ortobalaganensis*, which had adapted to living in total darkness—was the deepest terrestrial animal ever found.

In 2012, Samokhin returned to Krubera and descended 170 feet (52 m) more, creating a second world record. Future explorers still have a great deal to find beneath the Earth—as Robert Ballard said: "The next generation of kids will probably explore more of Earth than all previous generations combined."

◁ **The eternal adventurer**
British adventurer Ranulph Fiennes has set numerous exploration records. He was the first person to visit the North and South poles by surface means only (1979–82), and the first to completely cross Antarctica on foot.

Retracing journeys

Not all of today's journeys plumb new depths—many put a 21st-century slant on places that have been visited in the past. Briton Tim Severin, for example, has retraced the steps of historic figures such as Genghis Khan and Marco Polo in an attempt to understand the past. Many individuals have set new records. American Matt Rutherford became the first person to sail solo through the Northwest Passage, which was first crossed by Roald Amundsen in 1906. In 2006, New Zealander Mark Inglis was the first double amputee to scale Mount Everest. In 2015, Briton John Beeden became the first person to row solo non-stop across the Pacific Ocean, from San Francisco, US, to Cairns in Australia. Charitable causes also spur on explorers. Ranulph Fiennes is only part of the way through his Global Reach Challenge, which aims to raise money for the Marie Curie organization that helps those with terminal illnesses. His goal is to become the first person to cross both polar ice caps and to climb the highest mountain on each continent. Turkish-American Erden Eruç began a similar adventure in 2003, when he embarked on his Six Summits Project, a bid to climb the highest peaks on each continent (except Antarctica) after reaching them by human power alone. In pursuit of this goal, Eruç made the first human-powered circumnavigation of the globe in 2012.

Advances in technology have shed a new light on places that are inaccessible or hard to see. Satellites have revealed traces of ancient civilizations beneath the deserts of Arabia, and drones make it possible for ecologists to study the impenetrable canopies of rainforests. And then, of course, there is space.

▽ **Reliving the past**
Tim Severin has recreated several historic or legendary journeys, such as the voyages of Sinbad the Sailor in a handmade replica of a medieval Arab boat in 1980–81.

New frontiers

The last man may have set foot on the Moon many decades ago, but plans to colonize Mars and dreams of superfast flight show that the desire to travel into space is as strong as ever.

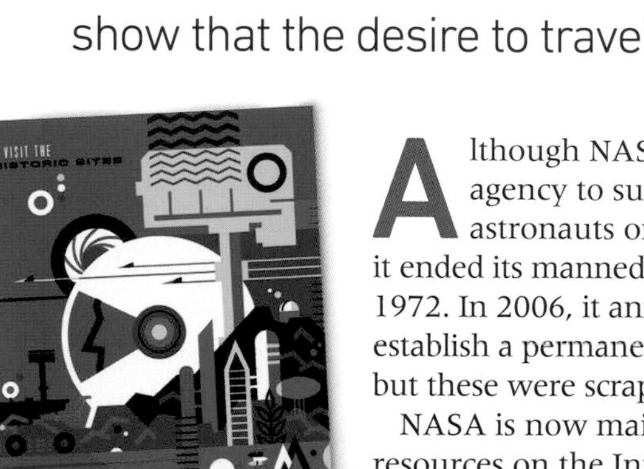

△ **Travel to Mars**
This poster, produced by NASA in 2016, imagines a future in which Mars is colonized. It also looks back at the milestones of Mars exploration, celebrated as "historic sites."

Although NASA was the first agency to succeed in landing astronauts on the Moon in 1969, it ended its manned missions there in 1972. In 2006, it announced plans to establish a permanent base on the Moon, but these were scrapped four years later.

NASA is now mainly concentrating resources on the International Space Station (ISS), which has had rotating crews drawn from 10 different nations in constant residence since November 2000. Mars is also a focus of attention, and NASA is trying to find out whether it might be habitable. Missions such as the Mars Rover program—the robotic *Curiosity* rover has been exploring the surface of Mars since August 2012—are providing important information about the geography and atmospheric conditions of the planet. However, NASA might not be the first to put a person on the Red Planet.

Colonizing Mars

In May 2012, a Dutch company called Mars One announced a plan to establish a human settlement on Mars by the year 2023 (this has since been revised to 2027). A privately funded project, Mars One aims to send a new four-person crew to Mars every two years to live in inflatable "life pods." The drawback is that there is no funding for a return rocket, so it would be a one-way ticket. That has not, however, deterred the 200,000 people who have so far applied to join the crew of the first launch.

Also in the race to Mars is Space X, an American company founded in 2002 by entrepreneur Elon Musk. The Space X program would involve spaceships

△ **International Space Station (ISS)**
The ISS is a space station orbiting about 205–270 miles (330–435 km) above the Earth. It is the largest artificial object currently in orbit.

" Where **we're going**, we **don't need roads**. "

DR EMMETT BROWN, *BACK TO THE FUTURE*, 1985

capable of carrying more than 100 passengers. Unlike Mars One, these spaceships would be able to take off from Mars and return to Earth again. However, Musk hopes that anyone who travels to the far-off planet will stay there, as he wants to establish a settlement. "I think there is a strong humanitarian argument for making life multi-planetary," Musk has said, "in order to safeguard the existence of humanity in the event that something catastrophic were to happen."

Travel on Earth

Musk has also come up with the concept of the Hyperloop, a vehicle that could radically speed up travel on Earth. Pod-like vehicles would be propelled through a vacuumlike tube at the speed of a jet aircraft. Musk claims that the Hyperloop could transport passengers the 350 miles (560 km) from San Francisco to Los Angeles in just 35 minutes, at an average speed of 600 mph (970 kph).

Sub-orbital aircraft

New technology could also drastically reduce long-distance flight times in the future. Several private companies around the world are investing in prototypes of sub-orbital aircraft. Part-rocket and part-aircraft, these would be launched to the top of the atmosphere, some 62 miles (100 km) above Earth. But rather than going into orbit around the planet, the aircraft would glide down to their destinations. A vehicle like this would be capable of taking passengers from Europe to Australia in 90 minutes, or from Europe to California in an hour.

Such a journey sounds exciting, but it would be extremely expensive. Then again, in 1939, a transatlantic airline ticket cost the equivalent of $90,000 (£73,000) in today's money. Nobody predicted that prices would plummet to such an extent that the transatlantic passenger liner would become obsolete, and that more than 8 million people would take to the skies every day.

IN CONTEXT
Outer space

When the Voyager 1 and 2 probes were launched back in 1977, Jimmy Carter had just been sworn in as US president, and the first *Star Wars* film was still in the cinemas. Four decades later, the probes are still exploring space. Both of them have flown by the giant planets, Jupiter and Saturn, and Voyager 2 has also made its way to Uranus and Neptune. The probes continue to monitor conditions in the outer reaches of the solar system, and are expected to be able to do so until around 2025. Often called the greatest feat of human exploration, the Voyager program is a wonderful example of just how far technology can travel.

AN ARTIST'S IMPRESSION OF VOYAGER 2

▽ **Mars One**
The Mars One project envisions colonists living on Mars in a series of linked transit modules, with large inflatable pods for living quarters. The technology is yet to be tested.

BIOGRAPHIES

A

▽ BENEDICT ALLEN

ENGLISH, 1960–

Writer, traveler, and adventurer Benedict Allen was born in Cheshire, UK. He studied Environmental Science in college, where his interest in travel was awakened by scientific expeditions to Costa Rica, Iceland, and Brunei. In 1983, he undertook his first major expedition—a precarious 600-mile (965-km) trek through the Amazon forest by foot and canoe. He is the only person known to have crossed the Amazon Basin at its widest point on his own. Since then, he has pioneered exploration of the Namib Desert in southern Africa, and became the first person known to have crossed the full width of the Gobi Desert using camels, not trucks.

Allen is best known for immersing himself completely in the culture of the indigenous people he meets. Further expeditions have taken him to Papua New Guinea, Borneo, Sumatra, Australia, Africa, and the Russian Arctic. He has made many television films of his travels, occasionally with the help of a camera crew, but more often doing the filming himself.

CAREER HIGHLIGHTS

1983 First expedition across Amazonia by foot and dugout canoe
1993 First person to cross the widest part of the Amazon Basin solo, a journey of 3,600 miles (5,790 km), without a compass or map
1995 Journeys 1,000 miles (1,610 km) across the Namib Desert
1996 First person to cross the Gobi Desert by camel

BENEDICT ALLEN ON THE SAND DUNES AT LANGEBAAN, SOUTH AFRICA

▷ ROALD AMUNDSEN

NORWEGIAN, 1872–1928

One of the great polar explorers of the 20th century, Amundsen was the first person to reach both the North and South Poles. Born in Norway into a family of ship owners, his parents wanted him to follow a career in medicine. In 1894, after the death of his mother, he left college and joined a sealing expedition to the Arctic. Then, in 1897–99, he served as first mate aboard the *Belgica*, which spent the winter in the Antarctic. From 1903 to 1906, he and a crew of six set out for the Arctic aboard the *Gjoa*; in 1905 they became the first to navigate the Northwest Passage.

In 1910, after a last-minute change of destination, Amundsen set sail for the Antarctic in an attempt to reach the South Pole before his British rival, Robert Falcon Scott. He dropped anchor in the Bay of Whales, and, on October 19, 1911, he and four companions set off on dog sleds. They reached the South Pole on December 14, 1911, a month before Scott. From 1918, Amundsen led further expeditions to the Arctic, including the first successful crossing of the North Pole by air, in the airship *Norge*, in 1926. He died in 1928, when his plane was lost in fog over the Barents Sea while attempting to find a friend's airship; the wreckage was never found.

NORWEGIAN EXPLORER ROALD AMUNDSEN, ON A JOURNEY TO THE ANTARCTIC, c.1911

CAREER HIGHLIGHTS

1897 Embarks on the first expedition to stay the winter in Antarctica
1905 Leads an expedition to cross the Northwest Passage
1910 Leads the first expedition to reach the South Pole in 1911, beating British explorer Robert Scott
1926 Makes the first crossing of the North Pole by air, in the airship *Norge*

▽ SALOMON AUGUST ANDRÉE

SWEDISH, 1854–97

Engineer, physicist, and polar explorer S. A. Andrée was born in Gränna, Sweden. He graduated from the Royal Institute of Technology, Sweden, in 1874 with a degree in mechanical engineering. He wrote articles about atmospheric electricity, heat conduction, and technology for various scientific journals, and took part in an expedition to Spitsbergen, where he recorded atmospheric electricity.

An enthusiastic balloonist, Andrée proposed a voyage by hydrogen balloon from Svalbard across the North Pole to Canada or Russia. After an abortive attempt in the summer of 1896, he and two other crew set off on July 11, 1897 in the *Eagle* from Dane's Island. The *Eagle* traveled for two days, then landed on Kvitøya, an island in the Arctic Ocean. The men never returned home, but took hundreds of photographs and made meticulous records, most of which were found with their bodies by a Norwegian expedition in 1930.

CAREER HIGHLIGHTS

1897 Attempts to fly across the North Pole in a hydrogen balloon

SALOMON AUGUST ANDRÉE AND HIS TEAM FLYING A FREE BALLOON, 1897

ROY CHAPMAN ANDREWS IN THE GOBI DESERT, MONGOLIA, 1928

△ ROY CHAPMAN ANDREWS

AMERICAN, 1884–1960

American explorer, adventurer, and naturalist Roy Chapman Andrews is best known for leading a series of expeditions into China, Mongolia, and the Gobi Desert in the early 20th century. Born in Wisconsin, he was a self-taught taxidermist and used funds from his hobby to put himself through college. He started working at the American Museum of Natural History as a janitor, and eventually became its director. In 1909 and 1913, he traveled to the East Indies and the Arctic respectively, to collect specimens.

From 1916 to 1917, he and his wife led expeditions to China, and in 1920 they began planning expeditions to Mongolia, famously driving a fleet of Dodge cars west from Peking. He led several more expeditions to Asia between 1922 and 1925. On one of these, on July 13, 1923, they found the first dinosaur eggs ever discovered. On the same journey, they found a skeleton from the Cretaceous period. Andrews made a final trip to Asia in 1930.

CAREER HIGHLIGHTS

1920 Leads the first of a series of four Central Asian expeditions across China into the Gobi Desert

1923 Part of the first expedition to discover dinosaur eggs

1926 Publishes *On the trail of the Ancient Man*, in which he predicts that the birthplace of modern humans will be found in Asia

1934 Appointed Director of the American Museum of Natural History

▷ NEIL ARMSTRONG

AMERICAN, 1930–2012

Best known for his work as an astronaut and as the first person to set foot on the Moon, Neil Armstrong was born in Ohio, and had his pilot's license by the age of 16, before he could even drive. He studied aeronautical engineering at college, then, in 1949, joined the US Navy as an aviator, first seeing action in the Korean War in 1951. He later served as a test pilot for the National Advisory Committee for Aeronautics before joining the NASA Astronauts Corps in 1962. Armstrong only made two flights into space: the first on Gemini 8 in 1966, which had to be aborted because of a technical fault; the second as commander of Apollo 11 in July 1969, the first manned expedition to the Moon. He resigned from NASA in 1971, and accepted a teaching position at the University of Cincinnati, leaving it in 1979. In 1985, he joined an expedition to the North Pole, saying he had only ever seen it from the Moon.

CAREER HIGHLIGHTS

1966 The first civilian astronaut to fly in space, on Gemini 8

1969 The first person in history to walk on the Moon

1972 Appointed Professor of Aerospace Engineering at Cincinatti University

B

▷ IBN BATTUTA

MOROCCAN, 1304–68

Battuta was one of the best-traveled people in history. He was born into a Berber family of Islamic scholars in Tangier, Morocco, and studied Islamic law as a young man. From an early age he was keen to make the hajj, the Muslim pilgrimage to Mecca, to see the Kabaa (Cube) in the Al-Masjid al-Haram mosque. He set off on the perilous journey in 1325 at the age of only 21, and

ASTRONAUT NEIL ARMSTRONG, COMMANDER OF APOLLO 11, TRAINING IN A SIMULATOR AT KENNEDY SPACE CENTER, 1969

EXPLORER IBN BATTUTA, DEPICTED IN THE 19TH-CENTURY NOVEL *DISCOVERY OF THE EARTH*, ILLUSTRATED BY LÉON BENETT

did not return to Morocco until 1349. Battuta traveled as far east as China, as far south as sub-Saharan Africa, and to Djenné in West Africa, visiting most of the Muslim world. He made the hajj no fewer than seven times, and worked as an Islamic judge in many of the places he visited. He also suffered numerous misfortunes at sea. When he returned home in 1354, the Sultan of Morocco ordered him to dictate his life's travels to the court poet, Ibn Juzayy. These were published as *Rihla* (*Travels*).

CAREER HIGHLIGHTS

1325 Leaves Tangier, Morocco, to start 29 years of traveling, during which he visits most of the Islamic world

▷ GERTRUDE BELL

ENGLISH, 1869–1926

An intrepid traveler, archaeologist, and mountaineer, Gertrude Bell was a rare example of a woman thriving in a man's world. She graduated from Oxford with a degree in history, then visited Tehran, Iran, with her uncle, who was the British Ambassador. Her first journey in the Middle East, in 1899, took her to Palestine and Syria. This was followed in 1905 by trips to Jerusalem, Syria, and Asia Minor. In 1909, she traveled down the Euphrates River to Baghdad, Iraq, and back up the Tigris to Turkey. Further trips in 1911 and 1913–14 took her to Ukhaidir in Iraq, to map ruins, and to Saudi Arabia. She spent many years working among the tribes of the Middle East, gaining knowledge of tribal leaders, as well as earning their respect. This relationship made her the ideal candidate to advise on the future administration of British territories in the region. She mastered no fewer than six languages: Arabic, Persian, French, German, Italian, and Turkish.

CAREER HIGHLIGHTS

1913 Awarded the Gill Memorial Award for geographical and archeological exploits in the Middle East

1914 Becomes only the second European woman to visit the oasis of Ha'il, Saudi Arabia, although she is placed under house arrest for doing so

1915 Joins the Arab Bureau in Cairo, working with T. E. Lawrence to assist British forces in Arabia

1921 Attends the Cairo Conference, where she and Lawrence persuade Winston Churchill to allow Faisal, the former king of Syria, to lead the new territory of Iraq

1926 The Baghdad Archeological Museum opens in June, displaying many of the artifacts that Bell had collected

▷ BENJAMIN OF TUDELA

SPANISH, 1130–73

Born in Tudela, in the Kingdom of Navarre, northern Spain, Benjamin of Tudela was a medieval Jewish traveler. He visited Europe, Africa, the Middle East, and Persia with the aim of finding safe passages from Spain to the Holy Land for his fellow Jews. In all, he went to more than 300 cities, and gathered information about many more areas. His book, *The Travels of Benjamin*, is a detailed account of his journey, in which he documents all the places along the routes where Jewish travelers could find hospitality.

Benjamin describes thriving Jewish communities as far east as Ghazni, in present-day Afghanistan, and gives a detailed account of urban life and the customs of all the people he encountered, both Jewish and non-Jewish. In contrast to the works of Marco Polo a century later, Benjamin always cites his sources. As a result, scholars consider his book an important document of medieval geography and ethnography. His account of the ruins near Mosul, in Iraq, includes one of the earliest descriptions of the site of Nineveh.

ILLUSTRATION OF BENJAMIN OF TUDELA

CAREER HIGHLIGHTS

1165 Sets out on his first pilgrimage to the Holy Land. After eight years, he returns to Spain in 1173

ENGLISH TRAVELER GERTRUDE BELL HAVING A PICNIC WITH KING FAISAL OF IRAQ, 1922

DANISH NAVIGATOR VITUS BERING STANDS WITH HIS DEPUTY, ALEKSEI ILYICH CHIRIKOV, IN PETROPAVLOVSK, RUSSIA. OIL PAINTING BY IGOR PAVLOVICH PSHENICHNY, 1938

△ VITUS BERING

DANISH, 1681–1741

Born in Horsens, Denmark, navigator Vitus Bering explored the northwest Pacific. In 1728, he was sent by Peter the Great of Russia to find out whether America and Russia were linked by a land bridge. He established that they were not, although he sailed so close to the Russian coast that he failed to see America, which was only 70 miles (110 km) away. In 1733, Catherine I, Peter's successor, commissioned Bering again, but this time to explore the American coast.

In 1740, after years of planning, the Great Northern Expedition set off with a large crew aboard two ships built specially for the purpose: *St. Paul*, commanded by Bering, and *St. Peter*. They reached America on July 18, 1841. On the return journey, the ships became separated, and *St. Paul* was forced to winter on what is now called Bering Island. Many of its crew died, including Bering. Only 46 men returned, but the reports and maps they produced set the course for Russian expansion into the east.

CAREER HIGHLIGHTS

1728 **Sets sail from Kamchatka Peninsula on his first expedition**

1740 **Embarks on the Great Northern Expedition to America**

▽ HIRAM BINGHAM

AMERICAN, 1875–1956

The son of missionaries, Bingham completed his study at Harvard in 1905 and became an academic specializing in Latin American history.

In 1906, Bingham retraced the journeys of Simón Bolívar, the 19th-century hero of South America's wars of independence, through Colombia and Venezuela. Inspired by this experience, in 1909, he traveled by mule from Buenos Aires, Argentina, to the ancient Inca capital city of Cuzco, in Peru.

When he returned to Peru in 1911, Bingham uncovered a major Inca site at Llactapata. He was informed by a farmer named Melchor Arteaga that the ruins of the Inca city of Machu Picchu (meaning "Old Mountain" in Quechua) were just a few miles away. Arteaga, Bingham, a translator, and an 11-year-old guide set off across the Urubamba river on a rickety bridge and entered the ancient city. Bingham later returned there twice, the first time to clear away the overgrowth, then to map the roads that the Incas used to reach the city.

CAREER HIGHLIGHTS

1911 **Becomes the first outsider to see the ruins of Machu Picchu**

1915 **Makes a final trip to Machu Picchu to map the area**

HIRAM BINGHAM ON A MULE, ON HIS EXPEDITION TO DISCOVER MACHU PICCHU, 1911

PHOTOGRAPH OF WIDELY TRAVELLED WRITER ISABELLA BIRD

△ ISABELLA BIRD

ENGLISH, 1831–1904

Explorer, writer, photographer, and naturalist, Isabella Bird was one of the 19th century's most remarkable travelers. Born in Yorkshire, UK, the daughter of a curate, she suffered from poor health for most of her life, but overcame this and traveled extensively, well into old age. Her travels took her around the world, from America, Hawaii, India, Kurdistan, the Persian Gulf, and Iran, to Tibet, Malaysia, Korea, Japan, and China. She climbed mountains and saw palaces and slums. She made great friends with people she met, but was occasionally attacked and chased. An accomplished rider, she rode thousands of miles on horseback.

Bird's subsequent travel books made her famous both at home and abroad, and she became the first woman to be elected Fellow of the Royal Geographical Society. She died soon after returning from a trip to Morocco, while she was planning a trip to China.

CAREER HIGHLIGHTS

1854 **Sets sail to the US to visit cousins**

1872 **Goes to Australia, Hawaii, and the US**

1886 **Starts studying medicine, and resolves to travel as a missionary**

1889 **Visits India, Tibet, Persia, Kurdistan, and Turkey**

1890 **Joins a group of soldiers in Baghdad**

1892 **Becomes a Fellow of the Royal Geographical Society**

1897 **Makes her final major expedition**

DANIEL BOONE

AMERICAN, 1734–1820

Considered to be one of the foremost frontiersmen in the US, pioneer, hunter, and woodsman Boone was the son of an English Quaker, Squire Boone, who settled in Pennsylvania with his family in 1713, then moved to North Carolina in 1750. Boone grew up on the frontier, so he had little formal education. As a young adult, he supplemented his income by hunting game and selling pelts. He served as a wagoner in the French and Indian war (1754–63), then, after hearing about the fertile land and abundant game in Kentucky, set off there in 1767, on a hunt with his brother.

In 1775, despite resistance from Native American tribes, Boone established Wilderness Road, the principal route used by settlers to reach Kentucky from the East. There, he founded Boonesborough, one of the first settlements to the east of the Appalachians. Boone served as a militia officer during the Revolutionary War (1775–83). He became a surveyor and merchant, but fell into debt, and in 1799, he moved his family to eastern Missouri, where he spent most of the last two decades of his life.

CAREER HIGHLIGHTS

1775 Establishes the Wilderness Road for the Transylvania Company
1787 Serves the first of three terms on the Virginia General Assembly

ROBERT O'HARA BURKE & WILLIAM JOHN WILLS

BURKE: IRISH, 1821–61
WILLS: ENGLISH, 1834–61

In 1860, Robert O'Hara Burke, a police inspector and emigrant from Galway, Ireland, and British surveyor William John Wills, led an expedition of 19 men across Australia from Melbourne in the south to the Gulf of Carpentaria in the north. The team set off on August 20, 1860, equipped with 26 camels, 23 horses, and six wagons.

The expedition was a disaster from the outset; it turned out that they were woefully ill-equipped. After a very slow start they split into two groups. Burke and Wills's party reached the halfway point—Cooper's Creek, the edge of the land explored by Europeans—in November. After waiting a month for supplies, on December 16 they decided to press on, but all but one of the party died, the sole survivor being cared for by Aborigines. Although the expedition was eventually successful, the bodies of Burke and Wills were not discovered until November 1861. They had probably died from starvation, dehydration, and exhaustion the previous June.

CAREER HIGHLIGHTS

1852 Wills emigrates to Australia, arriving in 1853
1853 Burke emigrates to Australia to work for the Victoria Police Force
1860 Burke and Wills lead the first expedition to cross Australia from south to north

▽ RICHARD BURTON

ENGLISH, 1821–90

Renowned for his travels in Asia, Africa, and the Americas, Richard Burton was a British geographer, translator, writer, cartographer, soldier, diplomat, and spy. He spoke some 29 languages, and is famous for disguising himself as an Arab and completing a pilgrimage to Mecca.

In 1856, Britain's Royal Geographical Society selected Burton to lead the East Africa Expedition to find out if the great lakes (Victoria, Albert, and Tanganika) in the center of Africa were the source of the Nile. Burton chose British Army officer John Hanning Speke as his companion.

By the time they arrived at Lake Tanganyika, Burton could hardly walk and Speke was almost blind. Speke traveled on alone and discovered Lake Victoria, which he claimed was the source of the Nile. Burton disagreed, and the two quarreled about the issue until 1864, when Speke died in a shooting accident. As it turned out, Speke was right after all.

Burton continued his explorations in South America, and later became British Consul in Damascus. He died in Trieste, Italy, and was buried in Mortlake, London. His tomb is carved in the shape of a Bedouin tent.

CAREER HIGHLIGHTS

1853 Undertakes the hajj
1854 Leads a Royal Geographical Society expedition in the Arabian Peninsula
1856 Leads the East Africa Expedition exploring the Great African Lakes with Speke
1883 Publishes the first English translation of the *Kama Sutra*
1885 Publishes an English translation of *The Arabian Nights*

19TH-CENTURY EXPLORER AND ORIENTALIST RICHARD BURTON

PORTRAIT OF LORD BYRON BY AN UNKNOWN ARTIST, 1830

◁ LORD BYRON

ENGLISH, 1788–1824

Romantic poet Lord Byron was born George Noel Gordon, the son of British Army officer John "Mad Jack" Byron, who changed his name to Gordon to inherit his wife's estate. After being deserted by his father, George lived in poverty in Aberdeen until he inherited the title Baron Byron of Rochdale in 1794. While studying at Trinity College, Cambridge, he began publishing poetry and took his seat in the House of Lords. However, adventure was in his blood, and in 1809 he embarked on the first of many journeys across Europe.

When he reached Athens, Byron began work on *Childe Harold's Pilgrimage*, a poetic travelogue that made him famous throughout Europe. He then journeyed through Greece and Turkey, where he swam the Hellespont, copying Leander of Greek myth, who made the journey for love.

After many affairs and a marriage, Byron left England forever in 1816. He befriended the Shelleys in Switzerland, settled in Italy, and became involved in revolutionary politics. In 1824, he died during his final adventure, fighting for Greek independence.

CAREER HIGHLIGHTS

1811 Publishes first canto of *Childe Harold's Pilgrimage*

1819 Starts publishing *Don Juan*

1823 Joins Greek insurgents fighting for independence

PEDRO ÀLVARES CABRAL

SPANISH, 1467–1520

King Manuel I of Portugal chose Pedro Àlvares Cabral as the successor to explorer Vasco da Gama, who had been the first European to reach India by sea. Cabral was tasked with spreading Christianity and establishing trading relations in India, by force if necessary.

Cabral's fleet sailed from Lisbon on March 9, 1500, intending to follow da Gama's route to India. However, it veered too far west and made landfall on April 23 on the coast of Brazil, which Cabral named *Ilha de Vera Cruz* (Island of the True Cross). The fleet then headed southeast for the Cape of Good Hope, but ran into a storm in which several ships were lost. The survivors discovered Madagascar, naming it *São Lourenço*, and, on September 13, they reached Calicut on the southeast coast of India. Cabral presented gifts to the ruler of Calicut, and in return, demanded trading privileges over the local Arab merchants. Cabral's remaining ships retraced their route home and arrived in Lisbon in July 1501, but only four of them made it back.

CAREER HIGHLIGHTS

1500 Becomes the first European to set foot in Brazil. Lands the first missionaries in India, and establishes treaties with the cities of Cochin (Kochi) and Cannanore (Kannuri)

KIT CARSON

AMERICAN, 1809–68

Famous frontiersman Christopher "Kit" Huston Carson was born in Kentucky. He left home at the age of 16, joining a caravan of fur trappers. In the 1830s, he lived with the Arapaho and Cheyenne, becoming fluent in Spanish and several tribal languages.

In the 1840s, Carson was hired as a guide by explorer John C. Frémont, who was mapping the Oregon Trail. He went on to guide two more expeditions in the American West with Frémont. Carson took part in the Mexican War and was celebrated for traveling to Washington D.C. to deliver news of victory to the US government.

He was taken on as an Indian Agent, but joined the Union army when the Civil War broke out. His fame spread throughout the US with newspaper reports and dime novels, the first of which, *An Adventure of Kit Carson: A Tale of the Sacramento* was printed in 1847. Named a brigadier general in 1865, Carson moved to Colorado after the war and became the commander of Fort Garland the following year.

EVLIYA ÇELEBI, BY AN UNKNOWN ARTIST

CAREER HIGHLIGHTS

1842 Joins his first expedition west, with Frémont, to map the Oregon Trail
1861 Is made colonel in the Union Army; promoted to brigadier general in 1865

▷ JACQUES CARTIER

FRENCH, 1491–1557

Born in Saint-Malo, France, Cartier was a cool-headed sea captain with a genius for navigating dangerous coasts, charting new lands, and surviving attacks by natives. Moreover, he did this without once losing a ship or facing a revolt from his men.

In 1533, he wrote to the high admiral of France, Philippe de Chabot, setting out his ambition to sail along the American coast in search of new treasures for France and for a trade route to the East. The following year, he crossed the Atlantic in just 20 days. In 1543, Cartier became the first European to map the Gulf of St. Lawrence, where the Great Lakes meet the Atlantic Ocean. He never found a trade route to the East, but "New France" proved to be of great strategic value to the French. He named the region Canada after the Iroquois word *kanata* (village), which he mistakenly took to be the Iroquois name of the country.

CAREER HIGHLIGHTS

1534 Spends three months exploring the Gulf of St. Lawrence and its surrounding coastline and islands
1535 Explores the St. Lawrence River in search of a trade route to the East
1541 Attempts to colonize the area around the St. Lawrence River

◁ EVLIYA ÇELEBI

OTTOMAN, 1611–82

Çelebi was an Ottoman explorer who traveled extensively throughout the lands of the Ottoman Empire for more than 40 years. He was born in Constantinople, now Istanbul, into a family attached to the Ottoman court. He received a court education, and although he was employed as a scholar and entertainer he refused any work that prevented him traveling. His early writings were on Constantinople and from 1640 he produced extended accounts of his travels, which took him to Europe, the Middle East, and Asia. He documented his journeys in a book called the *Seyahatname* (*Book of Travel*). His notes remain a useful guide to the culture and way of life of the 17th-century Ottoman Empire.

CAREER HIGHLIGHTS

1640 Journeys to Anatolia, the Caucasus, Azerbaijan, and Crete
1648 Visits Syria, Palestine, Armenia, and the Balkans
1655 Visits Iraq and Iran

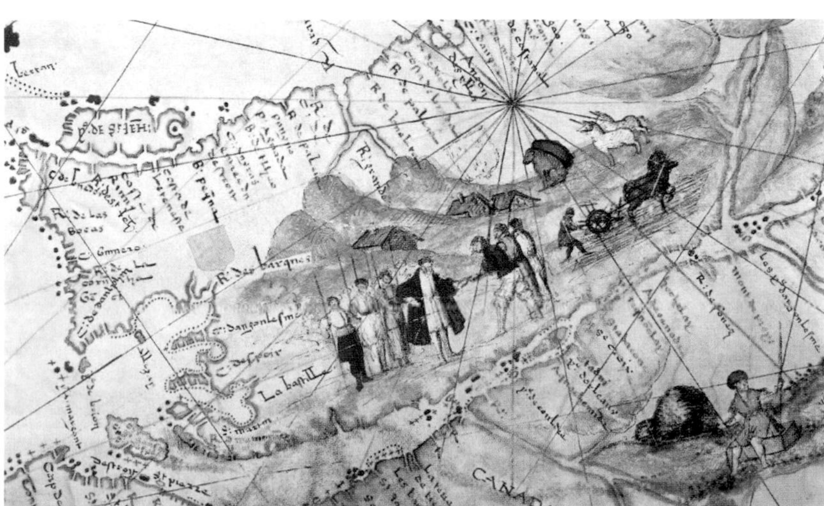

FRENCH EXPLORER JACQUES CARTIER IN CANADA, IN A DETAIL FROM A MAP MADE BY PIERRE DESCELIERS

SAMUEL DE CHAMPLAIN

FRENCH, 1580–1635

Soldier, navigator, and geographer Samuel de Champlain was born in western France into a seafaring family. After a period in the army of Henri IV of France, he followed in his father's footsteps, learning his craft aboard his uncle's ship, which was chartered to carry Spanish troops to the Caribbean in 1598.

Champlain went on to make voyages of his own to North America, exploring and mapping the rivers and lakes around the St. Lawrence River, including one that was named after him. Searching for a river route to the Arctic, he forged alliances with one of the local tribes, learning everything he could about this new land. He also fought battles with the Iroquois, the sworn enemies of his new allies.

From 1604 to 1606, Champlain sailed south to the area now called Massachusetts, and in about 1609, he founded the first permanent French settlement of New France on the site of Quebec city.

CAREER HIGHLIGHTS

1603 Makes his first expedition to New France, looking for a settlement site
1604 Sails south down the coast of Massachusetts
1608 Establishes the settlement that would become Quebec City
1615 Explores the shores of Lake Huron and Lake Ontario

CHRISTOPHER COLUMBUS AT THE ROYAL COURT OF SPAIN, IN AN ILLUSTRATION BY VÁCLAV BROŽÍK, 1884

▽ BRUCE CHATWIN

ENGLISH, 1940–89

Travel writer, journalist, and novelist Bruce Chatwin was born in Sheffield, UK. At the age of 18, he went to work at Sotheby's auction house, in London, where he gained an extensive knowledge of art and antiquities, and eventually became a director. He also began traveling, both for his job and for adventure.

In 1965, Chatwin made a trip to the Sudan, where he became intrigued by the way of life of a nomadic tribe. In 1966, he started studying archaeology at the University of Edinburgh, but gave it up after two years to pursue a writing career. He traveled the world interviewing political figures, but in 1974 he set off for Patagonia. He spent six months traveling and gathered stories about the people who had settled there. In 1983, Chatwin returned to the topic of nomads and decided to focus on Aboriginal Australians, describing their way of life in his book *Songlines*.

CAREER HIGHLIGHTS

1966 Promoted to junior director of Sotheby's, London
1977 Publishes his first book, *In Patagonia*
1987 Publishes *Songlines*, a book about Aboriginal Australians
1988 Publishes *Utz*, which is shortlisted for the Man Booker Prize

BRUCE CHATWIN IN PARIS, FRANCE, MAY 1984

△ CHRISTOPHER COLUMBUS

ITALIAN, c. 1451–1506

Genoese navigator Christopher Columbus became the most famous explorer in history, but little is known about his early life. By 1485 he was in Lisbon, Portugal, where his brother Bartolomeo was a map-maker. The two men hatched a plan to sail west, rather than east, in search of a sea route to Asia. To that end, in August 1492, Columbus departed from Palos, Spain, with a fleet of three ships, but without Bartolomeo.

The expedition sailed west, and on October 11 they discovered land—but it was the Bahamas rather than China. By Christmas Day, they had explored the islands, one of which Columbus named La Española (Hispaniola), and on it they built the town of La Navidad.

Columbus returned to Spain on March 15, 1493, bringing gold and cotton with him from the New World. A second expedition of 17 ships set off a few months later, with 1,000 new colonists. Columbus made a third voyage in 1498, and became the first European to set foot in

South America. This was followed by a fourth voyage in May 1502, which took him to Panama, but there he was forced back by local tribes. Columbus was rescued off the coast of Jamaica, and returned to Spain in 1504. He was wealthy, but his health was poor and his reputation in tatters.

CAREER HIGHLIGHTS

1492 Becomes the first European to sight land in the Americas. Establishes La Navidad, the first European colony in the Americas
1493 Is given the title Admiral of the Oceans by the Spanish royal court
1498 Becomes the first European to set foot on South America
1502 Leads the first Europeans to explore Central America

▽ JAMES COOK

ENGLISH, 1728–79

A skilled navigator, cartographer, and explorer, Cook was born in Yorkshire, UK. He started out in the British Merchant Navy, but volunteered for the Royal Navy in 1755. In 1768, Britain's Royal Society appointed him to lead an expedition to Tahiti in the South Pacific. On August 25, 1768, Cook set sail on HMS *Endeavour* and arrived on Tahiti on April 13, 1769. He then sailed south, following orders from the British Admiralty to establish if there was an undiscovered continent there. In October 1769, Cook arrived in New Zealand and surveyed the North and South islands, then sailed west. On April 19, 1770, the expedition landed in Australia and surveyed the eastern coastline before returning to Britain.

In June 1772, Cook set out to explore even further south. He crossed the Antarctic Circle in January 1773, and discovered the island of South Georgia in the southern Atlantic. In 1776, a third voyage took him to the Arctic Ocean. Searching for the Northwest Passage, Cook's crew became the first Europeans to land on the Hawaiian Islands. Cook returned to Hawaii in 1779, only to be killed by locals.

CAREER HIGHLIGHTS

1769 Records the transit of Venus across the Sun from the island of Tahiti and confirms that New Zealand is composed of two islands. Brings Polynesian cultures into contact with Europeans for the first time
1770 Arrives in Australia and claims land for the British crown, naming it New South Wales
1778 Discovers the Hawaiian Islands, naming them the Sandwich Islands

▷ HERNÁN CORTÉS

SPANISH, 1485–1547

Born in Medellín, Spain, to an impoverished noble family, Cortés chose to pursue a life in the New World. He set sail for the Caribbean Island of Hispaniola in 1504, and soon became a successful planter. Ambition led him to join an expedition to conquer the neighboring island of Cuba, after which he became one of the most powerful men in the colony.

Toward the end of 1518, Cortés led a relatively small expedition of just 500 men to Mexico. They landed in Tabasco in March 1519 and fought off an attack by local tribes. Impressed by the prowess of his opponents, Cortés turned to diplomacy. He formed alliances with any tribes who were opposed to the Aztecs, and managed to overthrow the Aztec Empire of 15 million people. He named Tenochtitlán, the Aztec capital, Mexico City, and claimed Mexico for Spain, opening the gates through which a tide of Europeans jostled to carve up the bounty of the New World. Cortés found fame, but did not receive the power and riches he thought he deserved. He died in Spain, in debt, but planning another trip to the New World.

CAREER HIGHLIGHTS

1504 Arrives in Hispaniola
1511 Joins Diego Velázquez de Cuéllar in an expedition to conquer Cuba
1518 Velázquez appoints Cortés leader of an expedition to the Mexican coast
1519 Enters the Aztec city of Tenochtitlán

HERNÁN CORTÉS, PAINTED IN THE LATE 16TH CENTURY

1521 Overthrows the Aztec Empire, which ruled over up to 15 million people, with only 500 men
1535 Explores the Pacific Coast of Mexico as far north as Baja in California

A TRAVEL POSTER FOR AUSTRALIA SHOWS CAPTAIN JAMES COOK LANDING AT BOTANY BAY

▽ JACQUES-YVES COUSTEAU

FRENCH, 1910–97

Although Cousteau described himself as an oceanographic technician, he was also a filmmaker, inventor, underwater explorer, conservationist, photographer, and author. Born in France, his family moved to New York in 1920. During summer camps spent at Lake Harvey, Vermont, he learned to dive. Cousteau returned to France in 1930 and entered the French Naval Academy. A serious car accident cut short his naval aviation career, but led him instead to follow his interest in the sea.

In 1934, Cousteau carried out his first underwater experiments in the Mediterranean Sea near his naval base. Along with two colleagues, in 1943 he invented the Aqua-Lung, which allowed divers to swim underwater for long periods for the first time. He went on to develop underwater living pods and two-person submarines, and pioneered deep-sea photography with cameras that could be operated at depths of 4 miles (7 km). Cousteau's experiments with underwater living not only improved diving technology, but also did much to inform the development of the NASA training programs.

CAREER HIGHLIGHTS

1943 Awarded prize for *Par dix-huit mètres de fond (18 Metres Deep)*, the first French underwater film made without breathing apparatus
1954 Wins the Palme d'Or at the Cannes Film Festival for his film *Silent World*
1957 Becomes Director of the Oceanographic Museum of Monaco
1962 Builds the first "Conshelf" (Continental Shelf Station), an underwater shelter in which divers could live for a week
1973 Founds the Cousteau Society for the Protection of Ocean Life
1985 Awarded the Presidential Medal of Freedom by Ronald Reagan

FRENCH OCEANOGRAPHER JACQUES-YVES COUSTEAU, c. 1969

▷ CHARLES DARWIN

ENGLISH, 1809–82

A geologist, naturalist, and biologist, Charles Darwin was born in Shropshire, UK, and showed an interest in natural history from a young age. He began training in medicine, and later for the Church, but throughout his studies, Darwin collected geological samples and carried out fieldwork.

In December 1831, he joined the voyage of HMS *Beagle* as an unpaid companion and geologist. The ship set out across the Atlantic, continuing around the coast of South America. It completed its circumnavigation via Tahiti, Australia, Mauritius, and the Cape of Good Hope, returning to the UK in October 1836.

PHOTOGRAPH OF BRITISH NATURALIST CHARLES DARWIN, 1878

Darwin spent most of the trip on land investigating geology, making notes on natural history, and collecting specimens. In total, he completed 15 notebooks and made more than 300 sketches. Darwin spent 20 years assessing his collection and notes, formulating his theory of natural selection. In 1858, he produced an abstract of his major work about evolution; the complete title, *On the Origin of Species*, followed a year later.

CAREER HIGHLIGHTS

1839 Publishes detailed travel notes as *The Voyage of the Beagle*
1859 Publishes *On the Origin of Species*, which set out his theory that species were not fixed, but developed under selection pressure from the environment

▷ ROBYN DAVIDSON

AUSTRALIAN, 1950–

A travel writer, Robyn Davidson is probably best known for her book *Tracks*, which describes her 1,700-mile (2,735-km) trek across the deserts of Australia. She was born on a cattle station in Queensland, Australia, and studied zoology at college. With plans to undertake a desert trek, Davidson moved to Alice Springs, in the Northern Territory, in 1975, to work with camels and learn the skills needed to survive in harsh climates.

In 1977, she set off for the west coast of Australia with a dog and four camels on a journey that took nine months. Along the way, Davidson encountered indigenous Australians who walked with her or led her to water sources. She went on to study and travel with nomadic peoples, looking at different forms of nomadic lifestyle in countries such as Australia, India, and Tibet. She has written books and papers about her experiences.

CAREER HIGHLIGHTS

1980 Publishes her first book, *Tracks*
2013 *Tracks* is adapted into a film of the same name

IPPOLITO DESIDERI

ITALIAN, 1684–1733

Born into a prosperous family from Tuscany, Ippolito Desideri was educated at a Jesuit school. In 1712, he was sent to reopen a Tibetan mission under the jurisdiction of the Jesuit Province of Goa, India. He arrived in Goa a year later, and then traveled across India, reaching Ladakh in June 1715. He arrived at the Jesuit mission in Lhasa in March 1716, where he was left in charge. Desideri began to teach Christianity and study Tibetan culture. He was considered to be the first European to understand the Tibetan language and culture, and between 1718 and 1721 he composed five works in literary Tibetan.

In 1727, Desideri was summoned back to Europe. He took with him his extensive notes on Tibet, but was banned from working on them any further. The manuscripts—the first accurate account by a European of Tibetan geography, government, agriculture, customs, and Tibetan Buddhist philosophy—were lost in the Jesuit archives, and did not come to light until the 19th century.

WRITER AND EXPLORER ROBYN DAVIDSON, PHOTOGRAPHED IN 2000

CAREER HIGHLIGHTS

1715 Becomes the only missionary in Tibet
1725 Moves to French Jesuit Malabar mission to learn Tamil
1955-57 *Historical Notices of Tibet and Recollections of My Journeys, and the Mission Founded There (Relation)* is finally published

▷ BARTOLOMEU DIAS

PORTUGUESE, c.1450–1500

Although a nobleman of the Portuguese royal household, little is known of Dias's early life. In 1446, Portugal's João II asked him to lead an expedition to investigate a trade route to India. Dias left in August 1487.

The flotilla reached the southern tip of Africa in early January 1488, but the weather deteriorated, so Dias ordered his ships further out to sea. In doing so, he discovered how to safely round the Cape of Good Hope by sailing wide of the dangerous currents. He reached present-day Mossel on February 3.

Dias wanted to continue to India, but his crew pressed him to turn back. It was on the return journey that he discovered the Cape of Good Hope. He never led another journey, but in 1497, Dias joined Vasco da Gama on a leg of his voyage to India. He sailed under the explorer Pedro Álvares Cabral and landed in Brazil in 1500. Dias died as they left Brazil when his ship encountered bad weather and sank.

CAREER HIGHLIGHTS

1488 Successfully rounds the southern tip of Africa, and discovers the Cape of Good Hope

STATUE OF BARTOLOMEU DIAS BY COERT STEYNBERG, 1934

AMERICAN AVIATION PIONEER AMELIA EARHART STANDS IN FRONT OF HER BIPLANE *FRIENDSHIP*, JUNE 1928

E

◁ AMELIA EARHART

AMERICAN, 1897–1937

Born in Kansas, aviation pioneer Amelia Earhart was the first woman to fly over both the Atlantic and Pacific oceans. She was taken for her first plane ride on December 28, 1920, by the pilot Frank Hawks, and within six months, she had bought her own aircraft. By October 1922, she had set a record for female pilots by rising to an altitude of 14,000 feet (4,270 m).

In June 1928, she undertook her first transatlantic flight, as a passenger of pilot Wilmer Stultz. Determined to set her own record, she once again crossed the Atlantic Ocean, in May 1932. She became the second person, and the first woman, to make the trip alone. She then gained the nickname Lady Lindy, after Charles Lindbergh, the first person to cross the Atlantic.

Earhart's next goal was to complete an around-the-world flight. On June 1, 1937, she set off east from Miami. She and her crew reached Lae, New Guinea, on 29 June, and then set off again on July 2, but they vanished and were never seen again.

CAREER HIGHLIGHTS

1922 First woman to fly to an altitude of 14,000 feet (4,270 m)
1923 The 16th woman to be awarded a pilot's licence by the Féderation Aéronautique Internationale
1928 Becomes the first woman to fly over the Atlantic Ocean
1932 The second person, and the first woman, to fly a solo flight over the Atlantic Ocean
1935 Becomes the first woman to fly over the Pacific Ocean

OLAUDAH EQUIANO

AFRICAN, c. 1745–97

Olaudah Equiano was kidnapped from West Africa at around the age of 11, and brought to Barbados as a slave.

On the ship that took him to the Americas, Equiano was renamed Michael, but his first owner called him Jacob. He was sent to Virginia in 1754, and sold to Michael Pascal, a lieutenant in the Royal Navy. Once again renamed, this time Gustavus Vassa, Equiano was taken to England by Pascal, and eventually sold to Captain James Doran who took him on a ship bound for the Caribbean.

Equiano's final owner was American Quaker Robert King who allowed him to trade on his own behalf and then to ultimately purchase his freedom. In 1767, Equiano returned to England, and worked for another 20 years as a seafarer, merchant, and explorer in the Caribbean, Arctic, and in South and Central America. In the 1780s, he became involved in the anti-slave trade movement in England, writing a book about his experience as a slave.

CAREER HIGHLIGHTS

1766 Purchases his freedom from slavery

1789 Publishes *The Interesting Narrative of the Life of Olaudah Equiano*. The book helped in the passing of the Slave Trade Act 1807, which ended the slave trade

▽ LEIF ERIKSON

ICELANDIC, c. 970–c.1020

The second of the three sons of Erik the Red, as well as the founder of the first Norse settlement in Greenland,

STATUE OF LEIF ERIKSON, BY ALEXANDER S. CALDER, IN REYKJAVIK, ICELAND

Leif Erikson is credited with being the first European to have discovered North America—centuries before Christopher Columbus. He was probably born in Iceland, and is thought to have visited Norway around 999–1000, where he was converted to Christianity by Olaf I, who then sent him back to Greenland to convert the settlers there.

According to the *Sagas of the Icelanders*, which was written around 1200, Erikson sailed off-course on the voyage and arrived in a place that he named "Vinland," because of the abundance of grapes growing there. Archeological evidence suggests that this was near the Gulf of St. Lawrence, in present-day Canada.

CAREER HIGHLIGHTS

c. 1000 Discovers North America—possibly the first European to do so

▷ GEORGE EVEREST

WELSH, 1790–1866

Born in Wales, George Everest joined the Royal Artillery in 1818. He was appointed as assistant to Colonel William Lambton who, in 1806, had started the Great Trigonometrical Survey of India—a project that aimed to take measurements of the entire Indian subcontinent with scientific precision. After Lambton's death in 1823, Everest succeeded him as superintendent of the project. He later became Surveyor-General of India.

Everest was instrumental in completing the 1,491-mile (2,400-km) section from Cape Comorin (now Kanyakumari), the southernmost tip of India, up to the Himalayas in the north. After 23 years, and despite numerous hardships, Everest finished his survey in 1841, but it took another two years for him to complete his calculations and compile his results.

Ill health forced Everest to retire from the project in 1843, and he returned to England. He became a fellow of the Royal Geographical Society, and was knighted in 1861.

CAREER HIGHLIGHTS

1823 Becomes superintendent of the Great Trigonometrical Survey of India

1830 Appointed the Surveyor-General of India

SIR GEORGE EVEREST

1862 Elected vice-president of the Royal Geographical Society

1865 Mount Everest named after him, despite his objections

F

AHMAD IBN FADLAN

ARABIC, c. 877–c. 960

Islamic scholar Ahmad ibn Fadlan is known for his remarkable 2,500-mile (4,000-km) journey from Baghdad to the River Volga, in Eastern Europe. Ibn Fadlan traveled from Baghdad as a secretary to an ambassador of Caliph al-Muqtadir, and was under instructions to teach the Volgas about Islam, and to construct a fortress against the Khazar people.

As his party traveled from the Caspian Sea to the East European Plain, ibn Fadlan kept a journal that remained undiscovered until 1923. He describes the tribes he met, including the nomadic Oghuz Turks, and some fair-skinned people he called the Rus, who may have been descendants of the Vikings. The journal also provides an insight into the cultures of Eastern Europe during the early medieval period, such as ibn Fadlan's account of a burial ritual in which a chieftain was laid out in a longship and burned, together with sacrificed slaves.

FAXIAN

CHINESE, 337–c. 422

Faxian is the spiritual name—meaning "splendor of dharma"—of a Chinese Buddhist monk who was originally named Sehi. He was born in the Chinese province of Shanxi, at a time when Buddhism was flourishing in China, and entered a monastery as a young child. Between 399 and 412, influenced by his profound religious faith, Faxian walked from Chang'an in the center of China to India, via Central Asia, to seek Buddhist texts.

He trekked across icy deserts, rugged mountain passes, and deserts with "scorching winds," entering India from the northwest. His journey took him to sacred Buddhist sites in Xinjiang in China, Bangladesh, Nepal, and India, as well as Pakistan and Ceylon (now Sri Lanka). After two years, he set off back to China by sea from Ceylon, taking with him copies of Buddhist texts and sacred images.

After many months, Faxian arrived in Mount Lao, northern China. He spent the last years of his life translating the Buddhist texts from Sanskrit into Chinese. Faxian recorded his journey in a travelogue, entitled *Foguoji* (*Record of Buddhist kingdoms*), filled with observations of the geography and history of countries along the Silk Road, as well as descriptions of the Buddhist sites and practices that he witnessed. The journal provides a fascinating insight into Buddhist India in the 5th century.

RANULPH FIENNES HAULS A SLED ON HIS EXPEDITION TO THE NORTH POLE, 1986

▽ PATRICK LEIGH FERMOR

ENGLISH, 1915–2011

The son of Sir Lewis Leigh Fermor, the director of the Geological Survey of India, Patrick was an intrepid traveler, an heroic soldier, and a writer with a unique style. In December 1933, at the tender age of 18, he set out to walk all the way from the Hook of Holland to Istanbul (or Constantinople, as he insisted on calling it).

In January 1935, he crossed the Turkish border at Adrianople and reached Istanbul. He then continued his travels to Greece and Romania. Leigh Fermor only returned home in September 1939, at the outbreak of World War II, to enlist with the British Army. He served with the Irish Guards and fought in Crete and mainland Greece, joining the Special Operations Executive (SOE) in 1941.

In the 1950s, he lived a nomadic lifestyle, not only traveling but also writing extensively. Leigh Fermor married in 1968. Although he and his wife continued to travel, they spent much of their time in Greece.

PATRICK LEIGH FERMOR, TRAVEL WRITER AND SOLDIER

CAREER HIGHLIGHTS

1943 Appointed a military OBE
1945 Made vice director of the British Institute in Athens
1950 Publishes his first book, *The Traveler's Tree*, which documents his postwar travels in the Caribbean
1977 Publishes *A Time of Gifts*, the first book of a planned trilogy about his trek across Europe at the age of 18
1986 The second volume of his unfinished trilogy, *Between the Woods and the Water*, is published
2004 Accepts a knighthood, which he had initially refused in 1991

△ RANULPH FIENNES

ENGLISH, 1944–

Born into an aristocratic family, Ranulph Fiennes is not only an explorer and holder of many endurance records, but also a prolific writer and poet. He spent eight years in the army, serving with his father's regiment, the Royal Scots Greys, as well as on secondment to the British Army's SAS (Special Air Service). However, disillusioned with the armed forces, he left to begin a remarkable career as an adventurer.

Fiennes was the first person to reach both the North Pole and the South Pole by land, and the first to cross Antarctica on foot. In 2000, he suffered severe frostbite in an unsuccessful attempt to be the first person to reach the North Pole solo and unsupported. He has led many expeditions in other parts of the world, such as his 1969 exploration of the White Nile, in Oman, on a hovercraft. Although Fiennes suffers from heart problems, in 2009, he became the oldest person to climb Mount Everest.

In 2016, at the age of 72, Fiennes began The Global Reach Challenge. This is an attempt to become the first person to cross both polar ice caps, and to climb the highest mountain on each continent.

CAREER HIGHLIGHTS

1979-1982 Undertakes the Transglobe Expedition—a journey around the world's Polar axis—using only surface transport

2000 Makesan attempt to walk solo and unsupported to the North Pole

2003 Completes seven marathons in the course of seven days

2009 Climbs Mount Everest at the age of 65

△ JOHN FRANKLIN

ENGLISH, 1786–1847

Franklin was a naval officer whose Arctic exploits made him a national hero in Britain, even though two of his three expeditions ended in disaster. In 1819, after taking part in an unsuccessful mission to find an open water route to the North Pole the previous year, Franklin was chosen to lead an overland expedition to find the Northwest Passage. The expedition was a disaster, and 11 of the 20 men died. There were even reports of murder and cannibalism.

From 1825 to 1827, Franklin led his second expedition to Canada, and the third to the Arctic coast. He explored to the east and west of the Mackenzie River, Canada. In 1845, he returned to the Arctic with the best-equipped expedition yet—only to become stuck in thick ice. The search for Franklin and his missing crew gripped the public imagination for many years afterward. A note that was found in 1859 finally revealed Franklin's fate; he had died in June 1847.

JOHN FRANKLIN ON AN EARLY VOYAGE TO AUSTRALIA, IN AN ENGRAVING FROM c. 1880

CAREER HIGHLIGHTS

1825-27 Successfully explores to the east and the west of the Mackenzie River in Canada's Northwest Territories

▽ XU FU

CHINESE, c. 255–c. 210 BCE

A Buddhist monk, explorer, and court sorcerer, Xu Fu was sent by Emperor Qin Shi Huang to spread Buddhism beyond China, and to search for the elixir of life. Xu Fu made two journeys between 219 BCE and 210 BCE. His fleet is thought to have included 60 barques (sailing ships), a crew of 5,000 men, and 3,000 boys and girls.

Xu set off in 219 BCE to look for the legendary Penglai Mountain, where the elixir of life was rumored to exist. The expedition was unsuccessful, and Xu claimed that a giant sea creature had blocked his path. His second mission began in 210 BCE, but Xu never returned from it. *Records of the Grand Historian*, a history of ancient China, suggests that he came to a place with "flat plains and wide swamps" and declared himself king. Other stories state that he landed in "Danzhou," but its whereabouts is not known. About 1,000 years after Xu Fu's expedition, a Japanese monk suggested that the explorer had landed in Japan. Those who support this theory credit Xu with introducing new farming techniques, as well as many new plants, to Japan.

PAINTING OF XU FU'S SHIP ON ITS VOYAGE TO FIND THE ELIXIR OF LIFE BY UTAGAWA KUNIYOSHI, c. 1840

VASCO DA GAMA ARRIVES IN CALICUT, INDIA, IN 1498

G

△ VASCO DA GAMA

PORTUGUESE, c. 1460–1524

Da Gama was the first explorer to link Europe and Asia by sea, after making a pioneering journey to India via the Cape of Good Hope. He was also perhaps the most ruthless explorer of the European Age of Discovery.

The son of the governor of Alentejo, a Portuguese province, da Gama spent his early years in military training and learning the skills of a mariner. In 1497, King Manuel I chose him to lead an expedition to find a trade route across the Indian Ocean. By doing so, da Gama made it possible to import spices and other eastern goods directly to the West for the first time. On the outward voyage, he sailed from Lisbon to Natal in southern Africa, making what was at the time the longest journey out of sight of land. On da Gama's second voyage, in 1502, he vigorously pursued Portuguese interests in India, and managed to force favorable trading concessions from the Zamorin (the ruler) of Calicut. At Cannanore, in India, he encountered a ship bringing Muslim pilgrims back from Mecca. He had the vessel looted, then locked all 400 pilgrims in the hold and burned them alive. In 1524, he made a third voyage to India, this time to consolidate Portuguese power, but died of malaria within three months.

CAREER HIGHLIGHTS

1497–99 **Sails from Lisbon to Calicut and back. Becomes the first European to visit Mombasa**

1502 **Returns to India with 20 warships and forces a local king to trade**

1524 **Returns to India to establish colonial administration**

▷ YURI GAGARIN

RUSSIAN, 1934–68

Born in a village near the town of Gzhatsk (renamed Gagarin after his death) in what was then the USSR, Yuri Gagarin was the first human to travel in outer space. After finishing school, he was drafted into the Soviet Army and was sent to First Chkalov Air Force Pilot's School. In 1960, he was chosen with 19 other pilots for the Soviet Space program. Gagarin was selected because he was extremely fit, and, at 5 ft 2 in (1.57 m), was small enough to fit inside the cramped cockpit of the spacecraft. In August 1960, all but three of his peers voted him the most suitable candidate to fly first.

In April 1961, Vostok 1 was launched with Gagarin on board. He became a hero of the Soviet Union and Eastern Bloc, and a worldwide celebrity. He then went on to spend several years designing a reusable spacecraft for the Soviet Union, and was made a Colonel of the Soviet Air Forces in 1963. In 1968, he was killed during a training accident.

CAREER HIGHLIGHTS

1961 **Becomes the first human in space, and the first to orbit Earth**

H

▷ HANNO THE NAVIGATOR

CARTHAGINIAN, c. 500 BCE

Originating from the Phoenician city of Carthage in present-day Tunisia, Hanno made the earliest

SOVIET COSMONAUT YURI GAGARIN IN THE CAPSULE OF VOSTOK 1, 1961

HANNO THE NAVIGATOR ENCOUNTERS "GORILLAI" OFF THE WEST COAST OF AFRICA

recorded journey down the west coast of Africa. The story was carved onto a stone tablet in Phoenician, but when the Romans razed Carthage to the ground in 146 BCE, the tablet was lost or destroyed. Thankfully, a Greek translation survived. This account describes an expedition to colonize the coast to the west of the Strait of Gibraltar, and a voyage that was made to what is probably the River Senegal. It tells of a fleet of 60 ships, each carrying 50 oarsmen and some 500 men and women, plus supplies.

Hanno probably kept close to the coast to allow settlers to disembark at regular intervals. Sailing up a great river, probably the Senegal, Hanno describes elephants, crocodiles, and hippopotamuses (or "river horses"), and reaching "an immense opening of the sea," which is thought to have been the Gambia estuary. Toward the end of the journey, Hanno descibes an encounter with a species of semi-human "gorillai" on an island off the coast: "We pursued but could take none of the males; they all escaped to the top of precipices, which they mounted with ease, and threw down stones; we took three of the females, but they made such violent struggles, biting and tearing their captors, that we killed them, and stripped off the skins, which we carried to Carthage."

CAREER HIGHLIGHTS

c. 500 BCE Sails from Carthage down the west coast of Africa

▽ HARKHUF

c. 2230 BCE

Harkhuf is the earliest recorded explorer. He was born into a noble family on Elephantine, an island on the Nile river, close to Egypt's border with Nubia (present-day northern Sudan), and served as a court official to two pharaohs of Egypt's 6th Dynasty: Merenra and Pepi II. Records from the wall of his tomb show that he made four expeditions to Nubia, traveling along the Nile to Yam, or Iyam, which archaeologists believe was the fertile plain south of present-day Khartoum, at the confluence of the Blue and White Niles.

On his first mission, Harkhuf traveled with his father, Iri, known as "Overseer of Interpreters," and befriended various Nubian chiefs. On subsequent missions, he led his own party. Merenra sent him on a third mission, bearing royal gifts to pacify warring Nubian tribes. After Merenra's death, Harkhuf traveled south again, returning with a pygmy for the new boy-pharaoh, Pepi II. Of the pygmy, Hanno wrote: "When he goes down with thee into the vessel, appoint excellent people, who shall be beside him on each side of the vessel; take care lest he fall into the water... My majesty desires to see this dwarf more than the gifts of Sinai and of Punt." No Egyptian traveled further south for another 800 years.

CAREER HIGHLIGHTS

c. 2230 BCE Made Nubian-controlled trade routes available for Egypt

THE TOMB OF HARKHUF, QUBBET EL-HAWA NECROPOLIS, ASSUAN, EGYPT

▷ ZHENG HE

1371–1433

Court eunuch and admiral Zheng He (whose birth name was Ma He) was born into a Muslim family in Kunyang (present-day Jinning), southwestern China. At the age of 10, he was captured by the Ming Army and, according to common practice at the time, was castrated and dispatched to serve at the Imperial Court in Peking.

CHINESE MARINER, EXPLORER, DIPLOMAT, AND FLEET ADMIRAL ZHENG HE

Between 1405 and 1433, Zheng He made six voyages and directed a seventh around the rim of the Indian Ocean, reaching as far as Malindi on the eastern coast of Africa. The voyages were remarkable not only for their attempt to assert Chinese dominance over the major trading ports of Southeast Asia, Arabia, and East Africa, but also for their colossal scale. Zheng He's first fleet is said to have been manned by 28,000 sailors, and included over 60 treasure ships, some of which were 450 feet (140 m) long. No larger fleet would be seen in the Indian Ocean until World War II. Zheng He was appointed Defender of Nanjing in 1425, but died shortly after his final voyage in 1433. As befitted an admiral, he was buried at sea.

CAREER HIGHLIGHTS

1405–09 Makes two voyages to Calicut, on the west coast of India

1409–15 Makes two voyages to Hormuz and Arabia, visiting the Maldives and reaching Jeddah, from where he continues to Mecca to complete his hajj

1421–22 Returns to Africa, sailing as far south as Malindi

1430–33 Completes a final voyage, but its route is unknown

▷ SVEN HEDIN

SWEDISH, 1865–1952

When he was growing up in Sweden, geographer, explorer, and travel writer Sven Hedin devoured the stories of explorers, both real and fictional, and was determined to emulate them. As a student, he traveled through Russia, the Caucasus, and Persia, and was caught out in a snowstorm in the Elburz Mountains and almost died.

He returned to the region in 1890 and set off along the ancient caravan route through Persia to Samarkand and Kashgar. In 1893, he set out again, this time for the Taklamakan Desert in Central Asia. The expedition almost ended in disaster when it ran out of water, but Hedin decided to press on, and eventually found the lost city of Dandan Uiliq, where he collected many artifacts. He repeated the journey again in 1899–1902, and in 1906–08, mapped unknown parts of Central Asia. A Nazi in later life, he was redeemed by saving many Danish Jews from concentration camps.

CAREER HIGHLIGHTS

1890 **Undertakes his first expedition in Persia**
1893 **Explores Central Asia and the Taklamakan Desert**
1899 **Returns to the Taklamakan**
1906 **Maps Central Asia**

SWEDISH EXPLORER SVEN HEDIN AND TWO COSSACKS ON AN EXPEDITION IN THE HIMALAYAS, c. 1900

AFRICAN AMERICAN POLAR EXPLORER MATTHEW HENSON

◁ MATTHEW HENSON

AMERICAN, 1865–1952

Matthew Henson is best known for having discovered the North Pole with Robert Peary. Henson's extraordinary life owes much to a chance encounter in a fur store in Washington, DC. An African American orphan from Maryland, he had sailed the seas for six years as a cabin boy before encountering Robert Peary, the polar explorer. Impressed with Henson's seafaring experience, Peary hired him first as a valet for a canal-building survey in Nicaragua in 1887, and then to join him in 1891 on an expedition to Greenland, the first of six expeditions to try and reach the North Pole.

Henson proved himself to be not only a skilled dog- and sled-handler, but also a hard worker, well able to withstand the cold. He also befriended the Inuit, learning their language and their survival skills.

Henson's achievement in having accompanied Peary on the expedition that the latter claimed took him to the North Pole in 1909 remained largely unrecognized—both by Peary and indeed the wider world. Henson later worked as a clerk in a customs house, and was only honored at the end of his life.

CAREER HIGHLIGHTS

1887 **First meets polar explorer Robert Peary in Washington, DC**
1891 **Makes the first of six expeditions with Peary to the polar regions, which continue until 1909**
1912 **Publishes his memoir, *A Negro Explorer at the North Pole***
1954 **Receives a presidential citation from President Eisenhower**

THOR HEYERDAHL ON THE OPEN SEA, CROSSING THE NORTH ATLANTIC FROM MOROCCO TO BARBADOS IN HIS PAPYRUS BOAT *RA II*, 1970

▽ THOR HEYERDAHL

NORWEGIAN, 1914–2002

Anthropologist Thor Heyerdahl was born in Larvik in Norway, the only child of elderly parents. A maverick, he completed several remarkable voyages on flimsy craft, hoping to find evidence that ancient peoples could have crossed the world's oceans. Some of Heyerdahl's theories about transoceanic contacts have failed to stand the test of time, but his voyages showed how it was indeed possible to sail the world using basic craft.

Heyerdahl's interest in this field began when, having abandoned his studies in Oslo, he spent time in the South Pacific in 1937 and became convinced that people had migrated to Polynesia not from Southeast Asia, as had been thought up until then, but from South America. In 1947, he set out to prove his hypothesis by sailing 4,000 miles (6,500 km) across the Pacific from Peru to French Polynesia on the *Kon-Tiki*, a simple balsawood raft that he had built himself.

He next tried to prove that ancient mariners could have crossed the Atlantic from Africa. Heyerdahl based his boat design on records from ancient Egypt, and named the craft *Ra*, after the Egyptian sun god. Battered by storms, *Ra* sank, but Heyerdahl succeeded with his second attempt, *Ra II*, in 1970. His final voyage was on a reed boat around the Arabian coast in 1978.

CAREER HIGHLIGHTS

1947 Crosses the Pacific on the wooden raft *Kon-Tiki*
1970 Successfully crosses the Atlantic on the papyrus-built *Ra II*
1978 Sails the reed boat *Tigris* around the Persian Gulf

▷ EDMUND HILLARY AND TENZING NORGAY

HILLARY: NEW ZEALANDER, 1919–2008
NORGAY: NEPALESE, 1914–86

When selecting climbers to reach the summit of the yet unconquered Mount Everest, the world's highest mountain at 29,029 feet (8,848 m), mountaineers Edmund Hillary and Tenzing Norgay were not the first choice. Two Britons had been chosen by the expedition leader, John Hunt, but they ran into difficulties 1,000 feet (300 m) from the summit and had to turn back.

Norgay was an experienced and formidable mountaineer but Hillary was, by his own admission, no "hot-shot rock climber." But the New Zealander had huge reserves of determination and, with the aid of bottled oxygen to help combat the effects of extreme altitude, the pair made it to the top of the mountain at 11:30 am on May 29, 1953.

There has always been some controversy over who reached the summit of Mount Everest first. Hillary maintained that both men arrived at the same time, but Norgay later revealed that Hillary had been ahead of him by a few paces. There also remains the issue of whether climbers George Mallory and Andrew Irvine had reached the top in 1924. However, since they both died on the mountain, the honor went to Hillary and Norgay.

CAREER HIGHLIGHTS

1953 Hillary and Norgay become the first recorded climbers to scale Mount Everest
1958 Hillary becomes the first person to reach the South Pole by land since Robert Scott in 1912

THOMAS HIRAM HOLDING

ENGLISH, 1844–1930

Until the start of the 20th century, camping was considered to be an uncomfortable necessity rather than a pleasant way to spend a holiday. The man who challenged that perception was an English traveling tailor.

Thomas Holding first developed his passion for camping when he crossed the United States with his parents in a wagon train in 1853, at just nine years old. In 1877, seeking an escape from smog-filled London, he camped with a canoe while in the Highlands of Scotland, and made a similar trip the following year.

Two books resulted from Holding's ventures. After a cycling holiday, he wrote *Cycle and Camp* in 1898. Then, in 1901, he formed the Association of Cycle Campers, the first camping club in the world. By 1907, it had merged with a number of other clubs to form the Camping Club of Great Britain. A year later, Holding published *The Camper's Handbook*, extolling the "charm and freedom of Camping."

CAREER HIGHLIGHTS

1878 Holding and others form the Bicycle Touring Club
1901 Forms the Association of Cycle Campers
1908 Publishes *The Camper's Handbook*

EDMUND HILLARY AND TENZING NORGAY ASCENDING MOUNT EVEREST, NEPAL, 1953

HUDSON THE DREAMER LANDING ON THE SHORES OF DELAWARE BAY, JEAN LEON GEROME FERRIS, 1609

△ HENRY HUDSON

ENGLISH, c. 1560–1611

Little is known of the life of Henry Hudson, but his fame rests on four expeditions that attempted to find a sea route from Europe to China through the Arctic Ocean.

Sponsored by the Muscovy Company of London, which sought a sea route to the east, Hudson set sail in 1607 for the Svalbard archipelago and Greenland, sailing further north across the Arctic Circle than any previous explorer. His second expedition, in 1608, attempted to find a sea route around the north of Russia, but pack ice halted progress at the Novaya Zemlya islands. Next, sponsored by the Dutch East India Company, he headed west in 1609, and explored a river in New York State that has since been named after him. In 1610, he set sail again, this time into a vast inland bay that also bears his name. Frozen in the ice and forced to stay the winter, his crew mutinied and cast him adrift, along with his young son and six others. They were never seen again.

CAREER HIGHLIGHTS

1607 Explores Svalbard and Greenland
1608 Travels further east to the Arctic islands of Novaya Zemlya
1609 Sails across the Atlantic to explore the Hudson River
1610–11 Makes his final voyage into Hudson Bay, where his crew mutinies and sets him adrift

▷ ALEXANDER VON HUMBOLDT

PRUSSIAN, 1769–1859

Born in Berlin to a prominent military family, Alexander von Humboldt was destined for a sober career (he studied finance and political science at college)—but his passion for scientific exploration took over. He undertook two geological journeys in Europe, but after the death of his mother in 1796, and his acquisition of a considerable inheritance, he resigned from his government post as Assessor of Mines and dedicated himself to science.

In 1799, Humboldt set off for Latin America, noting on the voyage that the rotation of the Earth did not affect the direction of sea currents. He also hypothesized that the two landmasses on either side of the Atlantic—Africa and South America—were originally one continent. In South America, on a four-month expedition that covered over 1,725 miles (2,776 km), he discovered the link between the water systems of the Orinoco and Amazon rivers. He also studied the fertilizing qualities of guano, which was later introduced to Europe as a result of his writings. After exploring Peru, he sailed to Mexico, and then met with President Jefferson in Washington DC.

On returning to Europe, Humboldt wrote up his theories and made a final 9,500-mile (15,000-km) journey across Russia. The first truly modern scientist of the natural world, Humboldt was also probably the last person to contribute to so many different fields of knowledge.

CAREER HIGHLIGHTS

1789 First geological tour up the Rhine Valley
1795 Makes a second geological tour, this time to Switzerland and Italy
1799–1804 Makes lengthy visit to Latin America, visiting Cuba, the Amazon basin, the Andes, and Mexico
1828 Crosses Russia
1845 Publishes the first volume of *Kosmos*, in which he attempts to unify all scientific knowledge

I

KURBAT IVANOV

COSSACK, UNKNOWN–1666

Born on an unknown date by the Yenisei River in Central Siberia, Kurbat Ivanov, a Russian Cossack, was one of the greatest explorers of Siberia, and its premier cartographer. Using information supplied by the explorer Ivan Moskvitin (the first Russian to reach the Pacific Ocean), Ivanov drew the very first map of the coastline of the Sea of Okhotsk in 1642. The following year, he set off with a team of 74 men—and a Tungus prince named Mozheul to guide them—to sail south up the Lena River, crossing the Primorsky Ridge to become the first Russian to see the vast Lake Baikal. Part of his team perished exploring the northern tip of the lake, but Ivanov returned safely to record his findings in *The Chart of Baikal, its Rivers and Surrounding Lands*.

It is unclear what Ivanov did for the next few years, but in 1660 he sailed to Cape Dezhnyov, the easternmost part of mainland Asia. On the basis of this and other expeditions, he made a map of Siberia and the Bering Strait, showing both the Diomede Islands in the strait and Alaska to the east, although it is doubtful that he saw those lands himself.

ALEXANDER VON HUMBOLDT, PIONEER OF EVIDENCE-BASED SCIENCE

CAREER HIGHLIGHTS

1642 Maps the Russian Far East coastline
1643 Discovers Lake Baikal
1660 Sails to east Siberia and maps the Bering Strait

MARGERY KEMPE

ENGLISH c. 1373–c. 1438

The largely overlooked English Christian mystic Margery Kempe deserves to be remembered for two reasons: her extensive travels in Europe and the Holy Land at a time when women did not travel, and her authorship of *The Book of Margery Kempe*, considered to be the first autobiography in the English language.

Kempe was born in Bishop's (now King's) Lynn in Norfolk, UK, the daughter of a merchant and member of parliament for the town. In about 1393, she married John Kempe, a town official, with whom she had at least 14 children. A devout Christian, she experienced visions of God and wept copiously in public as she begged for forgiveness for her sins.

In 1413, Kempe left England on the first of many pilgrimages, traveling to the holy places of Palestine. She later made a pilgrimage to the shrine of St. James in Santiago da Compostela in Spain. When she returned, she dictated her story to a scribe (she was probably illiterate), describing her visions, her travels, her sexual temptations, and her trials for heresy. These heresies were in fact in the minds of her accusers, and on each occasion she was acquitted by the church authorities.

CAREER HIGHLIGHTS

1413 Undertakes a pilgrimage to Jerusalem
1417–18 Makes a pilgrimage to Santiago da Compostela in Spain
1433 Travels to Danzig and Aachen in Germany

▽ MARY KINGSLEY

ENGLISH, 1862–1900

As was usual for a middle-class English Victorian girl of her day, Mary Kingsley received no formal education. However, she read widely, and devoured the newspapers her father, a doctor, brought back from his travels. When her parents died in 1892, she was free to travel, and by then, she was desperate to flee the restrictions of Victorian society. For the sake of respectability, she obtained a commission from the British Museum to collect "fetishes," or artifacts of African religion.

Mary's first expedition took her to Angola and inland through the Congo and Gabon. She returned two years later, in 1895, determined to explore the little-known Ogowé River of Gabon. She narrowly escaped death when she fell into an animal trap, encountered a village of cannibals, and climbed the volcanic Mount Cameroon. A fervent champion of racial equality, she treated Africans with great respect, and uniquely traveled either alone or with an entirely African crew.

CAREER HIGHLIGHTS

1893–94 Sails from Nigeria to Angola, and then through the Congo and Gabon
1895 Returns to Africa to explore Gabon and Cameroon
1900 Dies in South Africa, nursing prisoners of the Second Boer War

MARY KINGSLEY, EXPLORER OF AFRICA AND CHAMPION OF RACIAL EQUALITY

PIROGUE RACES ON THE BASSAC RIVER, FROM DOUDART DE LAGRÉE'S POSTHUMOUS *ATLAS OF A VOYAGE OF EXPLORATION IN INDOCHINA*

L

△ DOUDART DE LAGRÉE

FRENCH, 1823–68

In 1866, the French colonial authorities in Indochina decided to mount an expedition to map the Mekong River and assess whether it could be used to connect the port of Saigon with the riches of China and upper Siam (Thailand).

The man they chose to lead this expedition was Ernest Doudart de Lagrée, a naval captain, and a keen entomologist. Born in Saint-Vincent-de-Mercuze, France, he attended the École Polytechnique, and then joined the navy. De Lagrée was plagued by ill health throughout his life. When he was asked to go on the expedition, he had hoped that the climate would improve his ulcerated throat. Instead, de Lagrée developed fever, amoebic dysentery, and infected wounds, the latter caused by walking barefoot once the supply of spare shoes had run out. By the time the expedition reached Yunnan province in southern China, he was too sick to move, and died of an abscess of the liver.

In all, the expedition traveled over 6,800 miles (11,000 km), sailing to Shanghai up the Yangtze River and then returning to Saigon. It failed to enrich France, but it filled in many of the blanks on contemporary maps.

WILLIAM LAMBTON

ENGLISH, 1753–1823

As British rule extended over India during the 1700s, the need for proper maps became imperative. Boundaries between regions had to be drawn, and distances—previously only guessed at—had to be measured accurately. To this end, surveyor William Lambton was employed by the British East India Company in 1802. His chief instrument was a theodolite—a rotating device featuring a telescope with which horizontal and vertical angles could be measured.

Lambton came from a poor background, but was skilled at mathematics and used his talent for surveying while serving in the American colonies in the 33rd Regiment. His initial task in India was to survey the width of the country from Madras to Mangalore. He measured it at 360 miles (580 km), which was 40 miles (64 km) shorter than previously thought. He then continued northward, beginning the process of establishing a "gridiron" of triangulation chains running from north to south and east to west across India. He did this for more than 20 years, until his death while at work in Central India. His successor, George Everest, surveyed into the Himalayas, the tallest of which bears his name. The Great Trigonometrical Survey of India was finally completed in 1871.

CAREER HIGHLIGHTS

1802–23 Works on the Great Trigonometrical Survey of India

▽ RICHARD LANDER

ENGLISH, 1804–35

Mapping the Niger river had been the great goal of British explorers ever since Mungo Park first caught sight of the river in 1796. The person who finally did so was Richard Lander.

Born in Cornwall, UK, the son of an innkeeper, Lander showed early promise as an explorer, walking to London at the age of nine and sailing to the West Indies at the age of 11. Later, he assisted English travelers in Europe and South Africa. His big break came in 1825, when he accompanied Hugh Clapperton on his second expedition to follow the course of the Niger. Clapperton died before the mission was completed, but Lander returned to London with Clapperton's papers and persuaded the British government to fund another mission. So he set off again in 1830, this time accompanied by his brother, and traced the river to its mouth in the Gulf of Benin. When he returned, he was awarded a Royal Geographical Society medal: "for important services in determining the course and termination of the Niger."

In 1832, Lander led a final mission, this time with the aim of establishing a trading settlement at the junction of the Niger and Benue rivers. However, he was attacked by locals while he was canoeing upstream, and died of his injuries on February 6, 1834.

CAREER HIGHLIGHTS

1825–27 Explores the Upper Niger with Hugh Clapperton
1830–31 Explores the Niger down to its delta with his brother John
1832 Is awarded the Royal Geographical Society's Founder's Medal for "determining the course and termination of the Niger"

RICHARD AND JOHN LANDER VISIT THE KING OF BADAGRY, LAGOS, NIGERIA

RICHARD LASSELS

ENGLISH, c. 1603–68

Richard Lassels was born in Lincolnshire, UK, around 1603. He studied at the English College in Douay, in what was then the Spanish Netherlands, becoming Professor of Classics in 1629. On March 6, 1631, he was ordained a Roman Catholic priest and became tutor to several members of the English nobility. He accompanied them on three journeys in Flanders, six in France, five in Italy, and one through Germany and the Netherlands.

Lassels' tour of Italy prompted his best-known book, *Voyage or a Complete Journey through Italy* (1670), in which he asserts that any serious student of antiquity, architecture, and the arts should travel in France and Italy. Indeed, he says that all "young lords" should make what he called the Grand Tour in order to understand the economic, social, and political realities of the world. The Tour soon became a rite of passage for young, upper-class Englishmen—or middle-class men who could find a sponsor. It remained so until the 1840s, when rail travel made such journeys possible for all classes of society, and helped to demythologize Europe.

CAREER HIGHLIGHTS

1670 Publication of *Voyage or a Complete Journey through Italy*

AN 18TH-CENTURY DEPICTION OF THE MYTH OF PONCE DE LEÓN AT THE FOUNTAIN OF YOUTH

△ JUAN PONCE DE LEÓN

SPANISH, 1475–1521

Much of Juan Ponce de León's life is a mystery, but we do know that he was a Spanish noble who saw that his future lay in the New World. After fighting to evict the Moors from Spain in 1492, he joined Columbus's second voyage to the Americas in 1493, landing in Hispaniola (modern-day Haiti and the Dominican Republic). He is next mentioned in 1504, playing a leading role in crushing a rebellion in Hispaniola. As a reward for this, he was made a provincial governor. In 1508, he sailed to Puerto Rico and amassed huge quantities of gold. He then returned to Hispaniola and was made governor of the colony—although his failure to quell a second revolt led to his dismissal.

In 1513, hearing of rich islands to the north, Ponce de León sailed to a land he called *La Florida* (Land of Flowers). Some say that he went in search of the mythological fountain of youth, but there is no evidence to support this. He claimed Florida for Spain, but was killed by locals when he returned to take possession in 1521.

CAREER HIGHLIGHTS

1493 Joins Columbus's second expedition to the New World
1508–09 Explores Puerto Rico
1513 Discovers Florida

CHARLES LINDBERGH PREPARES TO FLY A CURTISS "PUSHER" MONOPLANE

▽ MERIWETHER LEWIS & WILLIAM CLARK

LEWIS: AMERICAN, 1774–1809
CLARK: AMERICAN, 1770–1838

In 1803, President Thomas Jefferson negotiated to buy a vast expanse of land west of the Mississippi River from France. This "Louisiana Purchase" cost a total of $15,000, and roughly doubled the size of the newly independent US. As the land was largely unknown, Jefferson sent out an expedition to map the new region and establish a route to the Pacific. Captain Meriwether Lewis led the mission, choosing William Clark as his assistant.

The expedition set off from Camp Dubois in Illinois on May 14, 1804, and headed up the Missouri River. The men spent the winter at the newly built Fort Mandan, where they recruited a French-Canadian fur trapper named Toussaint Charbonneau and his Shoshone wife, Sacagawea, who served as an interpreter. Sacagawea proved invaluable when she acquired the horses they needed to cross the Rockies from the Shoshone people.

Lewis and Clark reached the source of the Missouri on April 12, 1805, then followed the Columbia River Valley all the way to the Pacific, which they reached on November 20. Returning to St. Louis the following year, the pair reported back on their successful expedition to President Jefferson.

ILLUSTRATION OF LEWIS AND CLARK IN *THE AMERICAN FRONTIER*, 1931

CAREER HIGHLIGHTS

1804–05 Outward journey from Camp Dubois to the Pacific coast
1805–06 Return journey back up the Columbia River
1806 Lewis and Clark split up; Lewis follows the Missouri River and Clark the Yellowstone River

△ CHARLES LINDBERGH

AMERICAN, 1902–74

On the morning of Friday, May 20, 1927, American Air Mail pilot Charles Lindbergh became a hero due to one flight. The unknown aviator took off from Roosevelt Field on Long Island, New York, in an attempt to win the Orteig Prize of $25,000 offered to the first airman to fly non-stop across the Atlantic in either direction. Flying the *Spirit of St. Louis*, a single-seat monoplane, Lindbergh flew 3,600 miles (5,800 km) in 33½ hours, landing at Paris's Le Bourget airport on 10:22pm on Saturday, May 21.

Lindbergh was immediately hailed as a hero on both sides of the Atlantic, but tragedy struck when his infant son Charles was kidnapped and murdered in 1932. After this "crime of the century," as it was called, the Lindberghs fled to Europe to avoid unwelcome attention. When they returned to the US in 1939, Lindbergh campaigned vigorously against American involvement in World War II. He was accused of having fascist sympathies for doing so, but when the US entered the war in 1941, he flew 50 combat missions in the Pacific against the Japanese.

CAREER HIGHLIGHTS

1927 Flies solo non-stop across the Atlantic Ocean
1935–39 After his son's kidnapping, flees with his family to Europe
1940 Becomes a spokesman for the anti-war American First Committee
1944 Flies in combat missions against the Japanese

▽ DAVID LIVINGSTONE

SCOTTISH, 1813–73

A national hero by the time of his death, David Livingstone rose from humble origins in Scotland to become a doctor, then a missionary, and finally an explorer in Central Africa. He was driven for many years by an obsessive search for the source of the Nile River. Although he failed in this venture, he left an enduring legacy in the places he explored, ultimately opening them for colonization by Britain. His humane treatment of Africans set an example that at least some of the colonizers would follow.

Livingstone's first expedition took him from Cape Town up into the interior to establish his own mission at Mabotswa, in Botswana. From 1850 to 1856, he crossed the continent from coast to coast along the Zambezi River. In 1858, he sailed back up the river in a steamship, and discovered that the Zambezi was not navigable along its entire length. In 1866, he undertook his final expedition, this

THE COVER OF A BOOK ABOUT THE LIFE OF DAVID LIVINGSTONE, c.1875

ELLEN MACARTHUR PHOTOGRAPHED IN FALMOUTH, UK, 2000

time to find the source of the Nile. He failed, although he was famously found by explorer Henry Stanley in 1871, who reportedly asked: "Dr Livingstone, I presume?" When Livingstone died, in Central Africa, his body was carried to the coast and returned to a hero's burial in Britain.

CAREER HIGHLIGHTS

1841–49 Travels north from Cape Town to found a mission, and discovers Lake Ngami in Botswana
1850–56 Crosses the continent to Luanda on the Atlantic coast, then returns sailing down the Zambezi to the Indian Ocean
1858–64 Sails up the Zambezi River and walks to Lake Nyasa
1863–73 Searches for the source of the Nile

M

△ ELLEN MACARTHUR

BRITISH, 1976

Many people enjoy sailing, but few have taken it to such extremes as Ellen MacArthur. Inspired by the *Swallows and Amazons* books of Arthur Ransom as a child, she bought a dinghy when she was at school, paying for it with three years' worth of saved dinner money. In 1995, she sailed a yacht single-handedly around the British Isles, and in 1997, competed in a solo transatlantic race. She sprang to prominence in 2000, when she set the women's record for crossing the Atlantic solo from east to west, a record which still stands. A year later, she came second in the Vendée Globe solo round-the-world race, setting the women's solo circumnavigation record, which also still stands. A further Atlantic record, this time from west to east, was set in 2004. Best of all, in 2005 she beat the world record for a single-handed non-stop circumnavigation by more than one day, sleeping for no more than 20 minutes at a time and staying on constant lookout. Now retired from sailing, she campaigns for a circular economy that reduces waste and avoids pollution.

CAREER HIGHLIGHTS

2000 Sets the women's record for crossing the Atlantic east to west
2000–2001 Comes second in the round-the-world Vendée Globe race, and sets the women's record
2004 Sets a new record for the fastest west-to-east crossing of the Atlantic by a woman
2005 Breaks the solo, non-stop round-the-world record

▽ FERDINAND MAGELLAN

PORTUGUESE, 1480–1521

Portuguese navigator Ferdinand Magellan began his career sailing for Portugal, but after being wrongly accused of trading with the enemy (Spain), he transferred his allegiance to the Spanish king, whom he convinced to sponsor him to find a westward route to Asia. Vasco da Gama had pioneered the eastern route to Asia around Africa, and Christopher Columbus had sailed west and discovered America. Magellan proposed sailing west to the Americas, and heading south along the coast of South America to find a western route through to the Pacific.

Magellan set out in 1519, and despite mutinous crews, foul weather, and starvation, he found a channel (later named the Strait of Magellan) that led through the tip of South America into the Pacific. Unfortunately, Magellan was killed while helping a local chief in a war in the Philippines, and his crew returned to Europe without him. However, the expedition had been a success, and was the first to circumnavigate Earth.

CAREER HIGHLIGHTS

1505 Joins a fleet of Portuguese warships, enforcing their trade monopoly around the Cape of Good Hope
1512 Takes part in an expedition to Morocco, but is falsely accused of trading with the enemy
1519 Working for the Spanish government, he sets sails from Seville with five ships
1520 Sails through the Magellan Strait into the Pacific Ocean
1521 Killed in the Philippines

FERDINAND MAGELLAN DISCOVERS A CHANNEL THROUGH THE TIP OF SOUTH AMERICA

▽ SAKE DEAN MAHOMED

INDIAN, 1759–1851

Bengali traveler, surgeon, and entrepreneur Sake Dean Mahomed was one of the first and most notable Indian immigrants to Europe. He was also the first Indian to publish a book in English. Born in Patna, Bihar (then part of the Bengal Presidency), Sake learned much about Mughal customs from his father, who worked for the British East India Company. After his father died when he was 10, Sake served in the Company army as a trainee surgeon, traveling widely.

Following his mentor Godfrey Baker to England, he wrote his first book, which begins with praise for the past conquerors of India, and then goes on to describe several important cities in India. In 1810, after moving to London, he opened the first Indian restaurant in the country. When this venture failed, he moved to Brighton and set up a commercial "shampooing vapor masseur bath." This was a great success, and Sake became known as Dr. Brighton.

CAREER HIGHLIGHTS

1783 **Moves to Britain**
1794 **Publishes *The Travels of Dean Mahomed***
1810 **Opens the first Indian restaurant in Britain**
1814 **Opens Britain's first commercial "shampooing" bath in Brighton**

SAKE DEAN MAHOMED, WHO INTRODUCED SHAMPOOING TO EUROPE

GERMAN PAINTER, ENGRAVER, AND NATURALIST MARIA SIBYLLA MERIAN

△ MARIA SIBYLLA MERIAN

GERMAN, 1647–1717

The Frankfurt-born naturalist and scientific illustrator Maria Sibylla Merian was one of the most important contributors to the field of entomology. Her depictions of the metamorphosis of a butterfly were unparalleled at the time, and she discovered many new facts about insect life. She was three when her father died, but in 1651, her mother remarried, bringing Jacob Marrel, a flower- and still-life painter into their lives. Marrel encouraged Maria to draw and paint, particularly the insects and plants that she found.

Merian's first book of nature engravings, *New Book of Flowers*, appeared in 1675, when she was 28. A book about insects—*The Caterpillar's Marvellous Transformation and Strange Floral Food*—was published in 1679. 20 years later, in 1699, Merian and her daughter Dorothea set sail for South America on a scientific expedition, making them perhaps the first people to make a journey purely for the sake of science. Malaria cut their visit short, but her detailed studies in Suriname led to her book *Metamorphosis Insectorum Surinamensium*, which subsequently made her famous.

CAREER HIGHLIGHTS

1675 **Publishes *New Book of Flowers*, her first book of nature illustrations**
1679 **Publishes *The Caterpillar's Marvellous Transformation and Strange Floral Food***
1699–1701 **Travels to South America**
1705 **Publishes *Metamorphosis Insectorum Surinamensium***

MANSA MUSA

c. 1280–c. 1337

Apart from his pilgrimage to Mecca, Mansa Musa Keita I of Mali ("Mansa" means "sultan" in Mandinka) is known as one of the richest people in history. During his reign, Mali was the largest producer of gold at a time of high demand. On his pilgrimage, Mansa Musa took 80 camels, each of which carried 50–300 pounds (23–136 kg) of gold dust, which Musa distributed to the poor he met along the route.

Mansa Musa came to the throne of Mali in about 1312 and greatly expanded its territories across what are now Mali, Mauritania, Senegal, and Guinea. As a committed Muslim, he fostered the growth of Islam within his empire and felt duty-bound to undertake the hajj—the pilgrimage to Mecca. Along with 60,000 men, including 12,000 slaves, each of whom carried 4-pound (1.8-kg) gold bars, and heralds who carried gold staffs, he traveled for two years, crossing the Sahara Desert. He stopped off in Cairo, then traveled south through Arabia to Mecca.

CAREER HIGHLIGHTS

1312 **Becomes Sultan of Mali**
1324–25 **Makes the hajj to Mecca**

▽ FRIDTJOF NANSEN

NORWEGIAN, 1861–1930

One of the greatest polar explorers of all time, Norwegian Fridtjof Nansen adopted Inuit methods of traveling (including dress), and was famous for his willingness to take "considered risks". As a boy in rural Norway, he had developed a great passion for the outdoors and learned to ski and skate.

Nansen went on his first Arctic voyage when he was still in college. He studied the sea currents when the expedition ship, *Viking*, became frozen in the ice and drifted for months. During this time, he also observed a piece of wood that was frozen in the ice, and hypothesized that it must have come from Siberia. Later, he found out that he was right.

In 1888, he and five others skied "the wrong way" across Greenland (from the little-known east coast to the west), to considerable acclaim. Five years later, he set out on an even more remarkable mission aboard the *Fram*, believing that once the ship was frozen in the ice, sea currents would float it across the North Pole. His theory turned out to be incorrect, but his two-man assault on the Pole in 1895, although again unsuccessful, took him closer than anyone had ever been to that elusive place.

CAREER HIGHLIGHTS

1882 **Travels to the Arctic Ocean**
1888 **Skies across Greenland from east to west**
1893–96 **Attempts to float across the North Pole aboard the *Fram***
1895 **Makes a two-man attempt to reach the North Pole**
1906–08 **Serves as Norwegian ambassador to London**
1922 **Awarded the Nobel Peace Prize for humanitarian work in World War I**

FRIDTJOF NANSEN (FRONT) WAVES GOODBYE TO HIS CREW BEFORE HEADING FOR THE NORTH POLE IN FEBRUARY 1895

ENGLISH TRAVEL AUTHOR ERIC NEWBY, PHOTOGRAPHED IN 1992

△ ERIC NEWBY

ENGLISH, 1919–2006

Eric Newby was born at the end of an era when travel was undertaken with purpose and intent rather than for pleasure. His many travel books were entertaining to read, but they included much serious reflection about the people and places that he visited.

Born in London and educated at a good public school, Newby joined an advertising agency in 1938, and then served in the Black Watch and Special Boat Section during World War II. After being captured during an operation off Sicily in 1942, he was held prisoner, but managed to escape shortly after the Italian armistice of September 1943. His experiences in Italy became the subject of one of his best books, *Love and War in the Apennines* (1971). After the war, he worked in women's fashion until he became travel editor of *The Observer* in 1964.

Newby's most famous book, *A Short Walk in the Hindu Kush,* an account of his expedition to climb Mir Samir in Afghanistan, appeared in 1958.

CAREER HIGHLIGHTS

1942 **Held prisoner for a year in Italy**
1958 ***A Short Walk in the Hindu Kush* is published**
1964–73 **Becomes travel editor of *The Observer***

▽ CARSTEN NIEBUHR

GERMAN, 1733–1815

Self-taught mathematician and cartographer Carsten Niebuhr came from an impoverished background. He qualified as a surveyor and, in January 1761, set off from Copenhagen on a scientific expedition under the patronage of Frederick V of Denmark. His traveling companions were two Danes (a linguist and a doctor), a Swedish ex-soldier, a German artist, and a servant. The team adopted Turkish dress to avoid being identified as Europeans and traveled to Alexandria and Cairo, then across the Red Sea to Jeddah, and by land down the Arabian Peninsula. The party was beset by disease, and three members died before they reached Mocha, in Yemen. The remainder sailed across to Bombay, in India, but only Niebuhr survived the journey.

Niebuhr set off back to Europe by land, reaching Copenhagen in November 1767. He had written copious notes about the people, geography, and artifacts of the places he had seen, which he published as *Travels Through Arabia and Other Countries*. Of particular interest are his maps of Arabia, his charts of the Red Sea and the Persian Gulf, and his numerous sketches of towns. Altogether, they made the greatest single contribution to Europe's knowledge of Arabia in the 18th century. In 1809, Niebuhr was made a Knight of the Order of the Dannebrog, one of Denmark's highest honors.

CARSTEN NIEBUHR, DISGUISED AS A DISTINGUISHED ARAB IN YEMEN

CAREER HIGHLIGHTS

1761 Travels through Europe to Egypt and remains there for a year
1762–63 Explores the Arabian peninsula
1764–67 Travels solo by land from Bombay to Copenhagen via Muscat, Persia, Palestine, and Turkey
1774 The first book of the four-volume *Travels Through Arabia and Other Countries* is published. The book remains in print long after Niebuhr's death

▷ ADOLF ERIK NORDENSKIÖLD

FINNISH, 1832–1901

Mineralogist and geologist Adolf Erik Nordenskiöld is best remembered for being the first person to navigate the Northeast Passage between the Atlantic and Pacific oceans along the northern coast of Russia.

Born in Finland, Nordenskiöld was the son of an eminent geologist and explorer, and studied geology at the University of Helsinki before moving to Sweden in 1857. In 1858, he joined an expedition to Spitsbergen (in the present-day Norwegian Arctic), and within a few years, he was leading his own. In July 1868, he set off to see how close it was possible to sail to the North Pole. He believed that by late summer the Arctic would be free of ice, but he was greatly mistaken. He only reached a latitude of 81°42'N—and that was by "blasting ice in many places," according to the ship's captain.

Ten years later, after failing to walk to the North Pole, Nordenskiöld sailed in a steamship from Karlskrona via Spitsbergen to Asia in two months. The expedition became icebound and had to winter in Kolichin Bay, then it returned to Sweden via the southern route. The team were greeted as heroes, having been feared lost at sea.

CAREER HIGHLIGHTS

1868 Leads an expedition to see how close he can sail to the North Pole
1872 Fails to walk to the North Pole, but sets up three Arctic observation stations
1878 Successfully navigates the Northeast Passage
1880 Returns to Sweden via the southern route via the Bering Strait, Far East, India, the Suez Canal, and the Mediterranean

▷ KAZIMIERZ NOWAK

POLISH, 1897–1937

Born and raised in Poland, Kazimierz Nowak was a keen traveler, writer, and photographer. After four long-distance cycling adventures in Europe between 1925 and 1930, he decided to travel across Africa. In November 1931, he set out from Tripoli, Libya, with his seven-year-old bicycle. He followed the River Nile to the Great Lakes of the Rift Valley, trading with native tribes as he went, and reached Cape Agulhas at the tip of South Africa nearly three years later. He then turned around and set off across the continent again, reaching Algiers in November 1936. In all, he traveled 25,000 miles (40,000 km) and became the first man to travel the entire length of Africa and back again alone. Disease and malnutrition took its toll and he died a year later. He took photographs, kept diaries, and wrote letters throughout, but the first photographs from his travels were not published until 1962, and his writings did not appear until 2000.

ADOLF ERIK NORDENSKIÖLD WITH THE STEAMSHIP *VEGA* IN KOLCHIN BAY

POLISH WRITER KAZIMIERZ NOWAK, WHO TRAVELED WIDELY IN AFRICA

CAREER HIGHLIGHTS

1936 **Becomes the first person to travel solo from the North African coast to South Africa and back**
1962 **Publication of *Across the Black Land*, a collection of his photographs selected by his daughter**

P

▷ PAUL OF TARSUS

TURKISH, c. 5 BCE–c. 67 CE

A Roman citizen born of a Jewish family from the city of Tarsus in Asia Minor, St. Paul was one of the most important figures of the Apostolic Age. He traveled the Mediterranean to spread Christianity, and founded several churches in Asia Minor and Europe. He underwent a conversion while on the road to Damascus and was temporarily blinded. He spent the next 10 years in relative obscurity in his home town, then traveled extensively, spreading the Christian faith. He took advantage of his status as a Jew and a Roman citizen to minister to both the Jewish and Roman communities.

Paul's journeys spanned some 10 years and are described in the Acts of the Apostles in the Bible. The first took him from Antioch (in Turkey) to Cyprus, then into southern Asia Minor. On the second, he traveled from Jerusalem around the Mediterranean. His third journey took him from Galatia, in Central Turkey, to Ephesus (then the center of Christianity), then Macedonia and Greece, before he returned to Jerusalem.

CAREER HIGHLIGHTS

c. 31–36 CE **Is converted to Christianity**
c. 45–46 CE **Begins his travels. With Barnabas, another apostle, he travels to Jerusalem to deliver financial support from the Antioch community**
c. 55–58 CE **Writes the first of his extant epistles, to the Romans**

COMPTE LA PÉROUSE

1741–c. 1788

Jean François de Galaup was a French naval commander. Born near Albi, Southern France, he was known as "La Pérouse," the title of the family estate. He went to naval college at the age of 15, then saw action against the British during the Seven Years' War, and rose to the rank of commodore. In 1785, Louis XVI of France appointed him to continue the cartographical work of Captain James Cook, open new trade routes, and increase French scientific knowledge.

La Pérouse sailed from Brest in two ships, taking leading French scientists with him. They sailed across the Atlantic and around Cape Horn and surveyed the North American coastline; for centuries, their findings stood as the most exact record of the flora and fauna of the region. The ships then crossed the Pacific to Macao, China, and sailed on to Australia. In March 1788, they set out from Botany Bay toward New Caledonia, but they never arrived. The wrecks of both ships were found on the Santa Cruz Islands in 1825.

CAREER HIGHLIGHTS

1781 **Leads the French frigate *Astrée* to victory against the British in the Battle of Louisbourg during the Seven Years' War**
1782 **Captures two British forts in Hudson Bay, North America**
1786–87 **Crosses the Pacific, and arrives in Macao, China, in January 1787, from where collections and journals are dispatched to Paris**
1788 **Reaches Botany Bay, Australia, on January 26**

PAUL OF TARSUS, THE FIRST GREAT MISSIONARY OF THE CHRISTIAN FAITH

FRANCISCO PIZARRO SEIZING THE INCA OF PERU, JOHN EVERETT MILLAIS, 1846

▽ IDA PFEIFFER

AUSTRIAN, 1797–1858

At a time when women did not travel widely, Ida Pfeiffer was a pioneer. Born into a wealthy Austrian family in Vienna, she wore boys' clothes, received a boy's education, and at the age of five accompanied her father on a journey to Palestine and Egypt. In 1820, she married the much older Mark Pfeiffer, who was a lawyer. For political reasons he was unable to find work, so Ida was forced to give drawing and music lessons to support her family. She dreamed of traveling, and after the death of her husband (in 1838) and her sons' coming of age, she did just that.

AUSTRIAN TRAVELER IDA PFEIFFER, ENGRAVED c. 1856

Her first expedition was down the Danube river and across the Mediterranean Sea to Egypt. The success of her published account of the journey enabled her to set out on more extended explorations. After a trip to Scandinavia, she made two trips around the world, spending considerable time in both the Americas and the East Indies, and then a final trip to Madagascar.

CAREER HIGHLIGHTS

1842 Travels down the Danube to the Black Sea, Istanbul, and Egypt

1845 Explores Scandinavia and Iceland

1848–51 Completes her first journey around the world

1851–54 Completes her second journey around the world

1857 Visits Madagascar, but is involved in a coup against the government and is expelled

△ FRANCISCO PIZARRO

SPANISH, 1471–1541

Illegitimate and illiterate, Francisco Pizarro was an unlikely conquistador. After arriving in Panama as a poor Spanish colonist in 1502, Pizarro worked his way up through colonial society to become a leading citizen. He had already taken part in several expeditions, accompanying Balboa to the Pacific coast in 1513, but now he was ready to set out on his own. His first expedition to South America ended in failure, but on his second, he learned about the gold of the Inca Empire to the south. With a royal commission from Emperor Charles V, Pizarro set off again in 1531. At the time, the Inca Empire was engulfed in civil war, so his timing was perfect. His small force of heavily armed troops sprang a surprise attack against Emperor Atahualpa at Cajamarca in 1532. Despite offering a ransom of a roomful of gold, the captured emperor was killed and the empire fell to the Spanish. They ruled the region for the next 400 years.

CAREER HIGHLIGHTS

1502 Arrives in Panama as a colonist from Spain

1513 Joins the expedition to the Pacific coast led by Vasco Núñez de Balboa

1524–25 His first expedition to South America ends in failure

1526 On his second expedition, he learns about Inca gold

1531–33 Overthrows Emperor Atahualpa and conquers the Inca Empire

▽ MARCO POLO

VENETIAN, 1254–1324

It was Marco Polo's great fortune to be born into a rich family of jewel merchants in the mercantile port of Venice. He was only six when his father and uncle took him on a trading expedition to Constantinople and the Crimea. From there, they traveled on to Bukhara in Central Asia, where they stayed for three years. The Chinese ambassador from the court of Kublai Khan invited them to China, where they stayed until returning to Europe as ambassadors of the Khan.

Two years later, the Polos set out again, crossing Central Asia to revisit the Khan. Marco made a striking impression on him, and was sent to explore southern China and Burma. After 17 years in China, the Polos returned home, but Marco was soon caught in Venice's war with Genoa and was imprisoned by the Genoese. He dictated his memoirs to a fellow prisoner, Rustichello da Pisa, but was accused of telling lies. To this he responded: "I have only told you half of what I saw." The account was published as the *Book of the Marvels of the World*, also known as *The Travels of Marco Polo*, c. 1300.

CAREER HIGHLIGHTS

1260–69 Makes his first visit to China in the company of his father and uncle

1271–95 Second lengthy visit to China

1296–99 On his return to Venice, he is imprisoned by the Genoese and dictates his memoirs to a fellow prisoner

▷ PTOLEMY

GREEK, c. 100–c. 170 CE

Little is known about the life of Ptolemy, other than he was a Greek, or possibly a Greek-educated Egyptian, with Roman citizenship, who was born, lived, and died in Alexandria in the second century CE. We also know that he wrote three hugely important works of science. The first of them, the 13-volume *Almagest*, is the only extant treatise on astronomy from the period. The second, the *Tetrabiblos* (meaning "four books" in Greek) is a work of astrology. The most important one is the third, the *Geographia*, which is a major investigation into the state of geographical knowledge at the time of the Roman Empire.

Over eight books, the *Geographia* discusses the science of cartography, provides a gazetteer of the locations of every place known to the Romans, outlines the different projections necessary to construct a map of the world (he was the first to project the Earth on a two-dimensional surface), and provides a series of regional maps. Ptolemy's invention of latitude and longitude—a global system of coordinates for locating places on Earth—revolutionized cartography. Ptolemy's *Geographia* remained highly influential for more than 1,400 years.

CAREER HIGHLIGHTS

c. 130–40 CE Writes the *Almagest* and the *Tetrabiblos*

c. 150 CE Probable publication date of the *Geographia*

AN ENGRAVING FROM GREGOR REISCH'S *MARGARITA PHILOSOPHICA*, 1508, SHOWS PTOLEMY, "THE KING OF SCIENCE," GUIDED BY THE MUSE ASTRONOMY

THE POLO BROTHERS ARRIVE AT HORMUZ ISLAND IN THE PERSIAN GULF, IN A SHIP LADEN WITH GOODS FROM INDIA

PYTHEAS

GREEK, c. 350–c. 285 BCE

Around 325 BCE the Greek traveler Pytheas, a native of the Greek colony of Massalia (modern-day Marseilles), in the South of France, set sail for northern Europe. The exact reason for his voyage is unknown, but he had probably been asked by rich merchants to look for trade routes to the northern lands.

Pytheas avoided the Straits of Gibraltar, which the Carthaginians had closed to shipping, then crossed through France and sailed up the Bay of Biscay and across the English Channel to Britain. There he visited the tin mines of Cornwall and learned of the amber trade with Scandinavia. Eventually, he reached Thule, an unknown land that might have been Iceland. On the way there, he became the first person to describe the Midnight Sun (the Sun not setting in summer) and discovered icebergs and other Arctic phenomena. He was also the first person to suggest that the tides were caused by the Moon.

Both a geographer and an explorer, Pytheas made a contribution to the ancients' view of the world. His account of his travels has not survived, but it was well known in ancient times, and is quoted by many writers, including Strabo.

CAREER HIGHLIGHTS

c. 325 BCE Undertakes an epic voyage north from the Mediterranean Sea to northern Europe

23 CE Strabo quotes extracts of Pytheas's now lost account of his voyage in *Geographica*

ZHANG QIAN

CHINESE, c. 195–114 BCE

Born in the province of Shaanxi, Central China, Zhang Qian is famed for his journeys through the deserts and over the mountains of Central Asia to lands previously unknown to the Chinese. He pioneered the trails of the Silk Road, forging new trade routes with the West. He entered the service of the Chinese Han emperor in about 140 BCE and undertook three main missions. In the first (138–125 BCE), he traveled west from Chang'an, but was captured and held for 10 years by the Xiongnu, a nomadic people hostile to the Han.

A second journey in 124 BCE took Zhang further west to Daxia, but again he was blocked by hostile tribes. His third and final mission of 119–115 BCE took him to Central Asia. He returned having made trade contacts as far south as India, and was made a Grand Messenger in the Han court. Descriptions of his journeys are recorded in the *Shiji* or *Records of the Grand Historian*.

CAREER HIGHLIGHTS

119–115 BCE Establishes trade contact with the West
115 BCE Honored with the post of Grand Messenger, which ranks him among the nine highest ministers of the Han government

R

FERDINAND VON RICHTHOFEN

GERMAN, 1833–1905

Credited as one of the founders of modern geography, von Richthofen is best remembered for coining the phrase "Silk Road." He studied geology at the University of Berlin, and after graduating undertook geological research in the mountainous Tyrol region of Austria. In 1858, he was invited by the Prussian government to join a trade and diplomatic mission to East Asia. He wanted to undertake an expedition to China, but political unrest prevented this. Instead, he embarked on a geological survey of California's Sierra Nevada, and discovered gold fields in the process. He finally left for Beijing in the autumn of 1871 and crisscrossed imperial China, gaining access to most provinces.

In addition to geological survey work, von Richthofen wrote prolifically on all aspects of China, from its culture, climate, and politics, to the Chinese Army. On his return to Germany in 1872 he compiled his findings in a five-volume study.

CAREER HIGHLIGHTS

1859–61 Travels with a trade and diplomacy mission around east Asia
1861 Journeys through Thailand and Burma to Kolkata (Calcutta) on his own
1863 Begins pioneering studies of volcanic rocks in California
1877 The first of von Richthofen's five-volume study of China is published

S

SACAGAWEA

AMERICAN, 1788–1812

Born in Idaho, Sacagawea was the daughter of a Shoshone chief. At the age of 12, she was kidnapped by an enemy tribe and then became the wife of Toussaint Charbonneau, a trapper. In November 1804, Meriwether Lewis and William Clark hired Charbonneau as a guide for their expedition into the American West. They took Sacagawea as an interpreter, knowing they would need to buy horses from the Shoshone to reach the Pacific coast safely. Her skills as a translator and her knowledge of the terrain were invaluable. With Sacagawea's help, Lewis and Clark traded with the Shoshone and reached the Pacific after an arduous journey. Sacagawea, Charbonneau, and their baby son remained with Lewis and Clark throughout the arduous trip and eventually settled in Missouri.

CAREER HIGHLIGHTS

1804 Joins the Lewis and Clark Corps of Discovery expedition
1805 Successfully negotiates with the Shoshone for horses for the expedition

▽ ROBERT FALCON SCOTT

ENGLISH, 1868–1912

Born in Devonport, Plymouth, Scott began his naval career in 1881 as a cadet at the age of 13, and by October 1883 was en route to South Africa as midshipman aboard HMS *Boadicea*. Scott's first experience of the Antarctic came when he led the National Antarctic Expedition of 1901–04, which included Ernest Shackleton as Third Officer. Scott's ship, the purpose-built research vessel *Discovery*, landed at Cape Adare on January 9, 1902.

Scott made the continent's first balloon ascent to look for a possible route to the South Pole. After sheltering for the Antarctic winter, one party headed west in search of the South Magnetic Pole, while Scott, Shackleton, and physician Edward

ROBERT FALCON SCOTT BY A CRACK IN A SNOWFIELD DURING HIS *TERRA NOVA* EXPEDITION, 1911

Wilson headed for the South Geographical Pole. They turned back 500 miles (850 km) short of their goal. Scott finally made it to the pole on January 17, 1912, only to find that Norwegian Roald Amundsen had arrived 36 days earlier. The British team attempted to return to their base, but died due to bad weather and lack of supplies just 11 miles (18 km) short of One Ton Depot.

The last entry in their journals was on March 29. Scott wrote: "Had we lived, I should have had a tale to tell of the hardihood, endurance, and courage of my companions which would have stirred the heart of every Englishman."

CAREER HIGHLIGHTS

1901–04 Leads the National Antarctic Expedition to Antarctica, and sets a record for the furthest south traveled
1910–12 Returns to Antarctica, but is beaten to the South Pole in 1912

ERNEST SHACKLETON (CENTER), WITH ROBERT FALCON SCOTT AND EDWARD WILSON IN THE ANTARCTIC, 1903

▷ ERNEST SHACKLETON

IRISH, 1874–1922

A charismatic and driven figure, Irish polar explorer Ernest Shackleton went on four expeditions to the Antarctic. His first visit was as a member of Captain Scott's 1901–04 National Antarctic Expedition, when he was on the team that traveled further south than anyone had ever traveled before. He and three companions then established a new "farthest point south" record during his second 1907–09 expedition to the Antarctic aboard *Nimrod*.

But it is for his third expedition that Shackleton is most famous. As Amundsen had already reached the South Pole, he proposed an expedition to cross the continent, a journey of 1,800 miles (2,900 km).

Shackleton bought the 385-ton ship *Endurance* and the 425-ton *Aurora* for the job, and selected a crew of 56 from 5,000 applicants. The expedition very nearly ended in tragedy as his ship, the *Endurance*, became trapped in ice, but, remarkably, the entire crew was rescued and managed to return home safely.

On his fourth expedition to the Antarctic, Shackleton had a fatal heart attack on the Island of South Georgia.

CAREER HIGHLIGHTS

1901–04 Scott's expedition to Antarctica
1907–09 The *Nimrod* expedition to Antarctica sets a record for traveling to the furthest point south
1914–17 Undertakes the Imperial Trans-Antarctic expedition aboard *Endurance* and *Aurora*
1921 A final voyage on *Quest* ends in his death

▷ NAIN SINGH RAWAT

INDIAN, 1830–95

Born in India's Johar Valley on the border with Tibet, Nain Singh was the first of the late 19th-century indigenous surveyors, known as pundits, who explored regions to the north of India for the British. After leaving school, he helped his father in the traditional trans-border trade with Tibet. For the sake of his work, he learned to speak the Tibetan language and got to know Tibetan customs and manners.

At the age of 25, Nain Singh was recruited by German geographers Adolf and Robert Schlagintweit for a mission to explore Tibet. In 1863, he joined the Great Trigonometrical Survey, which, under the auspices of the British East India Company, measured the entire Indian subcontinent. Explorers were trained to record distances and went about their task disguised as monks or traders. Nain Singh undertook many journeys, traveling for months at a stretch, collecting intelligence, exploring, and mapping Tibet. He also trained surveyors and explorers.

In recognition of his achievements, Nain Singh was honored with many awards by London's Royal Geographical Society. In 1877, the Government of India bestowed two villages to him as a land grant.

CAREER HIGHLIGHTS

1855–57 Recruited to assist with a survey expedition in Tibet
1863–75 Employed on the Great Trigonometrical Survey
1877 Awarded Gold medal by the RGS

INDIAN EXPLORER AND CARTOGRAPHER NAIN SINGH RAWAT

▽ FREYA STARK

ITALIAN–ENGLISH, 1893-1993

Freya Stark was one of the first European women to explore the Hadhramaut, a remote desert area of southern Arabia. A cartographer and author, Stark explored freely, exploiting the fact that a lone woman traveler in the 1930s was an enigma. Stark described her journeys in evocative prose, producing more than 24 travel books and several volumes of letters and autobiographies.

Born in Paris to liberal-minded parents, Stark grew up in Italy and in Devon, England. In 1929, after learning Arabic and Persian, she made her first solo journey to Baghdad, Iraq. Two dangerous treks into the wilderness of Lorestan, in western Persia, followed. Here, Stark recorded the topography and local names for landmarks and villages. On her third journey, she located the fabled Valley of Alamut, known as "the Valley of the Assassins," in northern Persia. Her expedition to the Hadhramaut, undertaken in 1934, was in search of the lost ancient capital city of Shabwa, but Stark contracted measles and had to be airlifted out. Nevertheless, she recorded an intimate portrait of the people and landscape. Stark explored remote parts of Turkey in her 60s, and continued to travel in Nepal and the Pamir Mountains, before retiring in her 80s to Asolo, Italy.

CAREER HIGHLIGHTS

1934 **Travels in Hadhramaut, Yemen, searching for Pliny the Elder's lost city of Shabwa**

1934 ***The Valley of the Assassins and other Persian Travels*** **establishes Stark's career as travel writer**

1936 **Stark writes about her time in the Yemeni highlands in *The Southern Gates of Arabia***

1939–45 **Works for the British Ministry of Information in the Middle East, creating propaganda to encourage Arabs to support the Allies during World War II**

1942 ***Letters from Syria*** **describes Stark's 1928 travels in the region**

1972 **Made a Dame of the British Empire**

MARIANA STARKE

ENGLISH, 1761–1838

Writer Mariana Starke was arguably the first person to realize that 18th-century travel guides to the Grand Tour of Europe were of little use to family groups and people of ordinary means. Early in the 19th century, she produced practical guides for travelers in Italy and France that included essential information on luggage, passports, food, and accommodation. These became the template for modern guidebooks. They even included exclamation-mark ratings, the forerunner of the modern-day star rating system.

Starke grew up in colonial Madras (present-day Chennai), India, and spent six years in Italy. A writer of less successful plays and poetry, Starke returned to Italy after the Napoleonic Wars and devoted herself to revising and refining the guides that had earned her celebrity status. Mrs. Starke, as she was known, in spite of the fact that she never actually married, features in Stendhal's novel *The Charterhouse of Parma*. Stendhal writes of a traveling British historian who "never paid for the smallest trifle without first looking up its price in the *Travels* of a certain Mrs. Starke."

CAREER HIGHLIGHTS

1802 ***Travels in Italy, Between the Years 1792 and 1798*** **is published**

1820 **Publishes *Travels on the Continent: written for the use and particular information of travelers***

1828 **Publishes *Travels in Europe Between the Years 1824 and 1828***

FREYA STARK RIDING A MULE IN JABAL AL-DRUZE, SOUTHERN SYRIA, 1928

STRABO AS DEPICTED IN A 16TH-CENTURY ENGRAVING

△ STRABO

GREEK, 64/63 BCE–24 CE

A geographer, philosopher, and historian living in Asia Minor in the transition between the Roman Republic and Roman Empire, Strabo is celebrated for his work *Geographica* (*Geography*), a descriptive account of the known regions of his world.

Born into a wealthy family in Amaseia, in Pontus (now Amasya, Turkey), Strabo moved to Rome around the age of 21, where he studied philosophy and learned about parts of the empire that were unknown to him. Strabo went on to explore widely around the Mediterranean and in the Near East, traveling as far west as coastal Tuscany, and as far south as Ethiopia. He visited Kush in Egypt and sailed up the Nile to Philae. Strabo's *Geographica* sheds light on the ancient world, and reveals his early understanding of geology. He suggested that sea shells were found in landlocked terrain and at high altitudes because earthquakes and volcanic eruptions also occurred below the sea, lifting whole continents above sea level.

CAREER HIGHLIGHTS

c. 20 BCE **Writes *Historical Sketches*, his first major work**

c. 25 BCE **Sails up the Nile as far as Philae, Upper Egypt**

1469 ***Geographica*** **appears in Rome as a Latin translation**

c. 1516 **First Greek edition of *Geographica* published in Venice**

T

▷ ABEL TASMAN

DUTCH, 1603–59

Sea captain Abel Tasman's 17th-century expeditions were little appreciated in his time. The Dutch East India Company commander tried and failed to find new trade routes to South America and Australia. Nevertheless, his voyages increased Dutch knowledge of the Pacific, and led to the discovery of Tasmania, New Zealand, Fiji, and Tonga.

Born in Lutjegast, in the Netherlands, in 1603, Tasman rose to commander in the Dutch East India Company and was sent to its base in Batavia (present-day Jakarta) in 1638. On his first major voyage in command of the *Heemskerk*, Tasman caught the prevailing winds to sail via Mauritius, and then traveled southeast. He planted the Dutch flag on what became Tasmania, naming it Van Diemen's Land after the Governor-General of the Dutch East Indies. On the return journey east, the crew set foot on New Zealand and chartered island groups in the Pacific.

In January 1644, Tasman set out to discover whether New Guinea and Australia were part of the same landmass, but missed the Torres Strait that separates them, mistaking it for a shallow bay. The Dutch East India Company was disappointed with Tasman's expedition, and further explorations were shelved. Until Captain James Cook arrived 126 years later, no European landed in Tasmania or New Zealand, and mainland Australia was visited only by accident.

CAREER HIGHLIGHTS

1642 Lays claim to Van Dieman's Land (later named Tasmania)
1644 Second voyage to find a passage to the eastern side of New Holland (present-day Australia)
c. 1690 The Tasman Map is completed, based on original charts from Tasman's first and second voyages

OIL PORTRAIT OF ABEL TASMAN WITH HIS WIFE AND DAUGHTER, 1637

▽ WILFRED THESIGER

ENGLISH, 1910–2003

The son of a British diplomat, Wilfred Thesiger was born in Addis Ababa, Abyssinia, in present-day Ethiopia. As an Oxford undergraduate, he traveled to Constantinople (now Istanbul) on a tramp steamer, and to Iceland on a trawler. He served in the SAS in North Africa and the Middle East during World War II. In 1945, as part of a UN study of locusts in Arabia, he spent five years exploring the Rub' al Khali, the Empty Quarter, coming to know its Bedouin people intimately.

On the first of two crossings, a circular 1,500-mile (2,400-km) journey by camel, he mapped the oasis of Liwa and became the first European to see the fabled quicksands of Umm al Samim. Thesiger traveled for the rest of his life: he spent seven years during the 1950s with the Marsh Arabs in Iraq, journeyed with the Bakhtiari nomads of Iran, and explored the Hindu Kush, Afghanistan, India, Kenya, and West Africa. Thesiger received a knighthood in 1995.

CAREER HIGHLIGHTS

1930 Invited to the coronation of Emperor Haile Selassie of Abyssinia
1933 Leads an expedition to explore the course of the Awash River in Abyssinia
1959 Publishes *Arabian Sands* about his travels in the Empty Quarter of Arabia
1995 Knighted by Queen Elizabeth II
2004 The Pitt Rivers Museum in Oxford acquires Thesiger's huge collection of photographs

WILFRED THESIGER WITH HIS CAMEL, PHOTOGRAPHED ON A JOURNEY FROM THE AS SARUQ SANDS TO ABU DHABI, DUBAI, 1948

BERTRAM THOMAS CROSSING THE EMPTY QUARTER, IN AN ILLUSTRATION FROM 1970

△ BERTRAM THOMAS

ENGLISH, 1892–1950

Bristol-born Bertram Thomas was working as Finance Minister for the Sultan of Muscat when he made plans to become the first European to cross the Rub' al Khali. The 620-mile (1,000-km) journey would start from the Oman coast, going through Saudi Arabia to Qatar. The notorious Empty Quarter is an uninhabited, shifting desert with sand dunes reaching 820 feet (250 m) high. Thomas had to abandon his first attempt because his mountain camels were useless in the desert sands.

In October 1930, he sailed (secretly, because he was in competition with other explorers) from Muscat to Salalah, only to find that warring tribes had closed the route. He made an alternative plan, traveling with Salih bin Kalut, a sheikh of the Rashid tribe who shared his dream, plus 30 men and 40 camels. The pair negotiated safe passage from local tribes, traveling from one water source to the next, and surviving sandstorms and blood feuds. After 60 days, they reached the northern edge of the desert, and then the Persian Gulf.

CAREER HIGHLIGHTS

1916 Posted to Mesopotamia in World War I

1928 Makes camel journeys from Muscat to Sharjah and Muscat to Salalah

1932 Publishes a book about his journey, called *Arabia Felix*

1944 First director of the Middle East Center for Arabic Studies in Palestine

ENGLISH EXPLORER AND WRITER COLIN THUBRON, 2008

▷ CHARLES WYVILLE THOMSON

SCOTTISH, 1830–82

The modern science of oceanography really began with the voyage of HMS *Challenger*, which was commissioned by the Royal Society of London between 1872 and 1876. The expedition was led by Charles Wyville Thomson, a Professor of Natural History at the University of Edinburgh.

Thomson was born in West Lothian, Scotland, in 1830, the son of a surgeon who worked for the British East India Company. He had a particular interest in marine biology, studying invertebrates and making deep-sea dredging expeditions to the north of Scotland. For his historic expedition, which began on December 21, 1872, Thomson had HMS *Challenger*'s guns removed to make space for two laboratories.

Over a journey of nearly 69,000 nautical miles (130,000 km), Thomson and a team of scientists measured the depths of the oceans and took hundreds of soundings, trawls, dredgings, and temperature readings. More than 4,500 new species of marine life were discovered. Heralded as a great advancement in the knowledge of the planet, Thomson's expedition findings were eventually collated into a mammoth 50-volume report.

CHARLES WYVILLE THOMSON ON SHORE DURING THE HMS *CHALLENGER* EXPEDITION

CAREER HIGHLIGHTS

1870 Becomes the Regius Chair of Natural History at the University of Edinburgh

1872 HMS *Challenger* sets sail for its groundbreaking exploration of the marine environment

1877 Knighted by Queen Victoria

1983 The ill-fated NASA Space Shuttle *Challenger* is named in recognition of Thomson's expedition

◁ COLIN THUBRON

ENGLISH, 1939–

Acclaimed travel writer Colin Thubron is often described as a traveler from another age. Born in London in 1939, the Eton-educated son of a brigadier is an intrepid chronicler of places that have obsessed him throughout his working life—China, the old Soviet Union, Central Asia, Afghanistan, Iran, and Turkey. Thubron's lyrical exploration of a country's history, landscape, language, and traditions spring from a respectful immersion in the people and their culture.

His first travel book, *Mirror to Damascus*, published in 1967, is a "work of love" for a city with a rich artistic, social, and religious inheritance. Thubron has written books based on his extensive lone travels in the Middle East, Russia, and the Far East. *Shadow of the Silk Road*, published in 2006, chronicles his 7,000-mile (11,300-km) journey in rickety rail carriages, buses, and cars from China to the Mediterranean. Thubron lives in London and is also the author of several novels, including *God in the Mountains* (1977).

CAREER HIGHLIGHTS

1987 ***Behind the Wall: A Journey through China*** **wins the Hawthornden Prize and the Thomas Cook Travel Book Award**
1999 **Publication of** ***In Siberia***, **Thubron's account of his 15,000-mile (24,000-km) journey across Siberia after the breakup of the Soviet Union**
2007 **Awarded the CBE (Commander of the Order of the British Empire)**
2009 **Becomes President of the Royal Society of Literature**

△ MARK TWAIN

AMERICAN, 1835–1910

One of America's greatest writers, Samuel Langhorne Clemens (later known as Mark Twain) grew up in poverty, the sixth child in a family of seven children living by the Mississippi River in Hannibal, Missouri. In 1857, at the age of 22, Clemens became an apprentice steamboat pilot, plying the great river between St. Louis and New Orleans. Writing more than two decades later, Twain set his *Adventures of Huckleberry Finn* on the Mississippi of his childhood. Huck's journey in the novel, in which he sails downriver with an escaped slave, was a dark satire of the barbarous reality of life before the Civil War in the South.

When the American Civil War ended the river trade in 1861, Twain went west to prospect for silver but with little success. He was a journalist in California when his first short story, *Jim Smiles and His Jumping Frog*, was published in 1865. This was followed in 1869 by the bestselling *The Innocents Abroad*, a novel about Twain's journey from Europe to the Holy Land with a group of American travelers. Twain's travel writing and lecture tours established him as an international celebrity. He had written 28 books by the time of his death in Redding, Connecticut, in 1910.

PHOTOGRAPH OF AMERICAN WRITER MARK TWAIN, 1890s

CAREER HIGHLIGHTS

1869 **Publishes** ***The Innocents Abroad***
1876 ***The Adventures of Tom Sawyer*** **is published**
1883 **Publishes** ***Life on the Mississippi***, **a memoir of his early years as a steamboat pilot**
1885 **Publishes** ***Adventures of Huckleberry Finn*** **and a biography of President Ulysses S. Grant**

U

▽ NAOMI UEMURA

JAPANESE, 1941–84

Japanese adventurer Naomi Uemura undertook solo exploration in the most inhospitable parts of the Earth. Born in Hidaka, the youngest son of a rice farmer, Uemura was a student when he began climbing—something he hoped would build his strength and self-confidence. Just 5 ft 4 in (1.6 m) tall, but with remarkable stamina, Uemura rafted up the Amazon alone, walked the length of Japan, and scaled many of the world's highest peaks before conquering North America's highest mountain, Denali (formerly Mount McKinley), in Alaska.

In 1978, Uemara was the first lone explorer to mush a dog team to the North Pole. At one point, he was forced to lie still while a polar bear invaded his camp, and he was also temporarily stranded with his dogs when an ice floe broke apart. During Uemura's second attempt to climb Denali, in the winter of 1984, he reached the summit in temperatures as low as –50°F (–46°C). Unfortunately, he disappeared on his descent and was never found.

CAREER HIGHLIGHTS

1970 **Reaches the summit of Mount Everest in the first ever Japanese expedition**
1970 **First solo ascent of 20,310-foot (6,190-m) tall Denali, Alaska**
1976 **Sets the record for a 7,452-mile (12,000-km) solo dog-sled journey from Greenland to Alaska**
1978 **First person to reach the North Pole in a solo 500-mile (805-km) expedition across Arctic sea ice**

NAOMI UEMURA DURING HIS SOLO TREK TO THE NORTH POLE IN 1978

HUNGARIAN EXPLORER ÁRMIN VÁMBÉRY WEARING HIS TRAVELING CLOTHES, c. 1890

△ ÁRMIN VÁMBÉRY

HUNGARIAN, 1832–1913

Central Asia had been off limits to Westerners for more than 250 years when, in 1861, Ármin Vámbéry began a perilous journey to Samarkand, in present-day Uzbekistan, disguised as a Sunni dervish.

Born into a poor Jewish family in Szentgyörgy, Hungary (now in Slovakia) and lame from birth, Vámbéry showed an early aptitude for languages. He became a tutor in Constantinople (modern-day Istanbul), mastering some 20 Turkic dialects, and studying the Qur'an in preparation for his journey to find the origins of the Hungarian language.

Assuming the name Dervish Reshid Efendi, Vámbéry traveled by donkey, camel, cart, and on foot from Constantinople, via Trabzon on the Black Sea, to Tehran in Persia, where he joined a group of dervish pilgrims. After detouring to Shiraz, near the Persian Gulf, they traveled to Khiva, Bukhara, and Samarkand. Foreigners were routinely imprisoned, and the ruler of Samarkand grew suspicious of Vámbéry's "bold behavior," and requested an audience with him alone. However, Vámbéry withstood all challenges to his disguise.

Vámbéry returned to Constantinople via Herat, Afghanistan, in 1864. After visiting London to arrange for a book about his travels to be published in English, he was much in demand in elite British society and was recruited by the secret service as a foreign agent in Turkey.

CAREER HIGHLIGHTS

1861 Begins a journey from Constantinople to Samarkand disguised as a dervish

1865 Publishes *Travels in Central Asia* in English

1865 Becomes Professor of Eastern Languages and Hungarian Oriental Studies at Pest University

▷ AMERIGO VESPUCCI

ITALIAN, c. 1454–1512

A man of science and commerce, Amerigo Vespucci became an explorer when he was middle-aged, attracted to the excitement of New World navigation in the late 15th and early 16th centuries. Born in a village outside Florence, in present-day Italy, Vespucci was working in shipping in Seville, Spain, for the Medici family when he secured a place as an astronomer and cartographer on a Spanish ship.

After changing ship in the Caribbean to sail southeast, Vespucci described coastlines of trees, dense vegetation, and a huge outflow of fresh water where the River Amazon flows into the Atlantic. A journey by boat from the twin mouths of the Amazon up the Great River took them into an "Earthly paradise" of colorful wildlife. The ship traveled as far as Recife, in present-day Brazil, then sailed back to Spain via Trinidad, Venezuela, and the Caribbean island of Hispaniola.

On a second expedition, which lasted from 1501–02 and was led by the Portuguese explorer Gonçalo Coelho, Vespucci claimed to have charted "nearly 2,000 leagues of continental coast and more than 5,000 islands." The actual discovery of the New World had of course been made by Christopher Columbus, but Vespucci's revelation that the land belonged to a previously unknown continent, rather than to the coast of Asia as had been thought, forever changed people's understanding of the globe.

CAREER HIGHLIGHTS

1499 Secures a position as astronomer and cartographer on the Spanish expedition of Alonso de Ojeda

1501 A second Portuguese expedition convinces Vespucci that he has reached a new continent

1507 German cartographer Martin Waldseemüller names the new continent America—the feminine form of the name Amerigo

WILLIAM OF RUBRUCK

FLEMISH, c. 1220–93

"As God gives us the different fingers of the hand, so he gives to men diverse ways." With these words, the Great Khan of Mongolia rebuffed Friar William of Rubruck's attempts to convert him to Christianity. In 1253, William, a Flemish envoy of King Louis IX of France, was charged with taking the Christian faith to the

AMERIGO VESPUCCI HOLDING AN ASTROLABE, IN AN ENGRAVING BY JAN COLLAERT II, c. 1600

Mongols and forging an alliance against the Saracens of the Holy Land.

Traveling by ox-drawn cart, the Franciscan monk's arduous three-year journey took him from Acre in Palestine, via Constantinople, to the court of Batu Khan, ruler of the River Volga. Batu refused to convert and sent William on to Möngke—the Great Khan in Karakoram. William recorded Mongol culture, and debated with Buddhists and Muslims before the Great Khan, but none were converted. On his return to the Crusader state of Tripoli, he presented King Louis IX with a 40-chapter account of his travels, now held to be a masterpiece of medieval geographical literature.

CAREER HIGHLIGHTS

1248 Accompanies Louis IX, the king of France, on the Seventh Crusade to the Holy Land
1253 Travels to Karakoram on his mission to the Mongols
1254 Stays at the court of Möngke Khan for seven months

▷ FRANCIS XAVIER

SPANISH, 1506–52

Noted for his religious fervor, Francis Xavier was a pioneering missionary for the Catholic Church who traveled extensively across Asia in the 16th century. In many of these places, he was the first Christian missionary to ever visit. His missions enjoyed limited success, but his letters offer vivid descriptions of places that were little known to Europeans.

Born in Navarra, Spain, Xavier set sail from Lisbon to Goa in 1541 to minister to Portuguese communities in southern India, and to seek new converts. He traveled on to the Indonesian Spice Islands, then back to Malacca, in present-day Malaysia. In 1549, he became the first missionary explorer in Japan, and although kept at bay by the all-powerful Buddhist and Shinto religions, he became an admirer of Japanese culture. On a failed final mission to China in 1552, Xavier was forbidden access to the mainland. Lodged temporarily on San Chan, an island trading post off the Canton coast, he died of fever the same year.

17TH-CENTURY PAINTING OF FRANCIS XAVIER ABOARD THE *SANTA CRUZ*

CAREER HIGHLIGHTS

1542 Made an apostolic nuncio, an official envoy of the church by Pope Paul III
1549 Takes a Chinese junk from Goa, India, to Japan, following a Portuguese trade route
1552 Xavier's convert, Bernard, arrives in Lisbon—the first Japanese person known to set foot in Europe
1622 Canonized by the Roman Catholic Church

XUANZANG

CHINESE, c. 602–64

The writings of Xuanzang, a Buddhist monk and scholar who embarked on a 16-year pilgrimage across the mountains and deserts of Central Asia to India, are the stuff of myth and legend. Born in Henan Province, China, Xuanzang joined a Buddhist order of monks at 13, was ordained at the age of 20, and began his pilgrimage in search of holy texts, or *sutras*, in 629. Although foreign travel was prohibited because of war, Xuanzang found a route across the Liangzhou and Qinghai provinces and on into the Gobi Desert. He followed the northern Silk Road, crossing the Kyzylkum Desert, to reach the major trading city of Samarkand, in present-day Uzbekistan, and then Afghanistan.

Arriving in India in 630, he traveled widely, visiting sacred sites such as the Buddha's birthplace in Lumbini, and Kushinagar, where Buddha died. Xuanzang returned home with more than 600 Sanskrit texts, which he then translated into Chinese.

CAREER HIGHLIGHTS

c. 630 Visits the Great Stupa in Gandhara—then the tallest building in the world
c. 1592 Xuanzang's adventures inspire a novel, *Journey to the West*, now better known to Western readers as *Monkey*

JOURNEYS

Africa

▽ NILE CRUISE

EGYPT

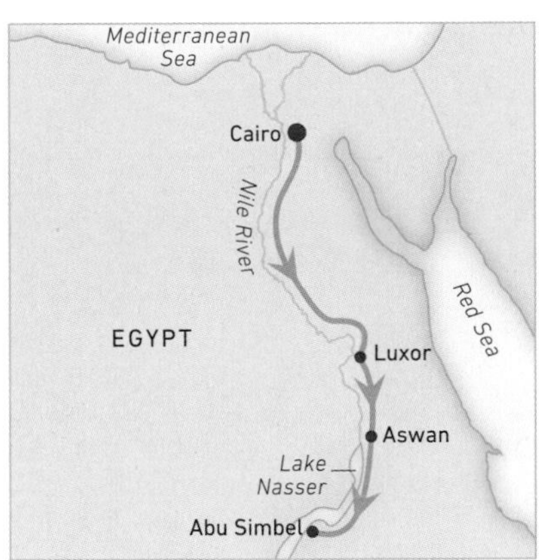

Some 90 percent of Egypt is desert and the only habitable parts of the country are the fertile Nile Valley and Delta. The Nile River nourished the ancient Egyptian civilization and it became a major trading route between the Mediterranean and the ancient kingdom of Nubia. Egyptians bartered their natural resouces of gold, papyrus, grain, and linen for tropical hardwood, precious metals, incense, and myrrh.

Long after the age of the pharaohs, monuments to these kings remained beside the river, which is why Thomas Cook led the first organized trip from Cairo to Aswan and back in 1869. Since then, a Nile cruise has been the quintessential Egyptian experience.

The traditional Nile journey begins with an excursion from Cairo to the Great Pyramid of Giza. Along with the necropolis of Sakkara, with its Stepped Pyramid, the pyramids are some of the most ancient and awe-inspiring monuments in Egypt, dating to around 2560–2510 BCE. Leaving Cairo, the boat heads upriver, making brief halts at Tel el-Amarna, site of the city of the heretic Pharaoh Akhenaten, and Qena, with its Temple of Dendara, before docking at Luxor.

Formerly known as Thebes, Luxor was the capital of Egypt at the height of pharaonic power. It remains a vast open-air museum, and boasts the greatest concentration of monuments in Egypt. On the east bank stand the Karnak and Luxor temples; the west bank holds the vast mortuary temples and valleys of royal tombs. The latter include the Valley of the Kings, where Howard Carter discovered the tomb of Tutankhamun in 1922.

The boat halts at three more temples on its way to Aswan, the last town before the border with Sudan. This hot, dry market town is a base for excursions to the late-period island temple of Philae (380–362 BCE) and the colossal temple at Abu Simbel, Lake Nasser, dedicated to Ramses II. Rapids hinder further travel south, so the boat turns around here and makes its way back to Cairo.

THE TEMPLE OF KARNAK, LUXOR

A CAMEL TRAIN PASSES THROUGH THE SAHARA DESERT, MOROCCO

△ THE TRANS-SAHARAN TRADE ROUTE

MOROCCO

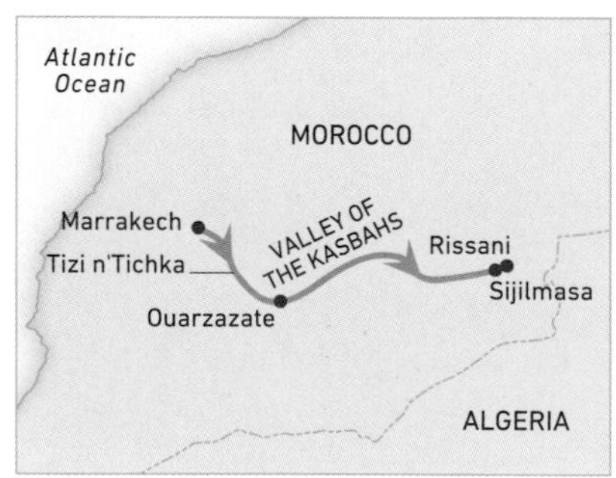

Today we think of the Sahara Desert as completely inhospitable—indeed, deadly to all those who enter it—but as long ago as the 4th and 5th centuries CE, it was criss-crossed by trading routes. The trade was conducted between the Berbers of North Africa, who lived in what are now Morocco, Algeria, and Tunisia, and the sub-Saharan Africans from Mali and the kingdom of Ghana. The latter would load their camel caravans with prized commodities such as kola nuts, hides, ostrich feathers, skins, slaves, and above all gold, while the Berbers supplied much-needed salt from the desert salt mines.

Today, it can be risky traveling to Mali, but it is still possible to get a flavor of the old caravan route. The town of Marrakech lies to the north of the Atlas Mountains, in Morocco. It began life as a trading post, and even today, its medina (town center) is still dominated by a sprawling souk. In this vast maze of narrow, shaded passageways, merchants set out their spices, brassware, silken garments, pottery, and maybe even the odd ostrich feather or egg. From the main southern gate of this still-walled city, a road strikes out across the dry plain and up into the mountains. It climbs over the Tizi n'Tichka Pass and snakes down again to the town of Ouarzazate, which is the gateway to the desert. From here, a lonely road runs east, through what the brochures call the Valley of the Kasbahs, after the tribal fortresses that line the route. Eventually, it comes to the village of Rissani, where a few ruins lie dotted among the palm groves. These are all that remain of Sijilmasa, a walled city that used to be the northern terminus of the trans-Saharan caravan route. Once an African El Dorado, it was destroyed in the 16th century, then rebuilt, and destroyed again by nomadic tribes in 1818. From Rissani, it is possible to drive a little further, then suddenly the road runs out and the giant, sculptural dunes of the Sahara loom up ahead. The next stop is Timbuktu, 620 miles (1,000 km) south.

▽ THE LIVINGSTONE TRAIL

SOUTH AFRICA, BOTSWANA, ZAMBIA

The Scottish missionary and anti-slavery crusader David Livingstone was one of the greatest explorers of Africa. Today, it is possible to visit many of the lands he passed through and to marvel at their beauty without having to endure the hardships that

THE *PRIDE OF AFRICA* CROSSES SOUTH AFRICA

he faced. As soon as Livingstone arrived at Cape Town, South Africa, in 1841, he traveled north to take up a missionary post in the interior. These days, it is worth stopping off in Cape Town. Table Mountain has beautiful trails to explore, and the vineyards of the Cape Winelands are only a short drive away, as are miles of beaches.

Regular bus and rail services lead from Cape Town into the interior, but the best way to travel is aboard the *Pride of Africa*, one of the world's most luxurious trains. It rumbles northeast through the heart of the country, and has a viewing car for appreciating the surrounding bush country. Stops are made at the diamond-mining town of Kimberley, and then Johannesburg and Pretoria. The route then heads north across the savannah and into Botswana. This is where Livingstone founded a mission at Kolobeng, before he set out on his career as an explorer, crossing the Kalahari Desert to reach Lake Ngami in 1849. The railway also crosses the Kalahari Desert before reaching the awe-inspiring Victoria Falls. In November 1855, Livingstone became the first European to set eyes on the Falls, which the native people called "smoke that thunders." They are still one of the natural wonders of the world today.

From the Victoria Falls, trains carry on into Zambia, a country that is closely associated with Livingstone, who famously followed the course of the Zambezi River all the way to the Indian Ocean. Just a few miles north of the river is the modern city of Livingstone, which was named after the explorer. From here, it is possible to carry on to Lake Tanganyika, where Livingstone spent the last years of his life searching, unsuccessfully, for the source of the Nile.

MONKS AT THE MAIN TEMPLE OF ANGKOR WAT, CAMBODIA

Asia

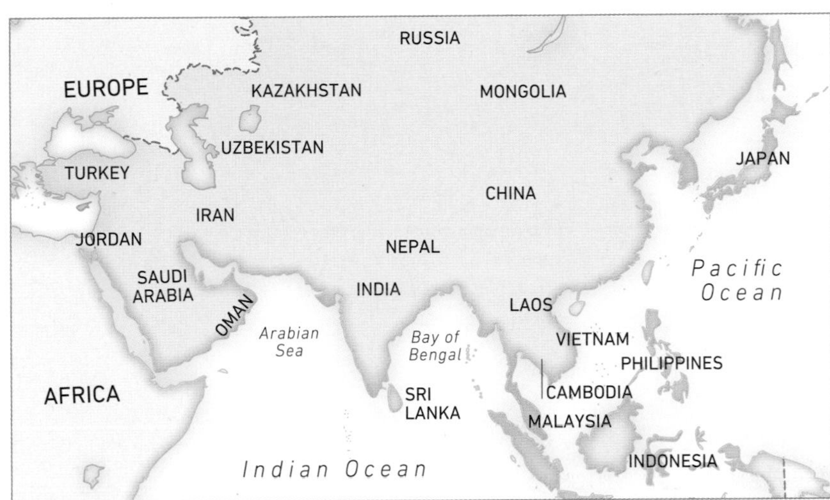

◁ ANGKOR WAT TO HO CHI MINH CITY

CAMBODIA, VIETNAM

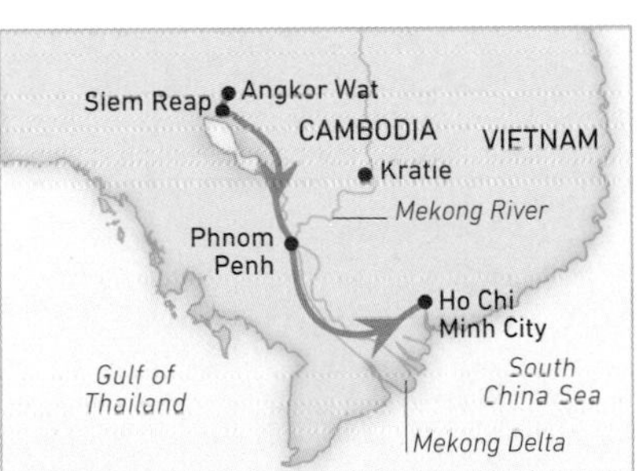

At 2,700 miles (4,350 km), the Mekong is the longest river in Southeast Asia, stretching from the Himalayan Plateau to southern Vietnam, and finally draining into the South China Sea. A stunning waterway, second only to the Amazon in terms of its wildlife, it was virtually unknown until a French expedition set off to explore it in 1866, hoping to prove that the river was navigable and could provide a vital trading artery between Saigon (now Ho Chi Minh City) and China.

The Mekong nourished the Khmer Empire, which bloomed in the 8th century, so the ideal trip starts at its former capital of Angkor Wat in Cambodia. A masterpiece of Khmer architecture, Angkor Wat is a vast temple complex originally dedicated to the Hindu god Vishnu. Its 12th-century lotus bud-like spires and walled compounds are covered with elaborate carved bas-reliefs depicting historical events and mythological tales. The temple was abandoned when the Khmer Empire declined in the 14th century, and disappeared beneath the encroaching jungle. It was virtually unknown in the West until French explorer Henri Mouhot found it in the mid-19th century. Parts of the complex have been left unrestored and the jungle is creeping back over it once more.

The resort town of Siem Reap is only a few miles from Angkor Wat and provides a base for exploring the temples. It is also the riverside port for boats that sail south across the great lake known as Tonlé Sap and to the Cambodian capital of Phnom Penh, which is on the Mekong River. The journey leads through floating villages and markets, and passes colorful pagodas and temples. From Phnom Penh, you can head north up the Mekong to Kratie, which is a good base for trekking through the jungle.

The alternative is to carry on south, crossing into Vietnam and passing through the Mekong Delta. This is an idyllic landscape of canals, streams, and bright green paddy fields. The final destination is Ho Chi Minh City. The city is now an appealing blend of French colonial landmarks and bustling 21st-century commerce.

▽ THE GREAT WALL OF CHINA

CHINA

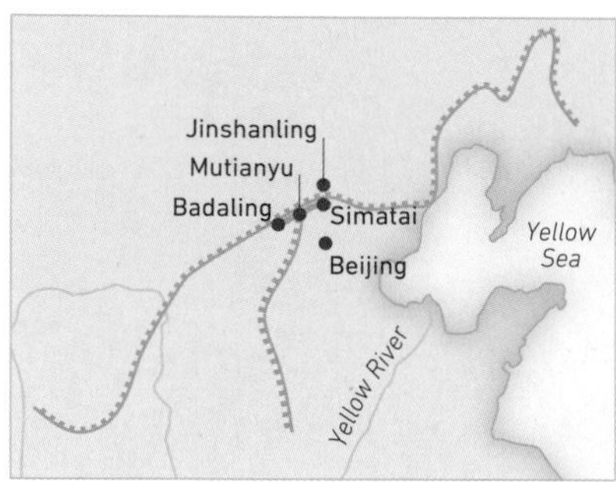

The Great Wall of China is the longest wall in the world and one of the most impressive structures ever built by humans. Visiting it is a journey in itself and many European explorers have traveled to see it with their own eyes.

An early form of the wall was built in 220–206 BCE, after the unification of the country under its first emperor, Qin Shi Huangdi, to prevent invasion and to protect Silk Road trade. Millions of soldiers, peasants, and prisoners toiled to build the wall, many of them dying in the process.

After falling into disrepair, the wall was rebuilt during the Ming Dynasty (1368–1644), and most of what survives today dates from that time. The Great Wall of the Ming Dynasty stretched for more than 5,500 miles (8,851 km) and ran from Xinjiang Province in the far west of China to the Yellow Sea in the east. Today, much of it has once again fallen into disrepair, and long sections of it are missing, but the historic structure has been restored to a semblance of its former glory.

The most popular section of the wall is at Badaling, 44 miles (70 km) west of Beijing. It was extensively renovated in the 1980s, and even has a zip line for those with a head for heights. More spectacular and less busy is Mutianyu, which lies 56 miles (90 km) north of Beijing. Here, a 7,380-foot (2,250-m) section of the wall snakes through numerous watchtowers as it winds through the hills. It can be reached by cable car or chairlift.

The best place to get a sense of the Great Wall in its unreconstructed state is Simatai, 68 miles (110 km) northeast of Beijing. It is the starting point of an 5-mile (8-km) trek along the wall to Jinshanling, and few tourists venture here. Parts of the wall are incredibly steep—the Heavenly Ladder has an 80-degree gradient—and in places the steps are worn and the towers are crumbling. However, for those fit enough to undertake the five-hour walk, the views amply reward the effort. Its highest point is Watching Beijing Tower, which stands at 3,235 feet (986 m). From here, at night, it is possible to see the lights of Beijing shimmering in the distance some 75 miles (120 km) away.

THE YANGTZE RIVER, PASSING THROUGH THE QUTANG GORGE

THE GREAT WALL OF CHINA AT SIMATAI, AT DAWN

△ THE THREE GORGES

CHINA

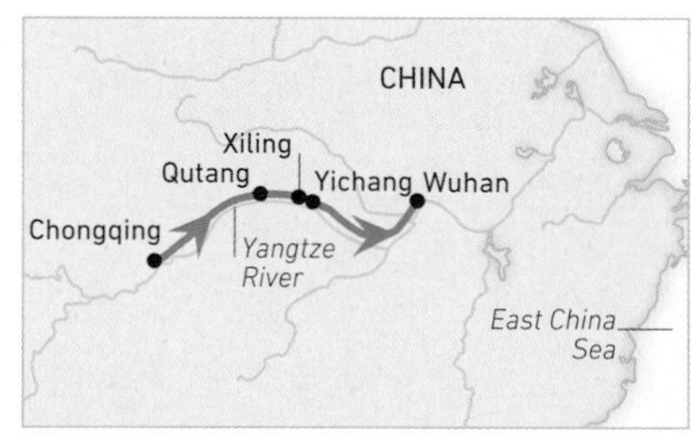

The Yangtze is the third-longest river in the world, stretching for 3,900 miles (6,300km), from the Tibetan Plateau in the west to the East China Sea. Connecting the interior with the coast, it is a major artery for China and one of the busiest waterways in the world, used for transporting coal, goods, and passengers.

The river is best known for a relatively short 120-mile (200-km) section in its middle reaches. Here, between Chongqing and Yichang, is an area of great natural beauty, known as the Three Gorges. As the Yangtze passes through the Qutang, Wu, and Xiling gorges, its waters squeeze between sheer, towering cliffs that are less than 328 feet (100 m) apart in the narrowest places. The approach view of the Qutang is so famous that it features on the Chinese 10-yuan note. Many cruise ships meander through the gorges, taking three days to complete the trip. A typical cruise makes several stops along the way, so that passengers can visit temples and other ancient sites. Passengers can also transfer to smaller boats to explore what are known as the Lesser Gorges—and then to even smaller boats, to venture up some of the Yangtze's many tributaries.

Since the 1990s, one of the most striking sights on the river has been the Three Gorges Dam, the largest dam project and hydropower station in the world, which was completed in 2006. Built in the Qutang Gorge, it generates electricity and reduces the risk of floods further downstream. By raising the level of the river it also broadens it, which increases the Yangtze's shipping capacity. The higher water levels make the surrounding cliffs and mountains seem smaller, but the area is still spectacular. Controversially, building the dam meant that some 1.3 million people had to be relocated. As a result, the boats now sail over "ghost towns" submerged beneath the water. In order to pass the dam, all shipping has to pass through a sequence of gigantic stepped locks, which is a dramatic experience in itself.

▷ THE DARJEELING HIMALAYAN RAILWAY

INDIA

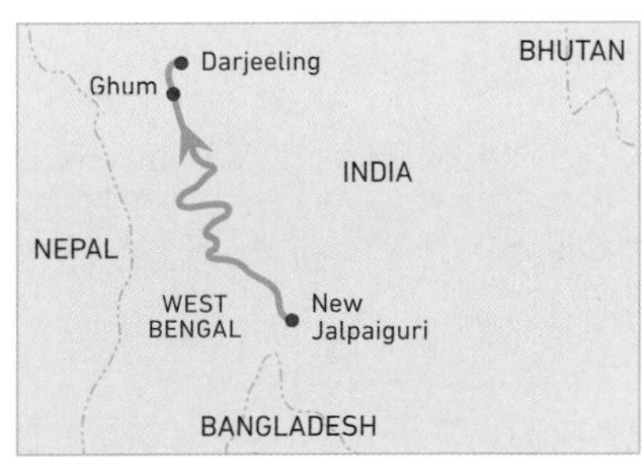

THE DARJEELING HIMALAYAN RAILWAY WINDS ITS WAY THROUGH THE HILLS OF WEST BENGAL

Many great railway journeys boast fantastic scenery, but the Darjeeling Himalayan Railway is unique. After taking the Toy Train from Siliguri to Darjeeling in 1896, the American author Mark Twain wrote that the journey was "so wild and interesting and exciting and enchanting that it ought to take a week." Covering just 48 miles (78 km), the journey is not particularly long, but over that modest distance the winding, single-track railway chugs uphill from around 328 feet (100 m) above sea level to some 7,218 feet (2,200 m). Its narrow-gauge tracks are only 2 feet (61 cm) wide and it is pulled by a tiny steam locomotive (hence its nickname, the "Toy Train"). Despite appearances, however, it is a genuine service that runs 16 trains each day—except when the line is blocked by landslides.

Like so many hill railways built by the British in India, the main purpose of the Darjeeling Himalayan Railway was to give them easy access to the cooler climes of the hills, to escape the heat of summer. Darjeeling itself, set amid the tea plantations of West Bengal, became a home away from home for many British expats who built colonial houses there. Completed in 1881, the railway connects the major rail junction of New Jalpaiguri with Darjeeling, and stops at 13 stations on the way. From New Jalpaiguri, the line climbs rapidly, gaining height with the aid of frequent reversing stations (Z-shaped lines of track that enable a train to shunt forward, backward, and then forward again, climbing a section of hill each time). The track is also looped in places to help the trains gain altitude quickly. The line runs alongside the equally vertiginous Hill Cart Road, which it crosses several times, the trains honking their horns at oncoming traffic. The full journey takes a painfully slow eight hours, but is well worth it for the scenery. The train crosses through semi-tropical valleys, tea plantations, lush forest, and villages where the shops almost tumble onto the tracks. The line's highest point, and the location of the highest station in India, is at Ghum, outside Darjeeling. Here, on a clear day, the dramatic panorama of the Himalayas is revealed, dominated by Kanchenjunga, the world's third-highest mountain.

▽ THE GOLDEN TRIANGLE

INDIA

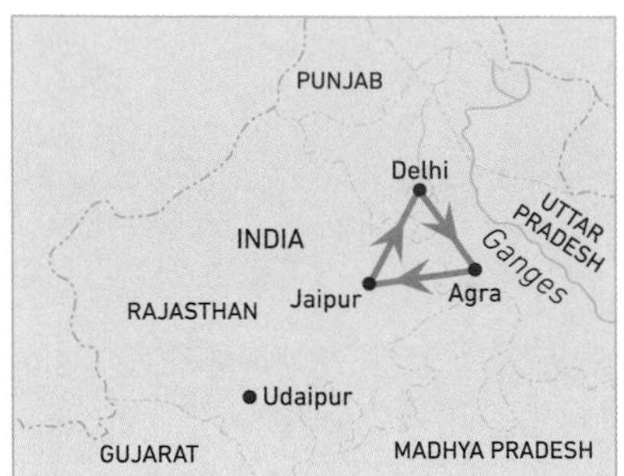

The Golden Triangle is formed of three of India's most memorable cities. They are relatively close together and are connected by good rail links or one incredible rail link, if you are prepared to pay for it. The Indian railways are the oldest in Asia, established by the British in the 19th century. The first major rail line, between Bombay and Calcutta, opened in 1870, and within three decades of that year, there were 40,000 miles (65,000 km) of track. London-based travel guide publisher John Murray published the first comprehensive handbook for travel in India in 1891. It noted that a trip there was no longer a formidable journey, and that "the Englishman who undertakes it merely passes from one portion of the British Empire to another."

The key sights, then as now, are the Golden Triangle of Delhi, Agra, and Jaipur—so called for the almost-equilateral triangle that the three cities make when plotted on a map, and the wonderful sights that they offer. Delhi boasts the towering 12th-century Qutb Minar and the Mughal Humayun's Tomb and Red Fort, as well as colonial buildings from the days of the British Raj, and the vast, teeming bazaars of Old Delhi. Agra is the location of the Taj Mahal and the Agra Fort. It is also the gateway to nearby Fatehpur Sikri, a magnificent fortified city that was once the capital of the Mughal Empire.

DAWN BREAKS OVER VARANASI ON THE GANGES RIVER

The third point of the triangle, the Pink City of Jaipur, is the ancient capital of the desert province of Rajasthan. A glorious city of palaces and bazaars, it is a good base for visiting the exquisite Amber Fort, high on a hilltop a few miles out of town.

All three cities can be reached fairly easily, using express trains or buses. There is also the luxurious *Palace on Wheels*. This award-winning train service visits all three locations, as well as the beguiling lakeside city of Udaipur to the southwest.

A CAMEL DRIVER CROSSES THE YAMUNA RIVER OPPOSITE THE TAJ MAHAL, AGRA

△ THE GANGES RIVER

INDIA

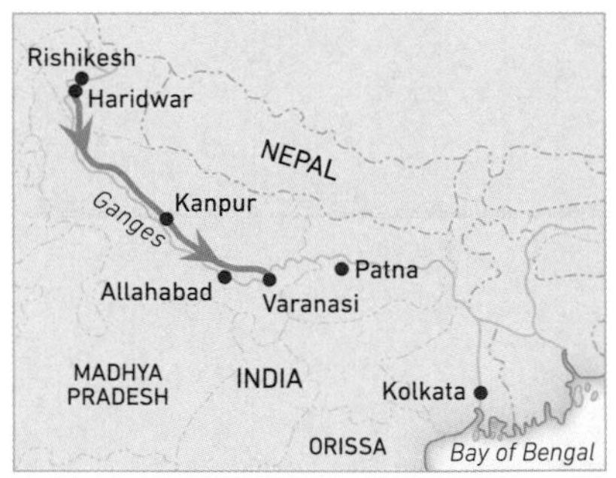

One of the greatest rivers on Earth, the Ganges has its source in the icy Himalayas and flows 1,569 miles (2,525 km) southeast to the Bay of Bengal in the Indian Ocean. It is sacred to Hindus, who worship the river as the goddess Ganga. The Ganges has drawn pilgrims to it throughout history, so to follow its course is to undertake a journey through the spiritual heart of India.

A good place to start is Rishikesh, in the Himalayan foothills. This is where the Beatles went in the late 1960s when they became followers of Maharishi Mahesh Yogi. The town is dotted with temples, both ancient and modern, and it is still a major center for studying yoga and meditation and is full of pilgrims clad in orange.

A more traditional Hindu city is Haridwar, which stands at the place where the Ganges emerges from the Himalayas. Here, pilgrims come in droves to bathe in the fast-flowing river at sunrise. It is especially busy during the pilgrimage season from May to October, when thousands of Hindus descend upon the city. The season peaks in July.

From Haridwar, there is a train to Allahabad, then a change for the most holy of all Hindu sites—Varanasi (also known as Benares), The city is famous for the ghats (stone steps) that line the Ganges. Every day, thousands of Hindus come to these ghats, to pray and to cleanse themselves of their sins in the sacred waters of the river. Two ghats are also used to cremate bodies on bonfires, tended by relatives and watched by the general public. When the pyres are burned out, the ashes are scattered in the river, in the belief that this will benefit the soul of the departed. One of the best ways to watch the scene is from a boat on the river, which gives a vantage point for seeing people going about their daily ablutions by day or torchlit activities by night. Varanasi enables visitors to experience what Hindu pilgrimage is all about.

▷ THE SPICE ISLANDS

INDONESIA

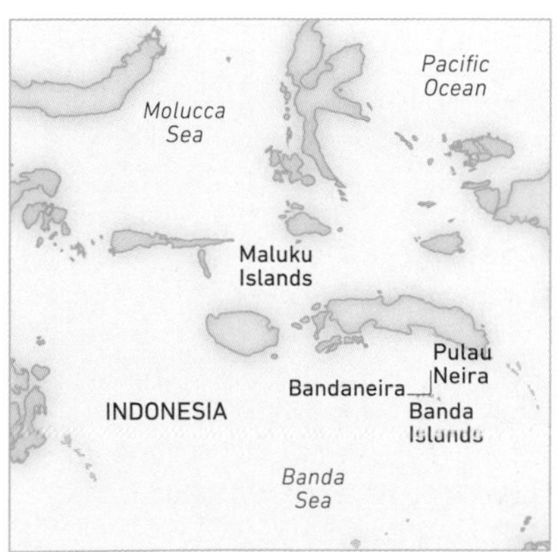

The recent history of the Maluku Islands (formerly known as the Moluccas) is not a happy one. They form an archipelago in Indonesia that split into two provinces in 1999, causing conflict between Muslim and Christian islanders, which resulted in half a million people being displaced.

This was not the first time that people had fought over the islands. Famed for the nutmeg, mace, and cloves that grow there, they had formerly been known as the Spice Islands. At a time when spice was worth more than gold, the islands were long sought after by seafaring Europeans. The Portuguese finally located them in the 16th century, but this only brought them into conflict with the Dutch and the English. The Dutch built forts throughout the islands and the English restricted themselves to the isles of Ai and Run. The islands' monopoly on spice was broken in the 18th century, and since then, Maluku has settled into gentle obscurity. Due to poor transporation, very few tourists go there, but regular flights from cities around Indonesia land in Ambon, the capital of Maluku. Here, the Dutch influence is still evident in the old colonial buildings that remain, and the fact that half of the population is Christian. The town also, famously, serves as a gateway to the nearby Banda Islands.

Reached by fast-boat service or a short hop in a 12-seater airplane, the 10 picturesque Banda Islands were once at the heart of the Dutch spice trade. The capital, Bandaneira, on the central island of Pulau Neira, is scattered with historic relics. These include Bentang Nassau, a fortress in which some 44 local leaders were beheaded and quartered by the Dutch in 1621. There are many other forts scattered among the islands, long since neglected and crumbling away. Old nutmeg smokehouses can also be found, nestled in nutmeg groves dotted with huge mango and almond trees. However, most people come for the paradisical white beaches, the underwater coral gardens, the jungle trails, and the striking scenery that includes volcanoes—one of which erupted as recently as 1988.

THE TINY ISLAND OF RUN, ONE OF THE MALUKU ISLANDS, INDONESIA

▽ JERUSALEM

ISRAEL, PALESTINE

Jerusalem has been a center of pilgrimage for Jews, Muslims, and Christians for thousands of years. Jewish pilgrims have been visiting since Solomon reputedly became the king of Israel and built the First Temple there in around 970–931 BCE. Jews believe that the temple was built over the foundation stone from which the world was created, on which Abraham prepared to sacrifice his son Isaac. The First Temple was destroyed, then rebuilt as the Second Temple, and then destroyed again in ancient times. All that remains today is the Kotel, or Western Wall, which is thought to be a section of the retaining wall of the Second Temple. It is considered holy by modern Jews because it is the closest they can get to their former place of worship.

The site of the temple has been a holy Muslim precinct ever since Islamic forces captured Al-Quds (Jerusalem) in 637 BCE. To Muslims, the temple site is the Haram ash-Sharif, or Noble Sanctuary, visited by the Prophet Muhammad on what is known as his "night journey," from Mecca to Al-Quds to heaven. The sacrificial stone that once lay at the heart of the Jewish temple is now covered by the Dome of Rock, the octagonal Islamic shrine with a golden dome raised in 691 BCE. The precinct has several other religious buildings including Al-Aqsa Mosque, which is used all year round, especially on the holy day of Friday and during the holy month of Ramadan.

Christians have been present in Jerusalem since the time of Jesus Christ. Their focus of worship is the Church of the Holy Sepulchre, built in about 325 BCE by Constantine, the first Christian emperor, over the cave in which the body of Jesus was supposedly laid to rest. Other sites around the city are linked with the Last Supper, Christ's route on his way to be crucified (the Via Dolorosa), and the crucifixion itself. All of the sites, whether Jewish, Islamic, or Christian, still attract thousands of pilgrims a year. It is not necessary to be religious, however, to appreciate the weight of history that bears down upon Jerusalem and its extraordinary architecture and culture.

THE DOME OF THE ROCK, LOCATED ON TEMPLE MOUNT WITHIN THE OLD CITY OF JERUSALEM

GOSHOJI TEMPLE, TEMPLE NUMBER 78

△ SHIKOKU PILGRIMAGE

JAPAN

Shikoku is the smallest and least populated of the four main islands of Japan. It is the location for the country's most famous pilgrimage route, a 745-mile (1,200-km) loop all around the island, known as the 88 Temple Pilgrimage. Thousands of Japanese undertake the circuit, or part of it, by tour bus every year. A smaller number of hardy souls does it on foot. Walking, which generally takes around 50 days, is truer to the spirit of the pilgrimage's founder, Kobo Daishi, a wandering holy man who helped to establish Buddhism in Japan, but it requires good physical fitness, as the route is long and hilly.

The circuit begins at Tokushima-ken, site of the first 23 of the 88 temples, and it is best to visit the temples in a clockwise direction, following the signs, to avoid getting lost. At each temple, the *henro* (pilgrim), dressed in a *hakue* (white jacket) and conical hat, performs a series of rituals that culminates in a chant of the Heart Sutra, a Buddhist prayer. One of the temple's monks then marks the pilgrim's book, which can be bought at the first temple, with a red seal, and writes down the name of the temple and the date on which it has been visited. Some temples specialize in blessings for ill health, passing exams, or getting pregnant (one of the temples, at a place called Uwajima, has a sex museum full of ancient fertility objects, as well as "adult" Japanese art). A highlight is Zentsu-ji, the 75th temple and the largest one on the route, which is where Kobo Daishi was born.

The route between the temples meanders through rugged terrain, but the path follows the coast and avoids the mountains, offering wonderful views of the Pacific Ocean. On the coast, at a place called Ishite, a giant statue of Kobo Daishi stares contemplatively out to sea. Local residents traditionally support pilgrims by offering them a bed for the night, but there are also guesthouses along the way.

▷ MOUNT FUJI

JAPAN

There is a Japanese proverb that says, "A wise man climbs Fuji once; a fool climbs it twice," because Japan's highest peak (12,388 feet / 3,775 m) is without doubt a tough ascent. It is not hard in the way that Everest is (climbers are unlikely to die), but the ascent is demanding and the views from the top are scant reward (that is, if the summit is not wreathed in clouds). Mount Fuji definitely looks at its most spectacular seen from a distance, so that you can appreciate the snow-capped profile of this near perfectly shaped volcano, but climbing it is a uniquely Japanese experience.

According to legend, Fuji was the abode of a fire goddess, who would display her displeasure from time to time by making the volcano erupt. On the occasion of the last eruption in 1707, ash covered the streets of Tokyo, some 60 miles (100 km) away. The combination of its conical form and power has meant that Fuji has long been revered as a sacred Shinto shrine. There are several routes up the mountain and the ascent is divided into sections known as stations. These days, most people take a bus to the Kawaguchi-ko, or fifth station, which is about halfway up. Here, a Swiss-chalet-style gift shop marks the end of the road. Traditionally, however, pilgrims would begin at Fuji-Yoshida, and pay their respect to the gods before embarking on a walk of around five hours just to get to Kawaguchi-ko. From here, it takes another six hours of steady walking in order to reach the summit. It is a Japanese tradition to climb the volcano at night, and watch sunrise from the summit.

There is a series of huts en route that provide restorative food and basic accommodation. At the summit, the crater has a circumference of some 2.4 miles (4 km), which takes about one hour to walk. There is a post office at the top of the mountain, and the Japanese like to post a letter so that it arrives with a Mount Fuji souvenir postmark. The peak times for climbing Mount Fuji are July and August, when the weather is at its mildest. Either side of these months, it can be extremely cold and snowy up at the top of Japan.

THE TOKYO-KYOTO BULLET TRAIN SHOOTS PAST SNOW-CAPPED MOUNT FUJI

THE OLD TOKAIDO ROAD IS PAVED WITH LARGE, FLAT STONES

△ THE OLD TOKAIDO ROAD

JAPAN

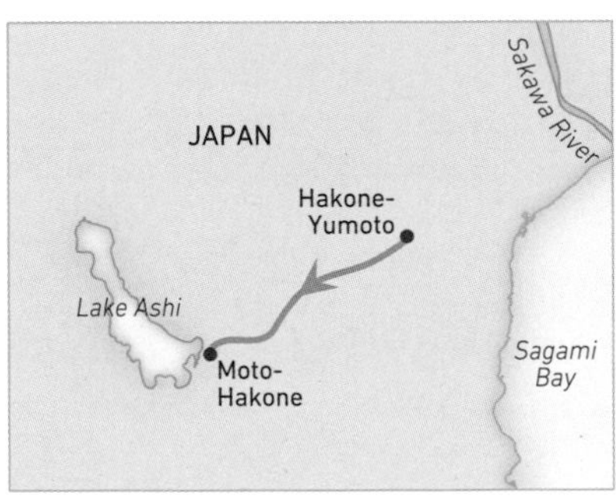

One of five important paved routes of the Edo period (1603–1858), the Tokaido Road connected Edo (present-day Tokyo) with Kyoto and followed the southeastern coast of the island of Honshu. It was an extremely busy route and was mostly traveled on foot, horseback, or, in the case of nobles, by *kago*, a type of palanquin which was carried by bearers. Famous for its spectacular views, the Tokaido was a popular subject in literature and art. Japan's most famous poet, Matsuo Basho (1644–94), wrote about his travels along it, and the artist Hiroshige (1797–1858) depicted the 53 rest stations along the road in a series of woodblock prints.

Today, the Tokaido is still a major thoroughfare, with two motorways and two railway lines—one of which carries the bullet train from Tokyo to Kyoto. Sections of the Old Tokaido road still exist though, meandering through some stunning Japanese scenery, and make ideal trails for trekking. The most popular section to walk is over the Hakone Pass. It is not far from Tokyo and can be reached by suburban train. Walkers start at the Hakone-Yumoto Station, from which it is a steep climb, on a road of large rough stones that snakes up and over hills densely forested with bamboo and cypress trees. On the way, the road passes the *amazake-jaya*, an old thatched wooden rest-house where travelers can stop for a drink of green tea.

Eventually, the road reaches the crest of a hilly ridge and descends toward the small town of Moto-Hakone, on the shores of Lake Ashi, a beautiful lake in an old volcanic crater with views of Mount Fuji. Before this, it comes to the Hakone Sekisho (Barrier). This was a government checkpoint often decorated with the crucified remains of criminals, but it is now the site of a small museum. There is a train back to Tokyo at Moto-Hakone. For an easier hike, it is best to follow the route in the opposite direction, so that most of the walking is downhill.

▽ PETRA AND WADI RUM

JORDAN

When 27-year-old Swiss explorer Johann Ludwig Burckhardt found his way into Petra in August 1812, he was the first European in over 600 years to visit the ruined desert city. Petra was once a wealthy trading center, home to 30,000 people, and the capital of the ancient Nabataean Empire. These desert dwellers operated a loosely controlled trading network, which centered on oases in what are today Jordan, Syria, and Israel. After the Nabataeans were conquered and absorbed by the Roman Empire, Petra fell into decline and was eventually abandoned and forgotten by everyone but the local Bedouins, who kept its presence secret from outsiders.

Today, visitors drive down from the Jordanian capital Amman to the small town of Wadi Musa, which is just a few miles from the entrance to Petra.

THE TEMPLELIKE TREASURY AT PETRA, CARVED OUT OF THE SANDSTONE ROCK FACE

The ancient site is approached by means of a narrow, winding, steeply sided gorge, known as the Siq. It emerges dramatically in front of the towering templelike Treasury building, and even the presence of other tourists cannot diminish the thrill of discovery.

The whole of Petra is carved from pinkish-red sandstone, with arches, columns, and doorways etched into the sheer rock faces. The haunting ruins that remain include temples and churches, a semicircular amphitheater, and a stunning clifftop monastery that is reached by an ancient rock-cut path with more than 800 steps.

A couple of hours to the south of Petra along the King's Highway (an ancient route that once ran from Heliopolis in Egypt to Palmyra in Syria), is Wadi Rum. This wild desert valley was also formerly occupied by the Nabataeans and there is a small temple here, but the ancient ruins are eclipsed by the overwhelming natural glories, which represent some of the most spectacular desert scenery in the world. Sheer-sided rocky outcrops loom up out of the desert, and erosion by the harsh desert winds and sand has created gigantic sandstone mushrooms, rock bridges, and canyons. The landscape is so eerie and otherworldly that it was used to represent Mars in the Ridley Scott movie *The Martian* (2015).

PRAYER FLAGS NEAR THE ANNAPURNA BASE CAMP

▷ THE ANNAPURNA CIRCUIT

NEPAL

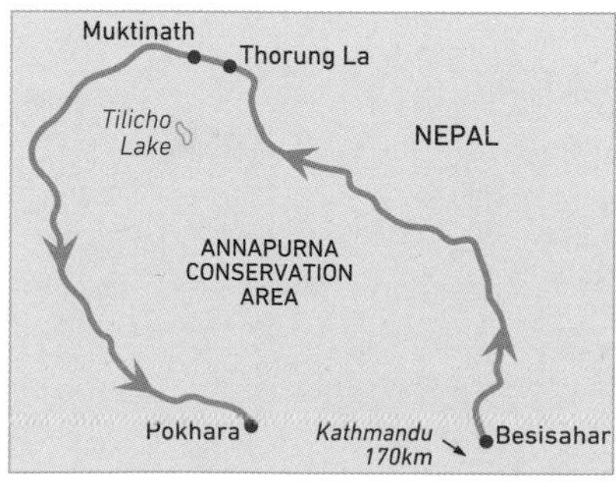

You do not have to be a mountaineer to experience the thrill of the Himalayas. There are spectacular trails in the lower reaches of the ranges that take trekkers to places that feel just like the top of the world, without the need for crampons and ice axes—the Annapurna Circuit, for example, which is regarded by many as the best long-distance trek in the world. It is a 128-mile (205-km) horseshoe-shaped route that circles around central Nepal's Annapurna Range, which includes one peak that is over 26,000 feet (8,000 m), and 13 peaks over 23,000 feet (7,000 m). The scenery is stupendous.

The trek begins after a seven-hour drive from Kathmandu at Besisahar in the Marshyangdi river valley and ends at the city of Pokhara, with tea houses and lodges all along the route. At the start, there are spectacular views of terraced paddy fields and subtropical forests, including several waterfalls, gigantic cliffs, and Nepali villages. The trek progresses through a tall, dense pine forest, from which there are occasional glimpses of the mountains ahead. On the way, there are constant reminders that the path follows an ancient trade route that is still very much in use today—trekkers can expect to meet caravans of donkeys laden with supplies of food and fuel being delivered to villages and stores. The trail finally emerges from the forest to a stunning view of lofty mountains all around, and a steady climb begins to the highest point on the circuit—the pass at Thorung La, which is 17,769 feet (5,416 m) in altitude. From here, the trail descends to Muktinath, a town sacred to both Buddhists and Hindus, where water shoots from 108 springs and a natural gas flame burns on top of water in one of the temples. Hindus believe that Muktinath is the only place on Earth where the five elements exist in their distinct forms. It sounds like nirvana, but from here there are still another four days of walking to complete the circuit.

EVEREST BASE CAMP AT DUSK

△ EVEREST BASE CAMP

NEPAL

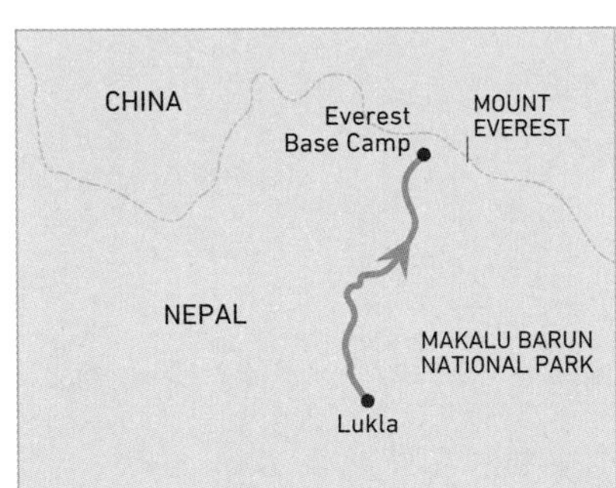

Mount Everest captivated the hearts of mountaineers when the first attempts on the summit were made in the 1920s. Since then, the names of some of those who have climbed the mountain—George Mallory, Edmund Hillary, Tenzing Norgay—have passed into history. Many thousands have followed in their footsteps, risking their lives just to stand on the highest point on Earth. However, there is an easier goal for travelers who simply want a really close view of the famous mountain, and that is a trek to Everest Base Camp (at which point, of course, they turn back). The base camp is where would-be climbers of Everest spend a few days acclimatizing to the height to reduce the risks of altitude sickness. It lies 17,598 feet (5,364 m) above sea level, some 11,430 feet (3,484 m) shy of the summit. There is not a lot to see there—it looks like a makeshift refugee camp in the snow, with lots of fluttering prayer flags—but there is a thrill to be standing at the foot of Everest with its breathtaking scenery. On the way in, there is also a taste of Sherpa culture, courtesy of several local monasteries and museums.

The adventure begins at Kathmandu, from where you fly to Lukla, a remote place with no roads or cars, which is located at an altitude of 9,383 feet (2,860 m). The Tenzing-Hillary Airport is literally an airstrip in the middle of nowhere, and often features on lists of the world's most dangerous airports. From there you walk from village to village along well-defined paths, sleeping in tea houses, where meals of *dal bhat* (lentil soup with rice) and plenty of water are served. Experts advise taking it slowly, walking three to seven hours per day, to give the body time to acclimatize. The entire trek usually takes 12 days in all: eight days (including rest days) to base camp, plus four to get back down. Many people who have completed it say that it is worth it just for the euphoria on the way down, because you feel lighter with each step as the altitude decreases. That, and the welcome prospect of a hot shower at the end of it all.

▽ OMANI FRANKINCENSE

OMAN

Arabia has been famously fragrant since the earliest of times. Greek and Roman authors wrote of an Arabia scented with spices and perfumes. Many of those fragrances were imported, but there is one that is entirely indigenous to the southern Arabian Peninsula: frankincense. It is an aromatic resin obtained from a particular type of tree, the boswellia, which is common in Somalia, Yemen, and Oman above all.

Even today, Oman is permeated with frankincense. The place to find it is the city of Salalah, in the southwest of the country, about as far from the Omani capital of Muscat as it is possible to go without crossing the border into Yemen. The souk here is full of frankincense (among other aromatics), which is bought by locals and burned in their houses, not only to make them fragrant but to keep pests away. It is burned at celebrations too, especially births and weddings. In Salalah, there is even a museum dedicated to frankincense.

FRANKINCENSE TREES IN WADI DAWKAH, OMAN

A TRANS-SIBERIAN TRAIN TRAVELING THROUGH RUSSIA IN FALL

The city is also a good base for visiting the frankincense groves in nearby Wadi Dawkah. Here, the spiny trees grow in a wide, stony valley, and it is possible to see how the resin is harvested. Hand-sized pieces of bark are cut from the trees, which makes the sap rise and congeal on the exposed surfaces. There, it hardens into milky blobs and beads that are then scraped off, creating frankincense.

Less than an hour's drive along the coast from Salalah lie the ruins of the ancient trading city of Sumhuram. As far back as the 1st century BCE, this was one of the major ports of southern Arabia, and was vital to the international frankincense trade; ships left here for Egypt and India. It was abandoned in the fifth century CE, perhaps due to the encroachment of a sandbar, so little remains to be seen, but it is in a lovely setting on a small hill above the tranquil waters of the Khor Rori creek.

△ THE TRANS-SIBERIAN RAILWAY

RUSSIA, ASIA

There is no one train called the Trans-Siberian; nor is there a single rail route with the name. The Trans-Siberian Railway is a vast Russian railway network that connects Europe with Asia. There are three main Trans-Siberian routes, all of which begin at Moscow's Yaroslavski Station. From there, the original Trans-Siberian route is served by a train called the *Rossiya* (the *Russia*), which departs every other day on a six-night, 5,752-mile (9,259-km) journey to Vladivostok in the far east of Russia. Many travelers, however, opt for either the Trans-Manchurian, which is a weekly service (aboard the *Vostok*) to Beijing via Manchuria, or the weekly Trans-Mongolian, which travels to Beijing via Mongolia and the Gobi Desert. Parts of these routes are also served by other railways.

The Trans-Siberian experience begins with settling into the small train compartment that will be home for roughly a week. For those who are sharing (most compartments have four beds) there is ample time to get to know their traveling companions, as well as the *provodnitsa*, the female attendant stationed in each carriage. There is little to do except watch the slowly changing scenery outside, make tea using the hot water from the samovar in the corridor, read, and doze. Keeping track of the time can be tricky as the train passes through up to seven different time zones. Passengers fall prey to a gently disorienting "train-lag," and end up sleeping at odd hours. An added complication is that all the timetables, station clocks, and train clocks in Russia remain on Moscow time and only revert to local time when in China and Mongolia.

All three trains call at many places along the way, but they are working services, not tourist trains, so the stops are never long enough to allow passengers to get off and explore. The Russians use the stops to stretch their legs and buy food from some of the itinerant vendors on the platform. For those who do want to break up the long journey and see something along the way, the most popular places are Yekaterinburg (for its rich Tsarist history), Irkutsk (for magnificent Lake Baikal), and Ulan Bator, the capital of Mongolia.

AN AERIAL VIEW OF MECCA

△ PILGRIMAGE TO MECCA

SAUDI ARABIA

Mecca has been the center of pilgrimage for Muslims since the Prophet Muhammad himself led the pilgrimage, known as the hajj, in 632 CE, the year of his death. The city is regarded as so holy that only Muslims can enter. Every Muslim must make the pilgrimage to Mecca at least once in their life, if they are physically able. The hajj begins on the eighth day of the Dhu al-Hijjah, which is the 12th month of the Muslim lunar calendar, and finishes on the 13th day. During this time, up to three million pilgrims pour into Mecca, to participate in the world's largest annual gathering of people. Most fly into the nearby coastal city of Jeddah and then travel to Mecca by road. The idea of the hajj is to remind Muslims that everybody is equal in the eyes of Allah (God). It is also meant to bring Muslims of all nationalities together, cleansing them of sin and bringing them nearer Allah.

The hajj begins at stations known as *miqat* just outside Mecca, which pilgrims cannot cross until they are appropriately dressed. For men, this means wearing just two white sheets, known as *ihram*, one wrapped around the waist, the other draped over the shoulder. For women, the only stipulation is to dress modestly. Pilgrims then recite the *talbiya*—a prayer to announce to Allah that they have arrived for hajj. There are then several days of prescribed rituals, the first of which is *tawaf*, in which pilgrims walk around the Kaaba, the holiest shrine in Islam, seven times in an anti-clockwise direction. Muslims believe that the origins of the rituals of the hajj go back to the time of the Prophet Ibrahim (Abraham). Other rituals include passing between the hills of Safa and Marwa in Masjid al-Haram, prayers behind the Station of Abraham, and drinking water from the spring of Zamzam.

▽ CAPPADOCIA

TURKEY

In the 1960s, when hippies set off from cities all over Europe in search of spiritual enlightenment in India, via the hash cafés of Afghanistan, the true starting point for their trip was Istanbul. It was here that Europe started to recede, replaced by a dreamy skyline of minarets, the floating calls of the *muezzin*, and clouds of dense, white smoke from the shisha-pipes in the coffeehouses on the Golden Horn. The first port of call was invariably a restaurant just up from the ancient Hippodrome called the Pudding Shop. This was the place to find like-minded company and pick up the latest information on the route ahead. The Pudding Shop is no more, but the restaurants on that same busy street, Yerebatan Caddesi, remain popular with visitors.

At Istanbul, it was just a brief ferry ride across the Bosphorus to reach Asia and then a bus onward across the heartland of Turkey. While some chose to travel the coast and drop out on some secluded beach, the aim for most

FAIRY CHIMNEYS IN CAPPADOCIA

VIEW OF THE MIRI-ARAB MADRASAH AND SKYLINE, BUKHARA

travelers was to make straight for Cappadocia. Today, most people fly direct from Istanbul. Arriving at Cappadocia is like landing on another planet—it is a geological oddity of rock towers, called fairy chimneys, shaped by natural erosion. Over the ages, people have bored into the soft stone to create cavelike residences inside the towers and across the barren countryside, riddling the area with fascinating cavern architecture. There are ancient churches and other historical sites, but most of the caves are still in use, serving as accommodation, restaurants, and bars. To get the best overview of this extraordinary fairytale landscape, numerous operators run balloon flights. The ideal time to take these is at dawn, when the rising sun casts an unearthly pink tinge over the scene.

△ THE SILK ROAD

UZBEKISTAN

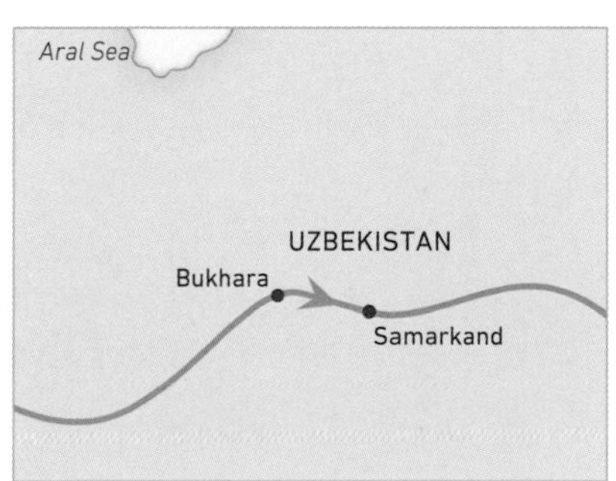

Dubbed the region that time forgot, Central Asia was once the middle passage for merchant caravans traveling along the ancient Silk Road, between China and Constantinople. They traded silk, tea, spices, silver, gold, and other goods, and the region grew rich as a result. Emperor Timur, also known as Tamerlane, used the money to fund military campaigns that extended his rule across Persia, Iraq, and all the way to Delhi. However, once the sea route around Africa was discovered in the 15th century, the trade wealth vanished and Central Asia dropped off the map.

Even today, thanks to their legacy as post-Soviet republics, the countries that now make up the region are seldom visited by outsiders. Yet, in Uzbekistan, the former Timurid cities of Bukhara and Samarkand are graced by some of the most exquisite medieval Islamic architecture to be found anywhere in the world.

Bukhara is a former center of Islamic learning with approximately 140 protected historic buildings—a collection, one visitor in 1938 wrote, that rivals "the finest architecture of the Italian Renaissance." Its slightly ramshackle, mud-brick center appears not to have changed much in two centuries, and it remains one of the best places to get a glimpse of what the world looked like at the time of the Silk Road.

In contrast, modern Samarkand is a Soviet-built sprawl of broad avenues and brutalist buildings, but it surrounds some magnificent monuments. Samarkand boasts the magnificent Registan, a grand public square that is flanked by three vast madrasahs (Islamic teaching schools), as well as the imposing Bibi-Khanym Mosque, Gur-e-Amir (Timur's mausoleum), and the hillside tomb complex of Shah-i-Zinda. All are covered by intricately patterned mosaic tiles and topped by domes of brilliant, shimmering turquoise.

Australasia

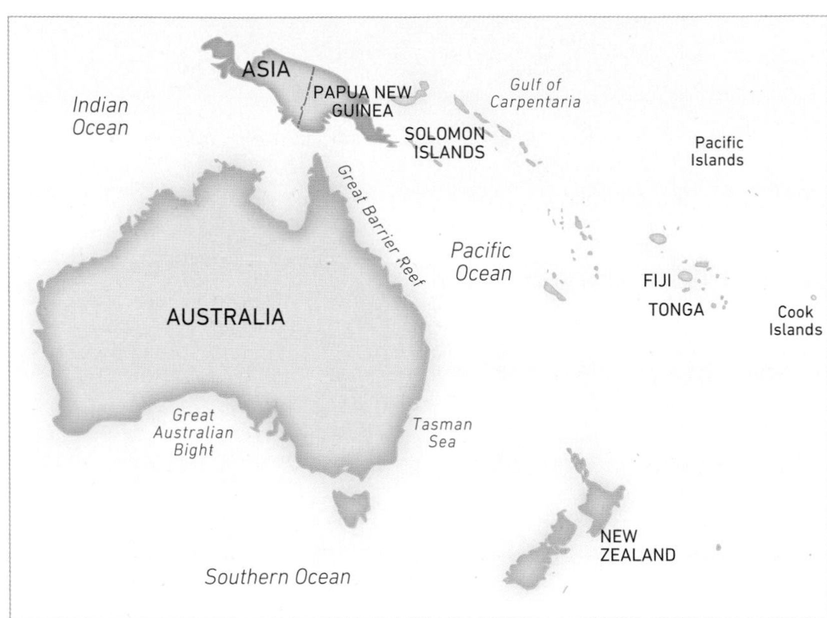

▷ THE BURKE AND WILLS TRAIL

AUSTRALIA

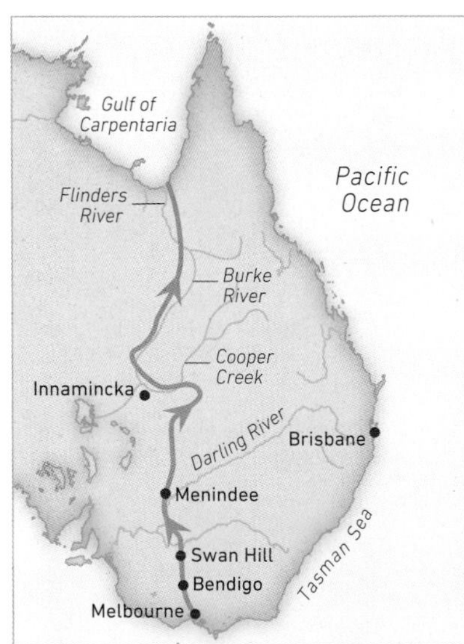

Burke and Wills's achievement—walking the 2,000 miles (3,220 km) across Australia, from Melbourne in the south to the Gulf of Carpentaria in the north—was such that it was another 150 years before anyone managed to repeat it. Historian Dave Phoenix did so, setting out in August 2008 and completing it the same year. He walked 114 of the 152 days the expedition lasted, and then wrote a guidebook so that others could follow in his footsteps. As Phoenix freely admits, the exact course taken in the original expedition is not known because the historical records are incomplete. Today, the best that anyone can do is approximate the journey. Also, to minimize the risk of death by dehydration or starvation, it should only be done in a four-wheel-drive vehicle.

From Melbourne, the freeway meanders out of the suburbs and climbs over the Great Dividing Range. On the other side, it crosses forests and farmland, and passes old homesteads and sparsely populated hamlets. A possible first overnight stay is at the former gold-mining city of Bendigo. From there, most of the roads are excellent until the town of Swan Hill; beyond this, they are little more than gravel tracks through vast empty landscapes. When it rains, these tracks become impassable, so it is vital to be mindful of the weather. Nevertheless, this is where the Outback adventure begins. The next stop is Menindee, a tiny town of fewer than 500 souls, but proud of its Burke and Wills heritage. It was here that Burke split the expedition party into two for the sake of speed.

It is a further 20 hours' drive to the tiny settlement of Innamincka, which is perhaps the most significant site on the trail. It lies on the banks of Cooper Creek (formerly Cooper's Creek), at the place where Burke and Wills died on their return journey. Their graves are there, as is the famous Dig Tree, where Burke buried his journal. Back in the vehicle, it is yet another 24 hours to the Gulf of Carpentaria, on the north coast, where Burke and Wills turned back.

▷ THE EXPLORERS' HIGHWAY

AUSTRALIA

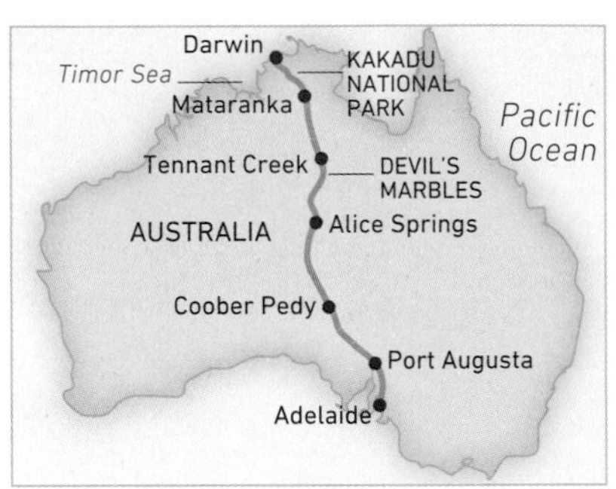

More correctly known as the Stuart Highway, this grand route runs from Darwin located in the tropical north of Australia, through the Great Australian Desert to Port Augusta on the south coast, a distance of some 1,761 miles (2,834 km). It was Australia's first transcontinental highway, and it is still often referred to simply as "The Track." Passing through great tracts of wilderness at the heart of the country, and providing a lifeline for impossibly distant communities, it is the Australian equivalent of America's

THE LAKES OF MENINDEE ON THE BURKE AND WILLS TRAIL

THE EXPLORERS' HIGHWAY SNAKES PAST THE FLINDERS RANGES

Route 66—a highway redolent of history, heroism, and romance. It is named after Scottish explorer and surveyor John McDuall Stuart, who was the first to complete a south–north crossing of Australia, in 1862.

The highway roughly follows the route that Stuart took. Most travelers drive from south to north, starting off in Adelaide, the laid-back capital of South Australia. This leads through a beautiful wine-growing region full of small vineyards, before reaching Port Augusta. It takes another day of driving over the rugged Flinders Ranges to reach the quirky opal-mining town of Coober Pedy, where generations of miners have carved out underground homes, shops, and hotels to escape the heat. The next stop is usually Alice Springs, a center of Aboriginal culture and the turn-off point for Uluru, the unmissable sandstone monolith formerly known as Ayers Rock.

Back on the road, it is a 10-hour drive to the Devil's Marbles, a group of finely balanced boulders which, according to Aboriginal myth, are the Rainbow Serpent's eggs. A further hour or so on is Tennant Creek, a gold-rush town, and Mataranka, with its warm thermal springs, is another six hours away. The Kakadu National Park, with its Aboriginal rock art, wetlands, and exotic flora and fauna is the reward for the long drive. The first glimpse of the Timor Sea is not long after, as the Stuart Highway winds into Darwin. This is Australia's only tropical capital city. It is a vibrant, bustling, cosmopolitan antidote to the 10 or 12 days of hard driving that it takes to get there.

▽ THE INDIAN PACIFIC

AUSTRALIA

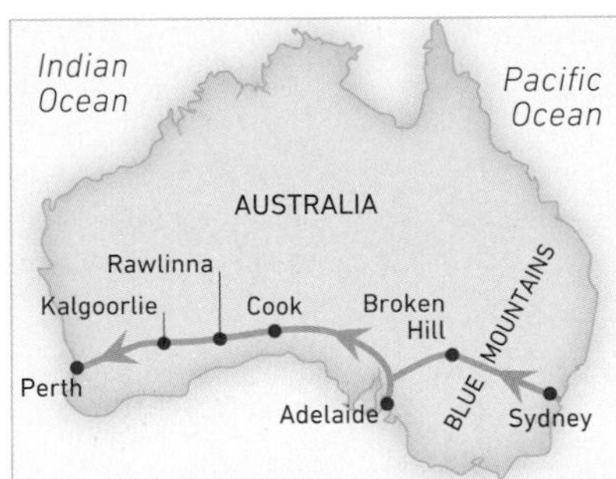

It has been called a trip across Australia through the middle of nowhere, but the Indian Pacific Railway is nothing if not epic. The line crosses the continent from Sydney on the Pacific Ocean to Perth on the Indian Ocean, a distance of 2,704 miles (4,352 km). Traveling it conveys a real sense of Australia's vastness that flying cannot replicate.

It is not an historic railway, as the line was only built in the 1970s and the first trains went into service in 1973. It is run as a private, luxury service, one that resembles a rolling hotel. Accommodation is in twin-berth compartments, although there is the pricy option of a Platinum Service, which offers real double or twin beds. A white-linen restaurant car offers some of the best meals found on a train, and there are several lounges for relaxing and watching the scenery.

The Indian Pacific leaves Sydney Central Station and winds through the suburbs before slowly climbing into the Blue Mountains. Beyond these is the Outback—a world of red earth studded by dark scrub and occasional gum trees. The train stops just long enough for travelers to go and explore the isolated mining town of Broken Hill; cosmopolitan Adelaide; the ghost town of Cook (population: four); the isolated siding of Rawlinna (which battles with Cook to serve as the definitive "middle of nowhere"); and Kalgoorlie, home of the country's biggest open-pit gold mine. The major milestone is Adelaide, after which the line crosses the hot, dusty, and extremely flat emptiness of the Nullarbor Plain (*nullus arbor* being Latin for "no trees"). At 297 miles (478 km), this is one of the longest stretches of straight railway line in the world. On the fourth day after departure, the train pulls into Perth, capital of Western Australia, and the welcome chance to rush headlong into the ocean waves.

THE THREE SISTERS OF KATOOMBA IN THE BLUE MOUNTAINS, NEW SOUTH WALES

THE COASTAL PACIFIC

NEW ZEALAND

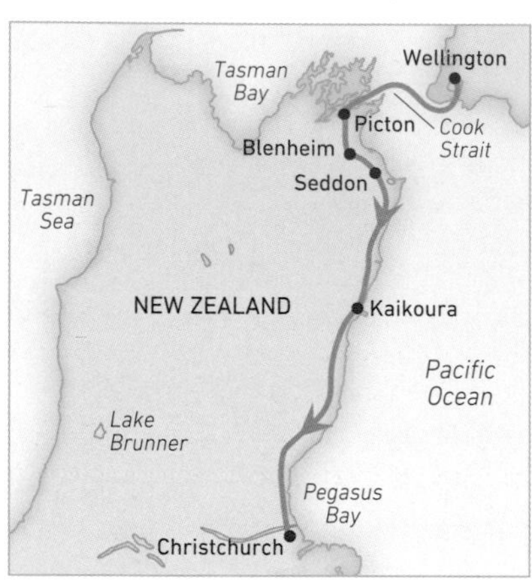

The Coastal Pacific Train (formerly known as the TranzCoastal) began life as the Main North Line and was primarily a means of connecting towns but became more of a summer tourist route due to the scenery. It operates from September to April between Picton on the northeastern tip of New Zealand's South Island and the city of Christchurch, approximately 211 miles (340 km) to the south. Earthquakes damaged the line between Blenheim and Kaikoura in November 2016 and the line was closed for repairs.

The journey is not particularly long, lasting just over five hours, but it is stunningly beautiful. The line follows the rugged Pacific coast against a backdrop of the Kaikoura Ranges, passing through 22 tunnels and over 175 bridges along the way.

Starting in the New Zealand capital of Wellington, on the southernmost tip of North Island, the three-hour crossing of the Cook Strait is one of the most scenic ferry rides in the world. On disembarking, Picton Railway Station is straight ahead. The train leaves Picton and curves around the valley out of town to the Marlborough wine-growing region. Vineyards stretch across plains and rolling hillsides. The train calls at Blenheim, the region's main town. Soon after, it climbs a long, gentle pass through grassy hills, and snow-capped mountains appear in the distance on the right. About an hour and a half into the journey, the line hits the coast and runs along it for the next 60 miles (100 km) or so. Seals and dolphins sometimes dot the surf. The train next stops at Kaikoura, South Island's main whale-watching and dolphin-swimming center. It is a good place to break the journey and stop over for a night or two. South of there, the train swings inland again, through green hills and valleys. It passes through the small towns of Waipara and Rangiora before entering the suburbs of Christchurch. The journey ends at the city's new station, which is a short shuttle-bus ride from the city center.

▽ FOLLOWING CAPTAIN COOK

PACIFIC ISLANDS

Given Captain Cook circumnavigated the world two and a half times, following in his footsteps is quite an undertaking. The journey begins in the English county of Yorkshire, where he was born, and proceeds to Plymouth, from where he set sail on the first of his voyages of discovery in 1768. Tahiti was Cook's first port of call on his earliest great voyage, and Hawaii the final point of his third trip (he was killed there). In between, Cook mapped the entire New Zealand coastline, and became the first European to make contact with the Maori people. Today, that meeting is commemorated in the Cook Landing Site National Historic Reserve in Gisborne, on North Island. This was where the Maori themselves first came ashore more than 400 years earlier. A fine statue of Cook, unveiled in 1932, can be found in Christchurch, on South Island.

Cook was also the first European to chart Australia's eastern coastline, landing at Botany Bay, now a suburb of Sydney. Today, the site is part of the Botany Bay National Park, with a Discovery Center dedicated to Cook. A full-scale, seaworthy replica of Cook's ship, HMS *Endeavour*, can be boarded at the city's national maritime museum. Further north, in Queensland, Cooktown is named after him. This is where the *Endeavour* put in for repairs after being holed on the Great Barrier Reef—an event commemorated in the town's James Cook Historical Museum. The marine and bird life, and botanical specimens ashore, that were recorded by Cook's crew match what it is possible to see today.

A true Cook enthusiast should also visit the Cook Islands. This remote group of 15 volcanic islands in the South Pacific Ocean was first settled in the 6th century by Polynesians, who had migrated across the ocean from Tahiti. Cook went there in 1773 and 1777 and originally named them the Hervey Islands, but the name was later changed in his honor. Fringed with palm trees, the islands are as beautiful as in Cook's day, with white sandy beaches and turquoise waters.

COOK'S BAY, COMPLETE WITH CORAL REEFS, ON THE FRENCH POLYNESIAN ISLAND OF MOOREA, NEAR TAHITI

Central and South America

△ THE GALÁPAGOS

ECUADOR

Countless places are said to be "inspiring," but few deserve the epithet more than the Galápagos—a group of 21 islands off the coast of South America where naturalist Charles Darwin conceived his theory of evolution. At just 26, he spent two and a half weeks studying the flora and fauna there in 1835, an experience that set him on the road to publishing his ground-breaking work, *On the Origin of Species*, in 1859.

Located in the Pacific Ocean, roughly 600 miles (1,000 km) off the coast of Ecuador, the Galápagos had received few human visitors by Darwin's day, and access today is controlled to minimize the impact of people on the environment. Only four of the islands are inhabited (San Cristóbal, Floreana, Isabela, in the order in which Darwin visited them, and Santa Cruz), and this is where visitors have to stay. No overnight stays are permitted on any of the other islands, although Darwin stayed on Santiago for over a week. Only five of the uninhabited islands are close enough to visit on individual day trips so these are the extent of what any visitor staying in a hotel can see. The alternative is to stay on a liveaboard boat, which enables visits to the more distant islands.

Whichever way, the abundance of wildlife on the Galápagos is overwhelming. The giant tortoises, flightless cormorants, and diverse variety of finches that helped Darwin to formulate his theories are still living there today. The pristine waters are home to unique marine iguanas, sea lions, turtles, and black-and-white-bellied manta rays, and the bird life ranges from clownish, blue-footed boobies to elegant, neon-pink flamingoes. Just as when Darwin visited in the 19th century, many of the animals are remarkably tame, as they have never learned to fear humans, so close-up encounters are common.

THE CHE GUEVARA TRAIL

BOLIVIA

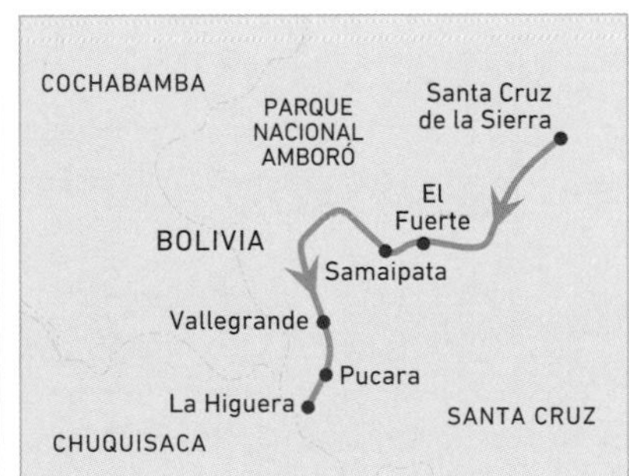

Thanks to the film *The Motorcycle Diaries*, people are now familiar with the story of how, in January 1952, the 23-year-old Ernesto "Che" Guevara and his colleague Alberto Granado set out on a nine-month motorcycle journey around Argentina, Chile, Colombia, Peru, and Venezuela.

Che then famously fought alongside the Castro brothers, overthrowing the administration of Batista in Cuba in 1959. Less well known is the time that Guevara spent in Bolivia in 1966–67.

MARINE IGUANAS ON SANTA CRUZ ISLAND IN THE GALÁPAGOS

This was a deadly serious mission to foment an uprising in Bolivia similar to the one in Cuba. It failed and ended in Guevara's execution in 1967.

Despite the fact that it was the Bolivian government that hunted, captured, and killed Guevara 50 years ago, the country's ministry of tourism now promotes a *Ruta del Che*, or Che Guevara Trail. The trek takes several days, and takes in the towns and forests where Che and his guerrilla fighters hid while trying to raise support for the revolutionary cause.

The trail leads by road from the lively capital city of Santa Cruz west to Samaipata, a small, sleepy town that was once overtaken by Che Guevara's *guerrilleros*. It is famous today as a base for visits to the mysterious pre-Inca hilltop site of El Fuerte nearby, and for trips into the Parque Nacional Amboró. The road continues to Vallegrande, where it is possible to visit the hospital laundry room in which Che's body was put on display to the public after his death. There is also the Che Guevara Museum and a memorial marking the spot where he and six of his colleagues were buried—until they were disinterred and removed to Cuba for reburial in 1997.

The road carries on south, through a small, picturesque village called Pucara, before reaching the village of La Higuera. This is where Guevara and his fighters were brought when they were captured on October 8, 1967. Guevara was held captive in a small school, which you can visit, and the following day he was taken outside and shot. Part Two of Steven Soderbergh's 2008 film, *Che: A Revolutionary Life* gives some background to the events that are commemorated on the trail.

HIKERS ON THE PERITO MORENO GLACIER IN LOS GLACIARES NATIONAL PARK, OFF THE PATAGONIAN HIGHWAY IN ARGENTINA

◁ THE PATAGONIAN HIGHWAY

ARGENTINA

Argentina's Ruta Nacional 40 (RN40), which locals call *la cuarenta* (the forty), is one of the world's great road trips. It runs for more than 3,106 miles (5,000 km), from the Bolivian border in the north to the Cabo Virgenes Lighthouse at the very bottom of Argentina. It skirts the far east side of the country, following the line of the Andes Mountains. In the north, at Abra del Acay in the Salta region near Bolivia, the road reaches an altitude of 16,404 feet (5,000 m) above sea level, while at its southern end it drops down to sea level. During this long, slow descent, the road crosses 20 national parks, 18 major rivers, and 27 passes in the Andes. The word "epic" hardly does it justice.

Driving the entire length of the RN40 is a serious undertaking. Many sections are little more than rutted tracks, and much of it crosses empty wilderness. Today, more and more of the road is being surfaced, but a four-wheel drive is still essential. It is also vital to stock up with provisions, with plenty of food, water, and reserve fuel. The rewards include some magnificent scenery, ranging from jagged Andean peaks to pristine plains and rivers. This must be what the American West looked like 150 years ago.

For those who are short of time, the best part of the RN40 is the Patagonian stretch, south of the Rio Negro province. There, highlights include the small towns of El Calafate and El Chaltén—both gateways to Los Glaciares National Park, with its blue-ice landscapes, and the 13,000-year-old rock art of *Cueva de las Manos* (Cave of the Hands). There are also isolated *estancias* (ranches), sheep farms, and the steppes to see, as well as the guanacos—llama-like natives of the Patagonian steppe—that occasionally stray across your path. At the end of the road lies the port city of Río Gállegos, near the Strait of Magellan. There, a lighthouse bears a sign reading "0 km," which marks the end of an amazing journey.

It is best to allow one to two months to do the trip, and to go between December and March, when the weather is finest. The journey will be quicker when the road has been paved, but something will also be lost. For now, the road's challenge is part of its charm.

▽ THE COPPER CANYON RAILWAY

MEXICO

Little known outside Mexico, *Barranca del Cobre* (Copper Canyon) is a canyon system in the state of Chihuahua that is larger and deeper than the Grand Canyon in the US. Part of the reason so few people know about it is that the area is incredibly remote and hard to travel around. The one exception to this is the Copper Canyon Railway, which runs right through the heart of the region.

The route was planned as a freight connection between Chihuahua and the coast. Completed in 1961, the line, known locally as *El Chepe*, took almost 90 years to construct. It runs 418 miles (673 km) from Los Mochis, by the Sea of Cortez, to Chihuahua, deep in the interior. Along the way, it barrels over 37 bridges and through 86 tunnels, often hugging tight to precipitous cliff walls. There are two daily trains each way—one a speedy trip for tourists, the other a slow stopping service for locals, which is perfect for hopping on and off. There are a few places well worth visiting. The first of these is Divisadro, the best place from which to explore the canyon on foot. Creel is an old logging town set among pine forests and strange rock formations. It is the base for hikes to the Cusarare Waterfalls or Basirecota hot springs, or for the bus to Batópilas, an old silver-mining town at the bottom of the canyon. Creel is also a place to encounter the local Tarahumara people, who wear distinctive multicolored clothing.

At the end of the line lies Chihuahua, the capital of Mexico's biggest state. It is a pleasant colonial city, with some beautiful buildings and a history of revolution that is celebrated in several museums, including a particularly colorful one dedicated to the guerilla leader Pancho Villa.

COPPER CANYON NATIONAL PARK VIEWED FROM CHIHUAHUA, MEXICO

▽ THE MAYAN ROUTE

MEXICO AND GUATEMALA

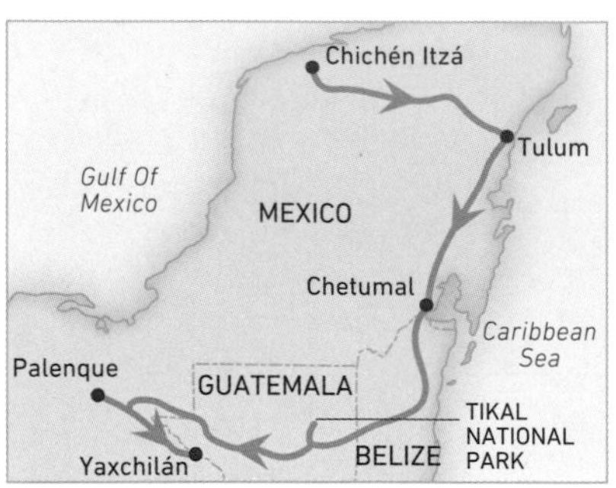

The Mayan sites of Central America have probably changed little in 500 years, though the crops and animals in the region were brought by Spanish conquerors of Mexico. When Hernán Cortés arrived on the coast of Yucatán in February 1519, the Mayan civilization was around 3,500 years old. By then, many of today's ruins had already been abandoned, and they received little further attention until they were rediscovered by Western explorers in the late 19th and early 20th centuries. Since then, people have become increasingly fascinated by what remains of this extremely enigmatic culture.

Mayan sites are scattered across several countries. Most of them are in Mexico, Belize, and Guatemala, but there are also several in El Salvador and Honduras. Although tourist brochures talk about *La Ruta Maya* (The Mayan Route), there is no such trail and travelers have to create their own itinerary. The big three sites are Chichén Itzá and Tulum in Mexico, and Tikal in Guatemala. The first two are popular because they can be seen on a day trip from the resort of Cancún. Despite the crowds, Chichén Itzá, in particular, is stunning, with a towering pyramidal temple with stepped sides called El Castillo. Tulum lies to the east of this, its crumbling towers standing atop 39-foot (12-m) cliffs on the Yucatán Peninsula. Tikal, called the "mother of all Mayan sites" because of its size, attracts significantly fewer visitors but is far more atmospheric.

West of Tikal, and back in Mexico, lies Palenque, a dreamlike landscape of jungle-swathed temples and tombs. Between Tikal and Palenque, right off the beaten track on the border between Mexico and Guatemala, lies Yaxchilán. The ruins here are several hours' drive from the nearest hotel, and can only be reached by boat along the Usumacinta River. Due to its remoteness, any visitors that manage to reach it are likely to have the site to themselves. As they push through the vines and giant leaves to discover ruins as far as the eye can see, it is like stumbling upon a secret kingdom, just as the explorers of old did.

THE MAYAN SITE OF TIKAL, GUATEMALA

THE RUINS OF THE INCA CITY OF MACHU PICCHU, PERU

△ THE *HIRAM BINGHAM*

PERU

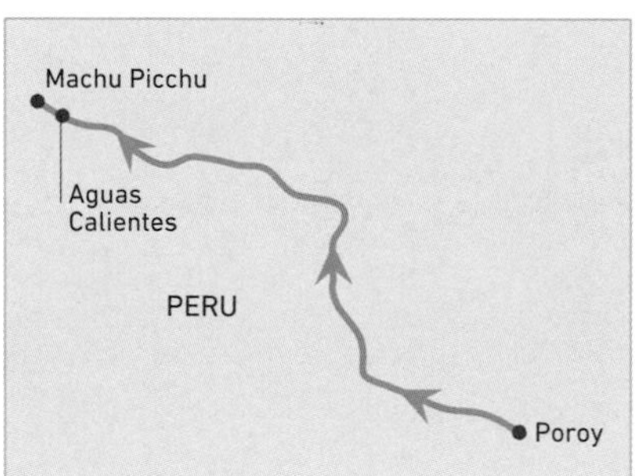

The mountain-plateau Inca ruins of Machu Picchu are celebrated as a wonder of the world, but getting there can be equally wondrous. A train called the *Hiram Bingham* (named after the American explorer who rediscovered Machu Picchu in 1911) runs from Poroy, just outside Cuzco, to Aguas Calientes, the town from which Machu Picchu can be reached by bus. The journey is hardly epic, covering just 57 miles (97 km), and takes a little over three hours, but the scenery is magnificent, with rugged mountains, deep gorges, rushing rivers, and dense forest. The *Bingham* is an unabashedly luxury service and is correspondingly expensive, but there is also a local train that operates the same route for a fraction of the price.

Anyone fit and able-bodied should also take the Inca Trail—a four-day, 27-mile (43-km) guided trek that follows a narrow, winding trail over the mountains. The trail starts between Cuzco and Aguas Calientes and passes through lush, colorful cloud forests that were laid out by the Incas themselves. It reaches 13,829 feet (4,215 m) above sea level at its highest point—the luridly named *Warmi Wañusqa*, or Dead Woman's Pass. The hike is taken at a steady pace, and there are plenty of stops to explore the lesser-known ruins along the way, including Phuyupatamarka, which has a series of ceremonial baths cascading with clear mountain water. The route approaches Machu Picchu from above, rather than from the main tourist entrance, and the first sight of the ruins below is unforgettable. To limit the impact of tourism on the environment, the number of people on the trail is strictly controlled, and applications for trekking permits have to be made many months in advance.

However, for those without an Inca Trail reservation, there are several other walking routes to Machu Picchu. These vary in length and difficulty, and include the 1-day Inca Trail, the 3–5-day Lares Route, and the 5–8-day Salcantay Route.

Europe

▽ LORD BYRON IN ALBANIA

GREECE AND ALBANIA

In 1809, years before he became a household name across Europe, George Gordon Byron—better known as Lord Byron—spent about 10 days traveling on horseback and on foot through Albania with a childhood friend named John Cam Hobhouse. Entering what was then a backwater of the Ottoman Empire, the two men, still in their early twenties, visited various ancient ruins and enjoyed the hospitality of a local despot, Ali Pasha.

They arrived in Greece at the port of Preveza, after a voyage from Malta, visiting the nearby Roman ruins at Nicopolis, before moving inland to the town of Arta, which was famous for its medieval bridge. From there, they rode north to the regional center of Ioánnina, and then to the small village of Zitsa—which Byron said had one of the most beautiful settings he had ever seen. Their next stop was Albania, which, thanks to the communist dictator Enver Hoxha, who closed off the country after World War II, is no better known today than it was in Byron's time. The landscapes are as unspoiled as then: mountainous, with abundant forests and lakes, and sparkling Adriatic beaches.

Once across the border, Byron and Hobhouse headed for the castle at Libohovë, of which only the ramparts remain for visitors to see today. Their goal was Tepelenë, where they stayed as guests of Ali Pasha. Byron described him as "a remorseless tyrant, guilty of the most horrible cruelties" (indeed, he roasted his enemies alive), "very brave, so good a general that they call him the Mahometan Buonaparte." A plaque celebrating the visit is fixed to a wall by a gas station. From there, the pair returned to Greece, where Byron began work on a poem that drew on his travels. Titled *Childe Harold's Pilgrimage*, it was published between 1812 and 1818. It gave the world the romantic "Byronic hero," and brought its author lasting fame.

THE ROMAN ODEON OF NICOPOLIS, NEAR PREVEZA, GREECE

▷ ROBERT LOUIS STEVENSON IN THE CÉVENNES

FRANCE

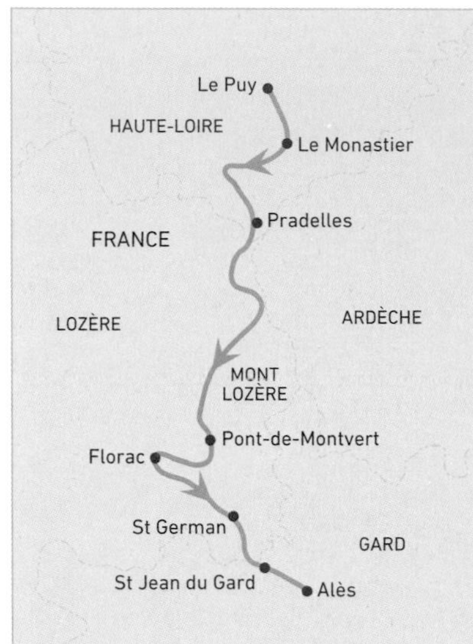

In 1878, the 27-year-old Robert Louis Stevenson was a struggling Scottish writer with a single obscure travel book under his belt (*An Inland Voyage*, published that year). Hoping to cure a broken heart, he moved to Le-Monastier-sur-Gazeille in south-central France, and from there, with a newly acquired donkey named Modestine, an egg whisk, and a revolver, he set out for the hills.

"I travel not to go anywhere, but to go. I travel for travel's sake," he wrote in his journal. "The great affair is to move; to feel the needs and hitches of our life more clearly." His account provided the basis for the book that became a minor classic of travel writing, *Travels with a Donkey in the Cévennes*. Its success gave Stevenson the encouragement and money to continue writing. His commitment was rewarded soon afterward with the publication of the novels *Treasure Island, Dr Jekyll and Mr Hyde*, and *Kidnapped* in quick succession.

Today, there is an official Stevenson Trail, designated GR70 on the French national network. It extends the route that Stevenson took and starts in Le Puy-en-Velay, which is to the north of Le Monastier, and ends 140 miles (225 km) to the south, at Alès. It takes about 12 days to complete, and you can even hire a donkey to ride on some stretches. The trail leads across a volcanic plateau and then through the Cévennes, one of the most rugged and least-populated areas of France, much of which is now protected as a National Park and is a haven for wildlife. The route drops down into pretty villages, such as Pradelles, Pont-de-Montvert, and Florac, where the locals still wear berets and play pétanque in the shady squares, as they did in Stevenson's time.

Travels with a Donkey was one of the first travel books to portray hiking and camping outdoors as something done for pleasure rather than necessity. Stevenson even had an early version of a sleeping bag especially made for him so that he could sleep under the stars, although it was so big and heavy he needed a donkey to carry it.

A PACK DONKEY IN THE CÉVENNES MOUNTAINS, FRANCE

▷ THE D-DAY LANDING BEACHES

FRANCE

Early on the morning on June 6, 1944, some 160,000 Allied soldiers landed along a 50-mile (80-km) chain of beaches in Normandy, in an operation to liberate France and ultimately drive the German army all the way back to Berlin. General Eisenhower called it a crusade in which "we will accept nothing less than full victory". The cost in lives was heavy, with more than 10,000 Allied troops killed or wounded, but by the end of that first day, the Allies had gained a crucial foothold, which was gradually expanded over the following weeks and months. By late August, Paris had been liberated, and Germany's surrender came soon afterward.

Now, more than 70 years later, the Normandy coast is peaceful, featuring lovely seaside towns and picturesque sandy beaches. Inland lies an ageless landscape of fields and farmhouses. However, the memories of D-Day are engrained in the environment, with monuments at almost every bend in the road and marking every bluff. Of the five beaches, two were taken by American forces; these were code-named Omaha and Utah. Omaha was the deadliest beach of all, and as testimony to that, the American Cemetery and Memorial at Colleville-sur-Mer, overlooking the beach, contains the graves of 9,387 American soldiers. Within walking distance from the cemetery, at Saint-Laurent-sur-Mer, is a monument dedicated to the "Big Red One," the US 1st Infantry Division. Nearby is the Omaha Beach Memorial Museum, which displays uniforms, weapons, personal objects, and vehicles from the campaign. To get an idea of what the landing forces were facing, visit the Musée des Batteries de Maisy—a preserved group of German artillery batteries and HQ with original field guns. An American Rangers monument also stands at the site.

Utah was the most westerly of the five beaches, and the site of massed airborne landings. Its story is told at the Airborne Museum, which is at Sainte-Mère-Église, a village that itself has numerous plaques explaining the operations of the US paratroopers. In the square, a mock parachute dangles from the church, commemorating what happened to one paratrooper who became snagged on the church's spire.

▷ THE ROMANTIC RHINE

GERMANY

Although a minnow compared with the Amazon, the Nile, or Mississippi, the Rhine is one of Europe's major waterways. Together with the Danube, it formed much of the northern frontier of the Roman Empire and has, since then, been a vital artery through Europe, carrying trade and goods deep inland. The many castles along the river are testament to its historical and cultural importance, both as a border and as a thoroughfare.

Rising in Switzerland, the river flows through Germany for most of its 760 miles (1,230 km), before emptying into the North Sea in the Netherlands. On the way, it passes through dramatic landscapes that have bewitched travelers for centuries. The 19th-century Romantics loved its craggy bluffs and Gothic ruins. One of their favorite spots was Drachenfels (Dragon's Crag), about which Lord Byron wrote: "the castled crag of Drachenfels frowns o'er the wide and winding Rhine." Visitors can follow in Byron's footsteps up the steep road to the ruins of the castle to enjoy views along the river to the spires of Cologne Cathedral. Other poets were here before Byron: the castle is named after a legendary dragon that lived on the hill and was slain by Siegfrid, hero of the medieval *Nibelungenlied*. The Middle Rhine, the 60-mile (100-km) section between Koblenz and Mainz, has about 40 such castles crowning vineyard-clad slopes, many of which were rebuilt in the 19th century to make them look more medieval.

Any Rhine tour should also include Assmannshausen, a village just west of Wiesbaden. It was a favorite place of the famous German poet and dramatist Johann Wolfgang von Goethe, the author of *Faust*. Not far away is Sankt Goarshausen, site of the towering cliffs of Lorelei, named after the tale of the beautiful siren who lured sailors to destruction on the rocks at the base of the cliff. Mark Twain included a verse poem about the Lorelei legend in *A Tramp Abroad* (1878), his account of his travels in the Rhine Valley, among other places. He claimed in this book that "Germany, in the summer, is the perfection of the beautiful"—high praise indeed.

STAHLECK CASTLE, ONE OF MANY FORTIFICATIONS OVERLOOKING THE RHINE

"LES BRAVES", THE OMAHA BEACH MONUMENT, AT SAINT-LAURENT-SUR-MER, FRANCE

SOME OF THE DORIC COLUMNS SURVIVE AT THE TEMPLE OF APOLLO, DELPHI

◁ ANCIENT GREECE

GREECE

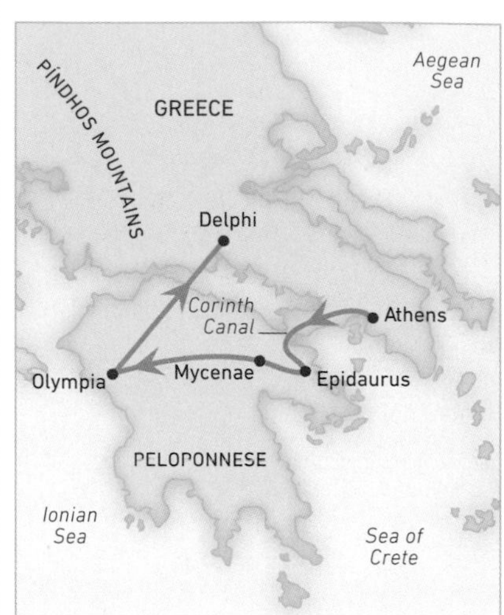

The ancient Greeks developed one of the most advanced civilizations in the world and their philosophy, learning, exploration, science, and mathematics laid the foundations of the modern world. They were also great travelers and architects, building temples, shrines, and open-air theaters in the places that were important to them. A journey around some of the most important ancient Greek archeological sites provides a fascinating insight into their ancient civilization.

The tour should start at Athens, which is the location of the Parthenon, the temple dedicated to the goddess from whom the city takes its name, Athena. It was constructed in 447–438 BCE, when the Athenian Empire was at the peak of its power, and it remains the most important surviving building of ancient Greece. It is a fine example of classical design, being rectangular with a single row of Doric columns on all sides.

From Athens, it is easy to drive west, cross the Corinth Canal, and head into the Peloponnese to visit Epidaurus, the site of a magnificent theater that was built in the 4th century BCE, and later extended by the Romans to hold 14,000 people. Nearby is one of the most impressive archaeological sites in the country: Mycenae, the seat of King Agamemnon, who led the Greek armies against the Trojans.

The route continues west to Olympia, the birthplace of the Olympic Games, visited by thousands of ancient Greeks. This was the site of temples dedicated to Zeus, the king of the gods, and Hera, his queen, as well as an ancient stadium. Following the destruction ordered by Theodosius II and the havoc wreaked by subsequent earthquakes, none of the temples are still standing, but the ruins do provide some idea of former glories, and the Olympic flame is still lit there today for the modern Games.

The next destination is the most evocative of the ancient sites, Delphi. This was the seat of an oracle whom the ancient Greeks consulted before all major undertakings. They considered the place the center of the Greek world. Delphi is unmissable, both for the historic significance of the ruins and the wonderful location on the slopes of Mount Parnassus.

▽ IN THE FOOTSTEPS OF ALEXANDER THE GREAT

GREECE, TURKEY, AND IRAN

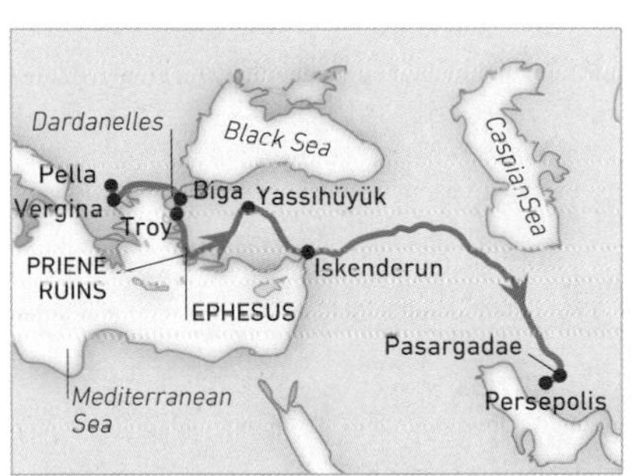

In the 4th century BCE, the young king Alexander of Macedon set off at the age of 22 on a grand expedition that led to him establishing the largest empire that the world had ever known in just 10 years. It stretched across three continents, from Greece and Albania in the west, to Egypt in the south, and India to the east.

A journey following in Alexander's footsteps could well start at Pella, in northern Greece, where he was born in 356 BCE, and which is today an archeological site with a museum. Nearby Vergina is where Alexander was proclaimed king following the assassination of his father, Philip II. Philip's tomb was discovered unlooted in 1976. The armor, the gold-plated quiver, and the ivory-and-gold shield with which he was buried are still on display to the public.

Alexander sailed from Greece, reaching Asia at the Hellespont, the modern-day Dardanelles in Turkey. He fought the Persians at the River Granicus, not far from the modern town of Biga, then traveled via Troy and Ephesus to Priene, where he paid for a new temple dedicated to Athena. The remains of the temple can be visited, along with the ruins of a structure known as the House of Alexander, where the king is said to have stayed during his time in the city. At this point, a detour north could head into the Anatolian heartland to the town of Yassıhuyuk, which stands on what was once Gordian, the capital of ancient Phrygia. It was here that Alexander slashed through the famous knot and proclaimed himself "master of Asia". A final stop in Turkey might be Iskenderun, a city founded by Alexander and named after him. It celebrates his defeat of the Persian army of Darius III at a site near here. Ideally, the journey would now continue across the border into Iran, to visit the ancient Persian capital of Persepolis, occupied by the Macedonian army around January 330 BCE, and now one of the world's most fascinating archaeological sites. It could also take in the first capital of the Persian Empire, Pasargadae, which was visited by Alexander.

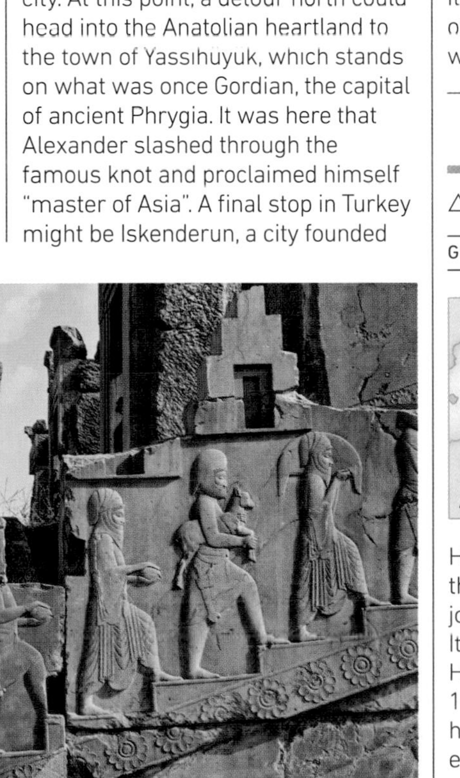

RELIEF SHOWING NOBLES CARRYING TRIBUTES TO THEIR KING, PERSEPOLIS

NAVAGIO BAY, ZAKYNTHOS, ONE OF THE IONIAN ISLANDS, GREECE

△ TRACING THE *ODYSSEY*

GREECE

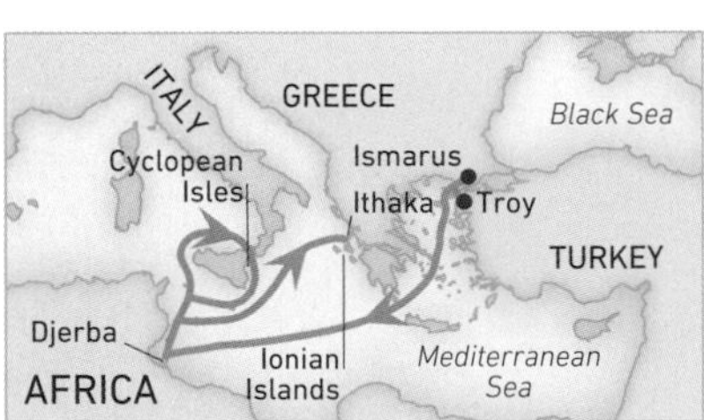

Homer's epic poem the *Odyssey* tells the tale of the hero Odysseus, and his journey home to his wife and son in Ithaca after the end of the Trojan War. He was waylaid in the attempt for 10 years, during which time he and his men wandered the Mediterranean, encountering many strange places and having numerous fantastical adventures. The *Odyssey* is a work of fiction, not a travelogue, but it may have had its foundations in true events and historians over the ages have speculatively linked certain geographic locations to some of the places the epic describes. All that is known for sure is that the journey began at Troy, which now lies in the province of Çanakkale on the Aegean coast of Turkey. Next, Odysseus and his crew sacked Ismarus, which may have been on the coast of Thrace, in what is now northern Greece. They sailed south but were pushed off course by the wind and currents, ending up in the Land of the Lotus-Eaters, "who live on a food that comes from a kind of flower." The Greek historian Polybius identified this place as the still seductive island of Djerba, off modern-day Tunisia. The island of the giant Cyclops is usually linked with Sicily, off the east coast of which the Cyclopean Isles lie, but by now, many scholars think, Homer's epic had entered the realms of fantasy.

Perhaps the best idea for anyone looking for the spirit of Homer is to visit the Greek Ionian Islands, the site of Ithaca and its neighbors. This is generally taken to be the home to which Odysseus was longing to return, and where his loyal wife, Penelope, was waiting for him. It is easy to understand his eagerness to get back. It is a place of pure enchantment, with a rugged coast fringed by deep blue waters, a mountainous interior dotted with olive groves, pine trees, and cypresses, and pretty villages. Some travel writers claim that it is the most beautiful island in Greece.

▽ VIA FRANCIGENA

SWITZERLAND AND ITALY

The Via Francigena is an ancient route that pilgrims took in medieval times from Canterbury, in England, through France and Switzerland to Rome, the resting place of St. Peter and St. Paul. Covering more than 1,200 miles (2,000 km), it would have taken about four months to walk the whole route. Not surprisingly, it fell out of fashion and the numbers of pilgrims dwindled. In 2009, however, the Italian government launched a project to reinstate the Italian leg of the route. Since then, it has been revamped and signposted, with a supporting website (www.viefrancigene.org) that is full of practical information and maps that can be downloaded.

The trail begins at the Great Saint Bernard Pass in the Great Western Alps in Switzerland, at the border with Italy. There is a hospice here, founded by Augustinian monks in 1049, which is legendary for its hospitality to travelers and its use of St. Bernard dogs for mountain rescues. The route descends rapidly to the plains of northern Italy, avoiding the big cities of Turin and Milan by sticking to minor roads, lanes between grassy banks and drystone walls, and forest paths. It winds down through Emilia-Romagna and into the golden hills of Tuscany. Again, the way skirts Pisa and Florence (although it would be worth making a detour to visit them) but it does go through medieval Siena and the hilltop town of Montefiascone, which overlooks Lake Bolsena in an old volcanic crater.

The Via Francigena offers a huge variety of vistas, from mountains and undulating vine-covered hillsides to coastal plains and stretches by the sea. The view that is perhaps most welcome, though, is the first glimpse of the dome of St. Peter's from the top of Monte Mario on the approach to Rome, the end of the journey.

THE STATUE OF SAINT BERNARD DOMINATES THE GREAT SAINT BERNARD PASS

THE COLOSSEUM AND THE RUINS OF ANCIENT ROME

△ ANCIENT ROME

ITALY

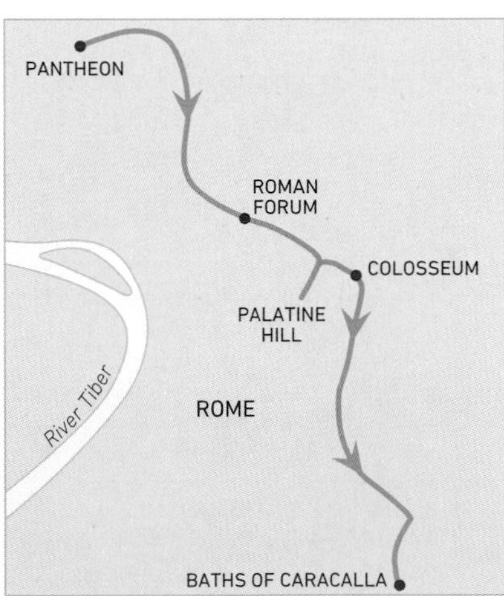

While there are many more recent glories of the modern city of Rome—St. Peter's, the Vatican, palazzos, and piazzas—it is still possible to track the vestiges of the classical city in a day's walk. Once the center of one of the greatest empires ever known, Rome's ancient monuments remain standing amid the urban sprawl.

Perhaps the most astonishing building is the Pantheon, a former temple completed by the Emperor Hadrian in around 126 BCE. Fronted by a huge portico, the main part of the building is circular and has a coffered concrete dome ceiling. Even nearly 2,000 years after it was built, the Pantheon's dome is still the world's largest unreinforced concrete dome. It is impossible to visit and not be humbled by the achievements of the Roman Empire. The Pantheon is also one of the best preserved buildings of ancient Rome, because it has been in continuous use throughout its history. It has been a church since the 7th century, and is still used as one today.

A few miles away, the Forum and Palatine were the centers of ancient Rome. Palatine Hill was the residence of emperors and senators, and the Forum combined the functions of marketplace, business district, and civic center. Today both areas are a maze of colonnades, terraces, and buildings that range from mere outlines in the ground to complete residences with vibrant frescoes.

Preeminent among the ancient monuments is the Colosseum. Half circus, half sports arena, Rome's most famous classical ruin has provided the blueprint for every stadium ever built since it was completed in 80 BCE. It seated over 50,000 people, from the emperor to the humblest citizen. Visitors today can explore the underfloor passageways through which gladiators and wild beasts made their entrances into the spectacular arena.

Further impressive Roman feats of engineering are on show at the Baths of Caracalla. Founded in 217 BCE, these baths incorporated two large gyms, an open-air pool, and several steam rooms of various temperatures, including a vast, domed extra-hot *calidarium*. The complex could host up to 1,500 people at any one time, and the towering ruins remain impressive for the modern visitor.

▷ THE GRAND TOUR TODAY

FRANCE, SWITZERLAND, AND ITALY

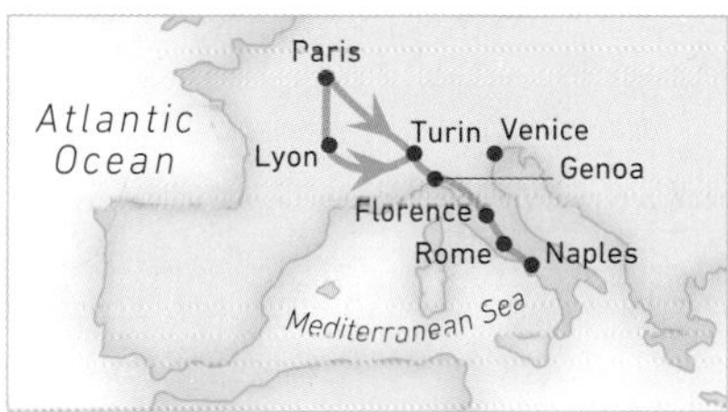

Although the 18th-century traveler on the Grand Tour could seek out art, culture, and the roots of Western civilization at his leisure, travelers today usually have to contend with both time and financial constraints, so are likely to have to select just a section of the original Grand Tour.

Paris is still the ideal starting point, including visits to the Louvre and Versailles. From there, one possible route is to take the train to Geneva in Switzerland and then on, again by rail, to Turin. A more intriguing alternative, however, is to travel from Paris to Lyon and transfer to a Turin train there. This travels on a line that goes through the Fréjus Tunnel in the Alps. Formerly known as the Mont Cenis Tunnel, this roughly follows the route that many Grand Tourists took, only they traveled by horse-drawn *diligence* (coach) in summer or by sledge in winter.

A highlight of Turin for visitors today, as it was to those who traveled two and a half centuries ago, is the Galleria Sabauda, the personal art collection of the Savoy monarchy, which was amassed over 400 years and is now housed in the regal Palazzo Reale.

THE COLORFUL CITY OF FLORENCE AND ITS CATHEDRAL

From here, most travelers of old pushed straight on for what then, as today, was a major highlight on the itinerary: Florence. Grand Tourists spent weeks or even months there, taking in the splendors of the Medicis' great Renaissance city, loitering on the Piazza del Duomo in the shadow of Brunelleschi's domed cathedral, visiting the many churches with their masterly frescoes and altarpieces, and paying homage to Michelangelo's sculptures. It was only the thought that Rome still lay ahead that pried them away.

In Rome, the favored haunt was the area around the Spanish Steps, where the English Romantic poet John Keats lived from 1820 until his death in 1821. As well as contemplating the ruins of the ancient city, grand tourists were also intent on seeing as much art by Michelangelo, Raphael, Botticelli, and Caravaggio as possible, which was in churches and galleries all around the city. Today's travelers can head straight to the Borghese Gallery, which houses one of the world's great art collections, and the Capitoline Museum. After Rome, those with more time can take the train to Naples, to see Vesuvius and to visit Herculaneum and Pompeii, which had only just been discovered at the time of the Grand Tour.

▽ CAMINO DE SANTIAGO

SPAIN

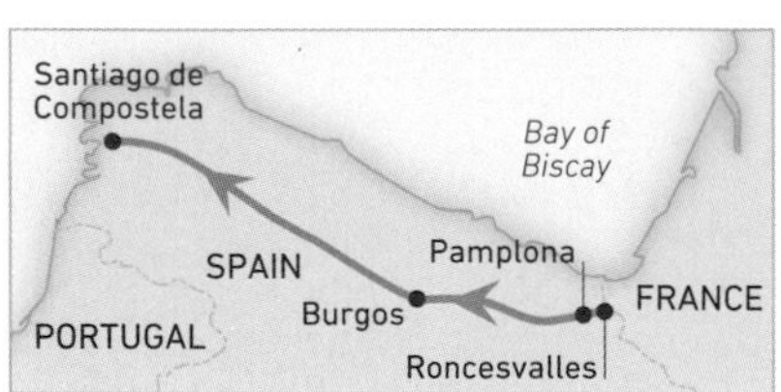

In the Middle Ages, Santiago de Compostela, a cathedral town in the far northwest of Spain linked with the biblical apostle James, was second only to Jerusalem and Rome as the most sacred center of pilgrimage. It still attracts over 100,000 people a year, many of whom walk or cycle across Spain on the *Camino de Santiago* (Route of St. James) to get there. Some are modern-day pilgrims making their own spiritual journey; others are simply taking pleasure in walking the high plains of Castilla and the hills of Galicia.

The *Camino de Santiago* has no single route or starting point, although many begin at Roncesvalles, a village in the Pyrenees, just a few miles south of the French border. From here, it is approximately 485 miles (780 km) to Santiago de Compostela, which equates to three or four weeks of walking, or about 10 days cycling. The trails west are marked with yellow arrows and scallop shells, a symbol of the pilgrimage. On the way are *albergues* (hostels) offering cheap accommodation for pilgrims. To prove their status, travelers carry a *Credencial del Peregrino* (Pilgrim's Passport), which is stamped twice a day along the *route*.

The walking is punctuated with plenty of opportunities for sightseeing, including the city of Pamplona, which is famous for the Running of the Bulls each July. Pamplona is also worth exploring for its beautiful cathedral, historic ramparts, and atmospheric Café Iruña, a favorite of the writer Ernest Hemingway. It is also worth making a short detour south to the striking Castle of Clavijo, which is visible for miles, and topped by a cross of St. James. Other worthwhile halts include the twin monasteries of San Millan de la Cogolla, and the provincial capital of Burgos. The striking Gothic cathedral there complements the soaring splendor of Santiago de Compostela's own Romanesque cathedral, which greets pilgrims at the end of the route.

HORESHOE ARCHES SUCH AS THESE IN CORDOBA, SPAIN, ARE A CLEAR REMINDER OF THE REGION'S ISLAMIC HERITAGE

THE BRIDGE OVER THE ARGA RIVER HAS BEEN USED BY PILGRIMS FOR CENTURIES

△ MOORISH SPAIN

SPAIN

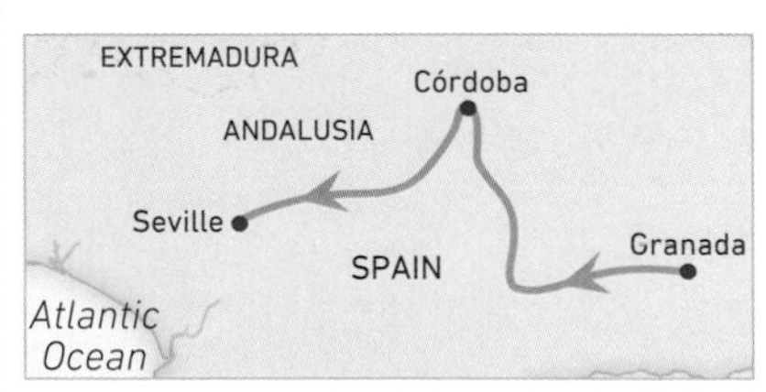

Many think of Europe as an almost wholly Christian continent historically, but that was not always the case. In 711, an army of Moors (North African Berbers and Arabs) crossed the Strait of Gibraltar to the Iberian Peninsula (Spain and Portugal). For about 800 years, about two-thirds of the Iberian Peninsula was ruled by Moors. Spain was a center of trade and thought, and more tolerant than elsewhere in Europe, so learned people traveled there from across the Muslim world and beyond to share ideas. The result was a unique civilization, with a distinct architectural legacy visible throughout the south of the Iberian Peninsula.

Muslim Spain was known as Al-Andalus, a name that lives on in Andalusia, the most southerly province of modern Spain, just across the Strait of Gibraltar from Morocco. Unsurprisingly, most of the vestiges of Spain's Moorish past can be found there. The lustrous blue ceramics, intricate plaster moldings, green-tiled roofs, and tradition of water gardens are redolent of the city's Muslim history, and give this sun-drenched region a highly individual character unlike anywhere else in Spain, or the rest of Europe.

Perhaps the high point of Moorish culture, and the place to begin a tour of Al-Andalus, is the Alhambra, the palace complex in Granada that tumbles down a hillside in a series of opulent fountain courts and garden terraces. Washington Irving, who lived in the Alhambra for a time, wrote of the palace: "Everything here appears calculated to inspire kind and happy feelings, for everything is delicate and beautiful."

Traveling west from Granada, there is a beautiful 10th-century mosque in Córdoba, with an interior of seemingly endless Arabic horseshoe arches. When the Spanish recaptured the city in 1236, they built a cathedral within the Islamic prayer hall.

Seville is a good place to finish a Moorish tour. Its walled palace, the Alcázar, is every bit as lavish and beautiful as the Alhambra, if a little smaller. Seville also boasts the Giralda, which now serves as the tower of the city's Gothic cathedral but was originally an Islamic minaret. Walking up the unique sloping ramp inside gives fabulous views from the top out over the city below.

▷ TOUR DU MONT BLANC

SWITZERLAND, ITALY, AND FRANCE

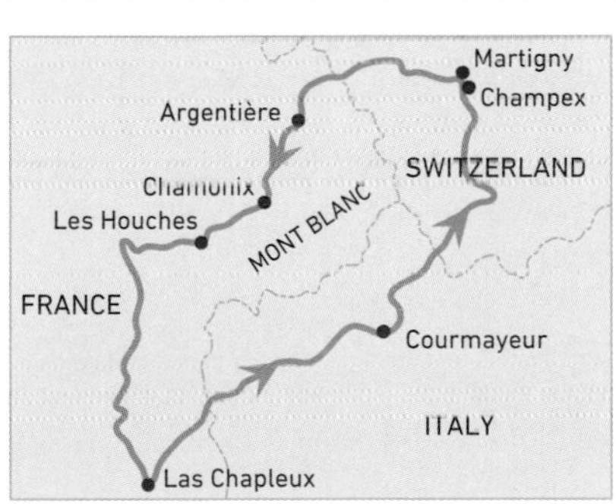

Europe's highest peak—Mont Blanc in the Alps—is where mountain climbing began. The challenge to reach its summit, laid down in 1760, kickstarted the sport that was, in the early days, known as "alpineering." However, there is no need to be an alpinist to appreciate Mont Blanc.

The Tour du Mont Blanc, or TMB, is a hiking route that circles the Mont Blanc massif, passing through parts of Switzerland, Italy, and France on the way. It covers a distance of roughly 110 miles (170 km), ascends at its highest point to 8,743 feet (2,665 m), and is one of the most popular long-distance hikes in Europe. The hike showcases the best of the Alps. Nowhere else can so many awe-inspiring peaks be seen in such close proximity. The scenery on the lower slopes is also beautiful, with clearly marked and well-maintained trails leading through the greenest of pastoral Alpine valleys. Also, because this route takes in three countries, it crosses an appealing mix of cultures.

The normal walking route is counter-clockwise, starting in any of the three countries: Champex or Martigny in Switzerland, Courmayeur in Italy, or Les Houches in the Chamonix Valley in France. Most trekkers take 11 days to complete the circuit, give or take a day or two.

It is worth factoring in a few rest days to linger in places such as the lovely Italian town of Courmayeur with its scenic cable car. There are also opportunities to ski and try out other outdoor activities, including ice-skating, in places such as Argentière in the Chamonix Valley. The route offers plenty of temporary accommodation, ranging from mountain huts and campsites to luxurious hotels, so the trail can be broken into segments of different lengths to suit everyone's preferred walking pace.

RIFUGIO BONATTI, ONE OF THE MANY LODGES ON THE TOUR DU MONT BLANC

▽ THE ORIENT EXPRESS

EUROPE AND TURKEY

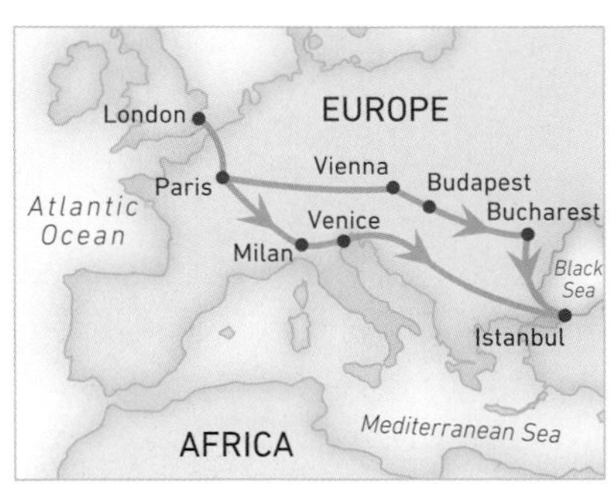

The original route for what was the world's most romantic railway journey, launched on June 5, 1883, was Paris to Vienna. Six years later, in 1889, the route was extended to Constantinople (Istanbul), and from that time on, Paris and Istanbul became the two cities synonymous with the service known as the Orient Express. The service would run, with occasional interruptions during war, right through until the 1970s. At different times, there were different routes. The Venice-Simplon Orient Express, for example, ran via Milan and Venice (that was the train on which Agatha Christie set her *Murder on the Orient Express*). However, the classic route was always Paris-Vienna-Budapest-Bucharest-Istanbul.

In 1982, the Venice-Simplon Orient Express was revived as a private venture. Using restored 1920s and '30s royal-blue carriages with brass insignia, the service still runs from London to Venice between March and November each year. The journey takes two days, with one night aboard, and is specifically targeted at wealthy nostalgists and leisure travelers (tickets cost several thousand dollars).

Passengers are carefully tended to by uniformed attendants in white gloves, and in the evening a four-course dinner is served in a wood-paneled dining car. Once a year, the company also offers a service from Paris to Istanbul (and from Istanbul to Paris). This includes three nights on the train, and a night each in Budapest and Bucharest.

A cheaper alternative, of course, is to make the journey using regular services. It is fairly straightforward to take a train from Paris via either Bucharest in Romania or Belgrade and Sofia in Bulgaria. Both routes take four nights, with a night spent in either Bucharest or Sofia. Possible additional city stops include Munich, Salzberg, and Vienna. Both trains have comfortable sleeping cars. Whatever the train, a copy of Graham Greene's novel *Stamboul Train*, which the author described as "the first and last time in my life I deliberately set out to write a book to please," makes essential reading. Booking a room at the beautiful Pera Palas Hotel in Istanbul, where Agatha Christie herself stayed, also gives a flavor of the past.

THE WOOD-PANELED DINING CAR OF THE ORIENT EXPRESS

▷ A MODERN CANTERBURY TALE

UNITED KINGDOM

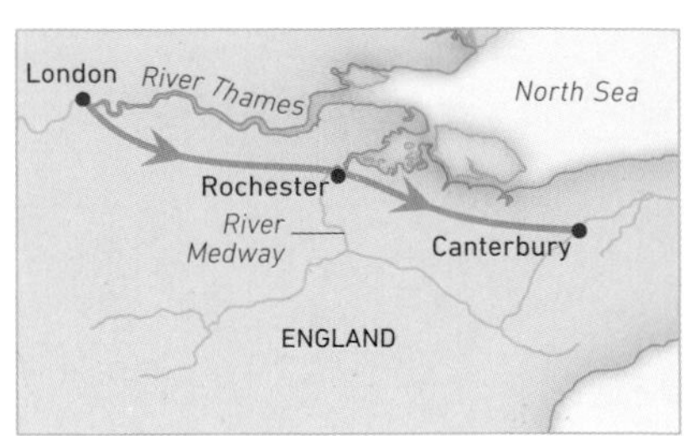

Chaucer's story of 30 pilgrims setting out from London to walk to the shrine of the martyred St. Thomas Becket in Canterbury is the most famous pilgrimage in English literature. At the start of the journey, an innkeeper suggests that during the walk each pilgrim should tell two tales to help pass the time, offering a free supper as a prize for the best storyteller on their return. The *Canterbury Tales'* cast of characters is drawn from all corners of 14th-century English society, and includes a knight, a monk, a clerk, a merchant, a prioress, and a very bawdy miller. The tales are variously moral, humorous, reflective, and rude, and tell us much about the nation at the time. There is plenty to enjoy in attempting to rediscover Chaucer's England, and one way is to follow in his pilgrims' footsteps.

A first stop could be at the British Library in London, which holds two editions of the *Canterbury Tales*, printed around 1476 and 1483 (roughly 80 years after Chaucer's death). The inn from which the pilgrims set out was the Tabard Inn, in Southwark, south London. It no longer exists, but the George Inn, now London's oldest pub, makes a good substitute. In a neighboring alley, a plaque marks where the Tabard used to stand. The high street beside the George is the old road to Canterbury and Kent, but a modern-day alternative is to take a train from London's Victoria Station to Rochester, where the pilgrims crossed the River Medway. The North Downs Way can be taken up there. This is a long-distance walking path that takes a scenic route through the Kentish landscape, following a similar trail to that taken by Chaucer's characters.

The distance from Rochester to Canterbury is 34 miles (55 km) or so. This makes a comfortable two- or

CANTERBURY CATHEDRAL, WHERE ST. THOMAS BECKET WAS MARTYRED

three-day stroll, spending the nights in small villages (such as Charing or Chilham) on the way. The route ends at Canterbury Cathedral, with its shrine to St. Thomas Becket. He was murdered there in 1170 while at prayer, after arguing with Henry II, the king of England.

▷ COAST TO COAST WALK

UNITED KINGDOM

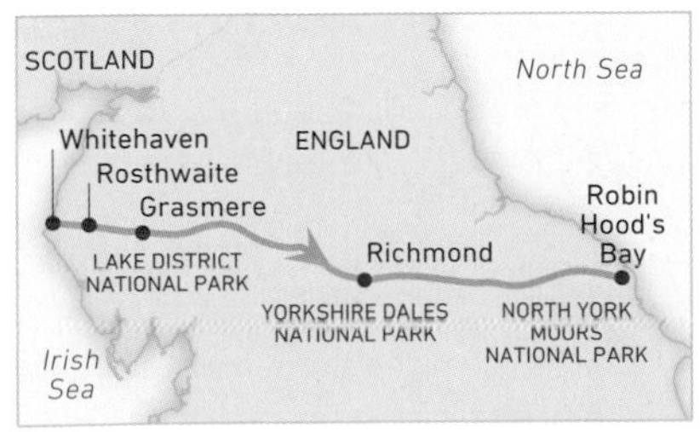

The Lake District is a stunning, rugged area of northwest England. Celebrated in some of the most famous verse of Romantic poet William Wordsworth, it is a region of emerald valleys, craggy fells (mountains) dotted with sheep, sparkling lakes, and drystone walls. Beatrix Potter lived and farmed there, and left all her land to the National Trust. In the 20th century, the area (which is now a protected national park) found a new champion in Alfred Wainwright, an accountant who devoted his life to walking and exploring the Lakes, and who produced a series of hand-illustrated walking guides to the region.

Wainwright was also the creator of the Coast to Coast Walk, which is 190 miles (305 km) long and runs from the west coast of Cumbria to the east coast of Yorkshire, producing his guidebook to it in 1973. The walk passes through three national parks with stunning landscapes: the Lake District, the Yorkshire Dales, and the North York Moors.

The walk is best made from May to October, and walking boots, maps, and a compass are essential. It is divided into 12 stages, each of which can easily be completed in a day, and ends in a village with places to stay overnight and usually a convivial pub that serves food and local beer. Including one or two rest days, the route makes a two-week vacation that takes in some of the finest English landscapes. Highlights include the dramatic mountain scenery on the walk through Ennerdale, and Rosthwaite, a hamlet of whitewashed cottages. In the pretty village of Grasmere lies Dove Cottage, the home of William Wordsworth, and the school where he taught (which is now a gingerbread shop). The Yorkshire Dales is an area of rolling hills, rivers, and pretty valleys, and a beautiful town, historic Richmond, which is full of cobbled streets and alleys. The North York Moors have vast expanses of rugged moorland covered in heather. The walk ends at the east coast with some dramatic scenery at Robin Hood's Bay, an old smugglers' village that is built into a fissure between two cliffs.

FELLSIDE NEAR ENNERDALE, THE LAKE DISTRICT, UK

North America

▷ THE VIKING TRAIL

CANADA

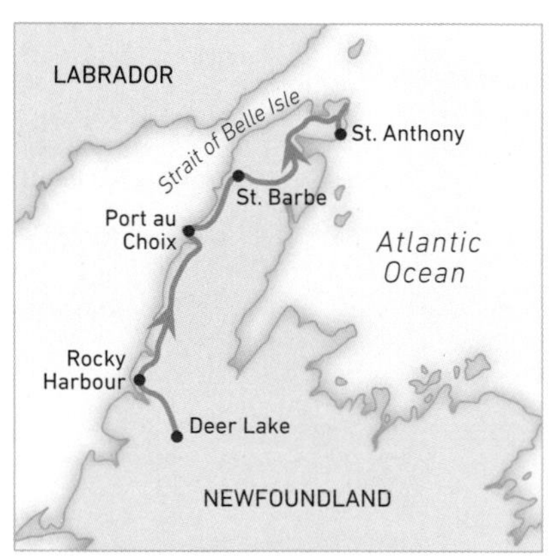

As well as being one of Canada's most beautiful scenic drives, the Viking Trail also passes a place of deep historical significance. It runs past the spot where Viking voyagers first settled in North America more than a thousand years ago—the only authenticated Viking site on the continent.

The road travels up the west coast of Newfoundland, covering a total distance of 258 miles (415 km), from the junction with Newfoundland and Labrador Route 1 at Deer Lake in the south to the whale-watching center of St. Anthony in the far north.

For most of its length, the road hugs the Gulf of St. Lawrence, with views over the water on one side and the Long Range Mountains on the other. Driving up from the south, the first stop most visitors make is at the town of Rocky Harbour, the gateway to the Gros Morne National Park. This is a UNESCO World Heritage Site with 697 sq miles (1,800 sq km) of dramatic landscapes and ancient geological wonders. About 20 marked day-trip trails run through the park, exploring its coastal and interior landscapes. In some parts it is even possible to spot wild moose and caribou. The road continues on past hamlets of colorful clapboard houses, often with lobster traps piled outside, through the historic fishing centers of Port au Choix, and on to St. Barbe, whichis the departure point for the Labrador Ferry.

Shortly before the route reaches its terminus at the town of St. Anthony, a turning leads to L'Anse aux Meadows National Historic Site. It is here, on boggy land beside the slate-grey Atlantic, that a group of Greenland Vikings landed around 1000 to establish a settlement, hundreds of years before Christopher Columbus arrived in America. The archaeological evidence for the Viking discovery was unearthed in a dig in the 1960s. The site now contains a recreation of a low, grass-roofed Viking longhouse, a replica Viking boat, and an informative visitor center displaying original excavated artifacts and hosting demonstrations of traditional crafts such as iron forging and textile weaving.

STEEP CLIFFS ALONG A FJORD IN GROS MORNE NATIONAL PARK

A HUSKY DOG TEAM ON BAFFIN ISLAND

△ THE NORTHWEST PASSAGE

CANADA AND THE USA

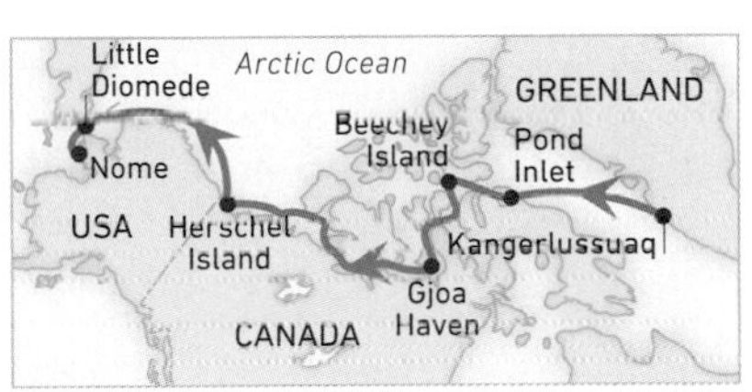

By the time that Norwegian explorer Roald Amundsen succeeded in becoming the first person to navigate the Northwest Passage in 1906, no one believed any longer that it could provide the long dreamed-of maritime shortcut between Europe and Asia. In recent years, however, melting polar ice caused by global warming has opened up Arctic waters, and in 2009 the passage that had been sought by sailors for centuries was finally clear for shipping. In 2013, a cargo ship that was too large for the Panama Canal made it through the Arctic Sea and around the top of North America. Taking advantage of the new sea route, global shippers are now planning to start regular services using the Northwest Passage.

However, it remains difficult for visitors to explore the region and chart their own course through the Northwest Passage. The only option is to take a sea cruise with a specialist operator. For those who can afford it, the journey offers the experience of a lifetime. The ships, which vary from the basic to the luxurious, usually depart from the transport hub of Kangerlussuaq in Greenland. They cross Baffin Bay to call in at Pond Inlet, on northern Baffin Island, Canada, a small Inuit settlement in a setting of snow-capped mountains, fjords, and glaciers. This is considered to be the gateway to the Northwest Passage. Another day's sailing west is Beechey Island, best known as the place where the doomed British expedition led by John Franklin wintered in 1845–46. After his two ships carrying 129 men sailed on from here, they were never seen again. A couple more days to the south is King William Island, at the heart of the Northwest Passage. On its southeast coast is Gjoa Haven, the name of which honors Roald Amundsen, who wintered there with his ship the *Gjøa*.

There is still another week's sailing, passing the old whaling station of Herschel Island and Little Diomede, an island at the edge of the International Dateline between Alaska and Russia, before the expedition docks at Nome, having completed a journey that eluded explorers for centuries.

▽ ROUTE 66

USA

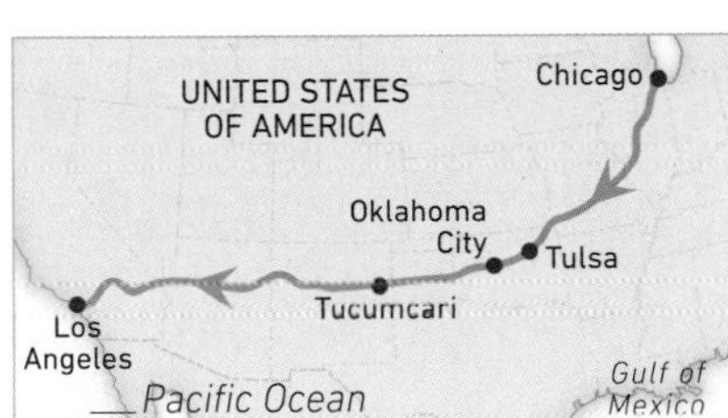

It may be a cliché, but there is a reason so many people choose to drive Route 66. It showcases much of what is best in the American West. The great cities of Chicago and Los Angeles are its starting and end points. Between them, if the corner of Kansas that the route just crosses is included, drivers pass through eight different states. There is scope for as much or as little planning as suits, because the number of places to stop off and things to do and see along the way is simply immense. Half the fun is just getting in the car and seeing what there is along the way, in the tradition of the Great American Road Trip.

Although stretches of the original Route 66 have been replaced by the modern highway network, the parts that remain make for interesting driving. Because the roads are smaller, the pace is slower, giving the chance to keep an eye out for old-school diners, restored gas stations, and towns that seem to be frozen in time, many with a vintage motel evoking a sense of classic Americana.

It is easy to find a motel each evening but checking in to the Campbell Hotel in Tulsa, Oklahoma, really makes the most of the trip. The hotel was built in 1927 and has 26 themed rooms, including the ultimate Route 66 Suite, complete with vintage road signs.

When passing from the plains and prairies of the Mid-West to the deserts of New Mexico and Arizona, the Grand Canyon makes a rewarding detour. This natural wonder has inspired generations with the sheer size and variety of its rock formations and its rich red color.

From the cornfields of Illinois to the golden sands of California, Route 66 offers drivers an abiding sense of the size, color, and contrasts of the US.

AN ORIGINAL SECTION OF ROUTE 66 WINDING THROUGH THE DESERT

HIGHWAY ONE CROSSES BIXBY BRIDGE IN CENTRAL CALIFORNIA

△ PACIFIC COAST HIGHWAY

USA

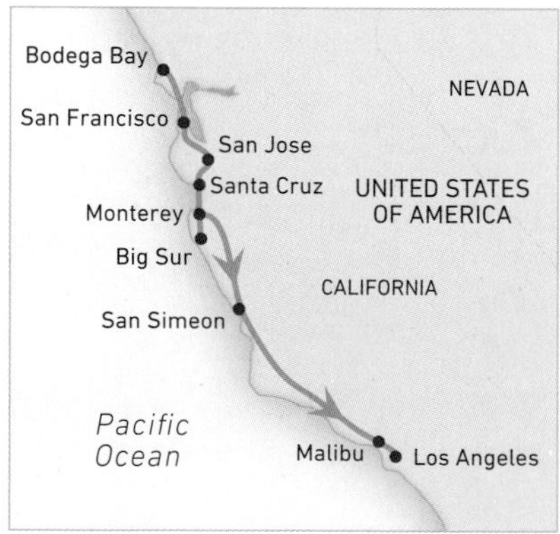

When it comes to American road trips, it is hard to beat the Pacific Coast Highway for sheer scenic beauty. Starting at California's northern border with Oregon and stretching all the way down to San Diego, the route runs for over 600 miles (1000 km). Although it could be driven in just two days, there is so much to enjoy that it is worth taking a week or two. It offers hours of cruising along bluffs overlooking the Pacific, with long stretches of beach, great restaurants and wineries, and some major towns and cities along the way.

The obvious northern starting point is San Francisco. However, rather than immediately heading south, there is an enjoyable detour north to Bodega Bay—a beautiful drive through two national parks and the chance to cross the Golden Gate bridge (twice). After leaving the Foggy City, Santa Cruz makes a good stop. Strolling along the Beach Boardwalk provides a taste of old-school Americana. A short drive south takes in Monterey and Carmel, after which a gentle uphill drive leads over photogenic Bixby Creek Bridge to the rugged, unspoiled stretch of coastline (often wreathed in fog in summer) called the Big Sur. This was a retreat for many bohemian writers and artists in the 1950s and '60s. There are many beautiful vistas here—such as Pfeiffer Beach, McWay Falls, Point Sur State Historic Park, and Ragged Point.

The next break from the wheel could be San Simeon, stop-off point for Hearst Castle and the Elephant Seal Rookery at San Piedras Beach. The "castle" was where newspaperman William Randolph Hearst lived, and was Orson Welles' inspiration for Xanadu in *Citizen Kane*. Equally extravagant is the Madonna Inn at San Luis Obispo. Next up are Santa Barbara and Ventura. Then, before hitting the low-rise sprawl of Los Angeles, there is one final stretch of glorious scenery as Route 1 skirts miles of incredible beaches around Malibu. Leaving the coastal highway, it is time to turn inland through the stunning Topanga Canyon. A pause at the top of Topanga Overlook gives a fabulous view over the San Fernando Valley. The final stop is Los Angeles.

▷ THE LEWIS AND CLARK TRAIL

USA

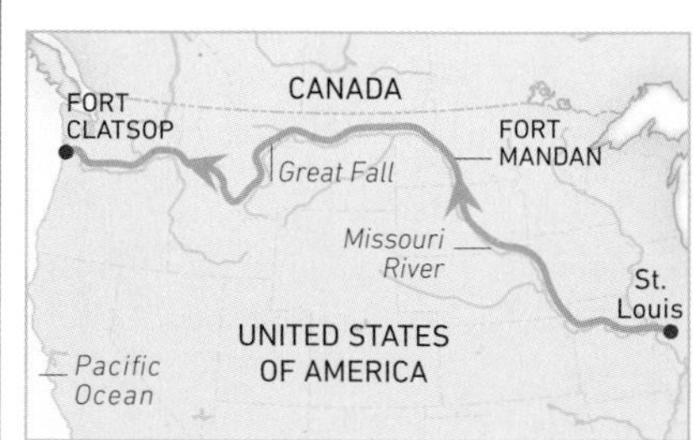

The journey taken by Meriwether Lewis and William Clark to find a route across central US to the Pacific in 1804 generally followed the Missouri River, from just north of St. Louis to the Missouri's headwaters in western Montana. From there, the expedition followed the Jefferson River (named by Lewis after the president who sent them) southwest before looping back north to the Clearwater River. Lewis and Clark followed the Clearwater west to the Snake River, which took them to the Columbia River, and finally to the Pacific. Today, their footsteps can be followed along the Lewis and Clark Trail, on which museums, parks, and memorials celebrate their historic adventure. These are all signposted by the National Park Service, and are documented on easily available maps.

A good place to start is the waterfront in St. Louis, where the Gateway Arch reflects the city's role in the westward expansion of the US—a story told in the Old Courthouse Museum. Also in Missouri is Fort Osage, a splendid reconstruction of the fort built by the expedition as a military outpost in the newly acquired Louisiana Territory. At Council Bluffs, in Iowa, the Western Historic Trails Center has material on Lewis and Clark and a nature trail that leads to a pristine spot on the river. One of the key Lewis and Clark sites is in North Dakota. A replica of Fort Mandan marks the spot where the expedition spent the 1804–05 winter, and met their interpreter, Sacagawea.

Great Falls in Montana is where the expedition faced its greatest hardship because the men had to carry their canoes and supplies around five waterfalls. Unfortunately, the falls have since been tamed by dams, but there is an outstanding Lewis & Clark Interpretive Center here. Nearby lies the Giant Springs National Park, a rare place where the land still looks as it might have done when Lewis and Clark saw it. Also in Montana, near the town of Billings, there is rare physical evidence of the expedition—William Clark's signature, which he carved into the rock known as Pompeys Pillar on his return trip in 1806. The tour ends at the Fort Clatsop National Memorial, near Astoria in Oregon. This is another replica fort, marking the place where the expedition spent the winter in 1805–06, before turning around and heading back east.

A MONUMENT TO LEWIS, CLARK, AND SACAGAWEA (PLUS CHILD) IN MONTANA

SUNRISE OVER MOUNT KATAHDIN, IN BAXTER STATE PARK, MAINE

△ THE APPALACHIAN TRAIL

USA

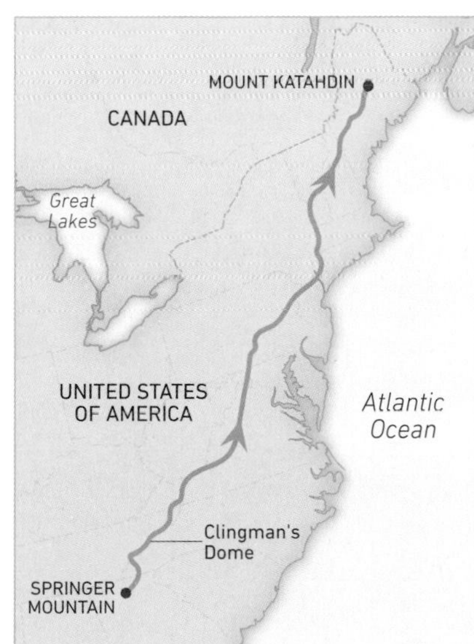

It is neither the oldest nor the longest long-distance footpath in the US, but the Appalachian Trail is the most user-friendly of the big three—the other two being the Pacific Crest Trail and the Continental Divide Trail. The trail was devised by a forester in 1921 for city-dwelling trekkers rather than adapted for walkers from a previous usage. It passes plenty of towns, and so is easier to plan than the Pacific and Continental trails. Still, it is no easy walk. Stretching from Springer Mountain in Georgia in the south to Mount Katahdin in Maine in the north, the trail follows the Appalachian range through 14 states, over 2,184 miles (3,524 km). Flat sections are few and far between. The trail's tallest peak, Clingman's Dome in the Great Smoky Mountains National Park, may only reach 6,643 feet (2,024 m) above sea level, but the constant ascents and descents add up to the equivalent of 16 ascents of Mount Everest.

That said, two to three million people every year hike a part of the trail although those that attempt the whole thing (known as "thru-hikers") number only around 2,500 a year (and three-quarters of these give up). To hike the entire trail would take 5–6 months, but life is made easier by the hostels, shuttle services, and hiker-friendly restaurants along the route that cater specifically for hikers.

It is easy to find the way too, as the entire trail is marked by white rectangles painted on trees and fence posts. There are also more than 250 garage-sized, three-sided sleeping shelters spaced about a day's walk apart from each other. These save carrying a tent—all that is needed is a ground sheet and a sleeping bag—and they give the trail a community feel.

The most challenging part of the trail is the most northerly stretch, the Hundred-Mile Wilderness, in Maine. Hikers heading north should stock up with provisions in the town of Monson before heading for the final destination—the summit of Mount Katahdin in Baxter State Park. Steep, and rising to 5,267 feet (1,605 m), this should only be attempted in good weather.

▽ THE *CALIFORNIA ZEPHYR*

USA

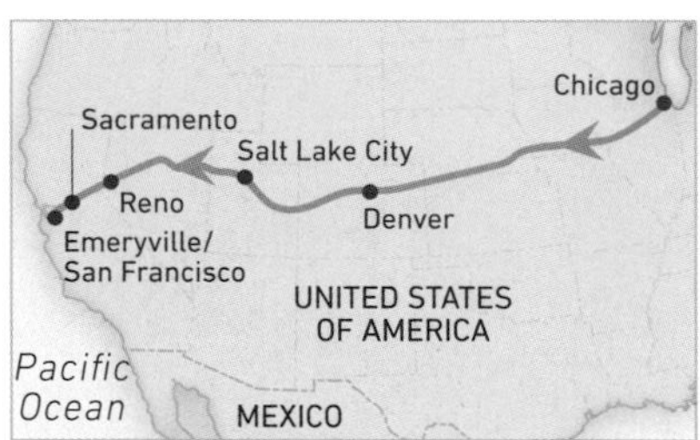

In 1869, railroad magnates hammered the final spike into the United States' first transcontinental railroad, finally linking the Atlantic and Pacific sides of the country. Today, the original line carries freight only, but the *California Zephyr* covers some of the same route and does the same job of connecting east and west coasts. It runs daily between Chicago and San Francisco, through seven states (Illinois, Iowa, Nebraska, Colorada, Utah, Nevada, and California), covering a distance of 2,438 miles (3,924 km). This is not quite the longest Amtrak route (that is the Chicago to LA *Texas Eagle* service), but it is the most scenic. Departing from Chicago, it crosses the Mississippi River as it passes from Illinois into Iowa, before coursing through the plains of Nebraska to Denver, across the Rockies to Salt Lake City, and then through Reno and Sacramento into Emeryville/San Francisco. The train has a Sightseer Lounge Car, in which the walls have been swapped for vast panoramic windows that give passengers fine, uninterrupted views of the scenery.

This is also an historic route: a train called the *California Zephyr* first took to the rails in 1949, and ran until 1970. Amtrak's modern incarnation takes two days and two nights, which can be done in a spacious coach seat or in a reserved roomette in a sleeping car. However, the train offers the chance of hopping off at one of its 35 stops and spending 24 hours (or more) in lots of secondary cities that most people would otherwise never get around to visiting.

Prime candidates for stop-offs include the "mile-high" city of Denver, Colorado, the casino and outdoor sports center of Reno, and maybe California's unheralded small state capital of Sacramento. Here, a visit to the California State Railroad Museum complements the train journey.

Even without any breaks before San Francisco, any passenger taking the full journey on the *California Zephyr* will have seen far more of the US than the average American.

▷ THE GREAT RIVER ROAD

USA

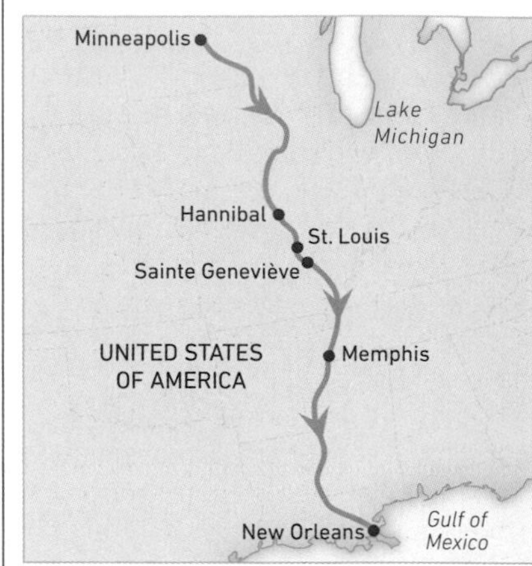

The mighty Mississippi River holds an almost mythical place in the American landscape. It was a highway used by

AMTRAK'S *CALIFORNIA ZEPHYR* WINDS ITS WAY THROUGH THE AMERICAN WEST

the early settlers of the country, and it marked where the American West began. It also gave the nation one of its greatest writers, Mark Twain, who made the river his most powerful character in books such as *The Adventures of Tom Sawyer* (1876) and *The Adventures of Huckleberry Finn* (1884). Today, sailing along stretches of the river in one of several replica steamboats is possible, but driving along the Great River Road (GRR) offers the chance to experience the kind of freedom Huck Finn would have approved of.

The GRR is not the single road the name might suggest, but a designated route along connected segments of other highways that passes through 10 states of the US (Minnesota, Wisconsin, Iowa, Illinois, Missouri, Kentucky, Tennessee, Arkansas, Mississippi, and Louisiana). Marked by green-and-white signs showing a steamboat inside a pilot's wheel, the GRR frequently changes direction, often crosses the river, and meanders through lots of small towns. It is not all pretty, and it isn't fast, but it rewards with plenty of local color.

To drive something approaching the whole route, it is necessary to start in Minneapolis and head south through small-town middle America, where attractions include La Crosse, Wisconsin, and Collinsville, Illinois. One essential stop is Hannibal, Missouri, for the Mark Twain Boyhood Home & Museum. St. Louis, Missouri, on the border with Illinois, is another option, while those who prefer to skip the bigger cities in favor of smaller places will enjoy visiting Sainte Geneviève, in Missouri, which is the only surviving French colonial village in the country. Founded in 1735, Sainte Geneviève is full of well-preserved old houses, antique shops, and cafés.

Further south, there is opportunity for immersion in music lore in Memphis, Tennessee, home to Graceland, Sun Studio, and the Stax Museum of American Soul Music. All too soon comes New Orleans, where the Mississippi spills out into the Gulf of Mexico. This is as good a place as any to park the car and follow the advice of the sage of the Misssissippi, Mark Twain, who once said: "Don't dream your life, but live your dream."

BRIDGES OVER THE MISSISSIPPI AT NEW ORLEANS, LOUISIANA

▽ ON THE ROAD WITH JACK KEROUAC

USA

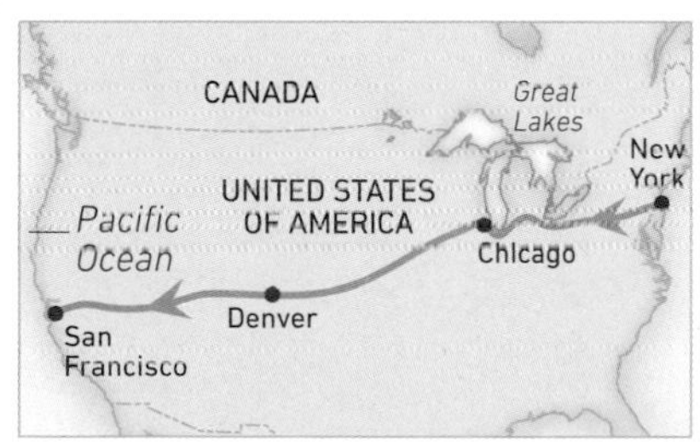

Although he is frequently heralded as the great American road-trip novelist, Jack Kerouac did not actually drive a great deal. He generally took buses and occasionally hitchhiked. New York is where his great book, *On The Road* (1957), starts and ends. Any Kerouac pilgrimage there should take in the Village Vanguard jazz club in Greenwich Village, where the writer performed Beat poetry in the 1960s. There is also the White Horse Tavern, another of Kerouac's hangouts, which was a center of Bohemian culture in the 1950s and '60s. After failing to hitch a lift, Kerouac caught a Greyhound bus to Chicago, rolling through New Jersey, Pennsylvania, Ohio, and Indiana, mostly in the dark.

The Chicago of his time was lively with jazz, particularly in the Loop, the central area wrapped around by the elevated train tracks. Today, the Loop is the financial district, and is totally dead at night. Heading Uptown to the Green Mill—a place Al Capone and other gangsters used to frequent in the 1920s, but which today is all about jazz—gives something of the city's old flavor. Kerouac then hitchhiked from Chicago to Denver, home to Neal Cassady, the model for *On the Road*'s hero, Dean Moriarty. The heart of Cassady's Denver was Larimer Street, which was full of "old bums and beat cowboys." Now gentrified, it is part of Lower Downtown, or LoDo, a hip area of restaurants, loft apartments, and microbreweries. Some places associated with Kerouac do survive: there is El Chapultepec, an old jazz venue that still has music most nights, and Don's Club Tavern, an old-school bar that has been around since 1947, and is said to have been one of Kerouac's old haunts.

After Denver, Kerouac took the bus to San Francisco. He stayed with Neal Cassady and his wife at 29 Russell Street on Russian Hill, an address where he worked on the manuscript of *On the Road*. The house still stands. San Francisco can claim to be the home of the Beat movement, its headquarters being the City Lights Bookstore on Columbus Avenue. The shop was opened by Kerouac's poet friend Lawrence Ferlinghetti, who, at the time of writing, is still alive—a last link to an America that now seems long gone.

THE CITY LIGHTS BOOKSTORE ON COLUMBUS AVENUE, SAN FRANCISCO

INDEX

A

B

C

D

H

I

N

P

T

U

V

Y

Z

Dorling Kindersley would like to thank the following: Contributors: Phil Wilkinson, Jemima Lord, Esther Ripley. Indexer: Helen Peters. Editorial assistance: Anna Fischel, Sam Kennedy, Sugandha Agarwal, Devangana Ojha. Design assistance: Rohit Bhardwaj, Devika Khosla, Vikas Chauhan. Chapter openers and design assistance: Phil Gamble. Jacket: Priyanka Sharma

The publisher would like to thank the following for their kind permission to reproduce their photographs:

Key: a-above; b-below/bottom; c-center; f-far; l-left; r-right; t-top

1 Dorling Kindersley: James Stevenson / National Maritime Museum, London. **2-3 Bridgeman Images:** Ira Block / National Geographic Creative. **4 Getty Images:** DEA / G. Nimtallah / De Agostini (tr). **5 akg-images:** Pictures From History (tl). **Alamy Stock Photo:** Lebrecht Music and Arts Photo Library (bc). **6 akg-images. Alamy Stock Photo:** Mary Evans Picture Library (br). **Getty Images:** MPI / Stringer (tr). **Rijksmuseum. 7 Alamy Stock Photo:** Contraband Collection (bl). **Getty Images:** Sky Noir Photography by Bill Dickinson (tr). **Library of Congress, Washington, D.C.** (tl). **NASA:** (br). **8-9 Getty Images:** Robbie Shone / National Geographic (t). **11 Bridgeman Images:** British Library, London, UK / © British Library Board. All Rights Reserved. **12 Getty Images:** DEA / G. Nimtallah / De Agostini (l); Science & Society Picture Library (c); DEA / G. Dagli Orti (r). **13 Alamy Stock Photo:** Uber Bilder (l). **Getty Images:** DEA / G. Dagli Orti (c); Marc Hoberman (cr). **14 Alamy Stock Photo:** kpzfoto (bc). **Getty Images:** DEA / G. Dagli Orti (bl); VCG (br). **15 Bridgeman Images:** Pictures from History (br). **Getty Images:** Fine Art Images / Heritage Images (bc); Too Labra (bl). **16 Alamy Stock Photo:** INTERFOTO (bl). **16-17 Alamy Stock Photo:** Peter Barritt (t). **17 akg-images:** Erich Lessing (clb). **Alamy Stock Photo:** Classic Image (br). **18-19 Getty Images:** DEA / G. Nimtallah / De Agostini (t). **19 Alamy Stock Photo:** INTERFOTO (c). **Dorling Kindersley:** Graham Rae / Hellenic Maritime Museum (bl). **Dreamstime.com:** Denis Kelly (br). **20 akg-images:** Hervé Champollion (cl). **20-21 Getty Images:** Leemage / Corbis (b). **21 Bridgeman Images:** Egyptian National Museum, Cairo, Egypt (cr). **Getty Images:** DEA / G. Dagli Orti (tc). **22-23 Getty Images:** CM Dixon / Print Collector. **24-25 Getty Images:** Science & Society Picture Library (b). **24 Science Photo Library:** Library of Congress, Geography and Map Division (tr). **25 Alamy Stock Photo:** The Natural History Museum (clb). **Getty Images:** Science & Society Picture Library (br). **26 akg-images:** Erich Lessing (bc). **Bridgeman Images:** Pictures from History (cla). **26-27 Getty Images:** DEA / G. Dagli Orti(t). **27 Alamy Stock Photo:** Anka Agency International (br). **28 akg-images:** British Museum, London. **29 Alamy Stock Photo:** imageBROKER (tc). **Getty Images:** DEA Picture Library / De Agostini (fbr, br). **30-31 Bridgeman Images:** Private Collection / Photo © Ken Welsh. **31 Alamy Stock Photo:** Science History Images (bc). **Dreamstime.com:** Olimpiu Alexa-pop (cra). **32-33 Dorling Kindersley:** Graham Rae / Hellenic Maritime Museum (b). **32 Alamy Stock Photo:** Charles O. Cecil (bl); North Wind Picture Archives (tr). **Getty Images:** DEA / G. Dagli Orti (cla). **33 Getty Images:** Marc Hoberman (cla). **American School of Classical Studies at Athens, Agora Excavations:** (cra). **34 Getty Images:** DEA / G. Dagli Orti / De Agostini (bl); Heritage Images (cla). **34-35 Photo Scala, Florence:** White Images (b). **35 Alamy Stock Photo:** kpzfoto (tl). **Getty Images:** Universal History Archive / UIG (crb). **36 Getty Images:** DEA / M. CARRIERI / De Agostini. **37 123RF.com:** Juan Aunin (bc). **Getty Images:** Universal History Archive (br). **Rex Shutterstock:** The Art Archive (cr). **38 Bridgeman Images:** Pictures from History (c).

38-39 Getty Images: VCG (t). **39 Bridgeman Images:** People's Republic of China (bc). **Western Han Dynasty Museum of the South Vietnamese:** (crb). **40-41 Getty Images:** DEA / G. Dagli Orti. **42 Alamy Stock Photo:** Granger Historical Picture Archive (cra). **iStockphoto.com:** sculpies (bl). **43 Alamy Stock Photo:** Granger Historical Picture Archive (cr); The Granger Collection (l). **44 Alamy Stock Photo:** Kenneth Taylor (clb). **Bridgeman Images:** The Israel Museum, Jerusalem, Israel / The Ridgefield Foundation, New York, in memory of Henry J. and Erna D. Leir (ca). **44-45 Alamy Stock Photo:** adam eastland. **46 Getty Images:** DEA / G. Dagli Orti (tc). **46-47 Dreamstime.com:** Robert Zehetmayer (b). **47 Dreamstime.com:** Axel2001 (crb). **Getty Images:** PHAS (ca). **48-49 Getty Images:** Photo12 / UIG. **50-51 Bridgeman Images:** Royal Geographical Society, London, UK (t). **50 Alamy Stock Photo:** Ken Welsh (c). **51 Dreamstime.com:** Marilyn Barbone (bc). **Getty Images:** Science & Society Picture Library (br). **52 Getty Images:** Fine Art Images / Heritage Images (t). **53 Getty Images:** Ann Ronan Pictures / Print Collector (cr); Fine Art Images / Heritage Images (tl); Universal History Archive (bl). **54 akg-images:** Album / Oronoz (c). **Alamy Stock Photo:** Granger Historical Picture Archive (r). **Getty Images:** Heritage Images (l). **55 Dorling Kindersley:** National Maritime Museum, London (cr). **Getty Images:** Stefano Bianchetti (c); Print Collector (l). **56 Getty Images:** Arne Hodalic / Corbis (bl); Kazuyoshi Nomachi (bc). **Science Photo Library:** NYPL / Science Source (br). **57 Alamy Stock Photo:** GL Archive (bc). **Getty Images:** Leemage / Corbis (br); Leemage (bl). **58 Photo Scala, Florence:** The British Library Board (t). **59 Bridgeman Images:** Pictures from History (bc). **Imaginechina:** (tl). **Rex Shutterstock:** Sipa Press (cra). **60-61 akg-images:** Pictures From History. **62 Alamy Stock Photo:** ART Collection (t). **Getty Images:** Heritage Images (crb). **63 Alamy Stock Photo:** www.BibleLandPictures.com (cl). **Dreamstime.com:** Viacheslav Belyaev (br). **Getty Images:** Heritage Images (cra). **64 Alamy Stock Photo:** Niels Poulsen mus (tr). **64-65 Getty Images:** Ullstein Bild (b). **65 Alamy Stock Photo:** Science History Images (cra); Sklifas Steven (br). **Bridgeman Images:** Ashmolean Museum, University of Oxford, UK (cla). **66 Getty Images:** Arne Hodalic / CORBIS (bl). **66-67 Alamy Stock Photo:** World History Archive (t). **67 Bridgeman Images:** Private Collection (br). **Rex Shutterstock:** Alfredo Dagli Orti (tr). **68 Dorling Kindersley:** National Maritime Museum, London (r). **Getty Images:** Bettmann (clb). **69 Alamy Stock Photo:** Charles O. Cecil (tl). **Getty Images:** Leemage (clb); Print Collector (br). **70 Bridgeman Images:** British Library, London, UK / © British Library Board (bc). **71 123RF.com:** Nickolay Stanev (bc). **Alamy Stock Photo:** Heritage Image Partnership Ltd (crb). **Getty Images:** Stefano Bianchetti (t). **72 Alamy Stock Photo:** ART Collection (tc). **72-73 Alamy Stock Photo:** Hemis. **73 Alamy Stock Photo:** Arctic Images (tc). **Getty Images:** Russ Heinl (cr); Universal History Archive (clb). **74 akg-images:** Jérôme da Cunha. **75 Alamy Stock Photo:** Josse Christophel (cr). **76 akg-images:** Album / Oronoz (b). **Getty Images:** Leemage (tc). **77 Alamy Stock Photo:** INTERFOTO (cl); robertharding (tl). **Getty Images:** Heritage Images (cra, br). **78-79 Alamy Stock Photo:** Granger Historical Picture Archive. **80 Rex Shutterstock:** Alfredo Dagli Orti (t). **81 Alamy Stock Photo:** The Granger Collection (cr); robertharding (clb); GM Photo Images (b). **82 akg-images:** Fototeca Gilardi (tr). **Getty Images:** Angelo Hornak / Corbis (cla); Fine Art Images / Heritage Images (br). **83 Getty Images:** Fine Art Images / Heritage Images. **84 Rex Shutterstock:** British Library / Robana (ca). **Science Photo Library:** NYPL / Science Source (bc). **85 Bridgeman Images:** British Library, London, UK (tr). **Getty Images:** DEA / M. Seemuller (tl). **86 Alamy Stock Photo:** GL Archive (bc). **Getty Images:** Leemage / Corbis (t). **87 Alamy Stock Photo:** Niday Picture Library (bl). **Bridgeman Images:** Pictures from History / David Henley (tr). **Getty Images:** Martin Moos (bc). **88 Alamy Stock Photo:** The Granger Collection (cla).**88-89 Getty Images:** Print Collector (b). **89 Alamy Stock Photo:** Pictorial Press Ltd (bc). **Bridgeman Images:** Private Collection / Pictures from History (tr). **90 Alamy Stock Photo:** D. Hurst (tr). **Dorling Kindersley:** Courtesy of Deutsches Fahrradmuseum, Germany (tc). **Rex Shutterstock:** Bournemouth News (cr).

90-91 123RF.com: Richard Thomas (c). **Dorling Kindersley:** Matthew Ward (b). **91 Dorling Kindersley:** A Coldwell (crb); National Motor Museum, Beaulieu (tl); Jerry Young (tc); R. Florio (tr); Jonathan Sneath (cb). **Nissan Motor (GB) Limited:** (br). **92-93 akg-images:** Roland and Sabrina Michaud. **92 akg-images:** Gerard Degeorge (bl). **94 Alamy Stock Photo:** The Granger Collection (ca). **94-95 AWL Images:** Nigel Pavitt (b). **95 4Corners:** Tim Mannakee (cl). **Alamy Stock Photo:** Ian Nellist (tr). **96 Bridgeman Images:** Private Collection / Archives Charmet (bl). **97 Alamy Stock Photo:** dbimages (crb). **Getty Images:** Heritage Images (l). **Württembergische Landesbibliothek Stuttgart:** (cr). **98-99 Bridgeman Images:** Bibliotheque Nationale, Paris, France / Index (t). **98 Getty Images:** Heritage Images (br); Universal History Archive (cl). **99 Library of Congress, Washington, D.C.:** G5672.M4P5 1559 .P7 (bc). **100 Alamy Stock Photo:** Stuart Forster (l); Visual Arts Resource (r). **Bridgeman Images:** Private Collection / Index (c). **101 Alamy Stock Photo:** Alberto Masnovo (cr); North Wind Picture Archives (l); Ken Welsh (c). **102 akg-images. Alamy Stock Photo:** North Wind Picture Archives (bl). **Getty Images:** Bjorn Landstrom (br). **103 Alamy Stock Photo:** Lebrecht Music and Arts Photo Library (bl). **Getty Images:** DEA / G. DAGLI ORTI(bc); UniversalImagesGroup (br). **104 Alamy Stock Photo:** Stuart Forster. **105 Alamy Stock Photo:** Chris Hellier (bl). **Bridgeman Images:** Pictures from History (cr). **Getty Images:** Chris Hellier (br). **106-107 SD Model Makers:** (b). **108 Getty Images:** Culture Club (ca). **Rex Shutterstock:** Gianni Dagli Orti (cla). **SuperStock:** Phil Robinson / age fotostock (br). **108-109 Photoshot:** Atlas Photo Archive (t). **109 Getty Images:** G&M Therin-Weise (bc). **110 Alamy Stock Photo:** North Wind Picture Archives. **111 Alamy Stock Photo:** Chronicle (clb); musk (br). **112 Alamy Stock Photo:** Granger Historical Picture Archive (tl). **Getty Images:** Leemage (tr). **112-113 Bridgeman Images:** Photo © Tallandier (b). **113 Alamy Stock Photo:** Mary Evans Picture Library (tc); The Granger Collection (crb). **114 akg-Images. Alamy Stock Photo:** Granger Historical Picture Archive (br). **Getty Images:** Fine Art Images / Heritage Images (c). **115 Alamy Stock Photo:** Chronicle (b); Prisma Archivo (tr). **116-117 Photo Scala, Florence:** bpk, Bildagentur fuer Kunst, Kultur und Geschichte, Berlin. **118 Bridgeman Images:** Private Collection / Index (t). **119 Alamy Stock Photo:** Colport (c); LMR Group (tr). **Getty Images:** DEA / G. Dagli Orti(tl). **120-121 Alamy Stock Photo:** The Granger Collection (b). **120 Alamy Stock Photo:** Chronicle (bc); The Granger Collection (tc). **Getty Images:** Bjorn Landstrom (cla). **121 Alamy Stock Photo:** robertharding (tc). **122 Alamy Stock Photo:** Lebrecht Music and Arts Photo Library (t). **Getty Images:** Stock Montage (crb). **123 Alamy Stock Photo:** Alberto Masnovo (cra). **Bridgeman Images:** Newberry Library, Chicago, Illinois, USA (bc). **124 Alamy Stock Photo:** Peter Horree (cra). **Getty Images:** DEA / G. Dagli Orti (cla). **124-125 Alamy Stock Photo:** Graham Prentice (b). **125 Alamy Stock Photo:** Granger Historical Picture Archive (tl). **Getty Images:** PHAS (cra). **126-127 akg-images:** Album / Oronoz (b). **127 Alamy Stock Photo:** Peter Horree (br); The Granger Collection (tc, c). **128-129 Getty Images:** Stock Montage. **130-131 Getty Images:** UniversalImagesGroup. **131 Alamy Stock Photo:** The Granger Collection (c). **132 Alamy Stock Photo:** Hi-Story (cl); Stock Montage, Inc. (tr). **132-133 Getty Images:** Leemage (b). **133 Alamy Stock Photo:** North Wind Picture Archives (crb). **Library of Congress, Washington, D.C.:** 02616u (ca). **134 Alamy Stock Photo:** North Wind Picture Archives (clb); The Protected Art Archive (cr). **135 akg-images. Alamy Stock Photo:** The Granger Collection (br). **Bridgeman Images:** American Antiquarian Society, Worcester, Massachusetts, USA (cr). **136 Getty Images:** DEA / M. Seemuller (bc); Robert B. Goodman (cra). **Mary Evans Picture Library:** (cla). **137 Getty Images:** Stefano Bianchetti. **138-139 Royal Geographical Society:** Jodocus Hondius Snr (b). **139 Getty Images:** De Agostini Picture Library (br). **Rex Shutterstock:** Harper Collins Publishers (cra). **140 akg-images. Şermin Ciddi**. **Getty Images:** Ullstein Bild (c). **141 Alamy Stock Photo:** Lebrecht Music and Arts Photo Library. **Bridgeman Images. 142 Bridgeman Images:** Pictures from History (bl). **Getty Images:** Historical Picture Archive / Corbis (bc); Universal Images Group (br).

143 akg-images: Fototeca Gilardi (bc). **Alamy Stock Photo:** North Wind Picture Archives (bl). **Getty Images:** (br). **144-145 Rijksmuseum:** (t). **144 Rijksmuseum. 145 Bridgeman Images:** Pictures from History (br). **146-147 akg-images:** Rabatti & Domingie. **148 Bridgeman Images:** Dutch School, (17th century) / Private Collection (cl). **Dorling Kindersley:** Mike Row / The Trustees of the British Museum (ca). **148-149 Nationaal Archief, Den Haag:** (t). **149 Wikipedia:** Bibliothèque François Mitterrand / TCY / CC license: wiki / File:Globe_Coronelli_Map_of_New_Holland (br). **150 Alamy Stock Photo:** Photo 12 (t). **151 Alamy Stock Photo:** Granger Historical Picture Archive (bl). **Getty Images:** MPI / Stringer (tc). **iStockphoto.com:** CatLane (br). **152 Alamy Stock Photo:** ClassicStock (bl). **Nationaal Archief, Den Haag. Pilgrim Hall Museum:** (br). **152-153 Getty Images:** The New York Historical Society (t). **154 Şermin Ciddi. 155 Getty Images:** DeAgostini (bl); DeAgostini (br). **The Walters Art Museum, Baltimore:** (cl). **156-157 Getty Images:** Historical Picture Archive / Corbis. **158 akg-images. Bridgeman Images:** Peter Newark American Pictures (cr). **159 Getty Images:** SSPL / Florilegius (cr). **Wilberforce House, Hull City Museums:** (b). **160 akg-images. 161 Alamy Stock Photo:** Granger Historical Picture Archive (clb); Uber Bilder (cr). **Bridgeman Images:** Peter Newark Pictures (cl). **162 AF Fotografie. Alamy Stock Photo:** The Natural History Museum (bl). **163 Getty Images:** Historical Picture Archive / Corbis (r). **Royal Pavilion & Museums, Brighton & Hove:** (cl). **164-165 Bridgeman Images:** Bonhams, London, UK. **166-167 Getty Images:** Anton Petrus (b). **167 Alamy Stock Photo:** AF Fotografie (tl). **Getty Images:** Fine Art Images / Heritage Images (br). **168 Alamy Stock Photo:** INTERFOTO (cl). **168-169 Alamy Stock Photo:** North Wind Picture Archives (b). **169 Alamy Stock Photo:** AF Fotografie (tl); INTERFOTO (br). **Dorling Kindersley:** Harry Taylor / Natural History Museum, London (tr). **170-171 Getty Images:** DeAgostini (b). **170 AF Fotografie:** (cl). **Getty Images:** Science & Society Picture Library (tr). **171 Alamy Stock Photo:** Granger Historical Picture Archive (tl); Granger Historical Picture Archive (tr). **172 Getty Images:** Universal Images Group (cla). **National Maritime Museum, Greenwich, London:** (ca). **173 The Trustees of the British Museum:** (tl). **Photo Scala, Florence:** White Images (b). **174 Getty Images:** Universal History Archive (tr). **Mary Evans Picture Library:** Natural History Museum (tl). **174-175 akg-images:** Private collection. **175 Alamy Stock Photo:** Granger Historical Picture Archive (tl). **National Maritime Museum, Greenwich, London. 176 Alamy Stock Photo:** The Natural History Museum (bl). **177 Alamy Stock Photo:** Florilegius (tl); The Natural History Museum (tr). **Mary Evans Picture Library:** Natural History Museum (bl). **178-179 Bridgeman Images:** Royal Collection Trust © Her Majesty Queen Elizabeth II, 2017. **180 Bridgeman Images:** English School, (19th century) (after) / Private Collection (t). **181 AF Fotografie. Bridgeman Images:** English School, (19th century) / Private Collection (br). **182 Bridgeman Images:** Civico Museo Sartorio, Trieste, Italy / De Agostini Picture Library / A. Dagli Orti (tr). **182-183 Bridgeman Images:** Christie's Images (b). **183 akg-images:** Fototeca Gilardi (tc). **184 Bridgeman Images:** Archives Charmet (bl). **Getty Images:** (cl). **184-185 Alamy Stock Photo:** Mary Evans Picture Library (t). **185 Bridgeman Images:** SZ Photo / Scherl (br). **186 Alamy Stock Photo:** Chronicle (cl); The Natural History Museum (cr). **186-187 State Library Of New South Wales:** (b). **187 National Library of Australia:** (tr). **National Archives of Australia:** (br). **State Library Of New South Wales:** Bequest of Sir William Dixson, 1952 (cl). **188 Bridgeman Images:** Alte Nationalgalerie, Berlin, Germany / De Agostini Picture Library (c). **Getty Images:** Science & Society Picture Library (l); Science & Society Picture Library (r). **189 akg-images:** ullstein bild (l). **Dorling Kindersley:** Gary Ombler / Christian Goldschagg (cr). **TopFoto.co.uk:** Roger-Viollet. **190 Getty Images:** Archive Photos / Smith Collection / Gado (bl); Hulton Fine Art Images / Heritage Images (br). **The Stapleton Collection:** (bc). **191 akg-images:** Universal Images Group / Underwood Archives (bc). **Bridgeman Images:** Keats-Shelley Memorial House, Rome, Italy (bl). **Thomas Cook Archives:** (br). **192 Bridgeman Images:** Alte Nationalgalerie, Berlin, Germany / De Agostini Picture Library. **193 Getty Images:** De Agostini Picture Library (br); iStock / andreaskrappweis (bc). **Missouri Botanical Garden:** Peter H. Raven Library (cr). **Zentralbibliothek Zurich:** (ca). **194 Alamy Stock Photo:** Hemis (tr). **Getty Images:** De Agostini / G. Dagli Orti(cl). **194-195 Bridgeman Images:** Pictures from History. **195 Bridgeman Images:** The Stapleton Collection (cr). **Getty Images:** Fotosearch (tc). **196-197 Getty Images:** Fine Art Photographic Library / Corbis. **198 Alamy Stock Photo:** North Wind Picture Archives (cla). **198-199 Alamy Stock Photo:** North Wind Picture Archives (t). **199 Alamy Stock Photo:** Don Smetzer (br); Granger Historical Picture Archive (cr). **Bridgeman Images:** Private Collection (bl). **200-201 Getty Images:** Fotosearch / Stringer (b). **200 Benton County Historical Society Museum in Warsaw, MO:** (bl). **201 Getty Images:** James L. Amos / National Geographic (br); MPI / Stringer (tl). **202 Getty Images:** Science & Society Picture Library (bl). **202-203 Getty Images:** Archive Photos / Smith Collection / Gado (t). **203 Getty Images:** Bettmann (br). **Library of Congress, Washington, D.C.:** (tr). **204 Alamy Stock Photo:** V&A Images (tr). **Getty Images:** Dea / G. Dagli Orti/ De Agostini (b). **205 Alamy Stock Photo:** John Baran (tl). **Bridgeman Images:** Keats-Shelley Memorial House, Rome, Italy (bc). **Wikipedia:** I.H. Jones (tr). **206 Getty Images:** GraphicaArtis (cl). **206-207 Bridgeman Images:** Historic England (b). **207 Alamy Stock Photo:** The Natural History Museum (cl). **Getty Images:** Science & Society Picture Library (br). **208 Historic England Photo Library:** (b). **208-209 Getty Images:** SSPL (tc). **209 Boston Rare Maps Incorporated, Southampton, Mass., USA:** (bc). **Getty Images:** Bettmann (br). **Penrodas Collection:** (tr). **210 Getty Images:** Hulton-Deutsch Collection / Corbis (cl). **210-211 akg-images:** ullstein bild (b). **211 Boston Public Library:** (tl). **Library of Congress, Washington, D.C.. 212-213 Alamy Stock Photo:** The Granger Collection (b). **212 David Rumsey Map Collection www.davidrumsey.com:** (tr). **Getty Images:** Time Life Pictures / Mansell / The LIFE Picture Collection (c); Universal History Archive / UIG (bl). **213 Bridgeman Images:** Pictures from History (tc). **214 Getty Images:** Photo12 / UIG (bl). **214-215 Bridgeman Images:** Royal Geographical Society, London, UK (t). **215 Alamy Stock Photo:** Mary Evans Picture Library (br). **Bridgeman Images:** Royal Geographical Society, London, UK (clb). **Getty Images:** The Print Collector (tr). **216 Getty Images:** Photo12 / UIG (tr); Science & Society Picture Library (b). **217 colour-rail.com:** (br). **Getty Images:** Bettmann (tc). **218-219 Dorling Kindersley:** Gary Ombler / Didcot Railway Centre (c); Mike Dunning / National Railway Museum, York (cb). **218 colour-rail.com. Dorling Kindersley:** Gary Ombler / The National Railway Museum, York (tr). **Getty Images:** Bettmann (cla). **Science & Society Picture Library:** National Railway Museum (br). **219 colour-rail.com. Dorling Kindersley:** Gary Ombler / B&O Railroad Museum (tl); Gary Ombler / Virginia Museum of Transportation (cb). **Getty Images:** SSPL (tr). **Vossloh AG:** (br). **220 akg-images:** Universal Images Group / Underwood Archives (b). **Alamy Stock Photo:** E.R. Degginger (tr). **221 Alamy Stock Photo:** Chronicle (bl); Granger Historical Picture Archive (br). **Getty Images:** GraphicaArtis (tr). **222 Bridgeman Images:** (bl). **Thomas Cook Archives. 223 Getty Images:** Hulton Archive / Stringer (l). **Thomas Cook Archives. 224-225 Getty Images:** Culture Club. **226 Bridgeman Images:** Bibliotheque des Arts Decoratifs, Paris, France / Archives Charmet (cra); Ken Walsh (bl). **227 Alamy Stock Photo:** Antiqua Print Gallery (tr). **Bridgeman Images:** Look and Learn / Barbara Loe Collection (br). **Getty Images:** Ullstein Bild (bl). **228 Alamy Stock Photo:** Amoret Tanner (bl). **Bridgeman Images:** The Geffrye Museum of the Home, London, UK (bc); Private Collection / Christie's Images (cla). **Dorling Kindersley:** Gary Ombler / The University of Aberdeen (cra); Jacob Termansen and Pia Marie Molbech / Peter Keim (tr). **Getty Images:** De Agostini Picture Library / De Agostini / G. Dagli Orti(tl); De Agostini / DEA / L. DOUGLAS (cb); Jason Loucas (crb). **National Museum of American History / Smithsonian Institution:** (tc). **Wellcome Images http://creativecommons.org/licenses/by/4.0/:** (ca). **229 Alamy Stock Photo:** Basement Stock (tr); Chronicle (tc); Caroline Goetze (cra); INTERFOTO (cla). **Getty Images:** Chicago History Museum (tl); Photolibrary / Peter Ardito (br). **230 Bridgeman Images:** Look and Learn /

Peter Jackson Collection (tr). **Getty Images:** The Print Collector (cl). **230-231 Getty Images:** Chris Hellier / Corbis (b). **231 Getty Images:** Chicago History Museum (br); Science & Society Picture Library (t). **232 Getty Images:** Universal Images Group (b). **NYCviaRachel:** (tr). **233 Bridgeman Images. Getty Images:** Don Arnold (tr); Joe Scherschel / National Geographic (tl). **234 Bridgeman Images:** Luca Tettoni (b). **235 Bridgeman Images:** Pictures from History (bc). **RMN:** Thierry Ollivier (cl). **236-237 Beinecke Rare Book And Manuscript Library/yale University**. **237 Bridgeman Images:** Peter Newark American Pictures (br). **238 Getty Images:** Daniel Mcinnes / Corbis (cr). **Mary Evans Picture Library:** SZ Photo / Scherl (cl). **238-239 Bridgeman Images:** Tallandier (b). **239 akg-images:** (tr). **Bridgeman Images:** City of Westminster Archive Centre, London, UK (cr). **Mary Evans Picture Library:** Pharcide (tl). **240-241 Tom Schifanella:** (all images). **242 Getty Images:** Science & Society Picture Library (l). **243 Bridgeman Images:** Royal Geographical Society, London, UK (c). **Getty Images:** Best View Stock (br). **Royal Geographical Society:** (tl). **244-245 Photo Scala, Florence:** White Images (b). **245 akg-images:** Fototeca Gilardi (tl). **Alpine Club Photo Library, London:** (tr). **Getty Images:** Kean Collection / Archive Photos (b). **246 Alamy Stock Photo:** Universal Art Archive (bc). **Getty Images:** Swim Ink 2, LLC / Corbis (cl). **247 The J. Paul Getty Museum, Los Angeles:** William Henry Jackson; I.W. Taber (tr). **248 Alamy Stock Photo:** Art Collection 2 (cl). **Thomas Cook Archives. 248-249 Alamy Stock Photo:** Old Paper Studios. **249 Bridgeman Images:** Cauer Collection, Germany (br). **Getty Images:** LL / Roger Viollet (c). **250 Getty Images:** DeAgostini (bc); Time Life Pictures / Mansell / The LIFE Picture Collection (cr). **Science Photo Library:** Natural History Museum, London (cl). **250-251 Getty Images:** Time Life Pictures / Mansell / The LIFE Picture Collection (b). **251 Alamy Stock Photo:** AF Fotografie (bc). **Getty Images:** Science & Society Picture Library (tc). **252-253 Alamy Stock Photo:** Vintage Archives. **254 akg-images. Getty Images:** General Photographic Agency (r). **255 akg-images. Alamy Stock Photo:** Lordprice Collection (l). **Dorling Kindersley:** Gary Ombler / Jonathan Sneath (cr). **256 Getty Images:** Bettmann (br); Cincinnati Museum Center (bl); Herbert Ponting / Scott Polar Research Institute, University of Cambridge (bc). **257 Alamy Stock Photo:** Contraband Collection (br). **Getty Images:** Time Life Pictures / Mansell / The LIFE Picture Collection (bc); Topical Press Agency / Stringer (bl). **258 Bridgeman Images:** United Archives / Carl Simon (bl). **The Trustees of the British Museum:** (c). **Getty Images:** Universal Images Group (cl). **259 akg-images. Museum of Ethnography, Sweden:** Sven Hedin Foundation (tl). **260 Alamy Stock Photo:** Lordprice Collection (br). **Getty Images:** Thinkstock (c). **The National Library of Norway:** Siems & Lindegaard (bl). **261 Getty Images:** Uriel Sinai (tr). **The National Library of Norway**. **Skimuseet i Holmenkollen:** Silja Axelsen (tl). **262 Dorling Kindersley:** Gary Ombler / Jonathan Sneath (tl). **Getty Images:** Cincinnati Museum Center (b). **263 AF Fotografie. Alamy Stock Photo:** Mary Evans Picture Library (bl); Universal Art Archive (tr). **Getty Images:** Bettmann (cl). **264 Alamy Stock Photo:** Marc Tielemans (tr). **The Camping and Caravanning Club:** (cla). **264-265 Country Life Picture Library:** (b). **265 Alamy Stock Photo:** AF Fotografie (tc). **Bridgeman Images:** Christie's Images (br). **266-267 Bridgeman Images:** Look and Learn. **267 Getty Images:** Sovfoto (tr). **Mary Evans Picture Library:** Illustrated London News Ltd (br). **268 Alamy Stock Photo:** The Granger Collection (br). **Getty Images:** Wolfgang Steiner (tl). **269 Alamy Stock Photo:** Chronicle (tl). **Bridgeman Images:** The Advertising Archives (b). **PENGUIN and the Penguin logo are trademarks of Penguin Books Ltd:** (tr). **270-271 Alamy Stock Photo:** Contraband Collection. **270 Alamy Stock Photo:** Universal Art Archive (tr). **271 akg-images. Alamy Stock Photo:** Contraband Collection (bl). **272 Getty Images:** Bettmann (tl). **Library of Congress, Washington, D.C.. 272-273 Library of Congress, Washington, D.C.. 273 Alamy Stock Photo:** Glyn Genin (br). **274 Getty Images:** Bettmann (cl); Roger Viollet (bc); VCG Wilson / Corbis (c). **275 Bridgeman Images:** Cauer Collection, Germany (r). **Photo Scala, Florence:** (tl). **276 Getty Images:** Bettmann (cl). **276-277 Alamy Stock Photo:** Universal Art Archive (b). **277 Getty Images:** Bettmann (tc); Universal History Archive (br). **278 Getty Images:** Herbert Ponting / Scott Polar Research Institute, University of Cambridge. **279 Alamy Stock Photo:** Uber Bilder (c). **Bridgeman Images:** Granger / Herbert Ponting (bc). **280 akg-images:** Sputnik (cr). **Getty Images:** Universal History Archive (bl). **281 Alamy Stock Photo:** Interfoto (cr). **Getty Images:** Bettmann (l); Time Life Pictures / Mansell / The LIFE Picture Collection (br, br); Time Life Pictures / Mansell / The LIFE Picture Collection (br, br). **282-283 Getty Images:** Bettmann. **284 Alamy Stock Photo:** Granger Historical Picture Archive (tr). **284-285 4Corners:** Susanne Kremer. **285 Alamy Stock Photo:** Granger Historical Picture Archive (tr). **Rex Shutterstock:** Eduardo Alegria / EPA (br). **286-287 Getty Images:** Bettmann (t). **286 Getty Images:** Topical Press Agency / Stringer (br). **287 Alamy Stock Photo:** John Astor (br). **Getty Images:** Bettmann (tr). **288-289 Getty Images:** Kirby / Topical Press Agency (b). **289 Alamy Stock Photo:** Danita Delimont (tl). **Getty Images:** Bettmann (cr). **Mary Evans Picture Library:** John Frost Newspapers (br). **290-291 Royal Geographical Society. 291 Getty Images:** arabianEye / Eric Lafforgue (tr); Universal Images Group (tl). **Royal Geographical Society. 292 Getty Images:** Roger Viollet. **293 Mary Evans Picture Library. 294-295 Alamy Stock Photo:** Royal Geographical Society (b). **294 AF Fotografie. Beinecke Rare Book And Manuscript Library/yale University. 295 Getty Images:** Roger Viollet (tr). **296 Affiliated Auctions:** (cra). **Getty Images:** Photo12 / UIG (bl). **297 Getty Images:** Bettmann. **The Granger Collection, New York:** National Geographic Stock: Vintage Collection (br). **Mary Evans Picture Library:** SZ Photo / Scherl (cr). **298-299 Alamy Stock Photo:** Contraband Collection. **300-301 Getty Images:** SSPL. **300 Getty Images:** SSPL (tr). **301 Getty Images:** General Photographic Agency (tr). **302 AF Fotografie. Getty Images:** Corbis / swim ink 2 llc (bl). **Mary Evans Picture Library:** Everett Collection (ftr); Onslow Auctions Limited (tr). **303 1stdibs, Inc:** (tc). **Alamy Stock Photo:** Vintage Archives (tr). **Canadian Pacific Railway**. **Getty Images:** Corbis Historical. **Mary Evans Picture Library:** Onslow Auctions Limited (tl). **304-305 Alamy Stock Photo:** INTERFOTO. **306 Alamy Stock Photo:** Dimitry Bobroff. **Getty Images:** Popperfoto (l). **Rex Shutterstock:** Turner Network Television (r). **307 Alamy Stock Photo:** A. T. Willett (cr). **Getty Images:** SSPL / Daily Herald Archive (l). **NASA. 308 Bridgeman Images:** Pitt Rivers Museum, Oxford, UK (bl). **Getty Images:** Fotosearch (bc). **Royal Geographical Society. 309 Getty Images:** Hawaiian Legacy Archive (bl). **NASA. 310 Getty Images:** Margaret Bourke-White / The LIFE Images Collection. **311 Getty Images:** Corbis Historical / Hulton Deutsch (tl); Stringer / AFP (cr); Photo12 / UIG (br). **Press Association Images:** (c). **312-313 Getty Images:** SSPL / Daily Herald Archive. **314 Getty Images:** Archive Photos (cl). **314-315 The Kon-tiki Museum, Oslo, Norway**. **315 Getty Images:** ullstein bild (br). **316 Bridgeman Images:** Pitt Rivers Museum, Oxford, UK (bl). **317 Bridgeman Images:** Pitt Rivers Museum, Oxford, UK (br); Pitt Rivers Museum, Oxford, UK (l). **Roland Smithies / luped.com:** (cr). **318 Getty Images:** Hulton Archive (bl); David Pollack / Corbis (cr). **318-319 Getty Images:** Museum of Flight / Corbis (t). **319 Alamy Stock Photo:** Collection 68 (bl). **Getty Images:** Bettmann (br). **Roland Smithies / luped.com:** (cr). **320-321 Alamy Stock Photo:** Tristar Photos (b). **Dorling Kindersley:** Gary Ombler / Brooklands Museum (cb). **320 Cody Images:** (cra). **Kristi DeCourcy:** (cr). **Dorling Kindersley:** Gary Ombler / Paul Stone / BAE Systems (clb); Martin Cameron / The Shuttleworth Collection, Bedfordshire (t). **321 aviation-images. com. aviationpictures.com:** (br). **Dorling Kindersley:** Peter Cook / Golden Age Air Museum, Bethel, Pennsylvania (crb); Gary Ombler / The Real Aeroplane Company (clb); Gary Ombler / De Havilland Aircraft Heritage Centre (cra); Dave King (tl). **National Air and Space Museum, Smithsonian Institution:** (tr). **322 Royal Geographical Society. 322-323 Royal Geographical Society. 323 Getty Images:** Moment Select / Jason Maehl (cr, c). **324-325 Getty Images:** Corbis / Hulton Deutsch. **324 Bridgeman Images:** Christie's Images (bl). **Getty Images:** Fotosearch (tr/1). **325 Getty Images:** Alfred Eisenstaedt / The LIFE Picture Collection (tc); Moviepix / Silver Screen Collection (br). **326-327 Getty Images:**

Sky Noir Photography by Bill Dickinson. **327 Getty Images:** Lonely Planet Images / Kylie McLaughlin (tr). **328 Getty Images:** Robert Alexander (tr); Alan Band / Keystone (cr); John Williams / Evening Standard (bl). **328-329 Getty Images:** AFP Photo / Philippe Huguen (b). **329 Dreamstime.com:** Tan Kian Yong (tc). **330 Getty Images:** Corbis Documentary / Ralph White (bc); Haynes Archive / Popperfoto (cla); SSPL (tr). **331 Rex Shutterstock:** Turner Network Television (bc). **World Wide First Limited:** Christoph Gerigk (c) Franck Goddio / Hilti Foundation (tr). **332 Getty Images:** Bettmann (tl); SSPL (tr); SSPL (bl); Blank Archives (crb). **333 Getty Images:** Business Wire (tr). **NASA:** JSC. **334 Alamy Stock Photo:** (bl); Profimedia.CZ a.s. (crb). **335 Getty Images:** Jack Garofalo / Paris Matc (b). **336-337 Getty Images:** Keystone / Hulton Archive. **338 Alamy Stock Photo:** Atlaspix (cra). **PENGUIN and the Penguin logo are trademarks of Penguin Books Ltd:** (cl). **Paul Theroux:** (bc). **339 Getty Images:** The LIFE Images Collection / Matthew Naythons (tr). **Magnum Photos:** Steve McCurry (b). **340-341 Getty Images:** CANOVAS Alvaro. **340 National Geographic Creative:** Mark Thiessen (bl). **341 Alamy Stock Photo:** (cr); Royal Geographical Society. **342 Alamy Stock Photo:** Futuras Fotos (l). **NASA. 342-343 Mars One:** Bryan Versteeg (b). **343 Getty Images:** Corbis (cr). **345 Alamy Stock Photo:** Adrian Arbib (bl). **Bridgeman Images:** SZ Photo / Knorr & Hirth (br). **Getty Images:** Apic (tc). **346 Getty Images:** Photo12 / UIG (tl). **NASA:** JSC (br). **347 Alamy Stock Photo:** AF Fotografie (tl). **Getty Images:** Culture Club (tr). **Mary Evans Picture Library. 348 Bridgeman Images:** Private Collection (tr); State Central Navy Museum, St. Petersburg (tl). **The Granger Collection, New York:** National Geographic Stock: Vintage Collection (br). **349 Getty Images:** Hulton-Deutsch Collection / Corbis (br). **350 Getty Images:** Fine Art Images / Heritage Images. **351 Şermin Ciddi:** (tc). **Getty Images:** DEA PICTURE LIBRARY / De Agostini (br). **352 Alamy Stock Photo:** Universal Art Archive. **Getty Images:** Ulf Andersen (bl). **353 Getty Images:** Fine Art Images / Heritage Images (tr); Hulton Archive (br). **354 Getty Images:** Hulton Archive / Print Collector (tr); Paul Popper / Popperfoto (bl). **355 Alamy Stock Photo:** PjrTravel (r). **Getty Images:** Fairfax Media (bl). **356 Getty Images:** New York Daily News Archive (l). **357 Alamy Stock Photo:** Dimitry Bobroff (bl). **Bridgeman Images:** Royal Geographical Society (tr). **358 Alamy Stock Photo:** Royal Geographical Society (tr). **Getty Images:** Ulf Andersen (bl). **359 Getty Images:** Universal History Archive (tc). **Photo Scala, Florence:** Museum of Fine Arts, Boston (b). **360 Alamy Stock Photo:** Pictorial Press Limited (tl). **Getty Images:** Sovfoto (br). **361 Alamy Stock Photo:** Chris Hellier (tr); Mary Evans Picture Library (tl). **Getty Images:** DeAgostini (bc). **362 Getty Images:** Bettman (bl); Ullstein Bild (tr); Ullstein Bild (br). **363 Getty Images:** Mondadori Portfolio (r). **364 Getty Images:** SuperStock (t). **365 Alamy Stock Photo:** Mary Evans Picture Library (br). **Bridgeman Images:** Granger (bl). **366 Bridgeman Images:** Bibliotheque des Arts Decoratifs, Paris, France / Archives Charmet (t). **367 Alamy Stock Photo:** Chronicle (bl). **Getty Images:** Hulton Archive / Stringer (tr). **368 Getty Images:** Bettman (tl); GraphicaArtis (bl); Universal History Archive (br). **369 Alamy Stock Photo:** Science History Images (br). **Getty Images:** Harry Borden (tl). **370 Alamy Stock Photo:** Granger Historical Picture Archive (tr). **Bridgeman Images:** British Library (bl). **371 Bridgeman Images:** Louis Monier (tr). **Mary Evans Picture Library:** Illustrated London News Ltd (bl). **372 Bridgeman Images:** Nationalmuseum, Stockholm, Sweden (br). **The Royal Library, Copenhagen:** (bl). **373 Getty Images:** Hulton Fine Art Collection / Heritage Images (r). **Kazimierz Nowak Foundation:** (tl). **374 Alamy Stock Photo:** Granger Historical Picture Archive (bl). **Getty Images:** Fine Art (t). **375 Alamy Stock Photo:** AF Fotographie (tr). **Getty Images:** Corbis Historical (bl). **376 Getty Images:** Herbert Ponting / Scott Polar Research Institute, University of Cambridge (br). **377 Getty Images:** Popperfoto (tr). **TopFoto.co.uk:** (br). **378 Alamy Stock Photo:** AF Fotografie (tr); Royal Geographical Society (b). **379 Alamy Stock Photo:** Uber Bilder (tc). **Bridgeman Images:** Pitt Rivers Museum, Oxford, UK (br). **380 Bridgeman Images:** Private Collection / Look and Learn (tl). **Getty Images:** Ulf Andersen (bl); Time Life Pictures (tr). **381 Getty Images:** Bettmann (tl). **National Geographic Creative:** Ira Block (br). **382 Alamy Stock Photo:** AF Fotografie (tl); Science History Images (br). **383 Getty Images:** DeAgostini / Lisbon, Museu De Marinha (tr). **385 Getty Images:** Oversnap (b). **386 Getty Images:** Dave Stamboulis (tl); David Lefranc (br). **387 Getty Images:** Peter Chrarlesworth (bl). **388 Alamy Stock Photo:** jejim120 (tr). **Getty Images:** real444 (bl). **389 Getty Images:** Steve Winter (tr). **390 Getty Images:** Douglas Pearson (bl); Instants (tr). **391 Alamy Stock Photo:** Joris Croesi (br). **392 Getty Images:** Joris Gorling / EyeEm (bl); JTB Photo (tr). **393 Getty Images:** GenPi Photo (r). **394 Alamy Stock Photo:** Robert Harding (tl). **Getty Images:** holgs (br). **395 Alamy Stock Photo:** Whit Richardson (tr). **396 Alamy Stock Photo:** National Geographic Creative (br). **Getty Images:** Jake Norton (tl). **397 Getty Images:** Wolfgang Kaehler (t). **398 Alamy Stock Photo:** Image Source (br). **Getty Images:** Issam Madkouk (tl). **399 Getty Images:** Tim Makins (t). **400 Getty Images:** Yury Prokopenko (b). **401 Getty Images:** Australian Scenics (br); Ian Waldie (tl). **402 Getty Images:** DeAgostini (br). **403 Getty Images:** Rodrigo Buendia / AFP (tr). **404 Getty Images:** Mario Tama. **405 Getty Images:** LightRocket / Wolfgang Kaehler. **406 Getty Images:** Gerig / ullstein bild (tr); Lonely Planet Images / Diego Lezama (bl). **407 Alamy Stock Photo:** Hercules Milas (b). **408 Alamy Stock Photo:** ImageBROKER. **409 Getty Images:** Arterra / UIG (bl); Heinz Wohner / LOOK-foto. **410 Getty Images:** Medioimages / Photodisc. **411 Getty Images:** Evgeni Dinev Photography (tr); Tuul and Bruno Morandi (bl). **412 Getty Images:** Arterra / UIG (bl); DEA / Pubbli Aer Foto / De Agostini (tr). **413 Getty Images:** Tim Graham. **414 Getty Images:** Education Images / UIG (bl); Geography Photos / UIG (tr). **415 Getty Images:** Lonely Planet Images / Glenn Van Der Knijff. **416 Getty Images:** Andy Shaw / Bloomberg (b). **417 Getty Images:** Moment Open / Angel Villalba (t); Moment / Joe Daniel Price (br). **418 Alamy Stock Photo:** Gaertner (br). **419 Getty Images:** LightRocket / Wolfgang Kaehler (tl); Photolibrary / Scott Quinn Photography (br). **420 Getty Images:** Mint Images / Frans Lanting. **421 Alamy Stock Photo:** Stephen Saks Photography (bl). **Getty Images:** Gallo Images / Robert C Nunnington (tr). **422 Getty Images:** Joe Raedle. **423 Alamy Stock Photo:** David R. Frazier Photolibrary, Inc. (tr). **Getty Images:** Moment / Joerg Haeske (br)

Endpapers: Emigrants Farewell: 20th August 1912: Emigrants wave their last goodbyes as the emigrant ship 'Monrovian' leaves Tilbury in Essex, bound for Australia. (Photo by Topical Press Agency/Getty Images) Credit: Getty Images / Topical Press Agency / Stringer

Cover images: Back: **akg-images:** Pictures From History fcl; **Alamy Stock Photo:** Granger Historical Picture Archive cl; **Getty Images:** Sky Noir Photography by Bill Dickinson fcr; **Photo Scala, Florence:** Christie's Images, London cr